Origins *of* Judaism

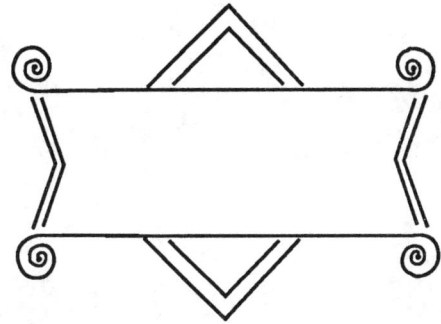

Religion, History, and Literature in Late Antiquity A Twenty-Volume Collection of Essays and Articles

Edited by
Jacob Neusner
University of South Florida
with
William Scott Green
University of Rochester

——— A Garland Series ———

Origins *of* Judaism

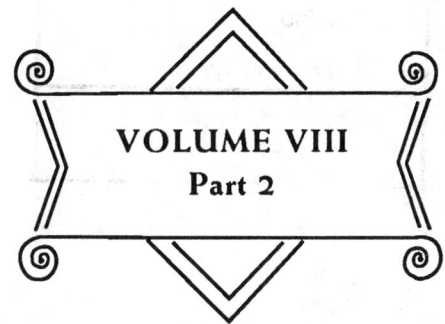

VOLUME VIII
Part 2

History of the Jews in the
Second through Seventh Centuries of
the Common Era

Edited with a Preface by
Jacob Neusner

—— Garland Publishing, Inc. • New York & London ——
1990

The volumes in this series are printed on acid-free, 250-year-life paper.
Printed in the United States.

Library of Congress Cataloging-in-Publication Data

History of the Jews in the second through seventh centuries of the
Common Era / edited by Jacob Neusner with William Scott Green.
p. cm. — (Origins of Judaism : vol. 8)
ISBN 0-8240-8179-X (alk. paper)
1. Jews—History—70–638. 2. Judaism—History—Talmudic period, 10–425. 3. Rabbinical literature—History and criticism. I.
Neusner, Jacob. II. Green, William Scott. III. Series.
BM177.075 vol. 8
[DS123.5]
296'.09'015 s—dc20
[296'.09'015]   90-13902

A complete list of articles in this series, indexed by volume and by
author, may be found at the end of this volume.

PREFACE

The history of the Jews in late antiquity is in two parts, divided by the destruction of Jerusalem and its Temple in 70 C E. That event marked the end of the Jews' mode of worship through sacrifice in the Jerusalem Temple and it further concluded the history of autonomy and self-government under a recognized, territorial authority that had begun so many centuries earlier. From 70 to the conquest by the Arabs bearing Islam in the seventh century, the Land of Israel/Palestine was ruled by territorial authorities other than those of the Jews. For their part, the Jews were ruled by an ethnic government, with the right to administer certain limited matters of purely local significance, hardly a political entity. So much for the Roman empire and the history of the Jews in it. On the other side of the international frontier to the east, Babylonia, where Jews lived from the sixth century B.C.E., was a province within the vast empire of Persia, which held that territory along with much else until the seventh century. Like the Romans, the Persians preferred to have their diverse populations ruled by their own ethnic leaders, who were responsible to the imperial government. In Babylonia the exilarch, or ruler of the exile, ruled the Jews in the Persian empire in the same ways as did the patriarch of the Jews in the land of Israel.

Great events in the history of the Jews in the Land of Israel are few. We take note of the war of 66–73 against Rome, the war of 132–135 against Rome, the latter led by Bar Kokhba, and not much else. A third important event, early in the fourth century, not noted in an explicit way in the Jewish writings, was the conversion of the empire to Christianity. A fourth, in 361, was the Emperor Julian's conversion from Christianity to paganism; he allowed the Jews to rebuild the Temple in Jerusalem, though nothing came of it. On the other side of the border, in Persia, there were no counterpart incidents that historians could describe. History is not made up of one-time events but rather of long-term trends.

In all, the period from the first through the seventh centuries, while rich in historical crises, produced for Judaism an essentially ahistorical canon. The traits of that canon tell us the conception of history of those who wrote it and perhaps also suggest ideas concerning history that were broadly familiar to those who received it, obeyed its laws, and adopted its theology. There are two ways of describing traits of historical sense characteristic of the authoritative writings of Judaism that emerged in that period. The first is to ask whether and how the canonical writings contain historically useful information. What kind of history can we locate within the principal writings of the age? The answer to that question will suggest the historical perspectives and doctrines of the authors of those writings. The sorts of information they chose to preserve, the ways in which through historical reflection and consequent narrative they represented and explained the world as they knew it—these will be contained within the way that events are represented. And one effective way for us accurately to assess the historical interest and perspective of a writing is to attempt to use that writing for historical purposes ourselves. That is why we do well to focus on an account of the type of historical data the canonical writings of talmudic times present, only then turning to the modes of historical thought and reflection revealed in the more important of those same sources. This gives us perspective upon the character of the historical writing in the essays collected in these volumes on the history of the Jews in late antiquity.

Talmudic history—that is to say, the kind of historical perspective found within the canonical writings of Judaism in late antiquity—cannot be said to deal with great affairs, vast territories, movements of men and nations, much that really mattered then. Even the bulk of the women and men of Israel, the Jewish nation wherever they lived, in the time of the composition of these canonical writings, by the testimony of the authors themselves fall outside of the frame of reference. To the sages most Jews appeared to ignore—in the active sense of willfully not knowing—those teachings that seemed critical to the authors. To use the mythic language, when God revealed the Torah to Moses at Mount Sinai, he wrote down part, which we now have in the Hebrew Scripture ("the Old Testament"), and he repeated the other part in oral form, so that Moses memorized it and handed it on to Joshua, and then, generation by generation, to the contemporary sages. Now, to the point, the contemporaries of the sages did not know this oral half of the Torah, only sages did, and that by definition. Only sages knew the whole of the Torah of Moses. So, it follows, the talmudic corpus preserves the perspective of a rather modest component of the nation under discussion. How could we define a subject less likely to attract broad interest: the opinions of a tiny minority of a nation about the affairs of an unimportant national group living in two frontier provinces on either side of a contested frontier? Apart from learning, from the modest folk of the time, some facts about life on the contested frontier of the ancient world—and that was only the one that separated Rome from Persia, the others being scarcely frontiers in any political sense—what is to be learned here that anyone would want to know?

Self-evidently, we cannot expect to find stories of great events, a continuous narrative of things that happened to a nation in war and in politics. The Jews, as it happens, before and after 70 constituted a nation and sustained a vigorous political life. But the documents of the age under discussion treat these matters only tangentially and as part of the periphery of a vision of quite other things. But if manifest history scarcely passes before us, a rich and complex world of latent history—the long-term trends and issues of a society and its life in imagination and emotion—does lie ready for our investigation. For the talmudic canon reports to us a great deal about what a distinctive group of people was thinking about issues that prove to be perennial and universal, and, still more inviting, the documents tell us not only what people thought but how they reasoned. That is something to which few historians gain access: the philosophical processes behind political and social and religious policy, class struggle, and popular contention. For people do think things out and reach conclusions, and for the most part, long after the fact, we know only the decisions they made. Here, by contrast, we hear extended discussions, of a most rigorous and philosophical character, on issues of theory and of thought. In these same discussions, at the end, we discover how people decided what to do and why. That sort of history—the history of how people made up their minds—proves particularly interesting, when we consider the substance of the story. The Jews in the provinces at that point adopted the policies put forward by the sages who wrote the sources we consider. The entire subsequent world history of the Jews—their politics, social and religious world, the character of the inner life and struggle of their community-nation—refers back to the decisions made at just this time and recorded in the Talmud.

The talmudic canon bears the mark of no individual authorship. It is collective, official, authoritative. Were it to hand down decisions without discussion, that collective character would not mark the literature as special. We have, from diverse places and times, extensive records of what legislative or ecclesiastical bodies decided. But if these same bodies in detail recorded how they reached their decisions, including a rich portrait of their modes of thought, then we should have something like what the Talmud gives us.

But the points of interest scarcely end there. The talmudic corpus stands in a long continuum of thought and culture, stretching back, through the biblical literature, for well over a thousand years. Seeing how a collegium of active intellectuals mediated between their own age and the authority and legacy of a vivid past teaches lessons about continuities of culture and society. For sages' culture had endured, prior to their own day, for a longer span of time than separates us from the Magna Charta and Beowulf. If these revered documents of our politics and culture enjoyed power to define politics and culture today, we should grasp the sort of problem that faced the Talmud's sages. For, after all, the Talmud imagined as normative a society that had little in common with the one confronting its sages. The ancient world was seen by them as isolated, independent, freestanding. But the sages' Israel was assimilated in a vast world-empire, subordinate and dependent upon others near and far. That problem of the conflict between ideal and reality is familiar even now .

The Talmud provides a striking example, for close analysis, of a problem of acute interest in historical debates even in our own day. We refer to the debates on how we study, not the individual, but human societies, organized groups, that engage historians from the Annales of the 1920s through social science history today.

How to proceed? In describing and interpreting the life of peoples, we seek to generalize about attitudes and shared conceptions, using the French word mentalité, for example, to explain that about which we speak. Specifically, we want to know how people form a shared conception of themselves, so as to see themselves as a group, and how, further, what they conceive in common relates to how they each, as individuals, confront and experience life. Louise A. Tilly frames matters in terms of shared emotions and, citing Lucien Febvre, founder, with Marc Bloch, of the Annales, quotes Febvre as follows:

[Emotions] imply relations between men, collective relationships. They are doubtless born within the organic depths specific to a given individual. . . . [B]ut their expression is the result of a series of experiences of common life, or similar and contemporaneous reactions to the shock of identical situations and encounters of the same nature. . . . [L]ittle by little . . . by linking many participants in turn as initiators and followers—[these] end by becoming a system of interindividual motivations that differ according to circumstances and situations . . . [and] a true system of emotions is built. They become something like an institution.

Febvre copes with the deep problems of how peoples' emotions so take shape as to fit a common pattern. That is why he speaks of experiences of common life, identical situations, encounters of the same nature. Now if we take up the same issue in terms framed not of feelings but of the ideas and doctrines that give expression to attitudes and feelings, we find ourselves raising exactly the same questions.

The thesis at hand, that collective relationships expressed through mutually comprehensible emotions emerge not from what is specific to the given individual but what is shared and common, pertains all the more so. Specifically, in the talmudic corpus we take up the social expression of attitudes. We turn then to matters of doctrines and institutions, and issues of governance of groups based on a compact of common values. These all together constitute politics, for the secular world, and theology, for the religious one. In the setting of Judaism, with its interest in what people do as much as in what they think, the whole reaches the surface of everyday life in what we call halakkah, the rules and laws of life. If, then, we can trace the context of consensus and the progress through which consensus is achieved, we find ourselves providing an exceptionally suggestive example for the inquiry into the interplay between the individual and the group, specifically the formation of collective attitudes out of individual experiences.

What sort of history then? Not manifest but latent, not political but interior, not public but the perspective of a single class of persons—specifically, sages. But the sages who wrote and preserved the books addressed a larger world, and, as a matter of fact, exercised a measure of influence and authority in that world. Accordingly, in the talmudic corpus we have the end result of half a millennium of the process of attaining concurrence, the achievement of what was at first a caste and class consensus but what was at the end a national compact and agreement. Israel, the Jewish people, in late antiquity produced a minority, the sages under discussion, which to begin with coalesced on its own, and then won adherence to its views, through coercion and persuasion alike, among the nation as a whole. So when we ask what sort of history we may expect from the sources, we find a remarkably relevant sort of discourse. We deal with an example of the long-term formation of collective doctrine, social theory shared among people in diverse times and places, subject to transmission, moreover, from the special circumstances in which the theory took shape to distant and wholly other conditions confronted by the Jewish nation later on. The sources come down from late antiquity because people agreed to copy and preserve them. They came to that agreement because what they found in the sources laid claim on truth and authority. The fundamental theses of the sources attained that status of utter self-evidence that made possible debate on everything but the fundamental issues. These were settled in late antiquity. Where, when, how they were settled, what sort of "experiences of common life, of similar and contemporaneous reactions to the shock of identical situations and encounters of the same nature," in Febvre's language, produced these components of a common consensus and endowed them with self-evidence—these are the issues before us.

In the conditions of contemporary debate on the nature of historical study, the interest in generalization and the analysis of collectivities, the concern for comparison of group to group, the interest in small details and how these typify large trends, the concern for politics and the influence of ideology—in these conditions the talmudic historian finds remarkably relevant what in itself is remote, particular, and rather special. What we have is a collective biography of a well-organized political and religious estate. But the constant reference to individual opinion characteristic of the sources allows for attention to the individual as well. The vigorous debate, the close study of modes of argument as much as of the substance, likewise allow us to address the formation of shared modes of thought. Self-evidence, in the documents, is not conferred by politics alone but is achieved by argument. Professor Tilly states:

The genius of social science history is twofold. First, its central method—collective biography of one kind or another—preserves individual variability while identifying dominant social patterns. Second, its focus on social relationships rather than psychological states remains our surest guarantee of reconstructing how ordinary people of the past lived out their days and made the choices that cumulate into history. Social science history, properly conceived, is the ultimate people's history.

So far as we wish to trace collective biography, our documents exemplify precisely the kind of sources that make that work feasible. So far as we take up the issues of social relationships, both within a social group and also between that group and the outsider, the sources of the talmudic canon address these precisely. That is why we claim that, by criteria of contemporary historical debate, the kind of history that bears the adjective "talmudic" and that emerges from a rather circumscribed body of sources indeed falls smack in the center of historical learning today. The studies collected in this volume take up many specific problems of the second and first centuries B.C.E. Biography, politics, social and cultural history—all come under sustained discussion. But, in all, these results of a historical character gleaned from documents of Judaism add up to what we may call "the ultimate people's history". how people agree to remember what has happened to them and collectively, publicly to portray their own past.

CONTENTS

VOLUME 8 (PART 2)

Contents

ACKNOWLEDGMENTS

Lieberman, Saul, "The Martyrs of Caesarea," Annuaire de l'Institute de Philologie et d'Histoire Orientales et Slaves, 1939–44, 7:395–446. Courtesy of Prof. Jacob Neusner.

Lieberman, Saul, "Palestine in the Third and Fourth Centuries," *Jewish Quarterly Review*, n.s., 1945–46, 36:329–70; 1946–47, 37:31–54. Reprinted with the permission of the *Jewish Quarterly Review*. Courtesy of Yale University.

Lieberman, Saul, "Roman Legal Institutions in Early Rabbinics and in the Acta Martyrum," *Jewish Quarterly Review*, n.s., 1944–45, 35:1–48. Reprinted with the permission of the *Jewish Quarterly Review*. Courtesy of Yale University.

Lieberman, Saul, "The Martyrs of Caesarea," *Jewish Quarterly Review*, n.s., 1945–46, 36:239–53. Reprinted with the permission of the *Jewish Quarterly Review*. Courtesy of Yale University.

Mann, Jacob, "Changes in the Divine Service of the Synagogue Due to Religious Persecutions," *Hebrew Union College Annual*, 1927, 4:241–310. Courtesy of Yale University.

Marmorstein, A., "Judaism and Christianity in the Middle of the Third Century," *Hebrew Union College Annual*, 1935, 10:223–63. Courtesy of Yale University.

Neusner, Jacob and Jonathan Z. Smith, "Archaeology and Babylonian Jewry," *Near Eastern Archaeology in the Twentieth Century, Essays in Honor of Nelson Glueck*, 1970, pp. 331–47. Reprinted with the permission of Doubleday & Co., Inc.. Courtesy of Yale University.

Neusner, Jacob, "Babylonian Jewry and Shapur II's Persecution of Christianity from 339 to 379 A.D.," *Hebrew Union College Annual*, 1972, 43:1–26. Reprinted with the permission of the Hebrew Union College-Jewish Institute of Religion. Courtesy of Prof. Jacob Neusner.

Neusner, Jacob, "Rabbis and Community in Third-Century Babylonia," *Religions in Antiquity: Essays in Memory of Erwin Ramsdell Goodenough*, 1970, pp. 438–59. Reprinted with the permission of E. J. Brill. Courtesy of Yale University.

Pawlikowski, John T., "Roman Imperial Legislation on the Jews: 313–438 C.E.," *Central Conference American Rabbis Journal*, 1970, 17(1):35–51. Reprinted with the permission of the Central Conference of American Rabbis. Courtesy of Yale University.

Segal, J. B., "The Jews of North Mesopotamia Before the Rise of Islam," *Studies in the Bible Presented to M. H. Segal, Publications of the Israel Society for Biblical Research*, 1964, 17:32–63. Courtesy of Yale University.

Wacholder, Ben Zion, "Chronomessianism: The Timing of Messianic Movements and the Calendar of Sabbatical Cycles," *Hebrew Union College Annual*, 1976, 46:201–18. Reprinted with the permission of the Hebrew Union College-Jewish Institute of Religion. Courtesy of Yale University.

Wallach, Luitpold, "Church and State in the Later Roman Empire," *Jewish Quarterly Review*, n.s., 1943–44, 34:261–62. Reprinted with the permission of the *Jewish Quarterly Review*. Courtesy of Yale University.

Weiss, Abraham, "The Third-Century Seat of Calendar Regulation," *Proceedings of American Academy for Jewish Research*, 1944, 14:267–76. Reprinted with the permission of the American Academy for Jewish Research. Courtesy of Yale University.

Zeitlin, Solomon, "Encyclopaedia Judaica: The Status of Jewish Scholarship," *Jewish Quarterly Review*, n.s., 1972–73, 63:1–28. Reprinted with the permission of the *Jewish Quarterly Review*. Courtesy of Yale University.

Zeitlin, Solomon, "Judiasm and Professors of Religion," *Jewish Quarterly Review*, 1969–70, 60(3):187–96. Reprinted with the permission of the *Jewish Quarterly Review*. Courtesy of Yale University.

Zeitlin, Solomon, "Spurious Interpretations of Rabbinic Sources in the Studies of the Pharisees and Pharisaism," *Jewish Quarterly Review*, n.s., 1974–75, 65(2):122–35. Reprinted with the permission of the *Jewish Quarterly Review*. Courtesy of Yale University.

Zeitlin, Solomon, "The Encyclopaedia Judaica: A Specimen of Modern Jewish Scholarship," *Jewish Quarterly Review*, n.s., 1973–74, 64: 74–91. Reprinted with the permission of the *Jewish Quarterly Review*. Courtesy of Yale University.

Zeitlin, Solomon, "The Plague of Pseudo-Rabbinic Scholarship," *Jewish Quarterly Review*, n.s., 1972–73, 63:187–203. Reprinted with the permission of the *Jewish Quarterly Review*. Courtesy of Yale University.

THE MARTYRS OF CAESAREA

The vast field of Talmudic literature fared ill at the hands of the historians. The historians were no Talmudists; the Talmudists were no historians. The former either entirely ignored the Rabbinic sources or misused them. Every single passage of Talmudic literature must be investigated both in the light of the whole context and as a separate unit in regard to its correct reading, meaning, time and place. Thanks to the modern methods of investigation which have begun to exert their influence on the work of the very small circle of Talmudic scholars, their researches often result in quite exact conclusions in the domain of history. The simple rule should be followed that the Talmud may serve as a good historic document when it deals in contemporary matters within its own locality. The legendary portions of the Talmud can hardly be utilized for thi‑ purpose. The Palestinian Talmud (and some of the early Midrashim) whose material was produced in the third and fourth centuries contains valuable information regarding Palestine during that period. It embodies many elements similar to those contained in the so-called documentary papyri. The evidence is all the more trustworthy since the facts are often recorded incidentally and casually. The Rabbinic literature has much in common with the non-literary papyri and the inscriptions.

Although the following paper cannot serve as a classical example of the above statement, since the nature of the subject-matter has sometimes compelled the author to resort to a probable conjecture, the reader can nevertheless learn that Talmudic literature is a valuable source for the events of its own time.[*]

I.

Our information on the life of the Jews in Caesarea in the third and fourth centuries is derived in the main from Rabbinic sources.

---

[*] Unless otherwise specified all the dates mentioned in this article are C. E. The English translations of the Greek text of M. P. are mainly borrowed from Lawlor and Oulton. In the translation of the Syriac version I followed in the main W. Cureton.

1

But the Rabbis did not write history; they did not intend to leave behind records of the events which affected Jewish life. They taught and explained the law; they instructed the people to behave morally and piously, and only incidentally mentioned facts and events bearing on Jewish life in Caesarea.[1] Thus any additional Caesarean source of that time may shed more light on this obscure period.

Happily we possess a contemporary literary work composed by an inhabitant of this city in which the writer reports facts and events of which he was an eye-witness, or had first-hand information. This is the work of Eusebius of Caesarea which is known by the name *De Martyribus Palaestinae*.

The shorter Greek recension[2] of this work follows the eighth book of Eusebius' Ecclesiastical History in most of the printed editions. A Syriac version of the longer recension[3] was published by W. Cureton in 1861 from a manuscript bearing the date 411.[4] The complicated and difficult problem of the relation of these two recensions to each other and to the *Historia Ecclesiastica*[5] is of no great importance for our subject. It should however be pointed out that the Greek original of the Syriac version was almost certainly written by Eusebius himself[6].

The longer version abounds in minute details which were of special interest and value to the people who were familiar with the scenes of action, and "it was written mainly for the instruction of the Christians of Caesarea"[7]. And what can be more valuable or trustworthy than an account written by a witness for people who were in a position to judge the facts by their own information? At least one aspect of the life of Caesarea, reflected in the treatment of the local Christians in the beginning of the fourth century, is fully available. The behavior of the Roman government, of its officials and their victims is clearly mirrored in these accounts. When we analyze

---

[1] See S. LIEBERMAN, *The Talmud of Caesarea*, p. 13 ff.
[2] Preserved in the group ATER of the mss. of the *Hist. Eccles.*
[3] Greek fragments were published in *Analecta Bolland.* XVI, 129 ff. and printed by Schwartz in his edition underneath the shorter Greek text.
[4] See CURETON's Preface, p. V, n. c.
[5] See N. G. LAWLOR, *Eusebiana*, p. 279 ff.; *ibid.* p. 285 ff.
[6] See LAWLOR, *ibid.* p. 179.
[7] LIGHTFOOT as quoted by LAWLOR, *ibid.* p. 180. This is, of course, true for the Greek original as well.

the information supplied by the Rabbinic sources of the time and compare it with the records of Eusebius we see how remarkably they supplement one another.

In the third and fourth centuries Caesarea was a center of Jewish learning. Many Jewish sages resided and taught there;[8] among them was the famous Jewish scholar, R. Abbahu, an older contemporary of Eusebius. He was the head of the Rabbinic academy in Caesarea and one of the pillars of the Palestinian Talmud. A learned and cultured person,[9] he was also an influential member of the community, who frequently came in direct contact with the government.[10] His connection with the government is particularly well illustrated in a passage in TP[11] where it is told that a woman named Tamar complained to the proconsul of Caesarea of the decision of the Tiberian Rabbinic court which condemned her. The Rabbis of Tiberias asked R. Abbahu to intercede in their behalf. He replied in a cryptic letter that he had already appeased three *lictores*[12] but had not succeeded in "sweetening" Tamar, who persisted in her "bitterness".[13] Thus, the connections of R. Abbahu with the *officium* of the proconsul in Caesarea are well attested.

---

[8] See BACHER, *Die Gelehrten von Caesarea* in MGWJ 1901, p. 302 ff.

[9] See his biography by S. G. PERLITZ in MGWJ 1887, p. 60 ff.; BACHER, *Die Agada der Paläst. Amoräer*, II, 88 ff.; *Jewish Encyclopedia*, I, p. 36; comp. also LIEBERMAN, *Greek in Jewish Palestine*, p. 21 ff.

[10] Comp. TB *Kethuboth*, 17a and parallels; BACHER, *ibid.* p. 94, n. 5 and n. 6.

[11] *Megilla*, III. 3, 74a.

[12] The text reads ליקטורין which was variously interpreted. See KRAUSS, *Lehnwörter* etc. p. 301 s. v. לאיקטור. Comp. also M. SCHWABE in *Tarbiz*, vol. I. fasc. 3, p. 111, n. 1. The explanation of Mussafia that the word means *lictores* was disregarded by Jewish scholars; but his interpretation can hardly be doubted. These *lictores* are members of the *officium* of the proconsul of Caesarea. They were in a position to withdraw the complaint of Tamar from the office before it came to the notice of the proconsul. The Rabbis frequently mention the officials of the *apparitio*. They know the *exceptor* (See KRAUSS, *Lehnwörter* etc. p. 410b), the *speculator* (*ibid.* p. 409b), the *quaestionarius* (*ibid.* 514b), the *commentariensis* (*ibid.* 510) and other members of the *officium*. These officials are very common in the documents of the Christian Martyrology (See E. LE BLANT, *Les persécuteurs et les martyrs* etc. p. 304 ff). The latter talk indiscriminately of the *spiculatores, lictores, exceptores* and *commentarienses* (*ibid.* p. 304-305). It is by way of bribing the *spiculatores* and the *exceptores* that the Christians obtained the protocols from the archives of the judge (*ibid.* p. 4, n. 3), and it is quite natural that R. Abbahu applied to the *lictores* for help in withdrawing the complaint of Tamar.

[13] It seems that the *lictores* agreed to withdraw the complaint on condition that Tamar should not object to it.

TB[14] bears witness to his good relations with the *Minim*. It is related there that R. Abbahu praised the great scholarship of Rab Safra before the *Minim*, whereupon the latter exempted him from paying taxes for a number of years. But when R. Safra failed to explain a difficult passage in the Scriptures they were annoyed with him. Herford[15] assumes that the *Minim* were Jewish Christians[16] and were therefore interested in the Bible. It is, however, hard to believe that R. Abbahu was on good terms with Jewish-Christian apostates. It is also unlikely that *Jewish* Christians, apostates from Judaism should grant a Rabbi exemption from taxes only because of his learning.[17] The simple meaning of the text is that the *Minim* were Gentile[18] Christians. Scholarly intercourse between Jews and Gentile Christians in Caesarea was practiced long before the time of R. Abbahu. Origen used to consult the Jews on Scriptural matters, and his contemporary R. Hoshaiah (of Caesarea) discussed religious questions with Christians.[19] In R. Abbahu's time the school of Christian instruction founded by Pamphilus functioned in Caesarea, where texts of the Scriptures were diligently studied.[20] Eusebius himself discussed his Biblical interpretations with Jewish authorities,[21] and he expressly mentions his Jewish teacher.[22] It is therefore no wonder that the Gentile Christians in Caesarea had a special respect for the Rabbis, who were well versed in the Scriptures.

But when did the incident with R. Safra take place? When were the Christians of Caesarea in a position (as contractors or collectors) to exempt a scholar from taxes? When did R. Abbahu have the

---

[14] *'Abodah Zarah*, 4a.

[15] *Christianity in Talmud* etc. p. 270.

[16] Comp. also his article in *Jewish Studies* (in memory of George A. Kohut), p. 359 ff.

[17] Herford's (*Christianity* etc., p. 268) suggestion that the *Minim* engaged R. Safra as their teacher has no basis whatever in the text of the Talmud. Nor is there any hint to the effect that the *Minim* engaged R. Safra as an assistant in collecting the imperial revenue, an opinion erroneously attributed by Herford (*Ibid.* p. 269) to Bacher.

[18] Comp. S. LIEBERMAN, *Greek in Jewish Palestine*, p. 141, n. 196.

[19] See BACHER, *Die Agada der Pal. Amor.* I, p. 92; KRAUSS, *JQR* V (1893), p. 139 ff.

[20] See below p. 421.

[21] See his com. *on Is.* XXXIV. 1, *Migne, PG* XXIV, 361b; *ibid.* XXII. 15.19, 249c. Comp. KRAUSS in *JQR* VI (1894), p. 84 ff.

[22] *Ibid.* XXXIX. 1, 361b.

friendly discussions with the Christians?[23] Since the activity of R. Abbahu in Caesarea was mainly concentrated in the time of Diocletian and his Caesars, it is pertinent to ask whether the incident with R. Safra occurred before, during or after the persecutions of the Christians by Diocletian and Galerius.

It is accepted among Jewish scholars that R. Abbahu died long after the Edict of Toleration was promulgated (311). Frankel remarks[24] that R. Abbahu was already "a great man" in 312, and it seems that he places his death much later than 312.[25] But there are few Rabbis whose death can be dated with such exactness as that of R. Abbahu.

Before we establish the time of his death let us try to estimate the approximate time of his birth. We read in the Midrash:[26] וימלוך תחתיו יובב בן זרח מבצרה. אמר ר' אבהו... כבר היתה מלכות עקורה מאדום ובאת בצרה וכיפקה לה מלכים וכו'. "And Jobab the son of Zerah of Bozrah reigned in his stead (Gen. XXXVI. 33). R. Abbahu said . . .'Kingship had already been uprooted from Edom (=Rome), whereupon Bozrah came and supplied her with kings, etc'." It is clear that this saying could be uttered not later than 249 when Philippus Arabs,[27] a native of Bostra, was still reigning in Rome jointly with his son. The "legal" dynasty of the Severi finished with the murder of Alexander Severus (235). The Thracian peasant Maximinus[28] usurped the purple, and was killed (238); the two emperors, Balbinus and Maximus, elected by the Roman Senate were murdered in their turn by the praetorians after a reign of three months. Gordian the Third did not occupy the throne more than half a dozen years; he was murdered by his own soldiers (244). What wonder then that the Jews saw in it a sign from Heaven, an

---

[23] Comp. BACHER, ibid. p. 96-98. The story told in TB ('Abodah Zarah, 28a) about a Christian physician who wanted to poison R. Abbahu seems to disagree with the Palestinian tradition (See TP ibid. II. 2, 40d).
[24] Mebo Hayeruschalmi, 63ᵇ.
[25] The writer in the Jewish Encyclopedia, I, 36a puts his death around 320.
[26] Bereshith Rabba, LXXXIII. 3, 998ᵉ.
[27] KRAUSS, Monumenta Talmudica, V, p. 61, correctly surmised that R. Abbahu referred to this king.
[28] On the social and economic situation of the Roman empire of that time see ROSTOVTZEFF, The Social and Economic History of the Roman Empire, p. 387 ff. 401 ff. and notes, ibid. p. 615; idem, Musée Belge, XXVII (1923), p. 236 ff.

omen that kingship was going to be uprooted from Edom (Rome)?[29] Bostra, on the other hand, supplied Rome with a king who intended to establish a new dynasty!

In the reign of Decius, when the purple returned to a Roman Senator, and especially during the subsequent anarchy, the remark of R. Abbahu would have had no justification. If we suppose that the latter was at least around twenty when he applied the verse of the Bible to the reign of Philippus we can place his birth about 229.[30] Thus R. Abbahu was more than seventy years old at the beginning of the persecutions (303), and it is natural to expect his death at that time or somewhat later.

Eusebius gives us the key to the solution of this problem. He describes a miracle that happened in Caesarea between the middle of November and that of December 309. He says:[31]

Αἰθρία ἦν καὶ λαμπρὸς ἀὴρ καὶ τοῦ περιέχοντος κατάστασις εὐδινοτάτη. εἶτα ἀθρόως τῶν ἀνὰ τὴν πόλιν κιόνων οἳ τὰς δημοσίας ὑπήρειδον στοάς, δακρύων τινὰ τρόπον οἱ πλείους σταλαγμοὺς ἀπέσταζον . . . λῆρος ἴσως καὶ μῦθος εὖ οἶδ' ὅτι δόξει εἶναι τὸ ῥῆμα τοῖς μεθ' ἡμᾶς, ἀλλ' οὐχ οἷσπερ ὁ καιρὸς τὴν ἀλήθειαν ἐπιστώσατο.

"It was fine weather, the air was clear, the state of the atmosphere very calm. Then all at once many of the pillars of the city which support the public porches let fall drop by drop as it were tears . . . I know well that my word will seem, perchance, idle talk and a fable to those who come after us, but not to those who have had its truth accredited on the spot." Eusebius' story is a report of a witness of the time and place of the miracle. The Syriac version[31a] states that "some of the people who saw it are still alive." The truth of the story is well attested. We find unexpected corroboration of the fact in Rabbinic sources. We read in the Babylonian Talmud:[32]

[32a]כי נח נפשיה דר' אבהו אהיתו עמודי דקסרי דמעי.   "When R. Abba-

---

[29] It was asserted that a similar feeling dominated the Roman soldiers when they heard that Caracalla was murdered, and they had no more Antoninus as emperor. *Ingens maeror obsedit omnium pectora, quod Antoninum in re publica non haberent, existimantium quod cum eo Romanum esset imperium periturum.* (Hist Aug. Diadum. I. 2).

[30] The period in which R. Abbahu's teachers, colleagues and pupils lived does not contradict this date.

[31] M. P. IX. 12.

[31a] Cureton, p. ו"ה.

[32] Mo'ed Katan, 25b.

[32a] So mss. See Rabbinovicz, *Var. Lect.* 87 n. 40.

hu died the pillars of Caesarea shed tears."[33] Some mediaeval authorities[34] interpreted the passage not as the account of an actual incident but as the phrase of a eulogist who bewailed R. Abbahu by calling upon the pillars of Caesarea to weep over his death. However the Palestinian Talmud disproves this interpretation. There it is stated:[34a] (read: אמרון) אמרין. אמרין דקיסרין עמודיא בכן אבהו ר' דמך כד (read: מדיעין) אמר לון ישראל ידעין אמר לון אינון אלא מריעין לית כוריא רחיקייא כמה דקריביא מריעין (read: מדיעין) (read: ידעון). "When R. Abbahu died the pillars of Caesarea wept. The Kuthim (= Samaritans) said: 'They are only perspiring.'[35] The Jews said to them: 'May the distant ones perspire as the near ones are perspiring".[36] The Palestinian Talmud cites it as a fact and not as a phrase of the eulogist.

It is very remarkable that Jewish scholars who noticed the passage of Eusebius took it only as a parallel to the Talmudic story. M. Joël[37] says clearly: "In der Deutung des Factums unterscheiden sich *die Zeiten* (my italics) und die Menschen." This seems also to be the opinion of Levy and Bacher.[38] Yet there is no doubt that both Eusebius and the Rabbinic source refer to the same facts.

From the words of the sources we see that the inhabitants of Caesarea took the drops of water on the pillars as a miraculous mani-

---

[33] The Syriac *M. P.* relates that the pillars emitted spots as if they were of blood; דרמא ... ורמא. הוא דמן כאפא ... בדמות דמעא שחלא הות. (Comp. also below n. 35). LAWLOR and OULTON (I, p. 375, n. a) emend (on the basis of the Greek and the Menaea) דטא into דט[ע]א. But TB *ibid.* tells (immediately after our passage): *At the death of R. Jose the roof gutters at Sepphoris ran with blood.* TP *'Abodah Zarah* (III. 1, 42ᶜ) *repeats the story and explains* : אמרין דיהב נפשיה על גזורתא. "Some say because he risked his life for the sake of circumcision" (See Tosaphoth Mo'ed Katan, 25ᵇ, s. v. שעמד). This is probably the source of *Midrash Tehilim* (IX. 19, ed Buber p. 89) which numbers R. Jose among the Ten Martyrs. Thus the miracle of the appearance of blood was associated with the sympathy of the inanimate objects with the martyrs, exactly the same as in the case of Eusebius.

[34] MEʾIRI and RAN *ad loc.* in the "*Harry Fischel Institute Publications*," pp. 143, 68. R. Salomo b. Ha-jathom (p. 119 bottom) explained that the pillars *perspired* (read: הזיעו instead of הזיפו) and looked like weeping.

[34]a *'Abodah Zarah ibid.*

[35] The Rabbis probably transmitted the words of the Samaritans literally, the verb as they used it. In the Syriac translation of Luke (XXII. 44) we read (*Palest. Syr. Lect.*, London 1899, p. 79) : ואתעברה דעתה : היך שליאן דאדם. Comp. below n. 39.

[36] I. e., let the Samaritans perspire like the pillars (which mourn and display sympathy over the death of R. Abbahu).

[37] *Blicke in die Religionsgeschichte* etc. I. p. 9.

[38] *Agada der pal. Amor.* II., 103 n. 3.

festation, as a phenomenon that was not known to them before, and
it is therefore impossible to admit that the same wonder occurred
twice in the same town within no more than a quarter of a century.
It is clear that the Jews and the Christians refer to the same occurrence. The Jews were sure that nature shed tears over the death of
R. Abbahu, the Samaritans (of whom R. Abbahu was the bitterest
enemy, see below) took them as drops of perspiration,[39] and the
Christians saw in them nature's reaction to the atrocities of the persecutors.

Now we can fix the death of R. Abbahu (at the age of approximately eighty) on a bright autumn day in 309.[40] R. Abbahu's connections with the government, with the men of the proconsul's officium, with Christian scholars and tax collectors should be placed
in the time before and during the persecution but not after them.

The Christians seem to have been numerous and powerful in
Caesarea in the time of Diocletian; their relations with the Jewish
leaders of the community were tolerably good. But there was another
minority problem in Caesarea at that time, one which reached its
crisis with the persecutions. The Samaritans constituted the largest
minority in that city.[41] This follows from TP[42] which implies that
only together did the Jews and the Gentiles form a majority over
the Samaritans.[43] The final break between the Jews and the Samaritans seems to have taken place at the time and as a result of the
persecutions.

----

[39] Among the omens which foretold the death of Commodus his biographer records (*Hist. Aug. Com.* XVI. 5) that *"In the Minucian Portico
a bronze statue of Hercules sweated for several days"*. (Herculis signum
aeneum *sudavit* in Minucia per plures dies). Comp. also *Pap. Ox. X.*
1242, l. 51-52 (ἡ τοῦ Σαράπιος προτομή... αιφνίδιον ἴδρωσεν)
and C. B. WELLES in the *Transactions and Proceedings of the American
Philological Association,* vol. LXVII (1936) p. 13. WELLES refers to
JOANNES LYDUS, *De ostentis, Proem.* 8. Comp. also *"The Itinerary of
R. Benjamin of Tudela"*, ed. GRÜNHUT (Hebrew), p. 91⁵. The existence
of this superstition does not invalidate the credibility of the Talmudic
sources and Eusebius. The contemporary evidence of the latter and the
life-like controversy of the Jews with the Samaritans recorded by the
Rabbis cannot be discredited. It may incidentally be noted that many of
the miracles recorded in the *Hist. Aug. ibid.* are very similar to those
related by JOSEPH. *Bel. Jud.* VI. 5. 3. 288-300. Comp. TAC. *Hist.* V. 13.
[40] See *Appendix,* I.
[41] A fact overlooked by scholars, as far as I know.
[42] Demai, II. 1, 22c.
[43] המינין האסורין בקסרין . . . הרי אלו שביעית היתר בשאר שני שבוע
דמאי . . . . . וזהו ודאי ? ישראל מתקנין וגוים פטורים. ישראל וגוים
רבים על הכותים .

8

Many diverse reasons have been offered for the excommunication of the Samaritans,[44] but the main reason is disclosed by the Palestinian Talmud:[45] עַל ידי עילא, "on a pretext." The formal reasons were only an excuse; there were intrinsic causes for it. As one of the formal grounds it was alleged that the Samaritans were suspected of worshipping a dove on Gerizim.[46] The Talmuds, however, did not take this charge seriously. TB quotes it in the name of a Babylonian Rabbi (III/IV c.) and TP ascribes it to "some one" (ואית דבעי מימר)! The Babylonian Rabbis probably drew the information from a polemical source. The Samaritans accused the Jews of practising idolatry in the Temple,[47] and the Jews retorted[48] by charging that the Samaritans worshipped idols on Gerizim.[49] The Palestinian Rabbis repeated this Babylonian opinion on the vague authority of "some one," but they themselves admitted that the Samaritans were outlawed ע"י עילא, "on a pretext." Among other reasons TP (ibid.) tells: ואית דבעי מימר כד סליק דיקליטינוס מלכא להכא גזר ואמר כל אומייא ינסכון בר מן יודאיי ונסכון כותייא ונאסר יינן "And some propose this explanation: When Diocletian came here he issued an edict decreeing: All nations except the Jews must offer libations. The Kuthim (Samaritans) complied and [therefore] their wine was declared forbidden." Graetz[50] remarked that the Talmud here refers to the persecutions of Diocletian, condemning the Samaritans because they did not suffer martyrdom for the sanctification of His Name. Halevy[51] justly objected to Graetz's view, contending that the Samaritans did not offer libations of their own accord but under threat of death, and in this case they do not deserve to be outlawed on account of their transgression of the Law. He, therefore, surmises that the Samaritans were in a position to avail themselves of the privileges of the Jews by identifying themselves with them. But they did not utilize the opportunity, and by offering libations they silently forfeited all claims to be regarded as Jews. This opinion

----

[44] TP 'Abodah Zarah, V. 4, 44d and TB Hullin 6ᵃ.
[45] Ibid.
[46] TP and TB ibid.
[47] See Montgomery, The Samaritans, p. 91. n. 32.
[48] [: ibid.; De es ita Sabba, LXXXI. 3, 974ᵃ.
[49] See Montgomery, ibid, p. 320.
[50] Geschichte, IV², p. 279, n. 1.
[51] Doroth Harishonim, IIᵃ, ch. 25, p. 340, n. 46.

is hardly tenable. The Samaritans did not worship idols. As a matter of fact they were very conservative and clung tenaciously to the
precepts of the Bible. They would have never failed to avail themselves of the *privilegia Judaica*, if they had been in a position to do
so. If they *willingly* worshipped idols under the very eyes of the
Jewish community in Caesarea, the Rabbis would not have had to
look for reasons to excommunicate them; they would never have admitted that the Samaritans were outlawed only on a pretext. It is
therefore evident that the local governors who frequently enforced
the imperial decrees at their own discretion and who knew the differences between the Jewish and Samaritan communities in Caesarea did not exempt the Samaritans from libations[52] to the gods of
the state. They sacrificed under duress, and the Palestinian Talmud
did not therefore regard these Samaritan libations as a serious reason
for their excommunication, and treated it merely as the opinion of
"some one." All the grounds for the break attributed here to the
"some one" are among the latest anonymous strata of the Palestinian
Talmud.

The item referred to in the Talmud is, according to Graetz,[53]
the promulgation of the fourth edict of Diocletian[54] in 305. It seems
more plausible that the Talmud referred to the enactment of the edict
in Caesarea, when registers of all the citizens were drawn up, and
heralds summoned all men, women and children to assemble in the
temples and offer libations to the idols (306).[55] The people of Palestine probably heard that the Caesar Maximin Daia visited Caesarea
shortly afterwards (November 20, 307), celebrating the birthday[56]
there with a beastly and gruesome spectacle.[57] The Jews subsequently confused Maximin with Diocletian who had already abdi-
cated at that time. At any rate it is hardly possible to admit that
Diocletian visited Palestine when his Fourth Edict arrived there.[58]

---

[52] See Montgomery, *ibid.* p. 93, but the reading of the text (Origen.,
Contra Celsum II. 13) he refers to is doubtful.
[53] Above n. 50. Comp. also Marmorstein, *Revue des Études Juives*, IIC,
p. 26. I cannot share his view.
[54] M. P. III. 1.
[55] *Ibid.* IV. 8.
[56] Of Diocletian. See the notes of Lawlor and Oulton, II. p. 327.
[57] M. P. VI. 1.
[58] See Lawlor etc. *ibid.*, p. 324, and comp. Lactantius, *de mort. persec.*
XVI.

Happily, another passage in TP, combined together with a Christian inscription, sheds light on this difficult problem. According to the opinion of R. Johanan,[59] the Jews are allowed to transact business with the heathen on the *Saturnalia* and *Kalendae* if the latter do not observe them. It seems that already in the time of R. Johanan (middle of the III c.) the heathen of Palestine were rather indifferent to the rites of idolatry and, therefore, the Jews were sometimes permitted to transact business with them on their festivals. This was especially true in Caesarea in the beginning of the fourth century. In a city where the majority of the population consisted of Samaritans, Jews and Christians the heathen appear to have entirely neglected the idolatrous ceremonies.

Eusebius[60] cites an order by Maximin (fifth edict, 309) to the effect "that care should be taken that all the people in a mass, men with their wives and household, *even babes at the breast*[61] {ὑπομάζιοι παῖδες) should offer sacrifices and libations . . . and the unbelieving heathen found fault with the absurdity of what was done, on the ground that it was harsh and unnecessary (for to their mind the thing was disgusting and burdensome)." Lawlor and Oulton[62] justly remarked: "It was a call to the heathen to observe the customs, so generally neglected, of their nominal religion. It may have been the part of the edict to which they objected as unnecessary and burdensome."

Now we shall be able to understand the obscure passage in the Palestinian Talmud to which it was referred above. It reads:[63]

ר' אבהו בעי והדא טקסיס דקיסרין מכיוון דסוגייא שמריין כפלחין היא צריכה[64] הדא טקסיס דרוקיס. The commentaries, dictionaries and mod-

----

[59] TP 'Abodah Zarah, I. 2, 39c. Comp. TB ibid. 8ª and 65ª.

[60] M. P. IX. 2-3.

[61] Comp. CYPRIAN de lapsis 25 and 26 (On the libation of minors, see *Texte aus Aegypten*, ed. Meyer, No. 15 l. 10). In a city like Caesarea, where the Samaritans formed the largest minority (see above), it was well understood, for the latter used to initiate their sucklings in religious rites. See Prof. A. Halkin's article in the *Proceedings of the American Academy for Jewish Research*, vol VII., p. 47 and my remarks in קרית ספר vol. XV., p. 57.

[62] Vol. II., p. 330.

[63] 'Abodah Zarah, I. 2, 39c.

[64] So Cod. Leyden, an obvious mistake for דרוקום. The usual spelling of dux, both in Aramaic and Syriac, is דוכום or דוכם but דוקום is also found. See PAYNE SMITH, Thesaurus, s. v. דוקאם and דוקום.

ern scholars completely misunderstood both the words and the meaning of the passage. Some scholars[64a] altered the word טפסים into טיכום,
τεῖχος, wall; some [64b] explained it to mean order, arrangement, and
some[64c] translated it "garrison." The word דוקים on the other hand
was understood as a name of a place.[64d] And after all these explanations the passage offers no sense.

But in truth the phrase needs no emendation whatever. We now
know from papyri, inscriptions and literary sources[64e] that in the
fourth century τάξις had quite a definite meaning, namely, *officium*. Thus it is clear that טפסים דקיס.יין means ἡγεμονικὴ τάξις, the
officium of the governor of Caesarea, and   טפסים דדוקום means the
δουκικὴ τάξις, the *officium* of the *dux Palaestinae*.

The correct translation of the passage is: "R. Abbahu said: 'The
[members of the] *officium* of Caesarea (i. e. of the proconsul), since
many of them are Samaritans,[65] are considered as people who observe the ceremonies [of Saturnalia and Kalendae] but the [status
of the] *officium* of the *dux*[66] is doubtful.'" Here R. Abbahu explicitly states that the Samaritans are worshippers of idols in the plain
sense of the word. This could only have had any meaning in the
time of the persecutions. The heathen were heedless of their ceremonies, and, according to the opinion of R. Johanan (see above),
the Jews could be allowed to transact business with the *officium* of
the proconsul on the Saturnalia and the Kalendae. But the Samaritan members of the *officium*, who were afraid of losing their positions and feared suspicion of their indifference to the State religion, did not disregard the required ceremonies and did not fail to

---

[64a] Levy II, 184, Kohut IV, 71 and others.
[64b] Krauss, *Lehnwörter* etc. 267 and *Additamenta ad librum Aruch Completum*, p. 206.
[64c] Jastrow 535.
[64d] See previous notes. Add ספר הישוב, Jerusalem 1939, p. 35. The word
טפסים is translated there (under a question mark) "holiday"!
[64e] See below n. 66.
[65] The Rabbinic sources usually call them "*Kuthim*," but the name   שמריין
is also employed (See TP 'Abodah Zarah, V. 4, 44d; Bereshith Rabba,
LXXXI. 3, 974²; ibid. XCIV. 7, 1178¹. ⁵ and elsewhere). The Samaritans
used this name for themselves, saying: "*We observe the holy Law and
are called Observers*" (Montgomery, *Samaritans*, p. 318. Comp. also
Z. Ben-Haim, *Tarbiz*, vol. X, p. 340 n. 38). R. Abbahu hinted here
with biting irony that the "Observers" are worshippers of idols.
δουκικη τας.ς. See Preisigke, *Wörterbuch* etc. vol. III (Aemter), p.
168ᵇ, Dessau *apud* Calder, *Expositor*, 1909 (vol. VII), p. 308, n. 2.

worship idols on these two festivals. Therefore R. Abbahu prohibited dealings with the *officium* (of the proconsul) on such days.

The decision may have concerned his own person. We have seen above[67] that he was on good terms with the officials of the proconsul and sometimes "appeased" them. In the interests of such relations R. Abbahu may have formerly (i. e. before the persecutions of Diocletian) followed the general practice of sending gifts to the *officium* of the proconsul on the Saturnalia.[68] But subsequently he had to decide against it because of the Samaritan officials who were to be treated like idol-worshippers of the old stamp.

But it is very interesting that the Caesarean Rabbi clearly realized the difference between the degree of duress under which the members of the *officium* of Caesarea (ἡγεμονική τάξις) worshipped and that of the *taxis* of the *dux* (δουκική τάξις). He is more lenient with regard to the latter than to the former. As a matter of fact the whole weight of R. Abbahu's statement seems to lie in his doubt regarding the status of the worshippers in the δουκική τάξις.

This distinction throws more light on the famous inscription of Julius Eugenius.[69] We learn from it that according to a late edict of Maximinus the Christian officials of the ἡγεμονική τάξις were ordered to offer sacrifices without the option of leaving the service; they had to remain therein.[70]

W. M. Calder has demonstrated by force of good arguments[71] that στρατευσάμενος and στρατεία in our inscription could refer only to military and not to civil service. The new edict of Maximin concerned only the army but the old laws regarding the civil officials remained in force; they were to be dismissed.[72] The distinction in

---

[67] P. 397.

[68] As the Christians did, see TERTULLIAN, de fuga, XIII (end); comp. also, idem, de idolatria, X. For the Jewish practice see TB 'Abodah Zarah, 64ᵇ (bottom), 65ᵃ.

[69] Monumenta Asiae Minoris Antiqua, ed. CALDER, I, 170. Comp. the bibliography in the Journal of Roman Studies, X, 1920, p. 44. Add: H. GRÉGOIRE, in Byzantion, VIII, p. 68-69.

[70] M. Ἰού. Εὐ[γέ]νιος Κυρίλλου Κέλερος Κοιησσέως βουλ. στρατευσ[ά]μενος ἐν τῇ κατὰ Πισιδίαν ἡγεμονικῇ τάξι... ἐν δὲ τῷ μεταξὺ χρόνῳ κελεύσεως [φ]οιτησάσης ἐπὶ Μαξιμίνου τοὺς Χρ[ε]ιστιανοὺς θύειν καὶ μὴ ἀπα[λ]λάσσεσθαι τῆς στρατεί[α]ς...

[71] Expositor, 1909 (vol. VII), p. 319 ff. Comp. also RAMSAY, Luke the Physician, p. 342 ff.

[72] See EUSEBIUS, Hist. Eccl. VIII. 2. 4; M. P., Introduction. The "scourging" mentioned by LACTANTIUS (de mort. pers. X) refers to the "household" of the palace.

the Palestinian Talmud between the *officium of Caesarea* and that
of the *dux* can be a distinction only between the civil and the military offices, for in those countries where the institution of *dux* was
introduced all the cohorts were under his command.[73] Under this
arrangement the offering of libations was absolutely incumbent only
upon the members of the δουχιχὴ τάξις. The members of the
ἡγεμονιχὴ τάξις could resign their posts and, as private citizens,
remain loyal to their faith. The Caesarean Rabbi ruled on the basis
of the respective status of the civil and military officials in connection with the character of their worship of idols.[74]

The officials of the governor would be dismissed if, as Christians
or Samaritans, they refused to offer sacrifices, but thereafter as private people could easily avoid the worship of idols on the Saturnalia
and the Kalendae. Since the Samaritan officials held on to their
posts despite their knowledge that as government officials they
would have to attend and participate in idolatrous rites and ceremonies, R. Abbahu regarded them as voluntary worshippers of idols.
On the other hand, the officials of the δουχιχὴ τάξις, as military officers, were *now* forbidden to leave the service, and consequently R.
Abbahu was unable to decide whether to regard their participation
in the festival rites as voluntary or not.

This explains the distinctly negative attitude of R. Abbahu towards the Samaritans. Their officials in Caesarea, afraid of losing
their posts, offered sacrifices and libations even when they had a
way of avoiding it (by resigning from their positions). They did it
for mercenary reasons. Not in vain did R. Abbahu reproach the
Samaritans:[75] אבותיכם לא קילקלו מעשיהם, אתם קילקלתם מעשיכם
"Your fathers did not corrupt their ways but you have corrupted
your ways." In face of the Christian acts of martyrdom the eagerness
of the Samaritan officials to cling to their positions seemed shameful and disgraceful. From their behavior the Caesarean public inferred that the Samaritans offered not compulsory but voluntary li-

---

[73] The ἡγεμονιχὴ τάξ-- of Pisidia, which apparently did not have a *dux*
at that time, included soldiers and military officers. See CALDER, *ibid.*
p. 309 ff.
[74] Since R. Abbahu died in 309, the question regarding the officials of the
δουχιχὴ τάξις was raised by him between 307 and 309. This may solve
the doubts of RAMSAY, *Luke the Physician*, p. 345.
[75] TP *'Abodah Zarah* V. 4, 44d.

14

bations. Hence the opinion of the "Some" (see above) in the Palestinian Talmud. The Samaritans were then finally outlawed and excommunicated by the Jews.

To sum up: Caesarea of the time of the persecutions had a small heathen minority; the overwhelming majority consisted of Samaritans, Jews, Christians and, probably, "Fearers of Heaven"(θεοσεβεῖς). The heathen minority was quite indifferent to the rites and ceremonies of its nominal religion. The social life of the community was complicated by the "Samaritan problem," the group with whom the Jews were on bad terms at that time. The relations between the heathen and the Jews and the Christians were tolerably good.

II.

A natural question arises. What was the attitude of the Jews at that time towards the Christian martyrs in Palestine? Eusebius twice[1] mentions that the Jews were present at the place where the Christians were tortured,[2] but he says nothing about a provocative attitude of the Jews towards the oppressed, persecuted Christians. If there had been any animosity on their part against the latter, Eusebius,[3] a contemporary eye-witness, would not have failed to mention it.[4]

We have good evidence to the effect that far from remaining indifferent to the fate of Christian martyrs in Caesarea the Rabbis approached this question from the point of view of Jewish law.

In the beginning of the fourth century Christianity was no longer the creed of Jewish heretics,[5] for it had long become the faith of the Gentiles. The persecutions of the Christians were not limited to the denial of Jesus,[6] but required actual worship of idols. In the

---

[1] M. P. VIII. 1 and the passage quoted in the following note.
[2] M. P., p. 52: הלך יהודיא בעלדבבא מצלא הוא. כגיאא גיר מנהון בהו עדנא
הה הוו בריכין . "He prayed for the Jews, the enemies, for many of them at that time stood around him." Comp. also M. P. VIII. 1, quoted below.
[3] He did not forget to record the behavior of the Smyrnaean Jews during the martyrdom of Polycarp in the II century (Hist. Eccl. IV. 15, 26-29, 41, 43), a fact which was known to him only from the Epistle of the Smyrnaeans. He would, therefore, not have overlooked any misconduct of the Jews of his own time and city if there had been any.
[4] Comp. Juster, Les Juifs dans l'empire Romain. I. 52 n. 4; 53, n. 1.
[5] Whose beliefs were a threat to the integrity of Judaism, and with whom no Jewish Rabbinic authority could compromise. These were always considered by the latter as the greatest enemies of Judaism.
[6] Comp. Just. Mart., Apol. I. 31; Euseb. Hist. Eccl. IV. 8, 4.

legal formulations of the previous edicts of persecution it was clearly stated that punishments would be directed against: *eos qui se cultores Dei confiterentur,*[7] "Such as professed to be *fearers of God.*"

The Jews saw simple "Fearers of Heaven" among the Christian martyrs. They were probably present at the Stadium of Caesarea[8] when Agapius of Gaza was tortured. They heard him expounding his views. In his long confession[9] there is only one single allusion to the life of Jesus; to all the rest any orthodox Jew could subscribe. The Jews saw him, a Gentile, refusing to offer libations to the idols, declaring: I am going to die in order "to bear witness to you all, to the end that you may know and worship the one and only God, Creator of heaven and earth[10] etc."

What were the feelings of the Jews in this and similar cases? Eusebius himself discloses them. He tells us[11] that in a certain town of Palestine[12] the Jews were present at the trial of the Christians. "They watched that amazing contest and surrounded the court of justice on all sides . . . they were the more agitated and rent in their hearts[13] when they heard the heralds of the governor crying out and calling the Egyptians by Hebrew names etc."[14] Eusebius is here a very trustworthy witness of the fact that the Jews were "agitated and rent in their hearts" at the terrible scene of trial.

Their feelings can be very easily understood. The Gentiles refused to sacrifice to the idols and suffered terrible tortures because of their refusal. What is the Jewish legal point of view? The question was brought before the Rabbinic academies. We read in TP:[15]

ר' אבונא בעא קומי ר' אימי גוים מהו שיהו מצווין על קידוש השם ...
ר' נסא בשם ר' לעזר שמע לה וכו' "R. Abuna asked R. Imi:[16] 'Are the Gentiles bound to sanctify His Name'[17]...R. Nassa in the name

---

[7] ULPIAN, *as quoted by* LACTANTIUS, Div. *Inst.* V. 11. *See* LE BLANT, *Les persécuteurs* etc., p. 51 ff.
[8] See above n. 1.
[9] M. P., ed. CURETON, n. ב"כ. Assem. and Menaea, but missing in the Greek short recension VI. 4.
[10] *Ibidem.*
[11] M. P. VIII. 1, according to the Syriac version and the Menaea.
[12] On the name of the town see below.
[13] CURET. p. כ"מ: הוי מצטרין ונפשתהון יתיראית דין הוו פקעין
[14] *Ibid.* In the sixth year of the persecutions, i. e. in 309.
[15] *Shebi'ith,* IV. 1, 35ᵃ and parallel. Comp. TB *Sanhedrin,* 74ᵇ.
[16] Rabbis of the III, IV c.
[17] I. e. to suffer martyrdom for the sake of the sanctification of His Name.

of R. Eleazar[18] learned it etc." The passage in TP comes from the
school of Caesarea.[19] It was not a purely academical question but a
problem coming directly from the stadium of that city.

Although the decision was that Gentiles were *not bound* to suffer martyrdom for the sanctification of His Name, it was only a release from a duty but not an order not to do it. What did the Rabbis
think of the Gentile who did not avail himself of the exemption and
did suffer martyrdom for His Name? All pious Gentiles were promised
their share in the future life;[20] those of them who suffered for their
good deeds were especially singled out,[21] and there can be no doubt
that the pious Gentiles who suffered martyrdom for their refusal to
offer sacrifices to idols were deemed deserving of one of the noblest
ranks in the future world. Moreover, it seems to me that we have a
direct allusion in Rabbinic literature to the status of those martyrs.

We first have to establish the correct name of the city where
"the Jews surrounded the court of justice on all sides and were rent
to their hearts etc."[22] The Greek[23] does not mention it; the Menaea
names this city Diocaesarea. But the Syriac version[24] records:

אית דין מדינתא חדא רבתא סגיאא באנשותא בארעא דפלסטינא וכולהון
עמוריה יהודיא הוו. ומתקריא בלשנא ארמיא לוד ויונאית מתקריא דיוקסריא.

"There is a certain great and populous city in the land of Palestine,
all of whose inhabitants are Jews. It is called *Lod* in the Aramaic
tongue, and in Greek it is called Diocaesarea." Cureton[25] is of the
opinion that Diocaesarea (= Sepphoris, צפורי) is a mistake for
Diospolis,[26] and that the scene took place in Lod (= Lydda).
Lawlor and Oulton[27] accept the reading Diocaesarea (= Sepphoris).

----

[18] This R. Eleazar is R. Eleazar the Second (See FRANKEL, *Mebo Hayerushalmi*, 111[b] and I. LEWY, *Interpretation des I Abschnittes des paläst.
Talmud-Traktats Nezikin*, Vorwort, p. 18, n. 2). He was a contemporary
of R. Nassa (See TP *Gittin*, V. 1, 46c), i. e. fl. in the first half of the
IV c.
[19] The preceding sentence in TP is explicitly recorded in the name of "the
Caesarean Rabbis." R. Nassa likewise was a Caesarean Rabbi. See
LIEBERMAN, "The Talmud of Caesarea", p. 11.
[20] *Tosephta Sanhedrin*, XIII. 2, 434[10] and elsewhere
[21] See TB *'Abodah Zarah*, 10[b]; ibid. 18[a]; *Midrash Tehilim*, IX. 13, ed.
Buber p. 89 and elsewhere.
[22] See above p. 410.
[23] *M. P.* VIII. 1.
[24] CURETON, p. ב"מ.
[25] P. 65.
[26] On p. ב"כ it is spelled: דייוספ׳ל
[27] II. p. 328-329.

17

They refer to the *Chronicle* (p. 320) from which it appears that the population of Diocaesarea was entirely Jewish. But the same source provides similar information about Diospolis. From Rabbinical literature we know that both cities had a predominantly Jewish population at that time.

However there seems to be internal evidence that the city in question was not Sepphoris but Lydda[28] as maintained by Cureton. Ninety-seven confessors, who were Egyptians sent from their native land to Palestine, had their fate foredoomed in advance. They were subsequently condemned to labor in the copper-mines of Phaeno. Since the way from Caesarea to Phaeno led via Lydda,[29] the proconsul Firmilian naturally passed through that city together with the assembly of the confessors on their way to Phaeno, and tried once more to break their determination by the trial in Lydda. This city was the crucial station on the ὁδὸς βασιλική from where the confessors could either return to Egypt as free people or continue to Phaeno as convicts. The choice of Lydda as the scene of the last trial[30] was based on psychological considerations. But to argue that Firmilian took ninety-seven men with him to *Palaestina Secunda*, to a Jewish town in Galilee, is to assume a hardly understandable procedure. There are therefore good reasons for accepting the reading Lod as the genuine one.

It seems that the trial of the confessors in Lydda and the terrible tortures they withstood before the eyes of the Jews who "surrounded the court of justice on all sides and were agitated and rent to their hearts" at that sight left its traces in the contemporary Rabbinic writings. We find a very obscure oracle in the Midrash:[31] ר׳ אחא

---

[28] The Syriac version uses the old Semitic names of the places more frequently than their Greek equivalents. M. P. I. 1 (ASSEM. See CURETON, p. 52) has אורשלם instead of the Greek *Aelia*. *Ibid.* (CURET. p. ד twice; *ibid.* p. ל׳ה twice): בישן instead of Scythopolis. *Ibid.* X. 2 (CURET. p. ל׳ח) : בית גוברין instead of Eleutheropolis (but p. ה׳ : אלותרפולס).

[29] See LIEBERMAN, *The Talmud of Caesarea*, p. 14.

[30] Ammian. Marcel. (XIX. 12.8) relates: "As the theatre of torture and death (of those who were suspected of high treason) Scythopolis was chosen, a city of Palestine which for two reasons seemed more suitable than any other: because it is more secluded and because it is midway between Antioch and Alexandria from which cities the greater number were brought to meet charges." (transl. of Loeb Class. Libr.). For these very two reasons (in our case publicity and not seclusion was desirable) we have to prefer the reading Lod.

[31] *Koheleth Rabba*, IX. 10, ed. Romm 24b.

הוה מתחמר למיחמי אפוי דר' אלכסנדרי. איתחמי ליה בחלמיה. הראהו
ב' מילין. הרוגי לוד אין לפנים ממחיצתם. ברוך שהעביר חרפתן של
לוליאנוס ופפוס ואשרי מי שבא לכאן ותלמודו בידו "R. Aha longed
to see the face of R. Alexandri [in a dream]. He appeared
to him in his dream and showed him *two*[32] things: There is
no compartment beyond that of the martyrs of Lydda;[33] blessed
be He Who removed the shame of Lulianus and Pappus and happy
is he who came here [to the next world] equipped with learning."[34]
The last part of the vision is quite understandable. R. Aha was comforted to hear that the man who dies in possession of learning, the
man whose doubts are solved by his learning, is happy in Paradise.
But the first part of the vision is very obscure. According to the
commentaries the martyrs of Lydda were Julianus and Pappus, the
famous two brothers who suffered martyrdom in the first half of the
second century; the "shame" refers to their martyrdom and the "removal of the shame" to the punishment of their persecutor.[35] It is
difficult to understand why the martyrdom of these two men was
styled "shame" and why R. Aha's mind was disturbed by a fact
which happened about two hundred years previously. However the
reading in our editions is a correction by the author of מתנות כהונה
who quotes it in the name of an old book. The genuine reading is
in *ed. pr.*:[36]

הראהו ג' מילין הרוגי לוד אין לפנים ממחיצתם בדור [37]שהעביר חרפתו
[38]של לוליאנוס ואשרי וכו' . "He showed him *three* things: There is

---

[32] Counting the martyrs and the "Shame" as one thing. (See below).
[33] I. e. nobody occupied a higher place than they in Paradise.
[34] In TB *Pesahim*, 50ᵃ, (and its parallel) a similar vision is ascribed to R.
Joseph the son of R. Joshua b. Levi (III c.), but the Palestinian *Ruth
Rabba* (Ch. III, beginning) does not mention the martyrs. This proves
that we have in TB a later combination of two different stories. *Koheleth
Zuta, ad loc.*, p. 122-123 follows the later tradition of TB. Comp. also
יהוסי הנאים ואמוראים s. v. לוי בן זכרי ed. FISHMAN, p. 56. The
author quotes our Midrash and not *Koheleth Rabba!* For further details see *Appendix III.*
[35] See *Megillath Ta'anith*, end, scholion, and the sources mentioned in
Prof. Finkelstein's article in *Essays and Studies in Memory of L. R.
Miller*, p. 38, n. 7.
[36] Pesaro and Constantinople.
[37] Read: ברוך במחיצתם.
[38] Ed. Venice 1545, f. 84ᶜ reads: הראה ב' מילין. הרוגי לוד אין לפנים;
מבהציתם בדור שהעבירו חרפתו של לוליאנוס ואשרי וכו' . BENVENISTE
(*Oth Emeth*, ed. Salonica, f. 114ᵇ) quotes the variant ברוך (to the
word בדור) but records no other variant to this passage.

no compartment beyond that of the martyrs of Lydda; blessed be
He Who removed the shame of Lulianus and happy is he etc.'" According to this true reading the martyrs of Lydda and the "shame"
etc. are two entirely different things. Moreover, there is no hint of
Pappus; only Lulianus is mentioned.[39] But who is this Lulianus,
and what is the shame connected with his name?

It seems to me that this Lulianus is none other than Julianus[40]
the Roman Emperor (361-363), and that the "Shame of Julianus" is
an abbreviated euphemism for the shame brought upon the Jews
by their consent to his decision to rebuild the Temple in Jerusalem.[41] Jewish scholars[42] frequently asked why the Rabbinic sources
did not explicitly mention Julian's promise to rebuild the Temple.
Graetz[43] correctly conjectured that the Rabbis were not too enthusiastic about the restoration of the former Jewish splendor by a
heathen emperor. The Third Temple will be rebuilt by the Messiah and not by a Roman heathen.[44] Our R. Aha seems to have
been of a different opinion; he maintained that the Temple will be
rebuilt before the advent of the kingdom of the house of David.[44a]
Bacher[45] correctly saw in it an allusion to his agreement to the undertaking of Julianus. It was after Julian's death (363), when it
was clear that his undertaking failed, that R. Aha saw the vision;
"Blessed be He Who removed the shame of Lulianus,"[46] for a Jewish Messiah will rebuild the Third Temple and not a Gentile king.
R. Aha himself subsequently formulated his opinion succinctly:[47]
דרך כוכב מיעקב. ממי דרך כוכב ועתיד לעמור מיעקב ‎ "There shall

---

[39] The wrong addition of Pappus to Julianus is quite understandable; these
two names are very frequently associated in Rabbinic literature, see
Bereshith Rabba, LXIV. 10, 710; TP *Shebi'ith*, IV. 2, 35ᵃ and above n.
35.

[40] See *Appendix*, II.

[41] See J. BIDEZ, *La vie de l'empereur Julien*, p. 306 and notes *ibid.*

[42] See BACHER in *JQR.* X, 1898, p. 168.

[43] See BACHER, *ibid.*

[44] Comp. *Pesikta Rabbathi*, ed. FRIEDMANN, f. 160ᵃ. See also *Rashi*,
Sukka, 41ᵃ (bottom), whose explanation is a quotation from *Tanhuma*,
as it follows from *Tosaphoth Shebu'oth*, 15ᵇ (top). For the expression
used by this *Midrash*, comp. *Sifre* II, 352, ed. FINKELSTEIN, p. 410² ff.

[44a] TP *Ma'aser Sheni* V. 2, 56ᵇ.

[45] *Ibid.* p. 169-170 and *Agada der Paläst. Am.* III, p. 111-112.

[46] Dr. JOHANAN LEWY demonstrated the motives and plans of Julian, which
dictated his decision to rebuild the Temple (Hebrew quarterly *Zion* vol.
VI. p. 22 ff.). I fully accept his conclusions and there is no wonder that
the Jews considered their consent "a shame."

[47] TP *Nedarim*, III. 12, 38ᵃ. Comp. BACHER, *ibid.*

come forth a star out of Jacob' (Num. XXIV. 17). Out of whom shall the star come forth and remain permanently? Out of Jacob." This saying was probably uttered after his vision.

Thus we see that two points of the vision were contemporary questions which disturbed R. Aha personally, and it is reasonable to seek the third point (the martyrs of Lydda) in the same direction. We can presume *a priori* that it was a hard and perplexing question which troubled the Jewish sage.

Our R. Aha was a Lyddan Rabbi,[48] born in the last decades of the third century. He may have had first-hand information of the trial of the Egyptian confessors (in 309) in his native town. Perhaps he himself, as a youth, was present at the terrible spectacle and witnessed the sympathy which the Jewish crowds showed towards the martyrs. The problem might have disturbed his mind for a long time.

He was very old when he saw the vision. The failure of Julian's promise was already known to him, and therefore the dream could not have occurred earlier than June 363, probably a few months later. Ammian. Marcell. relates[49] that comets were seen at Antioch in broad daylight (*et visa sunt interdia sidera cometarum*) shortly after the death of Julian. He talks as an eye-witness, for he says that he was in Antioch at that time, and he tries to explain the phenomenon. At any rate this was the rumor current then in the orient. The Palestinian Talmud[50] records: "The star (Mercury?) was seen at midday when R. Aha died."[51] If we take these legends seriously[52] we may assume that the death of R. Aha shortly followed that of Julian. The "shame of Julian" has just now been removed, the

---

[48] See TP *Sanhedrin*, I. 2, 18c-d and elsewhere. Comp. BACHER, *Agada etc.*, III p. 106 ff.

[49] XXV. 10. 2.

[50] *'Abodah Zarah*, III. 1, 42c.

[51] ר' דפך בר. אחא איתחמי כוכבא בטיהרא. Comp. also TB *Mo'ed Katan*, 25b and RABBINOVICZ *ad loc.* p. 87 n. 50.

[52] A similar legend is related on another occasion. We read in the *Hist. Aug.* (Pert., XIV 3): *"On the day before he died, very brilliant stars were seen near the sun in the day-time"* (Stellae etiam iuxta solem per diem visae clarissimae ante diem quam obiret). Comp. also the Christian legends in MIGNE PG XXXIII, 1169; *ibid.* 1176 ff.; H. GRÉGOIRE, *Revue de l'Université de Bruxelles*, vol. 36 (1931), pp. 254-255.

doubts of R. Aha regarding the martyrs[53] of Lydda were finally solved, and he was comforted to see the last part of his vision: "Happy is he who came here equipped with his learning."

III.

The history of the Jews in Palestine is rich in martyrs and martyrdoms. In the time of Antiochus Epiphanes the Jews, though suffering tortures and death, remained faithful to the precepts of the Law. After the destruction of the Second Temple the Jewish prisoners endured tortures and death and did not utter a single word contrary to the law.[1] In the time of Hadrian they did not betray the Law in the face of threats of death and tortures of vengeance.

The Jews took their martyrdom calmly and as a matter of course. They tried to avoid it, going so far as to disguise their nationality by dressing as non-Jews.[1a] But when they were discovered and had to face the worst, they submitted to martyrdom quietly. They sanctified His Name by showing that they loved Him with all their soul (see Deut. VI. 5). The names of the simple people who suffered tortures and death for the sanctification of His Name are not known. The dates of the martyrdom of the great, learned Jewish leaders were not transmitted to posterity (we find them only in the later writings). The Jews did not commemorate those days; there was no martyr-cult in Israel.

Apparently there were no Jewish martyrs in Palestine during the persecutions by Diocletian and Galerius. Yet the Jewish victims in the time of Hadrian, according to the Rabbis of the II-IV centuries, suffered tortures very similar to those described by Eusebius in M. P. The martyrs of both religions were tormented in the same

---

[53] The original has הרוג "the slain." The Egyptian confessors were not slain, but "they were deprived of the use of their left feet . . . their eyes were dug out with the sword and then finally destroyed by fire." (Comp. LACT. de mort. pers. ch. XXXVI.). The term הרוג could easily be applied to them (Comp. TB Hullin, 35b and parallels).

It goes without saying that the interpretations regarding the Martyrs of Lod and the Shame of Julianus are entirely independent. Whereas the former is only a probable conjecture, the latter is almost a certainty.

[1] JOSEPH., Contra Ap. I. 8. 43: ἤδη οὖν πολλοὶ πολλάκις ἑώρανται τῶν αἰχμαλώτων στρέβλας καὶ παντοίων θανάτων τρόπους ἐν θεάτροις ὑπομένοντες ἐπὶ τῷ μηδὲν ῥῆμα προέσθαι παρὰ τοὺς νόμους καὶ τὰς μετὰ τούτων ἀναγραφάς.

[1a] Bereshith Rabba, LXXXII. 8, ed. THEODOR-ALBECK p. 984*. Comp. also SUET. Domitian. XII.

city (Caesarea), by the same Roman government. The difference of almost two centuries did not change conditions greatly in the pro-cedure of the *apparitores* in Caesarea.

S. Krauss published two useful articles bearing on our subject. One, in which he collected much material from the Talmuds and Midrashim, deals[2] with the tortures of the body mentioned in an-cient Rabbinic literature.[2a] In the other he presents the Talmudic and Midrashic material bearing on the tortures of the famous "Ten Martyrs."[3] In the latter he made an attempt to compare the Rab-binic records on the Jewish martyrs with those of the various Chris-tian *acta martyrum*. However, Krauss did not discriminate well be-tween Tannaitic (II c.), Amoraic (III-V c.) and later Midrashic sources. His investigations are mainly concentrated around the later Midrashim. These have little historical value for our purpose, since they utilized material from earlier Midrashim concerning individual martyrs, which they related to the traditional number of the Ten Martyrs and embellished them with the usual Aggadic elements.[4] The only trustworthy accounts are those of the Tannaitic and Amo-raic works. It is to be highly regretted that the Tannaitic sources have only very scanty material on this subject.[5] The stories of mar-tyrdom are reported by them occasionally and incidentally, only for the purpose of teaching a moral lesson,[6] and their silence on details is not decisive. The Amoraic writings provide more ample informa-tion.

------

[2] Hebrew quarterly דביר, I. p. 88 ff.
[2a] KRAUSS (p. 104) quotes the Rabbinic Aggada which charged Manasseh with the assassination of Isaiah by means of sawing his body, remarking that this kind of torture as an actual punishment is not referred to any-where else in Rabbinic literature. This statement is not correct. In *Bereshith Rabba* (LXV. 22, 742') this cruelty is mentioned. Comp. also LE BLANT, *Les persécuteurs* etc., p. 295, n. 4 and the figure *ibid*. For the torture by means of a copper   μίλιον (KRAUSS, *ibid.*, p. 110) see LE BLANT, *ibid.* p. 292 and the figure on that page.
[3] השלה Vol. XLIV (1925), p. 10-22, 106-117, 221-233.
[4] See Prof. FINKELSTEIN's article on the Ten Martyrs in *Essays and Studies in Memory of L. R. Miller*, p. 29 ff. Comp. n. 33, above ch. I.
[5] See *Mekhilta Bahodesh*, VI. ed. HOROVITS, 277'; *ibid. Mishpatim* XVIII, 313' (and parallels in *Aboth deR. Nathan*, ed. SCHECHTER, p. 114 and *Semahoth* ch. VIII. Comp. *Appendix* IV); *Sifre* II, sect. 307, ed. FIN-KELSTEIN, p. 346 and *Tosephta Sota*, XIII, 319'. See also *Midrash Hag-gadol*, Genes., p. 510 (Comp. the wording of R. Hiyya B. Abba's state-ment with that of *Shir Hashirim Rabba* II. 7).
[6] Comp. *Mekhilta Mishpatim, ibid.*

However, the difference between them and the Tannaitic presentation of such stories is very instructive. We read, for instance, in Sifre:[7]

כשתפסו את ר' חנינה בן תרדיון נגזרה עליו גזירה לישרף עם ספרו.
אמרו לו נגזרה עליך גזירה לישרף ועליך עם בפרך ... אמרו לאשתו נגזרה
על בעלך גזרה לישרף ועליך ליהרג ... אמרו לבתו נגזרה גזרה על אביך
לישרף ועל אמך ליהרג ועליך לעשות מלאכה ...עמד פילוסופוס[8] על
אפרכיא[9]‏   שלו אמר לו מרי אל תזוח דעתך ששרפת את התורה
שממקום שיצאת הזרה לה לבית אביה, אמר לו למחר אף דינך כיוצא
באלו, אמר לו בשרתני בשורה טובה שמחר יהא חלקי עמהם לעולם הבא

"When R. Haninah b. Teradyon was seized [while teaching the Law] sentence was passed on him to be burnt with his Book (i. e. the Torah). They informed him: 'Sentence has been passed upon you to be burnt together with your Book'... they informed his wife: 'Sentence has been passed upon your husband to be burnt with his Book and on you to be executed' ... they informed his daughter: 'Sentence has been passed on your father to be burnt, on your mother to be executed, on you to "do work"' (i.e. to be prostituted)[10] ... Then one philosopher stood up before the proconsul[11] and said: 'My master do not become proud [of the fact] that you burnt the Scroll of the Law, for it has returned to the place whence it was issued, to its Father's house.' He said to him: 'Tomorrow you will be punished like them.' He retorted: 'You have announced good tidings to me; tomorrow my share will be with them in the future world.'"

The final redaction of this text took place either at the end of

---

[7] *Ibid*. The story is related quite incidentally on account of the verses cited by the martyrs.
[8] The majority of mss. read: פוליסופוס. πολύσοφος, very wise.
[9] An Aramaic form o איפרכוס‎. Comp. *Koheleth Zuta*, VIII. 4 (*Yalkut* ibid. 989): איפרכיא באיש‎.
[10] *Midrash Haggadol* Gencs., ed. Schechter. p. 420, quotes from the Sifre: שיעדיך ביך מלאכה בשבת‎; the *Exempla* of the Rabbis (Gaster, p. 41) read · ועליך למעשות מלאכה בשבת‎ "On you to do work on Saturday"! The Yemenite sources misunderstood the expression מלאכה‎. This word when used in connection with a woman had a definite meaning, as above, in Palestine. It meant: [σώματι] ἐργάζεσθαι. This is clearly evident from *Bereshith Rabba*, LXXXVII. 7, 1072². The parallel sources state explicitly that the daughter was condemned to a house of infamy. Comp. however TB *Megilla* 12ᵇ.
[11] Literally: "before *his* proconsul". The philosopher was a member of the *consilium* over which the proconsul presided.

the second or at the beginning of the third century. Thus, the source used by the Sifre was most probably contemporary with the event (during the fourth decade (?) of the second century), and is most authentic as regards the details of the execution. If we analyze the single elements of the story we find there nothing unusual in the Roman practice. R. Hanina was sentenced to be burnt alive (together with his book)[12] for having taught the Law. This penalty was frequently inflicted on the Christian Martyrs.[13] His daughter was condemned to prostitution, a punishment often mentioned by the Christian Church Fathers.[14] Finally a certain "philosopher" expressed sympathy for the martyr, and was threatened with death—nothing unusual.

But the Babylonian Talmud[15] describes in detail the execution of our saint. Three elements attract our attention in the account recorded in TB: first, that the Jewish sage was consumed by a slow fire and had wet tufts of wool placed over his heart; second, that his disciples advised him to open his mouth in order to let the fire enter the inside of his body, but he refused; third, that the executioner voluntarily threw himself into the fire.

The first detail was frequently practiced on the Christian martyrs of Palestine at the beginning of the IV c.[16] Urbanus, the governor of that country, had the feet of Apphianus wrapped in cotton soaked in oil and set them on fire.[17]

The second detail is very interesting. Le Blant[18] has already called attention to the habit of Christian martyrs tortured by fire of opening their mouths in order to put an end to their sufferings.[19]

---

[12] Comp. Mekhilta, Bahodesh, VI: מה לך יוצא לישרף על שקראתי בתורה "Why are you being lead out to be burnt? Because I read the Tora." Comp. also TP Ta'anith VI, 69ᴬ and our conclusions at the end of this chapter.

[13] Comp. Le Blant, Les persécuteurs etc., p. 65 ff.

[14] See Le Blant, ibid. pp. 171, 176, 206; Lawlor and Oulton, Eusebius, II, p. 326; F. Augar, Die Frau im römischen Christenprocess, p. 40 ff. Our source shows that this sentence was practiced under Hadrian.

[15] A "Baraitha" in 'Abodah Zarah 18ᴬ.

[16] See M. P. III. 1; Krauss in השׁלח XLIV (1925), p. 228.

[17] M. P. IV. 12; Krauss, ibid.

[18] Mélanges d'archéologie et d'histoire, V (1885), p. 102 ff.; idem, Les persécuteurs etc., p. 239 ff.

[19] M. P. XI. 19; Prudentius. Peristeph. Hymn. III, 159-160. Hananiah, Mishael and Azariah in the furnace are portrayed in the early Christian pictures as standing with open mouths amidst the flames; see Le Blant, ibid., p. 291. Comp. also Lucian, de morte Peregrini 21 (end).

However, R. Hanina did not open his mouth to the flames; he preferred to endure the terrible pains and not to return the deposit of the King until He Himself chose to take it.

As to the third scene, the death of the executioner, there is an open divergence between the Sifre [20] and the Talmud.

From the comparison of the two scenes portrayed in the above sources it may seem that the later one is colored by the contemporary procedure. However, there is no doubt that the display of cruelty of the Caesarean *apparitores* did not change much during the almost two centuries separating the Jewish from the Christian martyrs.

The great R. 'Akiba was beyond any doubt the most famous and the most popular Jewish martyr. Many legends have been woven around his death;[21] we shall however quote only the oldest records of his martyrdom. We read in the Palestinian Talmud:[22]

ר' עקיבה הוה מיתדין קומיטונוס (ט)רופוס הרשע אתת ענתה דקרית
שמע שרי קרי ונחך, אמר ליה סבא, סבא או חרש את או מבעט בייסורין
את וכו' "R. 'Akiba was tried[23] before the impious Tineius Rufus.[24] The time for reciting the Shema' arrived. - He commenced to recite it and became very joyful. 'Old man, old man', said he (i. e. Rufus), 'art thou a magician or dost thou defy torture'?[25] etc." He was detained in prison for a long time. According to a later source[26] he was confined there for *two*[27] years. During

---

[20] Here it is the philosopher, a member of the *consilium* (above n. 11), who protested against the sentence. Some hundred and fifty years later (298) St. Cassianus, the shorthand-writer of the court, threw down his note books in protest of the sentence pronounced over St. Marcellus. He declared to the judge: *iniquam eum dictasse sententiam.* (RUINART, *Acta Sincera,*[2] p. 305).

[21] See *Midrash Mishle,* IX. 2, ed. BUBER, p. 61 and the sources referred to by KRAUSS, *ibid,* p. 108.

[22] *Sota,* V. 7, 20c and parallel.

[23] but TB *Berakhoth* 61b records: והיו סורקין את בשרו במסרקות של ברזל "And they combed his flesh with iron combs." This seems to have been the most common torture in Caesarea at the beginning of the IV c. The Syriac version of M. P. mentions these cruel סרקא very frequently. See ed. CURETON (translation),pp. 6[18], 15[31], 22[28], 28[29], 38[11], 40[28], 41[8], 45[18] and 47[23].

[24] See SCHÜRER, *Geschichte,* I[4], p. 467.

[25] The Christian martyrs were also accused of defying torture by means of sorcery. See LE BLANT, *Les Persécuteurs* etc., p. 217.

[26] *Midrash Shir Hashirim,* ed. GRÜNHUT, f. 5b.

[27] The text has: ב' . . . . ., as noted by the editor *ad loc.* The scribes have subsequently resolved the abbreviation to עשרים (see below there). The earlier sources (*Tosephta Sanhedrin,* II. 8, 417[2]) seem to imply three years, but the meaning is not quite clear. See TB *Sanhedrin,* 12a.

that time his disciples had access to him,[28] and he contrived to teach them the Law there. Even the governor himself used to conduct discussions with R. 'Akiba,[29] in which he was always worsted by the wisdom of the latter. Subsequently the treatment of R. 'Akiba became harsher, and the Rabbis had to outwit the guards in order to get legal decisions from him.[30] When the difficulties increased four hundred denarii had to be expended in order to obviate them.[31]

The great saint breathed his last in prison during the month of Tishri[32] and by a miracle his body was removed from there and brought to eternal rest in the vicinity of Caesarea.[33] TB[34] is the first source to inform us that he died of being tortured by means of iron combs at the hands of the proconsul of Caesarea.

Pamphilus, the teacher of Eusebius, was undoubtedly the most distinguished and learned man among the Christian martyrs of Caesarea.[35] He founded a school of Christian instruction in that city, collected a big library and was particularly interested in the establishment of the authentic text of the Bible; he created a center of Christian learning, and copies of the Bible were brought there from different churches for the purpose of fixing the correct text.[36] He was thrown into prison around November (the latter Teshri), 308 and kept there about two years.[37] During his imprisonment the governor Urbanus "made a trial of his wisdom by questions and answers"[38] or "tested his knowledge of rhetoric and philosophy."[39]

---

[28] See TB 'Erubin. 21b, Pesahim, 112a (in the name of a "Baraitha", probably of the III c.).

[29] Bereshith Rabba, XI. 5. 92s; TB Sanhedrin, 65b; Pesikta Rabbathi, XXIII, ed. FRIEDMANN, f. 119v; Tanhuma Terumah, 3; ibid. Tazri'a, ed. BUBER, p. 35 (all the sources apparently not earlier than the IV c.). There is, however, no hint in the sources that the discussions took place during R. 'Akiba's imprisonment.

[30] See TP Yebamoth, XII. 6, 12d; Comp. TB ibid. 105b (the sources are not later than the III c.).

[31] TB ibid. 108b (not later than the III c.).

[32] Midrash Mishle, IX. 2 (ed. BUBER, p. 62); Halakhoth Gedoloth, ed. HILDESHEIMER, p. 194 (on the time of the source see the following note).

[33] Midrash Mishle, ibid. (original source not earlier than the IV c.).

[34] See above n. 23 (The source seems to be a later "Baraitha", III c.?). Comp. also TB Menahoth, 29b.

[35] M. P. VII. 4-5.

[36] See M. P. V. 2; ibid. ed. CURETON, p. 37 ff.; SCHWARTZ in PAULY-WISSOWA, Real-Encyclopädie, VI. 1372, 1373; J. STEVENSON, Studies in Eusebius, p. 23 ff.; LAWLOR and OULTON, Eusebius, vol. II, p. 331-332.

[37] M. P. XI. 5. On the exact time see LAWLOR, Eusebiana, p. 199.

[38] M. P. Syriac version, ed. CURETON, p. 25¹³.

[39] Ibid. Greek version, VII. 5.

All that time he continued his regular activity of transcribing and correcting the Scriptures,[40] and his pupils were able to visit him.[41] This tolerant attitude on the part of the Roman officials did not save him from the tortures of the combs.[42] He was executed[43] in 310, and his body was buried in honor after having been miraculously preserved from carnivorous wild beasts.[44]

What a striking parallel to the account of R. 'Akiba's life and death in the prison of the same city![45]

However, although the tortures and the means of executions of the Christian and Jewish martyrs (during the Hadrianic persecutions) were very similar, the judicial procedure in the trial of these two groups differed considerably. Mommsen[46] maintained that originally no special law was in force against Christianity and that the Christians were nominally charged under the *Lex Majestatis* with refusal to render the religious honor due to the emperors, but actually prosecuted under the vague power of *coercitio* which entitled prefects, governors and other high officials to act summarily against any person considered to be dangerous.

Other scholars[47] are of the opinion that a special law against Christianity was issued by Nero, which read something like: *Non licet esse Christianos*. Tertullian[48] states that the Roman law said: *Non licet esse vos*. Origen[49] asserts: *Decreverunt* (reges terrae) legi-

---

[40] See LAWLOR and OULTON, *Eusebius*, vol. II, p. 224-225; ibid. p. 331. Comp. also H. B. SWETE, *An Introduction to the Old Testament in Greek*, p. 77.

[41] See STEVENSON, *Studies in Eusebius*, p. 54 ff.

[42] M. P. VII. 6.

[43] Ibid. XI. 7.

[44] Ibid. XI. 28.

[45] The most important details of R. 'Akiba's martyrdom are provided by third century sources, and therefore could not be influenced by the narratives about the Christian martyrs under Diocletian. On the other hand, the details of Pamphilus' martyrdom are well attested by authentic contemporary sources, and they could not be borrowed from the description of the death of the great Jewish Martyr. We may therefore conclude that we have here two independent accounts which display the similar procedure of the Caesarean *apparitores* during almost two centuries.

[46] In his famous article "The Crime of Religion in Roman Law", *Historische Zeitschrift*, 1890, vol. LXIV. p. 389 ff.

[47] See, for instance, PAUL ALLARD, *Histoire des persécutions pendant les deux premiers siècles*, p. 163 t..

[48] Apol. IV.

[49] Homil. IX in Jos.

bus suis ut *non sint Christiani*. The Edict of Toleration[50] declared: denuo *sint Christiani*.[51]

It is clear that in the second century the mere name of Christian was already a crime (*nomen crimen est*) regardless of the moral behaviour of the bearer. But unlike all other criminals the Christian had the choice of repentance. If he sacrificed to idols or to the statue of the emperor he was immediately acquitted, in accordance with the special rescript of Trajan[52] (in 112). This was the regular practice[53] of the judges, as can be seen from the various *acta martyrum*. They disregarded the confession of the Christians if the latter followed their prompting to recant. A few grains of incense were enough to dismiss the case.

But what was the legal formulation of the persecutions of the Jews during the reign of Hadrian? Mommsen's theory[54] that the Jewish nation was dissolved after the revolt (in 70) was totally refuted by Juster.[55] The Jews continued to be recognized as a nation and not only as *collegia cultorum*. The question then is, did the anti-Jewish laws of Hadrian proscribe the name Jew, reading something like: *Non licet esse Judaeos?* Or did they abrogate the *privilegia Judaica*, declaring the Jewish religion a *religio illicita* and punishing the transgressors in conformity with the imperial law? The answer is provided by the Rabbinic sources.

From both Jewish and non-Jewish sources it appears that Hadrian's prohibition of circumcision preceded the Jewish rebellion,[56] a view accepted by modern Jewish and non-Jewish scholars.[57] Schürer[58] rightly observed: "The prohibition of circumcision was not limited to the Jews and was not immediately directed against them. When, under Antoninus Pius, the Jews were again allowed

----

[50] LACT., *de mort. pers.* 34.
[51] ALLARD *ibid.*, p. 165 nn. 3, 4, 5. Comp. also n. 2.
[52] PLIN., *Epist.* X. 97.
[53] From the second century on.
[54] *Historische Zeitschrift*, 1890, p. 421 ff.
[55] *Les Juifs dans l'empire Romain* II, p. 19 ff.
[56] *Mishna Shabbath* XIX. 1; TB *ibid.* 130a. TP *ibid.* 17a, TB *Yebamoth* 72ª; SPART. *Hadr.* 14. Comp. S. RAPOPORT, 'Erekh Millin s. v. Adrianus.
[57] SCHÜRER, *Geschichte*, I³, p. 674 ff.; JUSTER, *Les Juifs dans l'empire Romain*, I, p. 226 and notes *ibid.*
[58] *Ibid.* English translation I. 2, p. 292.

to circumcise their children, the prohibition still stood good against non-Jewish peoples. It was therefore originally a general order. The special feature of this legislation was not that it aimed at the rooting out of Judaism, but that it placed circumcision on the same level with castration and punished its practice accordingly (under *lex Cornelia de sicariis*). The prohibition was not, therefore, first of all directed against Judaism, but it is at the same time quite evident that Judaism would receive from it a deadly wound." There can be no doubt that the prohibition was one of the causes which stimulated the Jewish rebellion.[59] It is after the full outbreak of the rebellion that the reaction of Hadrian resulted in the proscription of most Jewish rites and practices.

We know that thereafter the Jews were forbidden to observe the Sabbath,[60] to eat unleavened bread on Passover,[61] to take the *Lulab* on *Sukkoth*, [61] to sit in the *Sukka*,[62] to read the scroll of Esther on *Purim*,[63] to light candles on *Hanukka*,[64] to observe the laws of tithes,[65] show-fringes,[66] *Tephilin*,[67] *Mezuza*,[68] mourning customs,[69] divorce,[70] marriage on Wednesday,[71] ritual immersion[72] (after menstruation), reading of *Shema'*,[73] study of the law,[74] and ordination of Rabbis.[75]

We have seen above that the prohibition of circumcision preceded the Jewish rebellion. It is pertinent to ask whether all the enumerated restrictions were enacted during and after the rebellion, or whether some of them were decreed prior to it.

It seems that not all of them were published simultaneously.

----

[59] This reason is given by Spartian. See above n. 56.
[60] *Mekhilta, Bahodesh,* VI; TP *Hagiga* II, 1. 77b; TB *Ta'anith* 18ᵃ and *Me'ila* 17ᵃ. Comp. Jos. *Bel. Jud.* VII. 3. 3, 52-53 (for an earlier period).
[61] *Mekhilta, ibid.*
[62] *Tosephta Sukka* I, 192¹⁹ and parallel.
[63] *Ibid. Megilla* II, 223¹⁵. Comp. 221⁵⁷ and parallels.
[64] TB *Shabbath* 21b, as correctly understood by Pineles, *Darka Shel Tora,* p. 47.
[65] *Mishna Ma'aser Sheni* IV. 11.
[66] *Vayyikra Rabba* XXXII, 1.
[67] *Mishna 'Erubin* X. 1; *Megilla* IV, 8; TB *Shabbath* 49ᵃ.
[68] *Tosephta Megilla* IV, 228⁴ (and parallels); TB *Yoma* 11ᵃ.
[69] *Semahoth* IX, ed. Higger 175¹, see variants *ibid.*
[70] *Mishna Kethuboth* IX. 9.
[71] *Tosephta ibid.* I. 260¹⁷ (and parallels). See Pineles *ibid.* (referred to above n. 64), p. 47.
[72] TB *Me'ila* 17ᵃ.
[73] *Tosephta Berakhoth* II, 4²¹.
[74] *Ibid. 'Erubin* VIII, 147²⁸, *Sota* XV, 322¹³, *Mekhilta Bahodesh* VI, *passim.*
[75] TB *Sanhedrin* 14ᵃ.

We read in Tosephta[76]: "Rabbi Meir said: We were once sitting before R. 'Akiba in the House of Study[77] and we recited the *Shema'* [in such a low voice] that it was not audible to our own ears, on account of a *quaestor* who was standing at the door etc". It is evident from this passage that the study of the Law was not as yet forbidden; R. 'Akiba met together with his disciples in the House of Study. The *quaestor* watched them only to prevent them from reciting the *Shema'* but apparently was not concerned with their study of the Law.

It seems, therefore, that the recitation of *Shema'* was forbidden before the other restrictions were enacted. The reason is quite obvious. The first verse of the *Shema'* (Deut. VI 4) reads: *God is our Lord, God is One.* This sounded like a direct challenge to the ambitions of Hadrian. At a time when discontent with the Emperor's religious policy began to brew in Palestine, the Jewish acclamation εἷς θεὸς μόνος acquired a revolutionary meaning. Hadrian may have seen in it a protest against his ambitions,[78] a watchword to defy his divine authority.[79] It is quite reasonable to assume that the prohibition to recite the *Shema'* was the precursor of the other restrictions.

We know further that in the time of R. 'Akiba it was already forbidden to teach the Law publicly.[80] But I doubt that it was then a prohibition *per se*. We read in the Babylonian Talmud[81]: "The wicked government once decreed against the Jews[82] that they should not engage in the study of the Law (publicly?). Pappus b. Judah came and found R. 'Akiba collecting assemblies and teaching them the Law." This is the reading of the editions. But the correct text is found in the best mss. of the Talmud:[83] "The wicked government once issued a decree that the Jews should not engage in the study of the Law, and that he who engaged in the study of the Law would

[76] *Berakhoth* II, 4[b].
[77] So *ed. princ.* and *Cod. Vienna.*
[78] On εἷς θεός as an acclamation see E. PETERSON, εἷς θεός, p. 227 ff., pp. 271 (εἷς Ἰουλιανός), 305, n. 1.
[79] The εἷς θεός acclamation was subsequently a regular feature in the Christian martyrology. See PETERSON, *ibid.* p. 183 ff., p. 189 ff.
[80] Minor tract *Kalla*, end: R. 'Akiba taught under an olive tree, *etc.*
[81] *Berakhoth* 61[b]. The source is a "*Baraitha*" of the second or the early third century.
[82] See RABBINOVICZ, *Variae Lectiones ad loc.*, p. 355.
[83] *Codd. Oxf. and Paris.* See RABBINOVICZ *ibid.*

be stabbed by the sword.[84] Pappus b. Judah came and found R. 'Akiba expounding [the Law] and collecting assemblies, etc."

At first glance the order of the sentence in the editions is quite logical: R. 'Akiba collected assemblies in order to teach them the Law. But the original and genuine reading of the mss.[85] implies that there were two transgressions: teaching of the Law and collecting assemblies.

One of the first measures preceding a general persecution was the prohibition of political associations. This was the course of action adopted by Pliny regarding the Christians.[86] It seems that the Talmud has preserved here the official terminology of the decree. In the Edict of Toleration[87] the Christians were accused of *per diversa varios populos congregarent*. Eusebius of Caesarea[88] renders it: ἐν διαφόροις διάφορα πλήθη συνάγειν, "They were collecting various assemblies in divers places." πλήθη συνάγειν is the exact equivalent of להקהיל קהלות of which the Rabbinic Sages[90] were accused. Both the Rabbis and Eusebius quoted the official terminology of Caesarea.

Thus we should divide the decrees of Hadrian into two categories. The first (the prohibition of circumcision, reciting of *Shema'* and collecting assemblies to teach the Law) emanated from Hadrian's general policy and were not immediately directed against Judaism. The second, comprising the restrictions issued during and after the Jewish rebellion when most of the Jewish rites were proscribed, aimed at the destruction of Judaism proper. The Roman government was aided by Jewish advisers who informed it of various

----

[84] It is noteworthy that the decree threatens with the sword and not with fire as was later the case. See above n. 12.
[85] It is also corroborated by the Yemenite tradition in the *Exempla of the Rabbis*, ed. GASTER, p. 16 and by TB *'Abodah Zarah* 17ᵃ in the editions and mss. Comp. also *Acta Saturnini, Dativi*, etc., 12.
[86] Epist. X. 96: post edictum meum, quo secundum *mandata tua hetaerias esse vetueram*. On the prohibition of associations, see the literature referred to by LEWY in *Zion* (Hebrew) vol. VIII, p. 63 ff., 66 n. 230 and p. 73.
[87] LACT., de mort. pers. 34.
[88] Hist. Eccl. VIII. 17.7.
[89] On πλῆθος = קהלה see M. SCHWABE in *Kedem* I, 1942, p. 92.
[90] R. 'Akiba and R. Hanina b. Teradyon, see TB *'Abodah Zarah* 17ᵃ.

details of the Rabbinic laws,[91] and the Jews were accordingly ordered to transgress them. The punishment was merciless and cruel, as we shall see presently.

Indeed the Rabbis employed different terms for the two different stages of the Hadrianic persecutions. The earlier was named סכנה, Peril. It is used in the Mishna[92] and is prevalent in the Baraithoth.[93] Although subsequently it was applied indiscriminately, it originally designated only the first stage of the persecutions. It was dangerous to perform the Law. Regular punishment in accordance with the Roman decrees was inflicted upon the transgressors. Because he collected assemblies to teach the law, R. 'Akiba was sentenced to death by sword.[94] But it so happened that before his execution the hour for the recital of Shema' arrived, and the saintly hero began to recite it in defiance of the special decree which proscribed it. It was a direct challenge to the divinity of the Emperor (see above), and iron combs were applied to prevent R. 'Akiba from his recitation.[95] He did not mind the tortures and gave up his ghost with the word אחד, εἷς.[96] The tortures were applied to him only as a preventive measure, to keep him from reciting the Shema'. The entire execution was performed in accordance with the unjust and cruel imperial law.

As pointed out above this stage of the persecution was styled Peril.[97]

The later term found in the Baraithoth and regularly used in the Talmudim and Midrashim is שמד, destruction, extermination. It designated both the eradication, extirpatio,[98] of the spirit and the

---

[91] TP Hagiga II 1, 77ª. The Roman governor himself was credited by the Aggada (Pesikta Rabbathi, ed. FRIEDMANN f. 120ª) with sound knowledge of Rabbinic law.
[92] Ma'aser Sheni IV, 11; Shabbath XIX.1; 'Erubin X.1; Megilla IV.8 and Kethuboth IX.9.
[93] Tosephta 4²¹, 147³⁸, 192¹⁹. 223¹², 228⁴, 260¹⁷, 374¹⁷, passim.
[94] The sword was the fate of the two earlier martyrs. See Mekhilta, Mishpatim XVIII (and parallels in Aboth deR. Nathan, ed. SCHECHTER, p. 114) and Tosephta Sota 319ª.
[95] See above n. 23.
[96] On εἷς as an acclamation see PETERSON. εἷς θεός, pp. 180 ff., 253, 271.
[97] EUSEBIUS (Hist. Eccles. VIII. 17. 8) renders the Latin of the Edict of Toleration pertaining to the persecutions of the Christians by: πλεῖστοι μὲν κινδύνῳ ὑποβληθέντες, Many indeed were subjected to peril.
[98] A regular Roman term for the uprooting of foreign religions. See LEWY in Zion vol. VIII, p. 82 and n. 8 ibid.

physical extermination, ἐξώλεια,[99] of the nation. The Jewish rebellion was drowned in fire and blood and all kinds of illogical pretexts were used to exterminate the nation physically.[100] Most of the Jewish rites and ceremonies were then forbidden and the most cruel tortures were applied to the Jews. There was no "legal" regulation of the penalties. Jewish life and property were entirely in the hands of the Roman proconsul and his officials. They acted summarily against all the Jews of Palestine under the power of *coercitio* and vented all their fury on the unhappy nation. There is no record from that period of sentences against the Jews involving exile,[101] imprisonment or work in the mines. The only sentence was death. This proves that the normal imperial law did not at that time operate in Palestine in respect of the religious crimes of the Jews. Everything depended on the arbitrariness of the local administration.

And herein lies the main difference between the persecution of the Jews at that time and that of the Christians. To be a Jew[102] was not a crime, and when a Jew confessed in court: *Judaeus sum*, he could not be sentenced for it, nor could he be condemned for his creed. Only the positive performance of a proscribed Jewish rite or ceremony was considered a crime. And although the performance of most of the Jewish rites and ceremonies became illegal,[103] it seems that specific edicts were issued to prohibit every important Jewish practice in particular, and different punishments were imposed for various practices.[104]

We read, for instance, in the Babylonian Talmud:[105] "The wicked government once decreed that whoever performed ordination should be put to death, as well as he who received ordination, the

----

[99] Apprian (*de bel. civ.* II. 90) calls Trajan: ἐξολλύντα τὸ ἐν Αἰγύπτῳ Ἰουδαίων γένος.

[100] See *Eka Rabba* III. 58, ed. Buber p. 139; ibid. p. 155.

[101] For the post-Hadrianic period comp. TB *Shabbath* 33b.

[102] For a man born in that faith.

[103] It seems that only the specifically Jewish practices or national festivals (like *Hanukka* and *Purim*) and civil institutions were proscribed, but prayer, celebration of holidays in a general way (rest from work, better meals) etc. were not forbidden. Only the typically Jewish "superstitions" were banned but not the general religious rites practiced by Gentiles as well in their heathen worship.

[104] *Mekhilta, Bahodesh* IV, end; *Vayyikra Rabba* XXXII. 1; TB *Shabbath* 49a.

[105] *Sanhedrin* 14a.

city in which the ordination took place should be demolished, and the boundaries wherein it was performed uprooted etc." The wholesale punishment of the crime is a typical example of the punitive measures applied under the power of *coercitio*, and is in accordance with the political character of the crime.[106] Indeed, when R. Judah b. Baba[107] was caught in the act of performing ordination, "the enemy did not stir from the spot until they had driven three hundred iron spear-heads into his body"[108], i. e. he was killed by the soldiers on the spot without even a nominal trial, an obvious application of military law on the field in time of war.

But what was the procedure at that time if the accused Jew was granted the privilege of a nominal trial in court? We turn once more to the unique, authoritative story referred to above. We read in the Babylonian Talmud:[109] "They brought R. Hanina b. Teradyon [to court]. They asked him: 'Why did you engage in the study of the Law?' He replied: '*As God my Lord ordered me*' (*Deut. IV 5*). *They immediately sentenced him* to be burned alive, his wife to be executed and his daughter to be committed to a house of infamy". The subsequent *Baraitha*[110] describes the terrible tortures which were inflicted on the martyr in course of his execution. We learn from these sources that, unlike the Christian martyrs, our saint was not offered the choice of recanting, but was sentenced to a cruel death *immediately* he confessed the crime. His answer: as God my Lord ordered me incensed the judge who saw in it a direct defiance of the authority of the Emperor, and he therefore condemned him to a cruel death and all his family to perish with him. The tortures of the martyr, unlike those of the Christians, were not admonitory but vengeful.

Our R. Hanina was not the only Jewish martyr on whom the Roman officials vented their cruelty. From the Palestinian Talmud[111]

---

[106] Ordination of Jewish judges granting them the right to impose fines on their correligionists.
[107] There is some doubt regarding the man (See *Tosephta Baba Kamma* VIII, 362¹⁶; TP *Sota* IX. 10, 24ᵃ and comp. Midrash *Shir Hashirim* ed. GRÜNHUT p. 5), but the truth of the story itself is not thereby invalidated.
[108] TB *Sanhedrin* 14ᵃ.
[109] TB '*Abodah Zarah* 17ᵇ, bottom.
[110] TB ibid. 18ᵃ.
[111] *Hagiga* II. 1, 77ᵇ. Comp. TB *Kiddushin* 39ᵇ.

we infer that the tongue of one of the Jewish martyrs was cut out.[112] This cruel act was performed both on Christian martyrs[113] and on political criminals.[114]

Although the Jewish sources do not explicitly record admonitory tortures during the Hadrianic persecutions,[115] it is hard to believe that the Roman magistrates did not in the long run avail themselves of cruelties for that purpose. After their thirst for vengeance was satisfied an alteration of method seemed a natural consequence. It is reasonable to assume that they attempted to eradicate the Jewish "superstition" by forcing the martyrs to abandon their faith.[116]

Moreover, Schlatter[117] noted that there is no clear evidence to the effect that Hadrian compelled the Jews to worship idols. He required of them only to abandon their Law, not actually to practice idolatry. This is partly true. No record exists in Rabbinic literature of a decree by Hadrian ordering the Jews to worship idols. The condemned Jewish leaders were not offered the alternative of sacrificing to idols, but there can be no doubt that the Roman officials, in their relentless efforts to destroy Judaism, tried to compel the Jews to do homage to the pagan gods or, at least, to offer divine honors to the emperor.

Indeed we read in *Tosephta:*[118] "Altars[119] which were set up by Gentiles during the persecutions may not be used even when the

---

[112] The stories mentioned in the later Midrashim are not taken into account here. Comp. however TB *Hullin* 123ᵃ, *'Abodah Zarah* 11ᵇ.

[113] Romanus of Caesarea. See EUSEBIUS M. P. 11. 3.

[114] SUET. *Calig.* 27 (end) and DIO CASSIUS LiX. 10. For tortures of political criminals see MOMMSEN, *Le droit pénal Romain* II, p. 239 seq.

[115] The story of Miriam and her seven sons (Midrash *Eka Rabba* I. 16; TB *Gittin* 57ᵇ and parallels) is borrowed from the accounts of the persecutions of Antiochus Epiphanes, as rightly observed by SCHLATTER, *Die Tage Trajans und Hadrians*, p. 8 ff. Comp. also TP *Shebi'ith* IV. 2, 34ᵃ (and parallel).

[116] R. Hiyya b. Abba (fl. in the last quarter of the third century) described (*Shir Hashirim Rabba* II. 7) the terrible tortures of the "Generation of the [Hadrianic] destruction". He added that he himself would readily give his life for the sanctification of His Name, provided he were executed immediately, but that he feared he would not be able to stand the tortures they endured. In the light of this supposed change of policy on the part of the Roman officials the meaning of this statement gains added importance. He was ready to sanctify His Name if death followed immediately, but feared that he might succumb to the demands of the Romans, if torture were applied. Comp. also TB *Kethuboth* 33ᵇ and *Tosaphoth ibid.*

[117] Ibid.

[118] *'Abodah Zarah* V, 468³⁰. Comp. also TB *ibid.* 54ᵃ.

[119] בימסיות, as in *ed. princ.* and *cod. Vienna.*

persecutions are over." Another statement provides even clearer
proof of Roman attempts to force the conversion of Jews. The
Mishna[120] teaches: "If a punitive expedition[121] has entered a town
in peace time all the open jars [of wine] are forbidden but the sealed
ones are allowed." Thereupon the Palestinian Talmud[122] observes:
"During the persecutions (literally: the destruction) all (i. e. both
open and sealed jars) are forbidden, for inevitably some Jew was
compelled to worship".[123] This clearly implies that during the persecutions the Gentiles erected special altars to compel the Jewish
masses to worship and to offer libations to idols.[124] The Romans
then followed the same procedure as during the persecutions of the
Christians.

But since the fragments of the Jewish *acta martyrum* preserved
in Talmudic literature do not record this Roman practice, and since
the above mentioned sources make no mention of the punishment
for the refusal to worship idols[125] it may be safely assumed that this
policy of compulsion was an arbitrary creation of the local authorities
who sought to break the "obstinacy" of the Jews by all the means in
their power. It was as a result of this same arbitrary policy and vague
authority of *coercitio* that a soldier threatened the disciples of R.
Joshua that he would compel them to worship idols, הריני משמד
אתכם.[126]

We conclude with the following summary. The legal basis of
the Hadrianic persecutions was provided by a series of decrees which
consecutively proscribed most of the Jewish practices by specific
mention of each rite and ceremony, and imposed various punishment for their transgression. Since most of the decrees were issued

----

[120] *Ibid.* V. 8.
[121] בולשת, διωγμῖται.
[122] *Ibid.* V. 8, 45ᵃ.
[123] I. e. to offer libations, with the result that even Jewish wine was then
considered like that of the Gentiles at that place.
[124] Comp. also TB *Shabbath* 130ᵃ; *Tosephta ibid.* 128ᵘ.
[125] It is possible that later on the authorities adopted an administrative measure of pacification by pardoning the Jew who was caught in the act of
observing the Law if he offered sacrifices to the idols.
[126] *Bereshith Rabba* LXXXII. 8, 985. To avoid the annoyance of the Romans
the disciples of R. Joshua dressed as non-Jews. Similarly, another Jew
sold pork in his shop (*Tanhuma Balak*, ed. Buber, p. 145 and parallels)
to pass as a non-Jew.

during and after the Jewish Rebellion, the Roman proconsul had
the right to act summarily against all the Jews of Palestine under
the power of *coercitio*. The Jews were not condemned either for
being Jews or for their creed, but only for the positive performance
and observance of Jewish rites. If a Jew was caught in the act of
fulfilling the Law he was convicted and no escape was *originally*
open to him. If he dared challenge the authority of the Emperor
cruel tortures were inflicted upon him, and, as a political criminal,
drew vengeance on his family as well. But the final aim of the
Roman authorities was to pacify the country. They adopted the usual
policy; after thousands of cruel executions they began to relax. They
resorted to admonitory tortures and similar measures. The Jew who
recanted was probably pardoned. The Romans themselves, weary
of the innocent bloodshed, inaugurated a period of so-called pacification, a time termed by the Rabbis שלפי השמד.[127]

Finally, a few words are in order about the attitude of the Gentiles towards the Jewish martyrs. It was stated at the beginning of
this chapter that the Jews took their martyrdom calmly and as a
matter of course. The simple Jew who was a victim of the Hadrianic
persecutions did not philosophise[127a] with his executioner but submitted to martyrdom quietly and untheatrically, ἀτραγῴδως.[128] The
Gentiles were unwilling to acknowledge the courage of the Jewish
martyr. In the initial act of accusation they tried to impute criminal charges to him,[129] a practice adopted by the Romans towards
the Christians as well.[130] They were subsequently able to allege
that the martyr died as a criminal.

---

[127] On שילהי see the Talmudic dictionaries *s. v.*

[127a] In one case it was the judge who challenged the Jew to argue (*Sifra Emor* IX. 5, 99d, and parallels), and the latter merely answered a question. Comp. also *supra* n. 115. Many retorts of Jewish martyrs during the persecutions of Antiochus Epiphanes have probably no more historical value than some of the discourses recorded by the early historians. On the defiant replies of the heathen martyrs to their judges comp. ROSTOVTZEFF, *The Social and Economic History of the Roman Empire*, p. 520, n. 17.

[128] On the attitude of the enlightened pagans towards the Christian martyrs see MARC. AUR. XI. 3. Comp. P. ALLARD, *Histoire des persécutions pendant les deux premiers siècles* etc. (Paris 1892), p. 393-394; A. D. NOCK, *Conversion*, p. 197 (comp. *ibid.*, p. 299).

[129] R. Eleazar b. Perata was accused of both being a teacher of the Law and a robber (*TB 'Abodah Zarah* 17b).

[130] See W. M. RAMSAY, *The Church in the Roman Empire*, p. 293-294.

It seems to me that an interesting fragment of a polemical source to this effect is preserved in Midrash Tanhuma.[131] We read there:[132] "The·[Gentile] people who witness [the execution of the martyrs] say: 'They (i. e. the martyrs) are *full of decay*, crimes are on their hands, and for this they are executed, and die because of their *corruption*',[133] but they do not know that the lot of the martyrs is in *the eternal life* etc." This Jewish view of the lot of the martyrs was known to the Gentiles. Tacitus[134] says about the Jews: *animosque proelio aut suppliciis peremptorum aeternos putant*. "*They believe that the souls of those killed* in battle or *by the executioner* (i. e. הרוגי מלכות) *are immortal*." The whole idea of interpreting the word חלד in Ps. XVII. 14 was probably suggested by the Gentile claim that the Jewish martyrs are μεστοὶ φθορᾶς, full of corruption.[135] To this the Jews cleverly retorted that the Gentiles do not know that the souls of the martyrs are ἄφθαρτοι,[136] immortal and eternal.

Appendices

I (to p. 402)

Eusebius[1] tells us: "The customary rains, indeed, and showers of the then prevailing winter season were withholding their usual downpour upon the earth, and an unexpected famine broke out, and on top of this a plague and an outbreak of another kind of disease. This latter was an ulcer, which on account of its fiery character was called an *anthrax*.[2] Spreading as it did over the entire body it used to *endanger greatly* its victims[3] . . . while the rest of the inhabitants of the cities under his rule were so terribly wasted by both the famine and the pestilence, that two thousand five hundred Attic

---

[131] *Ki Thavo* 2. The translation follows the *ed. pr.* Comp. ed. BUBER, V, p. 47, n. 19. The editor totally misunderstood the text.
[132] The author of the statement is a sage of the third century.
[133] An interpretation of *Ps.* XVII. 14: בְּמֵתִים מֵחֶלֶד.
[134] *Hist.* V. 5.
[135] Comp. MAXIMUS THE GRAMMARIAN's epithets of the Christian martyrs (*Augustin. epist.* XVI. 2.).
[136] On the play of these two Greek words in ancient literature see R. REITZENSTEIN, *Historia Monachorum etc.* (Goettingen 1916), p. 26, n. 3.
[1] *Hist. Eccl.* IX. 8.
[2] The Syriac translation (ed. WRIGHT p. 368) calls it גמורתא.
[3] ἄνθραξ προσαγορευόμενον . . . σφαλεροὺς ἐνεποίει τοῖς πεπονθόσι κινδύνους. The Palestinian Talmud (*Shabbath*, XIV. 4, 14d and parallel),

drachmas were given for a single measure of wheat (ἑνὸς μέτρου πυρῶν)[4] . . . and others again injured their bodily health, and died from *chewing small wisps of hay*[5] etc."

From the description of the season of the rains it is evident that Eusebius talks of Palestine, or at any rate includes Palestine among the lands stricken by hunger and plague (in the winter of 312-313). Lawlor and Oulton[6] seem to question a few of Eusebius' assertions. They remark: "The famine cannot have been due to the failure of the winter rain. Scarcity from that cause would not take place till the harvest of the following year etc." This argument is not sufficient to refute the clear statement of Eusebius: absence of the customary rains creates an immediate panic. The peasant and the grain dealer instantly withdraw the grain from the market in expectation of the future hunger, and scarcity and famine break out directly after the drought.

They further remark[7] about the price of 2500 drachmas for a measure of wheat: "The sum mentioned here would therefore be about £100, which seems an impossible charge for a measure of wheat—however large the 'measure' may have been." The learned authors lost sight of the fact that the famine took place at a time of inflation.[8] Two thousand five hundred drachmas were equal to 2500 denarii,[9] which at that time (313) had the value of something more than one *aureus*.[10] The "measure"[11] which Eusebius mentions was probably a small part of an artaba, and the price of more than an *aureus* for "a measure" of wheat[12] in time of a famine is not surpris-

———

in a passage apparently taken from the Caesarean academy, refers to this disease הרא גומרתא סכנה. *"This anthrax* (comp. the preceding note) *is a dangerous disease."*

[4] The Syriac translation (ed. Wright, p. 369) reads: דחר מ ו ד י א דחמא. בחרין אלפין והמשׁמאא מ ע י ן מתיהב הוא . Bar Hebraeus, *Chronography*, (ed. Budge, vol. I. 58) writes: *"God admonished the earth with famine and pestilence [so severely] that a modius of wheat was sold for two hundred and fifty měnin."*

[5] σμικρὰ χόρτου διαμασώμενοι σπαράγματα.

[6] *Eusebius*, vol. II, p. 297-298.

[7] P. 298.

[8] On the traces of this inflation on Palestine see Lieberman, *Greek in Jewish Palestine*, p. 5. Comp. also *Tanhumah, Terumah*, ed. Buber, p. 92.

[9] See A. Segrè, *Byzantion*, XV, (1940-1941), p. 249, n. 1.

[10] See Segrè, *ibid.* p. 263.

[11] See above n. 4. Comp. Julianus, *Misopogon*, 369a-b.

[12] Comp. Segrè, *ibid.* p. 261. See also Joseph., *Ant.* XIV. 2.2 (28).

ing at all. Moreover, the record of Eusebius that people used to eat "hay" at that time is corroborated by a contemporary of his. We read in the Midrash:[13] אמר ר' יצחק על הדורות הללו הוא אומר ואכלת את עשב השדה שאדם משליף משדהו ואוכלה עד שהיא עשב. "R Isaac (III-IV c.) said: [The verse] *Thou shalt eat the grass of the field* (Gen. III. 18) refers to the present-day generations, when a man plucks from his field and eats it while it is still herbage."

TP[14] relates that in the time of R. Abbahu the Jews had to offer prayers for rain. This statement does not disprove the clear evidence that R. Abbahu was not alive any more at the time of the previously mentioned famine. Absence of rain at the beginning of the season was not infrequent in Palestine, and prayers for it do not prove that there was a drought during the whole season. In the case of R. Abbahu the prayers seemed to have been answered.[15] Nor was drought accompanied by pestilence very rare in that country.[16] It is, however, probable that our case of plague and drought is referred to in TB,[17] where it is related that "In the time of R. Judah the Prince (III-IV c.) there was distress;[18] he ordered thirteen fast-days but their prayer was not answered etc." The personalities who figure in this case[19] were active in 313, and the tradition tells us[20] that the prayers to remove the misfortune were ineffective.

II (to p. 413)

In TP[21] it is recorded:

והא לולינוס מלכא כד נחת לתמן נחו' (read: נהתון) עמיה מאה כ' ריבוון. "When the Emperor Lulianus *came down* to Babylonia[22] (lit. "to there") there *came down with him*[23] one hun-

---

[13] *Bereshith Rabba,* XX. 10, 194.
[14] *Ta'anith,* I. 4, 64a.
[15] See TP *ibid.*
[16] See TB *ibid.* 8b.
[17] *Ibid.* 14a-b.
[18] This "distress" meant something additional to the drought (plague?). See Tosaphoth ad loc. and מראה הפנים ad TP *Ta'anith,* I. /, s. v. באילין. Comp. the reading in GINZBERG's *Genizah Studies,* I, p. 406, 1. 3.
[19] R. Judah III and R. Ami etc.
[20] TB *ibidem.*
[21] *Nedarim,* III. 3, 37d.
[22] = Persia.
[23] See below n. 34.

dred and twenty myriads [of people]." Zunz[24] correctly surmised that the Talmud refers to the expedition of Julian against the Persians, an opinion subsequently supported by Bacher.[25] However, Graetz[26] preferred the reading of the parallel passage in TP[27] which records דוקליטיאנוס, Diocletian, instead of לוליינוס, Lulianus. His opinion was accepted by modern scholars.[28]

But there is no doubt that the reading Lulianus is the only genuine one.[29] In addition to the arguments adduced by Bacher, there is internal decisive evidence in favor of this reading. The army which Diocletian's Caesar, Galerius, led to Persia was comparatively small;[30] its numbers could hardly impress the orientals. On the other hand the expedition of Julian against the Persians included an army almost three times greater[31] and was led by the emperor himself. The orientals greatly exaggerated its number. The "Syriac Stories,"[32] describing the different parts of this army and their numbers, set the total at about four hundred thousand.[33] The narrator adds that these numbers did not include the people of the villages who joined the army when *it came down* to Persia.[34]

Although these stories have little historic value for the time of Julian, they afford good evidence of the exaggerated estimates of Julian's army, which circulated among the Orientals at the beginning of the VI century, the time of the composition of the Roman,[35] and probably also during the V century. They talked about immense hosts of people who *came down with Julian to Persia.*

---

[24] *Die gottesdienstlichen Vorträge der Juden*, ed. BRÜLL, p. 56.

[25] JQR X (1898), p. 172.

[26] *Geschichte*, IV³, p. 459.

[27] *Shebu'oth*, III. 9, 34d.

[28] KRAUSS, *Monumenta Talmudica*, V, p. 59. But comp. *ibid.* p. 79 note.

[29] In Syriac texts of the VI c. the emperor Julian is called לוליינוס ; see the Index of HOFFMANN, *Julianos der Abtruennige*, p. XIII, s. v. לולינוס ; LOEW apud KRAUSS, *Lehnwörter*, II, p. 310.

[30] About twenty five thousand. See GIBBON, *Decline and Fall etc.* I, ch. XIII, p. 678. Comp. KRAUSS, ibid.

[31] *Zosim.* (III. 13.2) gives the number of 65.000.

[32] Edited by HOFFMANN. See above n. 29.

[33] *Ibid.* p. 162: והוא מנינא דחילא דאתסים למעבר עם קסר לארעא דפרסיא תלתמאא ותשעין ותשעא אלפין. "And the number of the host ready to pass into the land of the Persians with Caesar was 395 thousand." Comp. also BAR HEBRAEUS, *Chronography*, ed. BUDGE, I, p. 62.

[34] . . . ספר מן חלומא דאתלויו להון כד נחתין . . . דלא עלו למנינא

[35] See NÖLDEKE, *Zeitschrift d. deutsch-morgenländ. Gesellsch.* XXVIII, p. 283; BAUMSTARK, *Geschichte der syrischen Literatur*, p. 183.

The Palestinian Rabbis got their information from Babylonian
(= Persian) sources; it is no wonder that the latter, desiring to em-
ᶜ phasize that they were greatly outnumbered by the Romans, swelled
the size of the enemy army to fantastic numbers.

Thus, the reading לוליאנוס is beyond any question, and the Talmud refers to the expedition of Julian into Persia. The name לוליאנוס
given in the vision of R. Aha is not only the same name but the
same person.

III. ·

'Ανελήφθη. 'Ο κοινωνὸς ὁ κατὰ τόπον.

איתנגיד. חבר עיר. חבר מדינה (!)

On p. 413, n. 34, the version recorded in the Palestinian Midrash
was prefered to that of the Babylonian Talmud. Since the incident
took place in Palestine it is reasonable to accept the testimony of
the Palestinian source. In support of our view a second Palestinian
Midrash was also quoted there.[1] Interestingly enough internal evidence further proves that the original wording of the story has been
preserved in the Palestinian source which does not mention the
martyrs in the vision of R. Joshua b. Levi's grandson. TB[2] records:

כי הדר,   דרב יוסף בריה דר' יהושע בן לוי חלש ואיתנגיד[3]
אמר, ליה אבוה מאי חזית? א"ל עולם הפוך ראיתי עליונים למטה
ותחתונים למעלה . . . ושמעתי הרוגי מלכות אין אדם יכול לעמוד
במחיצתן וכו'. "R. Joseph the son of R. Joshua ben Levi fell sick and
gave up the ghost.[4] When he recovered his father asked him: 'What
did you see'? He said: ' I saw an inverted world;·the exalted were
low and the low were exalted . . . And I heard that none can stand

---

[1] Ibid.
[2] Pesahim, 50ᵃ.
[3] See RABBINOVICZ, Variae Lectiones, ad loc.; idem, Baba Bathra, p. 45,
n. 300. Comp. the Geonic Responsa, ed. HARKAVY. p. 179 and the Commentary on the Sepher Yezirah by R. JUDAH of BARCELONA, p. 24 and
p. 25, Pirkei de-Rabbi ed. GRÜNHUT p. 48, ed. SCHÖNBLUM f. 26ᵈ.
So RASHI: גוע ופרחה רוחו. R. HANANEL (and other commentaries):
כאילו פרחה נשמתו "As if he gave up the ghost," i. e. fainted (Comp.
Aruch Completum s. v. נגד I and נגד V.). The word איתנגיד is used as
a euphemism for the death of the righteous by the Targumim ·of the
Pentateuch (Gen. XXV. 8, 17; XXXV. 29; IL. 33). Comp. TB Baba
Bathra, 16ᵇ (bottom) and Nahmanides ad Gen. XXV. 17. Pirkei de-
Rabbi (ibid.) translated איתנגיד with נמשך לאותו העולם. Comp. below
n. 30. It is noteworthy that this word does not occur (in our sense)
in the Palestinian Talmud and the early Midrashim.

within the compartment of those martyred by the State.'" The text
in the Palestinian Midrash[6] reads:

ר' מיאשה בר בריה דר' יהושע [בן לוי][6]   נשתקע שלשה ימים
בחליו לאחר שלשה ימים נתיישבה דעתו. אמר לה אבוי, הן הוית?
אמ' ליה, בעולם מעורב הייתי. אמר ליה, ומה המית תמן? אמר ליה
הרבה בני אדם ראיתי כאן בכבוד ושם בבזיון.

"R. Meyasha the grandson of R. Joshua b. Levi was made un-
conscious by his illness for three days. After three days he regained
consciousness. His father said to him: 'Where were you'? He replied: 'In a confused world.' He asked: 'What did you see there?'
He answered: 'I saw many people who were held in honor here and
are in disgrace there.'" The Midrash does not mention the martyrs
at all.

As for the text, it is defective. The complete passage was preserved by R. Samuel Jama[7] who records:[8]

ר' מיאשה בר בריה דר' יהושע בן לוי נשתקע בחולי' אנליפתין
ג' ימים לאחר ג' ימים נתיישבה דעתיה וכו'

The words ג' ימים ;אנליפתין—'Aνελήφϑην for three days—were omitted by the scribes (of the manuscript, or manuscripts, from which
our printed editions were published) in accordance with their usual
practice in case of foreign words.[9] What does אנליפתין ἀνελήφϑην
mean here? No Talmudic dictionary lists it. Perles[10] explains it to
mean "he recuperated."[11] This explanation is totally untenable. It
requires considerable alteration of the following sentence of the
text. Secondly,[12] the passive of ἀναλαμβάνω never occurs in Greek
in the sense of recovering. It may above all be asked why the Rabbis employed an inflected form of a Greek verb in the middle of an
Aramaic sentence? It has already been observed[13] that "Almost every
foreign word and phrase have their *raison d'être* in Rabbinic literature." The use of ἀνελήφϑη in this passage could be justified only

----

[5] *Ruth Rabba*, III. 1.
[6] See below.
[7] XII. c.
[8] In his אגור, *Jubelschrift* . . . *Grätz*, Hebrew part, p. 25.
[9] See LIEBERMAN, *Greek in Jewish Palestine*, p. 152 and n. 43 *ibid*.
[10] *Festschrift Adolf Schwarz*, p. 294.
[11] Previously accepted by me in *Hayerushalmi Kiphshuto*, I, p. 187.
[12] *Greek in Jewish Palestine*, p. 6.
[13] As I learn from Prof. GRÉGOIRE.

if it could be proved to have been an every-day technical term conveying a well-known concept.

A very instructive article by Prof. H. Grégoire sheds light on this passage. He[14] elucidated certain words and phrases which he shows to have belonged to the Montanist terminology. He has republished[15] an inscription of the sixth century, found near the Lydian Philadelphia which reads:

'Ανελήμφθη ὁ ἅγι[ο]ς Πραΰλι[ος]
ὁ κοινωνὸς ὁ κατὰ τόπον. . .

We shall subsequently return to this inscription; let us first deal with the term ἀνελήφθη. Prof. Grégoire pointed out[16] that, in addition to this occurrence, the term is found only twice among the thousands of Christian inscriptions. The oldest is the inscription of Julia Euaresta[17] which mentions: μετὰ τῶν ἁγίων ἀνελήμφθη. De Rossi[18] designates it as *antiquissima* (i. e. third c.). The second is found in Dioskomè:[19] ἀνελήμφθη τὸ πεδίον 'Αντίπατρος etc.[20]

The first two of the inscriptions quoted above display their Montanistic character clearly, and H. Grégoire after convincing argumentation concludes that the last is also of Montanistic origin. Thus the existence of ἀνελήφθη as a technical term (= died)[21] on Montanist grave inscriptions is a well established fact.[22] The term was not invented by them. It occurs very frequently in Jewish Greek texts and especially in the Apocalyptic literature.[23] But subsequently the term disappears almost entirely from Jewish sources. It is therefore reasonable to assume that it was rather current among the

----

[14] *Byzantion*, II. 1925, p. 329 ff.
[15] *Ibid.* p. 330.
[16] *Byzant.* X, (1935), p. 248.
[17] Found in Rome on the Via Latina. De Rossi, p. CXVI.
[18] *Ibidem.*
[19] Ramsay, *Cities and Bishoprics* etc. II, p. 561.
[20] Fifth century? See Ramsay, ibid.
[21] Grégoire (*Byzantion*, II, 331) takes the formula ἀνάληψις Πέτρου (*Recueil*, I, 260) as the death of Peter. In the *Ps. of Solomon* (IV. 20) ἀνάληψις is applied to the death of the wicked. But the word seems to be either a mistranslation from the Hebrew or a scribal error. Comp. the notes of Ryle James *ad loc.*
[22] The opinion of Peterson (*Römische Quartalschrift*, XLII, 1934, p. 173 ff.) notwithstanding. Prof. Grégoire calls my attention to Eusebius (*Hist. Eccles.* V. XVI, 14.) who expressed himself about Theodotus, the Montanist: ἀναλαμβανόμενον εἰς οὐρανούς.
[23] See the long list by Charles, *The Apocalypse of Baruch* (1896), p. 73, n. 7.

Judeo-Christians, who were always under the influence of the Jewish Apocryphal and Apocalyptic writings. True to their general
practice[24] the Jews ceased to use it after it was monopolized by the
Christians. The Montanists borrowed it from their Judeo-Christian
brethren, just as they did in the case of the Heavenly Jerusalem[25]
(Pepouza).

Since R. Joshua b. Levi had Judeo-Christian neighbors,[26] he
and other Jews of the neighborhood could naturally be expected to
be familiar with the term ἀνελήφθη.[27] The original narrator in the
Midrash happily used this current term in his neighborhood instead
of "died" because it suited his idea perfectly; the subject of the little
tale did not actually die. He was taken up, ἀνελήφθη,[27a] but returned. The Midrash resorted here to the current terminology of
the locality.

The translation of ἀνελήφθη by איתנגיד[28] is quite correct. Ps.
Jonathan (Gen. V. 24) renders the Ἀνάληψις of Enoch:[29]
איתנגיד וסליק לרקיעא. It is also noteworthy that איתנגיד (designat-

----

[24] A. Aptowitzer (*Tarbiz*, II, 270ff.) has shown that the vision of the
heavenly Jerusalem and Temple which will in the future be established
in this earth is a purely Jewish idea, yet it does not occur in any early
Rabbinic source; according to him it was eliminated by the Rabbis because it was exploited by the Christians. It reappears in later Rabbinic
sources compiled in Moslem countries. Similar examples can be found
in my "*Yemenite Midrashim*" (Hebrew), p. 15 ff. Comp. also *Greek in
Jewish Palestine*, p. 189. n. 30.

[25] Comp. preceding note.

[26] TB *Berakhoth* 7ᵃ and TP *Shabbath* XIV. 4, 14ᵈ.

[27] Although the Judeo-Christians of Palestine spoke Aramaic at that time,
the prayers and the biblical lessons were recited in Greek (as appears
from Eusebius, M. P. ed. Cureton, p. 4. See *Greek in Jewish Palestine*,
p. 2), and, of course, the same language was utilized for the sacred terminology which was employed on the tomb-stones.

[27a] A good illustration of the use of our word in this *Midrash* is offered by
a Greek fragment of the *Ascension of Isaiah* (ed. Charles, London
1900, p. 142). It records that Isaiah fell into a trance (ἐν ἐκστάσει)
and he was thought to be dead, but when the king took his hand he
learned that he did not actually die, but was taken up (οὐκ ἀπέθανεν,
ἀλλ' ἀνελήφθη). Comp. also Hieron., *Epist.* XXII. 30 (Migne PL
XXII. 415): Cum subito *raptus in spiritu* ad tribunal iudicis pertrahor.
"Suddenly I was spiritually taken up and dragged before the tribunal
of the Judge" (ed. Isid. Hilberg, CSEL LIV [1910], p. 190, 8).

[29] TB *Pesahim*, 50ᵃ. Comp.*Pirkei de-Rabbi*, quoted above n. 4.

[30] In Greek we should render it: ἀνελήφθη καὶ ἀνέβη εἰς τὸν οὐρανόν.
It should be noted that וסליק לרקיעא has no equivalent in the Hebrew
text.

ing "died") reappears on the fifteenth century tombs of the Yemenite Jews[30] who frequently preserved ancient traditions.[31]

Thus, it is clear that איתנגיד is a translation of ἀνελήφθη but
not the reverse. The original is preserved in the Palestinian Midrash;
this proves the authenticity of that source. It does not record the
question of the Martyrs in the vision of R. Joshua b. Levi's grandson. We can reaffirm our statement that the vision about the Martyrs
was not connected with the name of R. Joshua b. Levi's grandson
(III c.) but only with the name of R. Aha (IV c.). The Babylonian
Talmud combined two different stories into one.

*
* *

Moreover, we may assume that the title of Praylios[32] κοινωνὸς ὁ
κατὰ τόπον is borrowed from the Jews. Prof. Grégoire[33] has elucidated the meaning of the Κοινωνός. The emperor Justinian banished the prelates and the priests of the Montanist church from
Constantinople. He mentions:[34] τῶν καλουμένων αὐτῶν πατριαρχῶν
καὶ κοινωνῶν ἢ ἐπισκόπων κτλ. H. Grégoire further refers to Je
rome[35] who writes: Apud nos apostolorum· locum episcopi tenent:
apud eos episcopus tertius est! Habent enim primos de Pepusa Phry-
giae patriarchas, secundos, quos appellant κοινωνούς[36] atque ita in
tertium, paene ultimum gradum episcopi devolvuntur. From the Latin
translation of the edict of Justinian we learn that the equivalent of
the Κοινωνός was socius.[37]

Thus, the Κοινωνός, socius, was a high dignitary in the Montanist church ranking next to the Patriarch. The title Patriarch was
most probably borrowed by the Montanists from the Jews, as sug-

---

[30] S. D. GOITTEN, Joseph Halévy's Journey in Yemen, Hebrew, p. 114;
Arabic, p. 61. It is very noteworthy that the Yemenite sources (Midrash
Haggadol Gen., p. 429; The Exempla of the Rabbis, ed. GASTER, p. 18)
read in BR LXV (end), 743²: ונפל איתנחנ instead of בחנב:ב, fell into
a trance.
[31] See Hayerushalmi Kiphshuto, I, p. 520; Yemenite Midrashim, p. 16 ff.;
Greek in Jewish Palestine, p. 189, n. 30.
[32] See above p. 439.
[33] Byzantion, II, 332 ff.
[34] Cod. Just. I. V. 20.
[35] Ep. XLI. 3 (ed. HILBERG, ibid,. p. 313, 14 ff.).
[36] Mss. caenonus AIID, cenonos B, cenonas ς.
[37] See GRÉGOIRE, ibid. p. 333-334.

gested by H. Grégoire.[38] It seems that the κοινωνός[39] similarly was taken from the same source.

The Rabbinic writings frequently mention the term חבר עיר.[39ᴬ] Ancient authorities[40] as well as modern scholars[41] disagree as to the meaning of this word. There is ample evidence in the Rabbinic sources that the phrase refers to a group of people in charge of religious and charitable functions;[42] the חבר עיר is then something like κοινὸν τῆς πόλεως. But, on the other hand, there is authentic evidence[43] that חבר עיר refers to an individual. And, indeed, the earliest authorities explain חֲבר עיר to mean the most prominent man in learning and wisdom, who exercises certain religious and social functions.[44] The term is therefore very similar to κοινωνὸς τῆς πόλεως.

In our opinion it is impossible to translate חבר עיר by the same word in all places. The existence among the Jews of an institution like κοινὸν τῆς πόλεως and an individual like κοινωνὸς τῆς πόλεως is quite certain. Both were called חבר עיר (perhaps differently vocalized), and both existed probably at the same time. The Κοινωνός of the Montanists seems to be the counterpart of the חבר עיר of the Jews, who was the religious (and to a certain extent the social) leader of the community.

We have now to reexamine the meaning of חבר in the famous inscriptions on the Maccabean coins, which read:[45]

כהן גדול והבר היהודים

Perhaps the exact translation would be: ἀρχιερεὺς καὶ κοινωνὸς τῶν Ἰουδαίων.

---

[38] Byzantion, VIII, p. 76.
[39] Κοινωνὸς ὁ κατὰ τόπον would be rendered in Aramaic: חברא דאתרא. Comp. מלבא דאתרא in TP 'Abodah Zarah I. 1, 39ᵇ.
[39ᴬ] Almost all of the sources which mention it are of the second century.
[40] See 'Arukh s. v. חבר.
[41] See Krauss, Jahrbuch der Jüdisch-Literarischen Gesellschaft, XVII (Frankfurt a. M., 1926), p. 195 ff.; Ginzberg, A Commentary to the Palestinian Talmud, III, p. 410 ff.
[42] See Ginzberg, ibid. p. 421-425.
[43] Tosephta Megilla, IV, 228².
[44] See Aruch Completum, III, p. 337ᴬ and n. 3.
[45] Madden, the History of Jewish coinage (London 1864), p. 62-77. The bibliography and the different commentaries were collected by Schürer, Geschichte etc. I⁴, p. 269 n. 25.

Finally, it should be noted that a grave and misleading[46] error crept in into Schulthess' Lexicon Syropalaestinum[47] s. v. ܚܒܪ. He lists חבר מדינא as meaning *civis*, πολιτικός. The only occurrence cited by him is from a fragment of the translation[48] of the vita S. Antonii.[49] The passage relates that S. Antonius' manners were not uncouth like those of a man who grew up and became old on a mountain, but that he was courteous and urbane. (Οὐκ... ἄγριον εἶχε τὸ ἦθος, ἀλλὰ καὶ χαρίεις ἦν καὶ πολιτικός). The Palestinian Syriac renders the last sentence: אלא מלא הוא חסד הבר מדינא. This makes absolutely no sense. There is an obvious mistake of one letter. The last two words have to be read כבר מדינא[50] and not חבר מדינא.[50a] The translation is: "He was full of grace like an *urbanus.*" The same connection between בן מדינה and πολιτικός is found in the Mishna,[51] where פוליטיקון (or פוליטיקין) provides a play of words in conjunction with בני מדינה.[52] The correction of the Syriac text is positively certain. We may conclude: The word חבר מדינא as quoted by Schulthess does not exist.

IV

בחיקו של אברהם εἰς κόλπον (ἐν κόλπῳ) 'Αβραάμ

On p. 417, n. 5, we referred to *Aboth deR. Nathan* and to the minor tract *Semahoth* where the stories of the martyrdom of R. Simeon b. Gamaliel and R. Ishmael are related. In the eighth chapter of *Semahoth* we have a collection of almost all the early martyrdoms mentioned in the *Tannaitic* and Talmudic writings. We do not know the original source (or sources) from which it drew, but the account agrees on the whole with the earlier, *Tannaitic*, sources; the details mentioned in the Talmud are missing there. It seems therefore that its readings are sometimes preferable to those

---

[46] See GINZBERG, *l. c.* (above n. 41), p. 426.
[47] P. 59.
[48] *Palestinian Syriac texts* by LEWIS and GIBSON, London, 1900, p. 104.
[49] MIGNE PG XXVI, 945ᴬ.
[50] A Hebraism for הוך בר.
[50a] It seems to be a mere misprint, for the editors have in the corresponding Greek text (p. 105): ὡς πολιτικός instead of καὶ πολιτικός of ed. MIGNE.
[51] *Terumoth*, II. 5.
[52] The explanations by Löw (*Flora der Juden*, II, 129) of בני מדינה and by SACHS (*Beiträge*, II, 195) of פוליטיקון are wrong.

of the Talmud. On the other hand it represents a later formulation than that of the *Tannaitic* works.

According to the above *Aboth deR. Nathan*[1] R. Ishmael said to R. Simeon b. Gamaliel: כשתי־ פסיעות ואתה³ נתון בצד אבותיך "In two steps and you will be at the side of your ancestors." Instead of בצד אבותיך *Semahoth*[4] *reads* בחיקן של צדיקים, "In the bosom of the righteous." This phrase seems to be borrowed from the later terminology of the martyrs. *Midrash Ekah*,[5] in relating the story of the Mother of the Seven,[6] tells us that the mother urged her youngest son to die for His Name, telling him ואתה ניתן בחיקו של אברהם אבינו[7], "Thou wilt be placed in the bosom of our father Abraham," εἰς τὸν κόλπον τοῦ Ἀβραὰμ τοῦ πατρὸς ἡμῶν.[8]

On the Christian epitaphs[9] the formula ἐν κόλποις (or εἰς κόλπους) Ἀβραάμ καὶ Ἰσαάκ καὶ Ἰακώβ occurs very frequently. It was already observed by Le Blant[10] that both the *Euchologium* and the Christian epitaphs used here the terminology of the Martyrs. But it appears that the Christians were wont to mention the bosoms of all the three patriarchs,[11] whereas the Jews referred to the bosom of Abraham only.

In the collection of M. G. Lefebvre,[12] among the dozens of inscriptions where the bosoms of all the patriarchs [13] are mentioned, one reads:[14] ἀνάπαυσον αὐτὸ[ν] ὁ Θ(εό)ς εἰς κόλιπον[15] Ἀβραάμ.

---

[1] Version II, ch. 41, ed. Schechter, p. 114.
[2] So in *Neveh Shalom*, ed. Tauszig, p. 39. Comp. also *Menorat Ha-maor* IV, ed. Enelow, p. 189.
[3] So Cod. *Parma*.
[4] *Ibid.*, ed. Higger, p. 153.
[5] I. 16, ed. Buber, p. 85. Comp. also *Pesikta Rabbathi* 43, ed. Friedmann f. 180b.
[6] IV *Maccab.* VIII. 3 ff.
[7] The term appears once more in Talmudic literature (TB *Kiddushin* 72b) in a different meaning (as appears from *Bereshith Rabba* LVIII 2, ed. Theodor, p. 620 and parallels). Comp. also *Pesikta deR. Kahana* in *Beth Talmud* ed. Weiss vol. V, p. 168; ed. Buber f. 25b n. 79.
[8] Comp. *Luke* XVI. 22 and "Kommentar" ibid.
[9] Especially in Nubia and Egypt. See Dumont *in Bull. de Corresp. Hell.* I, 1877, p. 321, and H. I. Bell, *Studies presented to F. Ll. Griffith*, p. 202.
[10] *Manuel d'épigraphie Chrétienne* etc., p. 87 n. 3, and p. 88 n. 1. Comp. also *ibid.* pp. 5, 83.
[11] See also R. James, *The Testament of Abraham*, Cambridge 1892, p. 128 ff.
[12] *Recueil des inscriptions grecques-chrétiennes d'Egypte*.
[13] NN 48, 67, 107, 541, 563, 564, 608, 623-625, 629, 635, 636, 641, 642, 645-647, 649, 652, 654, 655, 657-661, 664-668, 790, 805, 1157, 1173.
[14] N 622.
[15] Comp. Lefebvre *ibid.* No. 625.

Thus, the "bosom" mentioned in *Semahoth* betrays the later martyr-terminology, which is still absent in the earlier *Aboth deR. Nathan.*

Finally we may add that not only do we find in Jewish and Christian martyrology parallel incidents and similar terminology but also the same slogans.

The Babylonian Talmud[16] records that R. Eleazar b. Perata was charged[17] with studying the Law and committing theft.[18] He was asked by the judge: "Why have you been studying [the Law] and why have you been stealing?"[19] Our sage pleaded innocent saying: אי סייפא לא ספרא ואי ספרא לא סייפא, "He who is a warrior is not a scholar, and if he is a scholar, he is not a warrior." Since the text is not vocalized it can also be translated: "If the sword, then not the book, and if the book, then not the sword."[20] R. Eleazar pointed to the inconsistency of the charge which accused him of being both a student and a robber, and he was acquitted.

Eusebius[21] relates that the Roman soldier Marianus, stationed in Caesarea, confessed himself a Christian.[22] He was given three hours for consideration, after which he was expected to make a definite statement regarding his views. Meanwhile the bishop of Caesarea, Theotecnus, took hold of him and brought him near the altar. He raised a little the soldier's cloak and pointed to the sword, then pointed to the book of the gospels, and bade him choose between the two. The sword and the book[23] are incompatible.

----

[16] *'Abodah Zarah* 17b.
[17] Probably in the fourth decade of the second century.
[18] The original Palestinian version most probably told that he was accused of being a λῃστής, a robber, the usual Roman name for the Jewish nationalist fighters.
[19] Διὰ τί ἐλῄστευσας; "Why did you become a robber?" was the question put by the ἔπαρχος to Bulla the Robber. (Dio Cassius (LXXXVI) LXXVII. 10. 7).
[20] Comp. *Sifre* II, 40 (end), ed. FINKELSTEIN, p. 84² and KNAUSS in *Haggoren* (Hebrew) IV, p. 28 and n. 9 *ibid.*
[21] *Hist. Eccl.* VII. 15.
[22] In the seventh decade of the III c.
[23] The play of words in the slogan rather suggests an Aramaic origin.

ABBREVIATIONS

b   — *ben, bar* (son of).

BR   — Midrash Bereshith Rabba.

JQR   — The Jewish Quarterly Review.

MGWJ   — Monatsschrift für Geschichte und Wissenschaft des Judentums.

MP   — De Martyribus Palaestinae, by Eusebius.

R.   — Rabbi.

TB   — Talmud Babylonicum.

TP   — Talmud Palæstiniensis.

S. LIEBERMAN.

PALESTINE IN THE THIRD AND FOURTH CENTURIES*

By SAUL LIEBERMAN

The Jewish Theological Seminary of America

I. PERSECUTIONS AND REBELLIONS

MANY so-called important historical facts have taken such deep roots in the field of Jewish history that they have gradually become common knowledge and serve as background for further constructions. Persecutions of the Jewish religion by the Roman empire (in the third and fourth centuries) on the one hand and rebellions of the Palestinian Jews against it (during the fourth century) on the other are considered well established facts and are generally accepted. Since the time of Grätz[1] Jewish scholars take the persecution of the Jewish religion by Constantius for granted. Some scholars maintain[2] that the Jewish religion was persecuted in the third century as well. It is likewise generally accepted[3] that the Jews revolted against Rome during the fourth century. "As a matter of fact," asserts a Jewish historian,[4] "both cities (i. e. Lydda and Sepphoris), but especially Sepphoris (Diocaesarea), were centers of Jewish rebellion in the fourth century until they were destroyed by Gallus (351). In order to cure the focal

---

* All the dates mentioned in this article are C. E.

[1] *Geschichte der Juden*, IV³, p. 313 ff. and p. 456, n. 30.

[2] I. Halevy, דורות הראשונים IIb, p. 315; A. Marmorstein, Les persécutions religieuses à l'époque d. R. Yohanan b. Nappacha, *REJ* vol. LXXVI, 1923, p. 166 ff.; *idem, Tarbiz* III, 1932, p. 167 ff.

[3] Graetz *ibid.* and his followers.

[4] *JQR*, vol. XXXVI, 1945, p. 165.

329

infection of Jewish resistance, and to deter the population from any inclination to conspire against Rome, the governor decided·to hold the trial against sedition in just such a center." Thus, the Jewish rebellion and conspiracy against Rome is "a matter of fact." However, both the above mentioned persecutions of the Jewish religion and the rebellion of the Jews against Rome are far from being established matters of fact.

Since the historians link the religious persecutions with the rebellions of the Jews and regard the former as the cause of the latter, we shall treat both events together. Let us first take up the alleged persecutions of the Jewish religion in the third and fourth centuries and examine the evidence for them. In the entire Palestinian Talmud and early *Midrashim* we find no direct allusion to שמד (destruction, extermination, *extirpatio*, ἐξώλειας[5]) during the third and fourth centuries, a matter which in itself is quite significant for our problem. The scholars rely mainly on the Babylonian Talmud. They quote the passage in *Ḥullin* (101b): אמר רבא שמדא הוה וכו'. "Rabba said: It was a time of religious persecutions etc." Grätz[6] and Frankel[7] place these events in the fourth century.[8] I. Halevy and Marmorstein[9] place them in the third century.[10] The early authorities[11] however explain that Rabba referred neither to his own time nor to that of R. Johanan but to the time of the *Mishnah*, to the Hadrianic persecutions. Indeed, it is very plausible that R. Johanan himself had in mind a

[5] On these terms see Lieberman, *Annuaire de I'Institut de Philologie et d'Histoire Orientales et Slaves*, VII (1939-1944), p. 427-428.
[6] Pp. 318 and 456 n. 29.
[7] מבוא הירושלמי, 98b.
[8] Their opinion is based on the explanation of R. Nathan in his *'Arukh* s. v. שמד.
[9] See above n. 2.
[10] Their opinion is based on the interpretation of *Rashi a. l.*
[11] R. Gershom *a. l.* Comp. the elaborate exposition in *Ritba, ibid.*

specific year when the rabbis were prevented from fixing the day of the New Year on account of these persecutions. It is stated[12] that the fixation (by the rabbis) of the Day of the New Moon is valid even if the rabbis under duress selected the wrong day (אתם אפילו אנוסים), — an allusion to the time of the Hadrianic persecutions.[13] It probably happened that the rabbis were not able to fix this day at all for a certain year, so that the Day of Atonement was celebrated without the previous legal proclamation of the rabbis, and R. Johanan made his statement in connection with this.[14] Hence this passage has nothing to do with the third or the fourth centuries.

The second proof is again drawn from the Babylonian Talmud.[15] A cryptic message by the Palestinian rabbis to Babylonia[16] states that the rabbis "wanted to establish a *Nezib* (i. e. an additional month to the year), but yon Edomite (i. e. Rome) did not permit it." Graetz[17] and his followers take this as an indication of a general persecution of the Jewish religion under Constantius.

We must bear in mind that no date for any Jewish festivals can be fixed without the computation of the calendar, and the prohibition of such computation is in general tantamount to an injunction against Jewish religious festivals. Yet, there is no hint in Palestinian literature of that time that the Jews were forbidden to celebrate their holidays. It is therefore evident that the Romans were not concerned with the practice of intercalation but with its procedure, which consisted of a meeting

[12] *Sifra, Emor*, ch. X. 3, ed. Weiss, 100a. Comp. *Tosephta Rosh Hashana* III. 1, 211₁₆.

[13] See Rabbi Kasher, *Torah Shelemah* vol. XIII (in press), סוד העיבור, ch. 'ו.

[14] Comp. *Ritba a. l.*

[15] *Sanhedrin* 12a.

[16] Around the middle of the fourth century.

[17] P. 317.

of the greatest rabbis in solemn circumstances.[18] The Roman
government usually looked askance at this kind of meeting.[19] It has already been noted by scholars that at times,
particularly during periods of hostility between the Roman
empire and Persia, the government objected to the despatch of messengers to the Jewish diaspora by the Patriarch.[20]

However, this explanation is not entirely satisfactory.
According to tradition[21] the Patriarch, owing to changed
conditions, was compelled to fix a permanent calendar
around the middle of the fourth century. It was not
customary for the Jews to submit readily to a decree which
had no logical justification and the purpose of which was
only to annoy them. The rabbis could have made their
calculations privately and then arranged an open meeting
where they might announce their decision six months in
advance. The information could have reached the Jewish
diaspora through legal channels. Why then abandon a
practice sanctified by hundreds of years?

It seems to me that the government of the Christian
emperors was prompted by some other motive for prohibiting the early computation of the calendar by the Jewish
Patriarch. According to Jewish Law[22] the decision regarding the intercalation of the year which involved the day
of the celebration of Passover had to be made before Nissan;
in practice it was arrived at even earlier, in order to enable
the messengers bearing the proclamation of the Patriarch
to reach the Jewish diaspora, and especially Babylonia,
before Passover. Many churches in the East used to

[18] See *TP Sanhedrin* I, 18c; *TB ibid.* 70b; *Pirke R. 'Eliezer* VII, ed.
R. David Luria 20a ff. and parallels.
[19] See *TP ibid.* 18c, bot.
[20] See now R. Kasher, *Torah Shelemah* vol. XIII, סוד העיבור, ch. 'ג.
[21] See below n. 35.
[22] *Tosephta Sanhedrin* II, 418 ff. and parallels.

celebrate Easter during the week of Passover.[23] The Council of Nicaea decided to do away with this "Jewish practice" and tried to achieve unity among the churches with respect to the date of Easter.[24] In his epistle to the churches Constantine also emphasized the Jewish element in the custom of the Eastern churches.[25] But the efforts of the Christian emperors failed. Some Eastern churches obstinately persisted in their adherence to the Jewish custom.[26]

Athanasius[27] tells us that these churches were located in Syria, Cilicia (probably the parts adjoining Syria) and Mesopotamia.[28] We further know that the Mesopotamian Audians of the fourth century quoted a διάταξις ἀποστό-λων (constitutio apostolorum) which read: "As for you, make no calculations (i. e. regarding the date of Easter), but celebrate it when your brethren of the circumcision do it. Celebrate it with them at the same time ... And if they err do not care."[29] This apparently was the general attitude of many dissident churches in the East; they associated Easter with a historic event which happened on the *Jewish* Passover and thought it proper to follow the date of the latter whether it was fixed correctly or not.[30]

[23] See the material quoted and referred to in the *Dictionnaire de Theologie Catholique* (Paris 1932) vol. XI, 1951 ff.; Cabrol, *Dictionnaire* etc., vol. XIII, pp. 1542, 1547, 1548.

[24] See Euseb. *Vita Const.* III. 5, *PG* XX, 1057d.

[25] *Ibid.* 18, 1076a: ἀνάξιον ἔδοξεν εἶναι τὴν ἁγιωτάτην ἐκείνην ἑορτὴν τῇ τῶν Ἰουδαίων ἑπομένους συνηθείᾳ πληροῦν κτλ. "It seemed very unworthy of this most sacred feast, that we should keep it following the custom of the Jews etc."

[26] See Socrat. *Hist. eccl.* V. 22, *PG* LXVII, 625b ff.

[27] De *synod.* 5, *PG* XXVI, 687b; comp. ibid. 1032c.

[28] οἱ μὲν γὰρ ἀπὸ τῆς Συρίας καὶ Κιλικίας καὶ Μεσοποταμίας ἐχώλευον περὶ τὴν ἑορτήν, καὶ μετὰ τῶν Ἰουδαίων ἐποίουν τὸ Πάσχα.

[29] Epiphan. *Haeres.* LXX, 10, *PG* XLII, 356c–357b: ὑμεῖς μὴ ψηφί-ζητε, ἀλλὰ ποιεῖτε, ὅταν οἱ ἀδελφοί ὑμῶν οἱ ἐκ περιτομῆς. Μετ' αὐτῶν ἅμα ποιεῖτε ... Κ'άν τε πλανηθῶσι, μηδὲ ὑμῖν μελέτω.

[30] See Socrat. *Hist. eccl.* V. 22, *PG* LXVII 629a: Ἰουδαίοις, καίτοι τὴν ἀκρίβειαν μὴ σώζουσι δεῖν ἕπεσθαι περὶ τῆς ἑορτῆς κτλ. Comp. ibid. 644.

Jewish law itself ruled[31] that festivals were legal even if
erroneously fixed by the proper Jewish authorities. The
above apocryphal *constitutio* was certainly current in Mesopotamia during the fourth century. The Audians asserted
that the practice according to the *constitutio apostolorum*
was the old one, and that Constantine changed it for
reasons of his own.[32]

It was therefore natural for the Christian emperors to
render a service to the church which they earnestly strove
to unify by forbidding the Patriarch to compute and
proclaim in advance the date of Passover; and especially to
despatch messengers, who had to take roads to the Jewish
diaspora in the East, which ran through Syria and Mesopotamia. The sectarian churches of these countries would
thus be deprived of information about the date of the
Passover.

The Jews, however, outwitted the government by inter-
calating the year far ahead of time and thus avoiding the
watchful eyes of the informers. Once the messengers were
apprehended on their way to Babylonia, but eventually
they arrived safely.[33] It seems that the government was
quite determined in its efforts to prevent the Patriarch
from sending information regarding the dates of the holidays, and the Jews perhaps were compelled to compute the
calendar for a cycle.[34] Realizing that this prohibition, unlike
any other, was conceived not to annoy the Jews but to
achieve that unity, of such vital importance to the Christian
government, the Patriarch concluded that the measure was
not a temporary one and consequently created a permanent
calendar.[35]

---

[31] *Tosephta Rosh Hashana* III. 1, 211₁₈ and parallels.
[32] See Epiphan. *ibid.* 9, 353b-c.
[33] See above n. 15.
[34] See *TP 'Erubin* III, end, 21c.
[35] See Graetz, p. 457, n. 31.

.However, we find explicitly stated in the Babylonian Talmud:[36] בימי ר' זירא הוה שמדא ונזר דלא למיתב בתעניתא וכו', "In the days of R. Zera[37] there was a *shemad*[38] and fasting[39] was [also] prohibited etc." Since we are concerned with the Roman persecutions of the Jews, this passage bears on our subject only if it refers to Palestine. In this case the Babylonian Talmud is not a direct source, but a secondary one. The original source might have used a different term.[40] But even from the passage in its present form it does not necessarily follow that there was a religious persecution of the Jews (which is very unlikely under the reign of Diocletian). It most probably refers to a *leitourgia*, to urgent compulsory work imposed upon the inhabitants of Palestine, which was a daily occurrence at that time.[41] The Jews resented it because it involved the violation of the Sabbath,[42] and they imposed a fast upon themselves. The government's interference was of course natural: the fast would both discourage and weaken the workers. The Babylonian Talmud could certainly style such a tax שמד,[43] but we can hardly classify it among religious persecutions.

Similarly, Graetz[44] found an allusion to religious persecutions in the mnemonic sign:[45] אתא ר' דימי אפקה. אתא רבין קטלה, which he interpreted to mean that R. Dimi came to Babylonia because he fled the danger of exile and Rabin did likewise because he fled the danger of execution. This

---

[36] *Ta'anith* 8b, ed. Malter, p. 27b. Comp. also דקדוקי סופרים *a. l.*

[37] Flourished during the reign of Diocletian.

[38] See above n. 5.

[39] As a prayer to avert the decree.

[40] See *Tosaphot* to *TB Rosh Hashana* 32b *s. v.* השמד. Comp. דקדוקי סופרים *ibid.* p. 96, n. 300.

[41] As a matter of fact, R. Ze'ira (=Zera) himself was once drafted for an *angareia*, see *TP Berakhoth* I.1, 2d bot. and *TB ibid.* 9b.

[42] See *TP Shebi'ith* IV. 2, 35a (and parallel) about R. Abuna Ze'irah.

[43] See above n. 40.

[44] P. 456, n. 29.

[45] *TB Ḥullin* 106a.

explanation can hardly be taken seriously. We have here a mnemonic sign alluding to a usual Mishnaic expression[46] יצא ליהרג, where the word יצא precedes the word ליהרג; in the same way, R. Dimi who came first was the author of the הוציאוה version, and Rabin who followed him was the author of the הרגוה version.[47]

These are all the passages in the Babylonian Talmud which are supposed to refer to religious persecutions of the Palestinian Jews during the third and fourth centuries. But Palestinian rabbinic literature has also been invoked[48] to demonstrate the religious persecutions of the Jews. For instance, it is stated:[49] ארסקינס אוקיד אוריתא דצנבראי. אתון שאלון לר' יונה ולר' יוסה מהו לקרות בספר ברבים אמר[ו] לון אסיר. לא דאסיר אלא מן גו דנפשהון עגימה אינון זבנין להון אחורי וכו'. "Ursicinus[50] burned the scroll of the Law[51] of the Sennabreans.[52] They came and asked R. Jonah and R. Jose: 'May one read from the [burned] scroll in public service?' They replied: 'No.' Not because it was contrary to law but in order that they might feel badly about it and buy a new one." Graetz saw in this a persecution of the Jews by Ursicinus.[53]

Z. Frankel,[54] however basing his arguments on contemporary rabbinic literature from which it follows that definitely friendly relations existed between the rabbis of Palestine and Ursicinus, reasoned convincingly that it is

---

[46] *Mishna Gittin* III. 4; *'Erakhin* I. 3; *ibid.* 4. Comp. also אהאפק למקטלא in *TP Gittin* VI. 7, 48a.

[47] See *Rashi a. l.*

[48] Graetz, p. 315.

[49] *TP Megilla* III. 1, 74a.

[50] On the time of the event see below.

[51] It is obvious from what follows that the scroll was only partly damaged.

[52] Sennabris is situated about four Roman miles from Tiberias, see Jos. *Bel. Jud.* III, 447. It is frequently mentioned in rabbinic literature.

[53] P. 315.

[54] *MGWJ* XVI, 1867, p. 150; מבוא הירושלמי, 98b.

very unlikely that Ursicinus deliberately burned the scroll
of the law.   Whoever is familiar with the style of the
Palestinian Talmud will agree with Frankel that the above
passage does not warrant the assumption that the scroll of
the law was burned intentionally.   It was most probably
damaged in the course of Ursicinus' actions, when fire was
set to the houses in which (Diocaesarean?) rebels were
caught.[55]

Thus, there is no reason whatever for questioning the
sincerity of the rabbis (as Graetz did) when they ordered
bakers to bake bread (on the Sabbath) for Ursicinus,
because "he had no intentions to force the Jews to transgress their religion, he only wanted to eat fresh bread."[56]
Moreover, we learn[57] that the rabbis ordered that "bread
be brought[58] for Ursicinus on the Sabbath because the
community might be in need of it (or of him)," i. e. they
gave their orders in advance, before it was requested by
Ursicinus, to avoid a possible danger.[59]

What was the reason for Ursicinus' punitive expedition
to Palestine?   Graetz and Frankel[60] appropriately called
attention to the reports of Aurelius Victor and the churchfathers[61] which assert that there was a Jewish uprising in
Palestine in 352 (or 353).[62]   However, if we analyze these
sources we are forced to doubt their authenticity.   Accord-

---

[55] See below.

[56] TP Shebi'ith IV. 1, 35a (and parallel): לא אתכוון מטסדרתון, ולא אתכוון
אלא טיכול פיתא חמימא.

[57] TP Bezah I. 6, 60c bot., according to the correct reading of the
Genizah Fragments, ed. Ginzberg, p. 170, l. 22.

[58] A medieval author read here: "baked," see Ratner a. l., p. 10.

[59] Frankel, in his time, had only the defective text of the editions and
therefore he concluded (ibid., p. 148, n. 7) that the passage is obscure.
Comp. also מבוא הירושלמי, p. 55b–56a.

[60] Ibid.

[61] See below.

[62] Additional sources are referred to by Juster II, p. 197 nn. 1, 2.
Comp. also ibid., p. 196, n. 3.

ing to Jerome,[63] the Jews rebelled and slaughtered the
soldiers during the night and took their arms, but Gallus
subsequently suppressed their rebellion and burned their
cities Diocaesarea (Sepphoris), Tiberias and Diospolis
(Lydda). Socrates[64] states "that the Jews of Diocaesarea
in Palestine took up arms against the Romans and overran
the adjacent places,[65] but Gallus completely vanquished
them and ordered that Diocaesarea be razed to its foundations." This is repeated by Sozomenus,[66] Theophanes,[67]
Nicephorus Callist.[68] and others, who speak only of Diocaesarea and not of Tiberias and Diospolis.

On the other hand, the extensive contemporary rabbinic
literature of Palestine does not say a word about the
destruction of the above three cities. The impression
gained from the Palestinian Talmud, the product of the
academy of Tiberias, is that the cities continued their
normal life.[69] It is only stated[70] that the people of Sepphoris
(Diocaesarea) were sought in the days of king Ursicinus;
they disguised themselves by putting a plaster on their
noses, but they were denounced and caught.[71] The destruction of the city is not mentioned.[72] From the work of Theo-

---

[63] *Chronicon, Olymp.* 282, ed. R. Helm, Leipzig 1913, I, p. 238.

[64] *Hist. eccl.* II. 33, *PG* LXVII, 296a.

[65] περὶ τοὺς τόπους ἐκείνους κατέτρεχον.

[66] *Hist. eccl.* IV. 7, *PG ibid.* 1124d.

[67] *Chronogr. A. M.* 5843 (343!), *PG* CVIII, 440c. The ninth century
historian also knows that the Diocaesarean Jews slaughtered, besides
the Romans, Greeks and Samaritans.

[68] *PG* CXLVI, 353d.

[69] See below p. 352.

[70] *TP Yebamoth* XVI.2, 15c; *Sota* IX.3, 23c.

[71] Probably outside of their city; perhaps in Sennabris, see above
p. 337.

[72] Graetz' reference (p. 456, n. 30) to the *Pesikta* (ch. VIII, ed. Friedmann, p. 29b) is irrelevant. The passage does not mention a repression
of a rebellion, but talks of the general oppression at the hands of Gentiles. Besides, the anonymous passage may refer to events which happened centuries later, as realized by Frankel *MGWJ ibid.*, p. 151,
n. 5.

doretus[73] we also learn that some twenty years after its supposed destruction Diocaesarea was inhabited by Jews.[74] Thus the biased report of the churchfathers ought to be taken with great caution.

Being aware of the silence[75] of the contemporary local rabbinic sources, Frankel[76] realized that the contradictory narratives of the churchfathers possessed little historical value. But, as he could not easily discount the testimony of the unbiased Victor,[77] he decided that the Jews rebelled in the South of Palestine, in Judea. He referred to *Bereshith Rabba*[78] where it is stated: .אם יבא עשו אל המחנה האחת והכהו אילו אחינו שבדרום. " '*If Esau come to the one company and smite it*' (Gen. 32.8) refers to our brethren in the *Darom*."[79] According to Frankel, the rabbis had in mind the occurrences under Gallus in the middle of the fourth century. But the following sentence in the Midrash disproves it. It says: אמר ר' הושעיה אפעלפיכן מתענים היו ע ל י נ ו[80] בשיני ובחמישי. "R. Hoshaia said: 'Yet[81] they used to fast in *our* behalf on Mondays and Thursdays.' " R. Hoshaia who referred to himself as a Daromite is most probably R. Hoshaia the Great, who flourished in the beginning of the third century. The text therefore evidently refers to the devastation of Judea under Hadrian.[82]

[73] *Hist. eccl.* IV.22, *PG* LXXXII, 1180c.

[74] See M. Schwabe in the *Jubilee Volume For David Yelin*, מנחה לדוד, p. 110 ff.

[75] Except for the incident with the Diocaesareans and the burning of the scroll in Sennabris, see above.

[76] *Ibid.*, p. 144 ff.   [77] See below.

[78] LXXVI.3, p. 899.

[79] =Judea or Lydda, see Lieberman, הירושלמי כפשוטו I, p. 458.

[80] This is the reading of almost all mss. including the best: *Cod. Vat.*

[81] *I. e.* although the destruction of the *Darom* was predestined by the *Torah*, the Jews did not give up hope.

[82] The later R. Hoshaia also flourished before the time of Gallus, and he likewise could not refer to the events under this Caesar, as realized by Theodor in his commentary *a. l.*

However, the testimony of Aurelius Victor can by no means be disregarded. He says:[83] *Et interea Judaeorum seditio, qui Patricium nefarie in regni specie[m] sustulerant, opressa.* "At that time a revolt of the Jews who nefariously raised Patricius to the royal power, was suppressed [by Gallus]." In my opinion, the short sentence of Victor means nothing more than what it says. The Jews (of Diocaesarea) raised (perhaps with the help of the Roman garrison itself) a certain Patricius to the royal power. This Patricius might have been a heathen Roman officer whom the Diocaesarean Jews preferred to the extremely cruel Gallus who, like the emperor, was a devout Christian.[84] The East had numerous aspirants with real or imaginary claims to the royal power[85] in the time of Gallus' caesarship. Of course, they and their supporters paid with their life and property, and in 353[86] Ursicinus was summoned by Gallus from Nesibis to sit as judge in the trials of high treason. Ammianus Marcellinus, who was personally attached to the staff of Ursicinus gives a detailed account of these trials.[87] He mentions neither the revolt of the Jews nor our Patricius, but he significantly adds at the end of the chapter that after the execution of the aspirants to the throne, Gallus tried many cases of this kind, but that he did not find it worth while to give an account of all these trials.[88] The revolt in Diocaesarea and "king Patricius" were probably too insignificant to be mentioned.[89]

[83] *De caesaribus* XLII. II.

[84] Sozom. *Hist. eccl.* V. 19, *PG* LXVII, 1273d. Comp. Seeck in PW *RE*, VII, 1097.

[85] See Ammianus Marcel. XIV. 1. 2.

[86] See the references given by Prof. Schwabe *ibid.* (see above n. 74), p. 110, n. 2.

[87] XIV. 9. 1 ff.

[88] *Ibid.* 9: Gallus ... multa huius modi scrutabatur. Quae singula narrare non refert etc.

[89] *TP Berakhoth* V, 9a relates that R. Jonah and R. Jose (these are the two rabbis who ordered the transgression of the Sabbath in order

Thus, the rebellion of the Jews against the *Roman Empire* (in 353) is a possible figment of imagination of later writers. We have instead a local insignificant incident of a Roman usurper supported by some of the Diocaesarean Jews (who, it may be noted, enjoyed the same reputation as the Alexandrians and Antiocheians regarding their character[90]). The incident had no serious consequences for the community in general, because the majority of the Jews were not involved, and perhaps because it could be claimed that the rebellion was not aimed at the emperor but at the Caesar who was subsequently executed by his orders. At any rate, it is quite clear that neither the Patriarch nor the rabbis were involved in any action against the Roman empire during the third and fourth centuries.[91] The rabbis repeatedly warned the Jews not to rebel against Rome,[92] and they suited their action to their words. In the troubled years of Sapor's success in the East, when the rabbis may have entertained some secret hopes, they refrained from any open act.[93]

Indeed, religious persecutions, the main cause which prompted the Jewish masses to revolt, did not exist in the third and fourth centuries. There is no doubt that some Jews would have achieved higher social and political standing if they had adopted the state religion. The preachers in the synagogues were proud of those Jews, who in spite of strong temptation, adhered to their religion; and they accordingly exalted the Jewish nation which spurned worldly benefits for the sake of its religion. Besides, in

to supply Ursicinus' troops, see above p. 337) came to Antioch to see Ursicinus. He rose in their honor when he saw them. It seems that the two rabbis came to see him in 353 to intervene in favor of some of the Diocaesareans.

[90] See Frankel הירושלמי סבוא, 4b. See also below nn. 242 and 338.
[91] Comp. also *TP Terumoth* VIII.10, 46b.
[92] See *TB Kethuboth* 111a, *Shir Rabba* and *Zuta* to *Cant.* II.7.
[93] See below ch. III.

their praise of the Jews,[94] they usually employed fixed
literary formulas of earlier times, and their sermons to this
effect can by no means be taken as an indication of religious
persecutions.

There is absolutely no direct reference in the entire rabbinic literature of the third and fourth centuries[95] from
which we might legitimately conclude that the Roman
government deliberately persecuted the Jewish religion
during this time. The conjecture of Marmorstein[96] that
the Palestinian Jews of the third century were compelled
to transgress the Sabbath, to worship idols[97] and to give up
the rite of circumcision is as remarkable as it is unfounded.
The Christian *acta martyrum* assert that in the third century
the Jews urged the persecuted Christians to adopt Judaism
and thereby escape the persecutions.[98] At the same time
whenever the rabbis speak of tortures during religious
persecutions they state clearly that they refer to the
דורו של שמד, the generation of the Hadrianic persecutions.[99]
They never mention Jewish religious martyrs (as victims
of the government) of the third and fourth centuries.[100]

There is no doubt that Constantine, and especially
Constantius, began to curtail certain Jewish rights,[101] but
the Jews were not forced to transgress their laws. Moreover, rabbinic literature of the time does not refer to the

[94] See *Pesikta Rabbathi* XXI, ed. Friedmann, p. 106b and comp.
Graetz, p. 306. The passage in the *Pesikta*, however, is an adaptation of
a parallel in the *Mekhilta* (*Shirah* III, ed. Horovitz, p. 127), which
refers to the Hadrianic times.

[95] Anonymous passages of *Midrashim* compiled in a later time are,
of course, irrelevant.

[96] In his learned article, *Tarbiz* III, 1932, p. 168.

[97] It is highly doubtful that the Jews were officially constrained to do
it even during the Hadrianic persecutions. See Lieberman, *Annuaire*
etc. (referred to above n. 5), p. 430 ff.

[98] See *idem, JQR* XXXV, 1944, p. 23, n. 150.

[99] *Idem, ibid.*, p. 17, n. 106 *passim.*

[100] Comp. *idem, Greek in Jewish Palestine*, p. 86.

[101] Graetz, p. 307 ff.; Juster II, p. 179 ff. and n. 1 *ibid.*

limitations of Jewish rights[102] imposed by the first two Christian emperors. These decrees had probably very little, if any, practical application in Palestinian localities thickly inhabited by Jews. The emperors were first of all interested in the collection of taxes, and did not want to excite the population. When Arcadius was asked (around 400) to order the destruction of the pagan temples in Gaza, Marcus the Deacon tells us,[103] he became angry and said: "I know that this city is full of idols, but it loyally pays its taxes and contributes much to the treasury. If we suddenly frighten them they will run away and we shall lose so much in taxes."[104] This report of Arcadius' reply is in line with the general attitude of the emperors in such situations.[105] Jews probably never ceased building synagogues in Palestine during the fourth century.[106] We can see from the description of Epiphanius[107] how difficult it was to erect a church in Tiberias in spite of the explicit authorisation of Constantine. In places inhabited either by Jews or by heathens the religious policy of the Christian emperors of the fourth century remained more theoretical than practical. True, Constantius seems to have been an exception, for he forbade sacrifices in real earnest,[108] but

[102] A. Schlatter, *Verkanntes Griechisch*, p. 60 s. v. קלוסיא, identifies קלוסיא (*TP Gittin* IV.6, 46a) with ἐκκλησία. If he is right, we find here an allusion to the status of slaves owned by Jews, who were converted to Christianity. However, the identification of Schlatter, although very plausible (I hope to discuss it elsewhere) is not altogether certain.

[103] *Vita Porphyrii* 41, ed. Grégoire-Kugener, p. 35.

[104] οἶδα ὅτι ἡ πόλις ἐκείνη κατείδωλός ἐστιν, ἀλλ' εὐγνωμονεῖ περὶ τὴν εἰσφορὰν τῶν δημοσίων πολλὰ συντελοῦσα. Ἐὰν οὖν αἰφνιδιάσωμεν αὐτοὺς τῷ φόβῳ, φυγῇ χρήσονται καὶ ἀπόλλομεν τοσοῦτον κανόνα.

[105] See the admirable chapter in the editors' Introduction *ibid.*, p. LXV ff.

[106] Comp. M. Schwabe (referred to above n. 74), p. 110 ff.

[107] *Panar haer.* XXX.12, ed. Holl, p. 348.

[108] See the Introduction to *Vita Porphyrii ibid.*

the *practical* application of his policy towards Jewish institutions in Palestine cannot be ascertained. After all, even the enforcement of the edicts against paganism depended on the public sentiment in the various provinces.[109]

Nevertheless, the reign of Constantius (337–361) was a dark period for the Jews in Palestine. Oppression and robbery by the officials and tax-collectors prevailed throughout the Roman empire,[110] and as soon as the Jews lost the full protection of the emperors, they easily became the prey of the tax-collectors and were at the mercy of the Christian officials. They were exploited not only as provincials but also as Jews.[111]

And herein lies the basic mistake of Jewish historians. Taking it for granted that the Roman government was continually persecuting the Jews for their religion, they explained both the corresponding incidents cited in rabbinic literature and the rabbinic complaints against the government as relating to these imaginary abuses. They accordingly placed them in times of supposed outbreaks of persecution, as we shall presently see. And, indeed, these incidents and complaints can hardly be understood without a short survey of the levies and taxation of the Palestinian Jews.

II. Taxation and Imaginary Religious Persecutions

We read in *Aboth deR. Nathan*:[112] ועבדת את אויבך אשר ישלחנו ה' בך ברעב ובצמא ובעירום ובחוסר כל. ברעב כיצד בזמן שאדם תואב לאכול פת שעורים ואינו מוצא אומות העולם מבקשין ממנו פת נקייה

[109] See W. K. Boyd, *The Ecclesiastical Edicts of the Theodosian Code*, p. 22 ff.

[110] See Ammianus Marcellinus XVI.8.13; XXI.16.15–18.

[111] See Julian's letter to the community of the Jews 396d ff. The authenticity of the letter was recently well established by M. Hack's (יבנה II, Jerusalem 1939–40, p. 118 ff.) and J. Levy's (ציון VI, *ibid.* 1940–41, p. 27 ff.) excellent analysis of its style and contents.

[112] XX, ed. Schechter, f. 36a.

ובשר שמן. ובצמא כיצד בזמן שאדם מתאוה לשתות טיפה של חומץ טיפה של
שכר ואינו מוצא אומות העולם מבקשין ממנו יין משובח שבכל המדינות.
ובעירום כיצד בזמן שאדם י כ א^{ני} ללבוש חלוק של צמר או של פשתן
ואינו מוצא אומות העולם מבקשין ממנו השיראין והכלך שבכל המדינות.
ובחוסר כל. בלא נר ובלא סכין ובלא שלחן *"Therefore shalt thou
serve thine enemies that the Lord shall send against thee, in
hunger and in thirst and in nakedness, and in want of all
things* (Deut. 28.48). How *in hunger?* While a person is eager
to eat even barley bread and cannot find it, the nations of
the world demand of him white bread and choice meats.
How *in thirst?* While a man desires to drink even a drop of
vinegar or a drop of beer and cannot find them, the nations
of the world demand of him the finest wines of all lands.
How *in nakedness?* While a man is eager to wear a garment
even of [coarse] wool or linen and cannot find it, the nations
of the world demand of him the silks and *kulk*[114] [imported]
from all lands. How *in want of all things?* Without light,
without knife, without table."[115] This picture reflects
admirably the general situation of the provincials of that
time, under the reign of the Severi.[116] These conditions
did not change for centuries with the only difference that
the people became more accustomed to them. About a
century later we find an almost identical picture of the
East in the portrayal by Lactantius.[117] The calamities were
not borne by the Jews alone.

Similarly, we read in the Palestinian Talmud:[118] עניות

[113] The editions have : יבא, read יאב.
[114] *I. e.* cloth made of the down found at the roots of goats' hair. See
Geiger *apud* Krauss, תוספות הערוך השלם, 223b.
[115] The passage is ascribed to various authorities (See Schechter's note
a. l.). Most likely it is an elaboration by a later anonymous rabbi of
an older and shorter statement. It is most probably contemporary with
the compilation of the source, the third century. Comp. also *Sifre,
Deut.* 317, ed. Finkelstein, p. 360.
[116] See the previous note and below nn. 125, 126.
[117] *De mort. pers.* XXIII and XXXI.
[118] *Nedarim* IX, 3, 41c.

מצויה. כהדא חד בר נש הוה בעל דיניה עתיר אתא בעא מידון קמי רב.
שלח רב בתריה. אמ' עם ההוא אנא בעי מיתי מידון כך [וכך]‏[19] אין
אתיין כל גמלייא דערבייא לא טעינן קורקסייא דאפותיקי' דידי. שמע
ומר מהו מתנאה דלא ליה תהא פחתה בה. מן יד נפקת קלווסיס סן
מלכותא דייעול הוא ומדליה לטימיון. אתא גבי רב א"ל צלי עלוי דו
נפשי תחזור. צלי עלוי וחזר עלוי‏[20]. "Impoverishment is common.
Thus, someone had a litigation with a rich man and he
wanted to be tried by Rab.[121] Rab summoned him (i. e.
the rich man). The latter replied: 'Shall I go and litigate
with that [pauper]? [May] thus and so [befall me] if all
the camels of Arabia could carry my leather bags (κώ-
ρυκοι) full of mortgage titles.'[122] Rab heard it and said:
'How dare he boast of what is not his? A curse upon it!'
Immediately afterwards an order (κέλευσις) was issued
by the government that the man and his property should
go to the fiscus (ταμεῖον). He came to Rab and said to
him: 'Pray for me that I myself should be released.' He
prayed for him and everything was returned."

Here again, the precariousness of riches at the beginning
of the third century[123] is well demonstrated. "Impoverishment is common" says the Talmud; the rich of today can
suddenly become paupers by the greed of the fiscus. It
is almost identical with Herodian's description[124] of the
state of the provincials under Maximinus (235–238):

[119] See Lieberman, *Greek in Jewish Palestine*, p. 123, n. 70.

[120] The author of the מעלות המרות, ed. Cremona 62a reads here correctly
כולה. The reading of the editions is a dittography of the previous עלוי.

[121] The incident occurred in Palestine in the first quarter of the
third century.

[122] It seemingly was a current phrase. See *Ps.-Jonathan* Gen. 24.10.
Eunapius (*Vitae phil. et soph.* 471) describes the "philosophers" who
carried bags full of wills and contracts of sales (διαθῆκαί τε καὶ ἀν-
τίγραφα τούτων, καὶ συμβόλαια περὶ πράσεως κτλ.) etc. which would
have laden many camels. Comp. also *TB Pesaḥim* 62b; 119a; *Ḥullin*
95b.

[123] See above n. 121.

[124] VII.3.3.

"Every day one could see the wealthiest men of yesterday beggars today. Such was the greed of the tyranny etc."[125] The rich Jew wishes only to retain his personal freedom. He is reconciled to the loss of his property, a faithful picture of the general state of affairs in the Eastern Roman empire of that time, amply illustrated by many sources.[126]

The burden of the *leitourgiai* of the third century is also well mirrored in rabbinic literature. R. Johanan said:[127] אם הזכירוך לבולי יהא הירדן בעל נבולך. "If thou hath been nominated for the bulé (βουλή) let the Jordan be thy nieghbor," i. e. be ready to cross the Jordan and take flight.[128] A curious episode of that time recorded in the Palestinian Talmud[129] is quite typical. We read there:

חנוותא[130] דכיתאי הוה לון צומות והוה תמן חד מיתקרי בר חובץ ולא סלק. אמרי מה אנן אכלין יומא דין אמר חד חובצין. אמריתי בר חביץ. אמר ר' יוחנן זה אמר לשון הרע בהצנע. בולוטיה דציפורין הוה להון צומות והוה תמן חד מתקרי יוחנן ולא סלק. אמ' חד לחד לית אנן סלקין מבקרה ל(ר')יוחנן יומא דין. אמרין ייתי יוחנן. אמר ר' שמעון בן לקיש זה אמר לשון הרע בצדק. "The guild[131] of flax (*or* linen) traders held a meeting,[132] and there was [among their members]

[125] ἑκάστης γοῦν ἡμέρας ἦν ἰδεῖν τοὺς ἐχϑὲς πλουσιωτάτους τῆς ἐπιούσης μεταιτοῦντας. τοσαύτη τις ἦν τῆς τυραννίδος ἡ φιλοχρηματία κτλ. See Rostovtzeff *SEHRE* p. 399 ff.

[126] See *ibid.*, pp. 435, 626₁₉, 606₁₁.

[127] *TP Mo'ed Katan* II, 81b and parallel. Comp. the following sentence *ibid.*

[128] See *The Economic Survey of Ancient Rome* IV, p. 234, n. 25 and p. 243 *ibid.*

[129] *Pe'ah* I.1, 16a.   [130] So cod. Leyden.

[131] This is apparently the meaning of חנוותא. Comp. אומנות (*Mishnah Baba Bathra* IX.4; *Tosephta Demai* VI.4, 56₂₁ and parallels. In *Midrash Tehilim* [CXIV, end] we read: אם ברח ראש האומנות ברחה כל האומנות "When the head of the guild takes flight the whole guild does the same") and אומנו (*TP 'Abodah Zarah* II.1, 40c bot.).

[132] צסח means to collect, to assemble (see Jastrow, *Dictionary* s. v. צסח II. Comp. also J. P. N. Land, *Anecdota Syriaca* IV, p. 200₁₀: הן מצטחין סיניא [דהוין]) and צומות seems to have been a technical term for meetings of the *collegia* for the purpose of distributing of *leitourgiai*, see Jastrow *ibid. s. v.* צומות.

a man by the name of Bar Ḥubaz who did not attend. They said: 'What shall we eat today?' One replied 'Ḥubaz' (i. e. cheese). [The official[133]] said: 'Let Bar hubaz be summoned.' R. Joḥanan said: 'This man made a hidden denunciation.'[134] The councilors (βουλευταί) of Sepphoris held a meeting and there was [a councilor] named Johanan who did not attend. Those present said to one another: 'Are we not going to pay a visit to Johanan today?' They (i. e. the officials) said: 'Let Johanan be summoned.' R. Simeon b. Lakish said: 'This man made a denunciation in [the disguise of] righteousness.' "[135]

R. Johanan himself[136] summarized the situation:[137] מלכות הרשעה שמכנסת עין רעה בממונו של אדם. פלן עתיר נעבדיניה ארכונטס. פלן עתיר נעבדיניה בוליוטיס. "[Here is the policy of] the wicked government which begrudges a man his money. 'This one is rich let us appoint him magistrate (ἄρχων), this one is rich let us appoint him councilor (βουλευτής).' " The rabbi refers here to "men" and not only to Jews.

Besides the liturgies, rabbinic literature of the time mentions a great number of taxes;[138] the rabbis sometimes deplore the *Jewish* sufferings under the heavy burden of taxes, but very often they complain as mere provincials. Graetz[139] quotes an interesting passage[140] to demonstrate

[133] The γνωστήρ?

[134] *I. e.* a denunciation by implication. The Jew was reluctant to state explicitly that Bar Ḥubaz was absent. He therefore shrewdly mentioned cheese (Ḥubaz) to remind the official of the absence of Bar *Ḥubaz*. The legal aspect of this kind of denunciation is discussed in *TP Baba Kamma* III.1, 3c (regarding the distribution of the burden of χρυσάργυρον in the fourth century).

[135] By suggesting to pay a visit to a supposedly sick person, but actually making the officials conscious of the absence of the councilor.

[136] Who resented the denunciation of the Jew, see above.

[137] *BR* LXXVI, 6, 904.

[138] See L. Goldschmid in *REJ* XXXIV (1897), p. 199 ff.; Marmorstein in *Tarbiz* III, 1932, p. 172 ff.

[139] P. 315.

[140] *Pesikta Rabbathi* X, ed. Friedmann, 33b.

the oppression of the Jews under Constantius. But from
the parallel sources it is obvious[141] that the passage refers
to the taxes of the third century and not to those under
Constantius. Marmorstein[142] indeed saw in it a hint of the
persecution of the Jews during the third century. But
this is what the passage says:[143] להדא סירתא דאת מפשר ליה
מן הכא והיא מתעריה מן הכא. כן הוא עשו הרשע מתהפך. אייתי
גולגלתך, דימוסייך, ארנונא. לית ליה קניס ליה. גלי ליה ומזמי ליה
"Like this thorn of which you disengage yourself here and
it entagles you there, so the wicked Esau (*i. e.* Rome)
molests continuously: 'Bring your capitation tax, the
public taxes ($τὰ$ $δημόσια$), the *annona!*' If he [says he]
has not, [Esau] fines him, robs him[144] and imposes penalties[145] upon him." There is no hint in this complaint of a
special oppression of the Jews;[146] the wicked Esau oppressed
all the provincials in the same manner; they all complained
of it in a similar way.[147]

Similarly, Graetz quotes[148] a *Midrash*[149] which demonstrates the crooked ways of the Roman legal procedure in
trying the Jews. He sees in it evidence of the persecutions
of the Jews under Constantius. But he overlooked the
fact that the same passage is available in earlier sources[150]

[141] See *Pesikta de R. Kahana* II, 11a, n. 12.

[142] *Tarbiz ibid.*, p. 175.

[143] I copy from the text published in *Beth Talmud*, ed. Weiss and
Friedmann, vol. V, p. 85.

[144] The words גלי ליה are missing in ed. Buber (11b, comp. n. 18 *ibid.*)
as well as in all the parallel sources. We should perhaps read: נלו, see
Brockelmann, *Lexicon Syriacum*, s. v. נלו.

[145] Or: מומי ליה (see ed. Buber *ibid.* n. 18), he adjures him.

[146] The *fiscus Judaicus* is not mentioned here; it was a negligible
trifle in comparison with the general taxes. This passage and the
similar ones were already correctly understood by Zuri (see below
n. 167).

[147] See Rostovtzeff *SEHRE*, p. 664. Comp. the petition of the peasants to Philippus, *ibid.* p. 622₄₂.

[148] P. 315.   [149] *Ruth Rabba*, Proem. 3.

[150] See Lieberman, *JQR*, XXXV, 1944, p. 24, n. 156.

where it is quoted in the name of a rabbi who flourished
in the third century. There the government is blamed for
its corruptness in legal procedure in general. And indeed
it has already been proved that these were the usual ways
of the Romans in their trials.[151] It, therefore, has nothing
to do with the persecutions of the Jews.

Again, we read in the Palestinian Talmud:[152] דיקליטיאנוס
עעיק לבני פניים. אמרין ליה אנן אזלון. א״ל סופיסטה לא אזלין לון
ואין אזלון לון חזרון לון. "Diocletian oppressed the inhabitants
of Paneas. The latter said to him (i. e. to Diocletian):
'We shall go away' (i. e. flee). A sophist said to him
[Diocletian]: 'They will not go away, and if they do they
will return.' " Frankel[153] inferred from this passage that
Diocletian persecuted the Jews.[154] J. Zuri,[155] however, has
pointed out that it is not at all certain that the reference is
to Jews.[156] But above all, the contents of the passage was
not properly understood by Frankel. We have here a
typical petition to the emperor, asking for the reduction of
taxes.[157] Lactantius tells us that during the reign of Diocletian the farms were abandoned by the husbandmen,
because they were exhausted by the enormous impositions
etc.[158]

The petition of the people of Paneas was probably worded
according to the usual formula: "We shall flee from our
homes and the treasury will suffer the greatest losses,"[159]

[151] See Lieberman, *ibid.*, p. 25 ff.

[152] *Shebi'ith* IX.2, 38d.   [153] מבוא הירושלמי, p. 3a.

[154] His conclusion that the event took place before Diocletian became
emperor cannot be taken seriously.

[155] ר׳ יוסי בר׳ חנינא מקיסרין, p. 27. Comp. also Klein in ספר הישוב I, p. 181,
n. 6.

[156] See Jones, *The Cities of the Eastern Roman Provinces*, p. 283.

[157] The facts are well known. The instances are given here only
exem. gratia. Comp. Zuri *ibid.*

[158] *De mort. pers.* VII, *CSEL* XXVII, p. 180: enormitate indictionum
consumptis viribus colonorum desererentur agri etc.

[159] Petition to Gordian by a Thracian village in 238 (Dittenberger

or: "We shall be forced to become fugitives etc."[160] However, a sophist advised Diocletian[161] not to mind the petition. The passage in *TP* has probably nothing to do with Jews and certainly not with persecutions.

Similarly, we read in the *Midrash*:[162] אמר ר' הונא עריקין הויגן מן קומיה גוניתיה בהדא בטיסא דטבריא. "R. Huna[163] said: We were fleeing from before the Ghoths[164] [and hiding] in the cave of Tiberïas.' " Graetz[165] and Bacher[166] invoke this passage to argue for a persecution in the time of Constantius. However, it has already been pointed out by Zuri[167] that the flight was probably on account of taxes. He associated it with a passage in the same *Midrash*[168] where a rabbi[169] pictured the hiding of the people[170] in caves on account of the tax collector (נבאי).[171] Hence this incident

---

*Sylloge*³ 888₅₅): φευξόμεθα ἀπὸ τῶν οἰκείων καὶ μεγίστην ζημίαν τὸ ταμεῖον περιβληθήσεται κτλ.

[160] φυγάδας <τε> γενέσθαι κτλ. The phrase is taken from a petition to Septimius Severus by the peasants of the imperial estates in Asia Minor. See Rostovtzeff, *SEHRE*, pp. 357, 606₁₆. Comp. also our quotations above nn. 104 and 131.

[161] Lactantius (*ibid.* XI, p. 185) relates that whenever Diocletian determined to do ill he used to call in many advisers that his misdeed might be imputed to other men.

[162] *BR* XXXI.2, p. 283.

[163] There were three rabbis who had this name. The second flourished under Diocletian, the third — under Constantinus and Constantius.

[164] The varaint גונדא has to be dismissed because it has no support in the best mss.; it is also the *lect. facil.*, since it occurs frequently in *TB*.

[165] P. 317.

[166] Die *Aggada der Palaestinensischen Amoräer* III, p. 276.

[167] ר' יוסי בר' חנינא מקיסרין p. 29. Comp. Lieberman, הירושלמי כפשוטו I, p. 370.

[168] *BR* XXIV, beginning, p. 229.

[169] Who flourished in the second half of the third century.

[170] בני המדינה, not only Jews.

[171] This interpretation finds good support in some mss. of the 'Arukh (See Krauss, תוספות ערוך השלם 82, s. v. בטס) which read in *BR* גוביתיה instead of גוניתיה. But this reading looks like the correction of a learned scribe. Perhaps גוניתיה (or גונתיה, גנייא see the variants *ibid.*) means ἀγένται (see *Thesaurus linguae Latinae*, ed. Teubner, *s. v.* agens),

too bears no relation either on persecutions or on Constantius.

Again, we read in the Palestinian Talmud:[172] ר' מנא כד
עאל פרוקלא בציפורי הורי מפקי נחתומיא בשוקא. "When Proclus
entered Sepphoris, R. Mana ruled that the bakers go out[173]
into the market." Graetz[174] connected it with the religious
persecutions under Gallus. But Frankel[175] justly realized
that R. Mana became the head of the court in Sepphoris
after the execution of Gallus,[176] and in all likelihood after
the death of Constantius.

I think it very probable that the purpose of Proclus'
entering Sepphoris is revealed in another passage of TP.
We read there:[177] ביומי דר' מנא הוות נומירה בציפורין והוון בניהון
דציפוריי מישכונין נבון . . . בנין ציפרייא דלא יחלטון בניהון. "In the
days of R. Mana a division of troops (νούμερος, *numerus*)
was stationed in Sepphoris, and the sons of the Sepphoreans
were pledged[178] to them [to the troops] . . . So that the sons
of the Sepphoreans would not be forfeited."[179] From the

frumentarii, the famous *agentes in rebus*, ἀγεντισηρίβους (Athanas.
Apol. ad Constantium, PG XXV 608b) see PW *RE* I, p. 776.

[172] *Sanhedrin* III.6, 21b.

[173] I. e. bring or bake bread on the Sabbath or Passover.

[174] P. 314.

[175] מבוא הירושלמי p. 115a.

[176] The father of our rabbi, R. Jonah, was still alive under Gallus'
(see above n. 89) punitive expedition; he died in the lifetime of his
colleague, R. Jose (*TP Ma'aser Sheni* IV.9, 55b), and our R. Mana
became then a member of the court of Tiberias (See *TP Kiddushin*
III.14, 64d). Hence our incident occurred still later.

[177] *Pesaḥim* IV.9, 31b. I copy the text according to Ms. readings, as
recorded by S. Lieberman, הירושלמי כפשוטו *a. l.*, p. 443 ff.

[178] משכן means to seize as well as top ledge, ὑποτίθημι, see the following note.

[179] חלט is a legal technical term (See Jastrow, *Dictionary*, s. v. חלט III,
467a–b) which corresponds to the Greek βεβαιοῦν. The Hebrew
לצמיתות (Lev. 25.23) is translated by the LXX: εἰς βεβαίωσιν and by
the rabbis לחולטנית (*Sifra a. l.*, ed. Weiss 108d and parallels in *TP* and
TB). On the connection of βεβαιοῦν with ὑποθήκη and ἀρραβών see
Deissmann, *Bibelstudien* (Marburg 1895), p. 101 ff. and *Neue Bibelstudien* (*ibid.* 1897), p. 56. Comp. the preceding note.

context of the passage which speaks of the pledge (or seizure) of the sons of the Sepphoreans[180] and their possible forfeiture it appears that the *numerus* came to Sepphoris to levy recruits or to collect the *aurum tyronicum*. R. Mana enacted a special emergency law which allowed the Sepphoreans to sell their houses even if occupied by tenants, so that they could afford to redeem their sons by paying the *aurum tyronicum*.[181] The Jews acted here like all other provincials. And it is to this effect that Ammianus Marcellinus said:[182] "The provincials are glad to contribute gold to save their bodies." Thus, the Romans certainly did not come to Sepphoris to persecute the Jewish religion or the Jews. It was of vital interest to the Jews to be on good terms with the troops, and for this reason the rabbi ordered to provide them with bread on the Sabbath or during the Passover.

Moreover, the rabbis were not unaware of the fact that the Romans tried to put a face of legality on their robberies.[183] A rabbi of the third century summarized it in the following phrase:[184] מלכות הרשעה הזו גוזלת וחומסת נראת כאילו מצעת בימה. "This wicked government robs and extorts and makes it appear as though it were holding court."[185]

---

[180] Comp. Lieberman, תלמודה של קיסרין, p. 59, n. 102.

[181] Eighty *aurei* for each recruit in the time of Valens (Socr. *Hist. eccl.* IV.34, *PG* LXVII, 553c). See Rostovtzeff, *Journal of Roman Studies* VIII, 1918, p. 28; G. Harper in the *Yale Classical Studies* I (1928), p. 157.

[182] XIX.II.7: arum quippe gratanter provinciales pro corporibus dabunt. Comp. *ibid.* XXXI.4.4.

[183] An excellent parody on the Roman legality is available in *TB* '*Abodah Zarah* 8b.

[184] *BR* LXV.1, 713, and parallels.

[185] Another rabbi of the same century said (*BR* IX, end, 73): יהנה טוב מאד זה מלכות הארץ . . . שהיא תובעת דיקיות של בריות "*Behold, it was very good* (Gen. 1.31) applies to the government on the earth . . . for it takes up the causes of men." (See Theodor's notes on the parallels and the expression לתבוע דיקיות. The latter is a literal translation of δίκας αἰτεείν). The better is, of course, the enemy of the good. The rabbis

An interesting discrimination between the arbitrary and the "legal" actions of the officials is noted in the following passage:[186] מהו לשכור רשות מן הפונדיק. ר' חיננא ור' יונתן סלקון לחמתה דגדר. אמרין נמתין עד שיבואו זקני הדרום לכאן. אתא ר' נתן דרומה ושאלון ליה ושרא. שמע ר' שמעון בן לקיש ואמר מאחר שהגוי בא ומוציאני לא עשינו כלום. שמעון בר אבא אמר ר' יוחנן בעי מעתה אין בתינו שלנו. ר' יוסטי בי ר' סימון בשם ר' בייתוס אין בתינו שלנו לדור עמנו הא לצאת אין מוציאין אותנו ובפונדק מוציאין אותנו. "Is it proper to rent[187] premises from an innkeeper [for the Sabbath]?[188] R. Ḥanina and R. Jonathan came to the Hot Springs of Gadara.[189] They said: Let us wait until the elders (= wise) of the *Darom*[190] come here. R. Nathan the Daromite came. They asked him [the above question] and he allowed it. When R. Simeon b. Lakish heard it he said:

likewise interpreted that "*very good*" applies to death (*ibid.* 70₁) and to the evil inclination, יצר הרע (*ibid.* 72₁). An interesting *Midrash* is quoted by the Medieval authorities (See *Tora Shelemah* IV, p. 1022, n. 143) עשו בגימטריא שלום. "The numerical value of עשו (Esau = Rome) is equal to that of שלום (peace), *i. e.* 376. (It is doubtful whether the source used by these authorities is the minor tractate *Kallah*, ed. Higger, p. 219). The *Midrash* adds that but for this name (Comp. Lieberman, *Greek in Jewish Palestine*, p. 189, n. 25) no creature would be left in peace by Esau-Rome. Is this a possible allusion to the *pax Romana*?

[186] TP '*Erubin* VI,4, 23c.

[187] According to Jewish law objects cannot be moved (on the Sabbath) from one room to another (or from the house to the courtyard) unless the entire property belongs to one person or to Jewish partners who share a common meal, etc. In case a Gentile holds some rights to the property, the Jew can avoid the above restriction on moving objects only by renting the rights of the Gentile to the property for the whole Sabbath.

[188] Since the tenants could still be removed from the hotel in spite of their having rented it.

[189] In Transjordania, near Hippos. The place was renowned even among non-Jews. Eunapius (*Vitae phil. et soph.* 459) asserts that the warm baths in Gadara are second only to those of Baiae in Italy with which no other baths can be compared (Γάδαρα, θερμὰ δέ ἐστι λουτρὰ τῆς Συρίας τῶν γε κατὰ τὴν 'Ρωμαϊκὴν ἐν Βαΐαις δεύτερα, ἐκείνοις δὲ οὐκ ἐστιν ἑτέρα παραβάλλεσθαι).

[190] See above n. 79.

Since the Gentile can come and remove us,[191] the renting is of no avail. Simeon b. Abba reports: R. Johanan asked: Does it follow that our houses do not belong to us either?[192] To this Yusti b. Simeon in the name of R. Boethus replied: [There is a difference between our private homes and an inn]; our homes are not our own [in the sense that the Romans may] lodge with us but do not drive us out, whereas from an inn we are liable to be ejected."[193]

It is obvious from the names of the rabbis who visited the Hot Springs of Gadara that the question was raised in the first half of the third century. The problem revolved around the fact that the Jewish guests might at any time be removed from the hotel. The same complaint is available in another anonymous text:[194] ‏ואני אקניאם בלא עם. אל תהי‎ ‏קורא בלא עם אלא בלוי עם אלו הבאים מתוך האומות ומלכיות ומוציאים‎ ‏אותם מתוך בתיהם‎. "And I shall provoke them with those who are not a people (Deut. 32.21), read not belo ʿam (with not a people), but bilway ʿam (with associates of a people),[195] [I shall provoke them with] those who come from among the nations and kingdoms and expel them from their homes." The Jews were particularly annoyed at being ejected from their homes by the various barbars,[196] namely the auxiliary troops supplied by the socii populi Romani.

Herein lies the main point of the discussion of the rabbis in the above passage of the Palestinian Talmud. In prac-

[191] So as to billet soldiers.

[192] I. e. because the Gentile can drive us out in case the house is required for quartering soldiers.

[193] See my notes on the readings and interpretation of this passage in ‏הירושלמי כפשוטו‎ a. l., p. 312 ff. Comp. also TP ibid., 23b: ‏ואכסנייא אינה‎ ‏אוסרת לעולם באילין דעיילין דלא ברשות‎.

[194] Sifre Deut. 320, ed. Finkelstein, p. 367. The text is probably of the beginning of the third century.

[195] I. e. the socii populi Romani from whom the auxiliary troops were drafted. Comp. Midrash Tehilim CIV.21, ed. Buber, p. 446.

[196] See the following sentence in Sifre ibid. Comp. below n. 200.

tice the Roman troops ejected the natives from their homes
in defiance of any law which might forbid it. But the
rabbis discriminated between an arbitrary ejection and a
"legal" one. A contemporary local inscription sheds light
on the discussion of the rabbis. Julius Saturninus, in his
reply to the inhabitants of Phaenae in the Trachonitis[197]
who complained of the oppression caused by billeting of
troops, confirmed this rule: "Since you have an inn you
cannot be compelled to receive guests in your houses."[198]
From the rabbinic text, combined with that of the inscription, we learn that "legally" the soldiers could not be
billeted in the houses of the inhabitants so long as inns were
available, and, further, that there was another distinction
between private homes and inns: space could be requisitioned in the former[198a] without prejudice to the right of
the owner or tenant to remain in them, whereas the latter
could be wholly requisitioned and the tenants expelled.
The point of view of R. Boethus is now perfectly clear: the
renting of the inn in Gadara is of no avail, since legally it
can be requisitioned and its guests ejected the moment
Romans arrive. For Gadara evidently shared the ill fate of
Scaptopara in Thracia; it was an excellent health-resort,[199]
and the results were probably the same as in the Thracian
warm baths: a permanent flow of Roman nobles and common soldiers. And if the residents manged somehow to
accommodate the Roman nobles they greatly resented the
intrusion of the commoners.[200]

[197] *I. e.* not far from our Gadara.
[198] Dittenberger, *Or. Gr. Inscr. Sel.* 609: καὶ ξενῶνα ἔχοντες οὐ
δύνασθε ἀναγκασθῆναι δέξασθαι ταῖς οἰκίαις τοὺς ξένους. See the
editor's notes.
[198a] See *Cod. Just.* XII. XL (XLI), *de metatis* etc.
[199] See above n. 189.
[200] Dittenberger *Sylloge³* 888₄₄ (a petition to Gordian in 238): ἐπι-
δημοῦσι δὲ ὡς ἐπὶ τὸ πλεῖστον διὰ τὴν τῶν ὑδάτων χρῆσιν οἵ τε
ἡγούμενοι τῆς ἐπαρχίας, ἀλλὰ καὶ οἱ ἐπίτροποί σου. καὶ τὰς μὲν

The Jews were in exactly the same situation as the other provincials. They were ejected from their places both legally and illegally, but in the latter case they could hope for some protection. During the military rule of the Roman empire in the third and fourth centuries the Jews could apply for help to their successful countrymen (mostly villagers) as all the provincials did.[201] The *Midrash*[202] quotes a parable which reflects the fright of the inhabitants when a Roman officer (שלטון) entered the city. It was a villager who intervened in their favor, declaring: "This officer is my friend, and I am accustomed to talk with him etc."[203]

Finally we shall discuss a curious passage regarding Roman charity at the expense of the provincials. We read in the *Midrash*:[204] מרבה הונו בנשך ובתרבית לחונן דלים יקבצנו. ואיזה הוא חונן דלים זה עשו הרשע. ועשו הרשע חונן דלים, עושק דלים הוא. כגון אילין אפוטרופיא דנפקין לקרייתא ובוזזין לאריסיה ועלון למדינתא ואמרין כנשון מסכניא דבעינן למעבד עמהון מצוה. מתלא אמר ניירי בחיזורין ומפלגין לבישייא. "He that augmenteth his substance by interest and increase, gathereth it for him that hath pity on the poor (Prov. 28.8). Who is it that has pity on the poor? It is the wicked Esau (= Rome). But does the wicked Esau have pity on the poor? Does he not rob the

---

ἐξουσίας συν(εχ)έστατα δεχόμεθα κατὰ τὸ ἀναγκαῖον, τοὺς (δὲ) λοιποὺς ὑποφέρειν μὴ δυνάμενοι ἐνετύχομεν πλειστάκις τοῖς ἡγεμόσι τῆς Θράκης, οἵτινες ἀκολούθως ταῖς θείαις ἐντολαῖς ἐκέλευσαν ἀοχλήτους ἡμᾶς εἶναι κτλ. The attraction of this health-resort is obvious from the further description (line 125 ff.): καὶ θερμῶν ὑδάτων λουτρὰ οὐ μόνον πρὸς τρυφὴν ἀλλὰ καὶ ὑγείαν καὶ θεραπείαν σωμάτων ἐπιτηδειότατα: Comp. Rostovtzeff *SEHRE* pp. 427, 623; *The Cambridge Ancient History* XII, p. 83, n. 3.

[201] See Rostovtzeff *ibid.* pp. 446 ff. 628, n. 67.
[202] *Tanḥuma* האזינו 2, ed. Buber V, p. 51.
[203] השלטון הזה הוא אוהבי ואני רגיל לדבר עמו.
[204] *Pesikta deR. Kahana* XI, ed. Buber, p. 95b. The parallels (*Tanḥuma* ראה 10, ed. Buber 6, p. 21; *Shemoth Rabba* XXXI, end; *Midrash Tehilim* X, ed. Buber, p. 95) have slight variants.

poor? [it alludes to people] like those *procuratores* (ἐπί-
τροποι) who go out to the villages, rob the tenants of the
land, come to the city and say: gather the poor, for we want
to distribute charity to them. The proverb says: They
prostitute themselves for apples and distribute them among
the poor." The passage is attributed to a rabbi who
flourished in the third and fourth centuries, but the earlier
source[205] does not mention Esau in the statement of this
rabbi. As it reads in the latter, the rabbi made a general
remark regarding ill-gotten riches which are distributed to
the poor. It is therefore evident that the later source
(probably of the middle of the fourth century) elaborated
on the statement of the rabbi in accordance with the conditions of the time. The late *Midrash Tehilim*[206] talks explicitly of a capitation tax the proceeds of which Esau
(Rome) distributed to orphans. Our source (*i. e.* the
Pesikta) suggests that the charity was distributed in the
cities out of the revenue which came from the villages.

Can we suspect the rabbis of inventing such a "charge"
against Rome?[207] We can probably find the answer in the
words of Sozomenus. He asserts that Julian abrogated the
laws in favor of the clergy and that "he even compelled the
virgins and widows, who, *on account of their poverty were
reckoned among the clergy,* to refund the provisions which
had been assigned to them *from public funds.* For when
Constantine arranged the status of the church, he distributed a portion of the taxes levied upon every city among
the clergy everywhere, which was sufficient for the pro-
curing of provisions."[208] Julian himself mentions the aboli-

---

[205] *Vayyikra Rabba* III.1.   [206] See above n. 204.

[207] There is, of course, no question of *Alimenta* in Palestine of the
fourth century. Comp. also *TB Baba Mezi'a* 70b and Rapoport ערך
טילין, *s. v.* שבור מלכא.

[208] *Hist. eccl.* V. 5, PG LXVII, 1228a: μέχρι τε παρθένων καὶ χηρῶν,
τὰς δι' ἔνδειαν ἐν τοῖς κλήροις τεταγμένας, εἰσπράττεσθαι προσέτα-

tion of the clerical privileges, and naturally accuses the Christian clergy of assigning everything to themselves.[209]

What the rabbis meant is that ill-gotten goods will not fall into the hands of a really charitable person (which may serve as some consolation), but will fall (in the form of taxes) into the hands of Esau (Rome) who also distributes charities. But the fact remains a fact. The rabbis admitted that Esau asked for the poor (or orphans) to give alms to them. Since the Jewish clergy enjoyed, at least for a time, the same privileges as the Christian,[210] the orphans and the widows of the former had the same rights as those of the latter, and may have been entitled to certain provisions derived from the taxes. But the Jews would still be very resentful of the fact that the distributors were Christians who might utilize it for missionary work, and they sarcastically pointed out the means by which the alms to be distributed were procured.

We conclude our short survey with the position of the Patriarch and the Jewish scholars in the Roman system of taxation. The role of the former in the distribution of the tax-burden[211] and his responsibility towards the government are not clear.[212] However, it is certain that the Patriarch had to pay vast sums to the government and offer gifts to the officials. The *Midrash* relates[213] that the Patriarch asked R. Simeon b. Lakish[214] to pray for him, because "the

ξεν, ἃ πρὶν παρὰ τοῦ δημοσίου ἐκομίσαντο. Ἡνίκα γὰρ Κωνσταντῖνος τὰ τῶν ἐκκλησιῶν διέττατε πράγματα, ἐκ τῶν ἑκάστης πόλεως φόρων τὰ ἀρκοῦντα πρὸς παρασκευὴν ἐπιτηδείων ἀπένειμε τοῖς πανταχοῦ κλήροις.

[209] Epist. ad Bostrenses 437a: τὰ πάντα ἑαυτοῖς προσνέμειν.

[210] See Graetz, p. 307, n. 2.

[211] See TB Baba Bathra 7b, passim.

[212] See Krauss, Antoninus und Rabbi, p. 19, n. 1; A. Gulak, ספר טננס, p. 101; idem, Tarbiz XI, 121 ff.

[213] BR LXXVIII.12, p. 931ₛ. Comp. Graetz, p. 228.

[214] Flourished in the middle of the third century.

government is very wicked," and this is demonstrated by the following episode: "A woman brought the Patriarch a small salver ($\delta\iota\sigma\kappa\acute{\alpha}\rho\iota o\nu$) with a knife on it. He took the knife and returned the salver to her.[215] Then a courier ($\beta\epsilon\rho\eta\delta\acute{\alpha}\rho\iota o\varsigma$, veredarius) of the government came and he *saw it, coveted it and took it.*"[216]

As for the scholars, there is enough evidence to show that they were at certain periods (during the third and fourth centuries) exempt from some taxes, and especially from *leitourgias*.[217] But it is unlikely that *all* scholars enjoyed the tax immunities.[218] It is much more probable that only the ordained scholars benefited from this privilege, scholars who could be placed in the category of priests, *sacerdotes*.[219] From the Palestinian Talmud[220] we learn that Simeon b. Abba[221] was not ordained because he happened to be in Damascus when an opportunity to ordain him presented itself. We also find that R. Jonah[222] refused to be ordained prior to his teacher, R. Zeminah.[223]

These incidents raise a serious question. According to

[215] Comp. *TP 'Abodah Zarah* I.1, 39b.

[216] חמתה וחמדה ונסבה, an excellent parody on *veni vidi vici!*

[217] See Marmorstein *Tarbiz* III, 1932, p. 177; Klein *MGWJ* LXXVIII, 1934, p. 169; *An Economic Survey of Ancient Rome* IV, p. 243, n. 80. Comp. also *Tanḥuma* וארא ed. Buber p. 20: שבטו של לוי היה פנוי לטרניה במצרים "The tribe of Levi was free of *leitourgiai* in Egypt." We must, of course, discriminate between taxes paid to the Jewish community and those collected by the agents of the Government.

[218] Comp. Juster II, 259 and nn. *ibid.* We are concerned only with impositions by the government.

[219] On the latter see Jones, *The Greek City* pp. 228, 354 n. 33. Physicians, teachers and philosophers were exempt from liturgies, but apparently only from the *personal* ones but not from the patrimonial liturgies. See H. M. D. Parker, *A History Of The Roman World* etc., pp. 125–126 and the sources referred to *ibid.*, p. 333.

[220] *Bikkurim* III.3, 65d.

[221] Flourished in the second half of the third century.

[222] Flourished in the first half and the beginning of the second half of the fourth century.

[223] *TP ibid.* Comp., however, *TP Ta'anith* IV.2, 68a.

Jewish law there is no limit to the number of rabbis that may be ordained at one time. Any rabbi qualified by his piety, character and knowledge of the law can be ordained. Why then was Simeon b. Abba never ordained?[224] This suggests that at times the Patriarch was probably careful not to exceed a certain number in the ordinations he conferred. It is well known that the quota of physicians and teachers who enjoyed immunities from personal liturgies was limited,[225] and it is likely that the number of ordained rabbis who enjoyed the above immunities was similarly limited. The Patriarch would certainly be tactful to stay within the quota alloted to him by the government. Indeed, the Palestinian Talmud[226] relates: רבי הוה ממני תרין מינויין[227] אין הוון כדיי היו מתקיימין ואין לא הוון מסתלקין. מדדמך פקיד לבריה אמר לא תעביד כן אלא מני כולהון כחדא. "Rabbi[228] used to confer two ordinations [each year].[229] If the ordained rabbis proved worthy they remained [in office]; if not, they resigned.[230] When he was about to die he instructed his son, saying: Do not follow my practice, but confer all the ordinations together." In the light of the suggestion made above, this obscure passage now becomes clear. R. Judah Hanasi was in the habit of conferring the privileges of ordination on two rabbis each year; if the appointees were

---

[224] We ought possibly to discriminate between official ordination (connected with some office in the academy or the court) which was conferred by the Patriarch and the permission to render decisions in matters of law, which was granted by the head of the court. See *TB Sota* 22a; *TP Megilla* IV.5, 75b; *Ḥagigah* I.7, 76c (and parallel); *TB Sanhedrin* 14a. Comp. also *TP ibid.* I.3, 19a and below n. 237.

[225] See Jones *ibid.* pp. 189–190 and 344 n. 65.

[226] *Ta'anith* IV.2, 68a. Comp. *Koheleth Rabba* VII.7.

[227] *Koheleth Rabba* adds: בכל שנה, each year.

[228] *I. e.* the Patriarch R. Judah the First who flourished at the last quarter of the second and the beginning of the third century.

[229] See above n. 227.

[230] *Koheleth Rabba ibid.* reads: דסכין (a mistranslation of מסתלקין) they died!

not worthy they had to relinquish their place to others.
But he instructed his son to discontinue this practice and
to fill the entire quota which carries tax immunity at
once. The instruction was obeyed,[231] and henceforth a
rabbi could be ordained only when a vacancy was
available.[232]

The later Patriarchs, being in need of money to supply
the government, adopted the practice of the age[233] and
began to sell ordinations occasionally to the highest
bidders.[234] Those among the rabbis who were known for
their poverty were sometimes denied ordination, not because they had no money to pay for it, but because the
privileges involved were not of much use to them.[235] The
rabbis violently protested against the practice of selling
ordinations,[236] and, at least theoretically, a ruling was
finally adopted that the Patriarch was not to ordain without
the consent of his court.[237]

It is natural to expect that not only the rabbis, but the
community as a whole would be vitally interested in the
ordinations which granted immunities. Indeed, we read in

[231] His son ordained many rabbis together. The pious R. Ḥaninah
agreed to be the *third in rank* (The meaning of תליתאי is obvious from its
parallel: תינין. Comp. also *TP Pesaḥim* VI.1, 33a). *TB Kethuboth* 103b
has a different tradition.

[232] Through the death of an ordained rabbi.

[233] See Jones, *The Greek City*, p. 228. On the rush to the Christian
clergy, when the latter were granted immunity by Constantine, and the
subsequent restrictions imposed on them, see W. K. Boyd, *The Ecclesiastical Edicts in the Theodosian Code*, p. 72 ff. and Jones *ibid.* pp. 198
and 346 n. 83.

[234] See *TP Bikkurim* III.3, 65d and *TB Sanhedrin* 7b. Comp. the
numerous references to Christian literature given by Juster I, p. 398,
n. 2.

[235] According to *TP ibid.*, Simeon b. Abba, who was never ordained,
did not have a loaf of bread to eat.

[236] See above n. 234.

[237] *TP Sanhedrin* I.3, 19a. The rabbi who recorded the decision
flourished around the middle of the third century. On his name see my
note *apud* Lewin סתיבות וספר חפץ, p. 138 (n. to p. 97).

the Palestinian Talmud:[238] ולמה לא מניתיה הוא. אמר ר' דרוסא
בנין דצווחין עלויי ציפוראיי. ובנין צווחה עבדין וכו'   "Why did not
he[239] ordain him?[240] R. Derossa said: 'Because the Sepphoreans *shout* against him.' Ought shouting to influence action?"[241]   We have here an explicit tradition that the
Patriarch did not appoint R. Ḥaninah because the mob of
Sepphoris[242] clamored against him.[243]   Our rabbi was a very
rich man.   Out of the proceeds, or profit, of one transaction
with honey he erected a school house in Sepphoris,[244] which
was called "the school house of R. Haninah."[245]   Tax immunity would be quite important to that rabbi, and the
famous Sepphoreans would naturally begrudge him the
exemption.   Although an anonymous authority in the
Talmud wonders how the clamor could influence the
Patriarch, the explanation of R. Derossa is quite valid.
The βοή[246] or the ἐκβόησις[247] of the masses very often
could not be disregarded.

It is clear that the Sepphoreans knew of the Patriarch's

[238] *Ta'anith* IV.2, 68a. The correct reading is available in the Genizah
fragments (published by L. Ginzberg in his *Genizah Studies* I, p. 427)
and Cod. Leyden.

[239] *I. e.* R. Judah Hanassi.

[240] *I. e* R. Ḥaninah. From the context it is obvious that this ordination involved an appointment in the adademy. But it is equally evident
that R. Ḥaninah was not appointed at all (see above n. 224) during
R. Judah Hanassi's lifetime.

[241] In the parallel *Koheleth Rabba* (VII.7) the question is elaborated:
"Now they may shout justly, but if we listen to them regarding this
we shall have to listen to them regarding that as well."

[242] On their character see above n. 90 and below n. 338.

[243] Comp. *TB Berakhoth* 55a. However, in our case it was a question
of an appointment in the academy.

[244] *TP Pe'ah* VII.4, 20b. Such a gift to the community would be
quite remarkable for the third century. See Bernhard Laum, *Stiftungen
in der griechischen und römischen Antike* vol. I, p. 8 ff. Comp. also *TB
Kethuboth* 67b, bot. Our rabbi kept up the tradition of his ancestors,
see *TP Pe'ah* VIII, end, 21b.

[245] *TP Megilla* IV.11, 75c.

[246] See Libanius, *Orat.* XLI, 1 ff.

[247] See H. Grégoire, *Anatolian Studies Presented to Sir W. M. Ramsay*

intention to ordain R. Ḥaninah, and it is likely that his nomination was announced in advance. This reminds us of the famous passage of Lampridius:[248] "Whenever he[249] wanted to appoint . . . governors to the provinces . . . he used to announce their names, urging the people in case anyone wished to bring accusations against them, to prove it by clear evidence . . . He used to say that, since Christians and Jews observed this practice in annoucing the names of those who were to be ordained priests,[250] it was painful that it should not be observed in the case of governors of provinces etc."[251] In this instance, Lampridius' report of the Jewish practice seems to be true.[252] The Patriarch had good reason to announce the names of the candidates for ordination in advance; the chances of denunciation[253] were thereby minimized. Here again, the Jews and their leaders were in the same situation as the rest of the provincials, with this difference that, as far as the rabbinic court was obeyed, the Jewish masses had probably the protection of the law against excesses in the distribution of the burden of taxes.[254]

pp. 157, 547. We may add the γραμματεῖον δημοτικῶν ἐκβοήσεων mentioned by Sozomenus, *Hist. eccl.* II.25, *PG* LXVII, 1004a.

[248] *Hist. aug.*, *Alex. Sev.* XLV.6: ubi aliquos voluisset . . . rectores provinciis dare . . . nomina eorum proponebat, hortans populum, ut si quis quid haberet criminis probaret manifestis rebus . . . dicebatque grave esse, cum id Christiani et Iudaei facerent in praedicandis sacerdotibus, qui ordinandi sunt, no fieri in provinciarum rectoribus etc.

[249] *I. e.* Alexander Severus.

[250] *Sacerdos* was the official term for the government. Comp. Ducange, *Gloss. med. et inf. Lat.*, s. v. *sacerdos*, and Payne-Smith, *Thesaurus Syr.* p. 3766, s. v. קשׁישׁ 4 and 5. Palladius (*Vita Chrysostomi* 15 *PG* XLVII, 51) charges the Jews of πωλεῖν καὶ ἀγοράζειν τὴν ἱ ε ρ ο σ ύ ν η ν. Comp. also Epiphanius, *Haer.* XXX.11, *PG* XLI, 424b.

[251] Comp. Momigliano, *Athenaeum* XXII (1934), p. 152.

[252] Comp. my note in *Tarbiz* III, 1932, p. 207.

[253] That the ordination was conferred only for the purpose of exemption from *leitourgias.*

[254] See A. Gulak (referred to above n. 212) and comp. *TP Baba Kamma* III.1, 3c.

Apart from the general oppression by the burden of taxes the Jews enjoyed long periods of comfort and security in the third century. The Patriarch and the Jewish community were well treated under the Severi,[255] and it appears that even afterwards they had a certain amount of freedom. We shall quote a few interesting texts. The Palestinian Talmud relates:[256] ר' יוחנן אמר לבר דרוסיי חות ותבר כל אילין צלמייא דנו דימוסין ונחית ותבר כולהון פרא חד. ולמה כן. א'ר יוסי בר' בון מפני שנחשד ישראל אחד להיות מקטיר עליו. "R. Johanan[257] said to Bar Derossai: 'Go down and break all the idols which are in the public bath.'[258] He went and broke all of them except one (παρὰ μίαν). Why so (i. e. why did he leave one)? R. Jose b. R. Bun said: Because one Jew was suspected of offering incense on it.''[259] The explanation offered by R. Jose is not altogether clear. If the Gentile, Bar Derossai, intended to demolish the idols altogether, why did he not destroy all of them?[260] Moréover, it is strange that R. Johanan did not give heed to the advice of his great namesake, R. Johanan b. Zakai,[261] who warned the Jews:[262] אל תבהל לסתור במות גוים שלא תבנה בידך, שלא תסתור של לבינים ויאמרו לך עשם של אבנים, של אבנים ויאמרו לך עשם של עץ.

---

[255] See Graetz p. 224 and Juster I, p. 394 ff. and nn. *ibid.*

[256] *'Abodah Zarah* IV.4, 43d, bot.

[257] Flourished in Tiberias in the second and third quarters of the third century.

[258] דימוסין, δημόσιον (scil. λουτρόν). On the use by the rabbis of the vulgar Greek suffix ιν for ιον, see Lieberman, *Greek in Jewish Palestine*, p. 57, n. 185.

[259] Probably in the time of the Hadrianic persecutions. See *TP ibid.* V.8, 45a. According to Jewish law it is not permitted to derive any benefit from idols or from their debris. But when a Gentile discards the idol the Jews are permitted to benefit from it. Obviously, Bar Derossai was a Gentile. However, if a Jew worshipped an idol, the latter can never be discarded.

[260] See the preceding note.

[261] Flourished in the first century.

[262] *Mekhilta ad Deut.* in *Midrash Tannaim* ed. Hoffmann, p. 58. Comp. *Aboth deR. Nathan* II vers. XXI, ed. Schechter, p. 66-67.

"Do not rush to destroy altars of Gentiles, lest you be compelled to restore them yourself. You might break an altar of bricks, and will be ordered to build one of stones; you might break an altar of stones and will be commanded to build one of wood."[263] Our rabbi, probably, had good reason to believe that the government would overlook the destruction of the idols.

Another passage in the Babylonian Talmud sheds more light on our incident. We read there:[264] בי ינאי מלכא חרוב. אתו נויים אוקימו ביה מרקוליס. אתו נויים אחריני דלא פלחי למרקוליס, שקלינהו וחיפו בהן דרכים וסטרטאות. איכא רבנן דפרשי ואיכא רבנן דלא פרשי. א'ר יוחנן בנן של קדושים מהלך עליהן ואנן נפרוש מהן "The palace of king Yannai[265] was in ruins. Gentiles came and set up Mercurii[266] there. Subsequently, other Gentiles, who did not worship Mercurius, came and removed them, and paved the roads and streets with them. Some rabbis refrained from walking on them while others did not. R. Johanan said: The son of the holy ones[267] walks on them, shall we abstain?" From the parallel passage[268] as well as from the name R. Johanan it was safely inferred that the

---

[263] R. Joḥanan b. Zakai's advice emanated from bitter experience. In his lifetime the Jews of Jamnia, in Judea, destroyed an altar hastily built of clay formed into bricks, the most common material (Philo, *Legatio ad Gaium* 30, 201, ed. Cohn-Reiter VI, p. 192₂₈: αὐτοσχέδιον ἀνιστᾶσι βωμὸν εἰκαιοτάτης ὕλης, πηλὸν σχηματίσαντες εἰς πλίνθους). But when the emperor was informed of it "he ordered that a much more costly and magnificent, gilded colossal statue be set up in the Temple of the metropolis (*i. e.* Jerusalem) in place of the brick altar which was erected as an affront [to the Jews]." (*Ibid.* 193₇: πλουσιώτερον καὶ μεγαλοφρονέστερόν τι ἀντὶ τοῦ πλινθίνου βωμοῦ τοῦ κατ' ἐπήρειαν ἀνασταθέντος ἐν Ἰαμνείᾳ κελεύει κολοσσιαῖον ἀνδριάντα ἐπίχρυσον ἐν τῷ τῆς μητροπόλεως ἱερῷ καθιδρυθῆναι).

[264] *'Abodah Zarah* 50a.

[265] See below, n. 270.

[266] See Appendix.

[267] *I. e.* R. Menaḥem b. Simai.

[268] TP *'Abodah Zarah* III.13, 43b. See R. Hananel *a. l.* and comp. Klein, *Neue Beiträge zur Geschichte und Geographie Galiäas*, p. 2, n. 8.

scene of action was Tiberias. S. Klein[269] has correctly identified the ruined palace of king Yannai mentioned in our
passage with that of Herod the Tetrarch[270] in Tiberias
which was partly destroyed by the Jews because it contained representations of animals.[271] He added that the
details of our passage were not sufficiently clear.

However our passage is well illuminated by a description
of Epiphanius. He says:[272] Ναὸς δὲ μέγιστος ἐν τῇ πόλει
προϋπῆρχε. τάχα, οἶμαι, Ἀδριανεῖον τοῦτο ἐκάλουν.
ἀτελὲς δὲ τοῦτο τὸ Ἀδριανεῖον διαμεῖναν τάχα οἱ πο-
λῖται εἰς δημόσιον λουτρὸν ἐπειρῶντο ἐπισκεύασαι.''
"There was a very great temple in the city (i. e. Tiberias)
which I think was perhaps called Adrianeion. Since this
Adrianeion remained unfinished the inhabitants endeavored
to convert it into a public bath.'' The *very great temple* in
Tiberias which was unfinished reminds us instantly of the
half ruined palace of Herod. Since Epiphanius himself is
not sure of the exact name of the temple, it is very possible that he confused Ἡροδεῖον[273] with Ἀδριανεῖον. In
reality, the name has no bearing on our subject, since the
most likely occasion for the reconversion of the palace of
Herod into a heathen temple was in the time of the Hadrianic persecutions; thus the name Adrianeion fits the temple
very well. Now the meaning of the above passage in the
Babylonian Talmud, which tells that "Gentiles came and

---

[269] *Ibid.*

[270] The fact that *TB* calls different rulers by the name Yannai is well
known.

[271] Jos. *Vita* 12, 65: ζῴων μορφὰς ἔχοντα. Comp. Jawitz תולדות
ישראל vol. V, p. 160, n. 5, referred to by Klein *ibid.*

[272] *Panar. haer.* XXX.12, *PG* XLI, 425b; ed. Holl, p. 347.

[273] A passage in *TP* (see above n. 268), although based on a different
version than both *TB* and the parallels in *TP* (*Berakhoth* II.1, 4b;
Shekalim II.7, 47a; *Mo'ed Katan* III.7, 83c), mentions אדורי צלמא (in
Berakhoth ibid. אהדורי צילמיא) which some scholars interpreted as the
statue (or statues) of Herod.

set up Mercurii in the ruined palace" becomes perfectly clear: Gentiles converted the palace into a heathen temple. However, as is known from rabbinic literature and from Epiphanius,[274] Tiberias was an exclusively Jewish town in the third and fourth centuries. The Jews, in their turn, subsequently converted part of the palace[275] into a public bath, δημόσιον λουτρόν.

It is to the statues of this δημόσιον that R. Johanan referred in his advice to Bar Derossai. Now we perfectly understand why one idol was left. The Gentiles did not want merely to demolish the statues, but to utilize them, to pave the roads with them.[276] Had the Gentiles included the idol, which a Jew was suspected of having worshipped, in the material they paved the streets with, the Jews would have found it impossible to use the road.[277]

But who were those "Gentiles who did not worship Mercurius"[278] and paved the roads and streets with its statues? I think we shall not err if we identify them with Christians. To take apart heathen temples and utilize the material for building purposes was a usual practice of the Christians under Constantius[279] and in the late fourth century.[280] On the first of November 397 Asterius the *comes orientis* was ordered to repair roads, bridges etc. with the material of the demolished temples.[281] Some years later Porphyrius of Gasa gave orders[282] to pave part of the street

---

[274] *Ibid.*

[275] The temple proper could not be used by the Jews; they most probably utilized the adjacent premises for bathing purposes. Hence the impression of Epiphanius that the inhabitants "tried" to transform it into a bath.

[276] As is obvious from *TB ibid.* [277] See above n. 259.

[278] Probably a generic term for idolatry, see Appendix, n. 19.

[279] See Libanius *Orat.* XVIII.126. Comp. Bidez et Cumont, *Juliani imperatoris epistulae et leges*, pp. 48–49.

[280] See Grégoire-Kugener, *Vita Porphyrii*, Introduction, p. LXVI.

[281] *Cod. Theod.* XV.1.36.

[282] *Vita Porphyrii* 102.

with the marble taken from the temple Marneion. The majority of the heathen, and particularly the women, refrained from the use of this paved part.[283]

However the paving of roads with statues of gods around the middle of the third century is quite remarkable. True, Herodian accuses Maximinus Thrax of melting down the votive offerings of the temples, the statues of the gods, the tributes to heroes etc.,[284] but this was a measure of extreme emergency. Even so, he apparently took only the mintable metals[285] and not the cheap material from the temples.[286] The public removal of the statues for the purpose of paving the streets indicates that the inhabitants were not afraid of punishment for ἱεροσυλία (temple robbery), which in itself is quite instructive. It is to be regretted, however, that we cannot establish the exact time of this occurrence. The rabbi who counselled the demolition of the idols was the chief of the Tiberian academy during part of the second and the entire third quarter of the third century. It is probable that our incident took place under Philippus Arabs. For although it is most unlikely that the latter was converted to Christianity it is certain that he assumed a definitely friendly attitude towards the Christians.[287] When this became known in Palestine, the inhabitants of the

[283] R. Johanan who insisted that the Jews may use the road paved with the stones of the statues was possibly anxious that it be actually used, for otherwise it might be considered as a token of respect (See also *Sam.* 5.5. Comp. the parallel in *TP 'Abodah Zarah* III.13, 43b) to the statues.

[284] VII.3.5.: ναῶν τε ἀναθήματα θεῶν τε ἀγάλματα καὶ ἡρώων τιμάς . . . πᾶν ἐχωνεύετο.

[285] See *The Cambridge Ancient History* XII, p. 76. Comp. also. A. D. Nock, *The Harvard Theol. Review* XXXII, 1939, p. 89 and n. 37 *ibid.*

[286] Cases of individual Gentiles who discarded their idols and utilized the material were not uncommon, as is evident from the many instances cited in *'Abodah Zarah* chs. III–IV. Even the paving of streets with the stones of Mercurius is cited as a theoretical example (*Tosephta ibid.* VI, 470₂, and parallels in *TB ibid.* 42a and 50a bot.), but there the singular נכרי (a Gentile) is mentioned, *i. e.* an individual..

[287] See PW *RE* X, 768 ff. and 770 *ibid.*

localities where there were few heathens acted as they did later, during the reign of Constantius.

We now summarize our conclusions. There is no evidence either for the persecution of the Jewish religion during the third and fourth centuries,[288] or for Jewish rebellions during that time. The only exception is an insignificant local insurrection of a part of the Sepphorean Jews. Even in this case it is not certain that the Jews rebelled against the Roman rule. There is no proof that the burden of taxes levied on the Jews was heavier[289] than that on the other provincials. The rabbis very often complain against the Romans, not as Jews but as oppressed citizens denouncing the lawlessness and wickedness of the rulers.

(To be continued)

[288] I omitted from my discussion the arguments of scholars which are based on wrong texts (See, for instance, Ratner אהבת ציון וירושלים on *Ta'anith,* p. 70-71) or on incorrect identifications of persons and places. Anonymous passages of *Midrashim* compiled after the fourth century are also excluded from my paper (except when it is obvious from the context or parallels that they portray an earlier period).

[289] With the exception of the time of Constantius, see above p. 349 and n. 146.

PALESTINE IN THE THIRD AND FOURTH CENTURIES

(Continued from *JQR*, XXXVI [1946], 329–370)

By Saul Lieberman

The Jewish Theological Seminary of America

III. Rabbbinic Parallels To The Thirteenth Sibylline Book

"When first I have come to the imperial throne, Gordian Caesar assembled a force of Goths and Germans from all of Rome (the Roman dominion) and made an inroad into Assyria against the Aryan empire and us, and there was a great battle in the Assyrian mountains opposite Mishika-man. Gordian Caesar was killed, the Romans made (proclaimed) Philipp Caesar. Then Philipp Caesar came to us asking for terms and having given us 500,000 denars as ransom for the life (of his friends) became tributary to us." So spoke Shapuhr the First in the Kaabah of Zoroaster inscription.[290] Although the "king of kings" greatly exaggerated his victory[291] the Persian success must have made a deep impression in the Orient. During the reign of Philip (244–249) there apparently were no military operations between Rome and Persia.[292] The contemporary Sibyl[293] says: "But when these shall rule[294] in war and

[290] Gr. ll. 6–10. *The American Journal of Semitic Languages* LVII, 1940, p. 360; The English translation by Prof. Sprengling *ibid.*, p. 363.

[291] See A. T. Olmstead, *Classical Philology* XXXVII, 1942, p. 255; M. Rostovtzeff, *Berytus* VIII, 1943, p. 23.

[292] See H. M. D. Parker, *A History of the Roman World*, p. 339, n. 1 and Rostovtzeff *ibid.*, p. 31, n. 39.

[293] See now the excellent analysis of its contents by Prof. Olmstead, *ibid.* p. 250 ff.

[294] *I. e.* Philip and his son.

31

become lawgivers,[295] there shall be respite from war, but not for long."[296] It was only shortly after the death of Philip that Persia undertook its real aggression, and Rome entered one of its darkest periods of history.

The Midrash tells us[297] to this effect: וימלוך תחתיו יובב בן זרח מבצרה אמר ר' אבהו ... כבר היתה מלכות עקורה מאדום ובאת בצרה וסיפקה לה מלכים אין לי עסק אלא עם בוצרה הה"ד כי זבח לה' בבוצרה וטבח גדול בארץ אדום " *And Jobab the son of Zerah of Bozrah reigned in his stead'* (Gen. 36.33). R. Abbahu[298] said ... Kingship had already been uprooted from Edom (= Rome), whereupon Bozrah came and supplied her with kings. I shall deal with none but with Bozrah. Thus it is written: *'For the Lord hath a sacrifice in Bozrah and a great slaughter in the land of Edom' "* (Isa. 34.6). For a short time it appeared as if the Philippi averted the danger from the empire. It was already on the verge of ruin, when Bozrah[299] came and supplied Rome with a dynasty[300] which saved the empire. Because she rescued the empire, the Lord will take revenge on her.

Our Sibyl also rages against the cities of Arabia, which obtained privileges from Philip,[301] but it singles out two of them: "And of all most eager for mathematics Bostra and Philippopolis that you may come in great sorrow."[302] The

[295] Comp. *C. A. H.* XII, p. 89.

[296] XIII.25 ff.: ἡνίκα δ' οὗτοι ἐν πολέμοις ἄρξουσι, θεμιστονόμοι δὲ γένωνται, ἄμπαυσις πολέμου βαιὸν ἔσσεται, οὐκ ἐπὶ δηρόν.

[297] *BR* LXXXIII.3, 998.

[298] Some mss. read here אבא instead of אבהו. But the reading of the editions is substantiated by the two best mss. of *BR* as well as by שכל טוב, p. 211. Comp. also below.

[299] See PW *RE* vol. X, p. 756 ff. That the *Midrash* referred here to Philip was correctly surmised by Krauss, *Monumenta Talmudica* V, p. 61.

[300] The two Philippi, the emperors, and Priscus, the brother of Philip, the *rector orientis.*

[301] XIII.64 ff.

[302] *Ibid.* ll. 67 ff.: ἐκ πάντων δὲ μάλιστα μαθηματικὴ περ ἐοῦσα Βόστρα Φιλιππόπολις <τε>, ἵν' ἔλθῃς εἰς μέγα πένθος.

sibyl wants to create the impression[303] that it is angry with
Bozrah for its practice of astrology.[304] It is doubtful, however, whether it disclosed its true reason. The author of
the sibyl was an admirer of Palmyra,[305] and his hostility
towards a prospective rival-center of the oriental caravan
trade is quite natural. The importance of both Palmyra
and Bozrah in the oriental trade[306] as well as their colonial
status[307] may have irked the Jews, who hoped for the
destruction of both of them.[308] The Jews were the more
vexed when during the reign of Philip the cities of Arabia
enjoyed his special protection[309] and the hated Shechem rose
to the rank of a colony.[310] The remark of R. Abahu regarding Bostra had meaning only during the reign of Philip
or immediately after. Subsequently, when Persia seriously
endangered the Roman East, R. Abbahu's comment that
Bostra saved the empire would be pointless.

    We further read in the Midrash:[311] ... דא"ר א ב ה ו[312]

[303] Ll. 69 ff.

[304] Comp. J. Geffcken, *Komposition und Entstehungszeit der Oracula Sibyllina*, Leipzig 1902, p. 59–60. It is noteworthy that the astrologer mentioned in *TP* (*Shabbath* VI, 8d) came from Bozrah (See Lieberman, הירושלמי כפשוטו, *a. l.*, p. 115). Approximately half the inhabitants of the city were heathens during the reign of Julian the Apostate (See Sozom., *Hist. Eccl.* V. 15, *PG* LXVII, 1257b).

[305] See the end of the book and Geffken *ibid.*, p. 61.

[306] See Rostovtzeff, *Caravan Cities*, 1932, pp. 33 ff. 51.

[307] See Jones, *The Cities of the Eastern Roman Provinces*, p. 457, n. 52 (Palmyra) and p. 457, n. 90 (Bostra).

[308] See *BR* LVI.11, p. 610 and parallels. Comp. also *TB Yebamoth* 17a.

[309] See above n. 301 and Olmstead *ibid.*, p. 259.

[310] See Jones *ibid.*, p. 436, n. 73; *C. A. H.*, XII, p. 88. Philip's name was apparently erased in the inscription of the synagogue in Dura Europos. See J. Obermann, *Berytus* VII, 1942, p. 102. Comp. Dittenberger, *Or. Gr. Ins. Sel.* 640, n. 9. The biographer of Aurelian (*Hist. Aug., Aurel.* XLII.6) counts Philip among the bad emperors like Vitellius, Caligula, Nero and Maximinus.

[311] *Pesikta deR. Kahana* V, 56a and *Pesikta Rabbathi* XV, ed. Friedmann 79a.

[312] So ms. Oxf. and *Pesikta Rabbathi*. The editions and *Yalkut* read אבין.

מי פורע לכם מהם שני בלקטורים‎[313]‎ מרדכי ואסתר ... מי פורע לכם
מיון בני חשמונאי ... מי פורע לכם מאדום נטרונא‎[314]‎ שנאמר והיה לכם
למשמרת ... כי זבח לה' בבצרה וכו'‎.‎ "For R. Abbahu said ...
Who will settle your account with them (*i. e.* with Haman
and his sons)? Two guardians (φυλάκτορες), Mordechai
and Esther ... Who will settle your account with Greece
(*i. e.* with the Seleucids)? The Hasmoneans ... Who will
settle your account with Edom (*i. e.* Rome)? Natrona, as
it is written (Ex. 12.6): '*It shall be unto you for keeping*' ...
'*For the Lord hath a sacrifice in Bozrah etc.*' (Isa. 34.6)."
Who is that mysterious Natrona? Our rabbi, as is well
known, was fond of indulging in enigmatic speech (לשון
חכמה), based on the double meaning of words.[315] He
especially liked to play with interchangeable letters;[316] in
our case the main stress lies in the word למשמרת "for keeping." Mordechai and Esther are keepers, guardians,
בלקטורין, פלקטורין‎[317]‎ and it is not impossible that the Aramaic Natrona is שמור‎,[318]‎ a play on the name שבור‎.[319]‎ The
rabbi hoped that שבור מלכא, Shapuhr I, would settle accounts with Rome.[320]

The Babylonian Jews definitely sided with Shapuhr.
Samuel, the famous Babylonian rabbi, was a great admirer
of Shapuhr; the two were often in personal contact with
each other.[321]   The Babylonian Talmud[322] admits that

[313] So ms. Oxf. *Pesikta Rabbathi* reads בלקטורים‎. *Yalkut*, ed. *pr.* and
ms. Oxf., reads כלקטירין‎. The editions read דלקטירין‎.

[314] So ms. Oxf., *Pesikta Rabbathi* and *Yalkut*.

[315] See Lieberman, *Greek in Jewish Palestine*, p. 21 ff.

[316] See *TB 'Erubin* 53b and comp. *TP Ma'asroth* II.7, 50a.

[317] The letters פ, ב and מ are often interchanged in the Palestinian
dialect. See Frankel סבוא הירושלמי 8a *passim*. But why is He not explicitly mentioned?

[318] Being a פעול formation like שקוד‎, נטור‎ etc.   [319] See above n. 317.

[320] See *TB Yoma* 10a. J. Levy, *Neuhebräisches ... Wörterbuch* III,
p. 384, explains that God is designated by Natronai (See *TP Ta'anith* I.1,
64a and *TB Megilla* 11a *passim*). But why is He not explicitly mentioned?

[321] See D. Hoffman, *Mar Samuel*, Leipzig 1873, p. 46 ff.

[322] *Mo'ed Katan* 26a.

Samuel did not rend his garments when word reached him that Shapuhr slaughtered many thousands of Jews in Caesarea Mazaca. Nobody will suspect the rabbis of falsely trumping up such a charge against Samuel.[323] The story is undoubtedly true. But since Samuel died in 254 (or 255)[324] the event must have taken place before that year,[325] and there is no reason to doubt the information provided by the rabbis.[326]

However, the feelings of the Palestinian rabbis about this misfortune seem not to have been identical with those of the Babylonian. We read in the Palestinian Talmud[327] that when R. Ḥaninah died, R. Johanan rent his garments and the Talmud remarks: "We do not know whether he rent his garments because R. Ḥaninah was his teacher, or

[323] The subsequent passage of the Talmud *ibid.* about the splitting of the wall of Laodicea is, of course, only a legend. A similar story was current about Nisibis (See *Tabari*, ed. Nöldeke, p. 32). Comp. also *TP Baba Bathra* II.3 (end), 13b. Perhaps R. Ami heard the legend from the Cappadocian Jews in Sepphoris, see below n. 335.

[324] See the Epistle of Rav Sherira, ed. Lewin, p. 82. *TB Berakhoth* 56a relates that our Samuel foretold to Shapuhr that he would see in his dream that the Romans would capture him and make him grind date stones in a *golden* mill. The dream of Shapuhr sounds like an echo of what he did to Valerian and like a kind of warning (See *Hist. Aug., Val. duo* I.1 ff. But the letters are certainly spurious). The accounts of Shapuhr's maltreatment of Valerian are very unlikely (See the sources referred to by Olmstead, *Classical Philology* XXXVII, p. 413, n. 148. Comp. *CAH*, XII, p. 137). The assertion of Lactantius (*De mort. pers.* V) and Victor (*Epit.* XXXIII.6) that Valerian had to stoop and to present his back whenever Shapuhr wanted to mount his horse is only a legend. (Perhaps a deliberate misinterpretation of the bas-reliefs. See *CAH* XII, p. 123. Comp. *TB Megilla* 16a, '*Ab. Zar.* 10b). Labor in a *golden* mill is much more appropriate even for the popular invention (See *Hist. Aug., Tyr. trig.* XXX.26; *Aurel.* XXXIV.3). But the capture of Valerian took place in 260 when our rabbi was already dead. We probably have here a pseudepigraphic anecdote. Comp. the preceding story in *TB ibid.*

[325] See Hoffmann *ibid.*, p. 48, n. 3.

[326] Comp. now Olmstead *ibid.*, p. 400, and Rostovtzeff *Berytus* VIII, 1943, pp. 32 and 40.

[327] *Baba Mezi'a* II, end, 8d.

because bad news (שמועות הרעות) reached him at that time."
Now, R. Ḥaninah apparently died in the fifties of the third
century,[328] and the definition of שמועות הרעות in both Talmuds[329] is "news that Jewish masses were slaughtered". As a
matter of fact, the Babylonian Talmud itself[330] at first
considered the news of the slaughtering of the Jews in
Caesarea Mazaca as an example of שמועות הרעות, bad news,
which require the rending of the garments.[331]   It is therefore
highly probable that the Palestinian Talmud had this
"bad news" in mind when it cited it as a possible reason for
R. Johanan's rending his garments.[332]

Our sibyl further tells us concerning that time: "Alas!
How many shall flee from the East (*i. e.* on account of the
Persian invasion) with their goods unto men of other
tongues!"[333] It was natural to expect that the Cappadocian
Jews would take refuge in Palestine. And indeed we read
in the Palestinian Talmud[334] that the Cappadocian Jews of
Sepphoris complained to R. Ami[335] that "they have no
friend [in Sepphoris] and nobody greets them."[336] The
blameworthy behavior of the Sepphoreans is at least partly
extenuated by their hatred of Rome. They blamed the

---

[328] See Graetz, p. 234.

[329] *TB Mo'ed Katan* 26a and *TP ibid.* III.7, 83b.

[330] Ibid.

[331] Although *TB ibid.* decided that the law of the tearing of the
garments applied only in the case where the slaughtered masses consisted of the majority of the nation, it was only a justification for the
behavior of Samuel; the Palestinian Talmud does not mention this
limitation. Comp. also the conclusion in *TB ibid.*: התם אינהי נרמי לנפשייהו.

[332] R. Johanan had no reason to be a Persian patriot. He certainly
hated the Palmyrenes (See *TP Ta'anith* IV, 69b and parallels. Comp.
above n. 308). Moreover, he was not sure of the permanence of the
Persian conquests, see his remark in *TB Kiddushin* 72a.

[333] XIII.113: αἵ, ὁπόσοι φεύξονται ἀπ' ἀντολίης γεγαῶτες σὺν
κτεάτεσσιν ἐοῖσιν ἐς ἀλλοθρόους ἀνθρώπους.

[334] *Shebi'ith* IX.5, 39a.

[335] See above n. 323.

[336] דלית לאילין עמא רחם ולא שאל שלם.

Cappadocian Jews for their taking side against Persia.[337] The feelings of the Sepphoreans, however, cannot be taken as an indication of the general attitude of the Palestinian Jewry.[338]

The author of the Sibyl concludes his oracle: "But a well horned stag (*i. e.* Macrianus) after him (*i. e.* Valerian) shall come, again another (*i. e.* the younger Macriānus), hungering on the mountains, striving to feed upon the venom hurling beast (*i. e.* the Persians). Then shall come one sent by the sun (*i. e.* Odenathus), a terrible and fearful lion, breathing forth much flame. Then too by great and shameless recklessness shall he destroy the well horned rapid stag (*i. e.* Quietus, the son of Macrianus) and the greatest beast, venom hurling, fearful, sending forth many piping sounds (*i. e.* the Persians), and the sidewise moving goat (*i. e.* Callistus), but after him (*i. e.* Odenathus) fame follows; he, however, sound, unhurt, and unapproached shall rule the Romans, but the Persians shall be weak."[339] The identification of the "well horned stag" ($\dot{\eta}\nu\kappa\epsilon\rho\omega s$ $\check{\epsilon}\lambda\alpha\varphi os$) with Macrianus is almost certain, for the Hebrew מקרן (Ps. 69.32, as translated by Symmachus) means $\kappa\epsilon\rho\acute{\alpha}\sigma\tau\eta s$. The symbol of the stag was probably suggested by the fame of its reputed fight with the venomous snakes which it devoured.[340] The identification of the other animals is not so certain but it is highly probably: Odenathus will destroy Quietus and Callistus and will defeat the Persians.

The rabbis[341] commented on the verse in Dan. 7.8 as follows: וארו קרן אחרי זעירא סלקת ביניהון. זה בן נצר. ותלת מן

[337] *TB Mo'ed Katan* 26a. Comp. above n. 323.
[338] See above nn. 90 and 242.
[339] XIII.162 ff. I copied both the translation and the identifications from Olmstead, *Classical Philology*, XXXVII, 1942, pp. 414 and 420.
[340] See Clermont-Ganneau, *Recueil d'archéologie orientale* IV, 321 ff.
[341] *BR* LXXVI.6, p. 903.

קרנייא קדמייתא איתעקרה מן קדמה זה מקרוס[342] וקרוס[343] וקרידוס[344]

" 'And, behold, there came up among them another horn, a little one,' this refers to Ben Nazor,[345] 'before which three of the first were uprooted' this[346] refers to Macr[ian]us, Carus (?) and Cyriades." The reading מקרוס or מקרון is quite sure[347] and its identification with Macrianus is almost certain (a play on קרן), as correctly observed by Jewish scholars.[348] The correction of קירוס into קידוס or קיטס[349] and its identification with Quietus is plausible. But that Cyriades was destroyed by Odenathus is not borne out by the information supplied by other sources.[350] However, in spite of the unanimous opinion of the scholars,[351] the above text of the Midrash does not warrant the interpretation that Odenathus destroyed all the three "kings." It simply says that he succeeded them.[352] The rabbinic source is thus well paralleled by our sibyl.

---

[342] Var. מוקדון, מקדוי, מקדון, מקרון.   [343] Var. קצרוס, קודוס, קירוס.

[344] Var. קרירוס, קדירוס, קרדידוס, קרדידוסי, קרדון, קרידונא, קדירונא.

[345] Νάσωρος Παλμυρηνός (Dittenberger, Or. Gr. Inscr. Sel. 642₃), Odenathus, as correctly identified by Graetz Note 28, p. 455. It is noteworthy that the Midrash apparently refers to Odenathus as אחי שבא עלי מכוחו של עשו, "My brother that advances upon me on behalf of Esau (= Rome)." Comp. also TP Terumoth VIII.10, 46b.

[346] The editions have here an addition: שנתנה להם מלכותם, but no ms. has this interpolation (The Yemen ms. referred to by Theodor is a copy from the printed editions. See Albeck's Introduction, p. 115 ff.).

[347] See the variants above n. 342.

[348] See Theodor's notes a. l.

[349] See the variants above n. 343. The scribes who believed that the letters קר are a component part of each of the three names (because of the play on קרן) corrected קיטס into קירוס.

[350] See now Rostovtzeff, Berytus VIII, 1943, p. 32 ff.

[351] See Theodor a. l.; Graetz ibid.; Krauss, Monumenta Talmudica V, p. 74 ff.; Marmorstein, Tarbiz III, 1932, p. 163 ff., and the articles referred to by Marmorstein ibid.

[352] איתעקרו מן קדמה meaning "they were uprooted [shortly] before his reign." As a matter of fact the subsequent comment of the Midrash on this verse clearly confirms our interpretation. The order of the names in our source is quite logical: The Macrianus family is mentioned first and then Cyriades is named.

We conclude with the report of the Babylonian Talmud on the *ludi Saeculares* [of 248]. We read there:[353] אמ' רב יהוד' אמ' שמואל עוד אחרת יש ברומי אחת לשבעים שנה . . . ומכריזין ואומ'[354] סך[355] קיר[356] פלסתר[357] אחוה דמרנא זייפנא.[358] מאי אהני ליה לרמאה ברמאותיה ולזייפא בזייפנותיה[359] דחמי חמי ודלא חמי לא[360] חמי ומסיימין בה הכי[364] ווי ליה לדין כד יקום דין. "R. Judah said in the name of Samuel: They observe yet another festival in Rome [which occurs] once every seventy years[361] . . . They proclaim and say: The reckoning (*or* summary) of the master is a forgery. The brother of our lord [is] the forger! Of what avail is his deceit to the deceiver and his forgery to the forger! He who sees it sees it; he who does not see it now will never see it. And they conclude thus:[363] Woe unto the one when the other will arise." S. Rapoport[364]

---

[353] *Abodah Zarah* 11b. I copy from the best ms. of this tractate: Cod. New York (a Spanish Ms. of 1290). I am indebted to my friend and colleague Prof. A. Marx for his calling my attention to this valuable ms.

[354] This is also the reading of R. Hananel *a. l.*, '*Arukh s. v.* סך, *Meiri*, p. 21, *Aggadoth Hatalmud* 127c etc.

[355] This is also the reading of the above sources, of the editions of the Talmud, of R. Joseph ibn Migas (responsa No. 8), '*Ein Jacob a. l.* etc. Cod. Munich reads mistakenly בר. The word סך means number, summary and reckoning. Comp. *Meiri ibid.* See however, the explanation of R. Hananel (= R. Joseph ibn Migas and *Aruk ibid.*).

[356] This word means "the master," but it is not impossible that Shapuhr was jokingly called (for his excessive aspirations to restore the ancient Persian empire) Cyrus by the Romans. See below.

[357] This word always designates the falsification of a document, see Krauss *LW* II, p. 461 ff. *s. v.* פלסטר and פלסטרון. Comp. the following note.

[358] The verb זוף usually designates the forgery of a written document. See Jastrow, *dictionary*, s. v. זוף I.3. Comp. the preceding note.

[359] The order of the sentences in the editions is different, but that of the Mss. (see דקדוקי סופרים *a. l.*) is the only logical one.

[360] The word לא was inserted by the scribe between the lines. It is extant in all the editions, mss. and medieval quotations.

[361] We should perhaps read: הכ' (=הכא), here, i. e. Persia.

[362] The Jewish *saeculum*.

[363] See above n. 361.

[364] *s. v.* ערך מילין איד.

was the first to realize that the Talmud portrays here the *Ludi Saeculares*, as is clearly indicated by the proclamation of the herald: "He who sees it etc."[365] It is likewise the unanimous opinion of scholars that the secular games referred to by Samuel are the *Ludi Saeculares* staged by Philip in 248.[366] But no satisfactory interpretation of the obscure content of the proclamations has hitherto been offered.

Now it is remarkable that the declarations made on the occasion of the secular games in Rome in 248 have been transmitted, in a Babylonian source only, by the Babylonian Samuel, who died in 255 (or 254).[367] We have seen above[368] that our rabbi was an intimate of the court of Shapuhr. The Persians certainly kept a watchful eye on Rome during Philip's reign, and it is not surprising that they received information of what was going on during the secular games, the symbol of Roman patriotism. Samuel, most probably, derived his information from a Persian source.[369]

We have seen above (at the beginning of this chapter) that in his inscription Shapuhr glorified his victory over Rome and the good terms he obtained. On the other hand, Philip assumed the title Persicus Maximus in 244 and that of Parthicus Maximus in 245,[370] by which actions he evidently challenged Shapuhr's interpretation of the agree-

[365] See Krauss, *Monumenta Talmudica* V, p. 163; Lieberman, *Greek in Jewish Palestine*, p. 145, n. 7.

[366] On the occasion of the thousandth anniversary of the foundation of Rome (according to the Varronian calculation). See *CAH* XII, p. 91 ff.

[367] See above n. 324.

[368] N. 321.

[369] The Aramaic of the proclamation is Palestinian. But the rabbis may have purposely used this dialect for the wording of a solemn declaration; or, perhaps, the informant of the Persians was a Jew from the Roman empire.

[370] See Olmstead, *Classical Philology* XXXVII, 1942, p. 256, n. 43.

ment. The terms of the treaty were certainly not observed.
Shapuhr in his inscription says: "And the emperor lied
again and unto Armenia he did injustice etc."[371] Prof.
Olmstead[372] associated it with the words of our sibyl which
says of Philip:[373] "But when the wolf makes faithful oath
against the white-toothed dogs but then deceives[374] etc."
Like Shapuhr, the Christian Sibyl accuses the Roman
emperor of not observing his treaty. Evidently the Roman
and Persian emperors indulged in mutual recriminations.

In the light of this, the proclamation of the Roman
herald makes good sense. He said: The reckoning (or
calculations) of the master[375] is a fiction[376] (referring to the
plans of Shapuhr). The brother of our lord (i. e. Shapuhr)[377]
[is] the forger![378] Of what avail is deceit to the deceiver
and forgery to the forger![379] And they conclude thus:[380]
Woe unto the one when the other will arise [to fight]!
The Persians were speedily informed of the remarks made
against them in Rome.

[371] Ll. 10 ff. *The American Journal of Semitic Languages* LVII, 1940,
p. 366: καὶ ὁ Καῖσαρ πάλιν ἐψεύσατο καὶ εἰς τὴν Ἀρμενίαν ἀδικίαν
ἐποίησεν κτλ.

[372] *Ibid.* p. 257.

[373] XIII.28: ἀλλ' ὁπόταν ποίμνῃ λύκος ὅρκια πιστώσηται πρὸς
κύνας ἀργιόδοντας ἔπειτα δὲ δηλήσηται κτλ.

[374] Literally: makes mischief.

[375] See above n. 356.

[376] See above n. 357.

[377] That Philip could have styled Shapuhr ἀδελφός in the treaty is,
of course, natural.

[378] See above n. 358. The subsequent remark of R. Ashi (*TB ibid.*)
makes very good sense in the light of our interpretation: The forger is
really Philip not Shapuhr.

[379] I. e. the forgeries of Shapuhr in his boastful proclamations will not
help him.

[380] See above n. 361.

APPENDIX (to vol. XXXVI, p. 366, n. 266)

מרקוליס, MERCURIUS, Μερκούριος AND 'Ερμῆς

The idol מרקוליס, Merculis, Mercurius, is mentioned in rabbinic literature more frequently than any other pagan deity.[1] The rabbis knew of the Mercurius on the Roman limes,[2] the trilithon[3] and its other forms.[4] Some of the trilithons in Palestine may have survived till modern times.[5] A Mercurius stood in the field of a Palestinian rabbi[6] until he ingeniously got rid of it.[7] From the Mishnah and Talmud it clearly appears that this idol was quite popular in Palestine.

Yet it is rather strange that this pagan deity was known to the rabbis by the Latin name Mercurius and not by the Greek 'Ερμῆς, which never occurs in rabbinic literature. True, we read in an Egyptian papyrus:[8] ἐν ταῖς Μερκουρίου βιβλιοθήκαις, which was usually understood as "the libraries [of the temple] of Mercurius,"[9] but Prof. E. Bickerman rightly suggested[10] that the reference is not to a temple[11] but to the archives of the Roman administration of granaries, ad Mercurium Alexandreae.

---

[1] See Krauss LW II, pp. 353–354.

[2] ἐνόδιος. See Sifra בהר IX.5, ed. Weiss 110b and TP 'Abodah Zarah IV.1, 43d.

[3] Mishnah 'Abodah Zarah IV.1; TB Baba Mezi'a 25b. Comp. the notes of Elmslie to his edition of 'Abodah Zarah, p. 62.

[4] See Elmslie ibid.

[5] Conder, Syrian Stone-Lore, p. 43 ff.; Palestine Exploration Fund 1885, p. 10; Comp. Elmslie ibid. p. 74. Comp. however, F. M. Abel, Revue Biblique XLI, 1932, p. 81, n. 3, who maintains that these dolmens have nothing to do with Mercurius.

[6] Who flourished in the second and third centuries.

[7] TP 'Abodah Zarah IV.1, 43d.

[8] Oxyrh. XI, 1382.

[9] See Schmidt, Gött. Gel. Anz. 1918, p. 124.

[10] Journal of Bibl. Lit. LXIII, 1944, p. 352, n. 59.

[11] "Why should this indigenous divinity have here a Roman name?"

However, an inscription dated 173, that was found in Ḥamon near Baalbek (Heliopolis) reads: Μερκουρίῳ δωμίνῳ κώμης Χάμωνος ἔτους δπυ'.[12] "To Mercurius[13] the god of the village Ḥamon of the year 484" (Sel.). The text of a second inscription,[14] found in Abila (in the vicinity of Ḥamon), is Μερκουρίου Μα[λ]χι[βή]λου.[15] A third inscription discovered in Heliopolis itself is dedicated: ΔΕΩΙ Μερκουρ[ίῳ].[16] The words ΔΕΟΣ and δώμινος clearly indicate that we are dealing with a Latin divinity and that even the Greek speaking population of Syria did not translate Mercurius into Ἑρμῆς but retained the Latin name. This is quite natural in a Roman colony like Heliopolis and its neighborhood. It is well known that the temple of Heliopolis was very popular in the Orient. Its fame certainly reached Palestine, and even the rabbis made a reference to it.[17] The Mercurius Heliopolitanus[18] was therefore known in Palestine, and it is no wonder that, thanks to the renown of the popular deity, the Greek speaking population of Palestine adopted the name Μερκούριος employed by the soldiers and did not render it Ἑρμῆς.

[12] Dussaud et Macler, *Voyage archeol. au Safâ*, p. 211; *L'Année épigraphique* 1903, p. 25.

[13] It may incidentally be noted that its priest was apparently a converted Jew or the son of a converted Jew, see Dussaud et Macler, *ibid.*, p. 214.

[14] Waddington 1875a.

[15] See Isidor Lévy *REJ* XLIII, 1901, p. 189; H. Seyrig, *Syria* X, 1929, p. 338, n. 4.

[16] M. M. Alouf, *History of Baalbek*[15] 1938, p. 123. The article of H. Seyrig "Heliopolitana" (*Bull. du Mus. de Beyrouth* I) in which he deals with a dedication to *Mercurius dominus* is inaccessible to me. I know of it only from the "compte rendu" in *Syria* XIX, 1938, p. 304. On the dedications in Latin to the Heliopolitan triad, see A. B. Cook *Zeus* I, p. 554, n. 1. He does not mention the above Greek inscriptions.

[17] TB *'Abodah Zarah* 11b, as correctly explained by Brüll, *Jahrbücher* etc. I, (1874), p. 139 and Isidor Lévy in his stimulating article *ibid.* p. 192 ff.

[18] See the long discussion of H. Seyrig, *Syria* X, 1929, p. 335 ff.

The frequent mention of Mercurius in rabbinic literature suggests that this name sometimes served the rabbis as a generic term for idolatry. As a matter of fact one tannaitic source[19] rules: "He who sees a *Mercurius* must recite etc.," while its parallel[20] reads instead: "He who sees an *idol* must recite etc." Mercurius in the first passage is obviously a synonym for idolatry.[21]

This raises another question. How much did the rabbis know about the various idols and their worship and whence did they gain this knowledge? A rabbi of the second century remarked:[22] אלו נפרט להם כל שם עבודה זרה, לא היה מספיק להם כל העורות שבעולם. "If the name of every idol were to be specifically mentioned, all skins (parchments) in the world would not suffice." The pagan gods and godesses,[23] semi-gods and semi-godesses, celestial and chtonian deities, minor gods and heroes[24] were innumerable. The type and character of pagan worship were widely diversified,[25] and the rabbis were fully aware of their own ignorance regarding the details of idol worship. R. Johanan[26] said:[27] אין אנו בקיים בדקדוקי עבודה זרה כיעקב. "We are not as versed in the details of idolatry as [our father] Jacob." The Babylonian rabbis put it even more plainly:[28]

---

[19] *TB Berakhoth* 57b. Comp. *Tosaphoth ibid. s. v.* הרואה.

[20] *Tosephta ibid.* VII, 14₂₀.

[21] See Petrus Alfonsi, *Dialogi* V, *PL* CLVII, 602d and the judicious remarks of Prof. H. Grégoire in *Annuaire de l'institut de philologie et d'histoire orientales et slaves* VII (1939-44), p. 464, n. 1.

[22] *Mekhilta, Baḥodesh* VI, ed. Horovitz, p. 224; ed. Lauterbach II, p. 240; *Sifre* Deut. 43, ed. Finkelstein, p. 97, see variants and notes *ibid.*

[23] See Petronius *Sat.* 17; Tertullian, *De idolatria* XV (CSEL vol. XX.1, p. 48₇ ff.).

[24] See A. D. Nock, *The Harvard Theological Review* XXXVII, 1944, p. 162 ff.

[25] See Nock *ibid.* p. 141 ff.

[26] Flourished in the middle of the third century.

[27] *BR* LXXXI.3, 973₃.

[28] *TB 'Abodah Zarah* 14b.

"There is a tradition that the [tractate on] idolatry which our father Abraham studied contained four hundred chapters; ours contains (literally: we have learnt) only five, and we do not understand what we are saying."[29]

Yet, early rabbinic literature, particularly the tractate of *'Abodah Zarah*, abounds in details about heathen rites and practices. The Jews had every opportunity of taking notice of these practices in the Greek cities of Palestine with their many heathen temples.[30] The rabbis, most probably, were not familiar at first hand with the *leges sacrae* of the various divinities, but they knew many of its regulations from personal contact with the Gentiles. When, for instance, R. Gamaliel said[31] to a Gentile: "Even if you were given much money you would not enter your temple naked or after suffering pollution"[32] he was referring to a common practice of the Gentiles in Palestine and Syria.[33]

---

[29] נמירי דע'ז דאברהם אבינו ד' מאה פירקי הויין ואנן חסשה תנן ולא ידעינן מאי קאמרינן.

[30] See Schürer, *Geschichte des jüdischen Volkes* II⁴, p. 27 ff. 108 ff.

[31] *Mishnah 'Abodah Zarah* III.4.

[32] The rabbinic בעל קרי means both ἀκάθαρτος (ἄναγνος) ἀπὸ γυναικός and ἀπὸ ῥύσεως νυκτός; it does not convey the idea of sexual offences. Comp. the following note.

[33] See W. M. Ramsay, *The Cities and Bishoprics of Phrygia* I, 1895, pp. 136-38, 151 ff.; Dittenberger, *Syl.*³ 1042; *Mon. As. Min. Ant.* IV Nos. 283, 285, 288, 289; *Suppl. epigr. graec.* VI Nos. 250, 251; E. Fehrle, *Die kultische Keuschheit im Altertum*, p. 26 ff. and p. 154. The same law was, of course, in force in the Temple of Jerusalem (See Deut. 23.11; *Mishnah Middoth* I.9, *passim*), but the rabbis discriminated clearly between Levitical impurity and filth. The Palestinian Talmud (*Pesaḥim* VII.11, 37b) remarks that the presence of a latrine in the basement of the Temple does not prove that this part of the Temple may be entered in a state of Levitical impurity, for "Excrement is not impurity but merely filth" (וכי צואה טומאה והלא אינה אלא נקיות) or, "An excretion is not a pollution but a purge." Yet, although there is no specific law which prohibits admission to the Temple in filthy clothes, it is obvious from the *Mishnah* (*Berakhoth* IX.5 and parallels) that such dress (even in the premises of the Temple) would be considered a mark of disrespect (Comp. also *Bemidbar Rabba* IV end and parallels)

109

However, it can be definitely stated that the rabbis of
the first and second centuries were well acquainted with
the πρᾶξις of sorcery and magic.[34] A long catalogue of
Amorite superstitious practices is preserved in the Tosephta.[35] Books of magic, ספרי קוסמין,[36] as well as many
formulas of incantations are mentioned in the Talmud.[37]
The practice of sorcery of which the Palestinian Talmud
accused the women[38] was not limited to the recitation of
magical formulas but very often consisted of the actual
offering (by Jewish women) of incense to demons,[39] an
act which closely bordered on idolatry.[40] The laws of
sorcery with which the rabbis were well acquainted un-

towards the Temple. Some *leges sacrae* of the pagans, apparently,
forbade entrance to the temples (and their premises) in dirty clothes
(ἐν ῥυπαροῖς). See Ramsay *ibid.*, p. 152 No. 52; Comp. also G.
Ryckmans, *Revue Biblique* XLI, 1932, p. 396 and R. Pettazoni, *Harvard
Theological Review* XXX, 1937, p. 6. From the previous note it is
apparent that the impurity is not necessarily associated with sin.

The rabbis, likewise, were aware of many other differences between
their *leges sacrae* and those of the Gentiles. The Jews were not allowed to offer libations of mixed wines (*Sifre* I, 143, ed. Horovitz,
p. 190₂. Comp. Plinius *Nat. hist.* XIV.23), such as they knew (*TB
'Abodah Zarah* 30a) the Gentiles (Greeks) to offer (See P. Stengel,
Hermes XVII, 1882, p. 329 ff.). Boiled wine was disqualified by both
Jews (*Mishnah Menaḥoth* VIII.6) and Gentiles (*TP Terumoth* VIII.5,
45c and parallels). Comp. also *TB Giṭṭin* 56a *passim*.

[34] *Tosephta Sanhedrin* XI, 431₂₄; *TP* and *TB ibid.* VII, end. Note
that all the rabbis mentioned there were devoted students of the
mystical מעשה מרכבה. Comp. also Rabbi Kasher's note in תורה שלמה
vol. V, p. 1384, n. ס״ה.

[35] *Shabbath* VII–VIII. See Lieberman, *Tosefeth Rishonim a. l.*, pp.
126–131. Comp. also H. Lewy, *Zeitschrift des Vereins für Volkskunde*
1893, p. 136 ff. and Boaz Cohen, *Mishnah and Tosefta*, p. 91.

[36] See L. Blau, *Das altjüdische Zauberwesen*, p. 30 and nn. *ibid.*

[37] Blau *ibid.*, p. 72 ff. Comp. Lieberman, *Greek in Jewish Palestine*,
p. 110 ff.

[38] *Kiddushin* IV, 66b (ed. Krotoschin 66c, bot.), *Sanhedrin* VII.19,
25d.

[39] *TB Berakhoth* 53a.

[40] See *TB Sanhedrin* 65a and parallel. Comp. *ibid.* 61b and Maimonides, *Yad Haḥazakah*, "Laws on idolatry" III.6.

doubtedly included the obligation to bring the offerings
mentioned in various magic books.

In the light of this we shall better understand the *Mishnah* in *'Abodah Zarah* (I.5) which reads: אלו דברים אסורים
למכור לגוים אצטרובלין בנות שוח ופטוטרותי⁴¹ ולבונה ותרנגול הלבן . . .
ר' מאיר אוטר אף דקל טב וחצדⁱ⁴ⁱ וּנקליבס וכו' "The following
articles are forbidden to be sold to the heathen:⁴² pine-
cones (στρόβιλοι), *Benoth Shouaḥ*⁴³ and *petotroth*,⁴⁴ frankincense and a white cock . . . R. Meir adds: *Dekel Tab,
Ḥaṣad* (see below) and Nicolaus [dates]." *Benoth Shouaḥ*
is explained by R. Johanan⁴⁵ to mean תאיני חיוראתא, "white
figs," by which all the dictionaries and commentaries⁴⁶
understood the regular white figs. But it is obvious from
the sources⁴⁷ that the *Benoth Shouaḥ* bear a very inferior
fruit which can hardly be identified with figs, as already
realized by the medieval authorities.⁴⁸ Moreover, both

---

⁴¹ Var. בפטוטרותיהם. See דקדוקי סופרים *a. l.*, p. 32, n. 300.

⁴¹ᵃ This is the reading of *TP* and Cod. Kaufmann. For its meaning
see below.

⁴² Because they are suspected of using them in rites of idolatry.

⁴³ See below.

⁴⁴ R. Johanan (*TB* and *TP a. l.*) explains (or corrects) the *Mishnah*:
בפטוטרותיהם, "with their *petotroth*." According to the context the word
probably means "with their stalks," as interpreted by early authorities
(See the *Geonic responsum* in הצופה מארץ הגר V, 1921, p. 74). R. Hai
Gaon in his מקח וסמכר X (according to the reading of תוספות רי"ד, *'Abodah
Zarah a. l.*, f. 43a) apparently explained it to mean "in their holidays,"
which cannot be reconciled with the reading in *TP ibid.* But he has
the important reading כ ו ל ן בפטוטרותיהן שנו, "the stalks" thus referring
to the στρόβιλοι as well. (Comp. *TB Shabbath* 57a *passim*). See below
n. 64.

⁴⁵ *TB ibid* 14a; *Berakhoth* 40b.

⁴⁶ Including Loew, *Flora* I, 242. Comp. however the commentary
of Maimonides *a. l.*

⁴⁷ *Mishna Demai* I.1; *TB 'Abodah Zarah* 14a. Comp. also *Tosephta
Pe'ah* I, p. 18 ll. 27 and 30.

⁴⁸ See *Tosaphoth a. l. s. v.* בנות שוח. The proofs cited there to show
that the *Benoth Shouaḥ* bear a superior fruit are all based on a wrong
reading (בנות שוח instead of the correct בנות שבע). See below n. 60a and
comp. also Theodor in his notes to *BR*, p. 141.

the explanation of *Benoth Shouaḥ* and the description of
their growth, as given in the Palestinian Talmud,[49] cannot
be applied to figs.

From the association of this tree with the pine which it
follows in our *Mishnah* and *Beraitha*,[50] it is apparent that
we have to do with a variety of pine. Indeed, among the
trees whose wood may be used on the altar, the Aramaic
fragment of the Testament of the Twelve Patriarchs[51]
lists: ואט[ר][ו][ב]לא ושוחא, corresponding to the Greek: καὶ
στρόβιλον καὶ πίτυν.[52] Thus we have here a Greek
translation of שוח: πίτυς, *Pinus halepensis* (Aleppo pine)
or *Pinus pinea* (stone-pine).[53] This translation is strikingly
confirmed by the Palestinian Talmud[54] which states:
מהו בנות שוח פיטיריה[55] "which trees are called *Benoth Shouaḥ*?
πιτύδια,"[56] ("small pines").[57]

The subsequent discussion of the Talmud also confirms
our identification. It says: מה בכל שנה ושנה הן עושות, או אחת
לשלש שנים? בכל שנה ושנה הן עושות, אלא שאין פירותיהן מגמרין אלא
לאחר שלש שנים "Do they bear fruit each year,[58] or do they

---

[49] See below.

[50] TB ibid. 14a, according to Cod. New York (see above n. 353):
ואיצטרובלין ובנות שוח.

[51] Ed. Charles, 1908, p. 248; *JQR* XIX, 1907, p. 573.

[52] In *Geoponica*, VII.20.5, these two trees also follow each other.

[53] I. Lévi (*REJ* LIV, 1907, p. 177, n. 1) emended שוחא to אשוחא, a
species of cedar (see *TB Shabbath* 157a). He also gave as an alternative the connection of שוחא with שוח בנות "a kind of fig which produces
white figs." But since the πίτυς is not a fig tree, his conjecture was
correctly disregarded; see Charles' notes a. l. and Loew, *Flora* III, p. 16.

[54] *Shebi'ith* V.1, 35d.

[55] Read פיטידיה. In many mss. the ר can hardly be distinguished
from the ד. The medieval authorities read פיטיריאה (See Ratner a. l.
p. 40), but the ד was preserved in the commentary of R. Isaac b.
Malchizedek (on *Shebi'ith* VI.1): פישידיאת, which is an obvious mistake
for פיטידיאה.

[56] It is clear that if שוח is πίτυς, בנות שוח are only πιτύδια.

[57] The compilers of all the dictionaries and commentaries, including
Loew *Flora* I, p. 242, completely misunderstood this word.

[58] I. e. it takes three years for the fruit to ripen. One third of the

bear the entire amount of fruit once every three years?
They bear fruit each year but the fruit do not ripen before
three years." When we compare this statement as given
by R. Hananel[59] with Pliny's account[60] of the *Pinus* we
find them identical.

(Plinius):

Habet fructum maturescen-
tem, habet proxumo anno ad
maturitatem venturum ac
deindo tertio.

(רבינו חנאל):

נמצאו בכל שנה נ' מיני פירות בזה
האילן מקצתן צמל, והן שחנטו
מקודם לכן כשנתים, ומקצתן בוחל,
והן שחנטו מדאשתקד, ומקצתן פגין,
והן [שחנטו] בזו השנה.

"It has (*i. e.* the *Pinus*)
upon it [each year] the fruit
that is hastening to maturity, the fruit that is to come
to maturity in the next year
and the fruit that is to ripen
in the third year."

"Thus, there are three
kinds of fruit on this tree
each year: some are fully
ripe, i. e. those which were
formed two years ago; some
are ripening, i. e. those
which were formed a year
ago and some are unripe, i. e.
those which were formed
this year."

Moreover, according to the tradition of the Babylonian
Talmud, the fig trees burnt on the altar are nothing but
תאיני חיורתא, "[non productive] white fig trees,"[60a] i. e. the

potential output grows each year so, that after the third year of its
maturity the entire output is upon the tree.

[59] *TB Rosh Hashanah* 15b.

[60] *Nat. hist.* XVI.44.107.

[60a] *Tamid* 29b (See the commentaries *a. l.* Comp. also Lieberman
Tosefeth Rishonim II, p. 258, n. 25). Both F. Goldmann (*La figue en
Palestine à l'époque de la Mischna*, p. 27 ff.) and I. Loew (*Flora* I,
p. 241 ff.) overlooked this passage. Our identification of בנות שוח with
πιτύδια leads us to the reexamination of the meaning of מקיצין את
המזבח. קיץ המזבח. According to J. Barth ((*Jahrbuch d. Jüd.-Lit. Ges.* VII,

πίτυς which the above mentioned Testament numbers among the trees whose wood was offered on the altar.

Hence, the identification of בנות שוח with πιτύδια is certainly established. R. Johanan, who explained this tree as תאיני חיוראתא, "white fig-trees" (and not figs!), apparently had in mind a popular name for the *Pinus halepensis*.[61]

Our *Mishnah* thus lists three articles used by the heathen in their idol worship: the cones of two kinds of pines, the white cock and frankincense. Although the use of each of these articles in pagan worship is well known, it is highly probable that the rabbis drew this list from the magic books. For instance, we read in the "Eighth Book of Moses:"[62] ... καὶ ξύλα κυπαρίσσινα, στροβίλους δεξιοὺς

Frankfurt a. M. 1910, p. 129) the latter is equivalent to מקיסין את המזבח, ק י ס המזבח, the wood of the altar, they supply the altar with wood. This interpretation seems to be disproved by the argumentation in *TB Shebu'oth* 12b, from which it is obvious that our קיץ was associated by post-Tannaitic rabbis with בנות שבע (This was the reading of *TB*. See R. Hananel and דקדוקי סופרים *a. l.*), a species of fig. However, the interchange of בנות שבע and בנות שוח is very common (See above n. 48). It was favored by the fact that both בנות שבע and בנות שוח were sometimes spelled בנות שוע (See R. Isaac b. Malchizedek's commentary on *Ma'as-roth* II.8; N. M. Nathan, *Ein anonymes Wörterbuch etc.*, p. 28 and Redak to I Chron. 3.5. Comp. also Krauss, הגרן X, 1928, p. 149 and Goldmann *ibid.* p. 28). The latter was sometimes understood as בנות שבע and sometimes as בנות שוח. Indeed, the source of the *Beraitha* in *TB*, *Sifre Zuta* (ed. Horovitz, p. 323, according to *Yalkut ed. prin.* sect. 780; comp. the editor's note) states: מותר התרומה [עולות] ועולות כבנות שוע למזבח. "The surplus of the *Terumah* [is devoted to burnt-offerings], and these are considered like Benoth Shou'a (*Yalkut cod. Oxf.* reads כבנות ש ב ע and the editions of *TB* read כבנות ש ו ה) on the altar." Thus, the ingenious interpretation of Barth cannot easily be dismissed; the phrase כבנות שוע למזבח might have meant in the original: "Like the πιτύδια burnt on the altar."

[61] A variety of this tree produced some fruit-like formations which some Greeks called "figs" (Theophrastus, *Hist. plant.* III.3.9. Comp. also Plinius, *Nat. hist.* XVI.19.44). This variety according to Theophrastus bears no fruit. For the taste of the fruit of the regular *Pinus halepensis*, see *ibid.* I.12.1.

[62] K. Preisendanz, *Papyri graecae magicae* II, p. 88. Comp. Festugière, *La révélation d'Hermes Trismegistos*, Paris, 1944, p. 288.

δέκα, ἀλέκτορας δύο λευκούς . . . Ἡλίου λίβανον. [And put on the earthen altar] cypress wood,[63] ten fresh(?)[64] pine-cones, two white cocks . . . [for] the Sun — frankincense."[65]

To the list in the anonymous *Mishnah*, R. Meir adds three more items: *Dekel Tab*, *Ḥaṣad* and Nicolaus [dates]. Of these only the meaning of נקליבס is known. The latter is very often mentioned in the Palestinian Talmud and *Midrashim*,[66] and the inhabitants of Palestine undoubtedly knew that נקליבס (נקלווס) meant a Nicolaus date. However, to the Babylonian rabbis the meaning of this word was not known. They cited [66a] the opinion of a Palestinian rabbi who explained it to mean קורייטי, [δάκτυλοι] καρυωτοί, nut-like dates.[67] This explanation is confirmed by Pliny's account of the Judean palms.[68]

[63] The LXX translates עץ שמן (Nehem. 8.15) ξύλον κυπαρίσσινον. This is also the equivalent of אץ משחא in the *Testament of the Twelve Patriarchs*, see Loew *Flora* III, p. 16. The עצי שמן were used on the altar of the Temple in Jerusalem (*Mishnah Middoth* II.3 and in the *Testament ibid.*). In *TB* (*Rosh Hashanah* 32a and *Baba Bathra* 80b) עץ שמן is translated אפרסמא, "balsam-tree." Loew, *ibid.* p. 15, maintains that this translation is based on a misunderstanding. However, a parallel papyrus (Preisendanz *ibid.*, p. 106) reads ξύλα κυπαρίσσινα ἢ ὀποβαλσάμινα "cypress wood or balsam-tree wood."

[64] δεξιός is apparently used here in a sense near to the Hebrew ימין, see Lieberman ספר היובל לכבוד קרוים, p. 306. It possibly means the same thing as ואיצטרובלין בטטולותיהן (the comment on our *Mishnah* in *TP a. l.* I.5, 39d) "and pine-cones with their stalks," see above n. 44.

[65] Comp. also Preisendanz *ibid.* I, p. 22: ἐπίθυε δὲ ἐπικαλούμενος λίβανον ἄτμητον καὶ σ[τ]ροβίλους δεξιοὺς δ[ώ]δεκα καὶ ἀλέκτορας ἀ[σ]πίλους β'. See also *ibid.*, p. 62, l. 694 ff. For the white cock see *ibid.* pp. 68, l. 36, 141 l. 2190.

[66] See Krauss *LW* II, p. 367.

[66a] *A. l.* 14b.

[67] It is true the rabbis admitted that they did not know what kind of a fruit *caryotae* was, but a *Babylonian* (see the correct reading of Cod. München in דקדוקי סופרים *a. l.*, p. 34) rabbi assured them that the word was used in Palestine whereas נקלס was not known (?).

[68] *Nat. hist.* XIII.9, 44: caryotae . . . in Judea . . . ex hox genere nicolai. Loew, *Flora* II, p. 321 refers to Plinius, but does not mention that he confirms the identification of the Babylonian Talmud.

But the Palestinian Talmud states:[69] דקל טב וחצד ונקלבים
וכו'. ר' חמא בר עוקבא אמר קוריוטה. ר' אלעזר בי ר' יוסי אמר מין
הוא ושמו חצדא. " *'Dekel Tab and Ḥaṣad* and Nicolaus [dates]
etc.' R. Ḥama b. 'Ukba said *caryotae*. R. Eliezer b. R.
Jose said it is a species whose name is Ḥaṣda." I am certain
that *caryotae* refers to *Dekel Tab*,[70] i. e. R. Ḥama explained
that not the tree but the fruit is designated by *Dekel Tab*.[71]
As to *Ḥaṣad* it is obvious that in the fourth century the
origin of this *hapax legomenon* (in rabbinic literature) was
not known to the rabbis; it was merely "a species."

Perhaps Ḥaṣda[72] is nothing but ἰσχάδας,[73] "dry figs."
Indeed, the magic papyri list as components of ink[73a] for
magic purposes: ἰσχάδας καρικὰς γ', φοινίκων Νικο-
λαίων ὀστέα ζ'.[74] "Three Carian[75] dried figs, seven
stones of Nicolaus dates." R. Meir, like the anonymous
Mishnah, might have drawn his information from magic
sources.

In this light we shall be able to understand the statement
of a *Beraitha* in the Babylonian Talmud. The *Mishnah*[76]
mentions a disproportionately large or small nose among.

---

[69] *A. l.* 39d.

[70] Literally "a good palm tree."

[71] See *TB a. l.* 14b. All the commentaries, including Loew, *Flora* II,
p. 321, took this word (in accordance with the tradition in *TB*) as an
explanation of נקלבסין. But it is obvious from the succession of the
comments in *TP* that *caryotae* refers to the word that precedes Ḥaṣɪd.
Besides, as said above, the נקלבסין (נקלוסין) were well known in Palestine
and required no explanation.

[72] The interpretation of this word in *TB a. l.* is based on the different
reading חצב instead of חצד. Comp. also the ingenuous interpretation of
Loew *ibid.*

[73] A very common metathesis. The native population turned it into
an Aramaic word.

[73a] A matter of special interest to our rabbi. See *TB Sota* 20a.

[74] Pap. I, 245, Preisendanz *ibid.* I, p. 14. Comp. also Pap. VII, 999,
ibid. II, p. 43. Pap. IV 3204, *ibid.* I, p. 176 adds to it: θαλλοὶ φοίνικος
ἀρσενικοῦ γ'. "Three leaves of a male palm."

[75] See Plinius, *Nat. hist.* XIII.10.

[76] *Bekhoroth* VII.4.

the blemishes which disqualify a priest from serving in the Temple. Thereupon a *Beraitha*[77] comments: כאצבע קטנה, "Like a little finger," *i. e.* the normal length of a nose must be equal to the length of its owner's little finger.[78] The question arises whence did the rabbis learn this fact which most probably could be observed only by a sculptor, painter or similar artist? We know that the pagan magical books sometimes contained this kind of information.[79] And indeed, in the *Jewish* mystical book שיעור קומה we likewise find:[80] ואורך החוטם כאורך אצבע קטנה. "And the length of the nose is like the length of the little finger."

Similarly, it has recently been shown[81] that the *Merkaba* mysteries contained a chapter on physiognomy which is already quoted in *Seder Eliyyahu Rabba*.[82] The great similarity between the contents of pagan, Jewish and Christian *visiones* has also been recently demonstrated.[83] The mystical books, their international character, their early spread among the Jews and their influence on Jewish literature deserve intensive investigation.

Now, since the *Hermetica* were very popular among the magicians, and Hermes was the familiar figure in magic, astrology and *lapidaria* as well as in later Jewish incantations,[84] he was quite naturally regarded by the Jews as the

[77] Cited in *TB ibid.* 44a.

[78] As correctly understood by R. Gershom *a. l.* and Maimonides in his commentary on the *Mishnah a. l.* See Lieberman שקיעין, p. 12.

[79] See *Isis*, vol. XXXIII, 1941, p. 72. I am indebted to my friend Dr. Solomon Gandz for calling my attention to this article at the time of its appearance.

[80] *Raziel* 38a; Salmon b. Yeruhim, *The Book of the Way of the Lord*, ed. Davidson, p. 123. See Maimonides' opinion on this book in שקיעין *ibid.*

[81] *JQR* vol. XXXVI, 1946, p. 323.

[82] XXIX, ed. Friedmann, p. 162. See *JQR ibid.*

[83] *Ginzberg Jubilee Volume*, Hebrew section, p. 249 ff.

[84] See Montgomery, *Aramaic Incantation Texts*, Index, p. 270, *s. v.*

typical pagan god. It is therefore a little surprising that
the name Mercurius has replaced Hermes in Jewish sources.
Perhaps Mercurius was the contemptible symbol of stone
gods, the despised emblem of the stone worship prevalent
in Syria.[85]

הרמיס, אירטיס. Comp. also *ibid.* p. 99 and W. Lueken, *Michael*, Göttingen
1898, p. 56. See also Krauss, הגרן VII (הרס'ח), pp. 31, 33.

[85] See H. Grégoire *Annuaire etc.* (referred to above n. 21), pp. 464-
465.

ABBREVIATIONS

B., b.   — ben, bar (son of).

BR   — Bereshith Rabba.

CAH   — The Cambridge Ancient History.

Graetz   — Geschichte der Juden IV[3], Leipzig 1893.

Juster   — Les Juifs dans l'empire romain.

LW   — Griechische und lateinische Lehnwörter im Talmud,
            Midrasch und Targum, von S. Krauss, Teil II, 1899.

MGWJ   — Monatsschrift für Geschichte und Wissenschaft des
            Judentums.

PG   — Patrologia Graeca.

PL   — Patrologia Latina.

PW RE   — Pauly-Wissowa, Realencyclopädie der classischen Alter-
            tumswissenschaft.

REJ   — Revue des études Juives.

SEHRE   — Social and Economic History of the Roman Empire.

TB   — Talmud Babylonicum.

TP   — Talmud Palaestinense.

ROMAN LEGAL INSTITUTIONS IN EARLY RABBINICS AND IN THE ACTA MARTYRUM

By Saul Lieberman

The Jewish Theological Seminary of America

In a previous paper[1] I made the following statement: "The simple rule should be followed that the Talmud may serve as a good historic document when it deals in contemporary matters within its own locality. The Palestinian Talmud (and some of the early Midrashim), whose material was produced in the third and the fourth centuries, contains valuable information regarding Palestine during that period. It embodies many elements similar to those contained in the documentary papyri." The so called *realia* which are abundant in rabbinic writings are sometimes obscure and unintelligible without the help of the papyri and inscriptions.

This circumstance makes it incumbent upon scholarship to utilize the rabbinic works on the one hand and the Greco-Roman papyri and inscriptions on the other for their mutual elucidation. But there is also a genre of Greek and Latin literature which can be very helpful in clarifying *realia*, popular concepts and practices referred to in the Palestinian Talmud and Midrashim, namely, lives of saints and acts of martyrs. Written in vulgar *koine* and vulgar Latin, this literature employs a wealth of popular terms and homely expressions which have their counterparts in

[1] *Annuaire de l'Institut de Philologie et d'Histoire Orientales et Slaves*, v. VII (1939–1944), p. 395.

1

rabbinic sources. And the more polished patristic literature proves exceedingly useful for our purpose when it deals with *realia*, popular concepts and practices.

To illustrate I shall quote three instances (one for each category) from only one chapter of the first tractate in the Palestinian Talmud. We read there:[2] אפיקרסין היה[3] לובש מבפנים, "He wore an *apikarsin* (or: *epikarsin*) underneath." The word is extant already in tannaitic literature, and is often spelled יפרקסין[4]. The dictionaries identified it with the Greek ἐπικάρσιον and explained it to mean: shirt, dress, sheet. But the Greek word means simply a striped garment, whereas our *epikarsin* has the special sense of "undergarment." Similarly in *Pesikta deR. Kahana*[5] it is described as דבוקה בבשר, "next to the skin." And indeed, Jastrow[6] took the word to mean (according to the context) underwear, shirt.

It seems to me therefore that we have here a metathesis of the Greek ἐπισάρκιον,[7] underwear, shirt. True, no Greek dictionary records this word, but I find it in the *Vita S. Nicephori*[8] (X century[8a]): μόνῳ τῷ ἐπισαρκίῳ ἀπῄει, "he went away only in his shirt." Thus, the word was extant at least in the vulgar Greek.

Likewise we find there[9] the expression דברנליה חריב וברנליה מתבני, "and by his foot it was destroyed and by his foot it shall be rebuilt." At first blush this looks like an imitation of Gen. 30.30, but further evidence shows that רגל

[2] Ber. II. 3, 4d.
[3] Cod. Rome אפיסרקסין. See below, n. 7.
[4] See Krauss *LW*, p. 113.
[5] Ed. Buber, f. 15b.
[6] Dictionary, p. 107.
[7] Comp. the reading of Cod. Rome (above n. 3).
[8] *Analecta Bollandiana* XIV, p. 137. The text is published there for the first time.
[8a] All the dates mentioned in this article are C. E.
[9] *TP* ibid., 5a.

"leg, foot" was commonly used in rabbinic times to express the idea of bringing good or bad luck. Thus we read in a parallel passage:[10] לא היה זה אלא רגלו רעה על ישראל, "he only brought bad luck[11] for Israel," or literally: "His foot was only bad for Israel."

Exactly the same expression occurs in a Palestinian Greek text:[12] κακοποδινός ἐστιν ὁ Πορφύριος τῇ πόλει, "Porphyrius' foot is bad[13] for the city." Thus, רגלו רעה, κακοποδινός, was a popular expression for a man who brings bad luck.

Further we read there:[14] שמואל אמר אנא מנית פרוחייה[15] ר' בון בר חייא אמר אנא מנית דימוסיא. "Samuel (II–III century) said: [When I prayed] I counted the birds. R. Bun b. Hiyya said: I counted the layers of stones."[16] It seems that it was difficult for these Rabbis to concentrate their attention upon the prayer and they sometimes adopted the practice of counting birds or layers of stones in order to dissipate distracting thoughts.

A striking parallel is found in the *Apology*[17] of Tertullian: alius (si hoc putatis) nubes numeret orans, alius lacunaria. "Let one (if you prefer so to regard it) count the clouds as he prays, another the panels of the ceiling."[18] The Rabbi

[10] Published by Grünhut in his edition of the *Yalkut Hamakiri, Mishle*, f. 103b.

[11] Comp. also TP 'Ab. Za. III.2, 42d; *Shemoth Rabba* XXXI. 17 and parallels.

[12] *Vita Porphyrii* XIX, ed. Grégoire-Kugener, p. 16.

[13] The editors (ibid., p. 95) refer to Jerome (read: Augustine, *Epist.* 44) who explained the Phoenician נעטפעטא as *boni pedis homo*. Comp. also Ibn 'Ezra on Gen. 30.30 and *Midrash Aggada*, ed. Buber, I, p. 79 and n. 17 ibid.

[14] *TP* ibid.

[15] So *Yerushalmi Fragments*, ed. Ginzberg, p. 104. Cod. Rome: פרחייה.

[16] = נרבכיא, see LXX ad Ezra VI.4.

[17] XXIV. 5.

[18] The notes in Migne *PL* I, 476–477 do not solve the puzzle.

who counted the layers of stones probably looked at the upper courses, with his eyes directed upwards.

A very important category of *realia* in Rabbinic writings is the political *realia*. An exact knowledge of Roman institutions, their functions and activities, and the dates of their first appearance is of the utmost importance not only for the understanding of the texts, but also for the establishing of the correct reading. Thus, for instance, we read in the Palestinian Talmud:[19] אמר ר' יהושע בן לוי בשעה שברח משה מפני פרעה נעשו כל אוכלוסין שלו אילמין ומהן חרשין ומהן סומין וכו'. "R. Joshua b. Levi said: When Moses ran away from Pharaoh *all his people* became dumb and some of them deaf and some of them blind etc." This reading involves an unnecessary exaggeration. In the parallel passages[20] the reading is אסכילי and איסקולין[21] (instead of אוכלוסין), σχολαί, the imperial guards. This is both the rarer and the more appropriate word, and is therefore undoubtedly correct.

But since the σχολαί were first established by Constantine[22] R. Joshua b. Levi (flourished in the middle of the third century) could not have known of it. We have therefore to read in TP: ר' יהושע ב ש ם ר' לוי, "R. Joshua[23] (flourished in the first half of the fourth century) in the name of R. Levi."[24]

Similarly, we read in *Sifre*:[25] ... ר' שמעון בן יוחי אומר

---

[19] Ber. IX, 13a.

[20] *Debarim Rabba* II, 29.

[21] *Shir Hashirim Rabba* VII.4. Comp. the readings in *Shemoth Rabba* I. 31 and parallels. See also *Mekhilta Jetro* I, ed. Horovitz, p. 192.

[22] See Mommsen, *Hermes* XIV, p. 223, referred to by Löw *apud* Krauss *LW*, p. 87.

[23] In *Shir Hashirim Rabba* ibid. is explicitly stated: ר' יהושע דסיכנין בשם ר' לוי. Comp. Albeck, *Indices to Bereshith Rabba*, p. 57a.

[24] Flourished at the end of the third and the beginning of the fourth century.

[25] I, 82, ed. Horovitz, p. 78.

לאנטיקיסר שהיה מקדים לפני חיילותיו מתקן להם מקום שישרו, כך השכינה מקדמת לישראל ומתקנת להם מקום שישרו. "R. Simeon b. Joḥai (flourished in the middle of the second century) said . . . Like a vice-roy who precedes his army and prepares quarters for them, so the *Shekinah* precedes Israel and prepares quarters for them." But this makes no sense. It is not the task of the ἀντικαῖσαρ to precede the troops and to prepare quarters for them. Accordingly, Joseph Perles[26] altered our word to אנטיקנסור, ἀντικένσωρ, *antecessor*, and referred to Ducange[27] who counts among the definitions of *antecessores*: qui exercitus antecedunt et loca idonea ad constituenda castra investigant, "who precede the troops and investigate suitable places for setting up the camps."[28]

He is undoubtedly right in identifying our word with *antecessor*, and as a matter of fact in a number of similar passages in the *Midrash Yelamdenu*[29] God is characterized as Israel's מיטטור, μητάτωρ (*metator*), which means precisely the same thing as ἀντεκήνσωρ. But Perles is not altogether right in altering the reading אנטיקיסר to אנטיקינסור. Our reading is absolutely sure,[30] it is ἀντεκέσσωρ, the correct form of *antecessor*.[31]

On the other hand, a parallel passage quoted in the *Midrash Haggadol*[32] reads here קינסור, κήνσωρ (probably a mistake for [אנטי]קינסור, ἀντεκήνσωρ), which betrays the

---

[26] *MGWJ* XXXVII, p. 378.   [27] *Gl. med. Gr.* s. v.

[28] See also Sophocles, *Greek Lexicon*, p. 177, who gives the sources for ἀντεκήνσωρ as quartermaster.

[29] As quoted in *'Aruch* s. v. מטטר.

[30] Ed. princ. אנטיקוסר; *Yalkut Shimeoni* ad loc. sect. 727: אנטיקסר. Cod. Berlin: אטיקיסר: *Yalkut Sikili*: איטקסיר. Cod. Oxford: אנייקיסר, an obvious mistake for אטיקיסר. This is the Semitic spelling for אנטיקיסר, see G. A. Cooke, *North-Semitic Inscriptions*, p. 312, n. 4. The spelling קטרון, *centurio*, is often met with in rabbinic writings, see Krauss *LW*, p. 529.

[31] See Sophocles referred to above n. 28.

[32] = Horovitz, *Sifre Zuṭa*, p. 266, l. 9.

later Byzantine pronunciation.[33] It is consequently highly
doubtful if the quotation in the *Midrash Haggadol* is taken
from *Sifre Zuta*.[34] Thus, knowledge of the correct title
of an official may help us in establishing the source of an
anonymous quotation.

Many more instances from the various branches of the
Roman administration may be cited, but we shall henceforth limit ourselves to legal *realia*.

* * *

In addition to the normal law-codes prevailing in Palestine, special regulations were enacted by the government
from time to time. They are styled: פרוסטגמא, פרוזדגמא,
$\pi\rho\acute{o}\sigma\tau\alpha\gamma\mu\alpha$,[35] command, ordinance; דיוטגמא, דיאטגמא, $\delta\iota\acute{a}$-
$\tau\alpha\gamma\mu\alpha$,[36] edict; כתבים,[37] $\dot{\epsilon}\pi\iota\sigma\tauo\lambda\alpha\acute{i}$, $\gamma\rho\alpha\varphi\alpha\acute{i}$ or $\gamma\rho\acute{a}\mu\mu\alpha\tau\alpha$,
letters, rescripts.

The edicts became law only after they were displayed[38]
in the public place ($\delta\eta\mu\acuteo\sigma\iota\alpha$) of the city. We read in the
Midrash:[39] לדיוטגמא שהיא כתובה ומחותמת ונכנסה למדינה אין בני
המדינה נענשים עליה עד שתתפרש להן בדימוסיא של מדינה.
"Like a $\delta\iota\acute{a}\tau\alpha\gamma\mu\alpha$ (edict) which has been written and
sealed and brought to the city, but in respect whereof the

---

[33] Comp. S. B. Psaltes, *Grammatik d. Byzantinischen Chroniken etc.*,
p. 81. I am indebted to Prof. Henri Grégoire for calling my attention
to this useful grammar.

[34] Compiled not later than the beginning of the third century.

[35] See Krauss *LW*, p. 483.

[36] Ibid., p. 196. On the difference between the king's $\pi\rho\sigma\tau\acute{a}\gamma\mu\alpha\tau\alpha$
and $\delta\iota\alpha\tau\acute{a}\gamma\mu\alpha\tau\alpha$ see the literature referred to by R. Taubenschlag,
Atti Del Congresso Internazionale Di Papirologia (Firenze, Aprile–
Maggio 1935 — XIII), p. 260, n. 8.

[37] *Bereshith Rabba* X. 7, p. 82; *Vayyikra Rabba* XI. 7; *Bemidbar Rabba*
XXIII. 1 passim.

[38] = promulgated. See below, n. 40.

[39] *Vayyikra Rabba* I. 10, in the name of R. Eleazar (flourished in
in the third quarter of the third century).

inhabitants of the city are not punishable until it has been *promulgated*[40] to them in the public place of the city."[41]

Vivid accounts of the attitude of the people when they read the edicts of the emperors are preserved in Palestinian rabbinic writings. *Midrash Vayyikra Rabba*[42] records: אמר ר' יצחק משל למלך ששלח פרוזדוגמא שלו למדינה מה עשו בני המדינה עמדו על רגליהם ופרעו את ראשיהם וקראוה באימה וביראה ברתת ובזיעה וכו'. "R. Isaac[43] said: Like a king who sent out his orders to a city. What did the people of the city do? They rose to their feet, uncovered their heads[44] and read it in awe, fear, trembling and trepidation etc."

An exact parallel to our parable is offered by Chrysostom[45] who compares the reading of the Bible to the reading of the Imperial rescripts (βασιλικὰ γράμματα) and says: "A profound silence reigns when those rescripts are read. There is not the slightest noise; every one listens most

---

[40] The word פרש, פרס, to display, to stretch out, was a technical term for the promulgation of an edict. See *Aruch Completum* s. v. דטונסא and פרוזדנסא; Prof. Finkelstein's additional instances in *JQR* XXXII (1942), p. 387, n. 1 and add: *Midrash Tehilim* CXIX. 46, ed. Buber, p. 499. The Semitic פרס (פרס) most likely translated the Latin [edictum] proponere, προτίθεσθαι (*Euseb., Hist.* Eccl. VIII. 5. Comp. also Sophocles, *Greek Lexicon*, p. 953). Eusebius frequently uses the expression ἀπλοῦν βασιλικὰ γράμματα, βασιλικὰ διατάγματα etc., (Ibid. VIII. 2. 4; 17.2; IX, beginning; X. 9. 8; *De Mart. Pal.*, beginning) which is literally the equivalent of פרס דיוטנסא. Indeed, the Syriac translation of Eusebius (published by Wright and Maclean from a dated manuscript of 462, see Preface, ibid. p. V.) renders this verb פרס (See ibid. pp. 324, 353-354 and 357. Brockelmann, *Lexicon Syriacum* 600[b], quotes only one instance from the late Julian Romance of the use of this verb in the sense of promulgation).

[41] Comp. E. Le Blant, *Les persécuteurs et les martyrs*, p. 140 and notes ibid.

[42] XXVII. 6 and parallels.

[43] In *Pesikta deR. Kahana*, 77a, the parable is ascribed to R. Berechia. Both rabbis flourished under Diocletian.

[44] We have here valuable information about uncovering the head when reading the king's decrees. Comp. the *International Critical Commentary* to I Corinthians 11.4, p. 229.

[45] Migne *PG* LIII, 112.

attentively to the orders contained in them. Whoever makes the slightest noise, thereby interrupting the reading, runs the greatest danger. All the more should one stand with fear and trepidation ($\mu\epsilon\tau\grave{\alpha}$ $\varphi\acute{o}\beta o\upsilon$ $\kappa\alpha\grave{\iota}$ $\tau\rho\acute{o}\mu o\upsilon$) etc. in order to understand the contents of what is read to you."[46] Le Blant[47] refers to this important passage of Chrysostom, but the rabbinic source is approximately a hundred years older.

Beside the faithful picture of the attitude of the Palestinians under Diocletian towards the imperial edicts, as recorded in this passage, a genuine fact of great importance is preserved in another Midrash. We read there:[48] למלך ששלח כתבים למדינה ומדינה ובכל מדינה ומדינה שהיו מגיעים כתביו של מלך היו מחבקים ומנשקים אותם ·ועומדים על רגליהם ופורעים ראשיהם וקורין אותם ביראה באימה ברתת ובזיעה וכיון שהגיעו למדינתו של מלך קראום וקרעום ושרפום. "Like a king who sent letters[49] to every city. In every city, when the king's letters arrived the people *embraced and kissed them*,[50] rose to their feet, uncovered their heads and read them in fear, in awe, in trembling and in trepidation. But *when they arrived at the king's own city the people* read them, *tore them* and burnt them.'' This parable illustrates the verse in Jer. 36.23, where it is stated that the king tore to pieces the scroll of Jeremiah and burnt it.

At first glance it is a little puzzling that the rabbis should use such an elaborate and complicated parable. For the

[46] The comparison is the same as in our Midrash, except that the rabbis argue the other way, stating that God is more lenient in His requirement in connection with the reading of His proclamation, the *Shema'*, than the human kings in the reading of their ordinances.

[47] *Les actes des martyrs*, p. 43, and *Les persécuteurs et les martyrs*, p. 140.

[48] *Esther Rabba*, Proem. 11 (I copy from the ed. princ.); *Vayyikra Rabba* XI. 7; *Tanḥuma Shemini* 9.

[49] $\gamma\rho\alpha\varphi\alpha\acute{\iota}$, see below, n. 54.

[50] The italicized words are missing in the parallel Midrashim, noted above n. 48.

illustration of the verse, the tearing of the king's letters is sufficient. As a matter of fact in *Bereshith Rabba*[51] the example is short and concise: "Like a king who sent his ordinance ($\pi\rho\dot{o}\sigma\tau\alpha\gamma\mu\alpha$) to a city. What did the people of the city do to it? They tore it and burnt it." The parable can be properly understood only if we suppose that our Midrash possessed authentic and detailed information of an actual fact, and applied it to our verse.

And indeed, Lactantius[52] relates: *Postridie propositum est edictum quo cavebatur, ut religionis illius homines carerent omni honore ac dignitate . . . deripuit et conscidit.* "Next day an edict was promulgated depriving the men of this religion (i. e. the Christians) of all honors and dignities . . . [a certain person] tore it down and cut it in pieces." Lactantius' story is short; he did not record the behavior of the people in other places. He related a fact which happened in his own city, in Nicomedia, where the emperors then resided. For our purpose the words of Eusebius, a Palestinian, and probably a contemporary of the anonymous homilist in our Midrash, are of much greater importance.

He tells[53] us that when the edict[54] was published in Nicomedia a Christian tore it, and he devotes a few words to emphasizing the fact that the outrage was committed in a city where the two emperors were present.[55] It is almost certain that the anonymous Rabbi refers to the same incident. He emphasizes the fact that whereas in all other cities the people *embraced and kissed the edicts*[56] of the

---

[51] XLII. 3, ed. Theodor-Albeck, p. 402.
[52] *De mortibus persecutorum* XIII.
[53] *Hist. Eccl.* VIII. 5.
[54] $\gamma\rho\alpha\varphi\dot{\eta}$. See above n. 49.
[55] $\delta\upsilon\epsilon\hat{\imath}\nu$ $\dot{\epsilon}\pi\iota\pi\alpha\rho\dot{o}\nu\tau\omega\nu$ $\kappa\alpha\tau\grave{\alpha}$ $\tau\grave{\eta}\nu$ $\alpha\dot{\upsilon}\tau\grave{\eta}\nu$ $\pi\dot{o}\lambda\iota\nu$ $\beta\alpha\sigma\iota\lambda\dot{\epsilon}\omega\nu$.
[56] The omission of "the kissing and embracing of the edicts" in the parallel Midrashim is quite instructive. There the passage concerning the treatment of the edict is a mere quotation from the earlier sources (see above n. 43). Ammianus Marcellinus (XV. 5. 18) reports that

emperors, in the own city of the latter their fate was alto-gether different.[57] This fact was certainly widely known among the Christians,[58] and it is no wonder that it reached the Synagogue.

The disobedience of the king's ordinances or of the regular criminal laws drew harsh punishment upon the transgressor. He was arrested and was kept in prison[59] until he was sum-moned before the judge.

The defendant is usually dressed in black and does not shave his beard. We read in the Palestinian Talmud:[60]

Diocletian was the first to introduce the *adoratio* (See also Heumann-Seckel, *Handlexicon* etc. s. v. *adorare*), the kissing of the purple. In the beginning of the fourth century the *adoratio* of the edict was an actual fact; see the following note and comp. Le Blant, *Les actes des martyrs*, p. 263. Our Midrash had later and better information than its ante-cedents.

[57] The *burning* of the edicts and the remainder of the conclusion of our Midrash are an adaptation of a historic fact to the verse in Jeremiah. True, there is a Christian legend (*Acta Sanctorum, Septembris*, vol. VI, p. 686d) that when a Christian martyr (in Egypt) wanted to see the edict of Diocletian, it was brought and adored (= kissed). Then the proconsul also rose up to his feet and embraced the edict (similiter et praeses assurexit et edictum amplexatus est). The Christian, however, took it, read it and threw it into the fire (accepisset ac legisset . . . imperatoris edictum in ignem coniecit). An exact repetition of our Midrash! But this Christian legend has no historic value; the only reliable information contained therein is the general treatment of the edict.

[58] The latter ascribe the tearing of the edict to various saints, but all of them are connected with the same occurrence. I find in the *Synaxaria Selecta* (*Synaxarium of Constantinople*, ed. H. Delehaye, p. 538. Comp. also ibid. p. 248 and *Acta Sanctorum, Martii* vol. II, p. 391) that a certain Menignus (in the time of the Decian persecutions), a fuller by occupation, after snatching away the king's letters from the hands of the judge and cutting them to pieces trampled them under his feet (Μένιγνος . . . τὰ τοῦ βασιλέως ἁρπάσας γράμματα ἐκ τῶν χειρῶν τοῦ ἄρχοντος καὶ εἰς λεπτὰ κατακόψας κατεπάτησεν). But this story also has no historical basis, as the miracles related there prove.

[59] בית האסורים, see Kassovsky, *Concordance of the Mishna*, p. 371c, passim; פילקי, φυλακή, see Krauss *LW*, p. 448; דייטי של קיסרין, *Esther Rabba*, beginning; comp. also *Mekhilta deRashbi*, ed. Hoffmann, p. 23.

[60] R. H. I. 3, 57b. The statement is cited in the names of rabbis who flourished in the first half of the third century.

בנהג שבעולם אדם יודע שיש לו דין לובש שחורים ומתעטף שחורים ומגדל
דינו יוצא היאך יודע שאינו זקנו. "Ordinarily, a man expecting
trial dresses in black, covers himself in black and lets his
beard grow,[61] for he does not know how his trial will end."

As the judge in criminal cases, rabbinic literature names
the king,[62] the איפרכוס,[63] ἔπαρχος, the הינמון,[64] ἡγεμών, the
ארכון,[65] ἄρχων and his Hebrew equivalent, the שלטון.[66] These
titles are often the designations of the governor of Palestine.
In the case of R. 'Akiba we even know the name of the
governor, טונוס (ט)רופוס,[67] Tίννιος 'Ροῦφος.[68]

It has been hitherto overlooked that we possess a very
important rabbinic fragment in which another governor of
Palestine is mentioned by name, apparently in the capacity
of judge.[69] It reads: (read דמושיט) דמושיט כל בהון כתיב הא

---

[61] This fact is well attested by many sources. See Mommsen, *Römisches Strafrecht*, p. 391 and notes ibid. See also Daremberg et Saglio, *Dictionnaire des antiquités etc.* I, p. 670, n. 44; A. Brüll, *Trachten der Juden*, p. 15, n. 1.

[62] Very frequently, see Ziegler, *Die Königsgleichnisse des Midrash*, p. XXXVII, passim. But it should be borne in mind that the rabbis often called the proconsul פלך.

[63] *Sifre* II, 307, ed. Finkelstein, p. 346. In *Bereshith Rabba* (XXII, ed. Theodor-Albeck, p. 215) we find: לאיפרכוס שהיה כהלך באמצע פלטיא מצא וכו' הרוג, "like an *eparchus* who was walking in the middle of the road and found a slain person etc." However, the reading איפרכוס has very little support in the manuscripts. The best of them read: נקרא פטרס, נקרי פטירס, נקרפטריס, נקר פטרים, נקרא פטרם. It is clear to me that we have here a metathesis of νεκρεπάρτης, *vespillo*, a remover of corpses. The word is extant in only one late source, in the *Catalogus Codicum Astrologorum* (referred to by Liddell and Scott's dictionary) vol. VIII (3) 110; ibid.(4) 215: περὶ νεκρεπαρτῶν . . . νεκροτάφους ἢ νεκροϑάπτας ἢ νεκρεπάρτας (Cod. Germanicus: νεκροπάρτους. The same reading is found in vol. VII ibid., p. 117). Our Midrash proves that the word was already current in Palestine in the fourth century.

[64] Tosephta Ḥul. II, 503 19.   [65] TP Ber. II, 5c; ibid. IX, 13b.

[66] TP R. H. I, 57b. Comp. also *Vayyikra Rabba* VI. 2.

[67] TP Ber. IX, 14b and parallels.

[68] See Schürer, *Geschichte*⁴ etc., I, p. 647.

[69] The fragment, one leaf of very old parchment, was discovered by Rabbi S. Wertheimer in the *Genizah* of Cairo and published in his לקט מדרשים, 2b.

יתהון לא יתרים ראשיה. אמ' ליה ודידי אינון לא דהדין קטילא אינון.
אמר אנה לא חשיב לי, מה דכתב לי מלכא אנא עביד. נתב (נסב :read)
יתיה וקטליה. ונהרג יהודה בן נקוסה הוא ובנו על ישראל באותו יום,
ואשתרית נזירתא לעידן דערובתא ולא הוה עידן די יבשלון
ביריאתא. מה עבדון נסבון ביעין לכל נפש לשמיה ד י ס ב ר ו ם
א י פ ט א ד ק י ס ר י ן. The fragment begins in the middle
of a sentence, and it is hard to reconstruct the whole passage. It refers to Esth. 8.14 and relates that the Jews
were saved from a נזירה, an evil decree, through the self-
sacrifice of Judah b. Nakossa and his son.

We shall, therefore, translate the text (after making
some slight emendations which are indicated in the notes,
and which have no bearing on the main topic of our subject)
as it is extant before us: "[The judge said]: Behold it is
stated therein[70] that whoever hands them[71] over after the
fixed term[72] shall be decapitated. [The accused] said to
him: Are they mine? Do they not belong to this dead
man? [The judge] said: This does not matter to me;
I do whatever the king orders me.[73] Thereupon he had
him seized and executed. And Judah b. Nakossa and his
son were killed on that day for the sake of Israel, and the
decree was revoked on Friday in the late afternoon. There
was no time for the people to cook; what did they do?
They took eggs for every[74] soul for the name of *Severus the
consul of Caesarea.*"

[70] I. e. in the king's letters.

[71] Apparently stolen or lost valuable objects.

[72] I make a very slight emendation of the text, reading לא' (=לאחריו,
i. e. after the fixed term, which was probably mentioned before, in the
lost text. Comp. TP B. M. II, 8c) instead of לא.

[73] This was probably the standard reply of the judge when he was
confronted with an irrefutable reply. In the *acta martyrum* we find
numerous instances of expressions in the same spirit uttered by the
martyrs, e. g., *acta Cypriani* I. 7: *fac quod tibi praeceptum est. Acta
Phileae* (Ruinart, *Acta Sincera* 1803, III, p. 161): *fac quod tibi iussum
est... quod tibi iussum est fac. Passio S. Irenaei episc. Sirm.* IV. 2
(Gebhardt, *Acta Martyrum Selecta*, p. 163): *fac quod iussum est.*

[74] Is there a small lacuna after the word לכל?

We have here a fragment which gives us accounts of a trial and of the martyrdom of Judah b. Nakossa and his son, a fact not known from any other source. Moreover, Severus a Governor[75] of Caesarea is explicitly named.[76]

As the place of the Roman trials the rabbis generally mention the basilica.[77] A permanent[78] elevated platform ($\beta\hat{\eta}\mu\alpha$), to serve as the seat of the judge, stood in the place where the trial was held. For the defendant was provided a movable[79] נרדון, *gradus*.[80] Although some of our dictionaries correctly identified the Hebrew נרדון with the Latin *gradus*, they did not explain the exact meaning of the word and the function of the *gradus*.[81]

From the *acta martyrum* we may see that the rabbinic *gradus* is nothing more than the *catasta* so frequently mentioned in the trials of the Christians. So, for instance, we read in the *Passio Perpetuae* VI.2:[82] *ascendimus in catastam.*[83] *interrogati ceteri confessi sunt. ventum est et ad me. et apparuit pater ilico cum filio meo, et extraxit me de gradu* etc. "We went up to the *catasta*. The others, on being

[75] It is the only occurrence in rabbinic literature, [where the governor is called איפטא, ὕπατος; usually he is named אנטיפיטה, ἀνθύπατος, proconsul, see Krauss *LW*, p. 70-71.

[76] Since Judah b. Nakossa was a pupil of R. Meir's disciples and a contemporary of R. Judah the Prince he could not have died under the Severi mentioned by Schürer, *Geschichte*[4] etc., I, p. 648.

[77] See Mishna 'Ab. Zarah I. 7; *Esther Rabba* I, end, passim. But trials of capital cases in the theatre and circus are also mentioned. See *Aboth deR. Nathan* XXI, ed. Schechter, p. 74 (see ibid., p. 145). Comp. Le Blant, *Les actes des martyrs*, p. 60 ff.

[78] See Tosephta Kelim, B. M. X, 589[4] and Lieberman, *Tosefeth Rishonim* III, p. 66.

[79] See Lieberman, ibid.

[80] Mishna 'Ab. Zarah ibid. mentions the basilica and the *gradus* (see TB ad loc.), the stadium and the $\beta\hat{\eta}\mu\alpha$.

[81] See below n. 96.

[82] Ed. Robinson, p. 70.

[83] The Greek reads: ἀνέβημεν εἰς τὸ βῆμα. Although $\beta\hat{\eta}\mu\alpha$ and *gradus* are etymologically the same, they usually designate two different objects. But the sources sometimes use them indiscriminately.

questioned, confessed. Then my turn came. And my
father appeared there with my child and drew me down
from the *gradus.*" Thus, the *catasta* and the *gradus* are
identical. Likewise, we read in the vision of Marianus:[84]
*illic erat catasta, non humili pulpitu nec uno tantum ascen-
sibilis gradu, sed multis ordinata gradibus et longe sublimis
ascensu.* "There was a *catasta,* whose floor was not low,
nor was *one step enough for the ascent,* but it had a succession
of many steps, and was of great height to climb." Hence,
the *catasta* was a small movable[85] platform, usually raised
one step, where the accused were questioned.

Rabbinic literature frequently mentions [86] עלה לגרדון in
the sense of being tried and questioned. It means *ascendere
gradum* which is the same as ascendere in catastam.[87] In
a parable in the *Pesikta deR. Kahana*[88] we read: נטלו ותלאו
בגרדון א'׳ל עבדך אנא וכו'. "He took him (i.e. the slave) and
had him suspended (or lifted) in the *gradus*; the slave confessed: I am your slave etc." Similarly, we read in the
Midrash:[89] נטל את השבאי ותלאו בגרדון, התחיל לצער אותו ואמר
למה עשית כך לבני, עם שהוא מצערו התחיל להודות וכו'. "He took
the captor and had him suspended (or lifted) in the *gradus,*
and asked him: Why did you do this to my son? When he
was tortured he began to confess etc." Again, the Palestinian Talmud[90] records: וכיון שלא הודו לו תליין בגרדון, "And
since they did not confess[91] he had them suspended (or

[84] *Passio Mariani et Iacobi* VI, ed. Gebhardt, *Acta Martyrum Selecta,*
p. 139.

[85] See above n. 79.

[86] See *Aruch Completum,* s. v. גרדון.

[87] Comp. also Le Blant, *Les persécuteurs et les martyrs,* p. 180, n. 5.

[88] Ed. Buber, 118b.

[89] *Tanḥuma Beshalaḥ,* ed. Buber, p. 56.

[90] Ta'anith IV, 69b, top.

[91] The parallel *Koheleth Rabba* (III. 16) tells that they were threatened
they would be lacerated there with iron combs (the common torture
inflicted on the martyrs, Jews as well as Christians), and then they
confessed.

lifted) in the *gradus*." This expression לתלות בגרדון is
nothing else than *suspendere* (or *levare*) *in catasta* frequently
met with in the Christian acts of martyrs.[92]

The previously mentioned slave was questioned while
suspended in the *gradus*;[93] the captor of the king's son and
the suspected Jewish murderers[94] were tortured in the
same manner for the purpose of extorting confessions from
them; the Christian martyrs were submitted to the same
fate in the hope of extorting denials from them.[95] All were
questioned and tortured *in the gradus*.[96]

The suspending and torturing were performed publicly,
in front of the βῆμα of the judge, as may be seen from the
acts mentioned above and many others.[97] The Midrash[98]
offers a parable of a woman who came to court to complain
of her son, and she saw the judge sitting and torturing[99]

---

[92] *Acta Capionis* 12 (*Acta Sanctorum Maii* vol. VI, p. 31b): *et S.
Capionem in catasta suspendi* etc. *Acta Dorotheae* 9 (ibid. *Febr.* vol. I,
p. 774b): *Tunc Sapricius iussit S. Dorotheam iterum in catasta levari.*
See also the numerous references to these expressions as well as to
extendere in catasta) in Cabrol's *Dictionnaire* etc. II, p. 2529 and notes
ibid. Comp. also Le Blant, *Les actes des martyrs*, p. 163; idem, *Les
persécuteurs et les martyrs*, p. 180, n. 5.

[93] Torture was the regular requirement when a slave testified.

[94] See above n. 91.

[95] Marianus (*Passio Mariani et Iacobi* V. 5. See above, n. 84), however, was suspended to extort a confession from him that he was a
deacon (see ibid. V. 3), and not a mere reader.

[96] This solves the question of Krauss in the Hebrew periodical דביר I,
p. 112.

[97] In *Mekhilta* (*Jethro* I, ed. Horovitz, p. 192) Moses is described as
being tortured on the platform (βῆμα. See above n. 83). In the *Acta
Carpi* etc., 23 (ed. Harnack, *Texte und Untersuchungen* III, 1888, p. 447)
we read: ἐκέλευσεν αὐτὸν κρεμασθέντα ξέεσθαι, "he ordered him to
be suspended and scraped" (Comp. notes ibid. and add: *Acta Pionii*
XX.1 in the *Archiv f. slavische Philologie* XVIII, 1896, p. 169). All this
was done publicly before the eyes of the judge and the crowd. Comp.
also J. Rambaud, *Le droit criminel romain dans les actes des martyrs*,
p. 68–69.

[98] *Vayyikra Rabba* XXVII. 6 (and parallels).

[99] The Hebrew דין often means to torture. See Tosephta San. XIII,
434₁₈; ibid. 434₂₄; *Bereshith Rabba* XI, 5, ed. Theodor-Albeck, p. 943;

---

people with fire, pitch and whips (חמת דיינא דיתיב ודיין
בנור ובזפת[100] ובמגלבין[101]). The judge here *publicly* applied
instruments of tortures.[102]

The tortures were many and diversified,[103] but it can
not always be ascertained whether the tortures were inflicted in the court or in the darkness of the prison.[104] In
case of religious persecutions the atrocities were generally
committed publicly.[105] Here we shall content ourselves with
one striking illustration of cruelties mentioned in the *acta
martyrum* and in a rabbinic text, which may help us to

ibid. LI. 3, 5351; TB Git. 57a, passim. Similarly, the passage in TP
(Ber. II, 5c) נסביה ורדניה ואודי is to be translated: he had him seized, tortured him, and [then] he confessed.

[100] *Oth Emeth* ad. loc. (on the authority of the 'Aruch s. v. אפקלין)
altered the words בנור ובזפת into במרזובתא, hammer. This reading was
also accepted by M. Sachs, *Beitraege* etc. II, p. 108. But the parallels as
well as Cod. Oxford of our Midrash support the reading of the editions.
Furthermore, boiling pitch is a common feature in the description of
the tortures of the Christian martyrs. See Eusebius, *Hist. Eccl.* VI. 5. 4;
Acta Bonifatii (Ruinart, *Acta Sincera*, 1802, II, p. 184); *Acta Cyrici
et Julittae* 4 (*Analecta Bollandiana* I, p. 198); G. Zoega, *Catalogus Codicum Copticorum*, p. 24; *Hist. Laus.* III, ed. Butler, p. 19; *Passio S.
Anastasiae virginis* (published by Delehaye in his *Étude sur le légen-
drier romain*, p. 254: καὶ πῦρ . . . καὶ πίσσαν) and many others. Comp.
also Cyprian, *Epist.* I, *ad Donatum*, 10.

[101] μαγγλάβια, whips. See Sachs, *Beitraege* etc. I, p. 114 seq.;
Brockelmann, *Lexicon Syriacum*, p. 117, s. v. מנלבא; S. Zeitlin, *Josephus
on Jesus* (1931), pp. 36 and 102.

[102] According to the parallel passage in *Yelamdenu* (quoted in 'Aruch
s. v. אפקלין), the judge sent officers (אפיקלין, *officiales*, ὀφφικιάλιοι)
and policemen (בלשין) to fetch the son of the woman. The Hebrew בלשין
is probably synonymous with the *officiales*. On the role of the latter as
investigators, searchers, torturers and arresters see the abundant material in Cabrol, *Dictionnaire* etc. II, p. 1111, n. 10. However, it appears
from TP ('Erubin III, 21b) that the Jews were more afraid of the common soldiers than of the *officiales* (ταξεῶται).

[103] On certain parallels of tortures mentioned in rabbinic literature
and in the *Christian acta martyrum* see Lieberman, *The Martyrs of
Caesarea, Annuaire de l'Institut de Philologie et d'Histoire Orientales
et Slaves*, v. VII, p. 417, n. 2a; ibid., p. 419, n. 16; ibid., 420, n. 23.

[104] Comp. *Ammian. Marcell.* XV. 7. 5: tamquam in *iudiciali secreto*
exaratis lateribus. "He had his sides lacerated as in a secret dungeon."

[105] See above n. 97.

establish definitely the reading in the latter. A Rabbi, who flourished under Diocletian, thus described the methods of torture during the Hadrianic persecutions:

ἐκέλευσε ... σφαίρας σιδηρᾶς πυρωθείσας ὑποτιθέναι ταῖς μασχάλαις αὐτοῦ.[107] ἐκέλευσε καλάμους ὀξυθῆναι, καὶ ἐμπαγῆναι εἰς τοὺς ὄνυχας τῶν χειρῶν αὐτοῦ.[108]	היו נותנין כדוריות של [ברזל מלובנות ב]אש תחת בית שיחיהם וקרומיות של קנה תחת ציפורניהם.[106]
"He (i. e. the governor) ordered that glowing iron balls should be applied under his arm-pits." "He ordered that reeds should be sharpened and driven into the nails of his hands."	"Glowing iron balls were applied under their arm-pits and pieces of reed haulm were driven under their nails."

We now proceed to a description of the court room. The Midrash[109] records: ‎והוא ישקיט ומי ירשיע. דרש‎ ‎ר' מאיר הוא ישקיט מעולמו ויסתר פנים מעולמו כדיין שמותחים בילה על‎ ‎פניו. ואין יודע מה נעשה בחוץ‎ *"When He is undisturbed, who can*

[106] *Pesikta deR. Kahana*, ed. Buber, 87b. The bracketed words are extant in the parallels: *Shir Hashirim Rabba* II. 7; *Midrash Tehilim* XVI, ed. Buber, p. 121; *Midrash Haggadol, Gen.*, p. 510. The Christian parallels support the text of the editions, see Buber's notes.

[107] *Synaxarium of Constantinople*, col. 819. Nothing is known of the time and place of the martyrdom (Justus of Rome). Comp. *Acta Sanctorum, Julii* III, p. 651 ff. Eusebius (*Hist. Eccl.* V. 1.21) relates: χαλκᾶς λεπίδας διαπύρους προσεκόλλων τοῖς τρυφερωτάτοις μέλεσι τοῦ σώματος αὐτοῦ. "Red-hot brazen plates were applied to the most tender parts of his body" (of Sanctus, under Marcus Aurelius).

[108] *Acta Bonifatii* (Ruinart, *Acta Sincera*, 1802, II, p. 182). The martyr is supposedly a contemporary (290) of our Rabbi. Eusebius (*Hist. Eccl.* VIII. 12.6) records: καλάμοις ὀξέσιν τοῖν χεροῖν ἐξ ἄκρων ὀνύχων τοὺς δακτύλους διαπειρόμενοι. "Sharp reeds were driven through their fingers under the tips of the nails" (during the persecutions of Diocletian). Comp. also Perles, *Etymologische Studien* etc. (1871), p. 88.

[109] *Bereshith Rabba* XXVI, beginning, ed. Theodor-Albeck, p. 334. Comp. *Vayyikra Rabba* V. 1.

then condemn (Job 34.29). R. Meir interpreted it: '[When] He is undisturbed about His world and hides His face from it, like a judge in front of whom a curtain (velum, βῆλον) is stretched, and he does not know what is happening without'."

A parallel passage[110] reads:[111] מה הדיין הזה משהן‎י‎ נותנין פליטי‎נ‎י‎ לפניו עוד אינו רואה מה נעשה. "Like that judge who as soon as they put curtains in front of him he no longer sees what is happening.". The wording[114] of our Midrash clearly indicates that the question is not of a trial *intra velum*,[115] *in secretario*, but of the deliberation of the judge about the sentence.[116] The trial was public; the judge could observe the reaction of the spectators, but as soon as the *velum* was drawn before him he no longer saw what was going on in the crowd, and he did not heed the possible

[110] Overlooked by the editor of *Bereshith Rabba*.

[111] *Midrash Tehilim* X, ed. Buber p. 95.

[112] So Cod. Halberstam.

[113] Cod. Halberstam reads: פלסין. *Yalkut* ad loc.: פסליון. From the parallel Midrash it is obvious that the word means curtain. Perhaps it is corrupted from *palla*. Prof. Henri Grégoire, whom I consulted on this point, suggests altering the reading of the *Yalkut* פסליון into פסטון (which is graphically very plausible: the ט was resolved into לי), παστός, curtain. Krauss and Löw (*LW* 473) overlooked the parallel in *Bereshith Rabba* and their interpretation is therefore impossible.

[114] The idea is here ascribed to the wicked, and it corresponds to *Vayyikra Rabba* V. 1. Basil. Magn. (Migne *PG* XXIX, 344b) combats the same idea in the same terms.

[115] See below.

[116] In the *Passio Sanctorum Scillitanorum* (180), ed. Robinson, p. 112, we read: in *secretario inpositis Sperato* etc. Likewise, the reading in Ruinart's *Acta Sincera* (1802, I, p. 192) is: *Adductis ergo in secretario Cartaginis apparitorum officio* (comp. *Acta Cypriani* I. 1) *Sperato* etc. But Prof. E. Bickerman (in an oral communication) contends that a better draft of the acts is preserved in Baronius' text (Ruinart ibid., p. 188) which does not mention the *secretarium*. The later acts mostly mention only the deliberation *intra velum*. So, for instance, *Acta Claudii, Asterii* etc. (Ruinart ibid. II, p. 142, n. 9): Lysias introgressus obduxit *velum* et post exiens ex tabella recitavit sententiam. Comp. Le Blant, *Les persécuteurs et les martyrs*, p. 219, n. 1. See also below p. 40, n. 11.

condemnation by the public. This is the description of the court by R. Meir (flourished in the middle of the second century).

But an anonymous passage in the Midrash[117] states: הוי רואה עצמך כאילו אתה נתון לפנים משבעה קנקנים ויושב ודן, ואני נדון לפניך. "Consider yourself as you are sitting in judgment behind seven[118] cancelli, and I am tried before you."[119] In this scene the defendant has already been tried within the cancelli (and vela).[120] It corresponds to the regular procedure of the fourth century.[121] A few acts of alleged victims of the Diocletian persecutions confirm this procedure. The Acta S. Eupli[122] record that when Euplus was outside the curtain of the court room[123] he declared himself a Christian. He was brought into the secretarium and questioned there.[124] But he was subsequently tortured outside the velum. Then the sentence was drafted within the velum and read outside of it.[125]

Before we proceed to describe the formal examination of the accused, we shall quote here a very important text

[117] Bereshith Rabba LXXIII. 8, ed. Theodor-Albeck, p. 926.

[118] The number is, of course, a round one. Comp. Aruch Completum s. v. קנקל II.

[119] The text is apparently of the fourth century. The statement of the sage mentioned there a little below does not refer to our passage, see Theodor's note a. l. and comp. ibid., p. 9053.

[120] Comp. also the collection of Midrash Debarim Zuta, ed. Buber, p. 4.

[121] Comp. Mommsen, Römisches Strafrecht, p. 359, nn. 1, 2, and especially p. 362, n. 3.

[122] Ruinart, Acta Sincera, 1802, II, p. 430.

[123] cum esset extra velum secretarii.

[124] In the late Byzantine period there existed a special place for questioning with torture— πρόοδος. See Appendix I.

[125] Calvisianus intra velum interius ingrediens, sententiam dictavit. et foras egressus, afferens tabellam, legit etc. Similarly, we read in the Acta Crispinae (Ruinart ibid. III. p. 65): in secretario pro tribunali adsidente Anulino proconsule, commentariense officium dixit etc. See on all this Rambaud, Le droit criminel romain dans les actes des martyrs, p. 55, nn. 1, 3, and comp. below n. 198. See also Passio SS. Montani et Lucii XXI. 7 (Gebhardt, Acta Martyrum Selecta, p. 159).

dealing with the persecutions of the Christians. We read
in Tosephta:[126] מעשה בר' ליעזר שנתפס על דברי מינות והעלו אותו

לבמה[127] לדון. אמ' לו אותו הגמון זקן כמותך יעסוק בדברים[128] הללו.

אמ' לו נאמן דיין עלי. כסבור אותו הגמון שלא אמ' ר' ליעזר אלא לו,

ור' ליעזר לא נתכוון אלא נגד אביו שבשמים. אמ' לו הואיל והאמנתני

עליך, אף אני כך אמרתי, איפשר שהסיבות[129] הללו טועים בדברים

הללן[130]]. דימוס הרי אתה פטור "Once R. Eli'ezer[131] was arrested for *Minuth*, Christianity,[132] and he was brought up[133]
to the tribunal for judgment. The ἡγεμών, governor,[134]
said to him: Does an old man like you occupy himself
with such [idle][135] things? He replied: I rely upon the
judge.[136] The governor supposed that he said this of him,

[126] Ḥul. II, 503₁₈. I quote from the best manuscript, Cod. Vienna.
The date of the compilation of the text is not later than the beginning
of the third century. The original source was most probably contemporary with the event. Parallels are available in *Midrash Koheleth Rabba*
I. 8 and TB 'Ab. Zarah 16b.

[127] *Koheleth Rabba* ibid. reads: על הביטה, βῆμα. TB ibid. reads: לנרדום,
gradus, see above n. 83.

[128] Both parallels read here: בדברים ב ט ל י ם הללו.

[129] Ed. pr.: שהסיבות. *Koheleth Rabba*: שישיבות = ששיבות. See Lieberman,
Tosefeth Rishonim II, p. 227. J. Derenbourg (*Essai sur l'histoire et la
géographie de la Palestine*, p. 359) and many others (see below) misunderstood this word and drew false conclusions from it.

[130] So ed. prin. and Cod. Erfurt. *Koheleth Rabba* reads: דברים
ב ט ל י ם הללו. Comp. above n. 128.

[131] Flourished in the second half of the first century and in the first
quarter of the second.

[132] As is shown by the following context where the name of Jesus is
explicitly mentioned.

[133] The usual term in TB is אתויי (TB. Git. 57b, seven times; ibid.
'Ab. Zarah 17b, twice; ibid. Sanh. 43a, five times, see Rabbinovicz,
Variae Lectiones a. l., p. 126), *applicare* or *adstare*, see Le Blant, *Les
actes des martyrs*, p. 152 ff.

[134] On his name see below, n. 152.

[135] See above n. 128. Our text proves that in the beginning of the second century Christianity was not as yet μωρία, ἀπόνοια, *stultitia, insania*,
in the eyes of the Roman government, but merely μάταια, *inania*.

[136] The Rabbi used here a fixed legal term. Comp. *Mishna Sanhedrin*
III. 2: נאמן עלי אבא, נאמן עלי אביך "I accept [my] father or your father
as trustworthy", i. e. I rely upon them. Herford's translation (*Christianity in Talmud and Midrash*, p. 137) is inexact.

but R. Eli'ezer had in mind only his Father in heaven.
He (i. e., the governor) said to him: Since you relied upon
me, I indeed thought: Is it possible that these gray hairs[137]
will err in [those idle][138] things?[139] *Dimissus*,[140] behold thou
art released."

This very important and authentic text bears on Trajan's
persecutions of the Christians, as correctly observed by
Herford,[141] and an analysis of it will be very valuable. The
source does not inform us how and under what circumstances R. Eli'ezer was seized. It appears from the text
that no accuser was present,[142] and it is very likely that the
denunciation was anonymous. We know of this practice
from the famous letter of Plinius:[143] *Propositus est libellus
sine auctore multorum nomina continens.* "A placard was
put up without any signature accusing a large number of
persons by name." Trajan[144] replied that such information
should not be admitted. Since our incident probably took
place two or three years before this rescript of Trajan,[145]

[137] Herford, ibid., translates: these *societies*! Comp. above n. 129.

[138] Comp. above nn. 130 and 135.

[139] The governor probably said: εἰ δυνατόν ἐστι ταύταις ταῖς
πολιαῖς ἐν τοῖσδε τοῖς ματαίοις πλανηθῆναι; According to the
Martyrium S. Cononis IV (Gebhardt, *Acta Martyrum Selecta*, p. 131),
the ἡγεμών said to Conon: τί πλανᾶσθε... παῦσαι οὖν τῆς τοιαύτης
μωρίας κτλ. But this was supposedly some hundred and forty years
later.

[140] The sentence was rendered in Latin even in Greek-speaking
countries. See Le Blant, *Les actes des martyrs*, p. 119–120, who refers
also to the rabbinic דימוס.

[141] Op. cit. p. 141.

[142] TB 'Ab. Zarah, after recording our story, cites (17b) two incidents
in connection with the Hadrianic persecutions of the Jews. In the first
case the Rabbi denied the charge, and when the accuser rose to accuse
him (קם חד לאסהודי ביה) he was miraculously prevented from doing so.
In the second case the Rabbi admitted the transgression of the Hadrianic
laws, and was immediately sentenced to death.

[143] X. 96.

[144] Ibid. 97.

[145] See above n. 141.

it is no wonder that the Rabbi was arrested on the ground of an anonymous denunciation.

The rabbis do not tell us what the judge first asked R. Eli'ezer. He undoubtedly began by asking him for his name, country[146] etc. The rabbis usually omitted these well known standard details. But as to the accusation proper, it is clear that the judge began with the reproach: "Does an old man like you occupy himself with such idle things!" He pretended to assume that the accusation was true. The same behavior is displayed in the two subsequent stories related in the Babylonian Talmud.[147] The judge began his examination with: מאי טעמא תנית ומאי טעמא גנבת . . . אמאי קא עסקת באורייתא. "Why did you study the Law and why did you rob?[148] . . . Why did you engage in the study of the Law?" The judge took the validity of the accusation for granted, he only inquired into the reasons of the crime. This method of incriminating questioning was very common in the Palestinian courts of the Romans in the examination of the ordinary crimes, as we shall presently see.

R. Eli'ezer's answer was evasive. The straightforward answer should have been a flat denial. Perhaps he refused to give a direct reply because of his fear of additional questions. If the Rabbi had allowed a discussion to develop the judge might have asked him for the reasons of his excommunication.[149] It might have involved an explanation of the intimate internal affairs of the academies. Had R. Eli'ezer refused to answer this question, once it was asked, the charge would naturally be confirmed.

True, the Rabbi could easily prove that he was not *now*

---

[146] See below Appendix I, n. 36.

[147] See above n. 142.

[148] See also *Tanḥuma* quoted above, p. 14; *Debarim Rabba* 1. 17. Comp. Lieberman, The Martyrs of Caesarea, *Annuaire* etc. (see above n. 1), p. 445, n. 19.

[149] TP M. K. III. 1, 81d; TB B. M. 59b.

a Christian by cursing Jesus,[150] but his past beliefs could not be disproved by it. According to the regular Roman laws of that time repentance for a religious crime did not

[150] This was the only way for a Jew to prove that he was not a Christian, for a Jew could not be compelled to perform a heathen ceremony. Most probably, there is an echo of the real state of affairs (in the third century) in the words of the *Acta S. Pionii* XIII. 1: Ἀκούω δὲ ὅτι καὶ τινας ὑμῶν Ἰουδαῖοι καλοῦσιν εἰς συναγωγάς. διὸ προσέχετε μή ποτε ὑμῶν καὶ μεῖζον καὶ ἑκούσιον ἁμάρτημα ἅψηται, μηδέ τις τὴν ἀναφαίρετον ἁμαρτίαν τὴν εἰς τὴν βλασφημίαν τοῦ ἁγίου πνεύματος ἁμαρτήσῃ. "I hear that the Jews call some of you to the synagogues. Wherefore take care lest even a greater and voluntary sin take hold of you, lest anyone commit the unforgivable sin of blaspheming the holy spirit." From this passage it appears that even Gentiles could escape death by cursing Jesus and affirming that they were Jews (the laws against conversion to Judaism were not always strictly applied in practice). This was probably the manner of escape for Domnus, who turned from Christianity to Judaism during the persecutions (Eusebius, *Hist. Eccl.* VI. 12. 1).

From the letter of Plinius (X. 96) we learn that the Christians were required both to sacrifice and to curse Jesus. But the wording of the prototype of our *Acta Pionii, the Martyrdom of Polycarp* (IX. 3), suggests that a Christian could sometimes save himself (even in the beginning of the second half of the second century) only by cursing Jesus. We read there: ὄμοσον, καὶ ἀπολύω σε. λοιδόρησον τὸν Χριστόν. "Swear, and I set you free. Curse Christ."

In the later, legendary *acta martyrum*, this behavior of the Roman judge is clearly stated. So we read in the *Acta Platonis* (*Acta Sanctorum, Julii* Vol. V, 233): *Agrippinus ... dixit: Acquiesce vel adhuc, Platon. et si non vis sacrificare diis abnega saltem illum qui crucifixus est et dimitteris.* "Agrippinus ... said: Anyhow agree to this, Plato. And if you do not want to sacrifice to the gods, at least deny him who was crucified and you will be set free." Another narrative goes even further. The *Acta Nerei, Achillei* etc. (ibid. *Maii* Vol. III, p. 11) record: *Dicebant autem omnes ad eam, et ipsi qui torquebant eam: Nega te Christianam esse et dimitteris.* "But they all said to her (i. e. to Felicula), even those who tortured her: Deny that you are a Christian, and you will be set free." There is no doubt that these fictitious *acta* preserved here echoes of genuine concessions on the part of the judge (in certain cases) to the Christians.

Valuable information regarding the judicial procedure during the religious persecutions of the Jews is preserved in a fragment of *Midrash Yelamdenu* quoted in 'Aruch s. v. צבע I. It is very probable that the picture is borrowed from the descriptions of the persecutions of Antiochus Epiphanes.

annul the crime,[151] and R. Eli'ezer would have run a certain
risk, even after he had demonstrated that he was not *now*
a Christian.

Fortunately, the governor himself was glad to dismiss
the case, and seized the opportunity to declare that he
wondered how a gray-haired man could err in such idle
matters. This incident, now understood in its proper
perspective, provides valuable information on the attitude
of the Roman governor of Palestine[152] towards the Christians during the Trajanic persecutions.

We shall now proceed to an analysis of the court-
examination of the ordinary criminal, as described by the
rabbis.

The defendant was first asked his name,[153] his country
and his social condition[154] etc. Then he was asked directly
whether he admitted the crime.[155] As stated above, the
rabbis usually omitted these standard questions in their
descriptions. But they have preserved a colorful picture of
the incriminating questioning in the course of the examination in the Roman court.

We read in a *Genizah* fragment of the *Yelamdenu*:[156]

[151] It is only after the above rescript of Trajan that the judges were
officially authorized not to pay attention to the defendant's past, but
to release the Christian when he publicly relapsed into heathendom.
And even as late as the second half of the second century the judges
sometimes were not fully satisfied with the relapse of the Christians.
See Eusebius, *Hist. Eccl.* V. 1. 33.

[152] Probably, Q. Pompeius Falco (See Schürer, *Geschichte*[4] etc. I,
p. 645 ff.) who seems to have been even more lenient than his friend,
Plinius.

[153] Τίς καλεῖται τὸ ὄνομά σου; Quis vocaris? See TP Ber. IX, 12b,
top, and below Appendix I, n. 36. Comp. also Le Blant, *Les actes des
martyrs*, p. 156 ff.

[154] See Le Blant ibid.

[155] So, *Tanḥuma Vayyeishev*, ed. Buber, p. 182: והדיין אוכר לו, אמור אם
הרנת אם לא הרנת "And the judge asks him: Say, did you kill or did you
not kill?"

[156] J. Mann, *The Bible as Read and Preached in the Old Synagogue* I,
p. צ"ט. See the parallel passages in *Bereshith Rabba* XXXVII.2, ed.

מה הנחש מעוקם, כך אף המלכות מעוקמת בדרכיה. אומרת לאדם:
מה את, אדם טוב או רע? והוא אום' לו: טוב אני. והן אומרים לו:
כמה בני אדם הרגת? ואו' לא הרגתי. והוא או' לו: ומי היה עמך, ובמה
הרגת אותו, בחרב או במקל או באבן? אינו זז עד שהוא נותן לו אפופסיס
והורגו. "As the serpent is crooked, so the [Roman] government is crooked in its ways. It asks the man (i. e. the
accused): What are you, a good man or a bad man? He
replies: I am a good man.[157] He is asked: How many
people did you kill? He answers: I did not kill. Again he
is asked: And who was with you,[158] and with which instrument did you kill — with a sword, stick, or stone?[159] He
(i. e. the judge) does not budge until he "gives him"[160] the
sentence (ἀπόφασις) and has him executed."

It is clear that the rabbis' testimony cannot be discredited.
They give a faithful description of Roman procedure in the
Palestinian courts. And indeed Philostratus[161] relates that
when Domitian examined Apollonius he asked him this

Theodor-Albeck, p. 345 (in the name of a Rabbi who flourished in the
second half of the third century); *Debarim Rabba*, ed. Lieberman, p. 18
and n. 18 ibid.

[157] In *Aggadath Bereshith* LVI, ed. Buber, p. 113, we read: לאדם שעלה
לביסה התחיל בוכה, אמרו לו מפני מה אתה בוכה אסר להן מפני שאני אדם טוב, ולא
עשיתי רע מימי "Like a man who ascended the tribunal (βῆμα) and began
to cry. He was asked : Why do you cry? He said: because I am a good
man and I have never done any evil." Likewise the first declaration
of Speratus was (*Acta Sanctorum Scillitanorum*, Ruinart, 1802, I, p. 189):
Nos minime aliquando malum fecimus etc. "We have not done the
slightest harm to anyone etc."

[158] Comp. also TP Ber. II, 5c. This, of course, was the most natural
question. In the Digest XLVIII.3.6 (*de custod. et exhib. reorum*) we
read: ut irenarchae, cum adprehenderunt latrones interrogent eos de
sociis etc. (quoted in full and translated below n. 190). Comp. also
Tertullian, *Apol.* II. 4.

[159] In the parallel *Bereshith Rabba* (see above n. 156) the question is:
[Granted] you did not steal, who stole together with you? [Granted]
you did not slay, who slew together with you? In *Debarim Rabba* ed.
Lieberman, p. 18, the wording is: Suppose (אפותיסיס, ὑπόθεσις) you did
not kill, with which instrument did you kill?

[160] Comp. *sententiam dare*, ἀπόφασιν διδόναι.

[161] *Vita Apollonii* VIII.5.

catch-question (ὑφέρπων τὴν ἐρώτησιν): "Tell me, you
went out of your house on a certain day and you travelled
in the country — to whom did you sacrifice the boy?"[162]
This way of examining was certainly not invented by the
author, but was copied from the court practice.

Similarly, we read in an account of an investigation in
the Roman court[163] that the first words of the judge to the
defendant were: "Tell me the truth before you are put to
torture: How did you commit the murder?"[164] The defendant flatly denied the accusation and, after being tortured, was acquitted. Again, according to the *Vita Eugeniae*
14,[165] the judge did not ask Eugenia whether she committed
the crime, but how she dared commit it.[166]

---

[162] εἰπέ μοι, ἔφη, προελθὼν τῆς οἰκίας τῇ δεῖνι ἡμέρᾳ καὶ ἐς ἀγρὸν
πορευθεὶς τίνι ἐθύσω τὸν παῖδα;

[163] Ephraem Syrus, *Opera omnia, graece et latine*, III, p. XXVIIb.
The source is most probably of the fourth century (i. e. contemporary
with our Midrash or a little later), see Le Blant, *Les actes des martyrs*,
p. 170.

[164] τοῦ δὲ ἄρχοντος ἐπερωτῶντος αὐτὸν εἰπεῖν τὴν ἀλήθειαν πρὸ
τῶν βασάνων πῶς τὸν φόνον πεποίηκεν.

[165] In all the versions: Migne *PL* XXI, 1114; idem. *PG* CXVI, 632,
Ch. 20; *Studia Sinaitica* IX, p. כ'ז (Syriac); Conybeare, *Monuments of
Early Christianity*, p. 175 (translation from Armenian); Goodspeed,
Journal of Semitic Languages and Literature XXI (1904), p. 54 (trans-
lation from Coptic).

[166] Despite its legendary character, the *Vita Eugeniae* preserves
some true features of the time to which it is ascribed (the reign of
Commodus), as noted by Le Blant, *Les actes des martyrs*, p. 207. According to this narrative (Ch. VIII. *PL* ibid. 1112; *PG* ibid. 624, ch. 13;
Studia Sinaitica ibid., p. י'; Conybeare ibid., p. 168; Goodspeed ibid.,
p. 52) the father of Eugenia who was then governor of Egypt, believing
that his daughter was dead, set up a golden statue in her likeness and
worshipped it. The Latin, Greek and Armenian versions do not mention
the place where the Egyptian governor set up the statue. The Syriac
clearly states that it was erected in the city (ואקימה במדינתא). This was
a common practice of the age (See Le Blant ibid.). But the Egyptian
(the Coptic) version states: "Her father commanded them to make
for him *an image in her image* and in her likeness. And they made it
and placed it in his house." A contemporary of the supposed date of

The accused was given the opportunity to defend himself and to avail himself of the aid of lawyers[167] in his defence. The judge often extended the time previously allowed to the lawyer for his speech. For instance, we read in *Bereshith Rabba:*[168] אמר ר' לוי חלף סידרה מלאה מים, כל זמן שהיא מלאה מים הסניגור מלמד, פעמים שהדיין מבקש שילמד הסניגור והוא אומר הוסיפו בתוכה מים. "R. Levi[169] said: The water-clock (κλεψύδρα) is full of water; as long as the water is in it the lawyer speaks;[170] sometimes the judge desires the lawyer to continue and says: Pour more water into it."[171]

The rabbis have preserved an interesting example of the introductory portion of the speeches of the lawyers. We read in the *Sifre:*[172] משל ללוטייר שהיה עומד על הבמה ונשכר[173] לאחד לדבר על ידיו ולא פתח בצרכי אותו האיש תחילה עד שפתח בשבחו של מלך. אשרי עולם ממלכו, אשרי עולם מדיינו, עלינו זרחה חמה, עלינו זרחה לבנה. והיו אחרים מקלסים עמו. ואחר כך פתח בצרכו של אותו האיש וחזר וחתם בשבחו של מלך. "Like an advocate (ῥήτωρ) who was standing on the platform (βῆμα) [because] he was engaged by someone to defend him. He did not turn to the discussion of his client's case, before he began with the

our narrative (R. Nathan, *Mekhilta, Pisha* XIII, ed. Horovitz, p. 44 and parallels) says of the ancient Egyptians: כיון שהיה הבכור מת לאחד מהן היו עושין לו איקונין ומעמידה בביתו "When the first-born of one of them died, they would make an εἰκόνιον (image or statue) of him *and set it up in the house*."

[167] συνήγορος, see Krauss *LW*, p. 404; παράκλητος, see ibid., p. 496; δικολόγος, see ibid., p. 211; ῥήτωρ, see below.

[168] IL. 12, ed. Theodor-Albeck, p. 514.

[169] Flourished under Diocletian.

[170] See Mommsen, *Römisches Strafrecht*, p. 428, n. 1. The fact is too well known to give additional examples.

[171] See Mommsen ibid., n. 6.

[172] II, 343, ed. Finkelstein, p. 394. The date of the text is not later than the beginning of the third century.

[173] Cod. London has a very interesting variant ונדרך, "and he was authorized." But the word אדרכתא, authorisation, is not found, as far as I know, in early Palestinian texts.

praise of the king: 'Happy is the world with its king!'[174]
Happy is the world with its judge!'[175] Upon us the sun
shines!'[176] Upon us the moon shines!' And the rest [of the
people] acclaimed [them] together with him. After that
he began to talk about the needs of his client, and in his
conclusion he again praised the king." This too is not a
fanciful composition by a homilist, but a true description
of what he saw and heard in the Roman court.

A detailed and faithful portrayal of the procedure in the
criminal court is offered in *Pesikta deR. Kahana*:[177] לליסטים
שהוא נידון לפני הקוסטינר בתחילה הוא קורא אנגלין[178] שלו [ואח״כ הוא
מכה אותו ואח״כ הוא נותן לו כמס][179] ואח״כ הוא נותן פרקולה[180] ואח״כ
הוא יוצא ליהרג אבל הקב״ה אינו כן אלא בתחילה הוא קורא אנגלין.

[174] Comp. the acclamation in the *Acta Fratrum Arvalium*, Dessau
No. 451 (year 213): o nos felices qui te impe(ratorem) videmus!   See
E. Peterson, Εἶς θεός, p. 143.

[175] It seems to me that the king and the judge are not one and the
same person. The advocate first acclaims the king in his absence and
then the judge. See Peterson ibid., p. 147. In *Bereshith Rabba* (I.3,
ed. Theodor-Albeck, p. 5) we read: בנוהג העולם מלך בשר ודם מתקלס
בדרינה וגדולי מדינה מתקלסין עמו, למה שנושאין עמו בטשואו "Ordinarily, when
a human king is acclaimed in the city, the city dignitaries are acclaimed
with him, because together with him they carry his burden [of govern-
ment]." *Debarim Rabba* (ed. Lieberman, p. 53) records: דוכסין ואפרכין
ואסרטטולין אינן מתקלסין כשם שהמלך מתקלס? א״ר חייא רבה כל אלו מתקלסין בחוץ
בפני המלך, שמא בפני המלך ובתוך פלטין שלו "Are not commanders (*duces*),
prefects (or governors, ἔπαρχοι) and generals (στρατηλάται) acclaimed as the king is acclaimed? R. Hiyya the Great (fl. in the second
and the beginning of the third century) said: All these are praised in
the absence of the king, but hardly in his presence and in his palace."
Comp. however *Midrash Tehilim* LVI, ed. Buber, p. 373 and ibid.,
p. 539.

[176] Comp. *Ammianus Marcellinus* XVI. 5. 14.

[177] Ed. Buber, 159b.

[178] Cod. Carmoli: אנגילין. Cod. Oxford and *Yalkut Hamakiri*, Hosea
(*JQR*, N. S., Vol. 15, p. 210): אנלין (ibid., p. 212 mistakenly: אבלין);
Yalkut Shimeoni, Hosea 532: אולינין.

[179] The bracketed words are omitted in the edited manuscript by a
homoioteleuton. They are extant in all the mss. and the sources referred
to above n. 178.

[180] *Yalkut Hamakiri* ibid.: פריקולא.

ועתה יוסיפו לחטוא ויעשו להם מסכה. ואח״כ הוא מכה אותם. הוכה
אפרים שרשם יבש. ואח״כ הוא נותן להם כמס. צרור עון אפרים צפונה
חטאתו. ואח״כ הוא נותן להם פרקולה. תאשם שומרון כי מרתה באלהיה.
ואח״כ הוא מחזירן בתשובה. שובה ישראל "Like a robber who is
tried before a *quaestionarius*.[181] At first he reads his *elogium*,[182]
then he flogs him,[183] then he gives him a hook (i. e. puts
a hook in his mouth),[184] then he gives the *periculum*[185] and
then he is led to his execution. But the Holy One blessed
be He is not like this. First He reads his *elogium*,[as it is
written]: *And now they sin more and more and have made
them molten images* (Hos. 13.2). Then He flogs them [as
it is written]: *Ephraim is smitten, their root is dried up*
(ibid. 9.16). Then He gives them a hook, [as it is written]:
The iniquity of Ephraim is bound up,[186] *his sin is laid up
in store* (ibid. 13.12). Then He gives them the *periculum*,[187]
[as it is written]: *Samaria will be declared guilty, for she
rebelled against her God* (ibid. 14.1). Then He brings them
back by [their] repentance,[as it is written]: *Return Israel"*
(ibid. 14.2).

We have here three "realia:" the *elogium*, the *hamus*
(hook) and the *periculum*. We shall try to establish the
exact meaning of these terms in rabbinic literature. The
first word had several varied meanings in criminal procedure.[188] In the acts of the Christian martyrs the *elogium*

---

[181] Probably in the *officium*.
[182] The reading אנלין = אנללין (see above n. 178) cannot be easily dismissed. Perhaps they had in mind ἐυλογεῖον, ἐλλογεῖον, *imputatio*.
In the *Corpus Gloss. Latin.* (ed. Loewe etc. II, p. 861⁴) we find: *inputat*,
ἐυλογεῖ. Comp. *Epist. ad Rom.* V.13.
[183] Tortures him to extort from him a confession or the circumstances
of the crime.
[184] See below, Appendix II.
[185] See below.
[186] I. e., having a hook in his mouth he cannot deny his sin any more.
[187] See below.
[188] See *Corp. Gloss. Lat.* VI, p. 382; Le Blant, *Les actes des Martyrs,*
pp. 46, 91, 115 ff.

is the word frequently used for the report of the prelim-
inary interrogation conducted by the magistrate, which
accompanied the defendant, to the proconsul or the legate.[189]
This report was the first document read in the court of the
proconsul (or legate) when the accused appeared there.[190]

From the rabbinic sources it is obvious that the *elogium*
was used in Palestine in the above sense. It accompanied
the defendants, and was read to the judge before he proceeded with his interrogation. So we read in the Midrash:[191]
משל לאחד שהיה אילונין שלו נקרא לפני הדיין אמר הדיין עד עכשיו הוא
קיים. "Like a man whose *elogium* was read before the judge.
The judge said: Is this man still alive?!"[192] Similarly,
Midrash Tanḥuma[193] records: משל למלך שעלה אחד לבימה שלו
לידון הוציא דבר מפיו במה שחייב את עצמו הניח המלך האילונין שלו
וחייבו מפיו. "Like a king before whose tribunal (βῆμα) a
man came up for judgment. He let a word slip from his
mouth by which he condemned himself. The king laid
aside his *elogium* and convicted him out of his own mouth."

---

[189] *Passio Mariani et Iacobi* IX.1. and 4 (see above n. 84); *Acta
Saturnini, Dativi* etc. III ff. (Ruinart, *Acta Sincera* II, p. 381). See
Rambaud, *Le droit criminel Romain dans les actes des martyrs*, p. 42,
n. 1.

[190] *Acta Marcelli Centurionis* III, IV (ed. Ruinart ibid., p. 215 ff.).
This procedure is attested by the Digest (XLVIII. 3. 6): *divus Pius . . .
proposuit ut irenarchae, cum adprehenderint latrones interrogent eos de
sociis et receptatoribus et interrogationes litteris inclusas atque obsignatas
ad cognitionem magistratus mittant. igitur qui cum e l o g i o mittuntur
ex integro audiendi sunt, etsi per litteras missi fuerint vel etiam per
irenarchas perducti.* "The divine Pius . . . promulgated that when the
police-magistrates arrest brigands they should question them about
their associates and shelterers and send the interrogation for the information of the magistrate in closed and sealed letters. Then, [the
accused men] who are sent with the *elogium* should again be subjected
to a complete examination, although they are sent with letters (i. e.
the *elogium*), or may even be accompanied by the police-magistrates."
See Le Blant, *Les actes des martyrs*, p. 47; Rambaud, ibid., p. 43, n. 1.

[191] *Shemoth Rabba* XXI.6.

[192] I. e. after what he has done. It is from the *elogium* that the judge
learned first of the doings of the defendant.

[193] *Shelaḥ*, ed. Buber IV, p. 96 and parallels.

A third instance is even more instructive, as we shall presently see. We read in *Shemoth Rabba*:[194] משל למלך שאמ'
לבניו הוו יודעין שאני דן דיני נפשות ומחייב הקריבו לי קרבן (דורון)[195]
שאם תעלו לפני לבימה שאעביר אולוגין שלכם (לאחֵר)[196] כך אמר הב'ה
לישראל בדיני נפשות אני הורג. ראו איך אני חס עליכם ברחמים בדם
פסח ובדם מילה. "Like a king who said *to his children*: Know that I am going to try capital cases and convict [people to death]; offer therefore a sacrifice to me, so that in case you are brought before my tribunal I may dismiss your *elogium*. So God said to Israel: I am now sentencing people to death (i. e. the first born of the Egyptians), mind I shall have pity on you through the blood of the paschal lamb and the blood of circumcision." If the parable were a fiction it would be tasteless and artificial. It is inconceivable that a king sitting as a judge in capital cases should declare in advance that he would issue wholesale convictions (as in the case of the Egyptians) and would ask his children to offer a sacrifice to him!

It seems to me, therefore, that the parable refers to an actual fact. Lactantius[197] tells us: *et primam omnium filiam Valeriam conjugemque Priscam sacrificio pollui coegit... arae in secretariis ac pro tribunali*[198] *positae, ut litigatores prius sacrificarent atque ita causas suas dicerent, sic ergo ad iudices tamquam ad deos adiretur.* "And first of all he (i. e. Diocletian) forced *his daughter* Valeria and his wife Prisca to be polluted by sacrificing... altars were placed in the council chambers and near the tribunal, that the

[194] XV. 12. I copy from Cod. Oxford 147, f. 191b.
[195] The word קרבן is missing in the editions. But in addition to our manuscript it is also extant in Cod. New York. It is therefore obvious that דורון is a gloss to קרבן and, as usual, the original was dropped and the gloss retained.
[196] The dots on the word apparently indicate that the word is to be deleted.
[197] *De mort. persec.* XV.
[198] See above n. 125.

litigants might offer a sacrifice before their cause could be heard. Thus, judges were approached as gods."

Some two hundred years earlier, Pliny[199] adopted the same course. He brought the images of the emperor and the gods into the court and ordered the Christians to sacrifice to them. Similarly, we read in Tosephta:[200] ביטסיות שהעמידו מלכים בשעת השמד. "Altars[201] that the governors (=judges) set up during the [Hadrianic] destruction etc."

The parable becomes perfectly understandable. In the wholesale condemnation of the Christians during Diocletian's persecutions, the emperor's own daughter[202] and wife were forced to sacrifice; otherwise they might be condemned. The point of the parable is that the Jews were similarly spared during the wholesale conviction of the Egyptians by offering the blood of the Paschal lamb and the blood of circumcision; their *elogium* was then dismissed. The *elogium* in our parable has the same meaning as in the two previous cases.[203]

The reading of the *elogium* in the court should possibly be dissociated from the reading of the ὑπομνήματα. The Midrash[204] records: הרי הוא יוצא. שלו נקרין [205]הרי איפוטנימתה

[199] *Epist.* X. 96.

[200] 'A. Zarah V, 46826 (according to Cod. Vienna and ed. prin.). Comp. also TB ibid 54a.

[201] Krauss (*LW* I, sect. 361, p. 209) quotes Bar Bahlul (*apud* Payne Smith, *Thesaur. Syriac.*, p. 468 s. v. בומסא) who asserts that בומסא, βωμοί, are a kind of images which are worshipped. And indeed, the worship of the βωμός was common in the Orient and was not unknown in the Occident. See A. B. Cook, Zeus I, p. 519 ff. (esp. n. 2 ibid.). The fact is also confirmed by TP 'A. Zarah IV. 4, 44a (Comp. טראה הפנים a. l.). See also TB ibid. 47b (and *Tosaphoth* a. l., s. v. בית), 53b, bottom, and TP ibid.

[202] Comp. also Eusebius, *Hist. Eccl.* VIII. 6. 1 ff.

[203] The other Rabbinic passages where the *elogium* is mentioned (See Krauss *LW*, p. 34) do not contradict the definition given above of the word.

[204] *Debarim Rabba* II.29.   [205] So ed. prin.

.ליהרג ... הרי איפומני[מ]טא[206] שלו נקרין הרי הוא יוצא לישרף וכו'

"Behold, his ὑπομνήματα are read, he is led out to be decapitated ...[207] Behold, his ὑπομνήματα are read, he is led out to be burnt alife etc." Here the ὑπομνήματα are read before the verdict is issued. They are nothing but the *acta, gesta*, the minutes of the process, which were read before the sentence was pronounced.[208] The *elogium*, on the other hand, was usually read at the beginning of the process. (The כמוס, χάμος, will be dealt with in a special Appendix (II).

As for the פרקולא the *consensus* among the majority of scholars is to alter the word into ספיקולא[209]. But this is against the *consensus codicum* all of which read פרקולה or פריקולא[210]. The meaning of the word is obvious from the context. The Midrash associates it with the verse in Hosea (14.1): תאשם שומרון, *Samaria will be declared guilty*. Similarly, we read in *Pesikta Rabbathi*:[211] בשר ודם משמוציא אפופסין[212] אינו יכול לחזור בו, אבל הקדוש ברוך הוא חוזר בו לאחר

---

[206] So correctly Krauss, LW, p. 39.

[207] This is the meaning of ליהרג here, as the context proves. In addition to decapitation three other kinds of execution are mentioned here (and in the parallel TP Ber. IX. 1, 13a): throwing to wild beasts, burning alive and throwing into the sea. Comp. also TB Ket. 30b and parallels.

[208] Comp. *Acta Crispinae* II (Ruinart, *Acta Sincera*, 1803, III, p. 68): *acta ex codice quae dicta sunt relegantur. Et cum relegerentur Anulinus proconsul sententiam de libello legit* etc. Comp. Le Blant, *Les actes des martyrs*, p. 110–111. On the identity of the acta, gesta and the ὑπομνήματα, see E. Bickerman in *Aegyptus* XIII, 1933, p. 346 seq.

[209] See the editor's note; Fürst, *Glossarium Graeco-Hebraeum*, p. 159; Krauss, LW, p. 408. Sachs, *Beitraege* etc. II, p. 181, n. 152 (followed by Perles, *Etymologische Studien*, 1871, p. 89) explains our word to mean *proloquium*; Kohut (*Aruch Completum* VI, p. 448): φραγέλλιον; Levy (*Wörterbuch* etc. IV p. 138): πρόκλησις; Jastrow (Dictionary 1240): furcula!

[210] The same word is also found in *Pesikta deR. Kahana* 159a, *Midrash Haggadol* Exod., p. 65, and is likewise altered by the editors into ספיקולא!

[211] Ed. Friedmann, f. 183a.

[212] Ed. princ. mistakenly: איספופסין.

אפופסיס‎[213] שנאמר תאשם שומרון כי מרתה באלהיה מה כתב אחריו שובה ישראל‎. "A human being cannot revoke a verdict (ἀπόφασις) after he issues it,"[214] but the Holy one blessed be He revokes the sentence (ἀπόφασις) after it has been issued, as it is written (Hos. 14.1): *Samaria will be declared guilty for she rebelled against her God.* What follows? *Return Israel*" (ibid. 2).

Since this parallel Midrash uses ἀπόφασις instead of our פרקולא‎, it is beyond doubt that the word is nothing but *periculum*, the written draft of the sentence.[215] *Periculum*, like *tabella*,[216] is synonymous with sentence.[217]

To sum up, the procedure in the Roman court in Palestine consisted of the reading of the *elogium*, the *interrogatio* (the catching-method often used), the questioning by torture (on the *gradus, catasta*), the reading of the *acta* (*gesta, ὑπομνήματα*), the inserting of a hook (χάμος) into the mouth of the defendant and the pronouncement of the sentence (*periculum*).

The rabbis supply us also with information regarding the procedure after the sentence was issued. They often mention the appeal to a higher authority, as noted by Ziegler.[218] We shall cite one passage which has not been

---

[213] Ibid.: אפוספים‎. ·

[214] Comp. Seneca the Elder, *Controv.* VII. 7: *iudex quam tulit de reo tabellam revocare. non posset.* On *tabella* in the sense of sentence see Forcellini, *Tot. Latin. Lex.*, s. v. *tabella*; Le Blant, *Les actes des Martyrs*, p. 111, n. 3, who quotes the above Seneca.

[215] The classical dictionaries cite the term only from Nepos (*Epaminondas* 8) and Cicero (*actio in Verrem* 2, 3, 79 § 183), but it is also extant in later sources, like Cod. Theod. IV. XVII (*De sententiis ex periculo recitatis*) and others. See Le Blant, *Les persécuteurs et les martyrs*, p. 219, n. 3; p. 220, n. 3.

[216] See above n. 214.

[217] On the use of the Latin terms by the rabbis, see above, n. 140.

[218] *Die Königsgleichnisse des Midrasch*, p. 113 ff.; Hebrew part, p. XL ff.

properly understood. *Midrash Tehilim*[219] records: קטנטין[220] שרודף את האדם קובל לאפרכוס, אפרכוס רודפו קובל למלך[221]. The explanation of the word קטנטין in our dictionaries[222] is quite untenable. It is almost clear to me that we must read קטנרין[223], κεντηνάριος, centenarius.[224] The translation of the passage is therefore: "If a *centenarius* prosecutes a person the latter complains to the praefect (ἔπαρχος), if the praefect prosecutes him he complains to the king."[225] The situation well corresponds to that which prevailed in the fourth century under the *iudices militares*.

If the appeal was rejected, the convict was led to his execution. The rabbis (of the third century) quote a proverb:[226] במקום שקיפח הליסטים שם צולבין אותו. "The robber is crucified in the place where he robbed." This clearly implies that the criminal was conveyed from the place of the trial to the scene of the crime[227] where he was executed. This is confirmed by what is told in the *Acta*

---

[219] LIV, ed. Buber, p. 299, quoted by Ziegler ibid., p. XL.

[220] Both *Yalkuts* (see below) read: קטנתן.

[221] In *Yalkut Shimeoni* ad loc. the passage is quoted in the name of ר' בנימין בר יפת בשם ר' ישמעאל. But in all the editions and manuscripts (which Buber used) of the Midrash as well as in the *Yalkut Hamakiri*, p. 299, the statement is anonymous. It seems that there is an omission in the Yalkut after the word ישמעאל (which is probably a mistake for יוחנן. Comp. *Midrash Tanḥuma Tazri'a*, ed. Buber, p. 36–37).

[222] See Krauss, *LW*, p. 526; Ziegler ibid., p. 114.

[223] The רי were combined into a ת, and hence the reading קטנתן, see above, n. 220.

[224] For the reading of קטנרין instead of קנטנרין, see above n. 30. The *centenarius* is not mentioned anywhere else in rabbinic literature. However, Agadath Shir Hashirim (ed. Schechter, p. 16) mentions a military officer (the head of legion) whose salary was sixty denarii daily, which is a little less than a hundred thousand sestertii yearly, the salary of a *centenarius*. But the date of the text is uncertain.

[225] From the parallel passages (See Ziegler ibid.) it is evident that our text deals with the legal appeal of a sentence.

[226] *Pesikta deR. Kahana*, f. 187a, and parallels noted in *Debarim Rabba*, ed. Lieberman, p. 82, n. 4.

[227] Within the province, of course.

Codrati:[228] τοὺς μὲν ἄλλους ἁγίους τοὺς σὺν αὐτῷ ἐκέλευσεν ἀχθέντας εἰς τὰς ἰδίας πόλεις ἐν ταύταις διαφόροις
κολάσεσι τελειοῦσθαι. "He (i. e. the proconsul) ordered
that the other saints who were with him be taken to their
own cities and *perfected* in these various punishments."
Another version of the same acts[229] reads: ἐκέλευσεν ἕνα
ἕκαστον ἀπαχθῆναι εἰς τὴν ἰδίαν πόλιν καὶ χώραν,
κἀκεῖσε ζῶντας αὐτοὺς τῷ πυρὶ παραδοθέντας τελειω-
θῆναι. "He ordered that each of them be taken to his
own city and land and there *perfected* by burning them
alive." The translation of the Armenian version[230] reads:
"He commanded that they should all be bound and taken
to their several villages and burnt alive."[231]

The criminal was often led to the execution with the
corpus delicti hanging on his neck. We read in *Midrash
Tanḥuma*:[232] משל לגנב שנתפס תולין הגנוב על כתיפו "Like a
thief who was caught on whose shoulders they suspend
the stolen object."[233] Similarly, according to the acts of
Euplus,[234] the latter was led to the execution with the gospels
hanging on his neck.[235]

The convicted criminal himself had to carry the instrument of his execution. We find in *Bereshith Rabba*:[236]
כזה שטוען צלובו בכתפו "Like him (i. e. the convicted) who
himself carries the cross on his shoulders."[237] This practice

[228] Supposedly under Decius and Valerian. I copy from the *Archiv
f. slavische Philologie* XVIII. (1896), p. 180.

[229] *Analecta Bollandiana* I (1882), p. 462.

[230] Ed. F. C. Conybeare, *Monuments of Early Christianity*, p. 208.

[231] The *acta* utilized by Le Blant do not mention this procedure
explicitly, but they imply it. See idem, *Les actes des Martyrs*, p. 113 ff.

[232] Cod. De Rossi, as quoted by Buber, Introduction to Tanḥuma,
p. 151.

[233] Comp. also Lieberman, *Greek in Jewish Palestine*, p. 163. Comp.
also *Sifre, Balak*, 131, ed. Horovitz, p. 169.

[234] Ruinart, *Acta Sincera*, 1802, II, p. 432.

[235] *Appensum est ad collum ejus Evangelium*.

[236] LVI. 3, ed. Theodor-Albeck, p. 598, and parallels.

[237] Comp. also TP Ber. II, 5c.

of the Romans is well known.[238] We shall however quote one more rabbinic text which has been totally misunderstood. We read in *Midrash Debarim Zuta:*[239] משל למדינה שנצטרכה ללחם צעקו הבריות על ה ח ש ב ן[240] עמדו שני נחתומין והיו טוחנין כל הלילה בקשו לעשות עיסתן כבה הנר ולא היו רואין מה עשו בללו את העיסה ואפו אותה והוציאוה ומלאו את השוק. בא ה ה ח ש ב ן וראה הפת מעורבת קיבר א'ל ראויין הייתם ליתן הקופיץ בצואריכם ולהחזיר אתכם בכל המדינה, אבל מה אעשה לכם ומלאתם את המדינה בשעת הציפצוף "Like a city which was in need of bread. The people complained of the λογιστής,[241] the market-commissioner. Two bakers went to work and ground all night. They wanted to prepare their dough, but the lamp was burned out and they could not see. What did they do? They kneaded the dough, baked it, brought it forth and supplied the market. The λογιστής[242] came and saw the bread mixed with shorts (κιβάριον, cibarium). He said to them (i. e. to the bakers): You deserve to have the axe[243] hung on your necks and to be made to go around with it over

[238] See Le Blant, *Les persécuteurs et les martyrs*, p. 292–293.

[239] It was edited by Buber in his collections of this Midrash, p. 3. We shall quote it from the *Yalkut* ed. prin. (Debarim sec. 808) and collate it with Cod. Oxford.

[240] So Cod. Oxf.

[241] This is the literal translation of חשבן. It is the predilection of the *Tanḥuma*-type *Midrashim* to translate the Greek words into Hebrew. *Tanḥuma Tsav*, ed. Buber, p. 12, explicitly mentions the λογιστής. But the parallel in *Bemidbar Rabba* XX, 18, renders it בעל השוק. In the Palmyrene bilingual inscriptions we read (Cooke, *North-Semitic Inscriptions*, p. 278) in the Palmyrene: הוא רב שוק and in the Greek: ἀγορανομήσαντα. The scholion to Aristophanes, *Acharn.* 720, states: ἀγορανόμους οὓς νῦν λογιστὰς καλοῦμεν (quoted by W. Liebenam, *Philologus*, LVI, 1897, p. 317, n. 115. Comp. also the sources quoted by M. Gelzer in *Archiv für Papyrusforschung* vol. V, p. 358). Rabbinic literature frequently mentions the ἀγορανόμος. See Krauss *LW*, p. 11.

[242] A declaration from the ἀρτοκόποι, bakers (who returned their stock), to the λογιστής (year 338) is available in the *Oxyr. papyri*, vol. I, 85, col. III (see p. 147 ibid.).

[243] See Mishna Sanh. VII.3; P. Allard, *Ten Lectures* etc., pp. 261, 281.

the whole city,[244] but what can I do: You supplied the
city [with food] in a time of scarcity."[245] But for this, the
poor bakers would have had to go around the whole city
with the instruments of the execution on their necks.[246]

It goes without saying that the rabbis offer us a description of the "legal" procedure in the Roman courts of Palestine, *not* as it ought to have been (according to the Roman
laws) but as it was practiced in fact, legally or illegally.
They recorded the actual "realia" of the Roman procedure.

[244] In the Hebrew: מדינה. Comp. Adon, *Martyrol.* 9 Jan. (quoted by
Le Blant, *Les actes des martyrs*, p. 142): *Deinde sanctus Martyr vinculis
ferreis arctatus per civitatem sub voce praeconis circumducitur.*

[245] To the two occurrences of צפצוף in the sense of scarcity quoted by
Jastrow, Dictionary, p. 1298, add our passage, the parallel to Men.
(quoted by Jastrow) in *Sifre* II, ed. Finkelstein, p. 421, and *Midrash
Tehilim*, ed. Buber, p. 105 (see n. 9 ibid.).

[246] TP Yeb. (XVI, 16c, bottom) tells of the possibility that a matron
may free a condemned criminal who is led to his execution. *Midrash
Tehilim* XLV. 5, ed. Buber, p. 270, implies the same possibility. Hein-
rich Lewy (*Philologus* vol. 84, 1928–29, p. 387) identified this matron
as a Vestal virgin. He refers to Plutarch (*Vita Numae*, 10) who asserts
that when a Vestal virgin "accidentally meets a criminal on his way to
execution his life is spared." We may add that the role of the king's
daughter in the martyrdom of R. Ishmael (*Bet ha-Midrash*, ed. A.
Jellinek II, p. 67; ibid., VI, p. 23) could be explained on the basis of
this identification. For the simpler version seems to be preserved in
Midrasch Schir Ha-Schirim, ed. L. Grünhut, f. 4b. There it is a matron
who saw R. Ishmael before his execution. She asked the executioners
to tell R. Ishmael to look at her whereupon she would save him. But
he, of course, refused. This was a great offense to the matron and she
urged the executioners to flay his face. If we accept Lewy's conjecture
about the matron (the name matron for a Vestal *virgin* in rabbinic
literature is not strange, for obvious reasons), I would suggest that our
text contains an allusion to a Vestal virgin who wanted to save R.
Ishmael, provided he looked at her (i. e. saw her just as she saw him).
It will have to be supposed then that the stories about the prerogatives of the Vestal virgins reached Palestine, which is, of course, not
impossible.

On the other hand, Prof. E. Bickerman, whom I consulted on this
point, expresses his doubts concerning Lewy's conjecture. According
to him we have here, instead, a legendary motif, popular in the Orient,
where a queen or a princess intervenes in behalf of the condemned and
saves his life.

APPENDIX I (to p. 19, n. 124)

πρόοδος

The existence of a special judicial institution πρόοδος is attested neither by the definition of the word by Liddell and Scott[1] nor by Sophocles in their dictionaries. Ducange[2] quotes two instances of πρόοδος in the sense of "tribunal, iudicium." The first is from a manuscript of Cyrillus of Scythopolis[3] which reads: καὶ βάλλει αὐτὸν εἰς τὴν δημοσίαν πρόοδον, ὅπου ἦν φυλακή. "And he throws him into the public πρόοδος where there was a prison." But ed. Schwartz[4] reads: καὶ βάλλει αὐτὸν εἰς τὴν δημοσίαν φυλακήν, "and he throws him into the public prison." The editor does not record any variant from among the many mss. he used. Nor does the Slavonic version of the Life of Saba[5] mention the πρόοδος.[6] It is therefore probable that this represents a later explanatory note interpolated in the manuscript of Cyrillus.

The second instance cited by Ducange is from the Chronographia of Theophanes (IX c.), A. M. 6022:[7] καὶ Πηγάσιος . . . σὺν τοῖς τέκνοις αὐτοῦ ἐν προόδῳ ἐξητάθησαν. "Pegasios . . . and his children were examined in πρόοδος."

Prof. Ernest Honigmann has called my attention to Brockelmann's *Lexicon Syriacum*[8] who quotes פרודון from

---

[1] There is only one reference to a mediaeval glossary.
[2] *Gloss. med. Gr.*, p. 1247.
[3] *Vita Sabae* 56. The author flourished in the middle of the sixth century.
[4] P. 150.
[5] Житіе Св. Савы, Санктпетербургъ, 1890, p. 315.
[6] The editor, in a note to the attached Greek text, remarks: *Al.* πρόοδον, ὅπου ἦν φυλακή. The edition of Cotelerius is not accessible to me.
[7] Ed. Migne *PG* CVIII, 416a.
[8] P. 593b.

a Syriac source and, following Ducange, translates it: "tribunal, iudicium." However, the source which is not earlier than the seventh century (as we shall presently see) does not justify the meaning of tribunal.

Happily, I found the word in a Greek text which is not later than the fifth century and is perhaps earlier. In Prochorus's version of the *Acta Joannis*[9] we read: καὶ λαβὼν αὐτοὺς ἐγὼ ἔβαλον ἐν τῇ φυλακῇ τρεῖς ἡμέρας. τῇ δὲ τετάρτῃ ἐγένετο αὐτῶν πρόοδος καὶ κατέθεντο πολλὰ ἀσεβῆ, φαῦλα πράξαντες. καὶ ἰδὼν ὁ ἄρχων τὸ πλάτος τῶν κακῶν ὧν κατέθεντο, ἀνέπεμψεν αὐτοὺς ἐν τῇ φυλακῇ, ὅπως ἐν ἑτέρᾳ ἐξετάσει ἀκριβέστερον μάθοι τὰ περὶ αὐτῶν. "And seizing them I threw them into prison[10] for three days. On the fourth day [the time of] their πρόοδος came and they confessed[11] that they had committed many acts of impiety and deeds of evil. And when the judge (ἄρχων) realized the scope[12] of the evils they confessed, he sent them back to prison, that he might learn more accurately of their doings in *another examination*." From the text it is clear that the ἑτέρα ἐξέτασις is the equivalent of the first πρόοδος,

[9] Ed. Zahn, p. 37. On the time of its composition see ibid., p. LIX–LX.

[10] In Caesarea of Palestine.

[11] κατατίθεμαι, as a legal term, means to deposit [in court], but the present context implies the meaning of confession. See also below n. 31.

It seems to me that Prochorus drew here from the *Constitutiones Apostolorum* (II. LII. 1) which describe the procedure of the Roman court as following: κἀκείνου συγκατατιθεμένου, οὐκ εὐθέως ἐπὶ τὴν κόλασιν αὐτὸν ἐκπέμπουσιν, ἀλλὰ πλείοσιν ἡμέραις ποιοῦνται αὐτοῦ τὴν ἐξέτασιν μετὰ συμβουλίου πολλοῦ καὶ παραπετάσματος μέσου. "And although *he* (i. e. the malefactor) *confesses* [his crimes], *they do not presently send him out to punishment; but for several days they make inquiry about him* with a full council and with the *veil* (see F. X. Funk's notes in his edition, p. 149 and comp. above, p. 18, n. 116) interposed."

[12] πλάτος, or πλῆθος, the mass, see the variants ibid.

namely, examination in court.[13] Indeed, a mediaeval Glossary[14] records: *Interrogatio*, ἐξέτασις, ἐπερώτησις, πρόοδος.

The word is extant in another Greek source. We read in the *Acta Sanctorum*:[15] ὅτι Φεβρονία ἡ μοναχὴ πρόοδον δίδωσιν δημοσίᾳ... ἡ ἀδελφή μου Φεβρονία πρόοδον δίδωσιν δημοσίᾳ ... οὐκέτι[16] κατήγαγεν τὴν Ἱερίαν εἰς τὴν πρόοδον. "That the nun Febronia was publicly subjected to examination[17] ... My sister Febronia was publicly subjected to examination ... He did not bring Hieria down to the examination." The corresponding Syriac text[18] reads: דפברוניא דיריתא קדם בים דדינא מתחדינא... חתי פברוניא לבית דינא נחתת... לאי[19] אחתה לאיריא לבית דינא "That the nun Febronia is tried before the tribunal (βῆμα) of the judge ... My sister Febronia went down to the court ... He did not bring Hieria down to the court." But the older Syriac manuscript[20] instead of לבית דינא נחתת reads[21] פרדון יהבא, πρόοδον δίδωσιν, and instead of לבית דינא it reads לפרודוף[22], εἰς τὴν πρόοδον. The later manuscript[23] rendered the foreign פרודון by בית דינא, which shows that at that time πρόοδος was used in the sense of tribunal. But פרדון יהבא of the seventh century manuscript (like the Greek πρόοδον δίδωσιν) could mean only the examination and not the tribunal.

[13] It is quite surprising that Zahn did not notice the meanings of πρόοδος and κατατίθεμαι in his text. He did not even record them in his Index, p. 255.

[14] *Corp. Gloss. Lat.*, ed. G. Loewe etc. II, p. 90, l. 30.

[15] *Junii* vol. V, p. 25.

[16] P. 30, ch. 30, ibid.

[17] Comp. δίκην διδόναι in Liddell and Scott's dictionary, s. v. δίκη, p. 430b, top.

[18] Bedjan, *Acta Martyrum et Sanctorum* vol. V, p. 592.

[19] Ibid. p. 603.

[20] Add. 14647, dated year 688, see below, n. 25.

[21] Bedjan ibid., p. 592, n. 2.

[22] Ibid., p. 603, n. 1.

[23] IX century, see below n. 25.

The Greek manuscript published by the Bollandists is of the tenth century, but another Greek manuscript[24] of our acts is explicitly dated 890.[25] Jean Simon[26] concludes that the story was originally composed in Syriac and subsequently translated into Greek.[27] At the same time he asserts[28] that it is impossible to find the name of St. Febronia before the seventh century; therefore the composition itself is no older than its oldest manuscript.

Hence, the existence of πρόοδος as a legal term in the Greek sources of the fifth century[29] and the Syriac sources of the seventh century is well attested.

It is also extant in Jewish Palestinian sources. The ספר המעשים[30] records: מי שהלך לאכסניא ועשה דברים רעים ונתפש לרשות השלטון ועמד בקינדינון ונידון בפרורום (= בפרודון) יהודהי[31] שמו ושם עירו וכו' "He who went abroad[32] and was seized by the authorities and was brought to trial[33] and was tortured[34] in the πρόοδος (examination)[35] until he confessed his name

[24] Deposited in Paris, Bibliot. Nat. 1470.

[25] Jean Simon, *Analecta Bollandiana* XLII (1924), p. 70. On the date of the Syriac mss. see ibid., p. 69.

[26] Ibid., p. 76.

[27] His arguments are quite convincing, but his remark (p. 71) that פרודון was frequently used in Syriac seems to be an overstatement, since no Syriac lexicon records it except from our text.

[28] P. 69, n. 1.

[29] See above p. 40, n. 9.

[30] Discovered by Dr. B. M. Lewin of Jerusalem and published for the first time in *Tarbiz* I, fasc. 1, p. 93. The date of the passage is uncertain; probably sixth or seventh century.

[31] S. Ch. Kook (*Tarbiz* II, p. 119) correctly read here והודה, and he confessed. Comp. also TP Ber. II, 5c: נסביה ודניה ואודי ליה (see above p. 15, n. 99).

[32] לאכסניא. This word is frequently found in rabbinic literature with the meaning of "abroad" (see Lewin in *Tarbiz* ibid., p. 87–88). It means ξενία (sc. γῆ). See Liddell and Scott, p. 1188b, s. v. ξείνια II.

[33] κίνδυνος in the sense of trial is not extant in the Greek dictionaries, but it is a literal translation of the Latin *periculum* which means trial, action, etc. ועמד בקינדינון is the exact equivalent of ועמד בדין.

[34] This is the meaning of ונידון here, see above, p. 15, n. 99.

[35] Comp. the wording of Theophanes, above, p. 39.

and the name of his city[36] etc." Thus, the use of πρόοδος by the Jews of Palestine is likewise attested.

We shall not, therefore, err, in identifying our term in another, much older Jewish source. We read in *Vayyikra Rabba*[37] (in the name of rabbis who flourished in the middle of the second century): נטלו והחזירו בכל ערי ישראל וישב לו בפרדיאמוס והרנו... וישב לו בפרדיאמוס והרנו "And he (i. e. Nebuchadnezzar) took him and paraded him in every city of Israel; then he sat in פרדיאמוס and executed him . . . he sat in פרדיאמוס and executed him." Many various readings for the word בפרדיאמוס have been transmitted,[38] but all of them contain the letters דימס and the majority of them include the letters פר as well.

The context implies that וישב לו בפראדימוס is equivalent to the Hebrew וישב לו בדין. I am therefore almost certain that פרדימס, or פרדי[די]מס, is nothing else than προόδῳ δημοσίᾳ. The regular phrase met with in the *acta martyrum*[39] is: ἐκάθισεν (καθίσας) δημοσίᾳ, and in our case it will be: ἐκάθισεν ἐν προόδῳ δημοσίᾳ,[40] "And he sat for the examination publicly." He dragged around the Jewish king from city to city and questioned him in every city publicly. This practice of the Roman judges is well attested in the acts of the Christian martyrs. They were dragged from city to city after the governor and were subjected to trials and tortures in every town they stopped.[41]

---

[36] See above p. 22 and n. 146 ibid.

[37] XIX. 6. I copy from Cod. Oxford.

[38] Ed. princ. and *Yalkut* (II Kings 249) read: בפרדימס. (They have the word only once, it being omitted in the second part of the passage). Cod. Vatic. reads ביפראדימס the first time and בפראדימוס the second. Cod. Munich (as quoted by Perles, *Thron und Circus des Königs Salomo*, p. 20) reads בורדימוס the first time and ברידימוס the second.

[39] See Le Blant, *Les actes des martyrs*, p. 146. Add: *Acta Codrati* in *Analecta Bollandiana* I, p. 499.

[40] Comp. above p. 41: πρόοδον δίδωσιν δημοσίᾳ.

[41] Le Blant, ibid., p. 109.

The Rabbis portrayed the procedure of the Roman judge in their description of Nebuchadnezzar's behavior.

To sum up, it appears from almost all the texts cited above that πρόοδος means only examination and not tribunal. However the variant reading in *Vita Sabae*[42] and the readings of the later Syriac manuscript of the *Acta Febroniae*[43] suggest that the place where the examination was held was also subsequently styled πρόοδος.

II (to p. 33)

χάμος

כמוס in our Midrash is identified by Krauss[44] with κημός, muzzle. But κημός would be spelled קימוס in Hebrew and not כמוס. Perles[45] correctly recognized χάμος in כמוס and quoted a reference by Ducange[46] to the *Acta SS. Timothei et Maurae* 2,[47] which is as follows: ὁ ἡγεμὼν εἶπεν ... χάμον περίθετε αὐτῷ ... αὐτὸς ἀποκρίνασθαι οὐκ ἐδύνατο διὰ τὸ περικεῖσθαι αὐτῷ τὸν χάμον. "The governor said ... put a χάμος on him ... He could not answer because of the χάμος which was put on him."[48] Ducange equated χάμος with κημός. In this he is supported by the *Synaxarium of Constantinople*[49] which has κημός instead of χάμος.[50]

But the *Acta SS. Timothei et Maurae* seem to be no more than a mere romance, as proved by Tillemont,[51] and were

[42] See above p. 39 and n. 6 ibid.
[43] See above p. 41.   [44] *LW*, p. 292.
[45] *Etymologische Studien* etc. (1871), p. 89.
[46] *Gl. med. gr. s. v. χάμος.*
[47] *Acta Sanctorum Maii*, vol. I, p. 741.
[48] Perles' German translation of the passage is to be corrected: κρεμάσαντες κατὰ κεφαλῆς does not mean "hänget ihn am Kopfe auf," but "suspended him with his head down."
[49] Ed. Delehaye, col. 651.   [50] See below, n. 76.
[51] *Mémoires pour servir à l'histoire ecclésiastique* vol. V, p. 727 seq.

written much later than the supposed event (beginning of
the fourth century).

A second instance is recorded by Sophocles:[52] "χάμος =
κημός. Theod. Icon. 172a." The text reads:[53] οἱ δὲ δήμιοι
τὸν χάμον κατὰ τοῦ στόματος αὐτῆς ἐπιδήσαντες ἀπή-
γαγον αὐτήν etc. "The executioners bound a χάμος on
her mouth and led her away etc." The manuscripts
of the *Epistle of Theodorus of Iconium* (which recounts the
Acta SS. Cyrici et Julittae) are of the eleventh century[54]
and the authorship of the Epistle is doubtful.[55] In truth,
the older *Acta SS. Cyrici et Julittae*[56] do not mention the
χάμος at all.

Thus, both occurences of our word, quoted by Ducange
and Sophocles, are of late and doubtful origin.

However, the word also occurs in a variant reading of a
text by an author who died at the beginning of the fourth
century. Peter of Alexandria in his *Canonical Epistles*[57]
writes: χάμον[58] λαβόντες ἐν τῷ στόματι. "Having a
χάμος put in their mouths" (for the purpose of pouring
wine down their throats).[59] Here the meaning of χάμος
is clear: it is the *hamus*,[60] hook,[61] which was put into the

He refers also to our χάμος and remarks that the saint talked after the
χάμος was put on his mouth.

[52] *Lexicon*, p. 1160.
[53] I quote from the text published in the *Analecta Bollandiana* I;
p. 206.
[54] See Migne *PG* CXX, p. 165; *Analecta Bollandiana* ibid., p. 201.
[55] See *Analecta Bollandiana* ibid., p. 193.
[56] Ibid., p. 198–199.
[57] XIV, ed. Migne *PG* XVIII, p. 505a.
[58] So Migne ibid. in the variae lectiones.
[59] See the commentaries of Balsamon and Zonaras ad loc.
[60] Prof. Henri Grégoire, whom I consulted on this point, surmises
that the Greeks blended *hamus* and χάνος (a yawn, a mouth wide
open). Indeed the printed text in Migne reads here χάνον. The same
reading is extant in the commentary of Balsamon ad loc. The word
χάνος (in the sense of hook) is not recorded in any dictionary.
[61] See the Latin translation ibid., p. 506c.

mouth of the Christian in order to keep it open for pouring wine into it. Similarly, we read in the Babylonian Tal-mud:[62] ר' יהודה אומר כלבוס של ברזל מטילין לתוך פיה ... ומשקין אותה בעל כרחה "R. Judah[63] said: An iron hook[64] is inserted into her mouth ... and she is forced to drink."

That a *hook* was put into the mouth of the criminal is clearly stated in another Talmudic passage. We read there:[65] אמר ר' ירמיה בן אלעזר ... מדת בשר ודם מתחייב אדם הריגה למלכות מטילין לו ח כ ה לתוך פיו כדי שלא יקלל את המלך "R. Jeremiah b. Eleazar[66] said ... In human relationship when a man is sentenced to death by the government a *hook* is inserted into his mouth in order that he might not curse the king."[67] According to the rabbis,[68] a *hook* was inserted into the mouth of Balaam that he should not be able to curse Israel.

Likewise, Eusebius[69] records: ובבלמא פומה וספותה מתרעין הוו "And they (i. e. the *officiales* of Caesarea) tore his mouth and lips with a muzzle." This בלמא was evidently a sharp hook for inserting in the mouth of the condemned, which was on hand, and of which the *officiales* availed

---

[62] Sota 19b.

[63] Flourished in the middle of the second century.

[64] See Löw *apud* Krauss *LW*, p. 288.

[65] TB 'Erub. 19a.

[66] Flourished at the beginning of the fourth century.

[67] In the *Acta Codrati* (*Archiv für slavische Philologie* XVIII, p. 176; *Analecta Bollandiana* I, p. 454) a member of the *officium* admonishes the governor: "If you allow Codratus to go on talking he will not shrink from reviling you and the Emperors, and he will bring not a small danger upon us." (ἐὰν τοῦτον οὕτως ἐάσῃς οὐκ ἀποκνήσει σὲ καὶ τοὺς αὐτοκράτορας ὑβρίσαι, καὶ προξενίσαι ἡμῖν κίνδυνον οὐ τὸν τυχόντα).

[68] TB Sanh. 105b. Comp. *Tanḥuma Balak*, ed. Buber, p. 141 and n. 103 ibid., L. Grünhut ספר הלקוטים IV, *Balak*, f. 69a-b.

[69] Syriac version of *De martyribus Palaestinae*, ed. Cureton, p. 16. It is not extant in the Greek version IV. 10.

themselves. Finally, Hesychius, the Alexandrian, in his lexicon states: "χαμόν. καμπύλον," crooked.[70]

Thus the employment of χάμος in the sense of a hook is attested only in Palestinian and Egyptian sources,[71] whereas all the other works (both classical and Christian),[72] which mention the practice of muzzling the convicted person who is led to execution, do not talk explicitly of a bridle in the form of a hook.

This fact implies that the author of the *Acta Timothei et Maurae* has preserved some authentic information[73] regarding the judicial procedure in Egypt.[74] Although the text of the Bollandists uses the verb περιτίθεσθαι (to put around) in connection with the χάμος,[75] it seems that the original verb was ὑποβάλλειν or ἐμβάλλειν.[76] The

[70] We have drawn attention (*Greek in Jewish Palestine*, p. 32, n. 21) to Hesychius (s. v. κύμβαλον) who records βαβούλιον (a kind of cymbals) which no modern dictionary lists. The Palestinian Talmud, however, cites the word from the vocabulary of the Caesarean theatre (see ibid.). Likewise, the word λυκίσκος (pulley) reported by Hesychius (not included in any modern dictionary) is also found in a Palestinian source, in Cod. Jerusalem of the *Vita Porphyrii* (bishop of Gaza), ch. 98, ed. Grégoire and Kugener, p. 75 (See n. 1 ad loc. and p. 140 ibid. For other instances of words found only in Hesychius and Egyptian and Palestinian sources see ibid., pp. 132 and 144). The "ὀνίσκος. τεκτονικὸς πρίων" ("small ass, a saw of a carpenter") recorded only by Hesychius is exactly the same as חמור של חרשים of the Midrash (*Bereshith Rabba* LXV. 22, p. 742: נתנו אותו בחמור של חרשים והיו מנסרים אותו "He was put in an 'ass of the carpenters' and was sawn." Comp. also J. Perles, *Etymologische Studien* (1871), p. 53, n. 1 and p. 88) The importance of the Palestinian writings (including rabbinic) for the knowledge of the sources of Hesychius is therefore obvious.

[71] The phrase of the only other source in which the word occurs, the *Epistle* ascribed to Theodorus of Iconium (see above p. 45), suggests that the χάμος was not a hook, but an ordinary muzzle.

[72] See Le Blant, *Les persécuteurs et les martyrs*, p. 247, n. 1.

[73] This is the opinion of Le Blant, *Les actes des martyrs*, p. 106 seq.

[74] The martyrdom supposedly took place in Thebaide. Comp., however, *Analecta Bollandiana*, XXVI, p. 272.

[75] See above p. 44.

[76] The *Synaxarium of Constantinople* (ed. Delehaye col. 651) reads:

author of the primary version of the narrative related that the χάμος was put *into* the mouth of the convicted and not around it. This is in complete accord with other, genuine, Egyptian and Palestinian sources which record this procedure by the Romans.

καὶ κημὸν ὑποβαλόντες τῷ στόματι αὐτοῦ. The *Synaxarium Basilii* (*Acta Sanctorum, Maii;* vol. I, p. 720) reads: καὶ ξύλον ἐμβάλλει εἰς τὸ στόμα αὐτοῦ.

THE MARTYRS OF CAESAREA

By Saul Lieberman

The Jewish Theological Seminary of America

BOTH the method and some of the conlusions of my long essay "The Martyrs of Caesarea"[1] were seriously questioned in this journal.[2] Since the problems involved are quite important I deem it necessary to analyze the objections of my critic point by point.

1. On the Christian martyrs in general I contented myself with citing a few words[3] of Eusebius, an eye-witness of the Diocletian persecutions in Palestine, who said nothing about a hostile attitude of the Palestinian Jews towards the persecuted Christians. If there had been any animosity on their part toward the latter, he would certainly not have failed to mention it.[4] Subsequently I dealt only with the possible "Fearers of Heaven" *among* the Christian martyrs. Citing a case[5] of a Gentile who refused to worship idols and suffered death for the glorification of the One and only God, Creator of heaven and earth, I said: "What were the feelings of the Jews *in this and similar cases*? Eusebius himself discloses them etc." Obviously, the summary of my views given in this journal[6] is well-nigh a pure figment of the imagination.

---

[1] *Annuaire de l'Institut de Philologie et d'Histoire Orientales et Slaves*, vol. VII (1939-1944), p. 395 ff. The article will be cited by the abbreviated title — *MC.*

[2] I. Sonne, The Use of Rabbinic Literature as Historical Sources, *JQR*, vol. 36, 1945, p. 147 ff.

[3] *MC*, p. 409. I do not give here my notes which substantiated my statements.

[4] See *MC*, p. 409, n. 3.

[5] *MC*, p. 410.   [6] P. 163.

2. Now for details. I quoted[7] the following passage
from Eusebius: "They [the Jews] were the more agitated
and rent in their hearts when they heard the heralds of
the governor crying out and calling the Egyptians by
Hebrew names etc." I took it to mean that the Jews
sympathized with some of the martyrs, particularly with
those who bore Hebrew names. The Jews "were rent in
their hearts" when they saw that Gentile "Fearers of
Heaven" were going to be tortured for their refusal to
worship idols. In place of my interpretation[8] another
explanation is offered:[9] "It now at once becomes clear
why the Jews were so much 'agitated and rent in their
hearts' when the Egyptians were called out by their 'Hebrew names,' since the Egyptians were prosecuted as
rebellious Jews, and not merely as convicted Christians."
What is the evidence for this important discovery? "Eusebius tell us,"[10] it is said, "that when they were asked

---

[7] *MC*, p. 410.

[8] I referred (*MC*, p. 409, n. 3) to Eusebius (*Hist. Eccl.* IV. 15. 26 ff. =
Mart. Polycarpi XII ff.) who records that when the herald declared
that Polycarp confessed to being a Christian, the multitudes of Smyrna,
heathen and *Jews* alike, began to shout with uncontrollable wrath etc.
In the third quarter of the second century the Christains could easily
be confused with the Jews (particularly in a town outside of Palestine),
and the most natural reaction of the Jewish multitudes would be, as it
indeed was in Smyrna, to join in protest with the heathen, thereby
dissociating themselves from the Christians for their own protection.
If the Jews had behaved in a similar way in Palestine in the time of
Eusebius, would the latter have overlooked it? (See my note *ibid.*)
Would he have contented himself with the vague phrase: "They were
the more agitated and rent in their hearts?" (פקעין הוו דין ונפשתהון מצטרין
הוי). Undoubtedly, in the fourth century, and particularly in Palestine,
the distinction between the Jews and the Christians was already well
marked; the Jews were neither afraid that they might be confused with
the Christians, nor that the *privilegia Judaica* would be withdrawn
from them (See *MC*, p. 403). This, of course, obviates the arguments
raised in the criticism, p. 165 n. 31a.

[9] P. 165.

[10] P. 164.

about their names they called themselves 'Elias, and
Jeremias...' Furthermore, when asked about their
country they replied 'Jerusalem'... The national-political
aspect of the trial is here expressly stated, which, of course,
sheds new light on the whole situation." This suggestion
is reinforced by the following anachronism:[11] "In fact,
it is quite possible that there were some Jewish Sicarii[12]
among the Egyptians."

However, the passage cited above from Eusebius was evidently misunderstood.[13] These are the words of Eusebius:[14]
"When he (i. e. the judge) heard instead of his *actual*
name[15] that of one of the prophets, and it was the same with
the others: they *exchanged* the names derived from those of
idols, which their fathers had given them, for names of
prophets: Elias and Jeremias... He made a second statement in harmony with the first, saying that Jerusalem
was his city etc." Thus, the Egyptians did not reveal
their *actual* names but assumed Hebrew names to puzzle
and annoy the judge; the same applies to their reply that
their city was Jerusalem, which is typical of the sort of
replies that Christian martyrs made[16] and that perplexed
and exasperated the judges. The Hebrew names of the
Egyptians were assumed names[17] and the city of Jerusalem

[11] P. 165.

[12] In the fourth century!

[13] I am not able to check the English translation of Eusebius used
by my critic (See p. 164, n. 30), but this is, of course, immaterial for
our purpose.

[14] *De mart. Pal.* XI. 8 ff. I translate the Greek almost verbatim.

[15] Both Greek recensions read: ἀντὶ τοῦ κυρίου ὀνόματος; The
Syriac reads: חלף הו שמא ש ר י א.

[16] See Le Blant, *Les actes des martyrs,* p. 234 ff.; idem, *Les persécuteurs et les martyrs,* p. 188 ff.

[17] Of course, Hebrew names like Benjamin, Elias, Nathanial, Isaias
etc., etc. were quite common among the Christian Egyptians in the second half of the fourth century. Comp. the Index in *Hist. Lausiaca,* ed.
Butler, p. II, p. 265 ff.

was the heavenly Jerusalem,[18] as properly indicated by Eusebius himself.

My alleged failure to see the importance of the Hebrew names[19] of the Egyptians was cited as proof[20] that "this is another case[21] in which Lieberman seems to have failed to pay due attention to the context." Due attention should, of course, be paid to the context, but the text also has some claim upon our attention.

3. It is further stated:[22] "The political character of the trial offers also a plausible explanation for the choice of a certain great and populous city in the land of Palestine . . . in order to cure the local infection of Jewish resistance . . . Thus, we do not need to resort to any complicated psychological motive for the choice of the city, as Lieberman does." The reader may gain the impression that I forced Eusebius[23] to *place* the trial in Lydda "for complicated psychological reasons." The fact, however, is that Eusebius himself states the name of the city. It is only a matter of choice between two readings: Lydda or Sepphoris. After quoting external evidence for the preference of the reading Lydda, I said:[24] "This city [Lydda] was the crucial sta-

---

[18] Comp. Johannes Chrysostomus, *Homil. in St. Lucianum* 3, ed. Bareille, Paris 1866, vol. IV, p. 205. The passage is referred to by Le Blant *ibid*. Abercius in his famous inscription styles himself ἐκλεκτῆς πόλεως ὁ πολείτης, "the citizen of the Chosen City," which probably applies to Jerusalem, as interpreted by many scholars, see A. Abel, *Byzantion* III, 1926, p. 357. The importance of Jerusalem for the Christian heretics is best illustrated by Pepuza of the Montanists.

[19] Of this incidentally I made the reader conscious (see my quotation in *MC*, p. 410), but, of course, for a different reason.

[20] P. 163.

[21] On the first case see below n. 56.

[22] P. 165.

[23] Note 31, p. 165, is, of course, meaningless for the reader who will not consult my paper.

[24] *MC*, p. 412.

tion[25] on the ὁδὸς βασιλική from where the confessors could either return to Egypt as free people or continue to Phaeno as convicts. The choice of Lydda as the scene of the last trial[26] was based on psychological considerations ... There are therefore good reasons for accepting the *reading* Lod as the genuine one." This is my "complicated psychological motive for the choice of the *city*."

The new light shed by my critic could, of course, not be seen by me, because there is no evidence whatever to the effect that there was any resistance movement against Rome among the Jews of Palestine under Diocletian. Events which supposedly[27] happened some half a century later are, of course, irrelevant.

WHO IS LULIANUS MENTIONED IN *Koheleth Rabba*[28]?

4. In the Midrash given above it is stated: "R. Alexandri appeared to R. Aḥa in his dream and *revealed*[29] to him three things. 1. There is no compartment beyond that of the slain of Lydda. 2. Blessed be He Who removed the shame of Lulianus. 3. Happy is he who came here equipped with his learning." Later editions read here "*two* things" (instead of "*three* things") and add the name "Pappus" to "Lulianus."[30] The commentators identify the "slain of Lydda" with Pappus and Lulianus. The difficulty is self-evident. In the same vision the identical people are

[25] On the way from Caesarea to Phaeno where they were supposed to proceed if convicted.

[26] A parallel from Ammianus Marcellinus is adduced in n. 30 *ibid.*

[27] In a forthcoming paper I hope to deal with the alleged rebellion of the Jews of Sephhoris against Rome in 351.

[28] IX.10.

[29] The verb חמי is here a *terminus technicus* of the *visiones*, which means either to show or to reveal. See TP *Mo'ed Katan* III.5, 83a; *Megilla* I.12, 72b; *Ma'aser Sheni* II.7, 53c *passim*.

[30] On the reading see *MC*, p. 413–414, n. 38.

first called vaguely "the slain of Lydda" and immediately afterwards expressly named. The commentators who read *"two* things" (instead of *"three* things") in the Midrash had no other course than to combine the first two parts in one and make the identification. The genuine reading "three," however removes this difficulty. In addition, it is incomprehensible why the rabbis omitted the brother-martyr of Lulianus who is always associated with him in rabbinic literature.[31] And as a minor point: it is strange that the rabbis who considered martyrdom a great privilege[32] should call it a shame.[33] It is therefore logical to assume that the reference is not to the famous martyr but to another Lulianus.

Yet, the only reason for my rejecting the traditional explanation is that,[34] "Lieberman finds it difficult to understand why R. Aḥa's mind was disturbed by a fact which happened about two hundred years previously,"[35] and this is adduced as a measure by which "to determine the value of Liberman's use of Talmudic sources." My critic, on the other hand, copies and apparently accepts the original reading[36] (which has *three* parts and does *not* mention Pappus) and at the same time sees "no reason for rejecting the plain interpretation of the old commentators" (p. 168), "viz. that the 'slain of Lydda' were the famous Jewish martyrs Lulianus and Pappus"! (p. 166).

---

[31] See *MC,* p. 414, n. 39.

[32] See TP *Berakhoth* IX, 14b and parallels.

[33] Possible allusions to Biblical expressions (see p. 168, n. 38) are in this case irrelevant.

[34] P. 166.

[35] It was not disclosed that the difficulty arose after assuming that the other two parts of the vision regarded contemporary events which would naturally concern any rabbi. The nature of the concern, the place of famous martyrs in the future world, is also to be taken in consideration (See *TB Pesahim* 50a).

[36] This was not hitherto noticed by Jewish historians.

5. It is further argued (p. 168): "The fact that in the corresponding version in the Babylonian Talmud only the two other sentences are given . . . must, of course, raise the question of its authenticity." It was not, however, revealed that I dealt quite at length[37] with this "corresponding" foreign source (as well as with other parallels).

6. As to "the slain of Lydda," I properly demonstrated[38] that they can hardly be identified with Pappus and Lulianus. Who these "slain of Lydda" were remains an open question. My suggestion that the "slain of Lydda" were "Fearers of Heaven" maimed in Lydda during the life time of R. Aḥa is, of course, only a conjecture,[39] because we know comparatively little of the events in Palestine during that time.[40]

7. Now, to the final point of this chapter. Who was that mysterious Lulianus mentioned in the vision of R. Aḥa? Since Bacher came to the conclusion[41] that our rabbi was concerned with the emperor Julian's promise to rebuild the temple in Jerusalem, it is very natural to expect that the Lulianus in the vision is the same person.[42] But it was asserted (p. 168): "If, however, we identify 'Lulianus' with Julian the Apostate, the construction of the phrase is, to say the least, very awkward."[43]

Nevertheless, whoever is acquainted with the commentary of Rashi on the Pentateuch knows the predilection

[37] MC, p. 413, n. 34 and pp. 437–439.
[38] See above No. 4.
[39] As noted a. l., p. 416, n. 53. Comp. also my warning to the reader at the conclusion of my preface, p. 395.
[40] On the historic value of the statement in the Chronicle of Hieronymus (referred to in MC, p. 412) we shall dwell, D. V., in a forthcoming paper.
[41] On the authority of other passages.
[42] For Lulianus = Julianus, see MC, p. 436, n. 29.
[43] This awkwardness compelled my critic to offer his own conjecture; see below, No. 17.

of the ancient rabbis for euphemisms, or as they themselves express it: כאדם שמקלל את עצמו ותולה קללתו בחברו, "It is like a man who names somebody else in a curse when he means himself."[44] The phrase: "Blessed be He Who removed the shame of Lulianus (instead of "the shame of Israel") is not "to say the least very awkward" but quite typical.

The Crying of the Pillars of Caesarea. R. Abbahu and the Samaritans

8. I surmised[45] that the rabbinic statement of the weeping of the pillars of Caesarea when R. Abahu died referred to the occurrence which was mentioned by Eusebius. To this the following objection is raised (p. 152): "Since the rabbinic report is silent with regard to the atmospheric conditions, it might have been a foggy day in which such a phenomenon was almost normal."

The text of both the Palestinian and Babylonian Talmuds which count this occurrence among many other extraordinary phenomena testifies that the rabbis considered it very unusual. The very language of the rabbis and Eusebius demonstrates that the references are to an identical fact.

9. We are informed further (p. 153) that there is a commentary on the Palestinian Talmud by R. Samuel Yaphe-Ashkenazi who makes acceptable emendations and sound interpretations and that, after emending the text, he explains מריעין to mean "shouting with joy."

This interpretation was ignored by me for the simple reason that the verb הריע in the sense of "shouting with

---

[44] *TB Sotah*, 11a, quoted in *Rashi* to Ex. 1.10. Comp. also the usual expression שונאי ישראל, "the enemies of the Jews," instead of ישראל, "the Jews."

[45] *MC*, p. 400.

joy" (without actual trumpets) never occurs in Palestinian literature. The original reading ידעין (read ידעון) is the *lectio difficilior* and needs no emendation.[46] The scribe who luckily misunderstood here the meaning of the word ידעין left it unchanged.[47] The rabbis who often like to quote verbatim[48] probably transmitted the words of the Samaritans literally.[49]

10. Likewise we are told (p. 153) that such rationalization (i. e. that the pillars merely perspired) put by me into the mouth of the Samaritans seems to be an anachronism.

As said above, I did not put it into the mouth of the Samaritans, but I translated the correct text. Furthermore, the rabbinic student will see no anachronism in such rationalization. So, for instance, when a rabbi was asked why the *incubatio* in a heathen temple helps the sick he did not deny the fact, but replied that when the time predestined by Heaven for the duration of the sickness expires the sick man must be cured even if he was in a heathen temple.[50] In other words, it did not matter where the patient happned to be when the time for his recovery arrived; if he had resorted to the heathen temple before this time arrived he would not be cured.

11. Further I am blamed (pp. 154–155) for quoting ע״י עילא, instead of ו ל א ע״י עילא of the text. For technical reasons I was not able to cite the complete passage from the Talmud. It reads as follows:[51] ר' אבהו אסר יינן מפי ר' חייה ור' אסי ור' אמי שהיו עולין בהר המלך וראו גוי אחד שהיה חשוד על יינן

---

[46] It may be noted that R. Samuel Yaphe remarks: ומריעין גרסינן ב,,ריש". He obviously read: מדיעין.

[47] Believing that it means "they know."

[48] See my note *apud* Ginsberg in *Tarbiz*, vol. V, 1934, p. 383, n. 14, end.

[49] See *MC*, p. 401, n. 35.

[50] See *TB 'Abodah Zarah* 55a. Comp. also *Debarim Rabba* ed. Lieberman, p. 75.

[51] *TP 'Abodah Zarah* V, 44d

‫אתון אמרון ליה קוטוי. אמ' לון ולא ע"י עילא‬. R. Abbahu forbade
their [the Samaritans'] wine *on the testimony*[52] of R. Ḥiyya,
R. Assi and R. Ami, who used to ascend the "*Har Ha-
melekh*," and who came and reported to him that they
saw [there] a *Goy*[53] who was suspected of using their
[Gentiles'] wine. He [R. Abbahu] said to them: Is not this
an excuse [sufficient to forbid their wine]?" The passage
states clearly that R. Abbahu forbade the wine of the
Samaritans on the ground that *one* man was suspected of
using forbidden wine. It is certainly only an excuse. This
is also the explanation[54] of R. Moshe Margulies, a scholar
who published a commentary on the entire Palestinian
Talmud. Whoever is familiar with the style of the *Yerushalmi* will not question this interpretation.

The assertion (p. 155), "we cannot help gaining the
impression that Abbahu was reluctant to take extreme
measures against the Samaritans, and that he yielded to
the pressure of Amme and Asse" is as unfounded as it is
remarkable.[55]

12. I am likewise charged with not paying due attention
to the context.[56] It is stated (p. 158): "But it must appear
still stranger when we read the question in the context.
The discussion starts with Johanan's statement ... The
statement is followed by a question of the 'colleagues' ...
It seems therefore very likely that Abbahu's question as
well as that of the 'colleagues' was raised in the Tiberian
academy when Johanan's statement was discussed ... This

[52] Comp. Kassovsky, *Concordantiae Totius Mischnae*, p. 1430, *s. v.* ‫פי‬.
[53] According to the explanation of the *Pene Moshe*, the *goy* designates
here a Samaritan. But ‫יוי‬ may possibly be a "correction" for ‫כותי‬.
[54] This was never questioned.
[55] *TB Ḥullin* 6a does not contradict the above tradition in TP; it
rather confirms it.
[56] See above n. 21.

would, of course, rather suggest the last two decades of the third century."[56a]

The sequence of statements of rabbinic sages in the Talmud proves absolutely nothing. An opinion of a rabbi of the end of the fourth century may follow directly the statement of a rabbi of the beginning of the third century, a well known fact. The last editor arranged them according to the subject-matter.

13. We must now deal with the "strange" item as we did with the previous one which was declared "still stranger." It is asserted (p. 158): "Now[57] it appears to us rather strange, that at that age Abbahu would have 'asked' a question, and would not have ventured to decide it."

No comment is called for on this argument.

BOZRAH AND ROME

14. "Kingship had already been uprooted from Edom (= Rome), whereupon Bozrah came and supplied her with kings etc."[58] Rome was in a bad situation when her

---

[56a] This, of course, suggests also that Palestine had a δουκικὴ τάξις at that time. It is argued further (p. 160): "It appears more likely that in our passage the "taxis" — "the officium" is taken as a unit, an entity which assumes the character, the qualification of the population which it is supposed to govern." This new explanation of the word τάξις was brought forth because "to send gifts to the officium" must, according to my critic, necessarily mean to send gifts to each member individually, and it is therefore "hard to understand how it could be answered collectively" (ibid.). Similarly, it is stated (p. 161): "Unless I misunderstood Calder etc." Whether Calder was understood or misunderstood is immaterial here. My statement (MC, p. 407) was certainly misunderstood. The reference to Calder applies only to his interpretation of the word στρατεία in the inscription. As for the dismissal of the higher civil officials I referred (ibid. n. 72) to Eusebius who states clearly that the Christian dignitaries became ἄτιμοι (and, of course, as infames could be subjected to torture in any examination. See Lact. De mort. pers. XI, XIII) and hence lost all their rights.

[57] I. e., if we accept the opinion that R. Abbahu was eighty years old when he raised the question.

[58] Bereshith Rabba LXXXIII. 3, ed. Theodor-Albeck, p. 998.

emperor was assassinated, and Bozrah supplied her with
a king (who saved her), just as she did when the king of
Edom (the genuine one) died. I stated:[59] "It is clear that
this saying could be uttered not later than 249, when
Philip the Arab a native of Bostra[60] was still reigning in
Rome jointly with his son ... In the reign of Decius ...
the remark ... would have no justification"; it would have
been merely pointless, as will be demonstrated in a forthcoming paper. How one could derive from it (p. 150) that
I seem "tacitly to assume that after Philip's death Bostra,
as a bastion of the Empire, disappeared from the range of
speculation of Jewish preachers" is entirely incomprehensible to me. But granted that I did assume it, what
evidence is brought against it?

15. "But such assumption[61] is contradicted by a sermon
attributed to Aḥa ... and will flee from them to Bozrah
etc." The sermon is attributed to R. Aḥa in *Midrash
Abkir*,[62] a late and peculiar compilation.[63] The names
mentioned in this kind of late compilations, and particularly in eschatological passages, have no historic value.[64]

Moreover, it was overlooked that the passage is apparently based on the Babylonian Talmud[65] (or *Yelamdenu*)
which reads: אמר ריש לקיש שלש טעיות עתיד שרו של אדום לטעות
דכתיב מי זה בא מאדׁם חמוץ בגדים מבצרה. טועה שאינו קולטת אלא
בצר והוא גולה לבצרה וכו' "Resh Lakish[66] said: The patron
angel of Edom is destined to commit three errors, as it is

[59] *MC*, p. 399.

[60] Philippopolis in the Trachonitis (Victor, *De caes.* 28.1).

[61] See the end of the preceding number.

[62] See Buber's *collectanea* of this Midrash, p. 8 (*Haschachar* XI, 1883,
p. 412).

[63] See *idem*, p. VII.

[64] See *MC*, p. 417.

[65] *Makkoth* 12a.

[66] The reading "Resh Lakish" is absolutely certain; it is supported
by the mss. and medieval authorities. No other reading is known to me.

written: '*Who is this that cometh from Edom, with crim-
soned garments from Bozrah?* (Isa. 63.1). For it is only
Bezer that gives asylum and he will flee to Bozrah[67] etc.''
This statement by a contemporary of Philip, who predicts
that the patron angel of Edom will flee for protection to
Bostra by no means weakens my argument but rather
strengthens it. I dismissed this point because it needs
further investigation. It was already pointed out[68] that according to Resh Lakish's opinion, as recorded in both Talmuds and in the *Midrashim*,[69] Bostra was a place of asylum;
hence the patron angel of Edom would make no mistake!
It is therefore possible that we have to agree with Horowitz[70]
that Resh Lakish referred here not to Bostra in the Trachonitis, the place of asylum, but to Bozrah in Edom.[71] He
took the Bozrah of Isa. 63.1 in its true sense. The mistake
of the angel of Edom would be that he would, like my
critic, pick the wrong Bozrah.

The Use of Rabbinic Literature as Historical Sources

16. My critic not only instructs us to use rabbinic
sources in a sober and conservative manner, but solemnly
declares (p. 149): "Measured by the classical standard of
source criticism according to which the authenticity of even
official documents must be critically ascertained the Midrashic evidence is rather dubious." "The classical stand-

---

[67] The passage in *Abkir* is defective, for the reply to the claim of the
patron angel of Edom makes no sense. It is to be supplemented by
the text from the Talmud. Comp. also the reading of *Aggadoth Hatalmud*, f. 123b quoted in דקדוקי סופרים, 11a, n. 50.

[68] See *Tosaphoth, Aboda Zarah* 58b. *s. v.* בצר.

[69] See Lieberman, *Debarim Rabba*, p. 61, n. 4 and p. 62 n. 17.

[70] *Palestine And The Adjacent Countries*, Vienna 1923, p. 170, *s. v.* II
בצרה.

[71] Now אל בוצירה. See Horowitz *ibid.*

ard of source criticism" applied in the criticism of my paper has already been sufficiently demonstrated, but we shall however discuss the first and last points, by which it is sought to prove that the "Midrashic evidence is dubious" and which aim "to point out the perplexities and vagueness of the rabbinic sources" (p. 169). The plain passage[72] "Bozrah came and supplied her (i. e. Rome) with kings" can only mean that a man born in Bozrah became emperor of Rome. However it is stated (p. 150): "The very identification of 'Bozrah' with 'Bostrah'[73] is doubtful . . . since Edom was generally identified with Rome (Roman empire in the west)[74] the identification of the parallel 'Bozrah' with the Roman empire in the east must have automatically presented itself as soon as the division of the empire took place under Diocletian."

It is admitted (p. 151) that there is no evidence whatever for the assumption that Bostra symbõlized the Eastern empire; why then violate the simple meaning of the text? Why blunt the point of the saying?

17. The last item is even more typical. After performing a serious operation on the text of the Midrash (p. 168) it is suggested[75] (true as a mere conjecture) that "blessed be He Who removed the shame of Lulianus"[76] was a benediction recited by the rabbi when a place was shown to him where idol worship was uprooted. The shame of Lulianus means the "Roman emperor worship which began with Caesar." Besides the flagrant defiance of the text, we have to change לוליאנוס, Julianus,[77] into לוליוס (or יוליוס), Julius,

[72] See above n. 58.
[73] This is very frequently mentioned in rabbinic literature. See Horowitz *ibid. s. v.* III בצרה. [S. L.]
[74] In the west only? [S. L.]
[75] N. 40 *ibid.*
[76] See above No. 7.
[77] See above n. 42.

and to credit a fourth century rabbi with the knowledge that Roman emperor worship began with Caesar![78] Rabbinic literature is certainly not so vague and perplexing if it is only handled by competent hands.

I conclude with a correction of one of my errors. In my essay I copied thus:[79] R. *Abbahu* said etc." I did not notice that some mss. have here the variant "Abba" (instead of "Abbahu"), a reading which, if true, would invalidate my argument. Although the reading of the edition (R. Abbahu) is probably the genuine one,[80] yet no variant, in such cases, should be omitted. I am indebted for the correction of this omission to Dr. Isaiah Sonne

[78] Note that the rabbi of the fourth century calls him Julius and not Julius Caesar!

[79] *MC*, p. 399.

[80] It is supported by the two best mss. of the Midrash and by *Sechel Tob* I, p. 211.

CHANGES IN THE DIVINE SERVICE OF THE SYNAGOGUE DUE TO RELIGIOUS PERSECUTIONS

By JACOB MANN, Hebrew Union College, Cincinnati, Ohio.

CONTENTS

INTRODUCTION*

RELIGIOUS persecutions, or rather persecutions directed
against the steadfast adherence of the Jewish people to its
conception of God and His teachings, naturally aimed first of all
at the divine service of the synagogue. There the Jewish people
gave public expression to its religious beliefs, its hopes and aspirations. The liturgy of the synagogue reechoed the doctrine of
Judaism, proclaimed the unity of God and the uniqueness of

*The following abbreviations, besides the customary ones for periodicals,
will be used in the subsequent pages.
'Amram = סדר רב עכרם נאון, ed. Warsaw, 1865; ed. Fr. = סדר רב עסרם הסלם, ed.
    Frumkin, Jerusalem, 1912.
Elbogen = Elbogen, *Der jüd. Gottesdienst*, 1913; the notes are cited from the 2nd
    edition.
'Ittim = Judah b. Barzillai, ספר העתים, ed. Schor, 1902.
Mann = Mann, Genizah Fragments of the Palestinian Order of Service (in
    Hebrew Union College Annual, II, pp. 269–338).
Nöldeke, *Tabarī* = *Geschichte der Perser u. Araber zur Zeit der Sassaniden.* Aus
    der arab Chronik des Ṭabarī übersetst u. mit ausführlichen Erläuterungen u.
    Ergänzungen versehn von Th. Nöldeke, Leyden, 1879.
S. E. R. = סדר אליהו רבה וסדר אליהו זוטא, ed. Friedmann, 1902.
Soferim = מסכת סופרים, ed. Müller, 1878.
Vitry = מחוור ויטרי, ed. S. Hurwitz, 1889.
או"ז = Isaac of Vienna, אור זרוע, Zhitomir.
תשובות הגאונים = נ"ל, ed. Musafia, Lyck.
ד"ס = R. Rabbinovicz, דקדוקי סופרים.
תשובות הגאונים חמדה גנוזה = ח"נ, Jerusalem.
תשובות הגאונים הלכות פסוקות = ה"פ, ed. Müller.
שבה"ל = Ṣedekiah b. Abraham, שבלי הלקם, ed. Buber.
ש"ש = Isaac ibn Gayyat, שערי שמחה, ed. Bamberger.
תשובות הגאונים שערי תשובה = ש"ת.
בית נכות ההלכות או תורתן של ראשתים = תש"ר, ed. Horowitz, 1881.

Israel, and reiterated the story of the Bible, the exalted orations of the Prophets and the soul-stirring outpourings of the Psalmists. Within the scheme of the order of divine service of the synagogue the preachers and interpreters found the opportunity of instructing and edifying the worshippers by the living word of the Torah.

Some of these doctrines, publicly proclaimed in the synagogue, were construed by the ruling religions as challenges to their own teachings. The arm of the state was wielded to proscribe these doctrines. The Jews had to bow to the *force majeure* without giving up in the least their cherished beliefs and without their spiritual leaders lacking in ways and means of how to nullify the edicts that violated their elementary rights of religious conviction. Changes had to be made in the service to meet the new conditions imposed by the power of the state and the traces of these changes remained even after the emergencies, that had called them forth, disappeared with the setting in of new eras in the history of the nations to whom the Jews were subject.

We propose to discuss here anew the data recording these changes in the service of the synagogue. The material available refers chiefly to the two great centers of Jewry at the beginning of the Middle Ages, to Palestine and to Babylon. The triumph of Christianity in the Roman Empire since the times of Constantine the Great (312 C. E.) till the conquest of the Holy Land by the Arabs (634–40 C. E.) had as a sequel the rising tide of intolerance towards the Jews in Palestine. In Babylon a change to the worse in the condition of her large Jewry set in towards the end of the reign of Yezdejerd II (454–5 C. E.) continuing with interruptions again to the period of the arrival of the Arabs (637 C. E.). The liturgy of the synagogue in both these countries received its more or less fixed form just during these periods when it had at the same time to withstand the pressure exerted by the ruling religions of Christianity and Zoroastrianism respectively. The records of this pressure and of the counteraction on the part of the Jewish spiritual leaders are scanty and often obscure. They are not contemporaneous but date chiefly from the Gaonic period when both Palestine and Babylon were already under Muslim sway. Yet they evidently are more or less based on trustworthy traditions that have come down from the times of trial and tribulation

The two great religious persecutions that visited the Jewish people in Palestine previously, the one of Antiochus Epiphanes (168 B. C. E. and following) and the other of Hadrian (135–138 C. E.) have left no recorded changes in the liturgy[1], in the first instance, and only a few cases, in the second one, for the good reason that during both of them the practice of Judaism as a whole had been prohibited. There was no question of modifying or eliminating certain features of the liturgy when the whole service of the Temple, in the former case, and of the synagogue, in the second one, had been proscribed as a part, indeed a prominent one, of the obnoxious religion of Judaism. Not so in the periods under discussion in this paper when Judaism as a whole had to be granted the right to existence and the state in Byzantium and in Persia respectively, at the instigation of the spokesmen of the ruling faiths, insisted only upon the elimination of certain objectionable features, which it had construed as public challenges on the part of the Jews to the doctrines of the respective religions supreme in the two empires then containing the predominant part of the Jewish people.

In Babylon these objectionable features consisted of the emphatic declaration of the unity of God (the Shema') as against the dualism of Zoroastrianism. A distinct polemic against the latter was also found in the exalted orations of Deutero-Isaiah that were used in the Haftarot (נחמות שביעיה). In Palestine more features of the liturgy found offence in the eyes of the church upheld by the Byzantine government. The Shema', the Trishagion (Ḳedushah), the 'Amidah (especially the twelfth benediction known as ברכת המינים), the preachings and teachings of the Rabbis (the Deuterōsis)—these were the offensive portions which the

---

[1] About the supposed introduction of the Haftarah owing to Antiochus' prohibition of the reading of the Torah, see *infra*, p. 282. About the change in the time of sounding the Shofar on Rosh Hashanah, stated to have taken place during the Hadrianic persecutions, see *infra*, p. 299 ff., and about the rite of Tephillin, *infra*, p. 296. The changes in several religious customs owing to the dangers (סכנה) during the Hadrianic persecutions are outside the scope of this paper which deals only with the service of the synagogue.

state tried to eliminate from the public service of the synagogue. These points will be discussed here seriatim adding for completeness sake other details of the divine service that called forth objections in the Gentile environment in which the Jews were living.

Since our data are not contemporaneous but emanate chiefly from the later Gaonic period they have to be taken with great caution. The question frequently arises whether they are not *post eventum* explanations of liturgical features that could not be accounted for otherwise and therefore the general hypothesis of having been due to שעת השמד[2] was conveniently advanced as their reason. Yet this general and oft repeated tradition of changes in the liturgy because of religious persecutions seems to be well-grounded and it would be hypercritical to dismiss it altogether as unhistorical. Anyhow the problem deserves to be traced and examined in its manifold ramifications.

I

CHANGES DUE TO THE OPPOSITION AGAINST THE SHEMA'.

It would not be in keeping with our theme to discuss here anew the origin of the Shema' in the service of the synagogue and to trace the successive stages through which the Shema' was formed into a composite whole consisting of three Biblical passages (Deut. 6.4–9, 11.13–21 and Numbers 15.37–41) introduced and concluded by benedictions (see Ber. 1.4)[3] The recital of the Shema' *twice daily*, morning and evening, was already an old established custom in the first century, C. E., still before the destruction of the Second Temple. The Shema' assumed its characteristic significance not only as a solemn theological asseveration of monotheism as against dualism, trinity or polytheism but by the very designation of its first section (Deut.

---

[2] The prototype for this general hypothesis would thus be the passage concerning the change in the time of sounding the Shofar in R. H. 32b בעצה נורה המלכות, the correct reading of which is בעעת העבר צו (cf. *Dikduke Soferim*, a. l.). See *infra*, p. 299, note 124.

[3] For the existing literature on this problem see Elbogen, *Der jüd. Gottesdienst*, p. 16, and notes (2nd ed.) pp. 513–515.

6.4–9) as "the acceptance of the yoke of heaven" (קבלת עול מלכות
יָמַיִם, cf. M. Ber. 2.2, Babli 13b, 14b) the Shema' had also a
political connotation as a challenge to the yoke of Rome, the
wicked mundane rule. The third section with its concluding
reference to the redemption from Egypt and the subsequent
Geullah benediction kept afresh in the minds of the people the
hope of the ultimate restoration of Israel when the eschatological
"kingdom of heaven" would become supreme on earth.

The Talmudic literature records the recital of the Shema'
only twice daily in accordance with the verse in Deut. 6.7 ובשכבך
ובקומך, cf. Ber. 1.3: בשעה שבני אדם שוכבים ובשעה שבני אדם עומדים).
It became a characteristic token of Israel that declares "the unity
of God twice daily with love."[4] Yet in the post-Talmudic
liturgy that has come down to us the first verse of Shema' recurs
several times in the service outside the scheduled place assigned
to the Shema' in the conjunction with the Tefillah of Shaḥarit
and Ma'arib. What were the causes of these insertions? Some
reasons advanced by the early authorities trace these insertions
to the times of persecutions (שעת השמד) and therefore claim our
attention here.

1. SHEMA' IN THE SECTION לעולם יהא אדם.

The portion of the morning service preceding ברוך שאמר,
which was usually recited by the individual Jew at home before
proceeding to the synagogue for the public worship,[5] contains the
first verse of Shema'. In the Palestinian ritual it is introduced

---

[4] Thus in the morning prayer, to be discussed forthwith: אשרינו ... שאנו
משכימים ומעריבים ערב ובקר ואומרים בכל יום הכיד ומיחדים את שמך ואומרים שמע וכו'
(this is the reading in 'Amram, ed. Fr., I, 51a, but Vitry, p. 60, has שמך ומיחדים
פעמים); in Ḳedushah of Musaph (to be discussed farther on, p. 251 ff.), יחון עם
פעמים באהבה (the phrase המיחדים שמו ערב ובקר פעמים באהבה שבע אומרים was attacked already by Ben Baboi (about 800 C. E.), see *infra*, p. 255, note 26); likewise in the litany of והוא רחום we read שכך פעמים בכל יום המיחדים אום וחון. See
also Cant. R. 7.11: ומיחדים שמו שתי פעמים ואומרים שמע וכו'. Cp. further S. E. R.,
pp. 13 and 15, and especially *infra*, notes 7 and 18.

[5] See the data discussed by Mann, *H. U. C. Annual*, II, p. 273, and cf.
also the account of Natan Ha-Babli (in Neubauer, *Med. Jew. Chron.*, II, 83):
וחזן הכנסת מתחיל ברוך שאמר וכו'.

boldly after the benediction for the Torah (Mann, 280, 293), but in the Babylonian rite it is to be found within the beautiful section beginning with לעולם יהא אדם ירא שמים בסתר and leading up to the privilege of Israel to declare the unity of God by the declaration of the Shema'. This verse is followed by a significant benediction emphasizing the sanctification of God's name in public and in conclusion the prayer for the restoration of Israel is expressed (see the version in 'Amram, ed. Fr., I, 51a). The whole section was evidently known to the author of Seder Eliyahu Rabba (c. 19, ed. Friedmann, 118) where it is cited in a greatly shortened form due to the copyists, who only indicated its beginning and its end (see Friedmann's notes, a. l.). It is questionable whether the whole section was originally composed by the author of this Midrashic work, as it is frequently assumed, because he introduces it with the formula מיכן אמרו.[6] The whole setting of this section suggests a time of religious tribulation and trial when the declaration of the unity of God could only be made in secret (בסתר), viz. in the home of the individual Jew and not at the public worship. The benediction praising *God* for sanctifying His name in public (by some manifest action of His) significantly alludes by contrast to a time that demanded of the Jew (a *mere human being*) a sacrifice in doing this publicly. With right intuition R. Benjamin b. Abraham 'Anav, brother of the author of *Shibbole Ha-Leḳeṭ* (13th century), explains that the author of S. E. R. referred to a period when the Shema' could not be recited at the public worship of the synagogue and hence he impressed upon his contemporaries the duty of acknowledging the kingdom of heaven privately.[7]

[6] The text there omits בסהר after ירא שמים but several authorities had this significant word as is evident from the discussion in שבה׳ל to be cited forthwith. Also 'Amram has it.

[7] שבה׳ל, ed. Buber, p. 6:

ורבינו שלמה ז׳ל (Rashi) הרגיל שלא לוכר .לעולם יהא אדם ירא שמים בסתר׳ ספני שתוהין לומר: וכי בסתר יהא אדם ירא שמים ולא בגלוי?... וגאון אחד כה.ב שדגון לאוכרו... ור׳ בניסין אחי נר׳ו כתב כראוי לוכר .בסהר׳ כלא אכרו אבא אליהו אלא כנגד דורו כל ככד כנזרו שלא לקרוא את שמע ולא היו יכולין להיות יראין בגלוי. על כן הזהירם חרזם לקבל עליהם עול כלכות שכים בסתר. תדע לך שכן הוא שאוכר .חייבין אנו לוסד לפניך הכיד שמע בכל יום כו׳ וסיחדים את שמך פעמים באהבה ואוכר ואוכר׳ read= ואוטרים) כמע ישראל כו׳׳. ועל כן אוסר .ברוך המקדש שמו ברבים׳ לפי שבשעה השסד אין שכו מקודש ברבים אלא בסתר, על כן אין אנו לסנות.

Elgogen (p. 91) thinks it not impossible that R. Benjamin
was right in his explanation and yet regards it more likely that
the first verse of Shema' was inserted there in order to not delay
the time set for its reading.   His evidence is 'Ittim (p. 253)[8]
which, in dealing with Sabbath morning, recommends that the
weekly Sidrah should not be gone over at home before proceeding
to the synagogue in order not to delay זמן ק"ש.   This offers no
proof whatever for Elbogen's preferred explanation of the insertion of Shema' at this juncture.   But there is another statement
(not cited by Elbogen) in a MS. Munich (given by Perles, M. G.
W. J., XXV, 370–71) which probably emanates from the author
of 'Ittim, R. Judah b. Barzillai, and which shows that this argument of the delay of זמן ק"ש was unknown and is therefore quoted
as "a great secret" (סוד גדול).[9]   The whole passage was written
by a critic of the Piyyuṭim and, as Judah b. Barzillai was such a
one (as is evident from 'Ittim, p. 251 ff.), we may suggest that our
statement is to be found in the missing part of 'Ittim dealing with
the early morning service.   Hence in the MS. the beginning
should read somewhat like ונמצא בספרו של [מה"ר יהודא סוד גדול וכו'.

Be that as it may, the whole argument is hardly cogent or
logical.   On the basis of the statement in Ber. 13b a reference to
יציאת מצרים, as the conclusion of the Shema', is supposed to be
found in the lectionary הודו where Ps. 81.11 is included.   But
this lectionary was recited in public (בצבור) after ברוך שאמר and
not ביחידות as the Shema' in לעולם יהא.   Moreover the whole
lectionary was not at all fixed in earlier times.   It is missing the
Siddurim of 'Amram and Sa'adya (see 'Amram, ed. Fr., I, 70a,
note in מקור הברכות).   It is also not found in the Palestinian
ritual though Soferim indicates its beginning (see Mann, p. 276).

All these passages, quoted by R. Benjamin, were evidently in his copy of S. E.
R. but were omitted by later copyists. Cp. also Friedm., מבוא, p. 80. See
also Tanya, ed. Hurwitz, p. 11.

[8] Thus more correctly than p. 249, given in his notes (p. 527), which contains nothing on this subject.

[9] מה"ר יהורא סוד נדול שלכך תקנו חכמים קדמונים לומר .אשרינו שאנו משכים ומעריבים
ואוכרים בכל יום שכע ישראל' משום דשמע זה ק"ש של ר' יהודה הנשיא (see Ber. 13b). וכתכם
דהוא ור' יהודה הנשיא) כהדר אשמעתא דיציאת מצרים כראיתא .כדי להוכיר יציאת מצרים
בזכנה' (see ibid.) תיקנו בפסוקי דזכרה .אנכי ה' המעלך כארץ מצרים' (Ps. 81.11)
שאם יאחרו ביוצרות ופיוטים סיקרא ק"ש שלא בזמנו די להם בראשונות כר' יהודה הנשיא.

Following therefore the more probable clue of R. Benjamin b. Abraham 'Anav the date and place of this עעת השמד should be considered. Krauss (*Studien z. byz.-jüd. Geschichte*, 146–7) regards in a haphazard manner S. E. R. to be a product of Byzantium and the religious persecution, alluded to in S. E. R., is referred to those of "a Leo the Isaurian (723), a Basileos (868)!" But this view collapses under the weight of the historical evidence at our disposal. How is it that the whole passage from לעולם יהא to בשובי את שבותיכם לעיניכם אמר י״י is entirely missing in the Palestinian ritual but was taken over in the Babylonian Siddur? Surely the Holy Land was nearer to Byzantium than the distant Babylon. Moreover the persecution of Basileos (868) can hardly be considered in view of the fact that 'Amram, whose eighteen years of Gaonate (the first ones of which were in rivalry to R. Naṭronai) fall between 862–80, already has the whole passage as a regular part of his Siddur sent to Spain. Needless to say passages from a Midrash, supposedly written in Byzantium, were not incorporated by the Geonim with such speed in their ritual. Moreover a careful examination of the contents of S. E. R. clearly shows that the author lived for a considerable time in Babylon and that in a good deal of his work he depicted conditions of Jewish life in that country (see Appendix at end of this paper, *infra*, p. 302ff.). He himself was arrested during a raid carried out by the Persian authorities at the instigation of the fanatical Magians. As a result of this arrest the author records a disputation of his with a learned Magian on controversial matters pertaining to Judaism and Zoroastrianism. The dates to be found in the work, which lead down to the 10th century,[10] were evidently changed by the copyist whose text became the prototype of our texts, to suit his own time when he had prepared his transcript.

---

[10] Pp. 6–7: בעוניתו חרבו נכנס עלינו שעבוד בחוך שני אלפים של יסות המשיח ויצא מהן יותר משבע מאות שנה leads down to a date after 940 C. E. (4700 A. M.) and p. 163: ומשחרב והבית השני) ועד עכשיו הרי תשע מאות brings us to 968. A third date gives an intermediate year, viz. 944 (p. 37: נמצא מיום שנברא העולם ועד עכשיו תשעים וס׳ ד׳ שנים (i.e. jubilees) וארבעה עולכים. The first date שנה מאות משבע יותר is cited in Yalḳuṭ Makhiri to Zechariah (14.7) as שנה וארבע ושמים מאות שש, viz. 904 (see Poznanski, Z.f.H.B., XIII, 132), which shows clearly how the copyists changed the dates to suit their own times.

The passage in S. E. R., reflecting the religious persecution under discussion with regard to the Shema', rather helps us to fix the time of redaction of the book, viz. not long after the fanatical outbreak against the Jews in Babylon and in Persia under Yezdejerd II (454–5) during which the recital of the Shema' was forbidden as being a challenge to Zoroastrianism, as is expressly reported by the Geonim (see *infra*, p. 256 ff.) in connection with the Shema' in the Ḳedushah. The arrest of the author (or redactor) and his discussion with a Magian should be fixed in this time of trial and tribulation. The Jewish authorities of the time at first impressed upon their coreligionists the duty of reciting the Shema' (at least the first verse) privately in their homes before proceeding to the synagogue for the morning service. In the course of the religious persecution they invented also the strategem of inserting the beginning and the end of the Shema' in the Ḳedushah. The whole beautiful section from לעולם יהא and onwards formed an impressive setting for the private acknowledgment of the unity of God and His kingdom. The author of S. E. R. quotes it as an anonymous composition of the Babylonian Rabbis of the time (מיכן אמרו). It was, however, not taken over into the Palestinian ritual, though the first verse of Shema' occurs therein before ברוך שאמר, either as a later compromise with the Babylonian custom or perhaps as a reminiscence of the custom of R. Judah the Patriarch.

The redaction of S. E. R. not long after 455 renders it pretty certain that it should be identified with סדר אליהו רבה and its supplementary part סדר אליהו זוטא, cited in Ket. 106a, though the story related there connects it with R. 'Anan, the contemporary of R. Naḥman b. Jacob (end of 3rd and beginning of 4th centuries). The author preferred to remain in obscurity citing several episodes and statements in the name of "Father" Elijah (אבא אליהו), the great personality in Jewish folklore since Biblical times. The legendary relationship between Elijah and R. 'Anan was seized upon by the Saboraim in the 6th century to attribute to the latter the already by then famous work Seder Eliyahu Rabba and Zuṭṭa.[11] Yet it is not out of question to

---

[11] In the story in Ket. 106a, top, the phrase דהוה סתני ליה סדר דאליהו seems to be a Saboraic gloss to explain the preceding sentence רב ענן הוה רגיל אליהו

assume that there were known in Babylon as well as in Palestine teachings and episodes relating to Elijah which the author, living in the second half of the 5th century, incorporated into his work giving it the peculiar phraseology and form that render it as one of the most interesting literary productions in the field of Midrash. The reason for his division of the work into two parts, Rabba and Zuṭṭa, is not clear. Who knows whether he himself did not use the legend concerning R. 'Anan as a means to hide his own identity? Hence the Saboraim were guided by genuine tradition to declare the work to contain the substance of Elijah's teachings to R. 'Anan.[12]

2. Shemaʿ in the Ḳedushah.

The Ḳedushah in Musaph on Sabbaths and Festivals in the prevalent rites contains the insertion of the Shemaʿ in a characteristic setting which again recalls a time of aroused religious feeling owing to outside opposition. After the actual Trishagion and its accompanying verse of Ezek. 3.12 (which will be discussed *infra*, p. 261ff.) the text turns abruptly to a plea for God's mercy on the people that declare His unity daily, morning and evening, "twice with love" proclaiming the Shemaʿ (citing the first verse). Then comes the emphasis that only "He is our God, our Father, our King, our Savior,"[12a] pleading again for His mercy to

---

עד דאפיק ליה as if סדר דאליהו existed even before R. 'Anan. Likewise, דאתי נביה סדריה seems to be an insertion—all in order to justify the Saboraic identification והיינו דאכרי סדר אליהו רבה, סדר אליהו זוטא.

[12] The general conclusions are given here reserving further discussion of the problem of S.E.R. for the Appendix (*infra*, pp. 302–10).

[12a] The juxtaposition of these attributes "Father, King and Savior" has evidently a polemical emphasis against Christianity which designated Jesus by the last two terms besides ascribing to him divinity ($\theta\epsilon\dot{o}s$). As is well-known, Jesus is styled in the N.T. King ($\beta\alpha\sigma\iota\lambda\epsilon\dot{v}s$) and savior ($\sigma\omega\tau\dot{\eta}\rho$). In the well-known hymn אין כאלהינו we have also the juxtaposition of the attributes God, Lord, King and Savior, stressing still more the emphasis against Christianity which designated Jesus as lord ($\kappa\dot{v}\rho\iota os$). This hymn is evidently modeled after the above passage in the Ḳedushah and perhaps would warrant the reading there אדונינו too instead of אבינו. The hymn is found in the Palestinian ritual for Saturday night with the proper beginning כי כאלהינו (see Mann, pp. 319, 324–5). In the light of the above remarks it probably dates from the

become manifest by the redemption of Israel when His divinity
will be proclaimed before all mankind, and concluding with the
last phrase in the Shema', viz. ‎אני יי אלהיכם‎. 'Amram (ed.
Frumkin, II, 50b) briefly indicates this insertion: ‎כהר יתנו לך, ומוסיף‎
‎(ש"ץ) .פעמים באהבה‎, ‎ואומרים (הקהל‎. ‎שמע ישראל"‎. ‎ויש מוסיפין .להיות לכם‎
‎'לאלהים אני ה' אלהיכם‎. ‎ובדברי קדשך וכו‎ (see also I, 139b, where R.
Naṭronai Gaon mentions ‎פעמים‎ and ‎להיות לכם לאלהים)‎. The
author of Pirḳe de R. Eliezer (c. 4, end) seems to allude to this
enlarged Ḳedushah when in conjunction with the Trishagion
recited by the angels above he adds: ‎וישראל גוי אהד בארץ שהם מיהדים‎
‎שמו תמיד בכל יום עונים ואומרים .שמע ישראל ה' אלהינו ה' אחד"‎. ‎והוא משיב‎
‎גו.לעמו ישראל .אני ה' אלהיכם" המציל אתכם מכל צרה‎ The author of this
Midrash probably lived in Palestine at the beginning of the 8th
century (as will be shown elsewhere).

This insertion of Shema' into the Ḳedushah formed the subject of a discussion already in the early Gaonic period. R.
Yehudai, Gaon of Sura (c. 760 C. E.), is the earliest authority
mentioned who traced it to a persecution in Palestine in the course
of which both the Shema' and the daily Tefillah were proscribed
by the government. The Jews were only permitted to assemble
in their synagogues on Sabbath morning to recite and to intone
the Sabbath 'Amidah with the Piyyuṭim connected therewith.
As a subterfuge the Shema' was inserted into the Ḳedushah, viz.
the Ḥazzan would intone the beginning and the end of the
Shema' in such a manner as not to be noticeable to the officials
watching the service (see also *infra*, p. 259, note 32). This prohibition ended with the overthrow of Byzantine rule in Palestine
in consequence of the arrival of the Arabs (634–40). This

Byzantine period. Who knows whether its composition did not take place at
about the same time as the passage in the Ḳedushah? Hence the hymn has
not been adopted from the mystics as found in Hekhatot R. (c. 4, beginning:
‎כי כמלכנו...מי כיוצרנו מי כה' אלקינו‎, see Bloch, *M.G.W.J.*, XXXVII, 311) but
rather the author of this mystical tract used the phraseology of this hymn in a
modified form.

‎גו‎ R. David Lurya in his commentary (p. 11b, note 62) rightly points out
that the concluding phrase "Who redeems you from all trouble," alludes to the
insertion of the beginning and the end of the Shema' into the Ḳedushah in
consequence of the religious oppression which involved the prohibition of the
recital of the Shema'.

historical information reads in the words of Ben-Baboi,[14] who
recorded it, as follows: וכן אמר מר יהודאי ז'ל עמרו שמד על בני ארץ
ישראל שלא יקראו קרית שמע ולא יתפללו15, והיו מניחין אותן ליכנס שהרית
בשבת לומר ולזכר16ז מעמדוה17ו, והיו אומרים בשהרית בשבת מעמד17ו וקדוש
ושמע במוסף18ו, והיו עושים דברים הללו באונס, ועכשיו שכילה הקב'ה מלכות אדום
וביטל מרותיה ובאו ישמעלי9ם1 ונתניחום לעסוק בהורה20ה ולקרא קרית שמע
ולההפלל אסור לומר אלא דבר דבור במקומו כתיקון הכז'ל תורה20ה במקומה
ואסור ההרא21 במק'22 והפילה וקריית שמע במקו'23ם וכל ברכה וברכה וכל דבר
ודבר כתיקון הכז'ל במק' ובזמנו.

[14] A substantial portion of Ben-Baboi's work, known as פירקוי דבן באבוי,
has been published by Mann, *R.E.J.*, vol. 70, 129 ff. (See also the additional
passage given by J. N. Epstein, ibid., vol. 75, 179 ff.). Our passage is found on
p. 133. See the discussion of this problem, ibid., pp. 122–128, which, however,
is augmented here in several points.

[15] Evidently because the Shema' was regarded as a challenge to the doctrine of the trinity and the daily 'Amidah contained ברכת הכיצים (12th benediction) with its reference to the Christians (ולונצרים) as is evident from the Palestinian version of the 'Amidah (see Schechter, *JQR*, X, 657, and Mann, *H.
U. C. Annual*, II, 296.

[16] ולומר is not a dittography of ולוכר but refers to the intonation of the
מעמדות, Piyyuṭim, by the Ḥazzan. See notes 17 and 21.

[17] מעכדות denote, as J. N. Epstein has rightly pointed out (*R.E.J.*, vol.
75, 183, note 2), the Piyyuṭim inserted into the first 3 benedictions of the
'Amidah (as born out by 'Amram, ed. Warsaw, 47b, bottom: ויורד ש"ץ ואומר
בכנן ובחיה והמלך הקדוש סעכד שיש בו ריצוי וסליחה). But מעכדות can also be Piyyuṭim inserted into the last 3 benedictions of 'Amidah as is evident from
the passage cited in note 21.

[18] בכוסף does not mean here "at Musaph," because in Palestine the Ḳedushah
was only recited at the Shaḥarit service (as Ben-Baboi emphasizes, ibid., vol.
70, 135), but denotes "in addition," viz. as an insertion similar to the phraseology of 'Amram (above, p. 252) ויש כוסיפין להיות לכם וכו' and וכוסיף פיצים באהבה.

[19] Read יצמעאלים.

[20] It is characteristic that the study of Torah was formerly, under Byzantium, proscribed. This refers to the problem of the Deuterōsis (discussed *infra.*,
p. 281) and hence the Piyyuṭim (מעמדות) would contain the very elements of the
Deuterōsis, viz. the Aggadic interpretation of the Bible (called here הורה) and
also the Halakhic instruction (called here אסור והתר).

[21] Cf. Ben-Baboi's elaboration of this point (ibid., p. 130):
וכל שכן שאסור לוכר אסור והתיר והגדה בטלש דאשנות ובטלש אחרתות, וכל שכן מעשה
מרכבה שאסור לוכר בצבור ואפילו ביחיד... וכל שכן שאסור לוכר .האל הגדול הגבור והנורא'
וספסיק שבהו שלקב'ה ומתחיל והוכר .ויבא עַמַלק' ו.איבה אבכה' וכל כיוצא בו.

[22] =בסקוסס.

[23] =בכקוכן.

R. Yehudai's account no doubt refers to the time from 629 and onwards when Heraclius, on his reconquest of Palestine from the Persians, broke his promise given to the Jewish leaders to grant the Jews amnesty for their having aided the Persians during their invasion and occupation of the Holy Land (614–628) and allowed revengeful excesses to be perpetrated on them.[24] The divine service of the synagogue was restricted in every way. Services on week days were prohibited because of the Shema' and the 12th benediction of the 'Amidah. The teachings and preachings of the Rabbis, known as Deuterōsis, proscribed already since Justinian's famous novella of 553 (see infra, p. 279ff.), could not be given to the people assembled in the synagogues on Sabbaths. But the Piyyuṭim had already become a substitute for the Deuterōsis and these were permitted to be recited and intoned on mornings of Sabbaths and Festivals, followed no doubt by the reading of the Torah but without the sermons of the Rabbis. It is rather strange that the Trishagion was at all allowed to be recited in view of the reports of its proscription because of its interpretation by Christian theology to denote the Trinity (as discussed infra, p. 263ff.). But it seems that the Trishagion by itself was not proscribed but only when with its Targumic paraphrase it had a distinct polemical emphasis against the doctrines of Christianity (as shown infra, p. 266 ff.). However, it may be that the expanded Ḳedushah also formed a part of the Piyyuṭim whose very origin is stated to have been a stratagem whereby to outwit the authorities in their prohibition of the Deuterōsis.

This whole limitation of the divine service of the synagogue need not have been an innovation of Heraclius but rather the reënforcement of the old intolerant interference with the Jewish service that had become especially rigorous since the time of Justinian. It could not be carried out during the occupation of the country by the Persians but after the reconquest it asserted itself anew. R. Yehudai, living about 120 years after the conquest of the Holy Land by the Arabs, had naturally a more direct tradition about conditions prevailing there during the last years

[24] See Graetz, Geschichte, v (4th edition), pp. 30 ff. and 414 ff.

of the Byzantine regime. He demanded the elimination of the
Shema' from the Ḳedushah in the Shaḥarit 'Amidah of the Palestinian ritual, now that under Muhammedan rule the Shema' in
its entirety had returned to its proper place in the Shaḥarit service on Sabbaths and Festivals prior to the 'Amidah. R. Yehudai's protest was of no avail nor was the vigorous denouncement
of this item in the liturgy by Ben-Baboi (beginning of 9th century), a disciple of Rabah who in his turn sat at the feet of Yehudai Gaon.[25] Ben-Baboi seemingly failed to extend his opposition
to the Shema' in the Musaph Ḳedushah, prevalent in his own
country Babylon (to be discussed forthwith), because perhaps
this insertion, preserved as a memorial of the times of religious
persecution in Babylon under the Persians, was not found to be
so objectionable at Musaph which formed a sort of a separate
service after the reading of the Torah and the Prophets. But it
may be that he looked with disfavor also on the Babylonian
custom as the logical conclusion would be from the passage cited
above (note 25). However, he denounces the phrase באהבה פעמים
as containing a boastful complaint before God—a rather cantank-
erous remark.[26] In spite of Ben-Baboi's attack the Palestinian
ritual adhered to its old custom except that in Jerusalem and in
other Palestinian cities, where Babylonian Jews had settled, the
Ḳedushah (whether with or without Shema' is not clear) became
a daily feature of the service and probably also of Musaph on
Sabbaths and Festivals—this concession being granted only
after dispute and dissension.[27] It is doubtful whether ultimately

[25] REJ, vol. 70, p. 134:

כל שכין זה שאוברין שמע בין קדוש לויכלוך כאין הוא לא עתו ולא בקוכו שתיקנו חכו׳ל כפ:י
שלא חיקנו חכז׳ל לקרוא קרית ככע אלא כחרית וערבית בלבד סן הכשנה וכן התלכור. אכ
אתה אוכר: שמע פכוק ראשין שהוא אוטר. עיקר קריית שמע פכוק ראשון הוא וכו׳.

[26] Ibid.: ועור כל שכין זה כאוכרים. פע:יב בזאהבה׳ שהוא כסניז דעתו כלפי סעלה
Yet in the וכהרעים ואוכר שאנו אוכרים פעמים בכל יום שהוא כבניס דעתו כלפי כעלה
time of R. Hai this phrase was omitted at his school in Bagdad (see the passages discussed by Mann, REJ., vol. 70, 123, note 1). See also Marmorstein,
ibid., vol. 73, pp. 98–9, and my remarks, vol. 74, p. 111.

[27] Ibid., p. 135: תדע לך שכן היא ותקנת כמד היא שאין אוכרים שמע בין קדוש לויכלוך
אלא בתפילת שחרית של כבת בלבד. אבל בכוספין ובמינחה וכל יכות השבת אין אומרים.
עד עכשיו אין אוכרים בארץ ישראל קדוש וטכע אלא בשבת או ביכים טובים בלבד. בשחרית
בלבד. חוץ כירושלים ובכל מדינה שיש בה בבלאין כעשו כריבה :מחלוקת שקיבלו עליהם

the Palestinian ritual ever became uniform in this respect with the Babylonian rite.

On the other hand Gaonic reports of the 9th century trace the insertion of Shemaʻ in the Ḳedushah to a prohibition of Yezdejerd II. The declaration of the unity of God was obnoxious to the ruling religion of Zoroastrianism with its dualistic conception of the deity. Hence the government forbade the reading of the Shemaʻ in its usual place in the service. As a subterfuge the Ḥazzan would intone in an unnoticeable manner (בהבלעה) the first verse of Shemaʻ as well as the conclusion (אני ה' אלהיכם) within the Ḳedushah of *every service*, both on week days and on Sabbaths and festivals. When this decree was annulled and the Shemaʻ could again be fully recited at its proper place, the insertion in the Ḳedushah was removed from all the services and was only retained at the Musaph of Sabbaths and Festivals as a memorial of the persecution. Sar Shalom, Gaon of Sura (849–53), in giving substantially the above account, speaks only in a general way of a persecution prohibiting the Shemaʻ.[28] That he referred only to the situation in Babylon is evident from the fact that the daily ʻAmidah could be recited because it would offer no objection to the Magians whereas in Palestine it had been proscribed owing to the benediction against heretics (ברכת המינים), as stated above (p. 254). But anonymous Gaonic responsa, cited in *Shibbole Halleḳeṭ*,[29] give a more specific description of the manner of the

---

לובד קדושה בכל יום, אבל בשאר כדינות ועירות שבארץ ישראל שאין בהם בבלאין אין אומרים קדוש אלא בשבה וביבים טובים בלבד. This custom is also borne out by a Gaonic responsum (cited in Tosafot, Sanh. 37b) which gives an Aggadic explanation for it found in מדרש ויכולו (see *REJ.*, vol. 70, p. 127, note 2).

[28] Sar Shalom's responsum is quoted first in ʻAmram, ed. Fr., I, 139b, and is repeated in Vitry, p. 99, סדור רש"י, p. 252, par. 504, ʻIttim, 280–81, או"ז, II, 11c (22a). The parallel in *Pardes*, ed. Ehrenreich, p. 312, will be discussed *infra*. p. 259. The general reference to the persecution is, כפני שכגזורה מרה על שונאיהם כל ישראל (a well-known euphemism for Israel) שלא לקרות ק"ש כל עיקר היה אומר אותה שליח צבור בהבלעה בעמידה בכל תפלה דשחרית בין בחול בין בשבת וכו'. Sar Shalom speaks here only of the insertion of the Shemaʻ in the Ḳedushah of Shaḥarit but the responsa, discussed in next note, clearly mention this insertion at every service.

[29] Ed. Buber, p. 38: ולכה נהגו לובר פעכים ולהיות לכם בקדושה? סצאתי בתשובות הגאונים ז"ל...לפי שביכוה רב נחמן גמר יוהנרד ויזדרד ר. סלך פרס שלא יקראו קריאת שמא ושמע. ר. לאלתר מה עשו חכמים שבאותו הדור? תקנו להבליעו בין כל קדושת וקדושה ר. בין בשחרית.

198

subterfuge to outwit the authorities by the insertion of Shema'
into Ḳedushah and also by mentioning the occasion as due to the
fanaticism of Yezdejerd II.

This ruler (438 or 439–457) was notorious for his intolerance
both towards Jews and Christians. Several sources of the Gaonic
period refer to a persecution against the Jews about 454–5 which
involved their being compelled to desecrate the Sabbath.[30] His
death is reported to have been caused by the bite of a snake. R.
Naḥman mentioned in the above responsum is the Amora R.
Naḥman b. Huna, head of the school of Sura, whose death is
reported to have taken place at about the time when Yezdejerd's persecution began. Hence Halevy may be right in suggesting (דו״ר, III, 93) to emend שבימות רב נחמן into שבמות רב נחמן in
accordance with the report of Sherira Gaon and others. Our
responsum adds another detail of the persecution, viz. the prohibition of the Shema' and the subterfuge of its insertion in the
Ḳedushah. Yezdejerd's death in 457 only brought a temporary
respite for the Jews. The rule of his son Perōz (459–484) was
fraught with still more severe trials resulting (especially from
469–70 and onwards) in the closing of all schools and synagogues

בין במוסף, בין במנחה, בין בחול ובין בשבת ובין ביום טוב. ומאי הבליעה? רישא: טבע, סיפא:
אני ה' אלהיכם. ולמה היקָנוה לאומרה בהבלעה? כדי שלא תשתכח טבע מפי התינוקת. ובקשו
רחמים מן השמים ובא תנין בחצי היום ובלע יזֹנגרד יהזגנרד .r) המלך ובית כשכבו ובבית משכבו
r) ובכלה הגזרה והיו מתפללין על הסדר ופירדו על טבע כתיקנה בפרהסיא ובקשו לסלקה
לאלהר שלא לאומרה, אסרו חכמים כבאיזהו הדור: לא נבטל אותה שלא לאומרה כלל כדי
שיתפרסם הנס לדורות אלא נקבע אותה בתפילת המוספין ובתפילת נעילה שאין שם קריאת
שמע כלל, וכן מנהג בתי ישיבות. Cp. also the passage from הקצועות 'ס, cited in ארו,
l.c., which also speaks of the original insertion of Shema' in the Ḳedushah at
every service (בכל צלותא וצלותא) and not only at Shaḥarit.

[30] The primary account is in Sherira's letter (ed. Lewin, p. 94): ובתריה
רב נחמן בר רב הונא ושכיב בשנת הכסי׳ו (= .Sel 454/5) תפל כסדרא וגזר ינדרד לבטולי שבתא
וגזרו רבנן תעניתא ואיתי קודשא בריך הוא בליליה עליה תנינא.
Another version adds: ובלעוה מן משכביה ובכלה הזרתיה. Cp. further Sherira's
remark, ibid., p. 96. There are several variants as to the date but the above
figure seems to be the most correct one. Cf. further the data given in the
several versions of סדר עולם זוטא and סדר תנאים ואמוראים (in Neub., *Med. Jew.
Chron.*, I, 177, 184; II, 246, 247, bottom; Marx, *Lewy Festschrift*, Hebrew
part, p. 172). Also a Genizah fragment in Cambridge (T. S. 8 K 22.11) reads:
שנת תסי״ים נאסף רב נחמן בן רב הונא וגזר ידנרד כלך פרסיים על אבותינו לחלל את השבה.
About the date see also Rappaport, ערך כלי׳ן (ed. Warsaw, I, 71 f.) and cf.
Schorr, החלוץ, II, 120.

and in kidnapping the Jewish youth by the Magians to initiate them into the religion of Zoroaster. And then the movement of the reformer Mazdak, which had its chief seat in Babylon, only added to the oppression of the Jews till its overthrow in about 528.[31] We may therefore assume that even when the Jews were allowed during these years of intermittent religious intolerance to meet for public service they could not openly proclaim their doctrine of the unity of God and had to make use of the subterfuge of inserting it in the Ḳedushah. Indeed, Sherira Gaon speaks of years of persecutions and troubles right down to the close of Persian period (ed. Lewin, p. 99: והויין שני עמד וצרות בסוף מלכות פרסיים ולא הוו יכלין למקבע פרקי ואחובי מתיבתא עד כמה שנין וכו'.
Hence the freedom of reciting of the Shemaʻ fully at its proper place was probably not regained by the Jews in Babylon till the arrival of the Arabs and not immediately after the death of Yezdejerd II, as the above mentioned responsa would seem to indicate.

We have thus two parallel accounts about this change in the liturgy referring to persecutions both in Babylon and in Palestine. The one in Babylon seems to have been the earlier one. Byzantium, copying its example from the Magian-ridden government of Persia, probably began to interfere with the Jewish divine service since the times of Justinian. The Jews in Palestine then made use of the same stratagem of inserting the Shemaʻ into the Ḳedushah as their Babylonian brethren did before them. With the beginning of the era of freedom under Muslim rule, however, this innovation was relegated in Babylon only to the Musaph service on Sabbaths and Festivals, whereas in Palestine it remained in the Shaḥarit service also on these days since the Ḳedushah was not recited there on weekdays. In Babylon too the prohibition of the Shemaʻ was the cause for its insertion into the passage לעולם יהא אדם (as discussed above p. 249 ff.).

In our analysis of the accounts we have endeavored to separate the data relating to Palestine and Babylon respectively in

---

[31] The troubles of the Babylonian Jews under Perōz (פירח רב·יעא) and in consequence of Mazdak's reforms are well known. See also Nöldeke, *Aufsätze zur pers. Gesch.*, pp. 106–7, 109, 112–14, and *Ṭabarī*, pp. 118, note 4, 141 ff., 162 ff., 455 ff., 465.

order to ascertain their historical veracity. Confusion has been caused by the passage in *Pardes* (ed. Ehrenhreich, p. 312)[32] where, inside the responsum of Sar Shalom, Rashi inserted a gloss, which was a reminiscence of the prohibition in Palestine, whereas Sar Shalom no doubt dealt with the one in Babylon (as demonstrated above, p. 256). This whole reminiscence is connected with the obstacle placed before the Jews in Palestine to recite the Trishagion (as will be discussed *infra*, p. 267 ff.). Halberstam (יטרון, VI, 1868, pp. 128–130) was on the right track in endeavoring to separate the various accounts and yet Graetz (*M. G. W. J.*, 1887, 550 ff.) follows entirely the version as given in Pardes, without considering at all Halberstam's data, and Krauss (*l.c.*, 33–34) certainly added nothing to the elucidation of the problem. Our above analysis,[33] based on all the reports now available, enables us to comprehend better the occasions that gave rise to the insertion of the Shema' into the Ḳedushah. Of course all the reports could be discredited by the hypercritical argument of convenient and late allusions to the general hypothesis of שעת השמד. But as long as no other contemporaneous explanation of this liturgical problem is available the later Gaonic reports should be accepted as furnishing us with a more or less reliable tradition.

3. Shema' at the Taking Out of the Scroll.

The custom of reciting the first verse of Shema' at the taking out of the Scroll is mentioned first in *Soferim* 14.8 ff.[34] The whole passage there makes it evident that in the ritual of

---

[32] After בעמידה בהבלעה (ק׳ס) אומרה היה ש׳ץ we read: וכל הצבור היו אומרים בלחש שלא יבינו המינין הם חרסיהי והלמידי on חטא) הנוצרי שנחברו עם היונים והיו מריעים לנו, ובסביל הפחד לא היו יכולים לוסר וקבלת (insert מלכות שמים בקול, כי האורבים היו כסהתים שם עד שלש שעות וארבע שעות כי ידעו עד ארבע שעות זכנה לקרות, ואחר ארבע שעות היו האורבים הולכים וישראל מתאספים יחד בסתר ובפחד והיו אומרים קדושה (it is קדושה דיוצר?) וסתהפללין, ואומרים קדושה וקדושה דעמידה .viz) ובתוך הקדושה היו אומרים פעמים באהבה וכו׳׳ הכל כפי שאנו אומרים עכביו בקדושה.

About Rashi's mention of these "watchers" (detectives) in the synagogues see also *infra*, pp. 259, with regard to the Ḳedushah itself, and p. 299, with regard to the blowing of the Shofar.

[33] See also Mann, *REJ.*, vol. 70, p. 125, note 1.

[34] הכפטיר בנביא הוא פורס על כבע. באי זו כבע אנרו? בשטע של ספר הורה. היכי פותח והמפטיר (viz.)? אמרי יושבי ביחך, זאח׳כ עומד המפכיר ואומר אין כבוך באלהים

the author of *Soferim* the taking out of the Scroll was the occasion
of a solemn ceremony including the proclamation of God's unity
and emphasizing the Trishagion in the same sense. The combination of the Trishagion with the Shema' had clearly a polemical point against Christianity (as will be shown *infra*, p. 270 ff.).
It is difficult to ascertain when and where this custom arose. If
the ritual of *Soferim* reflects that of Palestine, which is not always
the case, then this whole custom goes back to an early time before
Christian Byzantium censored the divine service of the synagogue. It may be taken for granted that when the state objected
to the reading of the Shema' altogether the ceremony of הוצאת ס״ת
had to be curtailed omitting at least the first verse of Shema'
and the following Trishagion. The very reading of the Shema' in
this connection was based upon a novel interpretation of the
Mishnah (Meg. 4.5: המפטיר בנביא הוא פורס על שמע) which seems
to have found little acceptance, the author of *Soferim* himself
mentioning the usual explanation that the Shema' there meant
the regular Shema' of Shaḥarit (14.13: וי״א פורס על שמע טיאמר
יוצר אור וקדושה, i. e. Ḳedushah of Yoṣer!)[35] The very fact that
Shema' at הוצאת ס״ת is connected with the Mafṭir shows that it
was only done on Sabbaths and Festivals. The custom originally
spread to Italy only for the three Festivals but Abraham, the
father of the author of שבה״ל, introduced it for all Sabbaths and
Festivals.[36] From there it was adopted in Bohemia (ארץ כנען)
but not in western Germany which in this respect was alike to
the French ritual where it is missing.[37] Also the Spanish ritual

___

י״י וכו' (citing several verses) ביד נכנס ואל ההיכל .viz) ואוחז המפטיר את התורה
ואומר שמע... פסוק הראשון בנעימה ואף העם עונין אותו אחריו. ואחר ואומר אחד אלהינו...
וצריך להגביה את התורה בשמע ישראל ובאלו יחודין שלשה ובנדלו לי״י אתי.

[35] See Müller's note 25 on p. 190.

[36] שבה״ל ed: Buber, p. 56, par. 77:

אבא כרי ר' אברהם זצ״ל הנהיג לומר בכל שבת וירם כשמוציאין ס״ת לקרות בו פסוקים של
שבחות: אין כמוך באלהים ה'. כלכותך מלכות כל עולמים. שמע ישראל וכו' כסדר הכתוב
בסדורים בשלשה רגלים עד ינדיל הורה ויאדיר, והיה הדבר נראה כורח צביר וקטה בעיניהם
על שני המנהג, וטאצאנו ספך וסעד במס' סופרים וכו'.

[37] *Or Zaru'a*, II, 19a: וכנהגנו בארץ כנען לאחר שנוטר כל הקדיש מחיל ש״ץ ואומר
בקול רם: אין כמוך כו'... ואחר שיקבל ס״ת הניחנה לידו פוהח ואומ' בקול רם שמע ישראל כו'
וענינן הצבור אחריו, ושוב אוכר אחד אלהינו וענין הצבור אחריו כו', ואח״כ אומר גדלו לה'

omits the Shema' at the taking out of the Scroll because it has not been mentioned by 'Amram whose Siddur became basic for Spain. We have thus a remnant of a polemical asseveration of the Monotheistic doctrines of Judaism limited to a certain time in Palestine and adopted only by a small part of the diaspora, probably only after its re-insertion in Palestine with the conquest of the Arabs.

4. SHEMA IN MA'ARIB.

It is not recorded what substitute for the Shema' in Ma'arib, which must have also been proscribed both in Babylon and in Palestine respectively just as in Shaḥarit, the Jewish authorities found it appropriate to suggest to the people needing guidance in the times of trial and intolerance. However, it is significant that in the Palestinian ritual for מוצ״ש there is a section of Taḥanunim at end of Ma'arib service including the first verse of Shema' followed by אחד אלהינו גדול אדונינו קדוש ונורא שמו just as is the case with the insertion of Shema' before ברוך שאמר in the same ritual (see Mann, p. 324, and cp. pp. 281 and 319). Who knows whether this whole liturgy did not originate at the time when the regular Shema' of Ma'arib was forbidden in Palestine and hence it was recited privately and later on it was retained in the public service? However, in the Babylonian and in other rituals it is entirely missing though some sort of Taḥanun accompanied by נפילת אפים was permitted by Sar Shalom Gaon (see 'Amram, ed. Fr., I, 193b, top, cf. also Elbogen, 105–6). The custom of Shema' at bedtime (ק״ש על המטה) does not seem to bear on the problem discussed in this paper and therefore it will not be considered here (see Ginzberg, *Geon.* I, 135 ff., and Mann, 287–88).

II

CHANGES DUE TO THE OPPOSITION AGAINST THE KEDUSHAH (TRISHAGION).

1. The Trishagion was invested with much solemnity in the divine service of the synagogue. Isaiah's majestic imagery of the

אתי כו׳... ובני דייום אין להם בנהג זה אלא כנונבר ס׳ץ הפילה אומר קדיש וכוציא ס׳ה ואוכ׳ נדלו לה׳ אתי כ׳׳ ובכס׳ כופרים יש סכך לבנהגו אלא כלכם כוסיף פכוקים הרבה וגם לכם כשכע כהספטיר היה אוכר כל אלו הפסוקים. ומשכע לבאורה דלאחר הקריאה הי׳ כנהגם. The last deduction is evidently incorrect.

angels proclaiming God's holiness three times in succession (ch.
6.3) suggested to have this sanctification proclaimed also on
earth in the synagogue of Israel. To this there was added the
sentence which Ezekiel during his vision heard the beings of the
Chariot proclaim in eulogy of God (ch. 3.12). The mystically
inclined in Israel used this idea of the parallel sanctification of
God both on high and on earth to weave around it dramatic
fancies depicting the great stir caused among the heavenly hosts
when Israel pronounced the Trishagion. The words of God's
sanctification uttered by Israel in its synagogues became the
material out of which the angels on high were weaving a crown
to be placed on the head of the Creator (cf. 'וכו כתר יתנו לך).
Already in Ḥullin 91b, bottom, the Ḳedushah of the angels is
stated to be dependent on the Ḳedushah of Israel (so in MS.
Munich: ואין מלה"ש אומרין שירה למעלה עד שיאמרו ישראל שירה למטה).[37a]
Three groups of angels are supposed to take their turn daily when
reciting the Trishagion, the first one starting with Sanctus, the
second repeating it twice and the third one three times finishing
off the whole verse as given in Isaiah whereas Ezek. 3.12 is recited
by the Ofanim and the Ḥayyot.[38] From this Talmudic passage it
would seem that the Trishagion in heaven was recited only once
daily and yet in the synagogue the custom developed to repeat
the Trishagion three times daily. Thus in Targum Sheni (to ch.
5.1) we read in Esther's prayer: דאין ישראל יבדון מן עלמא, מן יימר
קדמך קדוש קדוש קדוש בכל יומא תלת זמין. This threefold recitation
is also mentioned several times in the mystical writings, cited first
by the Geonim but probably dating from earlier times (the so-
called Hekhalot writings).[39] Of these three occasions two would

---

[37a] In the so-called Pirḳe of R. Eliezer (in *Pseudo-Seder Eliahu Zuta*, ed.
Friedmann, p. 47) this statement is attributed to R. Eliezer the son of R. Yose
the Galilean.

[38] Cf. Ḥullin 92a top ברוך' אופנים הוא דאמרי לה... See 'Amram, ed. Warsaw,
I, 4b, where the passage is attributed to R. Ishmael and where it ends והאופנים
וחיות הקודש עונין אחרייהם ברוך וכו, and 10b.

[39] See Hekhalot Rabbati (in Eisenstein's אוצר מדרשים, I, 111b ff) 3.2; 3.3:
שלשה פעמים בכל יום... שפותחין פיהם לומר קדוש בשעה שישראל אומרים לפניו קדוש;
ch. 9. 2-3: ברוכים לשמים יורדי מרכבה אם האכרו ותגידו לפני כה אני עושה בתפלת שחרית
ובתפלת המנחה וערבית בכל יום ובכל שעה שישראל אומרים לפני קדוש... נ' פעמים
שאהם אומרים לפני קדוש (the parallel passage in 'Amram I, 4a, rightly omits

be the Ḳedushot of Shaḥarit and Minḥah[40] whereas the third is dubious. Actually the Babylonian ritual has in the daily Shaḥarit alone three Ḳedushot, viz. קדושה דעמידה, קדושה דיוצר and קדושה דסדרא, which with the Minḥah Ḳedushah increase the occasions to four. On Sabbaths, including the קדושה דסדרא recited on מוצ״ש, the number grows to six.[41] This increase is traced to times of persecution and will be discussed forthwith after considering first the importance of the Trishagion in the Christian liturgy.

2. In the Christian liturgy the Trishagion (or Tersanctus) also has a prominent role. It is interesting that in the Eastern liturgies[42] the proper Trishagion has the following remarkable form: Holy God, holy strong, holy immortal, have mercy upon us (ἅγιος ὁ θεός, ἅγιος ἰσχυρός, ἅγιος ἀθάνατος, ἐλέησεν ἡμᾶς). Drews (in Herzog-Hauck, *Realienencyklopädie f. prot. Theol. u. Kirche*, 3rd ed., XX, 125 ff.), while rightly arguing that the Trishagion was taken over by the Church from the Jewish liturgy going back to the earliest times (ibid 127, l. 19 ff.)[43], has difficulty in explaining the above form of the Trishagion (ibid., p. 128). A legend connects its origin with an earthquake in Constantinople

the word וערבית; see also שבה״ל, ed. Buber, p. 19); ch. 10, end; 11.3: בכל יום ויום בהגיע עלות השחר; 11.4: בכל יום ויום בהגיע תפלת המנחה; 18.3. The theme of the Ḳedushah of the angels being dependent on the Ḳedushah of Israel is further developed ibid., p. 122b, 123a, b. Another mystical text (ibid. 110a) speaks of angels reciting the Trishagion from morning to evening while others repeating ברוך from evening to morning. This idea is found already in S.E.R., ed. Friedmann, pp. 34, 84, 163, 193. Cf. also Midr. Ps., c. 19, ed. Buber, p. 166. Already in the book of Enoch (39.12) we read of angelic "watchers" ("those that never sleep" = עירין) who recite the Trishagion before God.

⁴⁰ See preceding note.

⁴¹ See Elbogen, p. 67.

⁴² Cf. the so-called early liturgy of James (in *Writings of Ante-Nicene Fathers*, VII, p. 538, col. 2) and the so-called liturgy of Mark (ibid., p. 553, col. 1). See also p. 537. Osterley in his new book (*The Jewish Background of the Christian Liturgy*, Oxford, 1925, pp. 142–147) has entirely failed to consider the problem discussed here.

⁴³ Drews (p. 127, ll. 50–51) is of course incorrect in assuming that the Trishagion was recited already in the time of Jesus in the first benediction before the Shema', hence the so-called קדושה דיוצר (see *infra* p. 274). The earliest Ḳedushah was the one in connection with the third benediction of the 'Amidah known as קדושת השם.

between the years 434–446.   Drews thinks that it is older than
the 5th century and yet cannot be granted much antiquity.   "It
is certainly not Jewish in origin because to call God ἀθάνατος is
not Jewish but Greek.   However why just this combination of
the attributes "strong" and "immortal" was chosen and why this
formula was afforded a place in the mass, is impossible to explain."

An examination of the Targumic paraphrase of Is. 6.3 will,
however, reveal the fact that the above form of the Trishagion is
a re-formulation of the Targumic form in the sense of the Trinity.
That Is. 6.3 was taken by the Christian divines to refer to the
trinity is well-known (so, e. g., Origen and Gregory Nazianzen).[44]
The trinitarian interpretation of the Trishagion is also evident
from the fact that all Eastern Christian liturgies have the end
of the verse of Is. 6.3 (מלא כל הארץ כבודו) in the form "heaven and
earth are full of Thy glory" (see Drews, ibid, p. 126, l. 15ff., who
offers no explanation for the leaving out of כל, πᾶσα).   It seems to
me that this was taken to refer to Jesus sitting in heaven at the
right hand of God.   It was at a time, when Christianity was not
yet triumphant in the Roman Empire so that "the *whole* earth"
could not yet be full of Jesus' glory, that in the Christian liturgy
this sentence was remodeled in a general way to denote "heaven
and earth are full of thy glory."   Be that as it may, Targum
paraphrases Is. 6.3 in the following threefold division: קדיש בשמי
מרומא עלאה בית שכינתיה, קדיש על ארעא עובד גבורתיה, קדיש לעלם ולעלמי
עלמיא, י״י צבאות מלוא כל ארעא זיו יקריה.   It is remarkable that in the
second sanctus reference is made to the earth "the work of His
power (δύναμις)" and in the third we have an allusion to his
everlastingness.   That the attributes "strong" and "immortal"
(i. e. everlasting) in the second and third Christian sanctus respectively are parallels to God's "power" and "everlastingness"
in the Targum is strikingly evident.   Of course in the Targum
these attributes are conceived in a sense of the absolute unity of
God whereas in the Christian formula of the Trishagion they
assume aspects of the Trinity.   Without going into a discussion
of the complicated development of the idea of the Trinity, it suffices to state that Jesus was regarded as the incarnation on earth

[44] See Diestel, *Gesch. d. Alten Testaments in d. Christl. Kirche*, p. 122.

of God's Logos and that the Holy Spirit formed a third element through the fellowship of which the believer became united with Jesus (see Hasting's *Encyclopedia of Religion and Ethics*, s. v. Trinity, XII, 458, col. 2, top.).[35] Now the Logos idea, was taken over from Philo who termed the Logos "the *power* ($\vartheta\acute{v}\nu\alpha\mu\iota s$) of God or the acting divine wisdom."[46] In Christian thinking Jesus became "the *power* and the wisdom of God" (so Paul in 1 Cor. 1.24: $\chi\rho\iota\sigma\tau\acute{o}\nu\ \vartheta\epsilon o\hat{v}\ \vartheta\acute{v}\nu\alpha\mu\iota\nu\ \kappa\alpha\acute{\iota}\ \vartheta\epsilon o\hat{v}\ \sigma o\varphi\acute{\iota}\alpha\nu$, see also verse 18). Hence in the second sanctus "holy strong" alludes to Jesus the embodiment of God's power (dynamis) while in the third "holy immortal" refers to the Holy Spirit by which the believers share in immortality.

    3. The above Targumic paraphrase has an evident polemical point. It has a distinct allusion of to the idea of God's "power" (נבורה, $\vartheta\acute{v}\nu\alpha\mu\iota s$) which was connected with the Philonic Logos.[47]

---

   45 See further Harnack, *Dogmengeschichte*, 4th ed., p. 213 ff.

   46 About Philo's idea of the Logos see Zeller, *Philosophie der Griechen*, 4th ed. (1903), III, 2, pp. 418 ff. See also p. 417 about Philo's idea of two chief forces immanent in the Supreme Being the one being His mercy and the other His power; the former being the creative, beneficient, gracious and merciful force, the second being the royal, legislative and punishing force. God's mercy is called $\theta\epsilon\acute{o}s$ while His power $\kappa\acute{v}\rho\iota os$. This is akin to the Rabbinic idea of מדת רחמים and מדת הדין the former being designated by the Tetragrammaton and the second by Elohim (see, e.g., Gen. R., c. 33: מדת ה' שנאמר מקום בכל רחמים ... בכל מקום שנאמר אלהים הוא מדת הדין.

About the various conceptions of the "great dynamis" of God, the Logos, see further M. Friedländer, *Synagoge u. Kirche*, pp. 9, 77, 84, 88, 90, 93, 129–30, 226 ff.

   47 Of course God is frequently spoken of in the Bible as "mighty" (נבור) and so also in the Talmudic literature; cf. e.g. the characteristic passage in Yoma 69b, as to what constitutes God's power (נבורה) in connection with the phrase at the beginning of the 'Amidah האל הגדול הגבור והנורא (cf. Deut. 10.17). But the allusion in Targum to the world as "the work of His power" (עובד נבורתיה) is evidently a reference to the "great dynamis," the Logos, which Philo regarded as the instrument by which God created the whole world. (See the references cited by Zeller, ibid., p. 420, note 1).

The influence of Philo's idea of the dynamis can also be detected in the attribute נבורה recurring many times in the Rabbinic literature as a synonym for God (see e. g., Makk. 24a, top: אנכי ולא יהיה מפי הגבורה שמענום; Sabb. 88b: כל דיבור ודיבור שיצא מפי הנבורה parallel to כל דיבור ודיבור שיצא מפי הקב״ה As is well-known the dynamis plays a role in the Ḳabbalah as one of the ten emanations (Sefirot). However, the matter cannot be discussed here in detail.

When it originated is difficult to say. Of course the Targum on the Prophets is traditionally attributed to Hillel's prominent disciple, Jonathan b. 'Uzziel (first half of 1st century, C. E., Meg. 3a). It is assumed that this Targum was adopted in Babylon in the third century as the official translation of the synagogue and that it was revised there to meet the linguistic pecularities of the Babylonian Aramaic. The Amora R. Joseph of Pumbedita seems especially to have devoted attention to this Targum, doing perhaps the revision work, and hence it is sometimes cited in his name (see Bacher, *J. E.*, XII, 61a, b). Whatever may be the veracity of the tradition assigning the Targum on Prophets to Jonathan, the above paraphrase could hardly emanate from him as it is unlikely that he already would allude to the Philonic Logos, not to speak of going further to combat the Christian idea of Trinity which was yet in its embryo. But it is evident that this paraphrase was used in the synagogue in connection with the Trishagion to combat the idea of the Trinity. It is significant that in the so-called קדושה דסדרא, whose origin is connected with a persecution prohibiting the recital of the Ḳedushah (to be discussed forthwith), Is. 6.3 is given in Hebrew together with this Targumic paraphrase (and likewise the accompanying verse of Ezek. 3.12). Already R. Naṭronai Gaon (6th decade of 9th century) was asked for a reason for this Aramaic translation of the Ḳedushah (נ"ל, No. 90) who, however, failed to give a satisfactory answer (as will be shown further on). The reason after our above discussion is self-evident. It was to emphasize the Jewish interpretation of the Trishagion as against the Trinity. Later on the Targumic paraphrase was recited softly (בלחש) as it was found in Christian countries advisable not to proclaim in a loud voice (בקול רם) such a manifest public declaration of faith.[48]

That the spokesmen of the church, powerful in Byzantium

---

[48] See Vitry, pp. 73–4: נ' כקראות הללו עובא ובא לציון. ואני זאת בריתי. וקרא זה אל זה: אומר ש"צ בפני עצמו כל אחד ואחד והציבור עונין אחריו על כל אחד ואחד...נ' סקראית הללו אומר כליח ציביר בקול רם והשאר בלחש עם הציבור. ומקבלין דין סן דין וכו' Graetz, *M. G. W. J.*, 1887, 553, rightly surmised the polemical point contained in the Aramaic paraphrase without, however, realizing its full significance. Yet he expressly threw out his suggestion for further examination by others (see p. 552, bottom).

which ruled over Palestine, should have objected to this Jewish
emphasis of the Trishagion is only natural. Indeed several
reports speak of the prohibition of the Ḳedushah a substitute for
which was found by the Rabbis in the קדושה דסדרא beginning
with ובא לציון in order to circumvent the decree of the government. The term קדושה דסדרא occurs only once in the Babylonian
Talmud (Soṭah 49a) without any indication of its contents. One
could argue that there the term means the Ḳaddish which, as is
evident from the phraseology of the Gaonim, also was connected
with the act of sanctifying God.[49] It would fit in there in the
context, viz. that after the study of a *Halakhic* theme (סדרא)[50]
in the synagogue the full Ḳaddish was recited beginning with
יתדל ויתקדש whereas after an Aggadic theme (אגדתא), viz. a
sermon delivered by the preacher, who usually concluded his
theme with a reference to the Redemption (גאולה or נחמה)
expressing his prayerful wish that it speedily arrive, the last word
of the speaker "Amen" would be taken up by the listeners with
the exclamation אמן יהא שמיה רבא וכו'.[51]

4. However, there is evidently a genuine tradition behind
the identification of קדושה דסדרא with the section known in the
ritual as ובא לציון, though the real meaning of the term seems to
me to have been hitherto misunderstood. Let us at first cite
what the authorities of the Gaonic period reported as to its

---

[49] See R. Naṭronai's responsum (in נ'ל No. 90): ח'ח כשהיו מתפללין ונופלין
על פניהן וסקדשין (=ואומרים ﬤ=אומרים קדיש)... ואח'כ בקדסן יבקדסין (read ועוסקין בהורה.
Likewise in 'Amram, ed. Warsaw, 18a: וכקדש ס'ק; 19a; וסקדש עד לעﬨֿⅼⅼⅸ. 25b:
וﬥⅴⅎⅅⅭⅾⅴ; 29b; ולאחר סיום הברכה סקדﬡⅹ; see also 30a, 31a.

[50] סדרא here would then mean סדר הלכוה. Thus a scholar who knew how
to present the Halakhot in order was called סדרן (סדרן, see Bacher, *Exegetische Terminologie*, II, 136). As is well known, in Babylon, before it had its
two organised schools in the 3rd century, the leader of the scholars in Nehardea
was called ריש סדרא (see Sherira's Letter, ed. Lewin, 78, 80).

[51] The full Ḳaddish after study of Halakhot seems to be indicated in
S. E. R., ed. Friedmann, p. 31: כיכן אמרו קורא אדם חורה ונביאים וכחיבים ויודע להשיב
בהם, יםכרם בידו ויברך ויגדל וירוכם ויקדﬡ לככו כל מי שאסר והיה העולﬤ, הקב'ה, ואין
בﬠﬤⅾ ﬤⅾⅰⅭⅾ. On the other hand cf. Kohel. R., 9.15: צריך לכי ﬡⅾⅾ הלכוﬤ
(cf. Midr. Prov. c. 10, ed. Buber, 66) and ﬤⅾⅰⅲ אחריﬤ אמן יהי שכו הנד:ל סבורך
still more explicitly in Midr. Prov., c. 14 (ed. Buber, 75): בﬠﬤ ﬡⅾⅼ נאספין
בבהי כסיוה ובבהי מדרשוﬤ ﬡⅾⅰⅴⅴ אגדה ﬤⅰⅼ חכﬤ, ואח'כ עחין.אמן יהא סﬤⅰ רבא סבורך.

meaning and its origin. On the one hand its origin is ascribed to
a persecution which involved the prohibition of the Ḳedushah.
Thus in a responsum evidently emanating from Ṣemaḥ b. Palṭoi,
Gaon of Pumbedita (872–890 C. E.), where it is not indicated
which Ḳedushah was proscribed.[52] The same account is found in
a more expanded form in Or Zaru'a (II, 11c) where it is cited as a
quotation from ספר המקצועות.[53] There is further an account,
evidently not Gaonic, which connected קדושה דסדרא with the prohibition of the reading of the Torah with its Aramaic translation[54]
—a seemingly absurd combination which, however, will be seen
further on to have its own explanation.

On the other hand R. Naṭronai of Sura tries to connect this
Ḳedushah with the former custom of extensive study by scholars
after the service which study had to be given up owing to economic reasons in order that the worshippers be not detained too

---

[52] לקוטי הפרדס, 9a, where the passage וכשאלתם seems to be a continuation of
the previous responsum by Isaac Ṣemaḥ (b. Palṭoi), Gaon of Pumbedita (971–
90). It reads: וכשאלתם: למה אוםרים קדושה דסידרא? פעם אחת מרה מרה מלכות הרשעה שלא
יאמרו ישראל קדוש, והיו יוסבין שלוחי מלכות עד שמסיימין התפלה והולכין, ואח״כ היו נכנסין לבתי
כנסיות היו פותחין בגאולה ואם׳ מאומרין (ר.) פסוקי דרחמי וכוללין קדושה באמצע כדי שלא תסתלק
מפיהם. The following passage, beginning with נראה לרבי, is Rashi's explanation,
who tried to unify the various accounts, as will be seen forthwith. This responsum
does not state which Ḳedushah was prohibited. Only Rashi explains that it
refers to the Ḳedushah of 'Amidah evidently taking the phrase כמסיימין התפלה
to mean the 'Amidah whereas it really means the whole service. Rashi's
explanation is also repeated in Vitry, 108; Siddur Rashi, 217–18; Pardes, ed.
Ehrenreich, 305–6. See also שבה״ל, p. 38. Also R. Isaac Ab-Bet-Din of Narbonne
(האשכול, I, 33) took over Rashi's explanation but for the Targumic paraphrase
gives an explanation that it was done for ignorami. He then gives another
explanation for קדושה דסדרא which shows how uncertain he was in understanding the whole matter.

[53] ועוד כתב בספר המקצועות דסדר קדושה נכי מרו מרה (ר.) מלכות הרשעה דלא למיטר
קדושה. כה עשו כשרים שבאותו הדור? כיון שהולכין שלוחי מלכות נכנסין לבתי כנסיות ומתחילין
פסוקי גאולה ובא לציון גואל, ואני זאת בריתי, ואתה קדוש, ואומר כעין קריאה וקרא זה אל זה
ואוכר קק״ק, וחוזרין ומתרגומין לה לקדושה ומקבלין דין סן דין ואמרין, ואומר פסוקי דקדושה
אחריתי עברי והרגום וכו׳.

[54] In Kobak's Jeschurun, Hebrew part, VI, 126–7, Halberstam edited from
a MS. a passage evidently emanating from R. Eli'ezer Roḳeaḥ, who first cited a
Gaonic responsum (מצאתי בתשובות הגאונים) about this Ḳedushah (similar to R.
Naṭronai's in נ״ל, No. 90) and then adds: ועוד שמעו שגזרה מלכות הרשעה שלא
יקראו בהורה ויתרגמו וקבעו חכמים שבדור לומר יענך ה׳ ביום צרה כל המזמור ולומר וקרא
זה אל זה, והשאני רוחי, ולתרגם אותם.

long in synagogue when due to attend to their making a living.[55]
The whole account does not explain in the least the insertion of
the Ḳedushah after the completion of the ordinary Tefillah whether
we consider the earlier custom or the later one and yet this has
been taken by modern scholars as a true explanation of קדושה
דסדרא.[56] Rashi tried to combine both accounts and only added
to the confusion of the problem. The two verses Is. 6.3 and Ezek.
3.12, to which R. Naṭronai clearly refers as having been retained
even after the reading from the prophets had been given up,
became to Rashi ובא לציון and ואני זאת בריתי whereas the Ḳedushah verses themselves were really due to a persecution.[57] The
same unwarranted combination of the different accounts we
have noticed above (p. 359) in connection with the insertion of
the Shema' in the Ḳedushah of the 'Amidah. Now if the Ḳedushah has also been prescribed by Byzantium, what becomes then
of the report of the insertion of Shema' within it by reason of gov-

[55] נ'ל No. 90: לרב נטרונאי: כשאלתם וקרא זה אל זה ואמר, ותשאני רוח, סה טעם יש עם
as if it could be called קרוח והרגם? וזה טעם קבעו אותם חכמים בסדר קדושה? וסדר קדושה
(without these verses) כך מנהג ראשיתם: מקום שיש עם ח'ח כשהיו מתפללין ותופלין על פניהם
ומקדשין, לאחר שענין אכן יהא כמיה וכו' מביאין נביא וקורין בו י' פסוקים, הן חסר הן יתר, וכהרנכין
אותן, ואח'כ אוכרים וקרא זה אל זה ואמר וסהרוסין כשם שהרומו אותה פרשה של נביא, ואומרין
ותשאני רוח וכהרנכין אותן כדי לסיים בשבחו של הקב'ה, ואח'כ מקדשין (וסקדשין r.) ו), ועוסקין
בתורה, הרוצה בכשה עוסק, הרוצה בתלמוד עוסק...ובין ערבתה עניות ודלות והוצרכו
תלמודים להתפרנס מטעשה ידיהם נסמכו על ההלמד בלבד ועזבו סקרא וסשנה...ועקרו
לקרות בנביא בכל יום אחר תפלה, ואע'פ שעקרו לקרות בנביא שני פסוקים לא עקרו
אחם ועדיין קבועים ועומדים. וכפני כה לא עיקרום סקדושה משלשת היא קק'ם וכלכוה נ'פ
בחפלה.

The same responsum is ascribed in ש'ת, No. 55, to Hai. See further Vitry, p. 26.

[56] See Elbogen, 79, and Ginzberg, Geonica, II, 299.

[57] Cf. the whole passage in לקוטי הפרדס, 9a: נראה לרבי שסדר הקדושה שאנו אומרים
בתוך ובא לציון בבקר בשעת השמד תיקנוה שמרו המטין בהם שלא לענות קדושה באגודה אחת
בתוך יח ברכות. ולאחר שעה שכבר הלכו כשם האורבים היו אומרים מקראות הללו של קדושה
<u>ליחד הם</u> (so Rashi realized the point against the Trinity). Then he begins
to recapitulate the other argument: ומתחלה היה להם כנהג שעה אחת בבית
הכנסת אחרי תפלתם וכו' אבל בבניא עקרו, ואעפ'כ היו קורין בבניא אלו שני פסוקים ובא לציון
גואל, ואני זאת בריתי שיש בהם מאין (ומעין read) קריאת התורה... ועדיין הם קבועים בסקומם...
עוד הסיפו לוטר בכל יום וקרא זה אל זה ואמר זה והטעם שאמרו (שאמרנו read) שלא היו
יכולין לוטר קדושה בתוך התפלה בחטיבה אחת מפני שהאורבים היו עם וכו'. See further
the parallel passages given above, note 52, end.

ernment prohibition? No wonder then that owing to this vicious
circle all the accounts relating to שעת השמד have been suspected
by modern scholars.

5. In my opinion קרושה דכדרא *originally* meant *in Palestine*
the Trishagion recited after the Shema' at the taking out of the
Scroll on Sabbath mornings for the purpose of reading the portion
(סדרא, סדר) of the respective week. That the weekly portion
of the Torah in the Triennial Cycle prevalent in Palestine was
known as סדרא is well established (see, e.g., the references given
by Bacher, *Exeget. Terminologie*, II, 134). What more appropriate psychological occasion could there be for emphasizing the
doctrine of the unity of God than at the taking out the Torah—
that very Torah which Christianity claimed to have been super-
seded by the new dispensation—to recite the first verse of the
Shema' and in connection therewith to reiterate the Trishagion
with its Targumic paraphrase as not indicating the Trinity but
rather being in accord with the strict Jewish conception of monotheism? Thus quite early in the Christian period the spiritual
leaders of Palestinian Jewry must have ordained to bring emphatically the basic principle of Judaism to the notice of the worshippers assembled for the divine service on Sabbath morning.
Then came the reading of the Torah with its Aramaic translation,
likewise the prophetic lesson with its Aramaic Aggadic paraphrase and finally on the basis of the Scriptural readings the
preaching and teaching of the Rabbis ending usually in depicting
the Messianic age or alluding to the coming of the redeemer to
Zion (ובא לציון גואל) which the worshippers would fervently take
up with אמן יהא שמיה רבא מבורך eulogising God as above all human
praises and pictures of consolation of Israel (לעילא מכל ברכתא
ושירתא, תושבחחא ונחמתא).[57a]

Now that some such introduction and conclusion of the
Scriptural readings were in vogue in the Palestinian ritual can
still be detected from the scattered data. Above (p. 259 ff.) the

---

[57a] These four words indicate the contents of the service preceding this
eulogy of God, viz. the various benedictions, the lectionaries from Scripture
and the other praises, which were recited from the beginning of the morning
service till the sermon of the preacher which contained 'consolations' (נחמות)
probably in connection with the Haftarah of the week.

insertion of Shema' at הוצאת ס"ח, preserved in *Soferim*, 14.8–9,
has been discussed. It was based on a characteristic interpretation of the passage in the Mishnah המפטיר בנביא הוא פורס על שמע.
Now *Soferim* continues to describe this ceremony of taking
out the Scroll by stating that after the Shema' the Maftir continues with a formula which resembles the Trishagion (14.10:
וחזר ואומר אחד אלהינו גדול אדתינו קדוש, אחד אלהינו רחום אדוניגו קדוש,
אחד אלהינו גדול אדונינו קדוש ונרא שמו)[58]. The author explains this
threefold sanctification to correspond to the three patriarchs
(כנגד שלשה אבות) but more correct is the alternative reason as
corresponding to the threefold sanctus (וי"א כנגד שלש קדושות)[59].
At the recital of the Shema' and the subsequent threefold yet
monotheistic sanctification of God the Scroll was lifted up to
make the ceremony still more impressive (14.11 end: וצריך להגביה
את התורה בשמע ישראל ובאלו יחודין שלשה ובנדלו ליי אתי.

The ritual in *Soferim* evidently represents already a modification by actually omitting the Trishagion with its Targumic paraphrase. This was the modified form already during the
Muslim period after the vicissitudes of the custom as a result of
the government proscription in the Byzantine period. For, such a
custom as suggested above must have strongly offended the
authorities when Byzantium became the champion of the Church.
It is difficult to ascertain when the government stepped in to
regulate the Jewish divine service according to its notions. The
first definite information dates from 553 when Justinian issued his
famous Novella concerning the Deuterōsis (though other inter-
ferences may be earlier). As a supplement of this edict then the
Shema' and Kedushah (קדושה דסדרא) at the taking out of the

---

[58] The usual editions of Mas. Soferim have shortened this threefold sanctification but one MS. and the quotation in *Or Zaru'a* have the full text (see
Müller's note 39 on p. 195) which is evident also from 14.11; אלו יחודין שלשה.
Interesting is the reference to God as "merciful" in view of the Christian
version of the Trishagion ending with "have mercy upon us" (above p. 263)!

[59] To explain that the author refers to the three Kedushot recited on
Sabbath morning (קדושה דיוצר, קד:שת שהרית וקדושה כוסף) would pre-suppose him
following the Babylonian custom for which there is no evidence. In Palestine
Kedushah was only recited in the Shaḥarit 'Amidah while קדושה דיוצר is also
missing in the Genizah liturgical fragments of the Palestinian ritual (see
infra, p. 274).

Scroll had to be omitted. With the preachings of the Rabbis also
proscribed, the subsequent Ḳaddish with אמן יהא שמיה רבא went
too. Hence the report in the name of R. Benjamin b. Abraham
'Anav (the same who reported about the insertion of Shema' in
לעולם יהא אדם, above p. 247) of a prohibition of the Ḳaddish in the
Hebrew language.[60] The reason given is not very convincing but
the tradition of a proscription of אמן יהא שמו הגדול מבורך seems to
have some plausible basis because it followed the preachings
(Deuterōsis) of the Rabbis.[61] Our explanation of קדושה דסדרא as
the Trishagion recited at הוצאת ס׳ת explains also its reported connection with the prohibition of the reading and the translating
of the Torah (above p. 268).

The ordinary Ḳedushah in the 'Amidah of Sabbath Shaḥarit
was probably not proscribed as it contained merely Is. 6.3 and
Ezek. 3.12 to which Christianity could not object as it too was
having the Trishagion in its liturgy. It was therefore used by the
Rabbis as a place wherein to insert the beginning and the end of
the Shema' which had been prohibited. It was done secretly and
slurred over in the intonation of the Ḥazzan (as described above,
pp. 252). But the קדושה דסדרא found now its place in ובא לציון
which was probably instituted at Sabbath Minḥah before קה׳ת.[61a]

---

[60] סבה׳ל, ed. Buber, p. 9: (cf. הגיא, ed. Hurwitz, p. 6d)I: ורבי בנימין אחי נר׳ו
כתב: שחחלת אמירהו היתה בלשון עברי כמו שאמרנו למעלה: ולא עוד אלא שבכל סעה שישראל
נכנסין לבתי כנסיות ולבתי מדרשות ועתין. אמן יהא שמו הגדול מבורך׳ ׳ברכיח, נ׳, ע׳א, ובכמה
מקומוה מצאתי באנדה נמצא בלשון הזה. וביני׳ עמד נזרו שלא יאמרו .שמו הגדול מבורך׳ לכך הנהינו
לאמרו בלשון ארמי שלא היו האויבים מכירין בו. ואע׳פ שבטלה (read ובכל) השמד, לא רצו
להחזיר הדבר ליצנו בלשון עברי כדי שלא ישתכחו הנסים והנפלאות וכדי לעשות פוטבי לדבר.
The French authorities did not know of such an explanation. Hence Tosafot
(Ber. 3a bottom) explains הקדיש נהקן בלשון תרנום בעבור ע׳ה whereas another,
rather mystical, reason is given on account of the "serving angels" (Pardes, ed.
Ehrenreich, p. 326: ואם ישאל אדם: לסה אוכרים בלשון ארסי הקדיש? כדי שלא ירדישו
פלה׳ס ששטו של הקב׳ה הוא חסר ססא יחרבו את העולם. לכך אנו אומרים בלשון ארמי כי אין
סבתין אלא לה׳ק בלבד וכו׳, see also לקוטי הפרדס, 7d, 8a). Cf. further Abudraham, ed. Prague 1794, 21b bottom, 22b.
[61] See also Pool, The Old Jewish-Aramaic Prayer, the Ḳaddish, 1909, p. 20.
[61a] With regard to ובא לציון on Sabbath Minḥah there was a difference of
custom in Babylon; in Sura and all over Babylon it was recited after the reading of the Torah whereas only in the school of Pumbedita this was done before
קה׳ת (see Genizah responsum cited by Mann, 317, note 108: בסנחה בשבת סני
מנהגין יש: בישיבה שלנו (i. e. Sura) ובבבל כולה קורין בתורה·ואחרי כן אשרי ובא לציון.

This service was not watched by the government as it contained nothing objectionable. The above whole ceremony in connection with the taking out of the Scroll was only at Shaḥarit as evident from the fact that it was assigned to the Mafṭir. There was no Hafṭarah in Palestine at Sabbath Minḥah (unlike Babylon, see *infra*, p. 282 ff.). Hence the authorities could be outwitted by having at Minḥah ובא לציון with Ḳedushah and its Targumic paraphrase. This explains the reports that people would assemble again in the synagogue (see notes 52 and 53), viz. for Minḥah service after having had their Sabbath meals soon after midday.⁶¹

Thus קדושה דסדרא was originally a Palestinian custom for Minḥah on Sabbaths. In Babylon there was no need for the whole ceremony at ס"ת הוצאת because her Jewry had not the same problem of emphasizing the unity of God in the Trishagion. The insertion of Shema‘ at the taking out of the Scroll was probably never adopted there because the Mishnah המפטיר בנביא הוא פורס על שמע was interpreted differently (see above p. 260). Moreover since Yezdejerd's prohibition of the Shema‘ (above p. 256) it was not found advisable to add it at the taking out of the Scroll as it might endanger the whole reading of the Torah. Hence it is not mentioned in the Babylonian ritual in this connection though אחד אלהינו גדול אדונינו קדוש ונורא שמו is still preserved in 'Amram (ed. Warsaw, p. I, 24a) as a relic of the Palestinian custom (or it may be it was taken over later on in the Muslim period). But קדושה דסדרא in ובא לציון, as it had been evolved in Palestine, found

ובישיבה פום בדיתא קורין כולא סידורא ובא לציון .viz) ובקדשין יאום' עד עושה וש]לום בתפלה זקורים בתורה וקקדשין (viz. end of Ḳaddish). It seems that Pumbedita followed here the Palestinian custom as was the case also with another liturgical item, viz. אהבת עולם and not אהבה רבה as the beginning of the second benediction before Shema‘ (see Mann, 291).

⁶¹ The custom of holding the Sabbath morning service till noon is reported by Josephus (*Vita*, 54, 279), in describing the political meeting held in a synagogue (proseucha) at Tiberias on a Sabbath (evidently in connection with the service) during his governorship in Galilee (67 C. E.) which grew excited and "had certainly gone into tumult, unless the sixth hour (i.e. noon-time) which has now come, had dissolved the assembly, at which hour our laws require us to go to dinner on Sabbath-days." Cf. further R. Joshua's statement with regard to Yom Tob (Beṣah 15b): חלקהו חציו לה' וחציו לכם. For this arrangement evidently the description of the service on 1. Tishri in Neh. 8. 3, 10–12, served as a model.

entrance in Babylon and it was even introduced for weekdays
after Shaḥarit. There set in a desire of having three times
Ḳedushah in Shaḥarit (viz. קדושה דעמידה, קדושה דיוצר and קדושה
דסדרא).[63] Altogether the Trishagion for mystical purposes was
more solemn in the Babylonian ritual than in the Palestinian.
Thus Abraham Maimuni reports that in the Babylonian synagogue in Fusṭāṭ the Ḳedushah of the 'Amidah was recited standing
whereas in the Palestinian synagogue sitting (see J.Q.R., V, 421–2).
This difference in custom evidently went back to earlier times as
prevalent in the respective countries Babylon and Palestine.[64]
Moreover in Palestine the Ḳedushah was at all omitted during
weekdays (see above, p. 255, note 37) though this may have been
a result of the proscription of the daily 'Amidah. Also Ḳedushah of
Yoṣer is missing in the Palestinian ritual and seems more likely
to be a Babylonian innovation (see Mann, pp. 289–90).

6. This seems to me to be the only plausible explanation of
this whole complicated problem of קדושה דכדרא. It reconciles the
various accounts and renders them more or less intelligible.
There remains only to discuss briefly the passage in Soṭah 49a
wherein this Ḳedushah is mentioned as a unicum. The Mishnah
(48a) contains a statement by Simon b. Gamliel, in the name of
Joshu'a b. Ḥananya, that since the destruction of the Temple no
day passes without some evil event (מיום שהרב בהמ'ק אין יום שאין בו
קללה) evidently referring to conditions in Palestine. Thereupon
Raba, head of the school of Meḥuza in Babylon (337–352 C. E.),
remarks that the curse of each succeeding day is greater than that
of the previous one (49a: בכל יום ויום מרובה קללתו משל חבירו). Now
conditions of Jewish life in Babylon were not so bad in his time.
It was the reign of Shāpūr II whose mother, Iphra Hormuzd (אפרא
הורמיז), especially befriended the Jews.[65] It is true that Raba

63 Cf. note 55, end.

64 Just the reverse was the custom with regard to the Shema' which the
Palestinians recited standing but the Babylonians sitting (see חלוף מנהגים, ed.
Müller, p. 10; Gaonic Responsa, ed. Harkavy, p. 399; Finkelscherer, Lewy
Festschrift, 255).

65 See B. B. 8a, bottom, and 10b, bottom. When Raba drew upon himself
the wrath of Shāpūr because a Jew, whom he had sentenced to be flogged, died
as result thereof, Iphra Hormizd dissuaded her royal son from prosecuting
Raba (see Ta'an. 24b and cf. Mann, הצופה לחכמת ישראל, X, p. 204–6).

complained of heavy expenses to keep the authorities in good
humor[66] but, compared to contemporaneous conditions in Palestine during the reign of Constantius, the Babylonian Jews could
regard themselves rather fortunate.   It seems therefore that
in commenting on the statement of the Mishnah, Raba was likewise thinking of conditions in the Holy Land.   He was well informed about them from the Babylonian scholars studying in
Palestine who had to come back to their native country right
from the beginning of Constantius' reign owing to persecutions.[67]
He too was informed of the difficulties which the Patriarch
was experiencing with regard to the fixing of the calendar
(Sanh. 12a).   How appropriate then was Raba's comment on
R. Joshua's remark about conditions in Palestine since the
destruction of the Temple that, as things were in his own time
in the Holy Land, the evil ('curse') seemed to grow from day
to day!

After Raba's comment we have the passage: ואלא עלבא אמאי
קא מקיים? אקדושה דסדרא ואידא שמיה רבא דאנדחא·שנא' ארץ עפתה כמו אפל
ולא סדרים איוב, י', כ'ב), הא יש סדרים ורש'י: סדרי פרשיות דתורה!) תופיע
מאופל.   It is evident that the "world" means here the Jewish
world and that there is a poignant allusion to the chaotic conditions in Palestine owing to the persecutions.   The question is
whether this passage is a continuation by Raba himself or is a
later addition by the redactors of the Talmud or even by the
Saboraim.   It seems to imply the proscription of קדושה דסדרא

---

[66] Hag. 5b, top: אסר (ורבא) להו (לרבנן): מי ידעיתו כמה מסדרנא בצעא בי שבור
?כלכא

Of course since 337 or 338, when Shāpūr started his long drawn war
against the Byzantine Empire, the Jews in Babylon were subjected to heavy
war expenses together with the rest of the population but of a religious persecution there is no evidence.   As a matter of fact while the Christian population
in Babylon was heavily punished for its loyalty towards Christian Rome
(since 339–40) the Jews were not molested (see Nöldeke, *Aufsätze zur pers.
Geschichte*, 98–99).   Cf. also Funk, *Juden in Babylonien*, II, 41–46, who, however, has overdrawn the picture and several of whose statements and supposed
references have to be used with caution.

[67] The so-called נחותי דמערבא.   Cf. Sherira's Letter (ed. Lewin, p. 61):
ובחר הכי אביי ורבא תפיש שמדא בא'י ואמעיבא הוראה תמן תובא, ונחית כן דהוה הכן
להכא דנחיתא נחותי וכלהו דיקי דרב רבין כנון בבלאי מן.   Cf. also Halevy, דוה'ר, 366 ff.,
455 ff., 467 ff., whose conclusions also need a critical sifting.

before the reading of the Torah and the Ḳaddish after the preachings of the Rabbis. These sanctifications of God recited under difficulties help to preserve the Jewish world intact. They seem to have been introduced already in Babylon, especially the form of קדושה דסדרא in ובא לציון as evolved in Palestine to outwit the authorities who prohibited it before the reading of the Law. In Babylon the קדושה דסדרא became a daily feature after the Shaḥarit service in connection with the study of the Bible and the Rabbinic tradition. If Raba is the author of this passage, we would have to assume the prohibition of קדושה דסדרא before קה"ת and its insertion in ובא לציון already in the time of Constantius for which, however, we have no direct evidence, though the general designation of his rule as time of שמד would render such an assumption possible. But it is more likely that the whole interference with the divine service of the synagogue dated from 553 in connection with Justinian's law about the Deuterōsis. Hence this passage in Soṭah 49a should be regarded as a later addition by the Saboraim, who realizing the significance of Raba's statement as reflecting conditions in the Holy Land in his own time, adjoined to it an item which resulted from Byzantine intolerance about two centuries later. By that time Babylonian Jewry too had undergone periods of persecutions under Yezdejerd II, under Perōz, and under Kavādh in connection with the movement of Mazdak. During these trials they saw their schools disbanded and their synagogues closed, the Shemaʿ proscribed as well as the Hafṭarot from Deutero-Isaiah (see *infra*, p. 282 ff.), the Sabbath desecrated and even their children taken away from them to be brought up by the Magians. Though in the second half of the 6th century the force of Magian intolerance was not so oppressive, the Jewish position seems to have been still insecure. Sherira in his Letter reports of troubles and persecutions right down to the close of the Persian period which prevented the schools from functioning properly and altogether hampered the pursuit of the study of Judaism.[68] Hence in Babylon too the Jewish world was declared to exist on קדושה דסדרא and אמן יהא שמיה רבא after the sermons. These sanctifications kept alive in the hearts

[68] See above, p. 258.

of the people the principle of monotheism and the hope of the Redemption. Thus the whole significant Talmudic passage in Soṭah 49a, when properly illumined, casts additional light on the problem of קדושה דסדרא as discussed in the previous pages.

III

OBJECTIONS TO THE DAILY 'AMIDAH.

1. The prohibition of reciting the daily 'Amidah in Palestine is expressly reported by Yehudai Gaon (above p. 253, cf. note 15), no doubt owing to benediction 12, the well-known ברכת המינים, which in the Palestinian version had a direct reference to the Christians (הנוצרים). It is not stated since when this proscription came into force. Though Yehudai probably speaks of the last period of Byzantine rule in Palestine (since its reconquest from the Persians by Heraclius, 629), the prohibition may have been older and was re-enacted after the reconquest (see above p. 254). Epiphanius, himself a native of Palestine, in his famous work against the heresies (the Panarion, begun in 374) refers to this benediction recited three times daily and likewise Jerome who lived many years in Palestine (after 385 till his death in 420).[69]

In the absence of any definite information we have to assume that the prohibition started under Justinian about the same time when the Shema' and the Deuterōsis were forbidden. But perhaps the references to this benediction by Epiphanius and Jerome caused the authorities to decree the proscription still earlier. What substitute was discovered by the Rabbis is also unknown. Should we say that the shortened 'Amidah, three versions of which have been preserved in the Palestinian ritual for Minḥah,[70] originally served as a substitute for the proscribed full 'Amidah? Later on in the Muslim period, when the full 'Amidah could again be recited, these shortened 'Amidot then were relegated to the Minḥah service. The direct reference to the Christians had in course of time to be omitted—as was only proper. How long the original form was preserved in Babylon is also difficult to say.

[69] See the passages cited by Schürer, *Geschichte d. jüd. Volkes*, 4th ed., II, 544, note 161. Cf. also Krauss, *JQR*, V, 130 ff.

[70] See Mann, 300–302, 309–11.

Only one version of 'Amram has a more or less similar formulation of the benediction to that of the Palestinian ritual.[71]   In
Babylon Jews and Christians were more friendly to each other
especially since they would frequently share the common intolerance of Magian fanaticism. Therefore it may be assumed that
the Jewish leaders found it advisable to leave out this obnoxious
reference.   The burden of the benediction was directed more
against lawbreakers within the Jewish fold—informers, apostates,
and heretics.[72]

   2. From the statement of the Church fathers it is evident
that the 'Amidah was recited in Palestine also at Ma'arib though
this was not obligatory (תפלת ערבית רשות).   Now a report that is
not earlier than the second half of the 13th century connects the
third section in Ma'arib after the Shema', viz. the one beginning
with ברוך יי לעולם אמן ואמן, with the prohibition of the 'Amidah.
This passage was supposed to consist of verses mentioning the
divine name 18 times corresponding to שמו'ע.[73]   But it is rather
strange that the Palestinian liturgy, as preserved in the Genizah,
has not at all this passage[74] though, of course, it could be argued
that it was omitted in the Muslim period when the 'Amidah was
reinstituted in Ma'arib.   The Geonim speak only in a general
way of the passage having been introduced by the later scholars
(רבנן בתראי), viz. of the Saboraic period.[75]   But Rashi was led into
evolving a theory of how the Babylonian scholars composed this
section and forwarded it as a gift to the sages of Yabneh in lieu of

----

   [71] See Marx, *Untersuchungen z. Siddur des Gaon R. Amram*, Hebrew part,
pp. 5-6.
   [72] The various forms of this benediction need not be discussed here. See
Berliner, *Raudbemerkungen zum tägl. Gebetbuche*, I, 50 ff., and also the literature
cited by Elbogen, 2nd ed., pp. 516, 519.
   [73] See שו"ת רשב"א, I, No. 14: ‏יש בה י"ח הזכרות ונחקנה ביפי‏‎ ...אבל ברכה המולך.
‏(insert י"ח הכמד כנגרו שלא להתפלל ועמדו והקנו אותה ברכה טיש בה י"ח ואוכרות כמו‏
‏ברכות שבתפלה, ואע'פ שבטלה מרה, נשארה אותה ברכה ביד הדורות.‏
Abudraham, ed. Prague, 43a, quotes the same in the name of בעל המנהגות, viz
Asher b. Saul of Lunel, author of כפר המנהגות, who lived in the 14th century
(see Gross, *Gallia Judaica*, 281) and hence after Rashba (who died in 1310).
   [74] See Mann, pp. 304–5, which is now modified by the present remarks.
   [75] See Naṭronai's responsum in 'Amram, ed. Warsaw, I, 25a, and 'Ittim,
pp. 172–3. See also 'Amram, I, 19a.

the שמוע received from them[76]—a theory that is impossible on the surface since the whole section is not mentioned in the Talmud at all. The Mishnah laying down the rule that at Ma'arib the Shema' should be followed by two benedictions (Ber. 1.4) would certainly not have overlooked the third section had it been already in the hands of the scholars of Yabneh. The Gaonic tradition of its later origin is correct though it need not have been composed in Babylon by the Saboraim but *in their time* in Palestine as a result of the prohibition of the 'Amidah, probably by Justinian, hence in the 6th century in the Saboraic period. This would be borne out by the report of Ibn Yarḥi (*Manhig*, p. 22b) who traces it to אנשי מערב, viz. the scholars of Palestine. The very fact that the sources speak of 18 אזכרות and not 19 (only Ibn Yarḥi has 19) would indicate a Palestinian origin where the 'Amidah consisted of 18 benedictions only. It is difficult to state certainties on this matter owing to lack of evidence but the Palestinian origin of ברכת המולך should not be ruled out of likelihood.[77] The section was taken over by the Babylonian Jews though they could recite the 'Amidah and hence it had been retained even later on whereas in Palestine it disappeared with the re-introduction of the Ma'arib 'Amidah after the conquest of the Holy Land by the Arabs. The report concerning the עמד, though mentioned first by R. Solomon ibn Adret, may go back to a much earlier source and need not have been invented by him especially as he was no doubt aware of the other explanations given for ברכה המולך.

IV

CHANGES IN CONNECTION WITH THE READING OF THE TORAH AND THE PROPHETS.

1. A restrictive regulation of the manner of reading the Torah and the Prophets was enacted by Justinian in the famous Novella 146 (in February 553). If we follow Juster's interpretation[78], the

[76] See the curious passage in *Pardes*, ed. Ehrenreich, 304, Vitry, 78, *Siddur Rashi*, 213–14, שבה׳ל, p. 21a (where it is expressly quoted in the name of Rashi).

[77] See Elbogen, p. 102–5, and notes (2nd ed.), p. 529, whose remarks on the problem are somewhat inexact.

[78] See Juster, *Les Juifs dans L'Empire Romain*, 1914, I, 369 ff. Juster (p.

dispute about substituting for the Hebrew reading with its Aramaic translation (Targum) a reading in the Greek language, as demanded by a number of Jews, gave the occasion to the Emperor, when the matter came to his notice, to regulate the divine service of the synagogue. While granting freedom to the worshippers to have the Bible read in the language understood by them, either in Greek in the translation of the LXX or in that of Aquila (but in no other version), or in Italian, he forbade at the same time the Deuterōsis, evidently meaning thereby the Oral Law which was the basis upon which the Rabbis developed their themes in addressing the worshippers after the reading of the Biblical lessons. In interpreting these lessons they would quote statements of the sages from Mishnah, Talmud or Midrash introducing them by a formula such as שנו הכמים or תנו רבנן, hence using the verb שנה (Aramaic תני) from which משנה = ϑευτερῶσις is derived.[79] The prohibition of the sermons meant that the people were deprived of Halakhic instruction and of Aggadic emulation, for these usually formed the themes of the sermons in connection with a Rabbinic interpretation of the Biblical lessons

370, note 3) argues (against Graetz) that the Greek was to supplant the Hebrew according to the demand of a minority section of the Jews. On the other hand Krauss (*Studien zur byz.-jüd. Geschichte*, pp. 58 and 60) follows Graetz's view that this demand, granted by the Emperor, meant only the elimination of the Targum and the substituting for it the Greek version side by side of the original Hebrew.

[79] In the writings of the Church fathers the term usually stands for Mishnah (see the passages cited by Juster, p. 372, note 6) which term denoted "the Oral Law and its parallel to מקרא, the term for Scripture and its study" (see Bacher, *Exegetische Terminologie*, I, 122). Cf. the interesting passage of Epiphanius (cited by Juster): Quantae traditiones Pharisaeorum sint, quas hodie vocant ϑευτερῶσιν, et quam aniles fabulae evolvere nequeo . . . . . Unde et doctores eorum σοφοί (=חכמים), hoc est sapientes, vocantur. Et si quando certis diebus traditiones suas exponunt, discipulis suis solent dicere: οἱ σοφοὶ ϑευτερῶσιν (= שנו חכמים, cf., e.g., Abot 6.1: שנו חכמים בלשון המשנה), id est, sapientes docent traditiones.

Krauss, p. 61, overlooked the fact that the sermons were based on the Deuterōsis and therefore jumped to the conclusion that Justinian ordered the closing of the schools for which there is no evidence. For other explanations see also Eppenstein, *Beiträge zur Geschichte u. Literatur im geon. Zeitalter*, 26, note 4, where various views are given.

read at the service. A reminiscence of the occasion of this prohibition we have in the phrase שלא יקרא בתורה ויתרגמו (in the
passage cited above, p. 268, note 54). Moreover the report of
Yehudai Gaon about conditions in Palestine prior to Arab conquest (above p. 253) clearly refers to a previous impossibility of
studying the Torah (לעסוק בתורה, i.e. the Arabs) (והג׳חום), viz. to
expound the Oral Law at the services, and it also indicates that
the מעמדות, i.e. the Piyyuṭim, were recited on Sabbath morning,
which contained the very elements of the sermons, viz. אכר ההר
(Halakhah) and Aggadah.

This statement of Yehudai Gaon can now be used as the
earliest account in connection with the modern theory of the rise
of the Piyyuṭ.[80] It corroborates the statement of *'Ittim*[81] in the
name of Gaonic authorities (רבוותא) that the Piyyuṭ was instituted at a time of שמד "when they (the Rabbis) could not mention
the words of the Torah (viz. the Oral Law) because the enemies
decreed upon Israel not to study the Torah (לעסוק בתורה)", exactly
the same phrase as in Yehudai's statement. Thus Elbogen's
argument[82] that Judah b. Barzillai's account is similar to that of
the apostate Samuel ibn Yaḥya al-Magrebi, who traced the origin
of the Piyyuṭ to the persecutions in Babylon and in Persia due to
the Magians,[83] falls to the ground. Either this apostate confused
the reports or it may be that during the troubles and persecutions
at the end of the Persian rule in Babylon, as reported by Sherira
(above, p. 258), the Jewish services were interfered with and the
Piyyuṭ was used as a substitute for the Rabbinic instruction.
But there is ground to believe that the Piyyuṭ as such originated
in Palestine as a result of Justinian's prohibition of the Deuterō-

---

[80] See Eppenstein, p. 26 ff., and cf. also Davidson, *Maḥzor Yannai*, XVI
ff., whose theory of the cryptic language of the Piyyuṭim may however need
still further substantiation.

[81] P. 252: יען שפיזפין אלו שנהגו העולם לפיסרינון חזי לנא לרבוותא שלא נתקן אלא בשעה
השמד בלחוד. מפני שלא היו יכולין להזכיר דברי תורה כי היו נוזרין האויבים על ישראל שלא
לעסוק בתורה. ועל כן היו חכמים שבתיהם בהקנין להן בכלל התחפלה להזכיר ולהזהיר לעכי
הארץ הלכות חג בחג והלכות ימים טובים והלכות שבתות ודקדוקי המצות בדרך שבחות והודיות
הרבות זפיזטים.

[82] *Der jüd. Gottesdienst*, 283.
[83] See Schreiner, *M. G. W. J.*, XLII, 221.

sis and that it took the place of the preachings of the Rabbis.[84]
It continued to flourish even after the era of religious freedom had
set in with the conquest of Arabs. R. Yehudai's criticism against
the מעמדות, the Paiṭanic insertions in the Sabbath 'Amidah containing אסור והתר and Aggadah and breaking the scheme of the
ritual, seems to have had little effect in Palestine. He could not
stamp out the Piyyuṭ even in Babylon, though he and several
other Geonim subsequently had tried to limit its extent.[85] The
Piyyuṭ spread from Palestine to the whole of Byzantium and to
Southern Italy, where Byzantine intolerance continued for a long
time, and from there to other European countries. However,
this is not the place to describe the growth and the spread of the
Piyyuṭ as the discussion here is only limited to the accounts of
its having found a prominent place in the divine service of the
synagogue as a result of persecutions (שמד).

2. On the other hand the report that the very reading of the
Hafṭarah from the Prophets having been a substitute for the
reading from the Pentateuch, which had been proscribed by Antiochus Epiphanes,[36] does not seem to have any historical basis.
In the persecution of Antiochus the whole existence of Judaism
was involved and not a mere item of the service such as the reading of the Torah. More credence, however, is to be given to the
reports concerning the Hafṭarot read in Babylon at the Minḥah
service on Sabbath which had to be abolished on account of their
proscription by the Persian government. This government action
(שמדא) is reported briefly without indicating its cause by R.
Naṭronai in a responsum which reads (*Geonica*, II, 302, No. XXVI):
בדורות ?(Sabb. 24a) וש' (=ובששאלהם) מהו המפטיר בנביא במנחה בשבת
ראשונים כשהיו קורין במנחה בשבת היו מפטירין בישעיה נביא (read והגביא,

---

[84] Cf. also the passage in Pardes, ed. Ehrenreich, p. 229: ולפי שכבר דל
ודלה (read החכמה ונתמעטה עכדו בכקום מדרש וקרובות| ופיוטי העגין. See also Epstein,
M. G. W. J., XLIV, p. 295–6, and Davidson, *l.c.*, XVI.

[85] See Ben-Baboi's objections (*REJ.*, vol. 70, 130–131, 133) based on
R. Yehudai's and see Eppenstein, *l.c.*, p. 39 ff. On the other hand see the
defence of the Piyyuṭim by R. Gershom Meor Haggolah (in שבה'ל, ed. Buber.
25–6), and *Pardes, l.c.*

[86] See Abudraham, ed. Prague, 52b, and Elijah Levita (השבי, s.v. פטר).
The latter has a report which ascribes to persecution to Antiochus Epiphanes.
See also Elbogen, p. 175.

וכולן בוהמות שבישעיה, ולא היו כוסיפין על י' פסוקין. ומרו פרסיים כמדא שלא
להפמיר, וכיון שסילקו (insert) מלהפטיר, סילקוהו.[87]

The original custom of Haftarot at Sabbath Minḥah is no doubt
Babylonian being in explicit contradiction to the Palestinian rite
as laid down in the Mishnah (Meg. 4.1: בב' ה' ובשבת במנחה קורין
שלשה...ואין מפטירין בנביא). Rab (who returned to Babylon about
219 C. E., as usually accepted) refers to the Haftarot at Sabbath
Minḥah in Babylon as well-established.[88]

[87] This responsum is also to be found in ח"נ, No. 95 (among other responsa
of Naṭronai) and is further cited in his name by R. Isaiah di Trani (המכריע, ס', ed.
Livorno, 20b, bottom). Rashi (to Sabb. 24a, s. v. הפמיר) cites it anonymously
and incompletely: בצאתי בתשובות הגאונים שהיו רגילים לקרוא בנביא בשבתות במנחה
עשרה פסוקים, ובימי פרסיים מרו גזרה שלא לעשׂ׃ת לעשׂ׃ת וכו'; thus leaving out the essential detail of נחמות שבישעיה which helps to ascertain the reason of the proscription by the government.

Graetz, *M. G. W. J.*, 1887, 554-55, wrongly explains the responsum in
ח"נ to refer to a Byzantine persecution, even suggesting that ובמי פרסיים is a
corruption, due to the censor, for ובכ:י רומיים. But the reading פרסיים is now
well-established by the Genizah text (in *Geonica*) which, needless to say, was
not subject to the whim of a Christian censor. Graetz's other arguments are
feeble as all ones *e silentio* are. Moreover in Palestine Haftarot at Sabbath
Minḥah were never in vogue as shown above in the text.

[88] Sabb. 24a bottom: דאמר רב אחדבוי בר רב כהנה אמר רב כהנה אמר רב
(so in MS. Munich) המפטיר בנביא במנחה בשבת א'צ להכיר של יו'ט כאלכלא שבת אין
נביא במנחה ביו'ט. This reading is also in '*Ittim*, 271, top. In Hai Gaon's
responsum רבא is evidently a misprint because R. Matnah was a colleague
of R. Yehudah b. Ezekiel (Ber. 11b). The French Tosafists indeed realized
the contradiction with the statement in the Mishnah (so R. Isaac הזקן in
Tosafot, ibid., s.v. כאלכלא) but the reply of R. Tam is wholly unsatisfactory.
He suggests that by "prophet" the Hagiographa are meant similar to the
custom in Nehardea to read passages from them at Sabbath Minḥah (Sabb.
116b: בנהרדעא פסקי סידרא בכתובים במנחא דשבתא). But the whole passage
there refers to study at the Bet Hammidrash and not to the service in the
synagogue as has been rightly pointed out by R. Isaiah di Trani (המכריע ס'
ואינו נראה לי דהאי פסקי סידרא לא כשבע התם אלא שהיו דורשים בכתובים או קרין:20c):
בהם במנחה בשבת כשלא היה להם זמן ביהם'ד כאחר שאכלו לא היו דורשים לרבים. R.
Isaiah after deducing evidence concludes (20d): אלמא פסקי סידרא לא כשבע
דרשה ולא הפטרה (read perhaps לענין) אלא לכדין. It is evident that R. Tam did
not know of the respective Gaonic responsa, which explicitly indicate Haftarot
from the Prophets, as otherwise he would not have made his fallacious suggestion. He also did not have the emendation יו'כ שחל להיות בשבת, which Judah
ibn Barzillai mentions ('*Ittim*, 271, top). It is evidently a later change by

The custom must have been in vogue in Babylon long before the Mishnah became there the accepted code and the object of intensive study in the schools since the times of Rab and Samuel, or else it would have been abolished by reason of its contraditcion with the proscription in the Mishnah. The exalted orations of Deutero-Isaiah, by which the נחמות שבישעיה are evidently meant,[89] were especially precious to the Jews in Babylon and in Persia since they dealt with conditions of the exiles in Babylon. Who knows whether their recital was not instituted in Babylon during the early Persian period before the conquest of the country by Alexander the Great?. Living in a social environment where Zorastrianism was predominant, how better could the Jewish spiritual leaders impress upon their people the monotheistic principles of their faith than with such a passage as Is. 45.1–7, especially verse 7: יוצר אור ובורא חשך עשה שלום ובורא רע אני ה' עשה כל אלה?[90] For a group living in a heathen environment and away from the center in Palestine, such as the Babylonian Jews were, the glowing fervor and exaltation of the chapters of Deutero-Isaiah indeed were admirably suited for public reading on Sabbath afternoons. The aim of these prophecies, in the words of Driver (*Introduction to the Literature of the O. T.*, 8th ed., pp. 230–31), "to arouse the indifferent, to reassure the wavering, to expostulate with the doubting, to announce with triumphant confidence the certainty

copyists against which already R. Zeraḥya Hallevi (מאור to Alfasi, Sabb. *a.l.*) protests.

[89] Though the Talmud (B. B. 14b) regards the whole of Isaiah as containing "consolations" (ישעיה כוליה נחמתא, cf. also Ber. 57b: ישעיה הרואה ובחלום ספר, וישעיה כוליה נחמתא, evidently referring to the cheerful visions to be found in chapts. 1–39 (e. g. 2.1–4; 9.1–6; c. 11–12; etc.), the term נחמות שבישעיה stood for sections chiefly taken from Is. 40 ff., though chs. 34–35 may have been included. It should be noted that the Hafṭarot for שבת נחמו and onward, the well known שבעה דנחמתא (to be discussed later on), are all taken from Deutero-Isaiah. About Isaiah, as the prophet of consolation, see also S. E. R., c. 16, pp. 82–3.

[90] About the insertion of this verse in a modified form (viz. ובורא את הכל for ובורא רע) in the morning service for the purpose of emphasizing monotheism against Zoroastrianism, see the attractive theory of Blau, *REJ.*, vol. 31, pp. 190 ff. Who knows whether originally the benediction יוצר אור did not end with ובורא רע? Cf. Ber. 11b where the change is explained to be due to a desire of using a more auspicious language (לישנא מעליא).

226

of the coming restoration"—held good for a long time after their first pronouncement.[91]

The Haftarot from the "consolations" of Deutero-Isaiah at Sabbath Minhah thus were probably continued to be recited in Babylon and Persia for several centuries till the Sassanids came to power in 226 in the time of Rab. As the Talmud does not mention anywhere of their having been proscribed by the new government, we may assume that the Jews followed their time-honored ritual throughout the Talmudic period. The prohibition, recorded by R. Natronai, probably took place during the fanaticism in consequence of the movement of Mazdak which brought great trials upon the Babylonian Jews towards the end of the 5th century and the beginning of the 6th. A verse like Is. 45.7 was regarded as a distinct challenge to the principle of dualism. Another objection may have been found by the fanatical Magians in the reference to Cyrus (Is. 44.28, 45.1) as achieving his glory for the sake of Israel (see Is. 45.4) since his memory was greatly revered by the Magians as the champion of Zoroastrianism. Altogether the great emphasis of Deutero-Isaiah on the nature of God as "the Creator, the Sustainer of the universe, the Life-Giver, the Author of history, the First and the Last, the Incomparable One" (in the words of Driver, ibid. p. 242) together with the glowing pictures of the restoration of Israel and the triumph of Zion must have been offensive to the spokesmen of Zorastrianism.[92] Hence these Haftarot recited at Sabbath

[91] But it should not be overlooked that Isaiah was a favorite book especially in Palestine for the Haftarot of the Triennial Cycle. Out of the 45 Haftarot to Genesis, 29 are from Isaiah and out of the 29 to Exodus, 18 are from this prophet (see Dr. Büchler's discussion of the problem, JQR., VI, 54 and 60). Several of these Haftarot are from ch. 40 ff. Were we to know the exact Haftarot in Babylon at Sabbath Minhah it would be of interest to trace how many of them corresponded to the Palestinian Haftarot from Isaiah at the morning service. Who knows whether the many Palestinian Haftarot eliminated in Babylon owing to the Annual Cycle had not found again their place in the Minhah services?

[92] Both Rappaport (ערך מלין, ed. Warsaw, I, 336) and Weiss (דדור, IV, p. 5, note 7) missed the right point in trying to explain the reason of the prohibition. Altogether Rappaport's remarks on this problem of the Minhah Haftarot have been rightly criticized by Schorr (החלוץ, II, 143–4).

Minḥah were proscribed and were not again re-introduced in
Babylon even after the intolerance had ceased, evidently because
of the fact that the Hafṭarah of Minḥah was against the Mishnaic
prescription.   Yet as late as in time of Hai Gaon there were still
distant congregations in Elam and in the islands of the Persian
Gulf, who retained the custom,[93] probably because the proscription of the central government at Ctesiphon in Babylon had no
sustaining power enough to reach these outlying communities
among whom then the Hafṭarot at Sabbath Minḥah had never
gone out of practice.[94]   The whole custom of Hafṭarot at Sabbath
Minḥah was one of the old differences in custom between Palestine and Babylon (as Schor in note 111 to 'Ittim, p. 271, rightly
pointed out) just as the difference of the Triennial and Annual
Cycles respectively.   The collection of differences (חלוף מנהגים)
between these two countries, emanating from the Gaonic period,
however, no longer mentions this item because at that time it had
already long been abolished in Babylon, the seat of the academies.

3. Since the readings from Deutero-Isaiah were proscribed in
Babylon, probably during the Mazdak movement, the question
arises with regard to the Hafṭarot from the 9th of Ab to New
Year, known as שבעה דנחמתא, which were taken exclusively from
Is. 40 ff. Dr. Büchler (J. Q. R., VI, 64 ff.) was on the right track
in suggesting that these Hafṭarot had originated in Palestine.
Elbogen (p. 178, see notes (2nd ed.) p. 545) has really no evidence
for his suggestion that they were ordained "probably in Babylon."
Dr. Büchler's theory is now strengthened by the remarkable
discovery of H. St. John Thackeray (The Septuagint and Jewish

[93] אבל הני לן לרבינו האיי גאון... ואלו הן הורף דבריו... שמנהג היה 'Ittim, p. 271:
בתחלה בסקוסות הרבה שמפטירין במנחה בשבת. ועדיין יש ספרי אפפרתא שיש בהם ענין לכנחה
לכל כנה וקורין לה נחכתא. אחר אפטרתא סחרית (read ודשחרית) כותבין נחמתא בישעיה,
נחמהא בירכיה.   ויש מקומות בארץ עילם ואיי הים של פרס פרנילין בה עד עכסיו.
'Ittim does not quote Hai's responsum fully (see the different version in המאור
to Alfasi, a. l.).   The phrase נחמתא בירמיה seems to me to be spurious in view of
the fact that in B. B. 14b the book of Jeremiah is described as כוליה חורבנא (cf.
also Ber. 57b: ירמיה ידאג לפורענות (בחלום ספר) הרו006), though of course there
are several passages that could have been selected containing consolations.

[94] This removes the difficulty raised by Dr. Ginzberg, Geonica, II, 298,
who likewise failed to realize the reason of the proscription of the Hafṭarah at
Sabbath Minḥah.

Worship, 1921, pp. 84 and 100) that the consolatory portion of Baruch corresponds more or less to these consolation Haftarot being dependent also on Deutero-Isaiah, just as the previous portions of this apocryphal book correspond to the three Haftarot of Punishment (ג' דפרענותא) preceding the 9th of Ab as well as to the readings on the fast day itself (from Jeremiah and Job). If Thackeray's ingenious theory be right, then the Haftarot of Consolation are much earlier than the date suggested by Dr. Büchler (ibid. p. 72), viz. the post-Talmudical times. However, in Babylon these Haftarot from the נחמות שבישעיה were never introduced simply because the local ritual used Isaiah's Consolations as Haftarot on every Sabbath at Minḥah including the seven Sabbaths between the 9th of Ab and New Year.[95] With the proscription of these Minḥah Haftarot towards the end of the 5th century it would have been dangerous to adopt the "Seven Consolation" Haftarot as the morning Haftarot during these seven weeks. This cycle of 7 Haftarot thus evidently found no entrance in the Babylonian ritual before the beginning of the Muslim period. Since the Minḥah Haftarot were not re-introduced, in spite of the removal of their proscription with the overthrow of the Sassanids, because of the explicit statement in the Mishnah that at Sabbath Minḥah there should be no Haftarah, the cycle of שבעה דנחמתא from Deutero-Isaiah was thus adopted in Babylon for these seven weeks in accordance with the Palestinian custom.

V

OTHER ITEMS.

In this section some items pertaining to the divine service of the synagogue will be discussed that underwent changes prior to the Byzantine and Sassanid periods respectively. The case of the Decalogue in the liturgy entails a change brought about by no

---

[95] Dr. Büchler writes (*l. c.*, p. 72, bottom): "the Babylonians were also apprised of the practice of reading the Haftarot exclusively from Isaiah" and as evidence he cites R. Naṭronai's responsum about the Minḥah Haftarot as if it referred to Palestine! He overlooked the end of the responsum which says clearly that these Haftarot were abolished בבני פרסײ, viz. the Sassanids, which can only refer to the Babylonian custom.

government interference but by the Jewish spiritual leaders in
Palestine in order to counteract the polemics on the part of Jewish
heretics.   The elimination of the recital of the Decalogue daily
in the service led to a change in the contents of the Tephillin.
This symbol in its revised form was a part of the practice of
Judaism, proscribed by Hadrian in consequence of the Bar-
Kokhba revolt, and did not regain for itself general observance
even after the Hadrianic edicts had been annulled.   Finally a
reminiscence from the Hadrianic persecution towards its close
we have in the change of the time set for תקיעת שופר on New Year
with which our discussion terminates.

1. The Decalogue in the Liturgy.

This problem needs only brief mention here in view of my
remarks elsewhere[96] in connection to the reappearance of the
Decalogue in the daily service at the Palestinian synagogue in
Fusṭāṭ in the Muslim period continuing right down to the 13th
century.   The Decalogue, recited daily in the Temple by the
officiating priests prior to the Shemaʻ, was eliminated in Palestine
from the service of the synagogue some time after the destruction
of the Temple (probably in the second century) because of
heretical claims that only the Decalogue was Divine the rest of
the Pentateuch consisting of later additions by Moses.   How
such claims could easily find acceptance among the people against
the Rabbinic conception of תורה מן השמים and the Oral Law from
Sinai is strikingly illustrated by the Nash Papyrus, being a
fragment of an early liturgy prevalent in Egypt, wherein the
Decalogue is followed by a Hebrew verse, not found in the Masso-
retic text but in LXX before Deut. 6.4 (the beginning of the
Shemaʻ), ואלה החקים והמשפטים אשר צוה משה את בני ישראל במדבר
בצאתם מארץ מצרים.   The elimination of the Decalogue prevailed
in Babylon where attempts in the Amoraic period to re-introduce
it in Sura and in Nehardea failed.   But in Egypt apparently the
Decalogue never disappeared from the liturgy.   Anyhow we find
it again in use in the Palestinian synagogue in Fusṭāṭ throughout

[96] See Mann, *Jews in Egypt and in Palestine under the Fatimid Caliphs*, I,
221–23, and especially *H. U. C. Annual*, II, 282–4.

the Gaonic period right down to the time of Maimonides and beyond (1211). Whether this was only a local Minhag in Egypt or whether in Palestine too the Decalogue was re-introduced in the Muslim period cannot as yet be ascertained.

2. TEPHILLIN.

The problem of the Decalogue in the liturgy has a bearing also on the contents of the Tephillin in early times. It is not within the scope of this paper to discuss fully the origin of the custom of Tephillin.[96a] Whatever may have been the original form of the Biblical אות and טוטפות[97] it is evident that in the course of the period of the Second Commonwealth the Tephillin became the outward symbol of קבלת עול מלכות שמים. The very name תפלה used in the Rabbinic literature for the phylactery seems to be connected with a ceremony at prayer-time. The modern explanation of the word from תפל (תפל=) to attach, to affix, is not very illuminating as a better noun could have been formed from the roots קשר or עד (viz. קֶשֶׁר or עֲנִידָה).[98] But even if this connotation

[96a] Rodkinsohn's work תפלה למשה (Pressburg 1883), while revealing the author's learning, basically suffers from lack of method and historical judgment. His theories need not, therefore, be dealt with here.

Schorr's article (החלוץ, V, 11 ff.) is indeed full of critical acumen but suffers from its too polemical tendency. While correctly realizing several features in the development of the custom, Schorr failed to obtain a clear view of the whole process. A radical fault of his was not to differentiate, when discussing the data, between the wearing of Tephillin at prayer only, and the whole day. Abraham Krochmal (עיון תפלה, Lemberg 1885, pp. 24–37), too, fails to give a clear picture of the history of the rite of Tephillin though some of his remarks are well worth while. He rightly surmised (p. 35) that there were once Tephillin containing five Biblical sections including the Decalogue but failed properly to understand this fact.

Blau's article (J. E. X, 26 ff.) is of a more informative nature than critical. In setting forth my own views it was not found feasible to enter into arguments on each point with the above authors but rather to let the data in their new construction speak for themselves.

[97] Cf. Hastings' *Dictionary of the Bible*, III, 869 ff., and J. E., X, 26, 28.

[98] Kohut in *Aruch Completum*, s. v. טטפת (vol. IV, 25–6) and תפל (vol. VIII, 258) and Jastrow, s.v. Cf. also the phraseology in Siphre (ed. Friedmann, p. 74b): וקשרתם אלו בקשירה וכו׳.

be granted, the expression תפלה (Aram. plur. תפלין to distinguish
it from תפלות, prayers) was purposely chosen because the symbol
had been originally meant to be used at prayer.[99] With the introduction of the Shema' in the daily service as an essential part of
it, the Rabbis thought it proper to symbolise this declaration of
the Unity of God by the Tephillin finding a support for this
symbol in the literal interpretation of the verses in Deut. 6.8,
11.18 (Ex. 13.9, 16). The symbol was ordained primarily at the
daily morning service. The reason why Tephillin were not put
on on Sabbath morning was rather due to the strictness of the
Sabbath observance and to the fear of carrying the Tephillin from
the home to the synagogue (הוצאה).[100] By analogy to the Sabbath
the Tephillin were not put on also at the service on the Festivals.
The usual explanation of Sabbath and Yom Tob being themselves symbols and requiring no further אות is later and more of
an Aggadic character.[101]

    The primary connection of Tephillin with the morning
service in conjunction with recital of the Shema' is also borne out
by the seemingly curious report of Jerome that the phylacteries
contained the Ten Commandments.[102] Jerome does not even

[99] So already in קול סכל, the polemical work against which Judah Leon
Modena wrote his שאגת אריה (in בחינת הקבלה, ed. Reggio, p. 39): ואהשוב כי מתהלה
היו כ׳ציבים אותם (והתפלין viz.) בשעת תפלה לבד, ולכן קראום תפלין, אח׳כ קצתם החסירו
יהר ללבשם כל היום וכו'.

[100] Cf. the cases of the Shofar, the Lulab and the Megillah when either
New Year, or the 1st day of Tabernacles or Purim happened to fall on a Sabbath (see R. H. 29b, Sukkah 42b-43a, Meg. 4b: גזירה שמא יטלנו בידו...ויעבירנו ד'
אכות ברה׳ר, והיינו כעמא דלולב. והיינו טעמא דמגלה.

[101] Cf. R. 'Akiba's statement (Men. 36b): יכול יניח אדם תפלין בשבתות וביכים
.ביביף ה׳ל: והיה לאות על ידך וכו' מי שצריכין אות יצאו שבתות וימים טובים שהן גופן אות
This really applies only to Sabbath (Ex. 31.17). See also Mekhilta of R. Simon
b. Yoḥai (ed. Hoffmann, p. 34). In the other Mekhilta (Bo. c. 17) the statement is ascribed to R. Isaac which seems more likely.

[102] See Jerome to Mt. 23.6 (in Migne, *Patrologia Latina*, vol. 26, col. 174)
hoc Pharisaei male interpretantes (sc. Dt. 6.8) scribebant in membranulis
Decalogum Moysi, id est decem verba legis, complicantes ea, et ligantes in
fronte, et quasi coronam capitis facientes, ut semper ante oculos moverentur.
Likewise to Ezek. 24.15 (ibid, vol. 25, col. 230, top): Aiunt Hebraei hucusque
Babylonios magistros, Legis praecepta servantes, *decalogum scriptum* in membranulis circumdare capiti suo, et haec esse quae jubeantur ante oculos et in
fronte pendere, ut semper videant quae praecepta sunt. Et quia Ezechiel

mention the Shema' in the Tephillin. But when we consider that originally the Decalogue preceded the recital of the Shema' in the service having been eliminated some time after the destruction of the Temple (probably at the beginning of 2nd century C. E.) in order to deprive the heretics of one of their arguments against the divine origin of the entire Torah, Jerome's account, becomes intelligible. We may safely assume that the Tephillin prior to the elimination of the Decalogue from the daily morning service really contained five Biblical sections, viz. the Decalogue, שמע, והיה כי יביאך and קדש, והיה אם שמע (Deut. 5.6–18, 6.4–9, 11.13–21, Ex. 13.1–10, 13.11–16). The section from Exodus was chosen because of the mention of אות and טוטפות and at the same time referring to the redemption from Egypt it well corresponded to the usual third section of the Shema', viz. Numbers 15.37–41, which likewise concludes with a reference to יציאת מצרים.[103] When, however, the Decalogue was eliminated from the service it had also to be eliminated from the Tephillin. Jerome may have seen such early phylacteries and looking only at the beginning of the strip of parchment within he noticed first the Decalogue. Had he read on he would have found there subsequently the Shema' and the other sections. It may also be that the Tephillin Jerome saw belonged to a heretic who disobeyed the ruling of the Rabbis.[104] The Mishnah (Sanh. 11.3) clearly reflects the time when the Tephillin included the Decalogue and hence had five sections in stating: חומר בדברי סופרים מדברי תורה. האומר אין תפלין כדי לעבור על דברי תורה פטור, חמשה טוטפות להוסיף על דברי סופרים חייב. Now what could these five Ṭoṭafot (viz. five compartments of the phylactery on the head) contain if not the Decalogue that pre-

---

sacerdos erat, nequaquam eum debere deponere coronam gloriationis, sed ligatam habere in capite. Hoc illi dixerint. The interpretation of פאר as Tephillin is reported in the name of Rab (Sukkah 25b, cf. Ber. 16b, top).

[103] The order of the Biblical portions in the Tephillin, given in Men. 34b, refers already to the time after the elimination of the Decalogue. See *infra*, note 106, about the position of the Shema' section.

[104] Cf. M. Megillah 4.8 about the different way of putting on Tephillin used by the Minim. Cf. also Blau, *J. E.*, X, 27, col. 2, who thinks that Jerome was incorrect in this account. But our explanation solves the whole difficulty. Nor is the Nash Papyrus with the Decalogue before the Shema' heretical as Blau seems to think (see above p. 40).

ceded the Shema'? The phraseology of the Mishnah makes the Tephillin containing four Biblical sections already Sopheric but the change only took place after the destruction of the Temple long after the so-called period of the Sopherim.[105]

One can even venture to suggest that the outward indication of the letter Shin on the head phylactery was ordained after this change to proclaim to all that the Tephillin began with Shema' (there being no room enough on the בית to write the word שמע in full, hence only letter ש was enough for the indication).[105a] Therefore the letter appears on one side of the capsule containing the Biblical sections in the usual form (שמע=ש) and on the other side with four tittles on the top (שׁ) indicating that there were only *four sections* inside![106] Later on the Shin on the head

[105] Interesting is the discussion in Siphre (ed. Friedmann, p. 74b), which reflects the earlier time when the Tephillin contained the Decalogue: ועדיין אני אומר: והרי קדש לי והיה כי יביאך שקידמום מצות אחרות הרי הם בקשירה, עשרת הדברות שלא קידמום מצות אחרות אינו דין שיהו בקשירה? אמרת קל וחומר וכו' Cf. also par. 34 (p. 74a) which also reflects the elimination of the Decalogue from the daily recital prior to the Shema' י' הדברות כלא קדכום מצות אחרות אינו ודין שיהו בשנן)

[105a] For a similar abbreviation cf. R. Judah's statement (Yer. Meg. 71a, 1. 20): אדר השני כותב תיו (=חתיין) ודיו. Cf. the different version in Meg. Ta'anit, end in Neub., *Med. Jew. Laron.*, II, 23). See also M. M. Sheni 4.11.

[106] This double form of Shin on the head phylactery is prescribed in the Gaonic work שמושא רבא (cited in Tos. to Men. 35a s.v. שין שלתפלין: צורה דשין דימינא ג' רישי ודשמאלא ד' רישי, ואי אפיך לית לן בה. This was an old tradition no longer understood. The ending permitting a reversal was due to the later shifting of the order of the Biblical sections (see end of this note). Originally, after the elimination of the Decalogue, the Shema' was purposely put on the right side of the capsule, outside of which was the letter שמע=ש.

The arrangement of the Biblical sections in the Tephillin underwent changes and was by far not fixed uniformly, as is evident from Men. 34b; ת"ר: כיצד סדרן? קדש לי והיה כי יביאך מימין, שמע והיה אם שמוע משמאל. והתניא איפכא? אמר אביי: לא קשיא, כאן מימינו של קורא, כאן מימינו של מניח, והקורא קורא כסדרן. The second version of the Baraita was evidently the original form. Formerly there was included the Decalogue too as in the daily service. After its elimination there remained 4 sections beginning with Shema' which took its place on the right side of the capsule where outwardly there was (and still is) the letter שמע=ש. Then followed קדש לי and והיה כי יביאך and והיה אם שמוע, the last being placed on the left side of the capsule outside of which we have the letter Shin in the form שׁ to indicate that there were only 4 sections. But the desire to have the sections in the order of their occurence in the Pentateuch resulted in a re-

phylactery was regarded as a law to Moses from Sinai (כין
שבתפלין הלכה למשה מסיני) because its real purpose was no longer
known.[107] The still later explanation of Shin as forming the word
שרי together with the knots of the head phylactery in the form of
ד and of the hand phylactery in the form of יוד need not detain
us long.[108] Beside its late origin it overlooks the fact that the
hand phylactery was worn covered and that even the knot of the
phylactery on the head was not always visible whereas symbols
are essentially instituted for outward appearance manifest to all.
All this only shows how successfully the Rabbis succeeded in
removing the traces of the earlier Tephillin containing five
Biblical sections so that the Tephillin in their new form became to

shifting of the sections. Even after this reshifting the section Shema' still
remained on the right side of the capsule (where Shin is marked on the outside) in many Tephillin and should be so according to R. Tam, who is supported by Garonic evidence (see Tos., ibid, s. v. והקורא: וכפרש ר'ת קדש והיה מימין של
(viz. on left side of the capsule) קורא וכשמאל של קורא הוי שבע כבהוץ ואחריה
והיה אם שמע מבפים וכו'.) Cf. also Maimonides instructive responsum on the
subject (קובץ תשובות הרמב"ם, I, No. 26, and in כסף כמנה to תפלין ה', ה' תורה, מענה,
3.5), where the reference to another Moses b. Maimon, of Cordova, who had
composed a work on Tephillin, is rather suspicious.

[107] Men. 35a: ואמר אבי שין של תפלין הלכה למשה כסיני. Bahya b. Asher
(כד הקמח, Lemberg, 1872, 116a) quotes similar statements of Abbaye with
regard to דל'ת של ת' and יו'ד של ת' but this reading is unwarranted (see note
108, end).

[108] Cf. the legendary account of the heated discussion between Moses
(sic!) and R. Tam about the knot in the shape of יוד on the hand phylactery
(given by Gedalya ibn Yahya, שלשלת הקבלה, ed. Lemberg, 1864, 69a, b, cf. the
MS. version given by Kaufmann, REJ., V. 274–5) which shows that the whole
combination of the three letters שרי is very late. אמר לו משה רבינו... שהקשירה של
יד ביד'ד לא צויתי לעולם ולא למדתיה, אכן חכמים הקנו אוהה בסברתם להשלים שם שרי,
ובשביל כך לא רצו לעשותה בראש שלא יבעו לוטר שציותים כך מאחר שאינה כצורפת עם הש'
ור'.

הלכה למשה Even with regard to קשר שבתפלין though it was regarded as קשר שבתפלין
מסיני (see Men. 35b), it is nowhere indicated in the Talmud that it had the shape
of דלת. Only later on the passage in the Talmud (ibid.): וראו כל עמי הארץ כי שם ה':
נקרא עליך וכו'. הגיא ר'א הנדול אומר אלו תפלין שבראש, suggested the combination of
a Divine name, viz. שרי. So Rashi: שם ה'... שכתוב בו רוב השם שין ודלת (cf. also
s.v. קשר) but Tosafot rightly objects to this: תראה דדלי'ת ויו'ד שברצועות לאו אותיוה
.גכורות הן ולא השיבי מן השם של שרי... ובכום דוכהא לא קרו להו כי אם קשר של תפלין
A still later explanation of letter ש as being רמז לשכינה is given by Bahya b.
Asher (כד הקמח, 115b, 116a).

be regarded as being of hoary antiquity and the outward indication such as Shin became a matter of guessing. All this was due
to their struggle against the Minim and to their desire to obliter-
ate as much as possible the details of this strife in order not to
arouse new controversies.

The symbol of Tephillin just as that of Ṣiṣit was employed
by the Pharisees as a means in their endeavor to intensify the
Jewish religious life and make it pervade everyday activities.
The Rabbis and their disciples began to wear Tephillin the whole
day, even after the divine service, in order to symbolize their
constant awareness of "the yoke of the kingdom of heaven" for
the acceptance of which the Shema' was the official declaration.
Of this custom first mention is made in Talmudic reports referring
to the 1st century, C. E. It combined both a religious as well as
a sort of political demonstration inasmuch as the spiritual מלכות
שמים was still staunchly hoped for by Israel though *de facto*
Palestine was under the mundane, wicked rule of Rome (see also
above, p. 246). Whereas the Tephillin of the Ḥasid in the time of
Simon b. Sheṭaḥ (Yer. Ḥag. 77d) probably were those used only
at prayer and likewise those of Shammai, which he had from his
maternal grandfather,[109] we hear of R. Yoḥanan b. Zakkai that
he constantly wore the Tephillin both in winter and in summer
and that his disciple R. Eliezer b. Hyrcanos followed suit.[110] The
whole account shows that this was regarded as an act of extreme
piety, especially in the summer when the heat made the wearing
of Tephillin the whole day very uncomfortable.[111] Needless to
say ordinary people, who had to labor either in the field, the

[109] Mekh. Bo., c. 17, end, Mekh. of Simon b. Yoḥai (ed. Hoffmann, p. 35,
top). In Yer. Erubin 26a this is reported in the name of Hillel and not of
Shammai.

[110] Yer. Ber. 4c, l.10; רבן יוחנן בן זכאי לא הווה תפילוי זעין מיניה לא בקייפא ולא
בסיתוא, וכך נהג ר' אליעזר תלמידו אחריו. R. Eliezer b. Hyrcanos wore his Tephillin
even on his death bed (see the story in Yer. Sabb. 5b, bottom, Babli Sanh. 68a,
Ab. de R. Natan, c. 25). Joshu'a b. Ḥananya, another famous disciple of R.
Yoḥanan b. Zakkai, also seems to have worn the Tephillin constantly as is
evident from the Sabb. 127b.

[111] Hence R. Yoḥanan b. Nappaḥa would wear the head phylactery the
whole day only in winter, ibid., l. 11: ר' יוחנן בסיתוא דהוה חזק רישיה הוי לביש
תרויהון, ברם בקייטא דלא הוה חזיק רישיה לא הוה לביש אלא דאדרעיה.

workshop or in the market place, could not follow this Pharisaic example of piety. In this respect Dr. Büchler (*Galil. 'Am-Haareṣ* p. 23, note 1) is right in emphasizing that only some scholars would practice this extreme symbolism of קבלת עול מלכות שמים. It was also regarded as a sign of piety to enlarge the phylacteries in size in spite of the discomfort of their heaviness in wearing them and hence the Pharisees are accused of doing this only to show off before people (Matthew 23.5), though it is not certain whether this refers to the phylacteries worn only at prayer or whether also during the whole day. The wearing of Tephillin the whole day as an act of piety naturally gave rise to abuses by hypocrites as is evident from the story in Yer. Ber. 4c top.[112] A foolish Ḥasid (חסיד שוטה) is illustrated by the example of his passing by a river and seeing a child drowning but delaying to go to its rescue till he takes off his Tephillin (in order not to desecrate them) while in the meanwhile the child is perishing.[113]

How far the common people practiced the custom of Tephillin even at prayer is difficult to ascertain. R. Meir is reported to say that "there is no man in Israel, who is not surrounded by Miṣvot, viz. Tefillin on his head and arm and other symbols (Tos. Ber. 7.25: אין לך אדם מישראל שאין מצות מקיפות אותו, תפלין בראשו והתפלין בזרועו, ומזוזה בפתחו וארבעה ציצית מקיפות אותו, cf. also Yer. Ber. 14d). Probably R. Meir meant here that at least some of these Miṣvot were kept by every Jew and should not be taken to reflect his actual experience of conditions in Palestine either before or after the Hadrianic persecutions. Moreover, this statement appears anonymously in quite a different form in Men. 43b.[114] Laborers in the field, or even in the homes of their

---

[112] עובדא הוה בחד בר נש דאפקיד גבי חבריה וכפר ביה, א'ל: לא לך הפנית אלא לאילין דבריך הפנית. Cf. especially Pes. R. c. 22 (ed. Friedmann, 111b): שלא ההא תפלין נושא וסליחך. עובף והולך ועובר עבירות.

[113] אי זהו חסיד שוטה? ראה תינוק מבעבע בנהר, Yer. Soṭah, 19a, l.14 ff: אמר: לכשאחלוץ תפילי, אצילנו. עם כשהוא חולץ תפיליו, הוציא זה את נפשו.

[114] Joshu'a b. Hananya characterises the 'Am-Ha-areṣ as not putting on Tephillin (viz. even at prayer), Ber. 46b, but in Soṭah 22a this statement is anonymous in reply to R. Meir, who had a more lenient view that the 'Am-Ha-areṣ be only stigmatised as such, if he does not recite the Shema'. This would show that R. Meir was fully aware of the fact that the laborers could not prac-

employers, early in the morning evidently recited the Shema' and
the Tefillah without putting on Tephillin (see Ber. 16a where
Tephillin are not mentioned at all). Whatever may have been
the extent of the prevalence of Tephillin before the Hadrianic
persecutions, the prohibition of Judaism in the years 135–138 (or
thereabouts) made the wearing of the Tephillin especially dangerous because of their conspicuousness and tended to bring about
laxity in the practice even after the removal of Hadrian's edicts
by Antoninus Pius. The danger of Tephillin during this time of
persecution is alluded to in M. 'Erubin 10.1 (ובסכנה מכסן הולך)
and in Sabb. 49a (also 130a) in connection with the story of
Elisha בעל כנפים.[115] Informers (à la Aḥer) probably pointed out
to the government that the Tephillin, like the Shema' contained
therein, had a special signifiance as a symbol of קבלה עול מלכות
שמים as against the rule of Rome.[116] On account of the obvious
danger people stopped putting on Tephillin even at prayer not to
speak of wearing them in the streets. Only a saint like Elisha
בעל כנפים would expose himself to the danger. The discontinu-
ance of the custom led to laxity even after Hadrian's time as is
characteristically admitted by R. Simon b. El'azar, a disciple of R.
Meir (Sabb. 130a).[117] On the other hand the scholarly refugees
from Palestine, who had sought safety in Babylon from Roman

tice this custom even at prayer. However, R. Meir's statement in Soṭah is
reported in Ber. in the name of Eli'ezer b. Hyrcanos.

[115] Schorr (החלוץ, V, 15) rightly suggests that בעל כנפים really meant a
member of the Ḥaberim, who observed Levitical purity (cf. Bekhorot 30b;
סקבלין לכנפים ואח'כ מקבלין למהרות), though his identification with the Essenes is not warranted. The explanation of the name in connection with the
miracle of the Tephillin in Sabb. 49a is of course legendary but the prohibition
of wearing Tephillin during the Hadrianic persecution reported there is quite
historical.

[116] Complete acceptance of this obligation (in the words of R. Yoḥanan,
Ber. 14b, bottom) consisted of Tephillin, Shema' and 'Amidah, הרוצה שיקבל
עליו עול מלכות שמים שלמה, יפנה ויטול ידיו ויניח תפלין ויקרא ק'ש ויתפלל, חו היא מלכות
שמים שלמה. Though R. Yoḥanan lived long after the Bar Kokhba period,
he no doubt reflects in this respect the sentiment maintained by the leading
Rabbis centuries before.

[117] תניא ר'ש בן אלעזר אומר: כל מצוה שמסרו ישראל עצמן עליה למיתה בשעת מרת
הפלכות ובטעת השמד (see ד'ס, a. l., better כנון ע'ז ומילה, עדיין היא מוחזקת בידם, וכל
מצוה שלא מסרו ישראל עצמן עליה כנון חפילין, עדיין היא פרופה בידם.

persecution, were especially zealous in spreading the custom in
Babylon, as is reported by Sherira Gaon (see *infra*, note 122).
But there too only some scholars would wear Tephillin the whole
day (like Rab and others.)[118]   This continued later on to be the
custom of the Geonim and the members of the academies.[119]   But
how far the ordinary people in Babylon made use of the symbol of
Tephillin even at prayer is not evident.[120]   Yet no doubt the insistence of the Rabbis gradually exerted its influence to make
Tephillin the regular feature for all daily worshippers in the
synagogues.

To sum up our discussion, the symbolism of Tephillin was
meant primarily to emphasize the acceptance of "The yoke of the
kingdom of heaven."   Originally connected with the recital of the
Decalogue and the Shema' in the morning, the symbol was extended
to the whole day by the Pharisees in their endeavor to make the
consciousness of their religious ideal the guide of their whole
daily life.   This extension was only meant for the scholarly class
but it had its reaction in the ordinary people being lax in using the
symbol of Tephillin even at prayer because the wearing of Tephillin the whole day became to be regarded as an act of extreme
piety.   The Hadrianic persecutions had their share too in weaken-
ing the practice of the symbol.   The Rabbis, especially in the 3rd
century C. E., would endeavor to emphasize the importance of the
symbol, some of them even resorting to the mystical fancy of God
too wearing Tephillin (see Men. 35b and Ber. 6a).   Their chief
aim was to establish firmly this custom at prayer (see Ber. 14b,
bottom, and 15a, top).   On the other hand the wearing of Tephillin the whole day by all and sundry was not encouraged.   It gave

[118] Among the ten points of extreme piety attributed to Rab (עשר מילי
דחסידותא) the 9th was: שהיה רגיל תדיר בתפלין ונהג רב ששת אחריו (ש"ח, No. 178).
The passage hints that the other disciples did not follow him in this practice.

[119] Cf. Gaonic Responsa ח"ג, No. 84, ש"ח, No. 153 (in responsum of Sar
Shalom); נ"ל, No. 3; חש"ר, I, 36 top, 46.

[120] Rab characterises a sinner as one who fails to put on Tephillin (R. H.
17a: פושעי ישראל בגופן. מאי ניהו? אמר רב: קרקפתא דלא מנח תפלין).   But other
readings have Simon b. Lakish instead of Rab.

cause to abuses by hypocrites. Hence R. Yannai (1st half of 3rd
century) came out with the statement that תפילין צריכין גוף נקי.[121]
He, no doubt, meant by it the wearing of them the whole day.
But it was interpreted by several people in Gaonic times to refer
even to Tephillin at prayer and it thus led to a general laxity of
practice. The Geonim, when asked about their opinion, were
eager to combat this tendency. Instead of clearly stating that R.
Yannai referred only to wearing Tephillin the whole day, they
explained away his statement to deal only with the time of persecution. They were misled by the gloss כאלישע בעל כנפים in Sabb.
49a (see note 121) to construe the whole statement of R. Yannai
as dealing with the time of the Hadrianic persecution.[122] The
obscurity prevailing about the meaning of R. Yannai's statement
contributed greatly to the general laxity of wearing Tephillin
even at prayer especially in Western Europe, viz. in France and
Spain. As late as 1235 R. Moses of Coucy during his travels in
the Provence and in northern Spain had to bestir himself to
impress in his sermons his audiences with the duty of Tephillin at
prayer.[123] This is the case with many a rite that in course of time

---

[121] Yer. Ber. 4c, 1.6: אמר רבי ייאי: תפלין צריכין גוף נקי. מפני מה לא החזיקו בהן
מפני הרמאין וכו'. It is doubtful whether from מפני is also by R. Yannai. In
Babli (Sabb. 49a, 130a) R. Yannai is supposed to illustrate his remark by the
example of Elishah בעל כנפים but in reality it seems a later insertion.

[122] See the responsum attributed to R. Yehudai (ה'פ, No. 62; ס'ח, No. 153
תש'ר, I, 45): ואם בא אדם לומר: תפילין צריכות גוף נקי כאלישע בעל כנפים, כך פי'
חכמים: במה דברים אמורים בשעת השמד. Still more instructive is Sherira's responsum (שבה'ל, ed. Buber, p. 382, cf. 'Iṭṭur, ed. Lemberg, II, 26d, where it is
ascribed to his son, Hai, the responsum probably emanating from father and
son combined): אמור רבנן פושעי ישראל בגופן... וכפרש ר' כמעון בן לקיש: פושעי
ישראל כן נינהו? קרקפתא דלא כנח תפילי. והאידנא מאי טעכא מזלזלי בהו רובא דעלמא?
(In 'Iṭṭur the reading is רבנן דעלכא which would then refer to wearing them the
whole day). אי משום דאלישע בעל כנפים, פירשו כבר הגאונים הראשתים ההיא בשעת
המרה. ויש מקומות שהתלמידים מניחין תפילין, מי מיחוי כיהורא או דילמא קיומא נד]מצוה עדיף?
(Here again it would seem that the point concerns the wearing of them the
whole day).
Sherira's reply was: (better נורה דנפישי כיון מימות הראבונים דבא'י חינא, הכין,
ודפיש סטדא, in 'Iṭṭur: ולא יכילו לאחותי ולאנוחי (better תפלין אשהכח מיניקין
בבבל וכנהון בבבל in 'Iṭṭur: המוהירים בהון וביותר יושבי מדרשות.

[123] About France see Tosafot to Sabb. 49a, s.v. כאלישע ואין חימה על
מה שמצוה זאת רפויה בידינו שנם בימי חכמים היתה רפויה. R. Moses of Coucy in
עשין, סמ'נ, par. 3, gives us fuller information about the laxity of observance:

lose their original symbolic significance and are practiced only by force of tradition. But even to rites the proverb הכל תלוי במזל can be applied. Some of them captured the imagination of the people and were scrupulously observed. Others, like Tephillin, had to go through a long time of neglect till they found a semblance of general observance.

3. The Time of Blowing the Shofar on New Year.

The most significant feature of the New Year celebration was the blowing of the ram's horn (Shofar). It should have therefore introduced the divine service of the day and yet it is connected not with Shaḥarit service but with the Musaph. This change of time is traced back to the Hadrianic persecutions. Thus R. Yoḥanan explains the direction of the Mishnah (R. H. 32b) for the reader of Musaph to initiate the sounding of the Shofar as due to an occasion at "the time of perseuction."[124] Rashi's explanation that government officials would wait in the synagogues till the completion of Shaḥarit about midday in order to enforce the prohibition of תקיעת שופר, whereupon after their departure the Shofar was clandestinely sounded at Musaph,[125] is hardly to the point

כך דרשתי פרשה זו בגליות ישראל להוכיח שכל אחד ואחד חייב בתפלין ומזוזות... עוד זאת
דרשתי להם כי יותר חפץ הקב"ה באדם רשע סיניח תפלין מאדם צדיק, ועיקר תפילין נצטוו:
להיות זכרון לרסעים ולישרם דרך טובה, ויותר הם צריכין זכר וחיזוק מאותם סנזדלו ביראת
סמים כל ימיהם... ויהי אחר ד"א והתקצ"ה שנים לבריאות עולם היתה סיבה מן השמים להוכיח.
ובשנת תתקצ"ו (1236) הייתי בספרד להוכיחם, ואמץ הקב"ה זרועתיו בחלוסות היהודים ובחלומות
הגוים וחזיונות הכוכבים, ויט עלי חסדו והרמז הארץ ותהי לחרדת אלהים ועסו תסובות נדולות
וקבלו אלפים ורבבות כצות תפילין כזוזות וציצית, וכן בשאר ארצות הייתי אחר כך ונתקבלו
יש מתרשלין במצות תפלין שאינן זהירין (115b): כד הקסח Cp. also דברי בכל הארצות
בהגחתן מפני שחוסבין שהתפלין צריכין קדוסה וטהרה יותר כדאי וכו'

124 (מסנה) העובר לפני התיבה ביו"ט של ר"ה הסני מתקיע... עמרא) מאי סנא הלל דבראסון
(ובסחרית viz. מסום דחריזין מקדיסין למצוח, הקיעה נמי נעביד בראסון מסום דחריזין מקדיסין
נזרת הכלכות For, נזרת הכלכות a phrase due to the צנו לכצות! אמר רבי יוחנן: בסעת נזרת הסלכות
censor, all Talmudic MSS. as well as other authorities have סעת הסמד (see ד"ס,
a.l.) which in the Talmud mostly means the Hadrianic persecution.
The Hif'il מחקיע indicates that the reader gave the direction for the sounding (by announcing תקיעה, etc.) to the בעל תוקע. Had he himself blown the Shofar, the Ḳal תוקע יקע would have been used.

125 Rashi (ibid., s.v. בסעת): אויבים מרו סלא יתקעו, והיו אורבין להם כל סס.
סעות לקץ תפלת סחרית, לכך העבירוה לתקוע במוספין. The same explanation is repeated in Vitry, p. 385 (cf. p. 352 in responsum of Joseph Bonfils), Or

because during the Hadrianic persecutions the whole Synagogal service was proscribed. Moreover, the authorities would no doubt be attracted by the sound of the Shofar. Rashi had in mind the details in connection with the prohibition of the Shemaʻ by the Byzantines (above, p. 259) when the rest of the Synagogal service was more or less permitted. Of course, during the Hadrianic persecution there were cases of clandestine fulfilling of תקיעת שופר by injecting the sound into a pit or a vat as is evident from the Mishnah (ibid. 27b, top)[126] But open services were altogether prohibited and there could be no alternative of תקיעת שופר at Musaph instead of at Shaḥarit.

With the help of the parallel passage in Yer. R. H. (59c, ll.48 ff.)[127] we can understand R. Yoḥanan's statement better. It was evidently towards the end of the persecution (known as שלפי השמד),[128] after Hadrian's death (138 C. E.) and at the beginning of Antonius Pius' reign, when the rigor of the persecution was relaxed and the local Roman authorities would allow the Jews in certain pacified districts to resume their religious practices while in other places, still under suspicion of harboring some turbulent elements of the population, watchfulness was still maintained. It would occur that the sounding of the Shofar caused excitement among the Roman garrison as a revolutionary signal especially when a multitude was assembled in one place, albeit in a house of worship.[129] This time of unequal conditions prevailing in Palestine at the end of the persecutions seems to be reflected in the

Zaru'a, II, par. 264, שבה״ל, ed. Buber fol. 143 a.b., Tanya, ed. Hurwitz, p. 160. Only R. Ḥananel rightly quotes Yer. for the proper explanation.

[126] התוקע לתוך הבור או לתוך הדות או להוך הפיכס, אם קול שופר שמע יצא, ואם קול הברה שמע לא יצא. Hai Gaon (cited in ש״ש, I, 35, bottom) rightly explains this passage: שהם (read המלכיות ומזרות) דברים הללו היו צריכין להם ביכי השמד והמלכיות מתיראים מהם מלתקוע בגלוי.

[127] רבי יעקב בר אחא בשם רבי יוחנן: מפני מעשה שאירע. פעם אחת תקעו בראשונה היו השונאים סבורין שכא עליהן הם הולכין ועסדו עליהן והרנום. מינו דאינון חסי לון קראו שכע ומצליין וקוראין באורייתא ומצליי והוקעין, אינן אמרין בימוסין אינון עסיקין. About the variants see Ratner (אהבת ציון וירושלים, to R. H., pp. 47–48). Several authorities (like Isaac ibn Gayyat in ש״ש and others) seem to have had in Yer. the following ending, ואע״פ שבטל השכד התקנה לא זזה ממקוסה.

[128] Cf. the meeting at Usha which took place בשלפי השמד (Cant. R. 2.5).

[129] Cf. Amos 3.6: אם יתקע שופר בעיר, ועם לא יחרדו

Baraita (Yer. R. H., 59d top) stating that in one place the actual sounding of Shofar would take place while in another only a benediction over the Shofar would be recited.[130] One such an occasion, when the sudden sounding of the Shofar on New Year caused a panic in the Roman camp at a certain place in Palestine and resulted in an attack on the Jews assembled for worship, is reported by R. Yoḥanan. Hence, to assure the Roman authorities, the Jews would assemble in their synagogues on New Year and first occupy themselves with the Shaḥarit service and the reading of the Biblical portions. The authorities, suspicious of the Jewish assemblies, would become convinced that they were purely religious gatherings and would not be alarmed when the Shofar was sounded. This new arrangement thus remained in force even after the conditions that had called it forth had long passed in the course of time.

In the absence of another tradition R. Yoḥanan's report deserves credence as he was informed in historical matters (see Bacher, *Ag. d. Pal. Amor.*, I, pp. 207–08). Only later on R. Alexander gave an homilectic reason for the new custom as if to justify its retention even after the echoes of the Hadrianic persecution had long subsided.[131]

CONCLUSION.

The details discussed above, disregarding those dealt with in the last section (V), illustrate the struggle of the synagogue of Israel in the Magian-ridden empire of the Sassanids and still more

[130] במקום אחד תוקעין ובכקום אחד מברכין, which *'Iṭṭur* (ed. Lemberg, II, 43b, middle) correctly interprets (probably on the basis of Gaonic tradition): וכסהברא ביטי הטבד כטתיראין להקוע בנלוי.

The question arises whether the whole benediction for הקיעת שופר was not instituted during the Hadrianic persecution as a substitute for the actual sounding of the Shofar which had been proscribed (see the discussion in Yer. R. H. 59d).

[131] See Pes. R. c. 40 (ed. Friedmann, 167b, 168a): אסר רבי מחס בשם רבי יהודה בן לוי בשם רבי אלבכנדרי: לסה אין תוקעין מן התפלה ראטונה אלא בהפלה כוספים? כדי שבשעה שהם עובדים בדין יהיו כצויין מליאי כצות הרבה ויוכו בדין וכו'.

Vitry, p. 385, correctly remarks that the retention of the custom later on was due to this homily: וכטבכלה המרה לא זה חז המנהג (read כסקומה וםכקובו) וסככו על האכור בפסיקהא וכו' (read,

in Palestine under the rule of Christian Byzantium. In essence
this struggle turned on the freedom of giving public expression to
the basic principle of Judaism, Monotheism, though other aspects,
such as the teachings of the Rabbis, figured therein. In the long
run the synagogue prevailed in obtaining this freedom. The
modification of such an item as ברכת המינים, to remove its direct
denunciation of the members of another faith, was a step in the
right direction leading towards the acquisition of this freedom.
The same applies to the adoration עלינו, on the whole a liturgical
composition of sublime aspirations, yet marred at its beginning by
a marked disparagement of the non-Jew.[132] These verbal dis-
paragements are echoes of the times of trial and tribulation when
amidst an environment of general religious intolerance the Jew
was out of all proportion wronged as against his own wrongs to
others. The protest of his outraged feelings found expression in
the Seliḥah and in the Ḳinnah—varieties of the Piyyuṭ that
seems to have been the outcome of Justinian's interference with
the divine service of the synagogue—rather than in the original
liturgy the bulk of which dated from before the era of religious
intolerance. It is this original liturgy, though modified in course
of the ages, that still forms the basis of the divine service of the
synagogue of today.

APPEENDIX (TO PAGES 249–51).

DATE AND PLACE OF REDACTION OF SEDER ELIYAHU RABBA AND ZUṬṬA.

The various views about the time and the place of the
authorship of this bi-sectional midrash are fully discussed by
Friedman in his מבוא (pp. 91–102) and need not be entered in
here again in detail. Theodor in his review of this מבוא (M. G. W.
J., vol. 47, 70–79), in criticizing Friedman's theory of assigning the
work actually to the time of the Amora R. 'Anan, offers no suggestion of his own on the problem. The last to discuss the work is

---

[132] About this adoration see Elbogen 80–81; cf. also Berliner, Rand-
bemerkungen, I, 47–8, 49–50. Its daily recital at the end of the service is dated
by Elbogen at about 1300. However, Vitry, p. 75, has it already with the

Eppenstein (*Beiträge zur Gesch. u. Liter. im Geon. Zeitalter*, pp. 182–3), who fastens himself on one detail, viz., the designation of the non-Jew as גוי, to come to the conclusion that the redactor did not live in a Muslim country but in a Christian environment, in Southern Italy, forgetting that if the work referred to conditions in Babylon in the Sassanid period, this expression גוי, even if granting Eppenstein's contention (already used by Güdemann) for argument's sake, would fit in well. G. Klein's curious theory (*Der Älteste Christliche Katechismus u. die Jüd. Propaganda-Literatur*, 1909, 68 ff.) that our work, in its original form, contained a program of proselytising for the heathens and was modified by a redactor living during the Crusades (sic!) need hardly be taken seriously. The writer is concerned with impressing upon *his own people* the ethics and morality of Judaism. The warnings against too intimate relations with the heathen (ed. Friedmann, pp. 45–48) are the best refutation of Klein's theory.

In discussing this remarkable Midrash the historical consideration of the general political situation of Jewry, as reflected in our work, is so often lacking. All scholars, who have assigned the redaction of this Midrash to the 10th century by reason of the late dates (see above, p. 249, and note 10), have overlooked the significant fact that nowhere is there mentioned the rule of Islām extending, as it did then, from Persia and the eastern provinces to Babylon, Syria, Palestine, Egypt and whole of North-Africa and reaching out to Europe by the occupation of Spain and also of Sicily. The great majority of the Jewish people were then living in this vast territory under the sway of the Muhammedans. The only reference in the work of the children of Ishmael, "over whom God permitted no nation to rule,"[33] evidently alludes to the more or less independent Arab tribes extending from the Arabian peninsula proper right to the confines of Babylon at the

indication to recite it quietly (ואומר בלחש עלינו לשבח) evidently because of its anti-Christian beginning. In the ritual of the English Jews before the expulsion in 1290 we find a long version also with a marked polemical allusion (*JQR.*, IV, 56–7). In the Palestinian ritual, as preserved in the Genizah fragments, עלינו seems to be given at the beginning of the daily service (see Mann, 276 and 325).

[33] Ch. 14, ed. Friedm., p. 65: ובכר יראה קמעא קמעא שירא ישמעאל את אביו לא נהן הקב״ה רצוה לכל אומה וכלכות שישלטו בבניו.

lower Euphrates. The author probably had specifically in mind the Arabs in the so-called kingdom of Ḥira (in the neighborhood of Kufa), the rulers of which, though vassals of the Sassanids, retained a good deal of independence.[134] Of the great change to the better in the political situation of the majority of Jewry, as compared to conditions under Christian Rome and Byzantium, that resulted from the tremendous political ascendency of Islām since the death of Muḥammad and onwards, there is no allusion in our book which occupies itself so much with the sad treatment meted out to Israel by the אומות העולם depicting so poignantly their oppression and tyranny (see ed. Friedmann, pp. 15, 20, 24–5, 110, 111, 117, 120, 123, 133–4, 180, 197.)

When the author speaks of the dominions, who had shared among themselves "the world," so that Israel might survive between them and not be persecuted in its entirety were there a united rule over it,[135] he clearly refers to the two great empires of his time, viz. that of the Sassanids and of Byzantium (as Friedmann rightly maintaied, p. 114, note 11, end מבוא, p. 82). Both these empires maltreated Israel in his time, as is evident from the re-iterated complaints of oppression, but fortunately a respite was given to the large Jewries in both empires, comprising the vast majority of the Jewish people, by the very fact that the oppressive acts occurred at different times, and were not guided by a united policy. This situation did not obtain at the time of R. 'Anan at the beginning of the 4th century (against Friedmann's theory) because conditions in Babylon were really tolerable after the first flush of victory of the Magian Persians under Ardeshir (226 and following) had subsided. Likewise in the Roman empire the Jews were then still fully enfranchised, their political and civic status becoming imperilled only since the triumph of Christianity

---

[134] About the Arab kingdom of Ḥira in the time of the Sassanids, see Nöldeke, Ṭabarī, passim, and further Rothstein, Die Dynastie der Laḥmiden in al-Ḥīra, 1898.

[135] Ch. 20, pp. 113–114: פ'א הייתי עובר ממקום למקום, מצאני זקן אחד. אמר לי רבי: ספני סה חלק הקב'ה את עולמו לשני נוים, לשתי ממלכות? אמרתי לו: אילכלא כל העולם כולו ביד נוי] אהד (וכמו insert) כנחריב מלך אשור ונבוכדנצר מלך בבל, עמדו ועשו בהם בישראל כרצונם. הא לא חלק הקב'ה את עולמו לשני נוים לשתי ממלכות אלא כדי לשבור את ישראל.

(since 312) and especially since the reign of Constantius (from 337).

Likewise such a situation does not fit in for the 10th century (and in fact from the middle of the 7th century and onwards) when the Jews under the rule of Islām were by far better treated than under Christendom in spite of occasional outbreaks of fanaticism on the part of the dominant Muhammedans. Moreover, no author or redactor writing in the 10th century, whether in Babylon or Palestine or in Italy, would speak of "the world" (viz. the one wherein the bulk of Jewry was concentrated) as divided among two nations and *two empires* (שתי ממלכות), when the Jews in Christian Europe belonged to different dominions (Byzantium, the German empire, France, etc.) and when the Muhammedan world was split up into three Caliphates, viz. the 'Abbasid Caliphate centered in Bagdad, the Fāṭimid one centered in Mahedia, near Kairowan, and then after the conquest of Egypt in 969, in Cairo, and the Omayyad one centered in Ċordova.

The political background of the Jewish situation, as evident from a close study of our Midrash, leads us to the second half of the 5th century when the large Jewry in the Sassanid empire began to experience real religious persecution since the fanatical outbreaks of Yezdejerd II in 454–5, followed by that of his son Perōz. This coincided with the chronic intolerance against the Jews prevalent in Byzantium and resulted in a general לחץ ישראל, in spite of which Israel was preserved, because in its vast majority it was under "two nations and two dominions," viz. Persia and Byzantium, so often at war with each other and not pursuing a unified policy with regard to the treatment to be meted out to the Jews.

There is further a clear reference to the Magians in Babylon and to their power in the state quite at the very beginning of our Midrash which those scholars, who assigned the work to the 10th century, ought to have first accounted for, in view of the elementary historical fact that the political power of the Magians came to an end with the overthrow of Sassanid Empire by the Muslims in 639. The author relates[136] of an official raid (evidently against

[136] Ch. 1, pp. 5–6: פ׳א הייתי מהלך בכרך נד:ל כבעולם, והייתה שם הסחורה, וחפכתי והכניסוני בבית המלך, וראיתי שם כסות מוצעות וכלי כסף וכלי זהב סכתחין... בא אלי חבר אחד

the Jews) in "a great city in the world" (probably Ctesiphon, the capital of the Sassanids) in the course of which he himself was arrested.   A Magian priest (חָבָר)[137] had an argument with him about matters of difference between Judaism and Zoroastrianism, viz. why God had created repulsive creatures (שקצים ורמשים) which, according to Zoroastrian teaching, would be the work of Ahriman, the god of darkness and evil, and about the symbol of fire (light) as emanating from Hormuzd (Ahuramazda).   This priest promised the captive his freedom, if he answered his questions, which indicates the political influence the Magians had on the government officials, whose raid probably was the result of the former's instigation.   Such a situation obtained in Babylon and in Persia under the Sassanids, especially under Yezdejerd II and Perōz, who were dominated by the powerful Magian priests, but certainly not under the rule of Islām, not to speak of Italy where such a situation does not apply at all.   The statement that "God created everything in His world except falsehood and iniquity" (Zuṭṭa c. 3, ed. Friedm. p. 175)[138] also seems to be directed against the Dualistic doctrine of Zoroastrianism that divided the creation between Ahuramazda and Ahriman.

Further indication of the author's familiarity with Jewish conditions in Babylon we have in the story of his visit to "a large city in the Diaspora of Babylon" inhabited entirely by Jews.[139]

ויאסר לי: כופר אההז אמרתי לו: כשהוא. אמר לי: אם האמר לי דבר זה שאני אומר ולדן לך לעולם. אמרתי לו: אמור. אמר לי: מפני מה ברא אלוה שקצים ורמשים?... אמר לי: אתם

אוסרים אש אינה אלוה, מפני מה כתיב בהורתכם ,אש הכיד'?

See also Friedmann, מבוא, p. 82.   Reifmann's emendation (cf. ibid 94, note 3, end) בכרך נדול שבעילם is unnecessary, as probably Ctesiphon, the capital of the Persian empire, is meant.

[137] About the fanaticism of these Magian priests, see the Talmudic passages cited in 'Arukh s.v. חבר (ed. Kohut, III, 339–40).

[138] .הכל ברא הקב'ה בעולמו חוץ ממידת השקר כלא ברא. ומידת עול שלא ברא

[139] Ch. 18, p. 100: פעם אחת הייהי מהלך בתוך נולה של בבל. ונכנסתי לעיר נדולה שכולה ישראל ואין בה נוים.   Graetz (Geschichte, v., 4th ed., p. 335, note 2) takes בבל in our book to denote Rome in order to assign the work to Italy.   But for this there is no proof.   The above story certainly applies better to the large Babylonian Jewry where there would be cities entirely inhabited by Jews.

Graetz's further remark that "the twice repeated phrase: Gog and Magog's punishing judgment has already befallen the peoples (c. 3 and 5) surely (sic!) refers to the devastating invasions of the Hungarians into Italy during 889–

The story of the ignorant Jew, who raised his voice at the recital of the Ḳedushah (p. 66), also refers to Babylon. In the passage dealing with the Messianic times (c. 20, p. 113) evidently the Jews of Babylon are meant who would leave for Palestine and will be maintained by their non-Jewish neighbors.[140] In Babylon the Jews would leave behind all their sins and return to the Holy Land in purity.[141] Altogether from the cryptic passage in c. 18 (p. 98 top) it appears that the view was prevalent that Elijah had first to go down to Babylon before the appearance of the Messiah.[142] The Messianic hopes possibly inspired the author to put his Midrash into the framework of an account of Elijah's experiences during his peregrinations amidst Babylonian Jewry. Of the ardent desire and hope for the restoration of Israel, voiced by the Jews of his time amidst the tribulations of oppression, there are several indications in our Midrash.[143]

The mystical manner of the book of presenting Elijah as perennially visiting Israel throughout the Diaspora (בכל מקומוה

955)" is entirely unwarranted, as the text speaks of the coming and the downfall of Gog in the Messianic times! See p. 15, top: דם ובצר נוג לעתיד לבוא על הרי ישראל. מקצח דם ובצר ובצר על לוהצינו בעולם הזה עינינו רואות תמיד בכל יום. and so on p. 24. By הרי ישראל the mountains of Palestine are meant (cf. Ezek. 36.1). Güdemann (*Geschichte des Erziehungswesens u. der Cultur der Juden in Italien*, p. 302) makes this passage to be a reference to the invasion of the Mohammedans into Italy. How theories are evolved out of misunderstood simple passages! (Cf. also Friedm., מבוא, 99, note 3).

If anything could at all be deduced from this general vague statement that Jewish oppressors are to be seen meeting with evil ends even at present, one could venture to find therein an allusion to the defeats of the Persians under Perōz at the hands of the Huns (or Haitāl) resulting in the death of this oppressive king in 492. Altogether the Huns were in the 5th century the most feared enemies of the Sassanids (see Nöldeke, *Tabarī*, 115, note 2, and 119 ff.).

[140] Ch. 20, p. 113: כל נדים העצארים בארץ (viz. Babylon) הולכין לארץ ישראל וסביאים בר לחם וסזון לתוך בתיהם של ישראל.

[141] P. 129: כל עוונתיהן של ישראל כניחין אותן בבבל זעולין כשהן טהורין לא'י.

[142] Ch. 18, p. 98 top: ורמז רכוחי לעולם שאני יורד חחלה לבבל, וא'כ יבוא משיח.

[143] Ch. 4 p. 19 top: כך כל חכם וחכם שיש בו דבר הורה לאמיהו וסתאנח על כבודו של הקב'ה ועל כבודן של ישראל כל ימיו, וסתאוה וסחבר וסצפה על כבוד ירושלים ועל כבוד בית הסקדש ועל ישועה שהצסיח בקרוב ועל כינוס גליוח.

See further pp. 53; 110: זכור כסה כסה זקנים וחקנות יש בהן בישראל שמשכיכין וסעריבין (repeated also לבית הכנסת ולבית הסדרש, כחסדין וסתאוין וסצפין ליישועהך בכל יום הכ'ד on p. 112).

משבותיהם) induced the author to clothe the accounts of his own
experiences of Jewish life in the form of Elijah having discussions
with the sages at בית המדרש הגדול in Jerusalem (pp. 49, 51, 80, 122)
and as hailing from Yabneh "the seat of sages and Rabbis."[144]
The "great school of Jerusalem" and Yabneh are only metaphors
of speech whereas really the Babylonian academies are meant.
This fact of the author's presentation of his own experiences in
the garb of Elijah's visit to Israel in the Diaspora is probably
also the cause for his abandoning the usual Midrashic style of a
mixture of Hebrew and Aramaic and composing his work purely
in a Hebrew, so full of choice and characteristic expressions (see
the list given by Friedmann, מבוא, pp. 118 ff.), which renders it so
unique in the whole Midrashic literature. Elijah, the prophet of
Biblical times, transplanted among the angels, who were not
supposed to understand Aramaic (according to a widely spread
tradition, cf., e.g., Soṭah 33a), naturally has to recount his
journeyings, arguments and experiences in Hebrew! That no
author in the Amoraic period could have written a work in such
choice Hebrew and would have only to employ the Hebrew-
Aramaic lingo found in the Talmud, is, of course, a weak argument that hardly requires a refutation (see the pertinent remarks
of Friedmann, מבוא, 131, bottom, and 132, top).

How haphazardly there was detected that "in the whole work
there blows, so to say, a European air" (to use Graetz's metaphor)
can be seen from the theories evolved from the references in the
book to trade and commerce and to the business relations between
Jews and non-Jews by Güdemann (*l. c.*, 53–54) and Eppenstein
(*l.c.*, 183), as if Italy was the only country in the world wherein
such conditions obtained among the Jews! In the Babylonian
Talmud there are many references to the occupations of the Jews
including their journeys for purposes of business. One has only
to refer to those who made sea journeys (נחותי ימא, Sabb. 20b,
21a, 90a, R. H. 21a, bottom, etc.) and to those who travelled to
distant Aḥwāz (בי החאי) which route it took a caravan to cover
there and back about 12 months (cf. B. Ḳ. 112b, bottom). Nu-

---

[144] P. 95: טיבה אני ממקום חכמים ורבנים, Zuṭṭa, c. 1., p. 168, top. The latter
title רבן may refer to the Patriarchs who were thus styled. It certainly should
not be construed in the sense of Rabbanites as against Ḳaraites.

merous data testify to their social and business relations with
non-Jews in Babylon. Several statements of the Babylonian
Amoraim reflect their observation of the standards of life of the
non-Jews in their country.[145]

The disputes, which our author had with people knowing or
accepting the Bible only but not the Oral Law, have rightly been
proved by Friedmann (מבוא, 93–98) to have no bearing whatever
on Rabbanite and Ḳaraite polemics, as Bacher and Oppenheim
had maintained. Our Midrash rather reveals the significant fact
that as late as the second half of the 5th century there were still
in Babylon people who opposed the Oral Law, and that this
skepticism towards Rabbinic Judaism probably continued sur-
reptitiously in the following centuries till it was organized into a
formidable movement since the times of 'Anan, the founder of
Ḳaraism.

The whole evidence thus gathered from a close study of the
work leads its origin back to Babylon in the Sassanid period (as
Friedmann rightly maintained), however, not to the time of the
Amora R. 'Anan but rather to the second half of the fifth century.
The complaint of the great oppression of Israel in both world
empires of that time, viz. Byzantium and Persia, reflect well
conditions in the latter country since the close of the reign of
Yezdejerd II (454–5). The item of the prohibition of the Shema'
(above, pp. 247 ff.) strengthens this conclusion still more. W.
Jabez[146] was on the right track in using the point of the prohibition of the Shema' as a clue for fixing the approximate date of our
Midrash but he soon went astray in explaining this prohibition to
have fallen in the time of Heraclius after his reconquest of
Palestine in 629. Hence our author became a Palestinian who
even alluded to the then leader of the Palestinian Jews, viz. no
less a person than Benjamin of Tiberias. Atlas (in הכרם, 96–102)
rightly refuted Jabez by realizing that this prohibition of the

[145] The whole matter cannot, of course, be entered in here. Cf. for the present
Gezow, על נהרות בבל, 34–35, 41–43, and Funk, *Die Juden in Babylonien*, I,
18–19, 26–27.

[146] In Rabbinowitz's כנסת ישראל, I (1886), 382–86. Cf. the analysis of his
arguments by Friedmann, מבוא, 98–102, but he, too, has no clear view on the
matter, even venturing to suggest (p. 101) that the passage in c. 19 (p.110)
הרי לך כמשיב על בנימין אחי refers to Benjamin of Tiberias!

Shema' should be connected with Yezdejerd's decree in 454–5.
But he, too, soon lost his clue to go astray in his own speculation.[147]

Our dating of the book places it prior to the conclusion of the
Babylonian Talmud which took place around 500 C. E.   Hence
the Mishnah is cited several times (שנו חכמים במשנה, see the enu-
meration of the passages by Friedmann מבוא, pp. 59–60) but
never the Talmud as such.[148]   Theodor's arguments (l. c., 77–78)
really do not explain this fact in the least.   Why not a single
Amora is mentioned by name seems rather to be due to the
tendency of the author to anonymous quoting.   Hence there are
found many quotations beginning with אמרו חכמים, מיכן אמרו, אמרו
(see the list, ibid. p. 60).   But while realising this tendency it is
not yet clear why he adopted this policy, though living at a time
when the work of the Amoraim in Babylon was practically completed.   But this is evident that had the Babylonian Talmud been
before him in a complete form, as the Mishnah was, he would
have used the expression שנו חכמים בתלמוד (or perhaps בגמרא) just
as he introduced his Mishnaic quotations with the formula שנו
חכמים במשנה.   This consideration militates further against assigning
the book to the 10th century when the Babylonian Talmud was
the common property of Jewry all over the Diaspora.   On the
other hand in the second half of the 5th century the Babli,
though arranged under the supervision of R. Ashi (d. 427) and
his colleagues, remained still the guarded treasure of the
Academies,[149] reaching its completion only about 500 and receiving
still further additions and finishing touches by the Saboraim in the
course of the 6th century.   Living in Babylon our author also was
not yet familiar with the Yerushalmi (supposedly concluded, or
more correctly interrupted, about 425).   A knowledge of the
Yerushalmi seems to have penetrated to Babylon only later
during the Gaonic period.

[147] Cf. also Friedmann's criticism, מבוא, 102, note 1.

[148] In c. 18 (p. 106) the expression תלמוד in the sentence: אף כל חכם וחכם
כיׂשראל ׂשיׂש בו דברי תורה לאמתו, יׂש בלבבו כאׂה כחׂשבות ׁשל מקרא כאה מחׂשבות ׁשל מׁשנה
תלמוד ׁשל תׁשובות מׂני ומאה means of course arguments deduced by means of the
Biblical exegesis (see Bacher, Exeget. Terminologie, I, 199 ff.).   On p. 68 (כׁשנה)
(מדרׁש הלכות ותלמוד ואנדות) the word תלמוד is evidently a gloss (cf. Friedm.,
מבוא, p. 60).

[149] Regardless of the mooted problem whether in an oral or written form

JUDAISM AND CHRISTIANITY IN THE MIDDLE OF THE THIRD CENTURY

A. MARMORSTEIN, London

I

RABBI Simon ben Lakish, who taught in Tiberias about 250 C.E., once raised his voice on behalf of the פושעי ישראל, Jewish transgressors, or Apostates. Neither the occasion nor the meaning of the defence of these peculiar people has been properly investigated, and yet, no doubt, for more than one reason, it deserves illumination. In so doing I am not guided by apologetic tendencies, but hope to contribute some details which should throw light on the darkness covering the relations between early Christianity and Judaism. Let us first turn to the saying of R. Simon ben Lakish. It reads: אין אור של ניהנם שולטת בפושעי ישראל קל וחומר ממזבח הזהב, מה מזבח הזהב שאין עליו אלא כעובי דינר זהב כמה שנים אין האור שולטת בו, פושעי ישראל שמלאין מצות כרמון דכתיב כפלח ברמון רקתך, אל תקרי רקתך אלא רקנין שבך על אחת כמה וכמה: The fire of Gehenna has no dominion over the Jewish apostates. This is a conclusion[1] a minori ad majus. If for so many years the fire had no rule over the golden altar which did not contain more gold than the thickness of a dinar, how much more the Jewish apostates, who are as full of Mizwot (commandments) as a pomegranate, as it is written:[2] "Thy temples are like a piece of pomegranate!" i. e. the empty ones in Israel are full of observances; consequently Gehenna cannot have power over them.

What induced this teacher to exempt the Apostates from the fire of Hell? Where did these Apostates "full of observances like a pomegranate" live and flourish? What does Rabbinic literature record of these Apostates in other sources and places? Finally, can one locate them in literary sources outside Jewish literature?

[1] B. Ḥag. 27a, b. 'Erubin 19a.
[2] Cant. 4.3. The preacher understood רקתך the empty one, i. e., as in Cant. r. ad. loc: הריקן שבכם רצוף מצות כרמון הזה ואין צריך לומר סבער לצמתך על הצנועין והסצוסתין שבכם.

223

These questions involve more than an idle inquiry into a more or less uninteresting episode of the past. They reveal an instructive attitude of the Rabbis towards intellectual and religious movements and developments, which are not without significance, and should serve as guidance in the problems facing us at present.

To begin with, there are many, favorable and unfavorable, references to the Posh'e Israel. The author of Psalm 51.15 aims at teaching transgressors (פושעים) God's ways, and hopes to convert sinners (חטאים). Sinners and transgressors belong together. In the book of the prophet Isaiah (1.28) they are included in the company of those that forsake the Lord (עוזבי ה'). Ps. 37.38 groups them together with the wicked (רשעים). Both are opposed to the righteous in the next verse. Similarly in Hos. 14.10. We can, however, derive only very scanty information about the nature of these different groups. In the period of the Hasmoneans the פושעי בתורה, the transgressors against the Torah, must have been well-known, highly detested figures in the then small commonwealth of Judea.[3] The School of Hillel opened the gates of the schools to all who longed to enter, for many transgressors had been in Israel who, through learning, drew nearer to the Torah and became ancestors of pious and righteous men.[4] The two schools also took another opportunity to discuss the final destiny of the Posh'e Israel.[5] R. Simon ben Lakish seems to contradict unequivocally the views of those schools, who condemn them to Gehenna, when he says: Gehenna has no rule over them! This is remarkable! Further, they do not draw a line between פושעי ישראל and פושעי או"ה, Jewish and gentile apostates. The same designations occur in a sentence of R. Eliezer ben Hyrkanos.[6] Finally, the Apostates together with the *Minim* figure in the special benediction of the Amidah, which similarly proves the existence of these people in the first century.[7] Apart from the bare names of these Posh'e Israel and *Posh'e ummot ha-olam*, very little information can be gained from our sources. The

[3] I Macc. 14.14, 2 Macc. 6.21.
[4] Abot R. Natan II, 9.
[5] B. R. H. 17a, Tosefta Sanh. ch. 13, 3, Abot R. N. I, ch. 41.
[6] Tos. Sanh. ed. Zuckermandel 434, b. Sanh. 105a.
[7] Pal. Ta'anit 65c.

School of Hillel draws a line between these Jewish and Gentile
elements on one side, and the Minim, informers, Epicureans,
those who deny the Torah and the belief in the resurrection,
those who separated from the ways of the community, those who
spread terror in the land of the living, and finally sinners like
Jerobeam b. Nebat on the other side. The Posh'e Israel must
therefore be distinguished from these eight more serious and
dangerous categories of sinners. None of the characteristic faults
and shortcomings of these eight groups applies to the transgressors. They are neither Minim in any sense, nor informers on
their fellowmen. They do not belong to antinomistic circles, they
do believe in the Torah and resurrection, are members of the
local synagogues and communities, they do not terrorize their
fellowmen in the land of the living, nor do they preach new
creeds and entice people to idol-worship. It would be tempting,
if space would permit such an attempt, to depict here the social and
religious conditions lurking in the background of this Baraita. Such
a picture would offer a dreary narrative of conditions prevailing in
the first century of the Current Era. In this chapter, however, I
limit my subject to the Jewish transgressors. In the first half of
the third century, at least in Babylon, the meaning of this term
פשעי ישראל בגופן and פשעי אומות העולם בגופן was not understood
by the students of the Baraita, and they frankly asked for the
meaning of these two terms. Rab interprets the first by referring
to a man (lit. קרקפתא a skull, head of a man) who does not put
on phylacteries, and the latter by referring to a gentile, who lives
in sin (i.e. an immoral life; עבירה, κατ' ἐξοχήν is immorality).
Though the leader of the school of Sura rightly estimates the
importance of the law and observance of Tefillin, it is surprising
that he would find no fault with the transgressor but the
transgression of this one law.

The author of the Seder Olam rabba could not have agreed
with Rab's opinion, when he defined the term פשעי ישראל; for he
interpreted the same, as we identified them, with people, who
transgress the Mizwot, or, according to a Geniza fragment, who
transgress Torah and Mizwot.[8]   This source judges the trans-

---

[8] Seder 'Olam r. ch. 3, cf. ed. A. Marx, p. 9.

gressors more strictly than Rab. The version of Seder Olam rabba differs from the Tosefta in other respects as well. The heretics of the alternative group include besides the Minim, Epicureans, and those who deny resurrection, the following new sets: apostates (משומדים), blasphemers, Boethoseans, those who despise the festivals, and who say that the Torah is not revealed from heaven. The latter can be classified with those who deny the Torah in the Baraita. There remain merely the informers unaccounted. Yet, some manuscripts of the Seder Olam have the מסורות.⁹ On the other hand, the Tosefta has Meshummadim, who are missing in the Baraita.¹⁰ Anyhow, all texts agree that the פושעי ישראל have to be distinguished from the others. Yet, even they are here temporarily subjected to the pains of Gehenna. R. Simon ben Lakish solemnly repudiated this teaching. Surely, he could not have done so without some cogent reasons, and for some weighty consideration. Was he the only one, who in his independence of judgment stood aloof from his contemporaries? He is not the only one who judged so leniently, and showed signs of otherwise unusual tolerance. R. Simon the pious (חסידא), who most probably lived in the age of R. Simon ben Lakish, said: Every fast day service, which is not attended by the פושעי ישראל is not a proper fast day.¹¹ Homiletically one can put into this sentence different ingenious meanings,¹² historically it must be taken at its face value. The "transgressors" have to join, or to be admitted to, the services held on public fast days. There, again, they are considered as belonging to the community in spite of their faults and blunders. Who and what are they?

One of their dogmas was that the Prophets and Hagiographa were not parts of the Torah, and they did not believe in them.¹³

---

⁹ *Ibid.*, p. 9, MSS. O and C.   ¹⁰ Ed. Zuckermandel 434, l. 21.

¹¹ B. Keritut 5b: כל תענית שאין בה מפושעי ישראל אינה תענית ריחה רע ומנאה הכתוב עם ממטני הקטרת. Cf. Maḥzor Vitry p. 45, r. ספריצי, cf. also Tos. Gittin 19a, Ginzberg *Geonica* II, 370.

¹² Cf. Wolf Jawitz, תולדות ישראל III, p. 93.

¹³ M. Tanḥuma ed. Buber 5, 19: פושעי ישראל אומרים שהנביאים והכתובים אינן תורה ואין אנו מאמינים בהם; also *Pugio fidei* p. 702. Ginzberg, *MGWJ*, 1913, p. 675, N. 2, rightly saw that the Haggadist did not have Samaritans in mind, but it will be seen in the course of this essay, that there is no reference to Sadducees either.

Secondly, they are depicted by contemporary preachers, skilled in coloring biblical narratives and events with the happenings and experiences of their own day, as indifferent to the fate of their nation and inclined to assimilate with their surroundings. They keep the law of circumcision, but they walk according to the statutes of the Gentiles.[14] This speaks for assimilation. Another indication of their indifference is in the next passage. There were פושעים in Israel, who got hold of Egyptian patrons, acquired fame, wealth and honor, and consequently did not care to leave Egypt with their brethren.[15] Thirdly, a complaint is made that these people discourage or weaken Israel in performance of the Mizwot.[16] Finally, they laugh and mock at the Messiah, who spends his time in prison.[17] Occasionally, it is reported that they deny the existence of God.[18] It is, however, doubtful, whether such statements can be taken literally, and if so, whether the report is not exaggerated, or biased.

This doubt arises partly out of the attitude taken by men of the type of R. Simon ben Lakish, and R. Simon, the Pious, as shown earlier, and partly by other reports in favour of these transgressors. An anonymous preacher expounded Ps. 31.24 and saw in the "faithful, whom God preserves" our Posh'e Israel, who forcefully utter their Amen, in fact they say: "Blessed be He who revives the dead."[19] Their chief doctrine was, therefore, belief in the resurrection, a belief which must have been exceedingly pleasing to the ears and minds of the Rabbis. They further firmly believed and eagerly expected the redemption of Israel, and set great hopes on the rebuilding of Jerusalem. They repeated the Eighteen Benedictions, but whether they understood the same things, the same ways and modes of salvation, and New Jerusalem or not, we will leave in abeyance for the present. As a

---

[14] Tanḥ. ed. Frkft. a.O. 22a: כופרים ופושעי ישראל והלכו בחקת הגוים והם מולין.
[15] Ex. r. 19; Tanḥ, f. 74a.
[16] M. Cant. ed. Grünhut 10a: שהיו מרפין ידיהם של ישראל מן המצות של תורה.
[17] Pes. r. 159b.
[18] M. Ps. 7b: פושעי ישראל שכפרו בהקב'ה.
[19] M. Ps. 240: אמונים נוצר אל, אלו פושעי ישראל שהם עונים אמן בעל כרחם באמונה ואומרים ברוך מחיה המתים. Cf. Marmorstein, *Religionsgeschichtliche Studien* I, 28. Note where I read בכל כחם.

matter of fact, it is recorded that they repaired morning and evening to the Synagogue.[20] It is seriously discussed and contemplated, whether sacrifices can be accepted from them, and the decision is in the affirmative.[21] Asked as to the attitude one should take, or manifest toward Jews, the פושע ישראל,[22] who was interrogated by Nekyomanteia[23] together with Titus and Balaam, the representatives of Rome and Gnosticism, when questioned as to who is honored in heaven and whether he should become a Jew, answered: Seek their good, and avoid their evil, for he who touches them is as if he had sinned against God.[23a] This friendly spirit to Jews and Judaism is most remarkable.

To sum up, we see that there were friendly and unfriendly views taken of these transgressors; they had manifested virtues and yet had shown peculiarities, which alienated the Rabbis from them; they surely did not give up their intimacy with the Synagogue, yet they loosened the tie of unity which held Jews together all over the world and through the ages. We find here in the third century a peculiar sect of Jews, who retain some laudable characteristics of Jewish religion and life, and yet, with one foot stand outside the camp.

II

This material, on which our knowledge of the Posh'e Israel rests, was collected by the present writer more than 20 years ago.[24] I suggested then that they represent Jews by origin and customs, who believed in Jesus. Since then I have searched in Jewish and Christian sources, and examined my thesis anew. I have found that the key for the understanding of these problems must be sought in external sources. The writings of the Church of the

[20] Cf. Yalkut Shime'oni's reading 88c.
[21] B. Hullin 5a, 'Erubin 69b, Lev. r. ch. 2.
[22] B. Gittin 57a; cf. Friedmann, *M. Onkelos und Akylos*, p. 97, who erroneously identifies the Posh'e Israel with Jesus.
[23] Cf. Marmorstein, "Die Nachrichten uber Nekyomanteia in der altrabbinischen Literatur," in *Zeitsch. für Neutest. Wissenschaft*, XXII (1923), pp. 290–304.
[23a] For the idea, cf. Mekilta 39a, Sifre Num. §84, ed. Horowitz, p. 81.
[24] *Religionsgeschichtliche Studien* I, 26–35.

first three centuries which hail from the East throw light on the subject. I studied first the *Clementine Homilies* and *Recognitions* which revealed to me the Posh'e Israel in their true character. Apart from the fact that the romance in which the Clementine writings are dressed is the mutual property of Judaism and Christianity[25] they possess many Jewish elements, and betray Jewish influence and Jewish workmanship. Jews and Judaism, Jewish lore and rite, Jewish thought and life, are the beginning and the end of the Clementines. There is something strange in the fact that these literary documents prefer the name "Hebrew",[26] whilst Rabbinic sources throughout favour the term "Israel" and only occasionally the name "Jehudi" is used, mostly in Aramaic fragments or when Gentiles are speaking of Jews. Mosaism and Christianity are identical, Moses and Jesus are the only true prophets. There is no suggestion of the abrogation of the law, as taught by Barnabas or Paul. One of the greatest New Testament and Patristic scholars of Germany, Prof. Carl Schmidt, says in his recent work on the Clementines:[27] "In der gesamten kirchlichen Literatur werden wir vergebens nach derartigen Gedanken über die Gleichwertigkeit des mosaischen Glaubens und des Christentums suchen." These Jewish-Christians celebrate Passover on the fourteenth of Nisan in the same manner as the Jews. They are strict in their Sabbath observance and most particular about the laws of ritual impurity. They adhere to the decree of the Apostles as to the dietary laws and perform the rite of circumcision.

There are plenty of proofs for these assertions. The Jewish-Christians gather in Jerusalem on the Jewish Pesach. Jerusalem

---

[25] Cf. the relations of the two stories in my article referred to above, note 23.

[26] Cf. *Rec.* 4.5, *Hom.* 8.5 f.: What, therefore, as a peculiar gift from God toward the nation of the *Hebrews*, etc. Since both to the *Hebrews* and to those who are called from the Gentiles, etc. Neither, therefore are the *Hebrews* condemned on account of their ignorance of Jesus, etc.

[27] *Studien zu den Pseudo-Clementinen, Texte und Untersuchungen* XLVI.1, Leipzig 1930, 251. I take this opportunity to express my deep indebtedness and sincere gratitude to this scholar for the help which I derived from his excellent work. I trust that by my treatment of the Rabbinic material his theory as to the origin and date of the Pseudo-Clementines will be verified.

is the centre of their unity.[28] They keep the seventh day, do not travel or make fire. Quid est ergo, quod nullum Judaeorum in illa die cogit genesis aut iter agere aut aedificare aut vendere obliquid aut emere.[29] The Ps. Clementines lay much stress on a propria quaedam nostrae religionis observantia, quae non tam imponitur hominibus, quam proprie ab unoquoque deum colenti causae puritatis expetitur.[30] They observed puritas, first of all according to the law of Leviticus (re menstruatae mulieri misceatur), secondly, etiam corpus aqua diluere, and thirdly the observantia castimoniae. They lived and thought as Jews, and were attacked by their fellow-Christians as Jews, and by Jews as apostates. Hence their ambiguous position!

III

The Syriac Didascalia preserved a number of the most hostile attacks of the "Catholic Church" against Jews who believed in Christ but could not sever their Jewish connections. The Didascalia appeals to Jewish-Christians not to be guided by the Jewish calendar and celebrate the Passover on the fourteenth of Nisan.[31] They should not imitate the ways of the Jews as far as the observance of the Sabbath goes.[32] The writer dishes up old[33] objections against the Sabbath: Why did the saints of old not observe the Sabbath? Why does God Himself not keep Sabbath? He is mightily upset and grieved that men and women in certain cases perform their ritual bath[34] or that Jewesses keep away from places of worship during the seven days of the menses.[35] The latter custom prevailed among Jews for many centuries and is still observed in many countries by non-Jews as well.[36]

[28] Cf. *Rec.* 1.44, further *Rec.* I, 10 = *Hom.* 1.13. Schmidt, *l. c.*, 324.
[29] *Rec.* 9.28.
[30] *Rec.* 6.10 f., *Hom.* 11.28.
[31] Cf. Achelis-Flemming 110.10; 114.10.
[32] *Ibid.*, 113.12 ff.
[33] Cf. Marmorstein, "Juden und Judenthum in der Altercatio Simonis Judaei et Theophili Christiani" in *Theologisch Tydschrift*, XLIX, pp. 360–383.
[34] 139, 1ff. 142, 1. [35] 139, 25ff.
[36] Cf. Marmorstein, "Spuren Karäischen Einflusses in der gaonäischen Halacha", in *Schwarz-Festschrift*, Wien 1917, p. 460f., Reprint p. VI.

Yet there were also some ideas common to the Jews of the Ps. Clementines and the Gentiles of the Didascalia. The latter urge the Jews to give up their Jewish practices, e.g. ritual bathing and dietary law, to which they still cling,[37] for only the Decalogue is binding, the rest of the Torah was given as a temporary law, as a punishment for the making of the golden calf, and was abolished with the advent of the true Prophet. The whole law is the Repetition of the Law, the curse of the Deuteronomy. This is one of the Didascalia's pet ideas. The term Repetition of the Law was not known to the Clementine writers, yet they must have stood in close relationship with similar ideas. They speak of the true prophet, i.e., Jesus. All the other prophets are not true at all. Consequently all Prophets and Hagiographa are rejected. Yet even parts of the Pentateuch, e.g. the sacrifices, are objected to. The whole institution of sacrifices is explained as a concession of Moses to his weak contemporaries, who built the golden calf, demonstrating that they were too much contaminated by Egyptian cults and examples, of which they could not rid themselves.[38] A similar idea is represented in the Haggada by R. Levi[39] who was somewhat younger than the assumed date of the Ps. Clementines' source. These points the Posh'e Israel shared with the Gentile-Christians. No wonder that even their zeal and loyalty to Jewish life and ritual were looked upon as half-hearted by the majority, and genuine or wholly worthy by only a few.

The Didascalia was written with the specific purpose of

---

[37] Didasc. chap. 26.

[38] Rec. 1.35ff. Meantime when Moses, the faithful and wise steward, perceived that the vice of sacrificing to idols had been deeply ingrained into the people from their association with the Egyptians, and that the root of the evil could not be extracted from them, he allowed them indeed to sacrifice, but permitted it to be done only to God, that by some such means he might cut off one half of the deeply ingrained evil, leaving the other half to be corrected by another, and at a future time.

[39] Lev. r. 22.5: משל לבן מלך שגס לבו עליו והיה למד לאכול בשר נבלות וטרפות אמר המלך זה יהיה תדיר על שולחני ומעצמו הוא נדור. כך לפי שהיו ישראל להוטים אחרי ע"ז במצרים והיו מביאים קרבניהם לשעירים וכו' . . . . יהיו מקריבין לפני בכל עת קרבנותיהן באוהל מועד ויהיו נפרשין מע"ז והם ניצולים. Cf. also Maimonides, Moreh III, 32, cf. I. Oppenheim, Heassif 6, 1894, 102.

frightening away Jewish-Christians from Jewish practices and usages. Owing to this tendency Jews and Judaism fare rather badly in that work. The author, whosoever he might have been, is in many instances indebted to Jewish, especially Rabbinic, teaching. Koraḥ is depicted as loving preeminence, coveting the High-Priesthood, and criticizing Moses' heathen wife, i.e. the Aethiopian.[40] Most probably the Didascalia is here indebted to some Gnostic critic, who took the part of Koraḥ, and sided against Aaron.[41] For the view that Manasseh's sins were forgiven, one can likewise find authority in the Haggadah of R. Judah ben Ilai of the second, or of R. Yoḥanan b. Nappaḥa in the third century.[42] The admonition to Christians not to let their hair grow, but to cut it,[43] has a striking parallel in a Baraita, which assumes that letting one's hair, or finger-nails grow, brings man into trouble, or leads to worry.[44] Didascalia as well as some of the rabbis at some periods evince hostile sentiments towards the books of the heathen.[45] There is no special purpose in pointing out some parallels in which Didascalia and the rabbis coincide in ethical and religious aspects, for they may have formed them independently, or these may go back to common experience or presumptions. Thus, when both teach to honour one's master as one honours God,[46] that sin brings forth sin,[47] that man should live in repentance, and live a clean life for he does not know his

[40] Didasc. chap. 23; cf. Tanḥ. ed. Buber IV, 96; *ibid.*, p. 85; Ps. Jonathan, Num. 12.1; Book of Yashar, chap. 46, and Chronicles of Yeraḥmeel, transl. by M. Gaster, London 1899, p. 114f. About Aaron's idolatry, R. Eleasar ben Pedat, b. Sanh. 7a; R. Jeremiah, Tanḥ. ed. Frkf. a.O. 124b; Exod. r. 37.2.

[41] Cf. Irenäus, *contra haeresos*, I, 31; my remarks *REJ* 54,190, and "The Background of the Haggada", *HUCA*, VI, 1929, 150ff.

[42] Didasc. chap. 2, M. Sanh. XI, 1 and parall. b. Sanh. 103a; cf. also Lev. r. 17, Num. r. ch. 14.

[43] Didasc. chap. 2.

[44] *Pirḳe Rabbenu haḳḳadosh*, ed. Grünhut ספר הליקוטים III, 18, p. 40. MS. Or. Br. Mus. Add. 22092a, 133b. S. Krauss, *Talmudische Archeologie* I, 191 and note p. 643 overlooked this passage.

[45] Chap. 2, cf. Joel, M., *Blicke in die Religionsgeschichte* I, 6.

[46] Didasc. ch. 9, cf. R. Eleazar b. Shamua, Abot IV, 12, Ned. 41b, Pesaḥim 22b, cf. already Didache 4.1.

[47] Didasc. ch. 6, cf. Ben Azzai, Abot IV, 2, or the well known phrase נעשה לו כהיתר or הותרה הרצועה.

exit from this world,[48] that a father should teach his son a handicraft which is suitable and leads to the fear of God,[49] this may prove that there are similarities between the Didascalia and the Rabbis. It is not impossible that the writer of the Didascalia was born a Jew, and as such indebted to the Rabbis in more than one instance. It would be futile to treat here at greater length the question of priority in spite of the many striking coincidences between the two groups,[50] yet it is of some importance for the date of the Didascalia that the similarities can be traced back to Tannaitic material. This agreement is in small matters, in trifles and petty points; the greater is the gulf between them in vital matters, when the author of the Didascalia comes to grips with problems which do matter, with questions of life and death, of being or not being.

The writer, who may or may not have sat at the feet of the masters of Usha or Sepphoris, Tiberias or Meron, finds cruel pleasure in teasing and taunting his poor fellow-congregants, that their brethren are a God-forsaken nation.[51] He was not the first to spread this cruel doctrine, and not the last. This teaching is one of the bitterest fruits of Paul's activity, which has embittered the relations between Jews and Gentiles, Judaism and Christianity, up to this day.[52]

[48] Didasc. ch. 6, cf. R. Eliezer, Abot II, 10, b. Šabbat 153a, cf. also Marcus Aurelius XII, 69.

[49] Didasc. ch. 22, cf. the views of R. Judah b. Ilai and of R. Meir on this subject p. Ḳid. IV, 12, b. Ḳid. 82b.

[50] Women have to cover their hair, Didasc. ch. 3, cf. Sifre Num. 11, b. Ket. 72a, b. Yoma 47a, pal. Yoma I, 1, Horayoth III, 3, Pesiḳta, Buber 174a, Num. r. 2.22, cf. 1 Cor. 11.3–15. Here again Krauss, *Talmd. Arch.* I, 195 and 652 has to be corrected. One should not go to heathen courts, or receive the testimony of heathens, Didasc. ch. 11. Cf. Mekilta of RSbJ, ed. Hoffmann p. 112. Didasc. ch. 13 is antagonistic, does not like people going to the theatre and circus, the same view is expressed by R. Meir, b. A. Z. 18b.

[51] Didasc. ch. 24, "God has left the nation and has filled the Church and has considered her the Mount of his habitation and the throne of glory, and the house of exaltation." Didasc. 23, "God has removed and forsaken the nation, as it is written in Isaiah, that he hath forsaken the people of the house of Jacob and Jerusalem is fallen, and their tongues are in iniquity, and they have obeyed not the Lord, and behold, your house is left unto you desolate."

[52] Cf. as to the early history of this teaching, N. Bonvetsch, *Der Schriftbeweis für die Kirche aus den Heiden als das wahre Israel bis auf Hippolyt,*

This taunt was born in the pagan mind at the sight of the numerous misfortunes and subjugations of the Jews, even before the final catastrophe in the year 70 C.E. How much more so after the destruction of the Temple and the devastation of the land. Cicero merely asserts that "while Jerusalem was flourishing, while the Jews were in a peaceful state, still the religious ceremonies and observances were much at variance with the splendour of this Empire, the dignity of our name and the institutions of our ancestors. And they are the more odious to us now because that nation has shown by arms what its feelings were to our supremacy. How beloved of the immortal gods that nation was, is proved by the fact that it has been defeated, that its revenues have been farmed out, and that it is reduced to a state of subjection."[53] Jews were consequently hated and forsaken by the gods. This impressed the victims very little and did not disturb them. Celsus[54] turns against Jews and Christians proving that the God of both must be very weak in allowing the slaughter of the whole military youth of his people, the burning of his city. Further he says:[55] "It is quite improbable that they are specially loved by God, or more beloved than others, or that special angels descended to them from Heaven, etc. For we saw with our own eyes which advantages, which preferences they and their country received!" Origen tells us[56] that Celsus foretold the ruin of the Jews, which is going to take place in the near future. He speaks in the manner of a prophet in prophesying their fate; overlooking all the care, which God bestowed upon the Jews, and the revered laws and institutions, which he handed down to them; he fails to notice that through their defeat the wealth of the pagans is increased. Celsus is mocking and laughing at God and his followers. Why does he not help you (Christians) and the

p. 1ff. Further. I. C. Mathes, *De Joden en het Christendom*, Amsterdam 1913, 1–10, and A. Marmorstein, "L'epitre de Barnabe et la polemique Juive", *REJ* 60, 1910, 213–220.

[53] Pro Flacc. 28, Oxford text §68: Quem cara dis immortalibus esset docuit, quod est victa, quod elocata, quod serva facta; cf. also Posedonium of Apamea at Diador Sic. 34.1. Photius p. 324, and Tacitus Hist. 5.8.

[54] Origenes, Contra Celsum IV, 73.

[55] *Ibid.*, V, 41.   [56] *Ibid.*, VI, 80.

Jews?[57] Rabbinic sources re-echo similar reproaches and this upbraiding on the part of pagans. R. Gamaliel II has a dialogue with a philosopher, who proves from Hos. 5.6 that God will never return to Israel.[58] R. Joshua ben Ḥananja has a pentomimic dispute with an Epicurean as to Israel's being forsaken.[59] Titus is credited with the saying that the God of the Jews has become old and weak, therefore he is unable to help them.[60] The defeats in 70 C.E. and 135 C.E. surely appeared to the pagan mind as an eloquent and undeniable proof that the God of the Jews lost his strength, that he forsook his people, as expressed in the Dialogue of Tinaeus Rufus with R. Akiba.[61] There must have been theologians, who taught that the withdrawal from Israel was merely a temporary one.[62] Paul and Barnabas adopted and adapted this dogma. They based their arguments on passages in the prophets, which contain unfavourable or condemning words about Israel. Paul[63] refers to Hosea 2.25, and Barnabas[64] to the story of the golden calf in order to teach that Israel was supplanted by the new Israel, or was forsaken by God, and that Israel never entered the covenant with God. The consequences of these teachings we see before us in the Didascalia. Their influence was most strongly felt by the teachers of the third century. The Tannaitic Haggada could not ignore the taunt that Israel was forsaken,[65] yet it was by no means so systematically and so often disputed as in the age of the Amoraim.[66] Most of the great apologists for Judaism in the third century dwell on the doctrine of God's unchangeable love for Israel on one side, and strongly repudiate on the other side the idea of Israel being forsaken by God. While doing so,

[57] *Ibid.*, VIII, 39 and 69.

[58] Cf. b. Yebamot 102b, Midr. Ps. 10, Midrash Haggadah Lev. 26.9, Bacher, *Ag. der Tannaiten* I, 82, 6. Büchler, A. "Die Minim von Sepphoris und Tiberias", Cohen's *Judaica*, Berlin 1912, 280.

[59] Cf. b. Ḥag. 5b.   [60] Gen. r. 10.8 and parall.   [61] B. B. B. 10a.
[62] Eth. Enoch 90.28f.   [63] Rom. 9.25f.   [64] Epistle ch. 9.

[65] Cf. esp. Büchler *l.c.* p. 279, as to R. Meir, p. 280, as to R. Joshua b. Korḥa, p. 281, Beruria the wife of R. Meir.

[66] Besides the Didascalia one ought to mention here also the Carmen Apologeticum of Commodian vv. 346–350, where this teaching is so emphatically underlined. Commodian must have written in a Jewish surrounding. The date is approximately settled, the origin still obscure.

they mention the latter view expressly as an assertion of the nations of the world, who are none else but Gentile Christians. The names of R. Hoshaja,[67] R. Jonathan b. Elieser,[68] R. Jannai,[69] Rab,[70] R. Joshua ben Levi,[71] R. Yoḥanan,[72] R. Simon ben Lakish,[73] R. Ḥanna b. Ḥanina,[74] R. Isaac,[75] R. Levi,[76] R. Samuel

[67] A contemporary of the Church-Father Origen who lived in Caesarea, b. Pes. 87b: א'ר אושעיא מאי דכתיב צדקות פרזונו בישראל צדקה עשה הקב"ה בישראל שפזרן לבין האומות. The exile is not a sign of Israel's rejection on God's part, but of God's love and justice.

[68] Ag. Ber. ed. Buber ch. 8, p. 22: א'ר שמואל בר נחמני א'ר יונתן איש הבירה אמרו מפני ישראל לאו'ה אומר אני לכם ב מ ה א נ ו מ ת נ ח מ י ן ולמה אנו יכולים בזעפו. ספכה אותנו וחוזר ס י ד ובורא אותנו ב ר י ה ח ד ש ה וכן ישעיה אומר (42.24) מי נתן למשסה יעקב, הרי כלו הרי נבוזו, אלא ח ו ז ר ס י ד ובוראם בריה חדשה, ומה כתיב אחריו (43.1) ועתה כה אמר ד' בוראך יעקב, לפיכך אמרו ישראל בדבר ז ה א נ ו ר ו א י ן ו מ ת נ ח מ י ן שבורא אותנו מיד [צ' להוסיף בריה חדשה] זה הוא שאומר ירמיה זאת אשיב אל לבי (Lam. 3.21). Israel's reply to the taunt of the nations is: God smites us, and creates us a new creature. The latter term might be used purposely as a retort against the Epistle to the Romans.

[69] Cf. M. Ps., ed. Buber, chap. 36.11.

[70] B. Ta'anith 20a: אמר ר' יהודה אמר רב לברכה כנדה מה נדה יש לה היתר אף ירושלים: יש לה תקנה, כאלמנה ולא אלמנה ממש אלא כאשה שהלך בעלה למדינת הים ודעתו לחזור עליה. Cf. also his saying b. Ber. 3a, God mourns because of Israel's absence and affliction.

[71] B. Sotah 38b, Pes. 85b, Pes. rabbati 85b: אפילו מחיצה של ברזל אינה מפסקת אמר ר' יהושע בן לוי למה נמשלו ישראל לזית, Menaḥot 53b: בין ישראל לאביהם שבשמים לומר לך מה זה זית אין עליו נושרין לא ביסות החמה ולא בימות הגשמים אף ישראל אין להם Cant. r. 1.5: ב ט י ל ה עולמית לא בעוה"ז ולא בעוה"ב ר' ברכיה וריב"ל למה נמשלו ישראל לנקבה. — כך ישראל משתעבדין וננאלין משתעבדין וננאלין וחוזרין וננאלין ושוב אין משתעבדין לעולם.

[72] Lev. r. chap. 6.5 (compromises) נתנו ביניהם שאינו ר' אחא בש"ר יוחנן הרבה צדיקים כופר בהם והם אינם כופרים בו Pesiḳta, ed. Buber 142a, העמידה בחורבנה יותר מצדיקים שהעמידה לי בבנינה. Israel produced more righteous men after the destruction of the Temple than before. How can such a nation be forsaken?

[73] God cares for Israel even in distress and in poverty, pal. Ber. 13b, and M. Ps. 4.2. God's love to Israel is expressed by three verbs: דבק, חשק and חפץ, Gen. r. 80, M. Ps. 22.22.

[74] B. Ber. 32a: אלמלא שלש מקראות הללו נתמוטטו רגליהם של שונאי ישראל. Cf. also b. Sukka 52b; the three passages are Micah 4.6, Jer. 18.6, Ez. 11.16.

[75] Eccl. r. 1.4: ישראל עומד לעולם, M Ps. 36.11, Pesikta 165a, Cant. r. 1.6: אור'ה מנין לישראל ואומרים אומה :: המירה כבדם. Cf. Marmorstein, Rel. Studien I, 17. God is with Israel even in exile, Ex. r. 15.16. The idea occurs also in the Haggadah of the Tannaites. M. Ct. ed. Grünhut 9B.

[76] Pes. r. 85b, Cant. r. 7.3.

b. Naḥmani,[77] and R. Abba b. Kahana[78] are witnesses for the
actuality and frequency of the Jewish defence against the charge
of the Didascalia.

Even more eloquent is the anonymous Haggada on this
question. The scoffers tell me: מי שהגלה אתכם שוב אין משיב אתכם
(He, who exiled you, will never bring you back, i.e., to Jerusalem!).[79] These people base their theory on the Scriptures, e.g.
Lam. 4.16. In this connection a religious persecution is spoken
of, forbidding circumcision, Sabbath and the reading of the law,
probably earlier than the Justinian prohibitions.[80] Israel was
accompanied by God into exile.[81] Job 39.27 is a reply to those who
assert that the Temple will never be built again.[82] A preacher expounded Ps. 3.3f. applying the verses to Israel. The nations of the
world (i.e. רבים, the many) rejoiced when Israel made the golden
calf, and spoke about them, saying: Hence there is no salvation and
existence left for them![83] Here we meet in the Haggada, not for
the first time as will be shown later on, the view that Israel lost
its claim on God, and God gave Israel up on account of Israel's
sin. In a homily on Ps. 4.3 God repeats the words of the nations
of the world who say: God has left them, forgotten them, and
He will never return unto them.   This argument is not true.
God has not forsaken and never will forsake Israel.[84]

The compiler of the Midrash on Exodus uses many older
homilies and fragments of Midrashic works in which this problem
was treated at greater length. In one passage we read: Israel

---

[77] Lev. r. 17, Cant. r. 8.7, Pes. r. 15b.

[78] Lam. r. 66b, Pes. Buber 139b.

[79] Midr. Psalm 495.

[80] Cf. Marmorstein, "Les persecutions religieuses a l'epoque de R. Jochanan
b. Nappacha, REJ. 77 (1923), 166–177, further, דורו של ר' יוחנן ואותות המשיח
Tarbiz, III (1932), pp. 161–180; cf., however, Graetz, Geschichte, V. 3rd ed.,
p. 20 f.

[81] Pes. r. 141a: מיד אמר להם הקב'ה אני אהיה ואני אעלה אתכם. Cf. also ibid., 143b,
144a, 162a.

[82] Pes. r. 10b: שאומרים הקב'ה אני בונה ביהמ'ק בנה אותו וחטאתם והחריב ועוד אינו בונה.

[83] Pes. r. 10b: אותה ששטעה מפי הקב'ה בהר סיני וכו' . . . יש לכם תשועה? אין ישועתה
אין לאלו עמידה ולא תשועה Pes. r. 39a reads. Tanḥ. Ex., Midr. Ps.
chap. 3. לו באלהים סלה.

[84] Pes. r. 147b: סה אתם מרדפים אחר דברים של ריקנות ואחרים עזבו הק' שכחו אין
שכינה חוזרת שם. Pes. Buber 134b, M. Ps. ch. 4.

dwelt in Zion, God was among them. When they sinned they were cast out. Yet, when he sees that they persevere in the performance of the commandments, then God repents what he wrought against Zion, and pleads Zion's case and contemplates the return of the exiles.[85] Secondly, when Israel was exiled from Jerusalem, and the enemies carried them away in chains, then the nations of the world said: God does not like this nation! as it is said: Reprobate silver they shall call them (Jer. 6.30). Silver can be melted and used for making vessels, once or twice, or more times, but finally one breaks it and it becomes useless; similarly Israel was talked of as a fallen people which had no hope to rise any more,[86] God having rejected them. When Jeremiah heard this, he said: "Lord of the world! hast Thou really rejected them?" (cf. Jer. 14.19, "Hast thou utterly rejected Judah? Hath thy soul loathed Zion? Why hast thou smitten us, and there is no healing for us?"). It is to be compared to a man, who was in the habit of beating his wife. Her *Shushbin* said to her husband: "How long are you going on like that beating her? If you want to drive her away, beat her to death, if not, why do you beat her?" He says: "Even if the whole of my palace is to be destroyed, I will not divorce her!" Thus says Jeremiah: "If you intended to drive us away, beat us to death (Lam. 5.22), if not, why do you beat us without healing?" God replies: "Even if I destroy my whole world I will not drive Israel away" (cf. Jer. 31.36. "If heaven above can be measured, and the foundation of the earth searched out beneath, I will cast off all the seed of Israel for all that they have done"). God will never sever his connection with his people. The author of this homily must have faced missionaries in Galilee, who propagated the Gospel of Israel's rejection, and of the Jews being forsaken by God, as taught in the Didascalia.

A third homilist preached on Ex. 25.1, and according to the way of preaching in his age, connected his text with Ps. 68.19.

[85] Ex. r. 30.8: כך ישראל היו בציון והקב"ה שרוי ביניהן, וכיון שחטאו טרפה אף הי"א השליכה בניה עליו וכשהוא רואה לישראל שעושים מצותיו מתנחם על מה שעשה בציון ומבקש לה זכות וכו'.

[86] Ex. r. 31.10: כן ישראל, היו אומרים and והיו או"ה אומרים אין הקב"ה חפץ באומה זו שאין להם תקומה שמאסן הקב"ה, cf. also Num. r. 16.23, Tanḥ. B. IV, 71.

Accordingly the words "and they bring me an offering" has a bearing on the verse in Psalms: "Thou hast ascended on high, thou hast led captivity captive!" How did the preacher accomplish his task? "Thou hast ascended," that is Moses (cf. Ex. 19.3 and 20.21). "Thou hast led captivity captive"; a king is grieved when his armies are led away captive. Thou wilt say that the same is the case with God? The text continues: "Thou hast received." When a man sells some of his property, he is grieved. (Perhaps the same happened with God?) Therefore it says: "Gifts of men." God said to them: I consider it as if I had given it to you as a present. The rebellious also: God spake to Moses: What do those idolators say: "will I not return to them because they worshipped idols" (cf. Ex. 37.8, Deut. 9.12)? No, even if they were rebellious I do not forsake (leave) them, and I do dwell among them, as it is said: God dwells among the rebellious.[87]

Let us turn to another compilation of homilies on Canticles,[88] in which the compiler of the Midrash collected many sermons on the same subject. To Cant. 8.14.[89] On the day the Temple was destroyed my Beloved fled, and became like a hart. Just as a hart runs from one end of the world to the other and returns to its place, so Israel, even though they are scattered in the whole world, they will in future return, cf. Hos. 2.9. Further in a parable to Cant. 6.2, we read: Israel is like a matrona, who rebelled against the king, and was divorced, driven out of the king's palace. People called her the divorced queen. She said: It is true that the king drove me out of his palace. Yet he did not repay me my dowry, and his name is still on me, i.e., I bear his name.[90]

---

[87] Ex. r. 33.2: ד'א ויקחו לי תרומה הה'ד עלית למרום שבית שבי, כל עלייך לא היה אלא מן הטרום ומשה עלה אל אלהים ומשה נגש אל הערפל שבית שבי מלך ב'ו בשעה שחיילותיו נשבים הוא מיצר תאמר אף כאן כך ת'ל לקחת. ובשעה שאדם מוכר הוא מיצר [תאמר אף כאן כך] ת'ל מתנות באדם. אמר להם כך אני מעלה עליכם כאילו מתנה נתתיה לכם. אף סוררים אמר הקב'ה למשה מה עכו'ם אוטרים שאיני חוזר עמהם על שעבדו עכו'ם שנא' סרו מהר, אפילו סוררים הן איני מניח אותם ועמהם אני דר שנא' אף סוררים וכו' Instead of מה עכו'ם one ought to read מה אומות העולם אוטרין, cf. Yalḳuṭ Makiri Psalms, ed. Buber p. 335, where the reading is או'ה.

[88] מדרש שיר השירים ed. Grünhut, Jerusalem 1897.

[89] P. 48b: אף ישראל אע'פ שנתפזרו בכל העולם עתידין לחזור שנא' אלכה ואשובה.

[90] P. 42b, the text is fragmentary, the application missing.

In a third place a sermon of R. Jochanan[91] is concluded with
Deut. 30.9 and 3, containing the promises of God to return the
exiles to the Holy Land.[92]

Anti-Jewish polemics did not stop short at this claim. "God
hates Israel!" is a saying attributed to the nations of the world
by a teacher of the third century, R. Shemaya.[93] They try to
sow hatred between God and Israel by their decrees and persecutions, by death and torture, yet they are unable to extinguish
the mutual love between God and Israel.[94] These accusations of
Israel's degradation and humiliation correspond literally to the
words of the Didascalia. The author of this document clearly
voices the feelings and expresses the attitude of Gentile-Christianity, with a double point, first of all against Jews, and secondly
against Jewish-Christians, the פושעי ישראל. The latter have been,
it is true, converted to the belief in Jesus. That is not enough.
They are under the curse of the law, especially the Repetition
of the law. Why is Israel forsaken? Hated? Rejected? On account
of the law. Paul and Barnabas could not find words strong
enough to condemn the law. The law was given as a sign and
as punishment for Israel's golden calf. The Didascalia follows
the teaching of these religious leaders most faithfully. Did their
teaching find adherents in the Jewish communities of Galilee, or
was their preaching restricted to the churches? Surely, this
latter was not the case, if our impression gained by the numerous
homilies on this subject conveyed through the Haggadic literature is right.

IV

In the sermons, anonymous and otherwise, cited in the previous
chapter, we could not avoid the feeling that the rejection of
Israel was due to the sin of the golden calf.[95] This view of the

[91] Cf. Pes. ed. Buber 139b, Pes. r. ch. 4, Lam. r.   [92] P. 21a.

[93] Agadat Bereshit, ed. Buber p. 27. R. Aḥa in his name: לפי שאו'ה מבקשין
לבא על ישראל שונא אותם הקב'ה נלך עליהם.

[94] Ibid., p. 164: כמה נתקעו אוו'ה להטיל שנאה בינו לבינינו ואין יכולין לבטל רבים אלו
האומות שנטשלו כמים. כמה אוו'ה' הורגין בישראל בשביל להחזירם מאחר הב'ה, וכנסת
ישראל אומרת להן אין אני יכולה לכפור בו. Cf. also Midr. Psalms 15. 4, ed. Buber 117:
סים רבים אלו אוו'ה לכבות את האהבה זה האהבה שבין ישראל לבין הקב'ה.

[95] Cf. notes 75, 83, 84, 87.

Didascalia was shared by the Church Fathers as well.[96] Here again, there is little to be gained from the Tannaitic literature on this subject; either the arguments were not known to them, or, if known, of no importance whatsoever. They are concerned with Moses' action in breaking the tablets, whether he did so at the command of God, or by his own will.[97] There are some, none too numerous sayings on this subject by Tannaim, which in style and tone differ greatly from those of the Amoraic period. Some of the former may be cited here. R. Akiba, who defended Moses for breaking the tablets,[98] seems to have pleaded also for Israel. He agrees with the School of R. Yannai, who ascribed the sin to the well-being of Israel; the abundance of gold and silver was the cause of the making of the golden calf.[99] R. Yose, the Galilean, remarks: Come and see how weighty the force of sin is. Before Israel committed that sin (i.e. the golden calf) there were neither people with issues, nor leprous among them, but afterwards there were.[100] In the days of the teacher of these sages, of R. Eliezer b. Hyrkanos, a wise woman asked a question about the three different punishments meted out to the worshippers of the golden calf, but there is in it no trace of the dogma taught by the Church Fathers.[101]

Turning to the teachers of the post-Bar Kokba period one

---

[96] Cf. esp. Tertullian, *adv. Judaeos*, ch. 1, cf. Justin, *Dial.* ch. 21, 22 and 27, Harnack, *Dogmengeschichte* I, 3, 579, Diestel, *Geschichte des A.T. in der christl. Kirche*, Jena 1896, 55. Die Hauptstrafe für diesen Abfall seien die Ceremonialgesetze.

[97] Cf. Abot R. Nathan ch. 2. R. Jose the Galilean, R. Judah ben Batyra, R. Eleazar ben Azarja, R. Aḳiba and R. Meir endeavour to explain Moses' extraordinary deed in breaking the two tablets. It is a veritable apology for Moses, but the burden of the accusation against Israel, as taught by the Church from the middle of the second century and onwards, is not yet discernible.

[98] Cf. previous note: לא שבר משה את הלוחות אלא שנאמר לו מפי הגבורה שנ' ואתפוש בשני הלחות בסה אדם תופס בסה שיכול.

[99] Cf. b. Ber. 32a, b. Yoma 86b, b. Sanh. 102, further Tos. Yoma chap. 4.19, cf. also the reading in Ginzberg's *Geonica* II, 374 l. 16ff., where the words כדר' ינאי דאמר ר' ינאי are omitted.

[100] Sifre Num. § 1, ed. Friedmann, 1b: בוא וראה כמה כמה קשה כחה של עבירה שעד שלא פשטו ידיהם בעבירה לא היו בהם זבים ומצורעים ומשפשטו ידיהם בעבירה היו בהם זבים ומצורעים.

[101] B. Yoma 66b, Gaster, *Exempla* No. 27, p. 20.

notices the same attitude towards this problem. R. Meir, who
defended Moses in his action,[102] has a word also for Israel. They
sinned whilst they were in a state of drunkenness.[103] This lame
apology was rightly refuted by R. Judah b. Ilai. Finally, R.
Simon ben Yoḥai confirms our observation distinguishing
between the Tannaitic and Amoraic treatment of this problem.
He, on the lines of R. Yose ha Gelili,[104] draws a psychological
difference between Israel before the sin and after. Before
they were fearless, afterwards they were frightened of Moses.[105]
In the time of the Mishna this agitation against Israel on account
of the golden calf was still so mild and insignificant that no
objection was raised to the reading and Targum of Ex. 32.1f.
Ex. 32.21f. was read, but not translated.[106]

How different is the outlook and the situation in the Amoraic
Haggada! .Here we again come across the same names, whose
bearers lodged a lively protest against the saying: God has forsaken,
or rejected Israel. We meet R. Hoshaya,[107] R. Joshua ben Levi,[108]

[102] Cf. above note 97.

[103] Cant. r. 2.13: אמרה כנסת ישראל הושלם בי יצר הרע ביין ואמרתי לענל אלה אלהיך
ישראל.

[104] Cf. note 100.

[105] Sifre Num. 1, p. 1b: בוא וראה מה כח עבירה קשה שער שלא פשטו ידיהם בעבירה
מה נאמר בהם וטראה כבוד ה' כאש אוכלת לא יראים ולא מזדעזעים משפשטו ידיהם בעבירה
cf. Num. r.; מה נאמר בהם וירא אהרן וכל בני ישראל והנה קרן עור פניו ויראו מנשת אליו

[106] M. Meg. III, b. Meg. 25b, pal. Meg. IV, 11, where in the Talmud
different portions are assigned to the second מעשה ענל.

[107] B. Ber. 32a: משל לאדם שהיתה לו פרה כחושה ובעלת אברים האכילה כרשינין
היתה טבעתה בו א'ל מי גרם ליך שתהא מבעטת בי אלא כרשינין שהאכלתיך. The defence is
on the same lines as that of R. Akiba and the School of R. Jannai, cf. above
note 99.

[108] Eccl. r. 4.5, in Ex. r. 41.12. Midr. Eccl. z. p. 100, the passage is quoted
in the name of R. Simon ben Yoḥai. Yet it is more probable that R. Joshua ben
Levi is its author. Moses did not move from his place until he was granted
forgiveness for Israel. A similar defence is put up by R. Abbahu, b. Ber. 32a:
אלמלא מקרא כתוב אי אפשר לאומרו מלמד שתפסו משה להקב'ה כאדם שהוא תופס את חבירו
בבגדו ואמר לפניו רבש'ע אין אני מניחך עד שתמחול ותסלח להם. In another saying R.
Joshua ben Levi pleads: לא עשו ישראל את הענל אלא ליתן פתחון פה לבעלי תשובה.
The story of the golden calf was not the source of a curse, i.e. the law, but an
immense bliss, to teach the sinner repentance. I wonder who is more human,
more enlightened, Paul, Barnabas, the Church Fathers on one side, or R.
Joshua ben Levi, who may have followed an older saying of R. Simon ben
Yoḥai? Cf. b. A. Z. 4b, cf. also Ex. r. 46.6

R. Joḥanan,[109] R. Eleasar,[110] R. Levi,[111] R. Isaac,[112] R. Samuel

[109] B. Ber. 32a: אמר רבי חייא בר אבא אמר ר' יוחנן משל לאחד שהיה לו בן הרחיצו
וסכו והאכילו והשקהו ותלה לו כיס על צוארו והושיבו על פתח של זונות מה יעשה אותו הבן?
This apology tallies with the view cited above from the Ps. Clementines,
note 38, and that of R. Levi, cf. note 39, cf. also Ex. r. 43.8, where the same
idea is expressed by R. Ḥona, in the name of R. Yoḥanan in a somewhat fuller
and clearer manner: משל לחכם שפתח לבנו חנות של בשמים בשוק של זונות, הסבוי עשה שלו,
והאומנות עשתה שלה, והנער כבחור עשה שלו, יצא לתרבות רעה, בא אביו ותפסו עם הזונה
התחיל האב צועק ואומר הורנך אני, היה שם אוהבו א"ל אתה איבדת את הנער ואת צועק כנגדו,
הנחת כל האומניות ולא למדתו אלא בשם והנחת כל המבואות ולא פתחת לו חנות אלא בשוק
של זונות, כך אמר משה רבון העולם הנחת כל העולם ולא שעבדת בניך אלא במצרים שהיו
עובדים טלאים ולמדו מהם בניך ואף הם עשו העגל. A similar apology is taught by
R. Abin in the name of R. Simon ben Yehozadak, Ex. r. 43.10, the application
of which reads: כך כשעשו ישראל אותו מעשה בקש הקב"ה לכלוחם אמר משה רבון העולם
לא ממצרים הוצאתם ממקום ע"ז ועכשיו נערים הם המתן מעט להם ולך עמהם ועושין לפניך
הוצאת מע"ט. R. Yoḥanan further asserts that God's vow was dissolved
by Moses, as a scholar annuls vows of people. Hence R. Simon ben Lakish
explains the fact that Moses was called איש האלהים, the man who annulled
God's vow, Ex. r. 43.5.

[110] Cant. r. 2.3 defends the worship of the calf by assuming that Israel was
not liable for punishment until the Law was expounded to them in the Tent
of Appointment: כך אע"פ שהתורה נתנה בהר סיני לא נענשו עליה עד שנתפרש להם באוהל.
Cf. Lev. r. 1.10: אע"פ שנתנה תורה לישראל מסיני לא נענשו עליה עד שנישנית מועד.
באוהל מועד—כך אע"פ שנתנה תורה לישראל לא נענשו עליה עד שנישנית להם באוהל מועד;
cf. also Cant. r. 3.4: שמשם נתחייבו ישראל (anonymously), further Cant. r. 8.2,
where R. Berakya says: זה סיני א"ר ברכיה למה קוראין לסיני בית שמש נעשו ישראל
כתינוק בן יומו? The idea is that the erection of the Tabernacle wiped off the sin
of the golden calf. Thus R. Berakya goes a step further in the defence of the
מעשה עגל.

[111] R. Levi defends the deed of Israel in different ways: God forgave
Israel and has not rejected his people, Lev. r. 1.3: בן אביתר שויתר הקב"ה על ידיו
מעשה העגל. Of a similar type is his saying in Lev. r. 27.7, כל פעולות טובות ונחמות
שהקב"ה עתיד לעשות עם ישראל אינם אלא בשביל פועה שפעיתם לפני בסיני ואמרתם כל אשר
דבר ה' נעשה ונשמע וכו' תועבה יבחר בכם אותה תועבה שכתוב עשו להם עגל מסכה מאותו
קרבן לפני הביאו התועבה. The very sacrifice shall remove the sin of the calf.
Ibid., 27.8, after a parable of a suspected matrona, R. Levi quotes the saying
of the nations of the world: כך אומות העולם מונין להם לישראל ואומרים להם עשיתם
את העגל' ובדק הקב"ה בדברים ולא מצא בהם ממש. Here R. Levi in his apologetic zeal
is inclined to treat the whole crime as a meaningless suspicion. This is surely
exaggerated; cf. however, Ex. r. 49.2, שחורה אני בשור שנ' וימירו את כבודם בתבנית
שור ונאוה אני בשור, שור או כבש או עז and Cant. r. 1.5. In a third homily R. Levi
preaches that God foresaw at the revelation at Sinai that Israel was going
to commit that crime of idolatry, Cant. r. 1.2: ר' פנחס בשם ר' לוי נלוי היה לפני
הקב"ה שעתידים ישראל להמיר כבודו באחר שנ' וימירו כבודם שלא יהא אומרים אלו הראנו את

א'ר לוי וכי לא היה נלוי לפני הסקום: Cf. also Ex. r. 29.4 כבודו ואת גדלו היינו מאסינים לו שאם הוא מראה כבודו לישראל שאינן יכולין לעמוד אלא צפה הקב'ה שהן עתידין לעשות עכום וכו' אוטרין והן יהו שלא. Ex. r. 41.3. R. Pineas b. Hama, cf. in the name of R. Levi: אלא שהיה צפוי וגלוי לפני הקב'ה שעתידין ישראל אחר מ' יום לעשות העגל וכו'.
Since no apology is attached to this sermon, which is somewhat surprising, most probably R. Levi elaborated an older saying. The term מקום for God corroborates such a suggestion. There is a long sermon in which the two ideas of Israel's rejection and the sin of Israel are defended, written either by R. Levi or by R. Simon b. Lakish, cf. b. Ber. 32b, cf. however Yalḳut Makiri Isaiah p. 179. There Israel says before God: Lord of the Universe! A man marries a second wife and remembers the first one. Thou, however, hast forgotten and forsaken me! God assures Israel that the whole universe was created for Israel's sake, how can He forget all the sacrifices of Israel in the wilderness? Since there is no forgetfulness before God perhaps he still remembers the deed of the calf. No, this is forgotten. Since there is forgetfulness before God He might have forgotten the Deed of Sinai? No, this I will not forget. The latter doctrine is ascribed to R. Hoshaya (cf. note 67) taught by R. Eleazar (cf. note 110). Finally in a homily of R. Levi we read: יסכר פיהם של או'ה שהיו אומרים לישראל שאין השכינה חחרת אלינו לעולם שנ' רבים אומרים לנפשי וני' אלו אלו עד שלא עשו את העגל בא הקב'ה ושרה אצלם משכנע עליהם אינו חזר עליהם. Tanḥ. f. 134a. The reply is again that the building of the Temple is an eloquent proof that God has forgiven Israel. Here, again, the rejection of Israel and the deed of the calf are closely connected, as in the Didascalia.

בשעה שעשו ישראל את העגל ביקש הקב'ה לכלותן שונאיהן של ישראל, א'ל Deut. r. 1.2: משה רבש'ע העגל הזה טוב הוא לסייע לך. א'ל הקב'ה מה מסייע לי? א'ל אם אתה מוריד נשמים הוא מפריח טללים אתה מוצא את הרוחות והוא מוציא את הברקים. א'ל הקב'ה אף אתה תועה בעגל? א'ל רבש'ע למה יחרה אפך בעמך. ולישראל אמר אתם חטאתם חטאה גדולה. The sin, alleged by the nations of the world to have broken God's covenant with Israel, is not so weighty as assumed. A similar homily is given in Exod. r. 43.6 from a source, which bears all the characteristic features of the Yelamdenu, scil. אלהים as the name of God, in the name of R. Neḥemya, reading: בשעה שעשו ישראל אותו מעשה עמד לו משה מפייס את האלהים אמר רבון העולם עשו לך סיוע ואתה כועס עליהם. העגל הזה יהיה מסייעך אתה מזריח את החמה והוא הלבנה. אתה הכוכבים והוא המזלות. אתה מוריד את הטל והוא משיב רוחות. אתה מוריד נשמים והוא מגדל צמחים. אמר הקב'ה משה אף אתה טעית כמותם והלא אין בו ממש א'ל אם כן למה אתה כועס על בניך הוי הי' למה יחרה אפך. Num. r. 2.15 copies merely a part of the homily, without mentioning either the name of R. Isaac, or that of R. Neḥemya: אמר לו משה זה העגל שעשו ישראל עכשיו הוא מסייעך הוא מוריד נשמים ואתה מפריח טללים א'ל הקב'ה וכי יש בו תחלת? א'ל משה ואם אין בו ממש למה ה' יחרה אפך בעמך וכו' מה כתוב אחריו וינחם. Cf. also Pes. rabbati 46a, Cant. r. on 1.6.
R. Isaac relates the following story: מעשה בקרתגית אחת שפחה שהיה לה שירדה: למלאת סן העין היא וחברתה אמרה לחברתה: חברתי למחר אדני מגרש את אשתו ונוטלני לאשה! אמרה לה: למה? בשביל שראה ידיה מפוחמות. אמרה לה: אי שוטה שבעולם ישמטו אזניך מה שפיך מדברת ומה אם אשתו שהיא חביבה עליו ביותר את אומרת מפני שראה ידיה מפוחמות

b.　Naḥmani,[113]　R.　Simlai,[114]　R.　Abbahu,[115]　R.　Judah

שעה אחת רוצה לנרשה את שכולך ספוחמת ושחורה ספעי אסך כל יסיך עאכו' כ כך לפי שאו'ה
סונין לישראל ואוטרים אוטה זו הסירו כבודם שנ' ויסירו את כבודם, אוטרים להם לישראל
עאכו'כ אתם נתחייבנו כך לשעה אנו אם ומה. Gentile-Christianity cannot reproach
Israel for "once" making an idol, since it is steeped in idolatry, cf. also a
fragment of a Midrash in Jellinek's *Bet ha-Midrash*, V, 160f.

[113] R. Samuel ben Naḥmani often recurs to this subject. He defends Israel
either in the name of his teacher, or in his own name. In the name of
R. Jonathan b. Eleazar he teaches, Ex. r. 43.1: הענל את ישראל שעשו בשעה כך
והוציאו השטן את ודחף עמד משה, עשה מה מבחוץ. עוטר ומשה בפנים ומקטרנ עוטר השטן היה
במקוסו ועמד לחוץ. R. Samuel b. Naḥmani expounds and develops this theory
even further by increasing and exaggerating the anthropomorphic tendency
of the Haggadah by saying: בדין עליהם הקב'ה יסב מעשה ישראל אותו שעשו בשעה כך
הקב'ה של ידו סתוך הלוחות את נטל משה? עשה מה דינן, נזר לחתום בא אלא עשה ולא לחייבם,
וכו' ושברן הלוחות את נטל מעשה ישראל שעשו כיון משה עשה כך חטאו. להשיב כדי.
It is obvious that R. Samuel b. Naḥmani availed himself of R. Jose the
Galilean's defence of Moses. Cf. note 93. Yet, there the defence of Moses'
deed, of his breaking the tablets, is the chief aim, here the defence of Israel
against the nations' verdict. This appears to me a most remarkable contrast
between the aims of the teachers who preached in the first decades of the
2nd century C.E. and the tendency manifested by those of the 3rd cent. C.E.
There is a full century between them, in which Christianity made full headway
in its opposition to Judaism. The second apology of this teacher is also most
remarkable in its tendency as well as in expression. It is a flat denial of Israel's
guilt. Israel did not at all commit that terrible crime for which the nations
of the world, Apostolic and Church Fathers, condemned their contemporaries
for alleged crimes of their ancestors. The latter are not responsible for the calf,
but the proselytes and strangers within their midst. R. Ḥuna and R. Idi say
in the name of R. Samuel b. Naḥmani: עשו שאילו מעשה, מאותו ישראל היו מוצלים
לישראל ואטרו עשאוהו עטהם עשלו הגרים אלא ישראל, אלהינו אלה לוטר להם היה הענל את
ישראל אלהיך אלה, Tanḥ. Lev. B. 94. Cf. also Lev. r. 27.7, Pesikta. In a
third homily, God's forgiveness is emphasized, contrasting God's character with that of a human being, Tanḥ. Frkft. 27a: ישראל שעשו אחר סוצא אתה וכן
הק' א'ל וכו', מזה לך עלה אל משה ד' ויהבר א'ל הקב'ה מה רחמים משה עליהם ובקש הענל את
אמר אם עשה ולא אומר סהו ויכזב. איש בו וחוזר מתנה ליתן שאומר כב'ו אני סשה
על וינחם אלא עשה ולא' סטני, הרף לטשה אסר שכן רעה להביא כעסו בשעת
הקב'ה א'ל כדבריך ד' סלחתי ויאסר אלא עשה ולא בהם אפי ויחר לי הניחה ועתה וכן הרעה
לעשותה ומתנאה רעה לעשות שאוסר ודם כבשר איני. I wonder whether R. Samuel
b. Naḥmani ever read the Epistle of Paul to the Galatians 3.15ff.: "Brethren,
I speak after the manner of men: Though it be but a man's covenant, yet if
it be confirmed, no man disannulleth, or addeth thereto, etc." R. Samuel
b. Naḥmani's words might have been directed against Paul. In a fourth
homily again the building of the Tabernacle is adduced to disprove that God
has not forgiven Israel for the deed of the calf: העולם לבאי היא עדות Tanḥ.

b. Simon,[116] R. Abba b. Kahana,[117] R. Ari,[118] and R. Judah bar Shalom,[119] most of them familiar to the readers of these pages.[120] Reviewing the teachings of these teachers, given fully in the footnotes, one is surprised by many quaint and unusual features. These teachers of the third century seem compelled to wipe off from Israel's history the sin of the golden calf. This whitewashing sounds strange, remembering the narrative of the Bible. The attempt to throw off all responsibility for that not too glorious deed and to lay the burden on the strangers who joined the camp of Israel sounds more like the fancy of a learned antiquarian and an eloquent preacher than true history. Even those Haggadists who do not shut their eyes to the truth are inclined to invent legends and situations proving the pardon granted by God to Israel. It cannot be denied that Christian fanatic polemics

---

Frkft. 136b. The term באי העולם is here intentionally used, to indicate the objections of the nations of the world; similarly in the application of the parable, where one reads: שוב אינו חוזר אליהם (או'ה) אמרו הגוים. Finally there is a fifth homily of R. Samuel b. Naḥmani, which cannot be understood without bearing in mind the anti-Jewish attacks on the part of the hostile Church. He says: בו ביום שעשו ישראל את העגל בו ביום ירד להן המן ולא עוד אלא שנטלו ממנו הקריבו לע"ז שנא' ולחמי אשר נתתי לך סלח וכו', Tanḥ. Frkft. 264b. Although Israel used the manna for idolatry, nevertheless God's gifts never ceased; so his covenant was not annulled, cf. also Tanḥ. Frkft. 123a f., where the homily is fuller than here, and Ex. r. 44.2 and 7.

[114] R. Simlai sees in Isa. 53.12 a characteristic of Moses: והוא חטא רבים נשא, b. Sotah 14a; consequently Moses achieved Israel's שכיפר על מעשה העגל atonement for the deed of the calf.

[115] Cf. above, note 108.

[116] Tanḥ. Frkft. 122a. The payment of the Shekel atoned for the sin of the calf. Num. r. 7.4 they were punished with leprosy for the deed of the calf. Cf. above note 100. M. Deut. Zutta, ed. Buber p. 11: כך כיון שחטאו ישראל שכעס עליהם הקב"ה וביקש לכלותם שנ' הרף ממני ואשמידם, also Ex. r. 43.9 in the name of R. Levi b. Parta.

[117] Cf. Lev. r. 10.3.

[118] Eccl. r. 9.3, 11: אין לך כל דור ודור שלא נטל אונקי אחת של עגל, Ex. r. 43.2, Lam. r. 1.20.

[119] Ex. r. 43.9, Tanḥ. Frkft. 148b.

[120] Sifra, Shemini 1.4: יבוא שור ויתכפר על מעשה שור יבוא עגל ויתכפר על מעשה. Sifre Zutta, ed. עגל הרעו שנתרצה המקום על עונותיכם עבירה שאתם מתיראים ממנה Königsberger, p. 1: נגד כל האומות שהם מרנגין אחריך במעשה העגל ואומרין שאין להם קמתי אני לפתוח, Cant. r. s.v. מחילה לעולם.

lurk behind these sayings. The dark clouds of misrepresentations, the gloomy spirit of fanaticism in the new sect or sects used the Bible for a cruel game of humiliation and subjugation, which poisoned and embittered the relationship between Judaism and Christianity. It is, naturally, impossible for a Christian to be quite impartial in judging that colossal fight between two religions, which are so near to, and yet so far from, one another. Yet, any impartial reader of the Bible will, nowadays, smile at the attack of the Church more than at the defence of the Hagga-dists. The latter, however unsatisfactory their views might appear from the historian's point of view, are nearer to the modern approach to the Holy Scriptures. This defence was the more vital among the Galilean Jews of the third century, since, with the acceptance of the theory that Israel was forsaken as a consequence of the golden calf, the doctrine of the abrogation of the Law penetrated into the hearts of Jewish-Christians and Jews. The traces of this struggle for the law will be the subject of the next chapter.

V

However humiliating the thought that God had forsaken Israel, the Shekinah being far removed from the community of the Jews, however teasing and annoying the impossible argument that Israel's covenant with God had been broken, or that it had never been effective, the calumny, and no milder word can be found for it, that the Law is a curse, the Law a cruel punishment, passes our comprehension. Could an impartial mind, one not blinded by hatred, a religious leader or teacher not perverted by selfish motives, really preach that the Law was closing the door to seekers after God? The author of the Book of Jubilees must have had in mind some such opposition to the Law even before Jesus and Paul arose, when he said that Israel's precepts and ordinances, moral and ritual alike, are not the ephemeral expres-sion of the moral consciousness of a particular age, but are valid for all eternity (2.18, 15.27). The eternity of the Law is taught also by other writers of Pseudepigraphical literature.[121] That these

---

[121] Cf. I Baruch 59.2.

writers were confronted by antinomistic tendencies can be shown
not by one but by many passages in their works.[122] It was left
to the writer of the Epistle to the Galatians to invent the theory
that the Law is of divine origin but was given as a punishment
to the Jewish people for their wickedness and sins.[123] Since Justin
Martyr[124] there is a tendency in favor of collecting Biblical
passages which show that God needs nothing, whence the proof
is deduced that all, or some at least, of the institutions of the
Jews cannot represent God's will. Here Justin coincides with
the old Jewish polemics against the gods and their needs on one
side, which have a close parallel with Epicurean thought, and
with Marcionite polemics against the Bible on the other side.
Some writers of Early Christianity point out the Sabbath, circumcision and dietary laws as ridiculous and laughable.[125] Tertullian
does not treat these matters in the frivolous manner of the
Alexandrian and Roman Antisemitic literature, but raises the
often trumpetted cry, how is it that people, who did not keep
Sabbath, or practice circumcision, were called friends of God?[126]
Clemens of Alexandria takes an exceptional stand in acknowledging the educational value of the Law,[127] which is, naturally,
not entirely denied by writers like Tertullian[128] and some others,
who became conscious that the earlier radical view of the abrogation of the Law was detrimental and contradictory to the teaching
of the Church about the divinity of the Holy Bible. Only later,
when the Gnostic flood abated, did the preachers and teachers
of the Church revert to their antinomistic attitude.[129] So much
so that after the consolidation of Christianity, Jewish ceremonies
and observances became a laughing stock on the part of clergy

[122] Enoch 94.3, Jub. 1.9, 1.20, 6.37, Baruch 41.3, IV Ezra 7.21–25; cf. also
Mark 13.31, Matt. 5.18.
[123] Gal. 3.19f. Baur, *Geschichte*, I, 111.
[124] Diestel, *Das AT in der Kirche* p. 85, cf. however earlier Enoch 45.3.
[125] Diogenet 4.
[126] Tertullian, *adv. Judaeos*, chap. II, Eusebius *Hist. Eccl.* I, 4, 8.
[127] Cf. Diestel, p. 56.
[128] Cf. Wirth, *Die Lehre vom Verdienst*, p. 26.
[129] Cf. Asterios of Amasea, Bretz, *Studien und Texte zu Asterios von Amasea*,
TuU. 40 I 84. Cf. Harnack, *Diodor von Tarsus*, p. 93: about the dietary law,
p. 92: Why are some animals clean, and others unclean? All are created by God!

and laity. The Church vied with the ancient satirists and come-
dians of Rome to satisfy the bias and keep alive the ancestral
hatred of the new converts. I cannot believe that there are many
bishops or professors of theology in Western Europe, who believe
today that Moses spoke in spirit, namely, in a spiritual sense,
but suggest that the Jews, as the writer of the Barnabas letter
asserts, were led into error by a bad angel and adopted the carnal
and literal meaning of the Mosaic laws and injunctions which
concealed the spiritual truths, and that thus the entire ceremonial
system was a result of a deplorable misconception.[129a] Yet,
nevertheless, I can point out some misconceptions of Christian
theologians about the Jewish attitude to the laws of Moses,
especially when Schürer teaches in his history:[130] "wie die Motive
im wesentlichen doch äusserlicher Art sind, so ist auch das
Resultat eine unglaubliche Veräusserlichung des religiösen und
sittlichen Lebens." On a similar misunderstanding is based the
opinion of Keim:[131] "Es wiederholte die jüd. Gesetzgebung, aber
je ernstlicher es ihren sittlichen Inhalt herauskehrte und die
geforderte Heiligung des äusserern und noch vielmehr des innern
Lebens schärfte, um so mehr überschritt es die notdürftigen
Buchstaben des Gesetzes, um so mehr ignorierte es jede rituelle
und ceremonielle Aeusserlichkeit." Here breathes Pauline spirit
and Marcionite bias against the law. Jewish-Christians, however,
taught differently and thought otherwise. The Epistle of James[132]
admonished Jewish-Christians in a spirit quite in agreement with
Rabbinic lore: "Whosoever shall keep the whole Law, and yet
offend in one point, he is guilty of transgressing all." Jewish
teaching and Rabbinic thoughts are repeated by the writer of
the Clementine homiles[133] when he says: "For he is a worshipper
of God, of whom I speak, who is truly pious, not one who is
such only in name, but who really performs the deeds of the law
that has been given him." "If he, who is of another tribe, keeps
the law, he is a Jew; but he who does not keep it is a Greek.
For the Jew believes in God and keeps the law." "But he who keeps

[129a] Barnabas Letter ch. X ff.
[130] *Geschichte* II⁴ 548.
[131] *Rom und Christentum*, 133.
[132] II, 10.   [133] Hom. XI, 16.

not the law is manifestly a deserter through not believing God;
and thus is no Jew, but a sinner." They are the Posh'e Israel of
R. Simon b. Lakish.[134] and of Simon the Pious.[135] The authorities
of the Church had a difficult task to entice Jews and Gentiles
alike from the Law. Synods and pulpits encouraged all their
incumbents and representatives to threaten and condemn with
hell fire above and disabilities of the Church below on earth all
those who adhered to the law of Moses and his successors.

How were these calumnies received by the Jews? And how
were they refuted by the teachers of the Synagogue? Apart from
the group, by no means small, of Posh'e Israel, who must have
been mightily disturbed by this fight against the Law which was
still sacred and dear to them, the community of real Jews deeply
felt this onslaught on the most vital fortress of their very existence.
Teachers of the second century raised their voices against the
doctrine that the Law was given to Israel as a punishment and
chastisement. No! the law was the most eloquent sign of God's
love for his people, Israel. The Tannaitic Haggada preserves a
number of sayings intended to bring home this truth.[136] The
Mizwot have no other function to man from God, than to
increase man's holiness. This was emphasized[137] by a teacher of
the second century, Issi ben Judah, who heard, or read that
some people taught abominable ideas about the law. R. Hananya

---

[134] Cf. above note 2.
[135] Cf. above note 11.
[136] Sifre Deut. § 36, 75b: חביבין ישראל שסובבן הקב״ה במצות תפילין בראש ותפילין בראש ותפילין
בזרוע מזוזה בפתחיהם וציצית על ד׳ כנפות כסותך. Cf. b. Menaḥot 43b, Tos. Berakot
ch. 1, b. Šabb. 130a, M. Ps. 6.1, Tanḥ. B. III,110 and IV,73. The latter sources
speak eloquently for the apologetic tendency underlying them. M. Ps. concludes
with a peroration against the Minim and Posh'e Israel, who deny the existence
of God; their share will be the fire of Hell. It is doubtful whether פושעי ישראל
is correct, perhaps it refers to apostates of a later period? Tanḥ. III has:
אם תקיימו מצותי מניח אני את העליונים וארד לשכון ביניכם. The law could not be so
bad, if God makes it a condition of His dwelling in Israel's midst. Tanḥ. IV
has the teaching that Torah and Mizwot assure Israel's share in the world
to come, זרע הקב״ה לישראל את התורה ואת המצות לישראל והנחילם חיי העולם הבא. God did
not leave a single thing without Mizwot. Surely not for punishment, or to
deprive them of future bliss, salvation, or nearness of the Shekina. Just the
reverse, in order to draw them near to the divine presence.
[137] Mekilta 98a.

b. Akasya, another sage of this time, said that the law was given in order to enable Israel to acquire merit.[138] The Babylonian Rab surely was moved by some special motive in teaching that God commanded the law in order to cleanse mankind.[139] It is remarkable that Rab considers the Mizwot binding and effective in the case of all creatures, without distinctions of race and creed, nationality and religion. Some copyists or editors of the Midrashim, e.g. that of Midrash Psalms,[140] Leviticus rabba,[141] Midrash Samuel,[142] read "Israel," yet in the Tanchuma the reading "creatures" coincides with that of Gen. Rabba.[143] These teachers must have been aware of the attacks made against the law, without or within the community, which could not be allowed to pass in silence. The law is not such an abomination as taught in the Churches, it is the means of cleansing and purifying of sins. It is not a source of contamination, but an ever fresh well of holiness and sanctification. Finally, a sign of love, and not of God's hatred.

Even more emphatic are the teachers of the third century (especially after 240), who protested against the Church Fathers' allegations that God forsook Israel, and that the sin of the calf still counted against them. They had to take up cudgels against the pernicious and perverted ideas which arose as a result of accusations against the Synagogue, now generally recognized as false. R. Jonathan ben Eliezer says: "Whosoever performs a commandment in this world, the same precedes him and goes before him in the world to come."[144] The Mizwah is an agent for salvation, and not for perdition. R. Jonathan ben Eliezer must have been upset by people who told him that the performance of the commandments deprives man of his future life. Where are these people to be sought, if not in the Gentile-Christian

[138] Abot R. N. 141, Makkot III, 16.
[139] Gen. r. ch. 41.1, ed. Theodor 424: לא ניתנו המצות אלא לצרוף את הבריות בהן.
[140] Ed. Buber 18.25, correct בריות to ישראל.
[141] Chap. 13.
[142] Ed. Buber ch. 4.
[143] Lev. שמיני ed. Buber §12, cf. however תזריע §7.
[144] B. Sota 3b. R. Samuel b. Naḥmani in his name: כל העושה מצוה בעוה"ז מקדמתו והולכת לפניו לעוה"ב.

camp? R. Joshua ben Levi faced the same antagonists of the
law, when he preached in his synagogue in Lydda: "All the
commandments that Jews perform in this world, will rise and
testify for them in the world to come."[145] Or, when the same
teacher uttered his saying: "He who performs Mizwot is as
if he had received the Shekina." Observances draw men near to
God, and do not drive them far away from Him.[146] These sayings
are closely connected with the anonymous teaching cited previously,[147] that God has sown Torah and Mizwot in order to
make Israel inherit a share in the future life. The preachers in
Tiberias in the sixties and seventies of the third century, R. Levi
and R. Isaac, show in some of their homilies and other utterances
a special predilection for our problem, which is shared by others
as well, e.g. R. Samuel b. Naḥmani, who says: "All the good
things and blessings, which the prophets saw in this world, were
the result of their obedience to the law."[148] On similar lines is
the teaching of R. Isaac: "He who performs a Mizwah as it ought
to be performed will never hear evil tidings, and if evil decrees
are passed on him God will nullify the same.[149] He further makes
God say to Israel: "I did not trouble you for observances."[150]
The observances are not given as a burden, as an unbearable
yoke, but as a joy. Similarly: "He, who loves Mizwot, never
gets satiated with them,"[151] i.e. the lover of commandments longs
for more and more; all the talk about precepts and ordinances
being a burden does not apply in reality to law-abiding and God-
fearing Jews. Let us now turn to R. Levi, in whose Haggadah
as we saw[152] the perverted theory of the golden calf was more
than once refuted. What good comes of observing the law and

[145] B. A. Z. 201: ‎כל מצות שישראל עושין בעוה"ז באות ומעידות להם בעוה"ב.
[146] Pal. Ḥag. 76a: ‎כל המקיים מצות כאילו מקבל פני שכינה.
[147] Cf. note 136.
[148] Eccl. r. 1.27: ‎כל טובות וברכות שראו הנביאים בעוה"ז לא לחינם באו אל ע"י שהיו
‎הונין ועושין מצות וצדקות.
[149] B. Šabb. 63b, according to MS. Brit. Museum Or. 1389, 4b, our text
has: R. Hinnana b. Idi. ‎ואפי' רעות בשורות! אותו מבשרין אין כמאמרה העושה כל
‎אם נוחרים עליו נזירה המקום מבטלה.
[150] Lev. r. 27.6, Tanḥ. B. IV,128.
[151] Deut. 218, Tanḥ. ad loc.
[152] Cf. above note 104.

doing good deeds?—seems to have been a question openly asked during the second half of the third century in religious meeting places of Tiberias.[153] Here again, just as in the saying of Rab.[154] the use of the term בריות "creatures," and not "Israel" is most noteworthy to the student of universalistic thought in Rabbinic theology. To the view of the Church that ceremonies and ritual commandments are a punishment for the making of the golden calf, the reply is given that the calf actually caused a shortening of many precepts and the omission of others, which were originally intended to be given to Israel.[155] Through the making of the calf they lost festivals and Mizwot, and it is not as the Fathers of the Church teach that these were imposed upon them. One may have one's own views as to this method of homoepathic apologetics, but one thing is sure, that R. Levi knew the theories attached to, or derived from, the Bible narrative of the golden calf.

The author of the Didascalia endeavors to convince Jewish-Christians, who, in common with those from whom the Clementine writings emanated, thought very highly of the Sabbath and its uniqueness, and who knew and kept the minutiae of its observance (*Rec.* 9.28), of the futility of this observance. The following are his two arguments: First of all, if the Sabbath was God's will, then, why were not the old saints of the Bible, before the revelation on Mount Sinai, entrusted with the same? Secondly, why does not God Himself observe this law.[156] These questions are of importance for the elucidation of many Haggadic passages and teachings. Yet, before turning to these, it may not be uninteresting to point out a few Christian writers who developed a similar rabulistic[157] with reference to the law of circumcision. In the dispute between the Jew Simon and the Christian The-

---

[153] Eccl. r. 1.4: מה הנאה יש לבריות אשר סכנלות במצות ובמע׳ט.

[154] Cf. note 139.

[155] Pes. r. 220b: אסר ר׳ לוי כך עלתה על דעתו של הקב׳ה ליתן לישראל רנל אחד בכל חורש שבקיץ בניסן פסח, באייר פסח קטן, בסיון עצרת וע׳י עבירות ומעשים רעים שעשו בעגל שהו בידן שלשה.

[156] Didascalia, *l.c.* 136.3ff.

[157] Cf. Carl Schmidt, *l.c.* 253. Note: "In echt rabulistischer Weise sucht er (the author of the Didascalia) etc." There is no reference in Schmidt's work to the authors mentioned above in the text.

ophilus,[158] which is contemporary with the Didascalia and the Clementines, the same objection is raised. Why are not Enoch, Noah, Job, or Malkizedek, or even Adam commanded this rite? Because all that God wants is the circumcision of the heart! The answer to this interpretation of the convenant, which is an old argument against Judaism, was given as early as the beginning of the second century C.E. by R. Ishmael and R. Akiba.[159] The anonymous Haggada enumerates a number of persons, among whom the aforementioned Biblical personages are to be found, who are said to have been born circumcised.[160] Why was the law of circumcision not given to Adam, or included in the Decalogue? was asked by heathens of many rabbis. So, by Tinaeus Rufus of R. Akiba,[161] by Akylas of R. Eliezer b. Hyrkanos,[162] by the Matrona of R. Jose b. Ḥalafta,[163] and by a philosopher of R. Hoshaya in Caesarea.[164] In another homily Abraham asks this question of God.[165] In any case we may see in this argument against the circumcision a pagan inheritance on the part of the Church, which lived a long life in the polemics against Sabbath observing Jewish-Christians, and Christians up to the turn of the fourth century. No wonder that the same argument is advanced by the author of the Didascalia against the Sabbath. Why did not the saints and heroes of the Bible observe the Sabbath? One reply can be found in the theory developed in the Haggada that the patriarchs of old kept all the minutiae of the law.[166] The Sabbath

[158] Cf. Marmorstein, "Juden und Judenthum in der Altercatio Simoni's Judaei et Theophilis Christiani" in *Theolog. Tijdschrift* XLIX, 1915, pp. 360–383.

[159] Cf. Marmorstein, *l.c.* p. 377.

[160] Cf. *ibid.*, p. 378, esp. note 1 and M. Friedländer, *Talmudische und Patristische Studien*, p. 73.

[161] Pes. r. 116b f. ?הואיל וחביבה היא המילה מפני סה לא ניתנה בעשרת הדברות

[162] b. B. B. 10a.

[163] Pes. r. 117a.

[164] Gen. r. ch. 11, ed. Theodor p. 94 and Pes. r. 116a (Rabbi).

[165] Gen. r. ch. 46, ed. Theodor p. 480.

[166] Cf. a fuller treatment of this Haggadic idea in my article: "Quelques problems de l'ancienne apologetique juive", in *REJ*, vol. 68, 1914, 161–174. Cf. further Num. r. 14.9. Joseph observed the Sabbath before the law. M. Ps. 52 ed. Buber. Adam was reprieved on account of the Sabbath; M. Ex. r. 5.18, Israelites kept the Sabbath in Egypt.

was not given as a burden, but, as all the observances for man's welfare and happiness, it increases holiness.[167] The second point of the Didascalia about God's observing Sabbath was raised by a Min, Gnostic Jew, who attended a Sabbath service in Rome, where and when R. Gamaliel and his colleagues from Palestine preached on the subject: Whatever God commands others to do, He does Himself. Thereupon the Min objected: Your God does not keep Sabbath![168] R. Akiba proves to Tinaeus Rufus[169] that nature rests on the Sabbath. An anonymous preacher exclaims in his sermon on the Sabbath: "Is it possible that God did work on Sabbath?"[170] These instances may suffice to show that both arguments against the Sabbath have been drawn by the author of the Didascalia from pagan sources. Further that they are preserved in the Haggada with a defence of the Jewish standpoint.

VI

Strenuous efforts were made by the Church to fight Jewish-Christians and also Christians who could not free themselves from the "yoke of the commandments." Whether the Rabbis defended the law against Christians for their sake or in order that the poison of antinomism should not penetrate into synagogues and schools is another question. All rabbis were not so tolerant towards the Posh'e Israel as were R. Simon b. Lakish and R. Simon the Pious, for in spite of their faithfulness to the Law, they succumbed in other respects, apart from their belief in Jesus. Their attitude towards the Holy Scriptures was not the correct Jewish standpoint as taught and dogmatized by the Synagogue. They, as we can see from the Clementines—and they are the most reliable witnesses for the doctrines and feelings of the Palestinian-Syrian Jewish-Christians of the third century— did not accept the Canon of the Holy Scriptures in its entirety. Even parts of the Pentateuch were eliminated as forgeries. Some objectionable stories in the life of the forefathers were simply

---

[167] Mek. 104a, Deut. r. 3.1, R. Ḥiyya b. Abba.
[168] Ex. r. ch. 30,6.
[169] Gen. r. ch. 11, ed. Theodor.
[170] Pes. r. 187a f.

ignored. A conception similar to the teaching of the Didascalia that the law of God comprises the Decalogue and the statutes issued before the making of the calf crept into the Clementines (*Rec.* 1.36). No adherent of the Jewish synagogue would go so far as to say: "Or, supposing the expressions in the Scriptures which are against God and are unjust and false, to be true, they did not know his real divinity and power" (*Hom.* 18.19). One notices in perusing the Rabbinic material that in the course of the Tannaitic and Amoraic periods various attitudes to the Holy Scriptures were manifested. First of all a distinction was made between the Decalogue and the rest of the Mosaic legislation, the natural laws on one side and the ritual laws on the other side. Some others accepted the Pentateuch with the exclusion of narratives and stories which for some reason or other did not appeal to them. A third group found it necessary, or convenient, to eliminate Prophets and Hagiographa. A fourth group accorded approval to the Canon of the Holy Scriptures, but did not accept the authority and binding power of laws and traditions outside these books.[171]

It is not surprising that R. Simon ben Lakish emphatically deduces from Ex. 24.12 that the Ten Commandments, the whole Pentateuch, all commandments in the Mishna, Prophets and Hagiographa, and the Talmud, all were given to Moses from Heaven.[172] Since we know R. Simon ben Lakish's relations to the Posh'e Israel, we can appreciate the motives underlying his elaborate defence of all parts of the Bible and post-Biblical literature. He surely wanted to convince these straying members of the Jewish community that their treatment of the Bible, their differentiation between the different parts of the Torah is not according to the spirit of the law. How far, or whether he succeeded at all with his persuasion and with his tolerance, is not recorded. Another teacher of this age, whom we know as spokesman on all problems affecting relations between Judaism and Christianity in the third century C.E., R. Joshua ben Levi,[173]

---

[171] For a fuller treatment of these movements cf. my article: "Ein fragment einer neuen Piska zum Wochenfest und der Kampf gegen das mündliche Gesetz", in *Jeschurun* XII, 1925, 34–62.

[172] B. Ber. 5a.   [173] Cf. above pp. 242 f.

affirms the same idea. Bible, Mishna, Halakot, Talmud, Tosefta, Haggadot, even a stray saying by a qualified pupil before his master, is of Sinaitic origin.[174] This saying, surely an exaggerated one, must be taken in the apologetic sense in which it was uttered. This teacher's life was, as we know,[175] made miserable by Minim, who wearied him with their Bible difficulties, blasphemies and taunting questions, all amounting to the one argument that the Torah has discrepancies, some of which cannot be reconciled. Thereupon, he made his declaration. In an anonymous sermon, R. Joshua ben Levi's teaching is deduced from Ex. 34.27 connected with Hos. 8.12, quoting the very words of the teacher in Lydda, without his name.[176]

A full treatment of this subject is contained in a Midrash, which was until lately buried in the dust of the Geniza. Dr. L. Ginzberg[177] published a Midrash fragment, which he furnishes with the title, "A Tanhuma-like Midrash to the section לך לך." He overlooked the fact that the author of the Or Zarua, R. Isaac ben Moses of Wien,[178] knew this Midrash. Further, that pages (a) and (b) belong to the Pesiḳta, a Cambridge fragment of which was discovered and published in an article quoted previously.[179] This Pisḳa, as far as it can be reconstructed, treats the following matters: (1) How many Torot are there? Answer: Two; (2) Differences between the two laws; (3) God offered the Torah to all the nations of the world; (4) (a) Israel accepted the Torah, consequently the covenant is made with them; (b) both are threefold (Pentateuch, Prophets and Hagiographa on one side, Midrash, Halakot and Haggadot on the other side), all are of Sinaitic origin.

So far the contents of the Pisḳa. No teacher or Haggadist is mentioned in our fragment, which may be a matter of accident owing to its fragmentary state, yet the date may be ascertained by reference to the problem which agitated the contemporaries

[174] Eccl. r. 1.29, 5.7, p. 104, pal. Pea 2.4, Ḥag. 1.8, Lev. r. 22.1.
[175] Cf. b. Ber. 7a, our text reads צדוק׳, MSS. have מינא.
[176] Tanḥ. B. II, 116, Ex. r. 47.1, Yalḳ. Ex. 405.
[177] *Ginze Schechter* I, 1928, pp. 18–22.
[178] I, 7a.
[179] Cf. note 171.

of the previous teachers, e.g. R. Joshua ben Levi and R. Simon ben Lakish. This century saw among Jews, or Jewish-Christians, a movement which had many forerunners as well as followers who picked and chose, according to their religious beliefs and theological preferences, among parts of the Scriptures, or within a section of them. Needless to say, the radical wing of these factions did away in its entirety with the Oral Law, although the Clementines as well as the Didascalia on the one hand and the Dialogues on the other hand seem to suggest that some Soferic or Rabbinic extensions of some of the laws were observed among the Jewish-Christians whose conduct was a thorn in the sides of some anti-Jewish writers. Yet, some kind of an opposition, most likely as a result of these agitations, crept into Jewish circles and groups, homes and schools.

There has to be mentioned a rather strange sentence of R. Adda b. Ḥanina according to the Babylonian version, or of R. Ḥunja according to the Palestinian version. The first reads[180] אלמלא לא חטאו ישראל לא נותן להם אלא חמשה חומשי תורה וספר יהושע שאילולי זכו ישראל לא היו, the second[181] בלבד שערכה של ארץ ישראל הוא קורין אלא חמשה חומשי תורה ה' ספרים בלבד. The former sentence implies that the books outside the Pentateuch and Joshua were given because of Israel's sin; the latter puts it that were Israel free from guilt they would read no more than the Pentateuch; Prophets and Hagiographa can be considered as punishment for Israel's sin. There can be no doubt, to judge from the passages cited previously, that the sin κατ' ἐξοχην was the sin of the calf. In spite of the differences between the two texts and the names of the teachers we can connect them with the teaching of the Didascalia which saw in the "Repetition of the Law" a punishment. These teachers[182] must have heard of the anti-Jewish teachings about the effect of the golden calf, and the law being a punishment. Just as the contemporary teacher, whose view was recorded before,[183] says that not Sabbath and festivals were the

[180] B. Ned. 22b.
[181] Eccl. r. 1.34.
[182] Cf. however Bacher *Agada Pal. Am.* III 655, who tries to identify them and saw in Eccl. r. 1.34 a modification of the talmudic passage.
[183] Cf. above note 155.

punishment, but the deprivation of additional festivals, so these teachers deny the doctrine of the repetition of the law, and consider the Prophets and other books, some of them the very basis and only justification of the Gospels and Epistles, the consequences of that sin. It may be taken for granted that the Posh'e Israel rejected Prophets and Hagiographa—the scarcity of quotations from these parts of the Scriptures in the Clementine writings bears out quite eloquently the observations of the Jewish teachers that these people ignored these parts of the Holy Bible.

As a result of our investigation, we may establish the following facts. Around the chief seats of Jewish learning and communal activities, like Tiberias and Sepphoris, Caesarea and Lydda, there were scattered about smaller or larger settlements of Jewish-Christians. These stood between two fires, on the one side Jews attacked them for their partly separatistic position, and Christian leanings, on the other hand they were condemned by Gentile-Christians for their Jewish observances and Jewish leanings. These latter consisted of more or less scrupulous observance of Sabbath and Festivals, circumcision and dietary law, purity and impurity in the first instance, for which they earned the highest praise in a Jewish teaching of the third century where they are called, "full of observances as a pomegranate." Their interest and attachment to their Jewish brethren is manifested by their longing to share the official fast-day services, of which, probably, some fanatics wanted to deprive them. They most probably took part in the ordinary public services as well as in Synagogue life. On account of all these virtues they were disliked by teachers and bishops of the Church, which is quite natural. The Didascalia follows herein the tradition laid down by Paul, and some of the more intolerant Apostolic fathers. The polemics against these Jewish-Christians developed in a straight line from Paul to the Didascalia, just as the Jewish-Christians kept to their old traditions from the earliest days of the Church. Here, however, our task is limited. We have to investigate and describe the position of the Jewish-Christians of the third century with regard to these peculiarities of the sect, namely their observances, around which revolved the three-fold attack of the Gentile-Christian Church, that the Jewish nation was forsaken by God, that the making of the calf deprived the Jews of the privileges granted to them and their forefathers in the Holy Scriptures, and, finally, that the Law was given as punishment and chastisement for the transgression and wickedness of the people. Our material shows clearly that on the whole these points of accusation and attack are a legacy of pagan anti-Jewish polemics and antisemitism, grown on the poison-breeding soil of Alexandria, Caesarea, and other Greek cities. They were adopted and adapted by Christian teachers, who supplied chapters and verses from the Bible. Jewish-Christians, rank and file, certainly disliked this method, and defended themselves, as Jews, against these highly pernicious, and, according to impartial judgment, quite unhistorical and unfair doctrines and views. There is not much preserved of their counter-actions, and what is left has come to us in a Gentile-Christian garb and shape. I mean the Clementine writings and the so-called Apostolic constitutions. They teach the very interesting fact that Jewish-Christians did not give way without struggle but held in reverence their old traditions and the hallowed forms of their ancestors' liturgy, until they disappeared, either returning to the Synagogue or assimilating with the body of Gentile-Christianity. Smaller or larger Jewish-Christian assemblies may have survived in Transjordania or in Syria for some generations, even after Christianity became the successor to pagan gods. We know nothing of them. Anyhow, this possibility accounts for the remarkable fact that preachers and luminaries of the Church harangued their audiences to refrain from visiting Jewish places of worship, from celebrating Jewish festivals, from observances, etc. The jealousy of the triumphant Church cannot be explained otherwise. Eloquent and honey-mouthed orators become stammerers, full of gall when they mention Jews or refer to Judaism in their pulpit utterances or letters. It is no wonder that the preachers of the Synagogue took up the cudgels in this fight for their sacred religion. Since at least some sayings evince interest in these stray members of the Jewish religion, one is right in assuming that teachers were not indifferent about the present attitude and future fate of these Jewish-Christian communities. They hoped to bring them back to the fold, and tried to prevent their drifting away. The misconception of Israel's relation to

God, and God's attitude to Israel, Jewish history and observances, Scriptures and expectations, could not leave them cold and indifferent. If the rabbis did not think of the partly alienated Jewish-Christians in the first instance, they perceived the gloomy danger looming in the near future for the whole house of Israel. The destroyer was not distant, but very near and able to carry discord and apostasy into Jewish family life and the Synagogues. Two independent witnesses bear out the historical fact that this agitation against which the teachers of Judaism fought, did not remain without serious consequences. A member of the distinguished family of Hillel, which nominally ruled in Judea and Galilea, was so much attracted by Christian doctrines or advantages accrued by professing them that he embraced Christianity and forsook the religion of his fathers. Similarly, another writer of the Church speaks of the conversion of noble and distinguished Jews about the middle of the third century, and of assisting a Bishop in his functions. These facts can easily be reconciled with the reports to be found in the contemporary Carmen Apologeticum which breathes pagan and Christianized hatred of Jews and Judaism because high-standing, influential Jews, either in Rome or in the provinces, agitated against Christianity. This must not be understood to mean that Jews instigated a movement for the persecution of Christians, but that they may have protected, or at least tried to safeguard, the best interest of their fellow-Jews against apostates and their satellites on the one hand, and against overzealous missionaries on the other hand.

In spite of this vehement opposition to Jewish customs and to the Law on the part of many foes and antagonists the attraction of Jewish observances prevailed for considerable time in Christianity, no matter whether they were the result of Jewish influence or a more or less shadowy legacy of defunct Jewish-Christianity. Every honest student of Rabbinic sources must be puzzled by a saying of R. Simon ben Lakish, whom we recognized as a protector and defender of the Posh'e Israel, namely Jewish-Christians, that a pagan who rests on Sabbath is deserving of death.[184] How could this teacher derive such a harsh law from

---

[184] B. Sanh. 58b, ואר'ל עובד כוכבים ששבת חייב מיתה שנ' ויום ולילה לא ישבתו, cf. Yalḳuṭ Gen. §61 where the full name is given.

Gen. 8.22 ("day and night shall never cease")? Who were those pagan and where are they to be found, who endeavored to solemnize
the Sabbath by resting? Finally, what real objection can be raised
to Sabbath observance on the part of Gentiles? The situation
becomes even more complicated if one consults R. Yoḥanan, the
leader of this age, and a colleague of R. Simon ben Lakish, whose
name has been mentioned more than once in the course of this
essay, and of whom a similarly strange and perplexing statement
about Gentiles engaged in the study of the Torah is recorded.[185] In
spite of this unfriendly attitude towards gentile students of the
Torah, which, by the way, must be taken as a proof that non-Jews
tried to learn the Torah, the Written and Oral Law, R. Yoḥanan
opposes R. Simon ben Lakish on the subject of the observation
of the Sabbath by Gentiles. One can further recall the strange
remark in the Epistle of Peter, that no one who is not circumcised
can study the Law,[186] which is paralleled by an exactly similar
saying of Akyla, in his Dialogue with the Emperor.[187] R. Yoḥanan
uttered the saying: "He, who observes the Sabbath according to
its rules, even though he be an idolator like the generation of
Enosh, is granted forgiveness of sin."[188] It is useless, for historical
and theological studies, to read new ideas into these quotations,
or to minimize their actual contribution to the knowledge of
contemporary religious conditions. It remains a fact that Sabbath
observance was popular even outside the Jewish communities in
Palestine as well as in the Diaspora, where it attained a special
significance for the Jewish communities.[189] This attraction of the

[185] B. Sanh. 59a: עכו״ם שעוסק בתורה חייב מיתה, cf. however b. Ḥag. 13a
R. Ami, a pupil of and a successor to R. Yoḥanan says: אין מוסרים דברי תורה
לעכו״ם; further the view of R. Meir about the pagan, who studies the Torah,
that he ranks higher than an ignorant High Priest, b. Sanh. 59a and parall.,
finally R. Jeremiah, Sifra on chap. 18, Warsaw 1866, p. 75b.

[186] Epistle of Peter to James, ch. IV: "we should not communicate the
books of his preaching . . . but to one who is good, etc., and who is circumcised and faithful."

[187] Tanḥuma, B. II, p. 82.

[188] B. Šabbat: 118b ר׳ חייא בר אבא בשם ר׳ יוחנן כל השומר את השבת כהלכתו
אפי׳ עובד ע״ז כדור אנוש מוחלין לו. Cf. M. Ps. 92.2. Pirḳe R. E. ch. 18, cf. Marmorstein, „Eine liturgische Schwierigkeit", Jeschurun, XII, 1925, p. 202.

[189] Cf. Marmorstein, שביתת השבת בגולה בסוף תקופת האמוראים in Hator (Jerusalem), VIII, 1928, No. 11.

Sabbath and the attitude of the pagan world to it was viewed from different points of view by these teachers of the third century. It may have been a matter of temperament, but more likely they were guided by actual events, considered and judged in the light of contemporary history. However that may be, we are surely right in assuming that Sabbath observance penetrated the not too wide boundaries of the Jewish congregations.

How popular the Sabbath was, can be deduced from the limi-tations of work on Sunday on the one hand, and the application of Jewish laws of Sabbath observance, which is condemned and considered as the crime of "judaizare," on the other. The time of Constantine emphasized the law of refraining from manual labour and work. In the year 538 the Jewish mode of observance by not riding on Sabbath, not preparing food or avoiding any adornments of the house, was opposed. Many synods and councils disapproved of the celebration of the day from evening to evening. Altogether the Christian Sunday retained or received a Jewish outlook, and was considered as a successor to the Sabbath of the Old Testament. Some went even further, and made of it a weekly Day of Atonement.[190] It shows clearly that the criticism of Early Christianity against the Law generally as well as particularly could not prevail since the Church had to tolerate, and fight the translation of the Jewish Sabbath into the Christian Sunday for nearly the whole of the first millennium of its existence. To Judaism the strict adherence to the law gave life and strength to endure, whilst for the Church in her war against her law-abiding sections, the victory meant return to barbarism and paganism.

---

[190] Hans v. Schubert, *Geschichte der christlichen Kirche in frühen M.A.* Tübingen 1920, p. 664. Attention may here be drawn to M. Friedländer, *Synagoge und Kirche in ihren Anfängen*, Berlin, 1908, pp. 34 ff., who offers convincing evidence that the observance of the Sabbath gained popularity among pagans in the third century C.E. which was looked upon with considerable disfavour by the teachers of the Church. May be that R. Simon ben Lakish and R. Yoḥanan also had occasion to express their views on this subject. Friedländer would have found confirmation of his theory in the material discussed in the text.

ARCHAEOLOGY AND BABYLONIAN JEWRY

Jacob Neusner

I

THE archaeological investigations of Professor Nelson Glueck, his disciples and colleagues, into the history of Israelite religion before 450 BC and of Judaism afterward, have no parallel across the Euphrates. The sites of the major Jewish academies and settlements remain unexamined. Peripheral areas, such as Dura-Europos, have shown that one may hope for important discoveries. Central Babylonia has, moreover, yielded significant finds of Parthian and Sasanian material. One might expect, therefore, that purposeful examination of the regions in which large numbers of Jews were settled might produce commensurate results. But that examination has yet to take place. In part, the reason was the neglect by archaeologists, until the 1930s, of Parthian and Sasanian strata in favor of older ones in Babylonian projects. While much has been done since to remedy that situation, the potential Jewish sites are not even catalogued, and surface examination has yet to take place. Strikingly, when Jacob Obermeyer wrote his *Die Landschaft Babylonien im Zeitalter des Talmuds und des Gaonats* (1929), he added the subtitle, "Geographie und Geschichte *nach Talmudischen, Arabischen, und Anderen Quellen*" (italics supplied). His stress lay primarily on literary materials, and this despite his own extensive travels in the region as teacher in the house of the Persian refugee-Prince, Abbas-Mirza-Naïb-aṣṣalṭanah. Obermeyer by no means stood alone in his attitude toward the artifacts of material culture. More recently, in commenting upon a passage in the Talmud (T.B. Berakhot 35b) relating to the agricultural calendar in Babylonia, the distinguished Talmudic historian Moshe Dov Beer provided extensive discussions of literary evidence on the climate of the Jordan valley. This, he supposed, is similar to that of the part of Babylonia between the Tigris and Euphrates along the Royal Canal where Jews lived. At no point did he turn to the various climatological or other studies readily available to explain the literary passage at hand.[1] Rather than speculation based upon literary evidence from another country, one might easily consult K. Mason, ed., *Iraq and the Persian Gulf* (1944), pp. 166 ff., 447–57, for a full account of normal meteorological patterns and consequent agricultural practices of the region.

How shall we account for the fundamentally anti-archaeological bias of past scholarship on Babylonian Jewry? First, "Talmudic history" is fundamentally a category of literary studies. Its purpose is not to illumine the life of the Babylonian Jewish community, but rather to investigate the sequence of generations of the Talmudic academies of the region.[2] The interest of Talmudic historians, to begin with, focused upon what happened in the rabbinical schools and among the sages. Further, since the life of the streets and the affairs of the schools were supposed to be pretty much identical, Talmudic historians saw little purpose in going beyond the pages of the Babylonian Talmud and later commentaries. One could find out not only whatever was important, but also whatever one wanted to know, in literary accounts. This bias depends upon the theological conviction that in the rabbinical schools, the "whole Torah" revealed at Sinai was preserved, both the written text as we now have it, as well as the oral traditions supposedly handed on alongside. No rational argument about the nature of the Babylonian Talmud as a *historical* source was ever thought necessary, for a fundamentally sacred text obviously contained whatever was so. The text did not merely yield history —it *was* history. What is noteworthy is the persistence of the effects of that conviction long after the belief itself has been set outside the realm of scholarly discourse. If, therefore, "Talmudic history" has on the whole neglected even the available results of archaeological studies, the primary reason was that, with the noteworthy exceptions of S. Krauss and S. Lieberman, the earlier scholars were really not interested in the kind of materials made available by archaeology or in the sort of broader questions that might be answered upon that basis. I do not suggest that where archaeological results could prove useful in the explication of one or another discrete text, for instance to explain the meaning or reference of a particular word or practice, Talmudists, including "Talmudic historians," proved disinterested. On the contrary, a work such as Joshua Brand, *Klei HaḤeres beSifrut HaTalmud* (1953), was welcomed by Talmudists. But "Talmudic history" was fundamentally a branch of literary studies, and not a very important one at that. In such a setting archaeology was likely to attract little sustained interest, so that even as eminent a geographer as Obermeyer could stress his use of Talmudic,

Arabic, and other sources to the exclusion of his own observations, in the title of his book.

The late Professor Erwin Goodenough frequently pointed out, moreover, that "philological method" generally predominated in Jewish scholarship. The appreciation of archaeological data was limited by almost exclusive concentration on texts as the source of all information, and upon the explication of texts—after they were critically edited—as the sole legitimate, authentic, scholarly task. Since modern Jewish scholarship followed the model of nineteenth-century German university science, it is quite natural that the methods and orientation decisive at the outset should prevail. What is not natural is that matters should have changed so little later on. Biblical studies constitute a striking contrast. There archaeological results are consulted by everyone, and both in the State of Israel and in Jewish centers of higher learning elsewhere literary studies constitute only one, though an important, aspect of biblical scholarship. The reasons for this exceptional situation are complicated. One of them is certainly the constructive influence of Professor Nelson Glueck and others of his generation, particularly Professor W. F. Albright, upon the study of the Bible under Jewish auspices. A second, applicable in the State of Israel, is the emotional attachment of Israelis to archaeology as the route by which their own roots in the country are uncovered. Hence the popularity—it has been called mania—of biblical archaeology. No similarly fruitful influence has yet affected archaeological studies of later Judaism, and no equivalent motive has led to equivalent researches in other lands where Jews have lived. Once again we see that the sociology of learning, as much as the inner momentum of research or the state of the evidence, shapes both our results *and* our methodology.

A third relevant factor should be briefly mentioned. Since 1948 it has not been possible for scholars of Jewish origin to pursue researches, whether archaeological or of any other kind, in 'Iraq. Hence, the field is closed to those who would be most interested in working in it.

To be receptive to the importance of archaeology one must first of all be willing to face the broader issues, answers to which are made more readily available by archaeological researches than otherwise. One must begin, I think, by supposing that literary evidence is important as one testimony, but only one among many, to the way things were. That evidence cannot be seen as an end in itself, still less as the measure by which archaeological data are to be evaluated and interpreted. (Editor's note: see above, pp. 64–80, for the same view from another perspective.) The disputed interpretation of the synagogue murals at Dura-Europos pro-

vides an excellent example of the dubious use of literary sources as a court
of higher appeal for the interpretation of archaeological data, as I have
suggested in *History of Religions* (4 [1964], pp. 81–102). Since I am
not qualified to offer an interpretation of the iconography or symbolism
of the Dura synagogue, it suffices merely to note that we have no scholar's
handbook of ancient Judaism, only what various groups later on chose
to preserve and hand on for our use. These groups, especially the Christian monasteries and the Rabbinical schools, had their particular purposes; to serve those purposes they selected some traditions, sayings, and
stories, or whole documents in the former case, and ignored or suppressed
others. If, as in the case of Dura, archaeology provides us with a new
corpus of data which otherwise we should not have had, then to begin
with we cannot suppose that those data are to be interpreted according
to the literary evidence transmitted for particular theological reasons
among wholly unrelated groups or parties. I cannot enter into the discussions of whether the Talmud, or Philo, or any other literary materials
offer the key to the Dura synagogue and the philosophy of the designer
of its murals. Professor Morton Smith has admirably summarized the
state of current thought—and, I think, greatly improved upon it—in his
"Goodenough's *Jewish Symbols* in Retrospect," *Journal of Biblical Literature,* 86 (1967), pp. 53–68. It is fruitless to debate matters in generalities,
and the time has come for specialists to take over, concentrating first of all
on the history of Dura-synagogue art as it is revealed in relationship to
other archaeological evidences.

                                          II

Having introduced the knotty problem of the relationship of literary to
archaeological evidence concerning the history of Babylonian Judaism,
I may cite one example of the complex difficulties yet to be considered.
The seventh-century AD magical bowls of Nippur, a town just east of
Sura, where the rabbinical school founded by Rav was located, contain
a number of references to a rabbi also mentioned in rabbinic traditions,
Joshua b. Peraḥiah. What is striking is that in these references the rabbi
appears as a magician. We shall review first the exempla provided by
Montgomery[3] and then the rabbinic traditions. Finally we shall see how
the two kinds of materials relate to one another.

The rabbi appears in bowls Nos. 8, 9, 17, 32 (=33), as follows:

No. 8: [That there flee from the house of this Geyônài bar Mâmâi
the evil Lilith . . . And again, you shall not appear to them in his

house nor in their dwelling . . . because it is announced to you, whose father is named Palḥas and whose mother Pelaḥdad—because it is announced to you] that Rabbi Joshua bar Peraḥia [sic] has sent against you the ban. . . . Thou Lilith, male Lilis and female Lilith, Hag and Ghul, be in the ban . . . [of Rabbi] Joshua b. Peraḥia, and thus has spoken to us Rabbi Joshua bar Peraḥia, A divorce writ has come to you from across the sea, and there is found written in it [against you] whose father is named Palḥas and whose mother Pelaḥ-dad . . . they hear from the firmament . . . Hear and obey and go from the house . . . And again, you shall not appear to them either in dream by night nor in slumber by day, because you are sealed with the signet of El Shaddai and with the signet of the house of Joshua b. Peraḥia and by the Seven which are before him . . .

There follow adjurations by the Strong One of Abraham, etc. On the divorce issued to Lilith from her victim, Montgomery comments, "This was a happy thought of the magicians, who thus applied the powers of binding and loosing claimed by the rabbis to the disgusting unions of demons and mortals. . . . The magical writ affects the same forms and formalism as that of the divorce court . . . The names of both parties are exactly given, hence the parents of the liliths are here specifically named."[4] In addition, the terms of the divorce are properly given, and properly served on the divorcée. Divine authority is invoked. The writ has come down from heaven, and so, like writs from abroad, special forms are included. The commissioners and witnesses are angels. The rabbi seals the divine decree.

Further references to R. Joshua are as follows:

No. 9: The bowl I deposit and sink down, and the work I operate, and it is in [the fashion of] Rabbi Joshua bar Peraḥia. I write for them divorces, for all the Liliths who appear to them . . .

No. 17: This day above any day, years, and generations of the world, I Kômêš bath Maḥlaphta have divorced, separated, dismissed thee, thou Lilith, Lilith of the Desert, Hag and Ghul . . . I have fenced you out by the ban which Joshua bar Peraḥia sent against you. I adjure you by the honor of your father and by the honor of your mother, and take your divorces and separations, thy divorce and thy separation, in the ban which is sent against you by Joshua b. Peraḥia, for so has spoken to thee Joshua b.P.: A divorce has come to thee from across the sea. There is found, you whose mother is Palḥas and whose father Pelaḥdad, you Liliths: And now flee and go forth and do not trouble Kômêš b.M., in her house and her dwelling. I bind and I seal with the seal of El Shaddai and with the seal of Joshua b. Peraḥia the healer . . .[5]

No. 32: . . . The bowl I deposit and sink down, a work which has been made like that of Rav Jesu bar Peraḥia sat and wrote against them—a ban writ against all the Demons and Devils and Satans and Liliths . . . Again he wrote against them a ban-writ which is for all time . . .

To the Jews in sixth and seventh century AD Nippur, therefore, the figure of R. Joshua b. Peraḥiah was associated with two anti-demonic prophylaxes, first, the ability to issue a legal bill of divorce against female demons, second, the pronouncement of a ban against demons. The divorce and the ban seem confused; in No. 8, the ban is announced, and then the proper formula for a divorce delivered from abroad is introduced, together with the necessary witnesses, signatures, and sealing, the last-named with the signet of God and Joshua's house. In Nos. 9, 17, and 32 the divorce is more clearly explicated, again in proper legal language. Lilith is adjured to receive the divorce, as is legally necessary.

III

Three questions require answers.

First, is the procedure of issuing a bill of divorce against demons to be located elsewhere in the Nippur bowls published by Montgomery? And if so, what authorities are associated with the procedure? Of the forty-two exempla, the figure of divorce appears in eight. Of these, Joshua occurs in all but three. Strikingly, in the exempla where Joshua is absent, the language includes an *explanation* of the divorce procedure, which we do not find in the Joshua-bowls:

No. 11: Behold I have written for thee (i.e., a divorce), and behold I have separated thee . . . [*like the demons*] *who write divorces for their wives and do not return to them.* Take thy divorce from . . . [Italics supplied]

No. 26: Again, bound and held art thou, evil Spirit and mighty Lilith. . . . But flee from their presence and take thy divorce and thy separation and thy writ of dismissal.

Similar language occurs in No. 18. Montgomery comments, "The additional thought appears here (No. 11) that inasmuch as demons divorce their spouses, divorce-writs must be as effective on them as among human kind."[6]

Yamauchi[7] provides Mandaean instances of the appearances of the word *GYṬ* in text 21, lines 10, 11:

> . . . *as the demons write a bill of divorce for their wives* in truth, *and may not return again* . . . Behold, take your bill of divorce and receive your oath . . . [Italics supplied]

PṬR appears in 21:9. *ŠBYQT* occurs in the meanings of "dismiss," "divorce," "forsake," and "leave" nineteen times, though not all usages signify the language of divorce-writs so far as I am able to tell. This brief survey shows that the use of divorce-magic was not unique to the Jews who invoked the name, ban, sealing, and magic of R. Joshua b. Peraḥiah. But it is equally clear that R. Joshua was associated only with such a technique, appearing in the context of ban and divorce alone. J. Z. Smith provides below further discussion of the scholarly literature.[8]

Second, do we find in rabbinic literature the use of a divorce, writ, or the language of a divorce, as an anti-demonic prophylaxis? I am not able to offer a definitive answer. I find no reference whatever to the use of a document of divorce as a means of protection from demons in Trachtenberg[9] or Ginzberg.[10] Since the Joshua-bowls refer consistently to Lilith, one might suppose that the use of a divorce to banish her was based upon her mating with Adam:

> She remained with him only a short time because she insisted upon enjoying full equality with her husband. She derived her rights from their identical origin. With the help of the Ineffable Name, which she pronounced, Lilith flew away from Adam, and vanished in the air. Adam complained before God . . . who sent three angels to capture her . . . The only way to ward off the evil [she does to babies] is to attach an amulet bearing the names of her three angel captors to the children . . .[11]

No reference to writing a bill of divorce is given by Ginzberg. While that fact cannot be offered as definitive, I think it highly suggestive. Similarly, Kohut makes no mention of such a prophylaxis in connection with Lilith.[12] We do have some instances in which rabbis drove off 'Igrath (=Lilith),[13] in particular b. Pesaḥim 112b. In both instances there, heavenly respect for the rabbi's learning (Torah) led to her being forced to accept his commands. Abaye thereupon said, "I order you never to pass through settled regions." Finally, we may note that Ludwig Blau[14] and Gideon Brecher[15] provide no reference whatever to divorcing Lilith. It is far easier to say what *is* in the Talmud and cognate rabbinic literature than what is *not* to be found there.[16] I can only tentatively suggest that while rabbinic literature knows Lilith well, at no point does a rabbi refer to *divorcing* her in the manner described by the magical bowls or in any other way.

One may suppose that the general, universal view that demons divorce their wives produced the specific, Jewish practice attributed to R. Joshua b. Peraḥiah of casting various spells, but especially, a legal bill of divorce, against the demon. One may, alternatively, interpret the explanatory clause, "like the demons who write divorces for their wives and do not return to them," as evidence that the exorcist supposed it to be an exceptional or strange practice, requiring an explanation (for the demon? for the Mandaean client?). The absence of a similar explanation in the Joshua-bowls may mean that the practice of divorcing demons was sufficiently well-known among Jews not to demand further comment. The absence— if it is absence—of attestation in Talmudic literature merely signifies that the rabbis did not recognize, approve, or care to preserve evidence about, such a practice. It does not tell us anything about the practice or knowledge of ordinary Jews.

Third, what other traditions about R. Joshua b. Peraḥiah existed in Palestinian and Babylonian rabbinical schools? First of all, as has already been noted, no passage suggests that R. Joshua b. Peraḥiah composed bills of divorce against demons. The extant traditions should be divided according to time and place. In the Tannaitic Midrashim, we find no reference whatever to R. Joshua. In the Mishnah, R. Joshua is cited twice, in Ḥagigah 2:2, on the ordination controversy, and in Pirqei Avot 1:6, which contains his saying in the chain of tradition, that one should provide himself with a teacher and a fellow-disciple, and judge people favorably. Nothing in the Mishnah of R. Judah the Prince suggests that R. Joshua was a magician. The Tosefta reveals a saying of his on purity laws (Makhshirin 3:4). The references in the two Talmuds deal with only two matters. First, in TB Menaḥot 109b, we find a *beraita*, citing R. Joshua b. Peraḥiah, that it is just as hard to accept high office as it is to leave it.

The other matter, however, is more important. (It occurs in TB Sanhedrin 109b, with a parallel in TB Sotah 47a. (The incident is further echoed in TJ Ḥagigah 2:2 and Sanhedrin 6:9, but there the rabbi in question is Judah b. Tabbai.) The *locus classicus* is fully discussed by Herford.[17] It is attached to a *beraita* that one should not too harshly repel penitents or potential converts to Judaism. R. Joshua b. Peraḥiah's treatment of Jesus is cited. When Yannai the King killed the rabbis, Joshua and his disciple Jesus fled to Alexandria. Šime'on b. Sheṭaḥ called them back when times proved more favorable. On route home they found a certain inn, where R. Joshua praised the hostess. Jesus disagreed, saying she had narrow eyes. Joshua then excommunicated him for looking too closely at the woman, saying, "Wretch, do you thus busy yourself?!" Jesus tried without success to repent. Finally, being repulsed, Jesus went and hung up a tile and worshiped it. At that time Joshua called on him to repent, without result. "So a teacher has said, 'Jesus the Nazarene practised magic and led astray and deceived Israel.'" Herford suggests that the story is based upon a Palestinian tradition. In any case, we may be sure that the legend of Joshua as a visitor to Egypt was known in the schools of both countries.[18]

IV

On the relationship between Joshua b. Peraḥiah in the magical bowls and the Talmudic passage, Montgomery comments:

> We find then in these magical bowls an independent tradition concerning an early hero of the Law, who appears as endowed with magic powers, and who furthermore was able to make the ascent of the soul to heaven. He was accordingly one of the earliest to attain that spiritual privilege . . . Joshua was possibly one of the good company of apocalyptists and our magic tradition may preserve a true reminiscence of his personality and claims.[19]

To this I may add another viewpoint, derived from my study of the social and religious role of the rabbi within Babylonian Jewry.[20] We must, first of all, regard the Joshua of the bowls as an authentic portrait of what some people, presumably Jews though not necessarily so, thought about the rabbi. They regarded him as both lawyer and magician. As a lawyer, he was expected to know the precise formula for a bill of divorce and to be able to issue a ban. Thus we noted in No. 9, Joshua b. Peraḥiah's divorces for all the Liliths who appear to them; in No. 17, both the ban spoken by Joshua and the divorce spoken (read) to Lilith by Joshua, in the appropriate legal language; in No. 32, a ban-writ against the demons. Now what we should not find unusual is that rabbis, whose effective legal jurisdiction extended mostly to matters of exchanges of property and personal status,[21] should be consulted on drawing up bills of divorce. What is surprising is that those legal documents were presumed effective, as in the Mandaean magical bowls, against demons. Here the second religious role of the rabbi becomes important, namely, his capacity, because of his mastery of Torah and his ability on that basis to exercise, independent of the wishes of heaven, the supernatural powers inherent in the Torah, to do works of magic against demons (among other miracles).

We noted above that Abaye, among others, was believed to be able to overcome demons because "in heaven his Torah was highly regarded." I have elsewhere cited considerable evidence that knowledge of Torah produced the capacity to do supernatural actions.[22] In the magical bowls, the two predominant roles of the rabbi are united in the figure of Joshua b. Peraḥiah. The law is effective—against demons. The rabbi carries out the law—for supernatural purposes. We find, however, little direct evidence that in the rabbinical schools of either Babylonia or Palestine such supernatural powers were attributed to R. Joshua. One can hardly argue that everyone who went to Alexandria came home a magician, despite the general reputation of the place.

What I find difficult to account for is the attribution of so central a magical role to R. Joshua b. Peraḥiah, who, as we have seen, played a relatively minor, and generally not-supernatural, role in rabbinic traditions of both Palestine and Babylonia. I may, with much hesitation, conjecture on why those who made the bowls selected R. Joshua above all other rabbis. Perhaps, as Montgomery suggests, his relationship to Jesus, believed by many Jews to be an expert magician, and by the rabbis to be R. Joshua's disciple, was sufficient also to distinguish R. Joshua as a magician. If the disciple was so puissant, how much more should the Jews, disciples of the rabbis and under their effective control by the seventh century, turn to his rabbinical master?

V

The R. Joshua of the magical bowls and the R. Joshua of the schools were not wholly unrelated, but they were also not closely correlated. The figure of the lawyer-magician is well-known to us in the Babylonian Talmud, but R. Joshua b. Peraḥiah was not singularly noted as such a figure. On the other hand, the bowls contain one important perspective on R. Joshua, that of the ordinary people who used them. Whether or not rabbis and those under their immediate influence and control also used magical bowls is not entirely clear. We know, of course, that the rabbis had other means of driving away demons. But those in no way exclude the use of the prophylaxes held in common among the various peoples of Babylonia, including other Jews. At any rate, we do know precisely what traditions on R. Joshua the rabbinical schools chose to preserve and to hand on as authentic and correct. For the most part, these are inconsequential. The striking tradition about the flight to Egypt brings us closest of all to the Joshua of the bowls, and provides at least a hint on why Joshua was otherwise so neglected. He was, to be sure, included *per force* in the sayings of Avot and in related sayings (cf. Ḥagigah 2:2 already cited), but otherwise almost wholly excluded. Only in the environment of the Amoraic schools in Babylonia was the apparently very old story of the trip to Egypt preserved, possibly for polemical purposes in a time marked by conversions of significant numbers of Jews to Christianity,[23] and now perhaps made useful by the more hospitable reception of magic in the later rabbinical schools, including that near Nippur itself.[24]

1. Moshe Dov Beer, *Ma'amadam HaHevrati veHakalkali shel Amora'ei Bavel* (1962), pp. 52–53. An even more striking illustration is J. Newman, *The Agricultural Life of the Jews in Babylonia* (1932), who seems not to have read a single current archaeological report, including work done in the 1920s on Ctesiphon, a city near which large numbers of Jewish farmers were situated, not to mention the studies of Assyriologists on earlier agricultural conditions. The single archaeological title in his brief bibliography is S. Kraus, *Talmudische Archaeologie*. Likewise S. Funk, *Juden in Babylonien* (1903), makes no mention of Nippur, near the town of Sura.

2. Yet, though one would suppose we should now have extensive histories of the Babylonian Talmudical academies, the opposite is the case. See my *History of the Jews in Babylonia.* III. *From Shapur I to Shapur II* (1968), p. 213, n. 1.

3. James A. Montgomery, *Aramaic Incantation Texts from Nippur* (1913).

4. *Ibid.*, p. 159.

5. Montgomery notes that No. 17 is a replica of No. 8, often incorrect, however.

6. *Ibid.*, p. 172.

7. Edwin M. Yamauchi, *Mandaic Incantation Texts* (1967).

8. Below, pp. 344–47.

9. Joshua Trachtenberg, *Jewish Magic and Superstition* (1961).

10. Louis Ginzberg, *Legends of the Jews* (1946). Since Lilith occurs in the magical bowls, one might surmise that a similar bill of divorce of Lilith might be referred to in Talmudic literature. Ginzberg refers to no such phenomenon. He does note in Vol. I, p. 66, that she was warded off by an amulet.

11. *Ibid.*, pp. 66–67.

12. Alexander Kohut, *Über die jüdische Angelologie und Dämonologie in ihrer Abhängigkeit vom Parsismus* (1866), pp. 86–89.

13. I here refer to Kohut's identification of 'Igrath with Lilith, but it was in fact rejected by both Ginzberg and Blau, with good reason.

14. *JE*, VIII, pp. 87–88.

15. Gideon Brecher, *Transcendentale, Magie, und Magische Heilarten im Talmud* (1850), pp. 47, 50, 54.

16. Nor do I find anything relevant in M. Margalioth's *Sefer HaRazim* (1967).

17. R. Travers Herford, *Christianity in Talmud and Midrash* (1966), pp. 51 ff.

18. See also J. Z. Lauterbach, *JE*, VII, p. 295, and A. Hyman, *Toledot Tannaim veAmoraim* (1910), II, pp. 647–48. Hyman notes that the Tosefta saying has to do with the ritual purity of Alexandrian wheat (perhaps the kernel of the legend of his flight from Palestine?). No tradition concerning R. Joshua b. Peraḥiah is found in Bereshit Rabbah.

19. *Op. cit.*, pp. 227–28.

20. I refer to my *History of the Jews in Babylonia* I (1965), II (1966), III (1968), IV (1969) and V (1970).

21. See II, pp. 251–87, III, pp. 195–338, for a review of the cases and evidence.

22. For further discussion of the rabbi as a holy man, see II, pp. 126–50, and III, pp. 95–191.

23. See III, pp. 8–29.

24. Further discussion of the rabbi as lawyer-magician will be found in IV, Chapter Five. My thanks are due to Professors Yohanan Muffs, Jewish Theological Seminary of America, and Morton Smith, Columbia University, for helpful comments.

ADDENDUM

Jonathan Z. Smith

THE earliest publication I know of is text No. 1 in A. H. Layard, *Discoveries in the Ruins of Nineveh and Babylon* (1853) in the translation of T. Ellis (pp. 512–13—Montgomery No. 11):

> This is a bill of divorce to the Devil, and to . . . and to Satan, and to Nerig, and to Zachiah, and to Abitur of the mountain, and to . . . and to the night monsters, commanding them to cease from Beheran in Batnaiun, and from the country of the north, and from all who are tormented by them therein. Behold I make the counsels of these devils of no effect, and annul the power of the ruler of the night-monsters. I conjure you all, monsters, . . . both male and female, to go forth. I conjure you and . . . by the sceptre of the powerful one, who has power over the devils, and over the night monsters, to quit these habitations. Behold I now make you cease from troubling them, and make the influence of your presence cease in Beheran of Batnaiun, and in their fields. In the same manner as the devils write bills of divorce and give them to their wives, and return not to them again, receive ye your bills of divorce, and take this written authority, and go forth, leave quickly, flee, and depart from Beheran in Batnaiun, in the name of the living . . . , by the seal of the powerful one, and by this signet of authority. Then will there flow rivers of water in that land, and there the parched ground will be watered. Amen, Amen, Amen, Selah.

Layard conjectures that this is the oldest of the seven inscriptions he has, dating it the third to second century BC (p. 525). Ellis gives the following commentary: ". . . there is one thing to which I wish to call the attention of Oriental scholars, namely the subject of the inscription of No. 1. It is a *letter of dismissal*, or *bill of divorce* to Satan and other evil spirits. The word here used to express this is *GYT'*, the very word found in the Talmud to express the same thing. . . . The ancient Jews supposed that the devils or evil spirits were propagated like mankind; that they eat, and drank, married, and it would seem quarreled with their wives, and divorced them."

Layard No. 1 is commented upon and re-translated by M. A. Levy, "Uber die von Layard aufgefundenen chaldäischen Inschriften auf Topfgefässen. Ein Beitrag zur Hebräischen Paläographie und zur Religionsgeschichte," *ZDMG,* 9, (1857), pp. 465–91; and D. Chwolson, *Corpus inscriptionum hebraicarum* (1882), I, pp. 103–20. M. Schwab, "Les coups magiques et l'hydromancie dans l'antiquité orientale," *Proceedings of the Society of Biblical Archaeology,* 9 (1889–90), p. 300, reprints the text and translation of Levy and offers no interpretation, in his full notes which follow (pp. 301–6), of the divorce, only noting (p. 300) that "un acte de divorce" is "en signe de répulsion." Although in the course of this article (pp. 292–342) he discusses a number of other magical bowls and inscriptions, no others have "divorce" of demons as a motif.

There is no mention of the divorce motif in the text or the discussion of R. Stübe, *Jüdisch-Babylonische Zaubertexte* (1895).

This exhausts the material prior to Montgomery known to me. Post-Montgomery, there are a few references to divorce in the texts published by C. H. Gordon—though none which contain reference to R. Joshua b. Perahiah in this practice. I believe the following references constitute a complete list:

(a) C. H. Gordon, "Aramaic Incantation Bowls," *Or,* 10 (1941), pp. 116–41 (pt. I):

Bowl No. 5 (p. 123 Louvre AO 1915): "Dismissed and divorced are all . . . ; bound by Zarhisi'el the star . . . (lines 1–2)—*SBYQT* is the term. Gordon has no comment.

(b) *Ibid.,* pp. 339–60 (Pt. III) Bowl, Iraq Museum No. 11113 a text with lacunae. Gordon translated (p. 351), "Lo I have written for thee thy bill of divorcement and I have dismissed, abandoned and banished (thee) . . . they do not return again; take thy bill of divorcement and re(ceive) thine adjuration."

(c) C. H. Gordon, "An Aramaic Exorcism," *ArOr,* 6 (1934), pp. 466–74 and Pls. XXII–XXV from a jar in the Iraq Museum No. 5497. The text is also printed in W. H. Rossell, *A Handbook of Aramaic Magical Inscriptions* (1953), pp. 107–9, No. 28. Gordon introduces his translation (p. 466) by noting, "The exorcism is intended to expel a harmful lilith named Hablas from the home of one Mazdewai and the latter's husband. The praxis here, to wit, that of banishing a lilith by serving a bill of divorcement on her, is already known from previously published texts . . ." The text of Gordon's translation follows:

(I.=Immā; I.S.=Immā Salmā)

p. 470 (1) In Thy name! Mazdewai, the daughter of Immā Salmā
(and) Beryl, the son of Immā, her husband. (2) In Thy name do
I act! Salvation from the heavens! Mazdewai, the daughter of I.S.;
Beryl, the son of I., her husband—that there may live and be preserved for her, sons and daughters (!) and that nothing bad whatsoever may injure them. In the name of the L(ord) and 'I am that I
am.' For the binding of Bagdānā (!) (3) who is the king; (to wit),
the king of demons and devil(s) and the great ruler of the liliths—I
adjure thee, O Lilith Ḥablas, the granddaughter of Lilith Zarnai, who
dwells on the threshold of this Mazdewai, the daughter of I.S., and
of this Beryl, the son of I. Amen. (4) (O thou) who fillest this habitation (?), smitest, strikest and castest down and stranglest and killest and castest down (?) both boy(s) and girl(s). *WMLR MṢY
WMR MYṢYT'*. I adjure thee that thou be smitten in the membrane
of thy heart and with the lance of Qatros, the mighty. And mayest
thou be uprooted. And again (5) mayest thou cease and be distant
from this Mazdewai, the daughter of I.S., from this Beryl, the son of
I., her husband—amen—from their sons and daughters, that they
have or will have, and from their house, from all their yard and from
all their threshold. *Lo I have written (a divorce) for thee, lo I have
dismissed thee (6) and lo I have abandoned thee and lo I have banished thee with a bill of divorcement Amen??? as demons and dev-
il(s) write and serve divorces on their wives and again they do not
return to them in their residence (?)*; so, thou wicked lilith—(7) (be
thou) male lili (or) female lili(th)—and strangler and daughter (of
demons) and ghost (?) and? and profane one—*take (thy) divorce
and thy document of dismissal and thy letter of banishment and flee
and take flight and go out and depart* from this Mazdewai, the
daughter of I.S. (and) from her husband Beryl (8) the son of I.

p. 471

—amen—from his sons and daughters and from all his yard. And
appear to them neither in visions of the day nor in impure fancies
of the night, in the shape of neither man nor woman, nor any??.
and do not approach them and do not molest (9) them and do
not devour their sons (!) and their daughters, that they have or
will have. Sealed with the great seal of the Holy One. *It is sealed
on thy divorce.* The Holy One, YH, holy is He, Hosts is His name,
YHYHYHYH, I am that I am, awful and holy, Amen, (10) amen,
amen, selah. *TL' KBL' TL'* in them *TL'*. "Even as the mountains
encircle Jerusalem, so the Lord encircles his people, from henceforth
and forever." "Beloved, cherished art thou (?), O Israel. Thy
amulet (?)—also (?) I shall bring thee up into the ark. Meat

with ? I shall feed thee, and wine (11) with ? I shall make thee drink." Again (?) salvation from the heavens for this Mazdewai, the daughter of I.S. Healed? in the name of the L(ord). I adjure thee, O Lilith Ḥablas the granddaughter of Lilith Zarnai, who smitest and strikest and killest—I adjure thee (that thou be smitten) in the membrane of thy heart with the lance of Qatros, the mighty. *Lo I have written (a divorce) for thee, lo I have dismissed thee as the demons write and serve divorces upon their wives and again they do not return to them. Now take thy divorce and receive thine adjuration and fly* (12) and flee and get out of the house, out of the yard, out of the threshold, out of the four (walls), (out of) the midst of the house, out of the body of Mazdewai, the daughter of I. Amen, amen, selah.

Gordon compares this text with Layard Bowl No. 1, Montgomery Nos. 11, 18 and with text No. 5 in M. Lidzbarski, "Mandäische Zaubertexte," *Ephemeris für semitische Epigraphik,* I (1902), pp. 102 f. (=Yamauchi No. 21, quoted above).

(d) *GYṬ'* occurs in a bill of divorce for demons on a bowl from the Iraq Museum No. 9737 published by Gordon, "An Aramaic Incantation," *AASOR*, 14 (1934), pp.411 f., lines 5–7:

Lo I have written [a divorce] (6) for thee and lo I have expelled thee, as the demons write divorce[s] to their wives and again they do not return. Take (7) thy divorce and receive thine oath and flee and take flight . . .

(e) In a bowl in the Jewish Theological Seminary, No. 950 in Gordon, "Aramaic and Mandaic Magical Bowls," *ArOr,* 9 (1937), p. 87, line 5, the demons are given a "bill of divorcement."

This, to my knowledge, exhausts the explicit references to divorce of demons in Aramaic materials outside Montgomery.

BABYLONIAN JEWRY AND SHAPUR II'S
PERSECUTION OF CHRISTIANITY
FROM 339 to 379 A.D.

JACOB NEUSNER

Brown University

For Krister Stendahl, in homage

THE Christian communities of Sasanian Iran, formed through both conversion of native Greeks, Semites, and Iranians, and Iranian deportations of Christians from the Roman Orient and Armenia, normally lived in tranquillity and peace from their beginnings in the second century to the middle of the fourth.[1] Then, in 339, Shapur II unleashed a ferocious per-

1 Abbreviations:

AB	*Analecta Bollandiana*
ASM	S.E. Assemanus, *Acta Sanctorum Martyrum Orientalium et Occidentalium*, I (Rome, 1748).
AMS	P. Bedjan, *Acta Martyrum et Sanctorum*. II. *Martyres Chaldaei et Persae* (Paris, 1891, repr. Hildesheim, 1968). IV. [No subtitle]. (Paris, 1894; repr. Hildesheim, 1968).
Bab. Tal.	Babylonian Talmud
BHO	*Bibliotheca Hagiographica Orientalis*, ed. Paul Peeters (Brussels, 1910; repr. Profondeville [Namur], 1954).
Braun	*Ausgewählte Akten persischer Märtyrer*, trans. Oskar Braun (Munich, 1915: *Bibliothek der Kirchenväter*).
History	Jacob Neusner, *A History of the Jews in Babylonia. IV. The Age of Shapur II* (Leiden, 1969). *V. Later Sasanian Times* (Leiden, 1970).
Hoffmann, *Auszüge*	George Hoffmann, *Auszüge aus syrischen Akten persischer Märtyrer* (Leipzig, 1880; repr. Nendeln, 1966. *Abhandlungen für die Kunde des Morgenlandes* vol. 7, no. 3).
Kmosko	Michael Kmosko, "S. Simeon bar Sabba'ē," *Patrologia Syriaca* I, ii (Paris, 1907).
Labourt	J. Labourt, *Le christianisme dans l'empire perse sous la dynastie sassanide (224–632)* (Paris, 1904).
Pat. Or.	*Patrologia Orientalis*
REJ	*Revue des études juives*
Wiessner	*Untersuchungen zur syrischen Literaturgeschichte I. Zur Märtyrerüberlieferung aus der Christenverfolgung Schapurs II* (Göttingen, 1967. *Abhandlungen der Akademie der Wissenschaften in Göttingen.* Phil.-Hist. Kl., 3rd series no. 67).

Further bibliography is given below, n. 33.

secution, which, for the next forty years, produced dissolution of Christian group-life, devastation of churches, and numerous martyrs. From 345 to Shapur's death in 379, for example, the metropolitan community of Seleucia-Ctesiphon did not dare to elect a catholicos, since consecration to that office served as a prelude to martyrdom.

Shapur II revised the antecedent Sasanian policy toward Christianity primarily because local Christians sympathized with his Christian enemies. Armenia had been converted in 301, Constantine in 311, and Iberia and Georgia in 330. Roman recognition of Christianity as the most favored religion was bound to cause difficulties for the Iranian church as soon as Rome and Iran resumed their continuing struggle for Armenia and Mesopotamia. Constantine's admonition to cherish the Christians "with your wonted humanity and kindness, for by this proof of faith you will secure an immeasurable benefit to both yourself and us,"[2] could not have enhanced Shapur's confidence in the local Christians' loyalty. To be told that the Christians, many of whom lived in Mesopotamia, Adiabene, and Armenia, where the struggle with Rome was to be waged, were subject to the special protection and concern of Iran's enemy could hardly have pleased Shapur.

Aphrahat's Fifth Homily, written in 336-7, provides a glimpse into the Christian mind of the day. Aphrahat assured the faithful that God decided what would happen: "All who glory will be humbled." Dan. 8:20-21 proves that "from the time that the two horns of the ram were broken until now were six hundred forty-eight years" (that is, the year 336-7). Now the ram's horns are broken:

> O ram, whose horns are broken, rest thou from the beast and provoke it not, lest it devour thee and grind thee to powder. . . O thou that art exalted and lifted up, let not the vaunting of thine heart mislead thee, nor say thou, 'I will go up against the rich land and against the powerful beast.' For that beast will not be slain by the ram, seeing that its horns are broken.[3]

The ram is Iran, the beast, Rome: "Rome is being kept safe for its Giver, and He himself will preserve it. . . That kingdom will not be conquered, for a mighty champion, whose name is Jesus, shall come with power and bearing as his armor all the power of the kingdom." Rome was under divine protection, the fit instrument for God's work. On the eve of Shapur's war against Constantine's sons, Aphrahat thus assured the Church of Iran that Rome would triumph over Shapur. Before the walls of Nisibis, Shapur indeed met disappointment. The largely Christian city did not fall into the power of the 'ram.'

---

2 Eusebius, *Church History*, trans. Ernest Cushing Richardson, in *Select Library of Nicene and Post-Nicene Fathers*, 2nd series, I (Grand Rapids, repr. 1961), pp. 543–4.

3 Trans. John Gwynn, *ibid.*, pp. 352–62.

When Shapur failed to take Nisibis, he would have seen things differently. Returning from the fruitless campaign of 337, he recalled that the bishop of Nisibis had led the defense, and that the Christians of his own empire had hoped for his defeat. He then decreed that the Christian community pay double the normal head-tax. This was part of his effort to raise funds for future campaigns. The tax would also test the loyalty of the Christians to his regime. But the Christians could not afford the tax. Many were nuns and monks, possessing no property at all. Nor would they pay it, for they regarded Shapur's wars as those of Satan, and the victory of Byzantium as the triumph of Christ. Simeon bar Sabba'ē, catholicos of Seleucia-Ctesiphon, the capital, professed his loyalty to the emperor but declined to collect the double-tax and declared the Christians neither could nor would pay it. In 341 or 344 he was martyred, and shortly thereafter, his successors likewise were put to death. In Adiabene, Beth Garmae, Khuzistan, as well as Babylonia (Beth Aramayē), the local Mobads, supported by the satraps, organized slaughters of Christian believers, particularly of the monastic communities. Nuns were offered the choice of marriage or death, and monks, of worship of the sun or death.

Jews appear in the stories of two martyrs, Simeon and his sister, Tarbo. Those two hagiographical traditions report that the Jews in Seleucia-Ctesiphon instigated the persecutions against the Christians. Hostility between Jews and Christians was already old and general. Presumably Jews would take advantage of the new policy to make trouble for the Christians. It was, however, a Sasanian persecution, mounted by the state with the willing cooperation of the Mazdean clergy, and ended by the state when it chose. Nothing other minority groups did could have brought on such a disaster, and nothing they did could have ended it.

Yet, after a certain point, nothing the Christians did mattered very much either. We find no hint of Christian treason in 363, when Roman armies under Julian stood at the gates of Ctesiphon. In no place in his narrative of Julian's campaign does Ammianus Marcellinus refer to Babylonian Christian cooperation with the invading armies. The Christian hopes for Byzantine success were based upon theological expectations alone and produced no political or military effect. Except through prayer, the local Christians did nothing to subvert the Persian government. To be sure, in besieged Roman cities they fought with special courage against Iran.

Once the persecution was unleashed, it took its own course, and whether originally issued for good reason or not, Shapur's decrees were obeyed long after the original provocation had been forgotten. The attribution of Shapur's persecution to the influence of Jews and Magi may be correct as to the episodes when the mob took over. But the persecution was to begin with Shapur's understandable reaction to defeat by a great Christian power, to his Christian subjects' obvious satisfaction at his defeat, and, perhaps, also to his feeling of encirclement by the Christian powers of Armenia, Iberia, and Georgia, as well as Rome.[4]

My purpose here is to examine the traditions on the Jews' participation in Shapur's persecution of Babylonian and Mesopotamian Christianity. Evidence on Shapur's persecution of Christianity derives from three sources. First, and most reliable, are Aphrahat's Demonstrations; second are the Syriac Acts of the Persian Martyrs, conventionally (but, Labourt has shown [pp. 51-55]; unreliably) attributed to Maruta, Bishop of Maipherqat and Roman envoy to the court of Yazdegird I in ca. 410; and third, the Byzantine and Christian-Arabic historians, in particular Sozomen.

I. APHRAHAT

Bishop of Mar Mattai, north of Nineveh, near present-day Mosul, Aphrahat wrote twenty-three demonstrations, the first ten in 336-7, the next thirteen in 344-5.[5] In Demonstration XXI, *On Persecution*, he sought to encourage the persecuted Christians and to explain to them that in suffering they were imitating Christ. Aphrahat was moved to write, he says, "because a Jew reproached the children of our people" (XXI:8). The encounter is described as follows:

> I have heard a reproach which has greatly troubled me, for the unclean [men] say, "This people which is gathered together from all the peoples [= the Christians] has no God."
> _ Thus say the evil [men], "If they had a God, why does he not exact the vengeance of his people?"
> Darkness still more thickens upon me when even the Jews reproach us and magnify themselves over the children of our people.
> It happened that one day, a man who is called 'the sage of the Jews' met me, and asked, saying, "Jesus who was called your teacher has written to you: If there shall be in you faith like one seed of mustard, you will say to this mountain, move, and it will move from before you; and [you may say] even, be lifted up, and it will fall into the sea, for it will obey you (Matthew 17:19; 21:22). Thus [he continued] there is not [to be found] among your entire people one wise man, whose prayer is listened to, who seeks from God that your persecutions should cease from you. Thus it is written to you in the word, There is nothing which you will be unable to do (Matthew 17:19)."
> When I saw that he was blaspheming and talking much against the [Christian] way, my mind was disturbed, for I knew that he would not accept the explanation of the words he was quoting to me. Then I also questioned him concerning words from the law and the prophets. I said, "You thus hope, that even though you are scattered, God is with you."
> He agreed with me: "God is with us, for thus God said to Israel,

4 See my *History*, IV, pp. 20–27.
5 See my *Aphrahat and Judaism: The Jewish-Christian Argument in Fourth-Century Iran* (Leiden, 1970).

Even in the lands of your enemies I have not abandoned you, and my covenant which is with you has not been annulled (Lev. 26:44)."

Again I said to him, "Very good is that which I hear from you, that God is with you. Against your words I also shall say something to you. Isaiah the prophet said to Israel [speaking] as from the mouth of God, If you pass through the sea I am with you, and rivers will not overflow you. And if you walk in fire, you will not be burned, and the flame will not scorch you, for the Lord your God is with you (Is. 43:2-3). Thus there is not a single man who is righteous, good, and wise among your entire people, who may pass through the sea and not be drowned [or pass through] a river but it would overflow him. Let him walk on fire, and let us see whether he would not be scorched, or whether the flame would not burn him. Now if you should bring me an explanation, I shall not be persuaded by you, just as you will not accept from me the explanation of the words concerning which you questioned me."[6]

II. THE SYRIAC MARTYROLOGIES

Jews occur only in the martyrologies of Simeon bar Sabba'ē and his sister Tarbo. I find no references to Jewish instigation of, or participation in, any other aspect of the persecution of Christianity by Shapur II.[7] The stories of

---

6 Trans. in my *Aphrahat and Judaism*, pp. 97–8.
The Chronicle of Arbela contains the following tradition (trans. E. Sachau, p. 75):

> Es wird gesagt, dass der König bereute, diesen harten Verfolgungsbefehl erlassen zu haben und ihn aufzuheben wünschte, aber Juden and Manichäer, die Feinde des christlichen Namens, hetzten die Magier auf an und brachten ihnen die Ansicht bei, sie sollten nicht zulassen, dass der König das täte. Sie legten ihnen dar, dass die Christen alle Spione der Römer seien, und dass nichts im Perser-Reiche vorgehe, das sie nicht ihren römischen Glaubensgenossen berichteten.

Sachau's translation (*Die Chronik von Arbela*, in *Abhandlungen der königl. preussischen Akademie der Wissenschaften* [Berlin, 1915]) is based upon A. Mingana, *Sources Syriaques* (Mossul, 1907). In the light of J.M. Fiey's study of the origins of the Chronicle of Arbela, "Auteur et date de la Chronique d'Arbèles," *L'Orient Syrien* 12, 1967, pp. 265-302, we can no longer make use of the Arbela Chronicle as a source for the study of early oriental Christianity. In this case, Mingana evidently used the Simeon-traditions, but, more likely, the Nestorian Chronicle (below, n. 33).

7 See I. Ortiz de Urbina, *Patrologia Syriaca* (Rome, 1965), pp. 194-6, and note also the critical discussion of Paul Devos, "Les martyrs persans à travers les Actes Syriaques," in *Atti del convegno sul tema, La Persia e il mondo greco-romano (Roma 11-14 Aprile 1965)*, (Rome, 1966: Accademia Nazionale dei Lincei), pp. 213-25.
The more important martyrologies of Shapur's reign are divided by I. Ortiz de Urbina into two groups, those executed first in 344-6, the second, in 376-7. Following Ortiz de Urbina's convenient, if *very* incomplete, list, let us review the references to Jews in the several martyrologies:
1. Simeon bar Sabba'ē - As given.
2. Tarbo – As given, Shahdost, 111 men and nine women, Barbashemin, 40 martyrs, Badema, Aqebshema, and associates: No reference to Jews. A Manichaean does occur in the martyrology of Aitillaha (Braun, pp. 132-3).
3. Adiabenians - No reference to Jews.

4. Miles, etc. – No reference to Jews. Barshabya was falsely maligned by "evil women" (*AMS* II, p. 281), and accused of sorcery.

5. *AMS* II, pp. 284-6 – No reference to Jews.

6. Captives of 362 – No reference to Jews.

7. Martyrs of Karka de Beth Selok – *AMS* II, 286-9, contains a list of the martyrs, with no reference to Jews.

8. Persian Soldiers – No reference to Jews.

9. Baddai – No reference to Jews.

For the sake of completeness, I further reviewed the martyrologies according to the full list of Paul Peeters, *Bibliotheca Hagiographica Orientalis* (Brussels, 1910). The following are the martyrs in the reign of Shapur II:

Abdas, Ebediesus – d. 374-5, *AMS* II, 325-347. No reference to Jews.

Abraham – d. 344, *AMS* IV, 130-1. No reference to Jews.

Acepsimas ['Aqebshema], Joseph, Aeithalas – d. 379, *AMS* II, 351-396. No reference to Jews.

Aeithalas and Apsees (Haphsai) – d. 354-5, *AMS* IV, 133-137. No reference to Jews.

Azad – d. 310, *AMS* IV, 248-254. No reference to Jews.

Badai – *AMS* IV, 163-5. No reference to Jews.

Badimus – d. 375, *AMS* II, 347-51. No reference to Jews.

Barbasymas (Barbashemin) – d. 346, *AMS* II, 296-303. No reference to Jews.

Barḥadbeshaba – d. 354, *AMS* II, 314-316. No reference to Jews.

Barsabias – d. 342, *AMS* II, 281-4. No reference to Jews.

Behnam, Sara, et al. – d. 352 (?) *AMS* II, 397-441; Hoffmann, *Auszüge*, pp. 17-19. No reference to Jews.

Berichiesius, etc. – d. 351, *AMS* IV, 166-9. No reference to Jews.

Dado – *AMS* IV, 218-221. No reference to Jews.

Daniel et Varda – d. 341, *AMS* II, 290. No reference to Jews.

Gobdelaas, Kasdoa, etc. – d. 332, *AMS* IV, 141-163. No reference to Jews. "Evil people" accuse Christians; Jews not mentioned.

Hananias, Arbelensis – d. 345, *AMS* IV, 131-132. No reference to Jews.

Iacobus et Maria – d. 347, *AMS* II, 307. No reference to Jews.

Ioannes b. Mariam et Jacobus Zelotes – d. 344, *AMS* IV, 128-130. No reference to Jews.

Ionas, Barachisius – d. 327, *AMS* II, 39-51. No reference to Jews.

Kardag – d. 367, *AMS* II, 442-507. See Abbeloos, *AB* 9, 11-103. No reference to Jews.

Martyres Beth Huzaini – d. 340, *AMS* II, 241-8. No reference to Jews.

Martyres Persae Variis in locis sup Sapore II – *AMS* II, 291-5. No reference to Jews.

Miles, Aborsam et Sinoi – *AMS* II, 260-75. No reference to Jews.

Narses, Joseph – d. 343-4, *AMS* II, 284-6. No reference to Jews.

Phusik (Posi) – d. 340, *AMS* II, 208-232. No reference to Jews.

Sabas Pirgusnasp – d. 362, *AMS* IV, 222-249; Hoffmann, *Auszüge*, pp. 22-8. No reference to Jews. Christians' accusers not specified (p. 225). Reference to Jews' crucifying Jesus, p. 226.

Sadoth (Šahdust) – d. 342, *AMS* II, 276-281. No reference to Jews.

Sapor, Isaac, Mana, Abraham, et Symeon – d. 340, *AMS* II, 51-56. No reference to Jews.

Sapor, Sanatruck, Hormizd et soc. – d. 351, *AMS* IV, 169-170. No reference to Jews.

Sultan Mahduct, Adurparva, et Mihrneses – d. 318, *AMS* II, 1-39; Hoffmann, *Auszüge*, pp. 9-16. No reference to Jews.

Symeon bar Sabbae, Abdhaicla, Hananias – d. 339, *AMS* II, 123-207 [see below].

Tharbo (Pherbutha), *AMS* II, 254-260 [see below].

Thecla, Marianne, Martha, Maria, Amai – d. 347, *AMS* II, 308-313. No reference to Jews.

Simeon bar Sabba'ē[8] and his sister Tarbo are as follows:

1) *Martyrium,* col. 738, line 25 — col. 739, line 21:

Now the Jews, our enemies, as was their custom, were accusing us and Simeon. For they are accustomed to find in such a time as this [occasion] for evil and not for good, as they clamored against Pilate when he killed the Messiah.

For they were blaspheming and saying, "If you, O King, should send impressive and wise letters from your empire and handsome gifts and precious presents of your majesty, they would not be accepted and much honored in the eyes of Caesar. But if this Simeon should send him a small and contemptible letter, he would arise and pay homage and receive it with both hands, and do the deed [asked by Simeon] in a worthy manner."

How similar is the false witness against Simeon to the evil testimonies which were against his Lord! They killed our Lord and were repudiated and scattered among the nations as aliens and hated [people]. They accused (QTRG) Simeon and were put to shame, and violence came upon them [lit.: arose over their heads] in many thousands by the sword which suddenly went forth upon them. For they had gathered together for the building of Jerusalem, and they had gone at the word of one who misled them [see no. 3].

2) *Martyrium,* col. 739, line 22 — col. 742, line 6:

[Simeon was thrown in chains and deported to Khuzistan, along with two of the elders of his court. When he was being led out of Seleucia] he besought them not to take him there [by way of his cathedral], for a few days earlier, it had been destroyed by the Magi in association (BHBRWT') with the Jews.

3) *Narratio de Beato Simeon bar Sabba'ē,* col. 806, line 20 — col. 811, line 9:

The Jews, people who always are against our people, those who killed the prophets, crucified the Messiah, stoned the apostles, and always thirst for our blood, found for themselves the opportunity to calumniate, for they [lit.: they had P'RRYSY'] had access to the queen. For she was of their way of thinking (BRT R'YNHWYN).

They began to calumniate against the victorious Simeon and were saying, "If you, the King of Kings, lord of all the earth, should send great and wise epistles of your empire and handsome gifts and precious donations of your honor to Caesar, they would not be honorable in his eyes. But if Simeon sent him one small and contemptible letter, he would rise and pay homage and receive it in both his hands, and he would speedily carry out his command. And under these circumstances there is no secret in your empire which he does not write and make known to Caesar."

8 Michael Kmosko, "S. Simeon bar Sabba'ē," *Patrologia Syriaca,* I, ii (Paris, 1927), pp. 661-1055. The translation is my own.
Martyrium: The Martyrdom [Testimony] of the Beatified Simeon bar Sabba'ē.
Narratio: The History of the Beatified Simeon bar Sabba'ē.

The Jews are accustomed to testify falsely at all times. Just as they testified falsely against our Lord, so also against the servant of the Messiah did they give false testimony.

For they testified falsely against our Lord. They were rejected and fell by the sword of the Romans when their city was destroyed.

Likewise they testified evil against Simeon. They fell by the sword at the hand of the Persians.

There they cried, "We have no king but Caesar," and they fell by the sword of Caesar.

Here they swore by King Shapur, and they were killed by him. And what it was that caused him to kill them? It is right that we should briefly tell.

Twenty-four years later, when Constantius and Constantinus, sons of Constantine the Victorious, had departed, Julian ruled the Romans. As soon as he became King, he sacrificed to idols; and to provoke the Christians to jealousy and to make a lie of the words of the Messiah which he prophesied over the ruin of Jerusalem, saying, There shall not remain in it stone on stone, which will not be thrown down (Matt. 24:22) − on this account he commanded the Jews of his whole empire to come up and build Jerusalem and the Temple and to sacrifice according to the commandment of the law.

Many went up and began to lay the foundations of Jerusalem. When these [things] were happening, a man of the imposters came to the land of the Persians and proclaimed to all the Jews, saying, "It is the time of the return of which the prophets prophesied, and I am commanded by God to announce to you the proclamation to go up."

This imposter came also to Maḥōzā, in Beth Aramayē and deceived myriads of Jews. They took and went forth from Maḥōzā because of the hope of the return, and they went three parasangs from the city.

When this matter was made known to King Shapur, he sent his forces, and they killed many thousands of them.

Concerning the slaughter, which took place among the Jews in the days of King Shapur, as best we can, we have briefly recorded.

Let us return to our account.

4) *Narratio,* col. 823, line 13 [Simeon addresses the priests to avoid sectarianism]:

"Keep yourselves far from traffic with the Jews, enemies of the Father, and haters of the Son, and adversaries of the Holy Spirit, who always murmur against the spirit of the Lord, as Isaiah the prophet testified; who spoke perjury against the highest, as David the Psalmist testified. They spoke ill against Moses and God; and as the Book of Kings teaches us. They killed the prophets and crucified the Messiah and stoned the apostles. They are the enemies of the Crucified one and envious of the salvation of nations and men. They calumniate our people and hand over the servants of God.

"Guard your soul from all heresies which I have already listed for you. Above all be watchful of the errors of the Jews and the teachings of Marcion . . ."

5) *Narratio*, col. 854, line 14:

[Shapur to Simeon]: "If you will not bow to sun, because it is dead, you should not bow to Jesus, who died when the Jews crucified him."

6) *Narratio*, col. 856, line 16 [Note also 858, 3-8]:

And the Jews envy the one who appeared, and not the one who did not appear they seized and crucified [meaning unclear].

7) *Narratio*, col. 902, lines 19-23 [Simeon]:

"Let me not to live and see the unclean people of crucifiers going and degrading your holy people and lifting themselves over your servants . . ."

8) *Narratio*, col. 907, lines 4-6:

He has taught us the mystery of the sacrifice of his body: Not by the Jews, but by the saints his servants, is he sacrificed in the churches.

9) *Narratio*, col. 939, line 3:

Remember, my brothers, that blessed Paul, who five times was scourged by the Jews with whips, and three times was smitten by the gentiles with staves . . .

10) *Narratio*, col. 942, line 22:

You are separate from the gentiles as they are from the Jews, they who killed our Lord Jesus and the prophets who were of them, and who persecute us . . .

11) *The Martyrdom of Tarbo*, her sister and servants (Bedjan, *AMS* II, p. 254) is as follows:

On that time by mischance the queen fell ill, and because her opinion was near [that of] the Jews, the enemies of the Cross, they said to her, as an evil accusation, as is their custom, "The sister of Simeon has placed you under a spell, because her brother was killed."

And when the word reached the king, Tarbo, a nun, and her sister, a holy one, and her maid, a nun, were all seized . . .

[The Mobad then interrogated the women.]

11a) The story of Tarbo further occurs in Greek Acts of the Persian Martyrs. The relevant passage is as follows:

During the time of our persecutions the Queen unexpectedly fell sick. But since her heart was full toward the Jews, the enemies of the cross, she gladly heard everything they said when they came to her: "Because the Bishop Simeon, with the surname Ionbaphaion, has been killed, his sisters have prepared a drug for you to kill you." As soon as this speech had reached the Queen, immediately Therbow with her sister and her maidservant were seized. Therbow was beautiful, but also the other two women led a beautiful life in Christ . . .[9]

9 Hippolyte Delehaye, "Les versions grecques des Actes des martyrs persans sous Sapor II," *Pat. Or.* 2, 1907, pp. 405-560. Text is on pp. 439-40. Note also p. 464 1. 28, p. 465 1. 26 contain references to Jews in the time of Jesus. Translation by Professor Horst R. Moehring, Brown University.

The narrative describes the interrogation of Tarbo by the Magian high priest. Jews do not recur in the passage, in which the leading participants are Tarbo and the Magi.

III. SOME ANCIENT AND MEDIEVAL HISTORIANS

1) *Sozomen*

Salaminius Hermias Sozomen, who came from Gaza and lived at Constantinople after ca. 405 A.D., wrote his history in ca. 450 A.D. His account of Shapur's persecution (II, 9, ff.) is as follows:

> When, in course of time, the Christians increased in number, and began to form churches, and appointed priests and deacons; the Magi, who as a priestly tribe had from the beginning in successive generations acted as the guardians of the Persian religion, became deeply incensed against them.
>
> The Jews, who through envy are in some way naturally opposed to the Christian religion, were likewise offended. They therefore brought accusations before Sapor, the reigning sovereign, against Simeon, who was then Archbishop of Seleucia and Ctesiphon, royal cities of Persia, and charged him with being a friend of the Caesar of the Romans, and with communicating the affairs of the Persians to him. Sapor believed these accusations, and at first, ground the Christians with excessive taxes, although he knew that the generality of them had voluntarily embraced poverty. He entrusted the exaction to cruel men, hoping that, by the want of necessaries, and the atrocity of the exactors, they might be compelled to abjure their religion; for this was his aim . . .
>
> About the same period, the queen was attacked with a disease, and Tarbula, the sister of Simeon the bishop, a holy virgin, was arrested with her servant, who shared in the same mode of life, as likewise a sister of Tarbula, who, after the death of her husband, abjured marriage, and led a similar career.
>
> The cause of their arrest was the charge of the Jews, who reported that they had injured the queen by their enchantments, on account of their rage at the death of Simeon. As invalids easily give credit to the most repulsive representations, the queen believed the charge, and especially because it emanated from the Jews, since she had embraced their sentiments, and lived in the observance of the Jewish rites, for she had great confidence in their veracity and in their attachment to herself . . .[10]

2) *Faustus of Byzantium*

By contrast, the brief account of Faustus of Byzantium (ca. early fifth century), contains no reference to Jews or to specific martyrs:

10 Chester D. Hartranft, ed., *The Ecclesiastical History of Sozomen. Comprising a History of the Church from A.D. 323 to A.D. 425,* in Philip Schaff and Henry Wace, eds., *A Select Library of Nicene and Post Nicene Fathers of the Christian Church.* Second Series, vol. II (Repr. Grand Rapids, 1957), pp. 264-7.

Sapor, roi des Perses, persécute les chrétiens

En ce temps-là, quand le prêtre Mari et les soixante-dix autres prêtres eurent subi le supplice de la mort, le roi Sapor suscita la plus grande persécution contre la religion chrétienne; il chargeait les chrétiens d'impôts onereux, leur infligeait des peines et des châtiments, après quoi il donna l'ordre de passer au fil de l'epée tous ceux qui, dans son royaume, portaient le nom de chrétien, sans aucune exception. A la suite de cet ordre, on massacra les chrétiens par milliers et par dizaine de milliers, pour qu'il n'en restât pas un seul dans les domaines du roi.[11]

3) *Theophanes*

The *Chronographia* of Theophanes for the year A.M. 5817 has the following, evidently following Sozomen:

In that year, when the Jews and the Persians saw Christianity flourishing throughout Persia, they brought before Sapor, the King of the Persians, accusations against Simeon, the Archbishop of Ctesiphon and Seleucia, to the effect that he was a friend of the Emperor of the Romans and that he informed him of the affairs of the Persians. Thus a great persecution broke out in Persia and the greatest number were arranged for martyrdom for the sake of Christ, among whom were Ousthazades, the pedagogue of Sapor, the Simeon the Archbishop, and in addition to many others a hundred clergymen and bishops were martyred in a single day . . .[12]

4) *Nestorian History*

The Nestorian History, written in Arabic by an anonymous author, who, according to Addai Scher, lived in the thirteenth century, alludes to the martyrologies attributed to Maruta, Bishop of Martyropolis (Maipherqat), and Akhi, the patriarch. The Christian persecution was instigated by the Magi:

During the thirty-first year of his reign . . . he [Shapur] attacked the Christians, destroyed the churches, and moved against Nisibis . . . The priests of the idols had said to Shapur, in behalf of their God, that if he exterminates the Christians, he would not die . . .[13]

On the martyrdom of Simeon, the Chronicle has the following:

Mais Satan, l'ennemi du Dieu des miséricordes, envia la sécurite, la paix, et la tranquillité de la chrétienté et de l'Eglise du Christ. Il se dit en lui-même, Je vais exciter Sapor à persécuter Siméon, comme j'ai excité Néron à persécuter Simon-Pierre . . . À la mort de Constantin,

11 Faustus of Byzantium, *Bibliothèque Historique*, IV, Chap. 17, trans. Jean-Baptiste Emine, in V. Langlois, ed., *Collection des historiens anciens et modernes de l'Arménie* (Paris, 1867), I, p. 255.

12 Ioannis Classen, ed., *Theophanis. Chronographia* (Bonn, 1839), pp. 36-7, in B.G. Niebuhr, ed., *Corpus Scriptorum Historiae Byzantinae*. Translation by Professor Horst R. Moehring, Brown University.

13 *Histoire Nestorienne (Chronique de Séert)*, ed. A. Scher. *Pat. Or.* 4, pp. 288-9.

dans la trente et unième année du règne de Sapor . . . Sapor fit ses préparatifs et vint attaquer Nisibe . . . Dieu envoya alors sur lui une nuée noire et des pierres du haut du ciel: il se retira vainçu et honteux; mais, semblable aux vipères, il vomit son poison sur les Pères et les fidèles qui étaient dans son royaume.

Sapor aimait beaucoup le métropolite Siméon; mais les Juifs, amis de Satan, connaissant ses mauvaises dispositions à l'égard des Chrétiens, le trompèrent en lui disant que Siméon, le chef de ces derniers, avait converti les princes des mages à la religion chrétienne, et que, chose beaucoup plus grave, il avait baptisé et converti à sa propre religion la mère du roil. Le père de cette princess était juif. Le Christ laissa ses brebis aux mains des ennemis, non par faiblesse ni en pure perte, mais pour leur utilité et leur sanctification . . .[14]

Jews do not recur in the Chronicle's martyrology of Simeon nor in the martyrdoms of Shahdost, Barbashemin, Qardagh, and others.

IV. MODERN HISTORICAL OPINION

Among the more important modern historians, Nöldeke and Peeters regard the story of the Jews' actions against Simeon and Tarbo as historically accurate and further conclude, following Sozomen, that the Jews participated in the persecution of Christians throughout the empire. Their opinions are as follows:

1) *Nöldeke:*

> Die Behauptung, dass die Juden gegen den Bischof Simeon bar Sabba'ē aufgehetzt hatten . . . gewinnt hierdurch an Wahrscheinlichkeit . . .[15]

2) *Peeters:*

> L'historien grec attribue principalement la colère de Sapor aux excitations des mages et des juifs. Il est pourtant probable que ces intrigues ont trouvé chez le roi un terrain bien préparé . . .
> Informé de la volonté expresse du roi, Syméon essaie de se dérober par de nouvelles excuses. Elles furent, on peut le croire, tournées en termes plus diplomatiques que l'homélie que la Passion nous donne à lire. Mais l'éffet n'en fut pas moins de mettre Sapor dans une colère que les ennemis des chrétiens surent habilement attiser. L'hagiographe paraît avoir eu de bonnes raisons d'en accuser surtout les juifs. Depuis le temps de la grande captivité, les juifs étaient demeurés nombreux en Babylonie. Ctésiphon était un de leurs principaux centres [sic!]. Là résidait le chef spirituel de leur colonie, le res galoutha, qui, à la cour du roi de Perse, exerçait une véritable puissance. Dans ce milieu actif et organisé, régnait traditionnellement une animosité antichrétienne, dont

---

14 *Pat. Or.* 4, pp. 296-305, *passim.*
15 T. Nöldeke, trans., *Tabari: Geschichte der Perser und Araber zur Zeit der Sassaniden* (Leiden, 1879), p. 68, n. 1.

le talmud fut la très authentique expression [sic!]. Les Passions des martyrs perses nous montrent fréquement [!] cette malviellance en plein exercice.[16]

Duval takes an agnostic view, and Kmosko and Labourt reject the stories of the Jews' complicity in instigating the persecutions:

3) *Duval*

Les poursuites furent motivées par le refus du patriarche de percevoir le double impôt de capitation que le roi avait édicté contre les chrétiens, à l'instigation des Juifs qui jouissaient de la faveur de la reine mère. Marouta se fait l'écho d'une accusation contre les Juifs, que l'on trouve répétée dans différents actes des martyrs de la Perse, mais qui peut n'être pas fondée. Quant à la reine mère, qui s'appelait Éphra Hormiz, elle était en effet favorable aux Juifs et avait une grande influence sur le roi, son fils, comme nous le savons par le Talmud.[17]

4) *Kmosko*

Acta enim testantur Iudaeos in causa S. Simeonis sycophantarum vice functos esse, et omnia, quae de Regina Iudaeis amicissima referunt ... cum Talmude accurate conveniunt. Certum autem est Iudaeos non fuisse causam nec unicam nec principalem persecutionis, sed Magos omnipotentes, qui tum ob religionis antiquae zelum, tum ob rationes mere materiales Regem contra Christianos excitasse omnia fere Acta testantur.[18]

5) *Labourt*

D'une part ils [the Jews] étaient en faveur auprès de la reine Ifra Hormizd; d'autre part ils détestaient cordialement les chrétiens, d'autant plus que Constantin n'usait guère de tolérance à l'égard de leurs co-religionnaires de Palestine. Aussi M. Nöldeke ... estime-t-il l'accusation de nos hagiographes tout à fait vraisemblable. M. Duval, au contraire, réserve son judgment ...

Une chose est du moins au-dessus de toute contestation; c'est que les Juifs, autant que les païens, se réjouirent des désastres que le cruauté de Sapor infligea aux Églises chrétiennes ...[19]

6) *Wiessner*

The most important historical-critical study of the problem is by Gernot Wiessner who states:[20]

The problems of the Jewish tradition[21] seem to be basically relatively easy to solve. This tradition seems to be the result of

16   Paul Peeters, "La date du martyre de S. Syméon," *AB* 56, 1938, pp. 125-8.
17   Rubens Duval, *La littérature syriaque* (Paris, 1900), p. 134.
18   Kmosko, *Pat. Syr.* I, ii, p. 694.
19   Labourt, p. 58, n. 2.
20   Gernot Wiessner, pp. 180-194, passim, Translated by Professor Horst R. Moehring, Brown University.
21   That is, the tradition concerning the Jews' involvement in the persecutions.

Christian-Jewish debates and polemics in the Mesopotamia of the fourth century.

During this period, Christendom, which had grown on Jewish mother soil, was about to work itself up to conscious independence. For this purpose it was necessary, first of all, to bring together the formerly independent congregations and to establish a Christian "central office" in the patriarchate of Seleucia Ctesiphon . . .

One of the main places of this controversy was probably Seleucia-Ctesiphon. Here the young patriarchate in Kōkē was confronted by a citadel of Jewish faith in Maḥōzā . . .

It is against this background of a close coexistence of the Christian and Jewish main centers within the city complex of Seleucia-Ctesiphon and the Jewish-Christian polemic connected with the fact, that we have to understand the tradition . . . which ascribes to the Jews the guilt for the death of Simeon (and Tarbo). The explicitly stated connection between the Jews and the royal Persian court and the mentioning of the Persian queen fit exactly into the picture known to us from Jewish tradition.

Regrettably, this Jewish tradition was later . . . covered by that other (tax) tradition and, with the exception of the traditional accusations against Simeon and Tarbo, can no longer be exactly recognized. Perhaps Simeon's death was already covertly described in this tradition; we even seem to have a small remnant of the trial against the ecclesiastical prince extant in *verbatim* . . . This circumstance and the fact that because of its language the Jewish tradition can be distinguished from the . . . [tax] make it most likely that it was available to the author of . . . [the tax-text] already in firmly fixed form, perhaps even in writing. It probably originated and was formed in Seleucia-Ctesiphon itself. Since here the Christian patriarchate and the main Jewish school stood face to face, it was most likely here that an anti-Jewish tradition developed which ascribed to the Jews the guilt for the death of Simeon. It will probably never be possible to clarify where this tradition rests upon an historical fact or whether it is merely the concrete expression of an easily understandable rumor. . .

The second tradition . . . we designated as the tax-tradition. Here Simeon's arrest and the subsequent events are explained with the order of the Persian king that the tax responsibilities of the Christians had to be changed somehow and with the refusal of the patriarch to accede to this demand. Because of this insubordination a trial is said to have been instituted against Simeon which . . . ended with the death-sentence against Simeon and which was followed by a general persecution of the Christians.

This tradition today almost completely covers the anti-Jewish thread of the narrative, so that of this only fragments can still be recognized . . .

I find myself in full agreement with Labourt and Kmosko. Labourt follows Aphrahat's view, that the Jews did not sympathize with the Christians. Kmosko stresses that the Jews could not have brought about the massive persecutions. Nöldeke did not critically study the talmudic stories about Ifra

Hormiz. Peeters' comments on the Talmud's "anti-Christianity" tell us that the great Bollandist in this respect did not take the trouble to find out the facts. As to Shapur's persecution, he was predisposed to believe that the Jews had done what the hagiographers claimed ("they had good reasons . . . "); but his sober judgment, that "the ground was well prepared," is more accurate. Wiessner's view, that we in the end cannot know what actually happened with Jews, Simeon and Tarbo, seems to me judicious. Whatever the case with Simeon and Tarbo, Jews evidently had participated in the martyrdoms of no other Christian witnesses known to us.

V. COMMENTS ON THE SYRIAC TRADITIONS

Aphrahat supplies the best evidence concerning the Jewish attitude toward Shapur II's persecution of the Christians. He wrote in 345; his testimony therefore comes at the very time of the events under discussion. He indicates that the Jews had no part whatever in instigating or carrying out persecutions of Christianity. They did regard the persecution as evidence of the false character of Christian belief, presumably did nothing to assist the Christians, and could not have regretted their unhappy fate.

Most Syriac martyrologies give the same picture. The Jews as a group and Jewish individuals simply do *not* occur in the stories of the Christian martyrs. In general the pattern is simple. The hagiographer gives the date of the martyrdom, the occasion for the arrest, and then, normally at great length, an account of the interrogation of the accused, his brave defense of the faith, and, occasionally, the disposition of his body after death. The arguments invariably are with the Mobads, never with the Jews. Only the highly literary, well-developed, and very elaborate accounts of Simeon b. Sabba'ē diverge from the picture. Here we are told the chief reason for the persecution: refusal to pay the tax. This theme recurs nowhere else. Alongside, as Wiessner stresses, is the quite separate motif of the Jews' accusations against Simeon and his sister Tarbo.

We see three elements in the Jewish part of the Simeon-martyrology, briefly given in the *Martyrium*, then greatly developed in the *Narratio*. First, as the narrator stresses the similarity between the death of Jesus and that of Simeon, so he also includes a reference to the Jews, who in both cases bore false witness, and in both cases received their just reward. The substance of the accusation takes for granted exchanges of letters between Shapur and Caesar and alleges that the letters sent by the king of kings were not properly received, while those from Simeon were appropriately accepted. This later on is developed into the accusation that Simeon was a Roman spy.

Second, the parallel between the destruction of Jerusalem in 70 and the destruction of Maḥōzān Jewry in 361-2 is drawn. The story is unattested elsewhere, but that does not mean it is not true. On the contrary, it seems a likely account, for the messianic hopes of Babylonian Jewry repeatedly came to the surface in Sasanian times.[22] That the occasion of Julian's call to rebuild the Temple provoked Jewish plans to emigrate – presumably with heavenly assistance – accords with what happened in the Roman empire at the same time and for the same reason. Shapur's reaction was understandable, for the 'deceiver' would have elicited the fear that Babylonian Jewry might support Julian in his projected Iranian invasion, and that may have been part of Julian's plan.

But for our narrator, the story takes for granted that the Temple was not rebuilt, the words of Jesus were not shown to be false, and Julian's effort in the end proved futile. The passage cannot be an interpolation. The point of including the story is clear, and articulated. So the whole serves to supply a date for the martyrology as we now have it (in both versions), namely, after 360, probably long afterward. Since Sozomen obviously had access to the Simeon and Tarbo materials, which are referred to accurately and in places *verbatim*, ca. 450 necessarily is the *terminus ante quem*. A reasonable guess is ca. 410, after the end of the period of troubles, but before Yazdegird's renewal of the persecutions of Christianity.

The third element is the poignant detail that Simeon did not wish to pass by his cathedral, which Jews had helped destroy. This seems to me credible, for the local Jews may well have done what the martyrologist claims, participating with the magi in the destruction of the Seleucian church.

The other references to Jews have nothing to do with the martyrdom of Simeon. They take for granted that Jews are "our persecutors," but give no further details. The speeches given to Simeon include reference to Jewish heresies, along with those of Marcion and others, and I assume Christians who followed Jewish beliefs in some respects were foremost in the narrator's mind. The other allusions to Jews are routine and inconsequential.

The claim that Jews were implicated in Tarbo's martyrdom lays stress on the fact that the Jews had a friend at court. The first Simeon-account knows nothing about a Jewish queen. The Jews are listened to because they make a good case against Simeon. It is taken for granted, to be sure, that they have access to the king. The developed account of the *Narratio* (no. 3) introduces the detail that the Jews had access also to the queen. She was a Jew or a sympathizer of Judaism. In Tarbo's story the same view of the queen occurs, in much the same language. The rest of the Tarbo-story follows the conventional lines of other martyrologies, stressing the interrogation and debate about religious beliefs. This motif next appears – besides in Sozomen – in the late Nestorian History, where it is explicitly stated that Shapur's mother was a Jew, converted to Christianity.

22 *History* II, pp. 27-57; III, pp. 17-24, 95-110, 192-94; IV, 44-56, 279-86, 400-402; V, 60-69, 95-112, 127-30.

Nöldeke in this connection first introduced the name of Ifra Hormizd and alluded to the several talmudic passages in which she is mentioned. From that time onward, it has been taken for granted that the Talmud "verifies" the martyrologies and supplies important information about the "Jewish queen" alluded to in them. This seems unlikely, for two reasons.

First, before the Nestorian Chronicle no one has heard about the Jewish queen-*mother*. The queen herself is Jewish or sympathizes with the Jews. And the Nestorian Chronicle explicitly states that the queen-mother's father was a Jew; but she herself was converted to Christianity by Simeon, so she cannot be the same as the queen-mother known in the Talmud as Ifra Hormizd, who there is not represented as a Jew, and who did not convert to Christianity.

Second, we do have stories about a Jewish queen, but in the time of Yazdegird, not of Shapur II. These stories, which were known to Iranian, but not rabbinic, historians, come at the very time of the composition of the Syriac martyrologies, after the death of Shapur II but before the Christian persecutions of Yazdegird. Let us now review both sets of stories.

1) *Ifra Hormizd*

Four stories relate that the queen-mother presented to rabbis three gifts and one question:

> Ifra Hormiz the mother of Shapur the king sent a purse of *denarii* to R. Joseph.
> She said, "Let them be for the performance of a great commandment."
> R. Joseph sat and considered, "What is a great commandment?"
> Abaye said to him, "Since R. Samuel b. Judah taught, 'One may not levy charity from orphans even for the redemption of captives,' one may infer that redemption of captives is a great commandment."
> (Bab. Tal. Bava Bathra 8a-b)

> Ifra Hormiz the mother of Shapur the king sent four hundred *denarii* to R. Ammi [in Palestine] and he would not accept them.
> She sent them to Rava, and he accepted them on account of keeping peace with the government.
> R. Ammi heard and was angry. He said, "Does he not accept the teaching of the Scripture, When the boughs thereof are withered they shall be broken off, the women shall come and set them on fire (Is. 27:11) [The meaning is,'When the gentiles have exhausted their merit, then their power will be broken, and charity adds to their merit'] ."
> And Rava ? On account of the peace of the kingdom.
> And R. Ammi for the same reason should have accepted them?
> [He was angry] because he ought to have given the money to the pagan poor.
> But Rava did give it to the pagan poor.
> R. Ammi was angry because they did not complete the report to him.

(Bab. Tal. Bava Bathra 10b-11a)

Ifra Hormiz mother of Shapur the king sent an animal sacrifice to Rava.

She sent word to him, "Offer it up to Him for the sake of Heaven."

Rava said to R. Safra and R. Aha b. Huna, "Go and put forward two [pagan] young men [of the same age], and see where the sea has thrown up alluvial mud, and take new twigs and make a fire with a new flint and offer it up for the sake of Heaven."

(Bab. Tal. Zevahim 116b)

Ifra Hormiz mother of Shapur the king sent blood to Rava.

R. 'Ovadyah was sitting before him.

He smelled it and said to her, "This is a blood of lust."

She said to her son, "Come see how wise the Jews are."

He said to her, "Perhaps it is like a blind man on a window [a lucky accident]."

She went and sent him sixty kinds of blood, and all he identified except the last one, which was lice blood, and he did not know it.

Fortunately, he sent her a comb which kills lice.

She said, "Jews! In the inner chamber of the heart do you live!"

(Bab. Tal. Niddah 20b)

The fifth story is of a different sort altogether:

A certain man was judged liable to the lash in the court of Rava because he had intercourse with a gentile [lit.: Samaritan] woman.

Rava had him lashed and he died.

The matter was heard in the court of Shapur the King.

He wanted to punish Rava.

Ifra Hormiz, the mother of Shapur the King, said to her son, "Have no dealings with the Jews, for whatever they ask of their Master he gives to them."

He asked her, "What would it be?"

She replied, "They pray for mercy and rain comes."

He said to her, "That comes because it is the normal time for rain, but let them ask for mercy now, in the summer season [lit.: in the Tammuz cycle], and let rain come."

She sent to Rava, "Concentrate, and beg for mercy that rain may come."

He prayed for mercy but rain did not come. He prayed before Him, "Lord of the world, Oh God, we have heard with our ears, our fathers have told us; a work you did in their days in the days of old (Ps. 44:2). But we with our own eyes have not seen it."

Rain came until the gutters of Mahoza emptied their water into the Tigris.

His father came and appeared to him in a dream and said to him, "Does anyone trouble heaven so much? Change your place!" He changed his place [for sleeping], and next morning he found that his bed was cut with knives.

(Bab. Tal. Ta'anith 24b)

As to the name Ifra ('YPR'), Nöldeke finds the name unclear, and no other sources report Shapur's mother's name as Ifra Hormiz(d). His father's name of course was Hormizd.[23]

The stories of Ifra Hormizd's gifts to R. Joseph and Rava are of two different kinds. The first two were told as the occasion for discussion of a legal issue, in the first case, What is a great commandment? and in the second, How would one rabbi justify declining a gift from the government, while another justified accepting it? The second story appears the least credible, for it is unlikely that the queen-mother would have had sufficient information about the Palestinian rabbis to send a gift to R. Ammi. That someone gave a purse of *denarii* to a very important Babylonian rabbi seems plausible.

The third and fourth stories, while different from one another, are preserved in a more narrowly historical framework. In neither is a legal discussion attached to, or caused by, the participation of Ifra Hormizd. The gift of an animal sacrifice to Rava has its parallel in the gift by an Arab of an animal sacrifice to Rav Judah in the preceding generation.[24] The consultation about the meaning of a vaginal flow does not appear unlikely, since the rabbis achieved a wide-spread reputation for their expertness in interpreting just such phenomena. But why a non-Jew should inquire I cannot say. The point of the story was that the rabbis were supernaturally powerful and should not be trifled with. This is the message of the narrative about how the queen-mother saved Rava from her son's punishment. We know that the Sasanians, as soon as they took power, checked up on Jewish courts, which administered physical punishment, and the case in which the prohibition was reported is similar to the one before us. R. Shila ordered lashes for a man who had intercouse with a gentile woman, and later murdered him because he suspected him of intending to inform the Sasanian authorities of Shila's contempt for them.[25] What is important in this story, however, is the belief of the queen-mother in the supernatural power of the rabbis, who could pray and bring rain, just as they could interpret the most subtle natural phenomena. The point is that the effectiveness of the rabbis' prayers and their wonderful knowledge of physiology won the admiration of the queen-mother, whose gifts to R. Joseph and Rava, including not only money but also an animal sacrifice, would have been a natural result. These traditions preserve a memory that Shapur II's mother did believe Jews were supernaturally powerful, therefore tried to win their favor by giving them gifts of money and animal sacrifices, and even warned her skeptical son against interfering in their affairs.

23 Nöldeke, *Tabari*, p. 52, n. 1, p. 68, n. 1; F. Justi, *Iranisches Namenbuch* (Repr. Hildesheim, 1963), p. 141, col. a.
    24 *History* III, pp. 30-31; IV, pp. 63-4.
    25 *History* II, pp. 32-3.

2) *The Exilarch's Daughter, Yazdegird's Wife*

Both later Iranian and Talmudic traditions hold that Yazdegird showed favor to Jews. Item 47 in Markwart's edition of *The Provincial Capitals of Iran*, reads as follows:

> The capitals of Shōs (Susa) and Shōstar have been built by Shōshāndukht (Shūshan), the wife of Yazdkert, the son of Shāhpuhr, since she was the daughter of the Rēsh-Galūtak, the king of the Jews, and the mother of Vahrām i Gōr.[26]

Markwart comments, "It is very probable that there were many Jews in the great cities Shōsh (cf. the Book of Esther) and Shōshtar, and that these had golden times during the reign of king Yazdkerd I, who had married Shōshandukht, but the attribution of its foundation to her influence is obviously a popular etymology."[27] Widengren shares this view.[28] Item 53, further, reads:

> The capital of Gay (Ispahān) was built by the accursed Alexander the son of Philip; there was a settlement of Jews there whom Yazdkert the son of Shāhpuhr carried there in his reign at the request of Shōshāndukht who was his wife.[29]

Of importance also is item 10:

> The capital of Khwarizm, was built by Narsēh the son of the Jewess.[30]

On this passage, Markwart states (p. 43), "Narsēh the brother of Bahram Gor (420-438), . . . was appointed by the king as governor of Khorasan, with residence at Balkh, and given the title of *Marzeban-i Kushan*."

Armenian tradition held that Shapur II resettled large numbers of Armenian Jews in Isfahan, as part of his general deportation of Armenian populations to Fārs.[31]

Clearly, these are several traditions giving somewhat similar facts. That someone, Shapur II or Yazdegird I, moved Jews to Isfahan is a view held unanimously by Armenian and Iranian traditions, but Talmudic ones on these

---

26 J. Markwart, *The Provincial Capitals of Erānsahr* (Rome, 1931), pp. 19, 96-98. See also his *Erānsahr, nach der Geographie des Ps. Moses Xorena'ṣi* (Berlin, 1901), p. 20 no. 54 on the city-lists: "The Jews were settled there [in Isfahan] by Yazdigird I at the desire of his Jewish wife."

27 *Capitals*, pp. 97-8.

28 Geo. Widengren, "The Status of the Jews in the Sassanian Empire," *Iranica Antiqua* 1, 1961, pp. 119-120, 139-142.

29 *Capitals*, p. 21.

30 See Widengren, *Status*, p. 120.

31 Vol. III, pp. 339-343. See especially Widengren, *Status*, pp. 134-5 for text and translation of the traditions of Moses Xorenaṣi and Faustus of Byzantium. Widengren gives the key sentence as follows: "At this time there arrived a command from King Šāhpuhr to destroy and pull down the fortifications of all the towns, and to carry away the Jews in captivity, and the Jews who were living according to the law of Judaism, in Van in Tosp . . . these Šāhpuhr caused to live in Ispāhān."

monarchs know absolutely nothing of that deportation. On the other hand, rabbinical traditions are certain that the mother of Shapur II was friendly to the rabbis. Ifra Hormizd would have been Yazdegird's great-great-great grandmother. Rabbinical traditions preserve no record of any exilarch's daughter's marriage to an emperor. This practically proves there never was one, since the rabbis would certainly have boasted of the connection.

We may take it as fact that Shapur II did move Jews to Isfahan. I think it is equally plausible that Yazdegird I was not hostile to the Jews. To both emperors were attributed women-folk who favored Jews, in the former case, his mother, in the latter a Jewish wife. Precisely how these traditions became garbled into the report that Yazdegird I built cities at the request of a Jewish wife or moved Jews to Isfahan for the same reason I cannot say. But I see no grounds to suppose they have the slightest basis in fact. What was fact was that strong Jewish communities were found in Isfahan in Islamic times.[32] For the rest, fanciful, probably garbled stories provided the necessary explanation.

3) *The Jewish Queen*

The Iranian account of Yazdegird's Jewish wife seems to me congruent to the Christian hagiographers' stories of Shapur's Jewish *wife*. But they are *not* similar to the Talmud's stories of Shapur's Jewish *mother*. The latter stress the queen-mother's high regard for rabbinical magic, a theme nowhere revealed in the Christian martyrologies. There the Christians are accused of sorcery, but the Jews neither make that accusation nor are made to bear it. Further, Yazdegird's persecution of Christianity, in a measure because of conversions of Iranian nobility to that religion, seems to me congruent to the Nestorian Chronicler's account of the conversion of Shapur's mother. But nothing in the talmudic stories makes Ifra Hormizd a Jew, let alone a Christian. The hagiographers, living in the time of Yazdegird, may well have known from Christian or Iranian sources the rumor of a Jewish queen at the Persian court; they would naturally have included her in the martyrdom of Simeon bar Sabba'ē. They knew nothing of a queen-mother sympathetic to Judaism or to the Jews, let alone to Christianity. The Iranian, not the rabbinic, traditions therefore lie at the base of the stories of Shapur's Jewish wife.

It remains to observe that no talmudic story of debates between magi and rabbis exhibits the depth or theological force of the Christian martyrologies.

---

32 Widengren, *Status*, p. 142, "From other sources we actually know that Ispāhān was an old Jewish site." At the time of the Arab conquest, one of the town's two quarters was called al-Yahudiyyah. See also S. Funk, *Die Juden in Babylonien* (Berlin, 1902) II, p. 146, who thinks "Djai" (or "Jei") = "Jehudia." It is a groundless supposition; and J. Darmesteter, "Texts pehlvis relatifs au judaisme," Part ii, *REJ* 19, 1889, pp. 41-83, in particular pp. 41-52.

Attributed to fourth-century rabbis are a few stories of dialogues with pagans, e.g., Rava and Bar Shishakh (Bab. Tal. 'Avodah Zarah 65a), and only one involving a Mobad, in the fifth century:

> A certain Magus said to Amemar, "From your middle upwards belongs to Hormiz, and from your middle downwards belongs to Ahormiz."
> He replied, "If so, how does Ahormiz permit Hormiz to send water through his territory?"
>   (Bab. Tal. Sanhedrin 39a)

This tells us what rabbis conceived would happen if they were to dispute theology with Magi. It does not suggest a profound disputation and reveals no knowledge of what would have been at issue between the two religions. By contrast, the Christian martyrologies supply long and thoughtful dialogues, entirely from the Christian viewpoint to be sure, between Magi and the Christian martyrs. This suggests that the Jews never were persecuted for their failure to worship the sun and to do the other things the Magi demanded of the Christians.

Judaism should have been persecuted on the same grounds as Christianity. It was largely ignored throughout Shapur's time, except for the incident at Maḥōzā. That fact calls into question the Christians' representation of the basis of the persecution in religious difference. The more likely reason Christians suffered and Jews did not was, as I said, the question of political loyalty.

VI. CONCLUSION

In my judgment, the absence of references to Jews in the martyrologies is extremely important. It raises the question, Why do Jews appear only in Simeon-Tarbo materials? The answer obviously is that it was not merely a convention of Iranian Christian martyrologies to include references to Jewish persecution. A historical fact therefore probably underlies the tradition concerning the Jews in Simeon's case. But exactly what happened is difficult to say. The author's portrayal of events was shaped by the intent to present Simeon as a second Jesus, which is made explicit in the Jewish parts of the Simeon-martyrologies. This accounts for the inclusion of anachronistic materials about the slaughter of Maḥōzān Jews by Shapur's troops. The reference to a Jewish queen, furthermore, evidently reflects the Iranian traditions about Yazdegird's Jewish wife, supposedly the daughter of the exilarch. So the whole Jewish section (and much else as well) represents matters as they were known at the turn of the fifth century. The hagiographer would seem to have had a tradition that Jews were involved in Simeon's arrest and in pogroms staged by Magi and Jews against Seleucian

Christians. This he reshaped according to the materials he took for granted: a Jewish queen, the Jesus-Simeon typology, and the slaughter of Jewish messianists.[33]

33 Further bibliography:

Abbeloos, J.B., "Acta Mar Kardaghi, Assyriae Praefecti, Qui Sub Sapori II Martyr Occubuit," *AB* lead 9, 1890, pp. 5-106, contains no reference to Jews' participating in the interrogation or martyrdom. Jews are referred to in connection with the crucifixion (Chapter 29, p. 37), in a speech in which Satan refers to "the Jews our companions" (ḥbryn hywdy').

Assfalg, Julius, "Zur Textüberlieferung der Chronik von Arbela," *Oriens Christianus* 50, 1966, 19-36.

Baumstark, Anton, *Geschichte der syrischen Literatur* (Bonn, 1922), pp. 52-7 ; on Marutha of Maiperqat, p. 57.

Chabot, J.B., ed. and trans., *Synodicon Orientale. Ou Recueil de Synodes nestoriens* (Paris, 1902: *Notices et extraits des manuscrits de la Bibliothèque Nationale et autres bibliothèques*, vol. 37). Chabot dates the collection at 775-790. The first part, which interests us, consists of a document transmitted by Maruta of Martyropolis (Maipherqat) in 410. The report of the synod of Mar Isaac, in 410, attributed to Maruta, alludes to the restoration of peace and tranquillity by Yazdegird and to the persecution of the churches in the preceding period. No reference to the Jews' part in those persecutions occurs. On the Jews in the *Syndicon orientale*, see my *History*, V, p. 121-2, n. 4.

Christensen, Arthur, *L'Iran sous les sassanides* (Copenhagen, 1936[1]), p. 262-3.

Classen, Ioannis, ed., *Theophanis, Chronographia* (Bonn, 1839). In B.G. Niebuhr, ed., *Corpus Scriptorum Historiae Byzantinae.*

Delehaye, H., "SS. Ionae et Barachisii, Martyrum in Perside. Acta Graeca," *AB* 22, 1903, pp. 395-407. The martyrdom took place in 327. Jews are not mentioned in the account.

———, "S. Sadoth Episcopi Seleuciae et Ctesiphontis. Acta Graeca," *AB* 21, 1902, pp. 141-47. S. Sadoth died in Shapur's persecution, after Simeon, who appeared to him in a dream. Jews do not occur in the martyrology.

Devos, Paul, "Commemoraisons de martyrs persans dans le synaxaire de Lund," *AB* 81, 1963, pp. 143-58.

———, "Les Martyrs persans à travers leurs actes syriaques," *Accademia Nazionale dei Lincei* 363, 1966 (*Problemi Attuali di scienza e di cultura* 76). *Atti del covegno sul tema: La Persia e il mondo greco-romano (Roma, 11-14 April 1965)*, pp. 213-25; on Shapur II, pp. 221-25.

———, "Notes d'hagiographie perse," *AB* 84, 1966, pp. 229-48, on the names of martyrs in Sozomen's account. On Aphrahat and the beginning of the persecution of Shapur II, pp. 246-8; Devos comments on the views of Peeters and Kmosko.

———, "Le R.P. Paul Peeters. Son ouvre et sa personnalité de bollandiste," *AB* 69, 1951, pp. I-XLVIII, with a bibliography of Peeters' works.

———, "Sozomène et les Actes syriaques de saint Syméon bar Sabba'ē," *AB* 84, 1966, pp. 443-56, discusses Sozomen's sources. Sozomen supplies a resumé of his Syriac source, which is, in fact, the text in *Bibliotheca hagiographica orientalis* (Brussels, 1910), No. 1117.

Duval, Rubens, *La littérature syriaque* (Paris, 1900), pp. 129-47.

Fiey, J.M., *Assyrie Chrétienne. Contribution à l'étude de l'histoire et de la géographie ecclésiastiques et monastiques du nord de l'Iraq* (Beyrouth, I, 1965; II, 1965; III, 1968).

———," "Auteur et date de la Chronique d'Arbèles," *L'Orient Syrien* 12, 1967, pp. 265-302.

Fiey here reviews the controversies surrounding the work of A. Mingana, and, with reference to his Chronicle of Arbela, states, "Je crois de moins en moins à l'éxistence de ce manuscrit hypothetique. L'étude des sources nous convainc que l'écrivain de la Chronique possédait une bibliothèque qui ressemble beaucoup à celle du professeur de ·riaque au Séminaire St.-Jean entre 1902-1907 [= Mingana]."

The Chronicle's author cannot be Meshiha-Zkha, about whom absolutely nothing is known. The author did not live in the sixth century (between 550 and 569), as Mingana maintained. The author did not live in, or come from Arbela. The author was not even a Nestorian.

In all, Fiey raises such serious doubts about the authenticity of the Chronicle of Arbela and about the accuracy of its attribution to a sixth-century authority that one can no longer make use of it as evidence of the period of which it claims to give testimony, but rather as a piquant document in the history of modern Syriac scholarship.

I regret I did not see Fiey's article when revising my *History of the Jews in Babylonia, I. The Parthian Period* (Leiden, 1965[1], 1969[2]). Had I known it, I should have deleted the references to Meshiha Zkha, I[2], pp. 182-3, and dropped references to Arbela as an early Christian center.

—————, "Diocèses syriens orientaux du Golfe Persique," *Mémorial Msgr. Gabriel Khouri-Sarkis* (1898-1968), (Louvain, Imprimerie Orientaliste, 1969), pp. 177-219.

—————, "Notule de littérature syriaque, le démonstration XIV d'Aphraate, "*Le Muséon* 81, 1968, pp. 449-54.

—————, "Topography of al-Mada'in (Seleucia-Ctesiphon area)," *Sumer*, 23, 1967, pp. 3-38.

—————, *"Vers la réhabilitation de l'Histoire de Karka d'Bét Slôḥ,"* AB 82, 1964, pp. 189-222; on Shapur's persecution, pp. 203-8.

Follieri, Enrica, "Santi persiani nell'innografia bizantina," *Accademia Nazionale dei Lincei 363, 1966 (Problemi attuali di scienze e di cultura 76). Atti del convegno sul tema: La Persia e il mondo greco-romano (Roma, 11-14, Aprile 1965),* pp. 227-42.

Funk, Salomon, *Die haggadischen Elemente in den Homilien des Aphraates, des persischen Weisen* (Vienna, 1891), pp. 10-14.

Garitte, Gérard, "La version georgienne de l'Entretien VI d'Aphraate," *Le Muséon* 77, 1964, pp. 301-36.

Gentz, Günter, *Die Kirchengeschichte des Nicephorus Callistus Xanthopulus und ihre Quellen* (Berlin, 1966: *Texte und Untersuchungen zur Geschichte der altchristlichen Literatur*, v. 98). *Überarbeitet und erweitert von Friedhelm Winkelmann*). The account of Nicephorus about the persecution of Christianity and the Persian martyrs depends upon Sozomen and Theodoret (p. 85).

Gray, Louis H., "Two Armenian Passions of Saints in the Sasanian Period," *AB* 67, 1949, pp. 361-76. Re Bardisoy: Jews do not occur.

Hasse, Felix, *Altchristliche Kirchengeschichte* (Leipzig, 1925), p. 94-111.

Higgins, Martin J., "Aphraates' Dates for the Persian Persecution," *Byzantinische Zeitschrift* 44, 1951, pp. 265-71.

—————, "Chronology of the Fourth-Century Metropolitans of Seleucia-Ctesiphon," *Traditio* 9, 1953, pp. 45-99.

The results are as follows:

Simeon died at 31 Sapor II = 344-5 A.D.

Shahdost – 345 A.D.

Barbashmin – 346 A.D.

Vacancy – 33 years.

—————, *The Persian War of the Emperor Maurice (582-602). Part I. The*

Chronology, with a Brief History of the Persian Calendar (Washington, 1939: *Catholic University of America Byzantine Studies* v. I), pp. 17-8, on the chronology of the Syriac Acts of the Persian Martyrs. Two systems of dating were followed, one beginning with I Tishri, following the Julian calendar, and second, a lunar year.

Lenain de Tillemont, *Mémoires pour servir à l'histoire ecclésiastique des six premiers siècles* (Paris, 1700), VII, pp. 76-101, 236-42, surveys the Byzantine sources. This work is used more widely than it is cited.

Nau, F., "Un Martyrologe et douze ménologes syriaques," *Pat. Or.* 10, 1915, pp. 7-26. The martyrology, in Syriac, comes from a Greek original, of the period before 411, possibly as old as 362 (p. 7), probably from Nicomedia. The Syriac translation is not exact. Among the Oriental martyrs are Simeon, Barbashmin, Shahdost, bishops of Seleucia and Ctesiphon. The list contains no stories or details of the several martyrdoms.

Ortiz de Urbina, Ignatius, "Intorno al valore storico della Cronaca di Arbela," *Orientalia Christiana Periodica* 2, 1936, pp. 5-33.

————, *Patrologia Syriaca* (Rome, 1965), pp. 194-96.

Parmentier, Leon, ed., *Theodoret Kirchengeschichte* (Berlin, 1954: *Die griechischen chrislichen Schriftsteller der ersten Jahrhunderte.* Bearbeitet . . . von Felix Scheidweler): The letter of Constantine, pp. 76ff.

Peeters, Paul, *Bibliotheca Hagiographica Orientalis* (Brussels, 1910, repr. 1954).

————, "La date du martyre de S. Syméon archevêque de Séleucie-Ctésiphon," *AB* 56, 1938, pp. 118-34: The date is 341, not 344 as maintained by Kmosko.

————, "Le début de la persécution de Sapor d'après Fauste de Byzance," in Paul Peeters, *Recherches d'histoire et de philologie orientales*, I (Brussels, 1951), pp. 59-77 (= *Revue des études arméniennes* 1, 1920-21, pp. 15-33). In Chapters 16-17, Faustus discusses Shapur's relationships to Armenian Christianity. He alludes to the martyrdom of Mari and others. He does not mention Jews. The Magi are the chief counsellors of Shapur. Procopius silently bypasses the massacre of the Ctesiphon priests and Shapur's persecutions. The data supplied by Faustus point toward the date of 339 for the beginning of Shapur's persecution.

————, "S. Eleutherios-Gehištāzād," *AB* 29, 1910, pp. 150-6, distinguishes between the Gehištāzād of the Simeon-martyrology and the one who is mentioned in the Passion of SS. Nerses and Josephus (343 A.D.) in Karka deBeth Seloq. The latter is Eleutherios-Azad. The two were not one and the same man. The former was a high dignitary at the court of Shapur, executed by his master's order, and the second was at the house of the governor of Adiabene, and was condemned for refusing to obey the edict of Shapur; a third St. Azad was massacred in the royal palace. The several martyrologies contaminate one another. Sozomen and the other historians confuse the three.

————, "Le martyrologe de Rabban Sliba," *AB* 27, 1908, pp. 129-97.

————, *Orient et Byzance. Le Tréfonds oriental de l'hagiographie byzantine* (Brussels, 1950).

————, "Une Passion arménienne des SS. Abdas, Hormisdas, Sahin (Suenes) et Benjamin," *AB* 28, 1909, pp. 399-415.

————, "Le 'Passionnaire d'Adiabène,' " *AB* 43, 1925, pp. 261-304, *re* Shapur's persecutions in Beth Garmai: it was primarily at Arbela, the capital. The persecution came at the same time in Adiabene as in Seleucia-Ctesiphon.

————, "Traductions et traducteurs dans l'hagiographie orientale à l'époque byzantine," *AB* 40, 1922, pp. 241-98; p. 256: Pherbutha of the Greek Acts of the Persian Martyrs is Tharbo of the Syriac Acts.

Pigulevskaja, N., *Les villes de l'état iranien aux époques parthe et sassanide.*

Contribution à l'histoire sociale de la Basse Antiquité (Paris, 1963); *re* the persecutions, pp. 169-73.

Sachau, Eduard, "Von den rechtlichen Verhältnissen der Christen im Sasanidenreich," *Mitteilungen des Seminars für Orientalischen Sprachen zu Berlin*, 10, ii (Berlin, 1907).

——————, "'Zur Ausbreitung des Christentums in Asien," *Abhandlungen der preussischen Akademie der Wissenschaften* 1919 (Phil.-Hist. Klasse 1), 1-79.

Séd, Nicolas, "Les hymnes sur le paradis de Saint Ephrem et les traditions juives," *Le Muséon* 81, 1968, pp. 455-501.

Theodoret, *Church History*, Book V, Chapter 39 (Cambridge, 1720), pp. 239-41. concerning the persecutions of Yazdegird, contains no reference to Jews.

Uhlmann, F., "Die Christenverfolgungen in Persien unter der Herrschaft der Sassaniden im vierten und fünften Jahrhundert," *Zeitschrift für die historische Theologie* 31, 1861, pp. 3-162, retells the stories of the various martyrs, without adding anything.

Vailhé, S., "Formation de l'Église de Perse, *Echoes d'Orient* 12, 1910, pp. 269-75.

Vööbus, Arthur, *History of Asceticism in the Syrian Orient . . . I. The Origin of Asceticism, Early Monasticism in Persia* (Louvain, 1958: Corpus Scriptorum Christianorum Orientalium, vol. 184, Subsidia vol. 14).

Wright, William, *A Short History of Syriac Literature* (London, 1894); on Simeon bar Sabba'ē's letters, pp. 30-1.

The author acknowledges with thanks the critical comments of Professors Horst R. Moehring, Brown University; Morton Smith, Columbia University; Geza Vermes, Oxford University; and Samuel Sandmel, Hebrew Union College–Jewish Institute of Religion. This study was undertaken with the support of Brown University, which granted the author a sabbatical leave in 1970-1971, and the American Council of Learned Societies, which provided a research fellowship in the same year. Brown University further bore research and typing expenses. For this support the author is especially grateful.

RABBIS AND COMMUNITY IN THIRD CENTURY BABYLONIA

BY

JACOB NEUSNER
Brown University

I

The Babylonian rabbis played no special role in the life of the synagogue. They exercised no sacerdotal functions. While some of them, notably Rav and Samuel, composed prayers, we have no way of knowing how widely, if at all, rabbinic liturgies were accepted in synagogues during their lifetimes. Many of these, for instance blessings to be said before eating various kinds of food, and the Grace after Meals, probably were initially recited in the school house alone, even there posing some complex difficulties for the students, as we shall see. In any event, the rabbis did not normally recite the services, read from the Torah, bless the people, or assume any other sacerdotal duties which set them apart from, and above, the people in the synagogue. While they quite naturally praised synagogue prayer, they held that *their* studies were more important. R. Ḥisda (late 3rd century), for example, explained (Ps. 87.2), "The Lord loveth the gates of Zion [ẓiyyon]" to mean that the Lord loves the gates distinguished [meẓuyan-im] through law [halakhah] *more* than synagogues and houses of study, and similarly we have the following sayings:

> Abaye said, "At first I used to study in my house and pray in the synagogue. Since I heard the saying of R. Ḥiyya b. 'Ammi in the name of 'Ulla, 'Since the day that the Temple was destroyed, the Holy One, blessed be He, has nothing in his world but the four cubits of the law alone,' I pray only in the place where I study..." Rav Sheshet used to turn his face to another side and study [during the public reading of the Torah], saying, "We with our [business], and they with theirs."
>
> (Bab. Talmud Berakhot 8a)

A contemporary of Rav Sheshet, R. Naḥman, said that he found it too much trouble to gather ten people in his home to permit him to engage in public prayer even there.[1] The rabbis' attitude was based

---

[1] Bab. Talmud, Berakhot 7b.

in part upon the theological presupposition, expressed many times from the first century A.D. onwards, that study of the Torah was the highest religious action, exceeding in sanctity the sacrifice of the Temple priests. Since Temple sacrifice had been replaced for the present age by synagogue worship, it was quite natural for the rabbis to regard their studies, particularly of law, as more important than synagogue prayer.

At the same time, it is quite likely that the rabbis in this period disapproved of aspects of synagogue affairs, but, possessing no power to change things to suit themselves, merely tolerated the status quo. We have a number of stories which indicate rabbinical objection to synagogue practices, not merely concerning which prayers were said at a given time, or whether the Torah was to be blessed before it was read, but more significantly, involving the presence in the synagogue of mosaics and statues. The chief sources are as follows:

> Was there not the synagogue which 'moved and settled' in Nehardea and in it was a statue [andarta[1])], and Rav and Samuel and Samuel's father used to go in there to pray...
>
> (Bab. Talmud Rosh Hashanah 24b)

> Rav happened to be in Babylonia on a public fast. The whole congregation fell on their faces, but Rav did not fall on his face. Why did Rav not fall on his face? There was a stone pavement there, and it has been taught, 'Neither shall you place any figured stone in your land to bow down upon it' (Lev. 26.1). Upon it you may *not* bow down in your land, but you may prostrate yourselves on the stones in the Temple. ...If that is the case, why is only Rav mentioned? All the rest should equally have abstained? ...
>
> (Bab. Talmud Megillah 22b[2])

> Rav once came to Babylonia, and noticed that they recited the Hallel on the New Moon festival. At first he thought of stopping them, but when he saw that they omitted parts of it, he remarked, 'It is clear that it is an old ancestral custom with them.'
>
> (Bab. Talmud Ta'anit 28b)

---

[1]) See Bab. Talmud 'Avodah Zarah 40b and Shabbat 72b (Sanhedrin 62b). In the latter discussion, bowing down to an *andarta* (carved image of a man) is not regarded as idolatry if the man did not regard it as a god. In the former, Samuel interprets the Tanna, R. Meir's prohibition of "all images" to include, quite explicitly, a royal statue. In any event, whether the rabbis permitted the placement of such a statue or not, it was clearly *not* they who instigated it, and the tenor of the Talmudic discussions leaves no doubt on that score.

[2]) Note that in the same source, it is reported Rav refrained from following the congregational practice in blessing the Torah. The geonic traditions *ad loc.*, say that later on, the synagogue floor-mosaics were covered up with dirt.

But we do not know what would have happened had Rav attempted to change their liturgy. In any event, it is possible that Rav did not approve of the mosaic, and quite clear that he would not prostrate himself upon it, but did not have the power to remove it. Despite the presence of a statue, Rav, Samuel, and Samuel's father prayed in a famous old synagogue in Nehardea, the town in which Samuel's father and, after him, Samuel himself were the rabbinical authorities. None of the three rabbis apparently had power over the synagogue's affairs. It stands to reason, therefore, that the synagogues in Sura and Nehardea were not subject to rabbinical control. And it was in these very cities that the rabbis lived, taught, and judged.

The situation in Palestine differed not at all. Sukenik long ago pointed out[1]) that pictorial representations of animals and human beings occurred with extraordinary frequency in Galilean synagogues and elsewhere:

> A theory was evolved that the synagogues found were the work of sections of Galilean Jewry which took a more liberal view of the matter than the orthodox authorities. It was realized, however, that so widespread a lack of discipline as is indicated by the number of such synagogues was rather extraordinary in Galilee, the centre of Jewish national and religious life in those times.[2])

Sukenik held that there were those who held a more lenient view of Exodus 20:4 and Deuteronomy 5:8; in such a view these verses prohibit the worshipping of images only, and the latitudinarian tendency prevailed in normal times, while in crisis, "particularistic and rigoristic views prevailed." Thus Sukenik held that "pictorial art had its ups and downs... a period of greater laxity being followed by a reaction..."[3]) Goodenough argued, however, that while the rabbis of a given period may have *permitted* one or another kind of ornament, the groups that *created* the art could not have been rabbis at all:

> Where are we to find the moving cause in the taking over of images, and with what objective were they taken over?...[4])
> Even if some rabbis tolerated such an image, the implication is that they were far from taking the initiative in introducing anything of this kind.[5])

---

[1]) E. L. Sukenik, *Ancient Synagogues in Palestine and Greece*, (London, 1934) being the Schweich Lectures of the British Academy for 1930, 61-67.

[2]) *ibid.*, 62.

[3]) *ibid.*, 63-4.

[4]) *Jewish Symbols in the Greco-Roman Period* (N.Y. 1953) IV, 10.

[5]) *ibid.*, 15.

The rabbis did not *prohibit* paintings on walls,[1]) and they did not *hinder* their contemporaries from making designs in mosaic.[2]) They were not however, the people who directed the design of murals for walls and mosaics for floors, as Goodenough said, "the decorations... express a mood and a religious attitude which rabbinic Judaism...at best only grudgingly tolerated, [but] never itself championed or advocated."[3])

The limited evidence cited above, all of which Goodenough knew, should suggest, however, that Babylonia was not so different from Palestine as he conceived.[4]) He thought that the Jews in Babylonia were dominated by the rabbis, and in some ways, as we shall see, they were. But it is quite clear that all the evidence we have, slight though it is, and tentative though is our reading of it, points in one direction: the 3rd century Babylonian rabbis controlled synagogue affairs, including their decoration, no more effectively than did Palestinian rabbis. Goodenough understood Dura to have been a representation of Judaism before the "halakhic reforms" of Rav and his colleagues. Yet these reforms took place well before the second paintings at Dura were completed in 246; Rav died, according to the Ge'onic chronology, in 247.

In fact Goodenough assumed, before he wrote volume XII of *Jewish Symbols*, a thorough-going dichotomy between Hellenistic and rabbinic Judaism. With this assumption in mind, he had to accept available descriptions of Babylonian Judaism as wholly rabbinic in the narrowest sense. Being unable to find a rabbinic center in the Greco-Roman world, he simply assumed it was, as the works he consulted said, on the other side of the Euphrates. His survey of rabbinic views of iconography[5]) should have suggested the contrary, and I think had he lived he may have revised his view of Babylonian Judaism, just as in vol. XII he modified his idea of the relationships between rabbinic and Hellenistic Judaism. He would, I think, have subscribed to the view of Professor Judah Goldin:

> This need not necessarily suggest that the Judaism reflected by midrashic-talmudic sources is unrepresentative of Judaism of the time, nor that the artifacts demonstrate the existence of a different kind of

---

[1]) Yer. Talmud 'Avodah Zarah 3.3.
[2]) Cit. by J. H. Epstein, *Tarbiz* 3, 1931, 20.
[3]) Goodenough, *Symbols*, IV, 24.
[4]) *ibid.*, I 13f.
[5]) *ibid.*, IV, 1, Ch. 2.

Judaism; but perhaps current interpretations of rabbinic sources are still too narrowly, too partially formed. Even the literary texts may reveal hitherto only partially understood details when the realities this art reflects are taken into account.[1])

An example of such a revision of the interpretation of literary texts in the light of archaeological realities will be found in Professor Morton Smith's *Image of God*.[2]) If one accepts the interpretation of the literary texts provided in *Image of God*, he must admit that the people who produced these texts might well have 'instigated' the sort of decoration found in the synagogues. Goodenough's assertion to the contrary is not completely convincing in the light of Smith's study. The texts he discusses show a very vivid verbal symbolism. Similarly, Goodenough never confronted the question of how the rabbis and their followers faced the existential issues of salvation and immortality, which the groups who made use of pictorial symbolism confronted in a mystical manner. Given the stress upon acquiring the world to come which one finds in Talmudic sayings, I find it difficult to distinguish the fundamental concerns of these groups. One cannot overstress, therefore, the importance of Goldin's statement.

Even if the texts cited above prove that the rabbis opposed synagogue decorations, as it seems to me they may indicate, they *still* have not been subjected to a form-critical study. These are, after all, sixth century collections of material about third-century rabbis. One needs to ask which traditions were preserved for what purposes, and which were purposefully, or accidentally, suppressed, lost, or revised. The notion that third-century rabbis must have disapproved of synagogue frescoes or incantation bowls is not, therefore, proven. I offer it as a working hypothesis, subject to considerable revision. I do not know how we shall achieve a history of the traditions without first composing, however tentatively, a history of the Babylonian Jews and the tendencies, issues, and ideas characteristic of each period in that history. Upon such a basis, one can isolate later tendencies which may have caused earlier traditions to be revised. A provisional history must be subjected to continual revisions, but it must, nonetheless, be attempted, if a history of the traditions is to emerge at all. So I have argued in "In Quest of the Historical Rabban Yoḥanan ben Zakkai" [*Harvard Theological Review*, Oct., 1966], and the same argument applies here.

---

[1]) Charles J. Adams, ed., *A Reader's Guide to the Great Religions* (N.Y. 1965) 209-210.

[2]) *Bulletin of the John Rylands Library* 40, 2, 1958, 473-512.

II

If the Babylonian rabbis did not play a special role in the life of the synagogue, being unable even to effect their wishes in the ornamentation of synagogue buildings, as is quite possible in Dura, Nehardea, and Sura, then what was the basis of their authority? Were they *ever* able to effect their policies? The question is not whether there was a widespread lack of discipline or not, but rather, In *which* areas of life were the Jews of Babylonia subjected to rabbinical discipline at all? And how can we know?[1])

Our only extensive source is the Babylonian Talmud, mostly a legal document, the Babylonian part of which consists mainly of discussions of the Mishnah. These discussions provide explication of Mishnaic and external traditions on given point in law, inquiry into the authorities for given laws, and, in part, comparison of the legal views of two or more authorities. None of this material can, on the face of it, be used as evidence concerning the sociology of Babylonian Jewry. Even legal questions asked in the academies do not necessarily reflect the social conditions of the time, for we have no way of knowing which questions were devised for, or emerged from, theoretical discussion, and which were actually the result of the circumstances of day-to-day life. One kind of evidence, however, is of inestimable value, the reports of cases decided in rabbinical courts, or of questions brought to the rabbis by ordinary people. Laymen cannot be supposed to have devised such inquiries for purposes of logical or rhetorical exercise, but rather asked them because they needed the answers for practical reasons. If we have no way of knowing how much of Mishnaic law, and the legal doctrines arising from it, actually influenced the life of the people, we have at least the corpus of cases and popular inquiries.

We are not helped by the language of the Talmud. I think it most likely that the rabbis used Hebrew to preserve and transmit fixed legal dicta, while Aramaic (apart from a few fixed, rhetorical forms) was most likely used for more practical matters; e.g. most of the case reports are in Aramaic. (My research, however, does not as yet justify the assertion as a fixed rule that Aramaic usage invariably connotes a practical decision.) Further, the language of the rabbis' discourse does not vary, whether the subject is theoretical or wholly practical. For example, late-third-century Babylonian rabbis held that heathens are to be

---

[1]) See my *History of the Jews in Babylon*, II. *The Early Sasanian Period* (Leiden, 1966) ch. 8, pp. 251–287.

executed for violating the seven Noachide laws;[1]) they discussed what
is to be done to the layman who sacrificed the Red Heifer, a rite not
carried out, quite obviously, after 70, and only a few times before then;
and numerous other very serious discussions on sacrifical laws and
Temple procedures took place. Further theoretical questions were
considered, for instance, "How do we know that when one offers a
sacrifice without proper intention, it is invalid?"[2]) Other laws, such as
the following, could not have been enforced even by a vast, totalitarian
government.

> Rav said, "A man who wilfully causes an erection is to be placed under
> the ban."
>
> (Bab. Talmud Niddah 13a)
>
> Samuel said, "The domestic and wild goose are forbidden copulation."
> (Bab. Talmud Bekhorot 8a)
>
> Rav said, "It is forbidden to sleep by day more than a horse's sleep."
> (Bab. Talmud Sukkah 20b)

The legal sources cannot, therefore, be used indiscriminately to
provide testimony about the conditions of daily life.

The rabbis and the exilarch whom they served (see below) did not
have at their disposal means of physical coercion, except in very clearly
specified areas of law. The Sasanians were not at all willing for the Jews
to govern themselves without imperial supervision. On the contrary,
at the very outset of their rule, they made it clear that the Jewish courts
would be closely watched, expected to explain their actions to the
government, and required to conform to Sasanian law. Moreover,
Jews could easily leave the Jewish community, and some did when
confronted with rabbinic excommunication for Sabbath breaking.[3])
None of this proves that the rabbis had no authority whatever. It
should indicate, however, that Goodenough's critique of the view
that the Palestinian patriarchal apostles governed the whole Roman
diaspora applies with equal force to the Babylonian rabbis' relationships to their community. Without armies or police, merely tolerated
by the new regime, the third-century Babylonian rabbis depended, in
the end, upon the actual willingness of Jews to obey the law, because it
had been revealed by God to Moses on Mount Sinai and was authori-

---

[1]) Bab. Talmud Sanhedrin 57a.
[2]) Bab. Talmud Zevahim 46b.
[3]) See my *History of the Jews in Babylonia, I. The Parthian Period*, (Leiden 1965)
147-8.

tatively exposited and applied by them; upon the inertial force of accepted authority; and upon the willingness of the Persian government to allow them to govern some specific areas of life. The issue of rabbinic authority is therefore considerably more complicated than has been recognized.

The matter is made more difficult still by the one-sidedness of our evidence. Rabbinic sources mostly suppress or report only by indirection actions contrary to rabbinic dicta, and where such reports occur, it is only because the rabbis tell how they punished a law-violator. The two great bodies of independent archaeological evidence from Mesopotamia, the Dura synagogue and the incantation bowls, provide striking evidence that the masses of people were not living entirely in conformity to rabbinic law, but engaged in religious and magical activities which the rabbis might at best have tolerated, but which they would never in the first place have approved. When we review their sermons, moreover, we find considerable evidence that people displeased the rabbis. That, of course, is nothing new, nor can we discount the preacher's love for hyperbole. But when the rabbis preach against those who defer payment of a worker's wages, withhold wages entirely, cheat on communal taxes, behave arrogantly, and so forth, it is difficult to believe that they had the power to do more than curse the sinner and encourage penitence. Living in Babylonia were Jews who did not put on phylacteries, who did not meet the rabbis' standards for ethical economic and moral behavior, and who did not even respect the rabbis. Rav said that the blessings of the world to come are denied—a fearful threat—to anyone who insulted a scholar.[1]) We rarely, if ever, hear what those insults were, or why the rabbis were so exasperated about them. If, as we are told, an inhabitant of Naresh kisses you, count your teeth; if a Pumbeditan accompanies you, change your lodging; if thieves in Pumbedita open many casks of wine, the wine is not prohibited as it would be if it had been touched by an idolator, because the majority of thieves there are Jews.[2]) Such people as these are obviously not described by Mishnaic laws or academic discussions. And we do not know about the masses, who were neither learned academicians nor criminals.

It is hardly reasonable, moreover, to talk of the 'halakhic reforms' of Rav as if these greatly changed, in a very few years, the ancient patterns of Babylonian Jewish life. The rabbis were few in number.

---

[1]) Bab. Talmud Sanhedrin 99b.
[2]) Bab. Talmud Ḥullin 127a, 'Avodah Zarah 70a.

They were concentrated in central Babylonia itself. Elam produced students, but no teachers. Mesene was in such a state that the rabbis prohibited intermarriage between Jews from the south and those in Babylonia. Few rabbis, if any, came from Adiabene (which may by then have been Christian) and Armenia. The very instruments for the propagation and application of rabbinic laws were probably unavailable in the outlying districts. I estimate that there were from 600,000 to one million Jews in Babylonia in this period. We know the names of a handful of rabbis; certainly there were many others, but students and teachers together could not have amounted to over a thousand. Later on, the influence of the rabbis spread, as the academies grew in strength, and as large numbers of people attended their semi-annual adult-study sessions. But for the third century I have found very little evidence that the great masses of Babylonian Jewry always or even mostly conformed to Mishnaic law as expounded by the rabbis.

How then can we know which halakhic sayings affected the life of the people? As I said, minimal, but highly significant, evidence is to be derived from case reports and popular questions addressed to the rabbis. There are numerous such reports, and these are by no means scattered at random in the legal literature. Naturally, none at all exist on the laws pertaining to the Temple cult. But some of the laws did yield court cases, and while none can argue that *only* that law was enforced which produced judicial records, I think it clear that *at the very least*, here are areas of the common life which the rabbis did supervise.

Some of the laws were obeyed because the people believed that they were commanded by God. I did not expect that among these would be the laws about separating priestly gifts, and it is probable that whatever tithes were set aside, tithing ended after 260.[1] But we have the story that Rav Ḥisda held in his possession the tithe of cattle,[2] which suggests that some people even later gave priests their due. Samuel, moreover, fined a man for disobeying the laws on mixed seeds[3] and Levi received a question, on 'mixed seeds' in a vineyard, asked by the citizens of Bashkar. The agricultural taboos would have been obeyed where they were explicit and well known, and held by the masses, contrary to Mishnah Qiddushin 1:9, to be valid even outside of Palestine. Hence a close study of such laws, as exposited by the rabbis, would be sociologically significant.

---

[1]) Evidence is cited in my *History*, II, chapter II.
[2]) Bab. Talmud Shabbat 10b.
[3]) Yer. Talmud 'Orlah 3.7.

Those laws which were actually enforced by the rabbis mainly concerned property matters. As a general rule, one can say that wherever exchange of property was involved, as in trade, real estate dealings, torts and damages, marriage and divorce, there the rabbis exerted full and unchallenged authority. It is, moreover, quite natural to suppose that this should be the case. What the farmers did on their farms would not normally come under the supervision of the rabbis, nor what the women did in their kitchens, nor what husbands and wives did in their beds (though, as we shall see, the menstrual taboos were widely observed). Transfers of property, in *any* form, were quite another matter. They had to be regulated by public authorities; documents had to be properly written and registered, and the rabbis and their scribes were the official registrars of such documents. Transfer of property required public authorization, recognition, and confirmation. It was the rabbis, acting for the exilarchate, who supervised property transfers. When the people came to them, the rabbis had a splendid opportunity to act as they thought proper. As judges, they had no difficulty in enforcing the law. Still they did not have an entirely free hand. Practices which the people accepted, such as the writing of a *prosbul*, could not be easily changed. (Samuel said that if he could, he would abolish it.[1]) He never did.) Where transfer of property was concerned, there people could find absolutely no way to avoid the rabbinical courts.

Transfers of inheritance and the execution of wills posed numerous knotty problems. Questions were addressed from outlying parts on the matter,[2] and many cases came to the courts.[3] There is no reason to doubt that the great corpus of civil law, in the tractates Bava' Qama', Bava' Meẓi'a, and Bava' Batra', mostly contains practical, not merely theoretical, law. Moreover, the rabbis' decisions on proper acquisition of property sometimes overrode ancient custom:

> A certain lady had usufruct of a date-tree...A man came and hoed underneath it a little, and claimed ownership. He asked Levi, who confirmed title to the land. The woman complained bitterly. He said, "What can I do for you, for you did not establish your title properly?"
>
> (Bab. Talmud Bava' Batra' 54a)

In this case, the woman had assumed she owned the tree for thirteen years, and until someone, probably better informed than she, challenged

---

[1]) Bab. Talmud Gittin 36b.
[2]) Bab. Talmud Bava' Batra' 127b and 152b, to Samuel, for example.
[3]) Bab. Talmud Bava' Batra' 143a.

her, no one assumed to the contrary. Hence it stands to reason that the average person identified usufruct with possession. The rabbis, (at least superficially) for exegetical reasons disagreed, and when they came to apply Mishnaic law, they were able by *force majeure* to sustain their decisions. For their part, they made great efforts to publicize the law, encouraging people to avoid purchasing lands under disputed title, publicly teaching how to acquire cattle, fields, trees, and so forth. Nonetheless, cases came before them daily,[1] dealing with land, claims for loss and damages,[2] and the like.

We have a number of instances, moreover, where a firm legal dictum was stated in the name of one or another of the rabbis, and challenged in dialectical argument, whereupon it was admitted that Rav or Samuel never made such a statement, but rather the disciples deduced what they *thought* was the rabbi's legal dictum on the basis of observation of an action. These cases invariably occur in matters involving transfer of property, mainly in civil and commercial law, rather than in liturgical, ritual, cultic or agricultural law. The legal sayings of the rabbis on dormant matters, such as the cult, or on theoretical issues, did not give rise to any such speculation upon the basis of an observed action. It was only where the law actually applied to daily affairs that the rabbis' actions could be subjected to close scrutiny. And these cases, for Rav and Samuel, all concerned civil law.

By contrast to the substantial number of civil suits reported by the Talmud to have been adjudicated by the rabbis, I know of not a single criminal, and certainly no capital, action reported as a precedent, described as a case at trial, or otherwise mentioned in a historically credible setting in the time of Rav and Samuel. There are two cases in which criminal action seems to be implied. In the first, a 'man wanted to show another's straw' to the government for taxation; in the second, a man had intercourse with a gentile woman. But these two cases provide no striking exceptions, for they actually involved political, and not judicial, policy, and prove (in the second case) that the Jews could not in fact freely inflict the death penalty once the Sasanians took power, although they could and did in Parthian times. (The former case entailed at best civil damages, but political circumstance transformed it into a more serious matter. This matter is fully discussed in my *History*, II. Ch. 2. i, pp. 27–35). We have many sayings on criminal law and procedure, but no cases showing that the rabbis' courts ever judged such

---

[1] Bab. Talmud Bava' Batra' 110b.
[2] Bab. Talmud Bava' Qama' 11a, Bava' Meẓi'a' 13b, etc.

cases. Since criminal cases must have arisen, we can best assume that the Sasanians' courts tried them for the most part.

Laws of personal status were enforced in the rabbinical courts, and I think the reason is the same as that given above: the legality of a marriage and the legitimacy (for purposes of inheritance, for instance) of offspring involved not merely private acquiescence but also public recognition, because the drawing up of documents and, frequently, property-transfers were involved. On the other hand, the rabbis' *obiter dicta* could not have meant much. For example, Rav preached that a barren marriage must be annulled after two and one-half years, but we have no case in which such a law was enforced.[1]) The rabbis did use their power to flog to enforce good public morals; they discouraged betrothal by cohabitation, or in the open street, or without previous negotation. Since they were believed to have accurate physiological and medical information, their judgments on the legitimacy of children were respected. Divorce procedures, in which property always was an issue, yielded many cases, though even here[2]) the peoples' pattern of behavior took precedence over rabbinic opinion in some matters. The rabbis' power, however, depended not upon popular acquiescence, though it was considerable, but upon the coercive capabilities of their courts, and upon the practical consequences of the decrees these might issue.

It was the Bible which shaped the religious life of the masses. The rabbis did not need to urge the people to keep biblical laws. Popular practice may have required rabbinical supervision over the ways the commandments were carried out. Where biblical laws and rabbinical interpretations were clear, well-known, and widely accepted, there the rabbis merely guided the affairs of the people, who brought them their queries. Where rabbinical injunctions were not widely accepted, there the rabbis relied upon coercion when they could, or upon public instruction in their view of the biblical requirements. The construction of 'eruvin, for example, was in the hands of the rabbis, and the laws pertaining to Sabbath-limits were therefore enforced by them.

This is not to suggest that the greater part of the people was so meticulously observant as the rabbis would have liked. Tension between a class of religious virtuosi and the masses of their followers is certainly a common phenomenon in the history of religions. But because they knew the Bible, the Jewish masses proved amenable to

---

1) Bab. Talmud Yevamot 64b.
2) Bab. Talmud Yevamot 102a.

the guidance of the rabbis, especially when the rabbis could base their decisions upon convincing Scriptural exegesis. Three kinds of ritual law were rigorously obeyed, those dealing with slaughter of animals, menstrual separation, and the Sabbath. In all three, the rabbis were frequently consulted. The menstrual taboos were probably universally observed because the Bible is explicit about them, and the rabbis were frequently consulted about how to keep them. The Sabbath was either publicly observed, or publicly profaned, and the rabbis did not have to wait to be consulted. They aggressively punished Sabbath breaking, and the people doubtless expected them to do so, because of the well-known biblical precedents. We do not know how the Sabbath laws were kept in areas not under rabbinical influence. We have, however, numerous inquiries from distant places, and from students who would have carried the rabbis' influence far beyond the academies. By contrast, since the rabbis had no special function in synagogue affairs, and no authority over them, they had to tolerate popular practice, which was based upon very ancient, tenacious, and widely accepted traditions.

Insight into the level of popular knowledge may be derived from the questions referred to above, of the citizens of Bashkar to Levi: "What about setting a canopy on the Sabbath, what about cuscuta in a vineyard, what about a dead man on a festival?" The first was prohibited, the second permitted, and the third elicited the reply that the burial of the corpse had to be held over to a weekday. These are fairly basic matters, and the simple inquiry would suggest that the people would have been unaware of other such laws.[1]) Unless they sent an inquiry or received a pastoral visit, the rabbis could not censure them. For the rest, as we have seen, the rabbis were relatively powerless:

> Rav saw a man sowing flax on Purim, and he cursed him, so the flax would not grow.
>
> (Bab. Talmud Megillah 5b)

Doubtless the rabbis' prestige far outweighed their powers of coercion, for people believed in the rabbis' curses.

On the other hand, the rabbinical viewpoint was quite easily enforced among their own students. Such laws included mourning and burial practice, blessings before and after meals, and the like. In these,

---

[1]) Yet I am not entirely persuaded that the "men of Bashkar" were not simply the local group of rabbinical disciples, rather than the leaders of the whole community.

we have questions addressed to the rabbis *only* by students, and the single case of enforcement of burial rites involved an academician. A student of Samuel had intercourse during a period of mourning; Samuel heard and was angry, and the student died. It is likely that many would prefer to obey a rabbi than to risk his curse or some worse results.

No legal system could depend for enforcement upon the success of curses, barren flax-seeds, and the like. The many stories in which a rabbi's curse was sufficient to bring down punishment upon the head of a recalcitrant Jew—invariably cases *not* involving property-transfers —reveal that in these matters, only the curse, and *not* court action, was available for enforcing the laws. The laws the breaking of which was punished by rabbinical curses were probably, therefore, those which rabbinical courts could not otherwise have adjudicated; or which were not subject to popular inquiries addressed to the rabbis about proper observance.

Reference has been made to liturgical dicta. Within their academies the rabbinical authority was unlimited. Hence we have numerous cases, all taking place in the school house or among disciples, in which a disciple made a mistake in saying grace, in which the proper posture during a given prayer was discussed and demonstrated, or in which some detail was elucidated for a questioning disciple. But we have only one liturgical case in which a non-academician was involved:

> Benjamin the shepherd made a sandwich and said, 'Blessed be the master of this bread,' and Rav said that he had performed his oligation.
> (Bab. Talmud Berakhot 40b)

Rav's judgment was very lenient, for he did not require the normal formula of the blessing. Since the rabbis' disciples found great difficulty in understanding and carrying out the laws of saying grace (Rav's students after his funeral lamented that they still had problems with them), it stands to reason that the common people would have found it quite impossible, without the elaborate education by precept and example provided in the academies, to do precisely the right thing. If this were so in the everyday act of blessing food, one may reasonably suppose that more difficult or unusual matters were quite remote from public comprehension, let alone observance.

As the students were trained and went to their homes, and as judges were sent out from the academies to various villages and towns, the legal doctrines of the rabbis radiated into the common life. This was not a process completed in one generation, nor was the transformation of the people's life effected by a few men alone. It took many centuries before Babylonian Jewry in the mass came to approximate rabbinical ideas of how religious, social, and personal affairs should be conducted. For my part, I do not knew precisely when it was the case that rabbinical law accurately described popular conduct. But it was not in the third century. One cannot conceive that before the foundation of Babylonian rabbinical academies, in consequence of the Bar Kokhba war, Babylonian Jewry possessed neither laws nor authoritative doctrines. During the six preceding centuries, indigenous traditions of law, exegesis, and probably doctrine, were surely cultivated. It could not have been otherwise. Babylonian Jews married, bore children and educated them, divided their estates and litigated their affairs, celebrated the festivals and Sabbath, and pursued the many matters which required legal adjudication, producing a rich corpus of precedents, long before the first rabbi appeared in their midst. What is remarkable therefore is that in the third century anything changed at all, for the inertia of earlier centuries must have made the process of social and legal change painful indeed. The available cases suggest that it was mainly where the rabbis were able to apply very specific judicial-administrative pressures that matters were influenced by them.

III

If so, then one must ask, What was the basis of the rabbis' power? The later, acute tension between the rabbis and the exilarch has obscured the obvious fact that in this period, most of the rabbis were agents of the exilarch, acting under his authority, and fully respectful of his person, his office, and his prerogatives. It is true that when Rav returned to Babylonia, he got into trouble with the exilarch for refusing to enforce his decree regulating market-prices; but Rav was the *agoranomos*, or market supervisor, by virtue of exilarchic appointment, and was forced, by imprisonment, to do just as the exilarch said. Samuel, for his part, recognized the superior status of the court of Mar'Uqba, exilarch of his time,[1] as well as its superior authority.[2] Samuel apparently regarded his chief function, however, as instructional, while Mar'Uqba's was judicial:

---

[1] Bab. Talmud Shabbat 55a. See my *History*, II, chapter III, pp. 92-125 and III, pp. 41-94.

[2] Bab. Talmud Qiddushin 44b.

When they were sitting together [at the school house] Mar'Ubqa sat
before him at a distance of four cubits, and when they sat together at
a judicial session, Samuel sat before him at a distance of four cubits, and
a place was dug out for Mar'Uqba where he sat on a matting so that
he should be heard. Every day Mar'Uqba accompanied Samuel to his
house. One day he was engrossed in a law-suit, and Samuel walked
behind him. When he had reached his house, Samuel said to him, 'Have
you not been rather a long time at it? Now take up my case!' He
realized that Samuel was angry, and submitted himself to 'reproof' for
one day.

(Bab. Talmud Mo'ed Qatan 16b)

Mar'Uqba cited Samuel's teachings on medicine, on judicial procedure, on the preparation of the 'eruv, and other matters, while Samuel
was guardian for the children of Mar 'Uqba after his death. The two
men got on well together. Samuel taught law to the exilarch, who
could not have had so extensive a legal training as the rabbi, while
the exilarch honored him and submitted to his pedagogical authority.
Mar 'Uqba had a good name for his generosity toward the poor, his
learning, and his meticulous honesty. Rav and Samuel both explicitly
stated that if a person wished to decide monetary cases without liability
in case of judicial error, he had to obtain the sanction of the exilarch.[1]
For his part, the exilarch employed Qarna, Levi, Rav, and Samuel in
his administration. Apart from the difference with Rav, based upon
the latter's adherence to Palestinian traditions (and, one supposes, his
ordination there), there is no evidence of tension between the exilarch
and rabbis, and certainly not with the rabbis as a group. The exilarch
was not an ignorant figurehead, but a powerful, learned man. As chief
judge, the exilarch was, by analogy to the *Erpatan Erpat* of the
Mazdean church, certainly head of the Jewish community.

To suppose, moreover, that the sages' rulings were based not upon
the authority of the exilarch, but upon their own, requires an absurd
postulate. One would have to conjecture that there were two separate
systems of Jewish government in the troubled times of early Sasanian
Babylonia, one run by the rabbis, the other by the exilarch. There was
no question in the Sasanians' mind that minority groups, including the
Jews, should continue to govern their own affairs. But their supervision of the Jewish courts suggests that they would surely intervene
if matters developed contrary to their will. If they approved the
continuing rule of the exilarch under specified conditions, it is hardly

---

[1] Bab. Talmud Sanhedrin 5a.

likely that they would have also permitted the development of a second competing administration. Their politics required hierarchical centralization, in their own chancery, of all power, and the careful parcelling out of authority where necessary to specified bureaus and officials. It is inconceivable that they would have allowed the Jews to be subjected to competing authorities, and not to a single, hierarchical regime like their own. And, as we have seen, the actions of the rabbinical courts depended upon the willingness of the imperial regime to back up their decisions in exclusively practical cases. If the rabbi's decisions on the transfer of property were to be enforced, they must have been made with the consent of the Persian regime. If they were free of the danger of having to make restitution, it was certainly with Persian *and* exilarchic approval. The contrary would have been impossible, for the aggrieved party could simply repair to the imperial court, which, if the action was unauthorized or illegal, would doubtless reverse the decision, and probably also punish the 'judge' who made it. Moreover, the Persians collected taxes not from individuals but by millets or communities. The exilarch was responsible for collecttion of these taxes, as was the Christian *catholicus*. The sages had to collect the poll-tax in their own towns, and they must have done so as agents of the exilarch. The only Jewish judges in Babylonia whose decision could have stood, therefore, were exilarchic appointees, as Rav and Samuel explicitly stated.[1])

At the same time, the rabbis acted far more than merely as agents of the exilarch. They clearly possessed a law-code regarded by them as bearing divine sanction, and they knew how to study and exposit

---

[1]) But their language is noteworthy. "If a man wishes to be free of liability for judicial error, *he should acquire permission* from the exilarch." They do not say, he should *seek appointment* (ordination). Part of the reason, of course, is that the exilarch, unlike the patriarch, did not bestow such appointment in this period, so far as we know. But it may well be that I am presenting too neat and simple a view of affairs. It is possible that in some places, a local learned man would be recognized as arbiter among the people, with or without exilarchic knowledge and permission. Such a man could issue judgments, and popular support, combined with the absence of a competing authority, would have rendered them effective. The language of the rabbis suggests that if a man does not care about possible liability for judicial error, he might as well go ahead and judge cases. Their words may well mean that such was the case. The very limitations upon the police power of the Jewish government would have made it quite feasible for local authorities to operate entirely beyond its control. The case cited below, in which a man is dissatisfied with the exilarchic court's decision, and therefore repairs elsewhere for judgment, would suggest that even in so central a settlement as Nehardea it was possible for a respected person to ignore the exilarch. But I cannot, in any case, envision the development, in this period, of a completely separate system of

the numerous traditions relating to it. Rav and Samuel were prepared to insure that the Mishnah would be the law of the Jewish courts, as in the following case:

> Once a man drowned in the swamp of Samki, and R. Shila' permitted his wife to marry again. Said Rav to Samuel, 'Come, let us place him under a ban [for he has acted against the law of the Mishnah]'. 'Let us first,' Samuel replied, 'ask for an explanation.' On sending to him their inquiry, 'If a man has fallen into limitless waters, is his wife forbidden or permitted (to remarry),' he replied, 'Forbidden.' They asked, 'Is the swamp of Samki regarded as water that has a limit or not?' 'It is regarded as water that has no limit.' 'Why then did the master act in such a manner?' 'I was really mistaken,' he replied, 'for I was of the opinion that as the water was gathered and stationary, it was to be regarded as water which has a limit, but the law is in fact not so, for owing to the prevailing waves, it might well be assumed that the waves carried the body away...'
>
> (Bab. Talmud Yevamot 121a)

This story indicates that Rav and Samuel were prepared to enforce conformity to Mishnaic law by means of the ban of excommunication. I doubt that the needs of the exilarchate impelled them to do so. If, moreover, they were acting as the exilarch's agents, they could well have used force, as did the exilarch against Rav himself. The issue was therefore, *Which* body of laws and precedents would be enforced in the Jewish courts? Rav, who had come from Palestine and was deeply committed to the enforcement of R. Judah's Mishnah, here appeared eager to demonstrate the authority of that law, even before the case was adequately clarified, but Samuel was no less anxious to enforce the same principle. Their failure to resort to an appeal to the exilarch is noteworthy. It would suggest that the latter would not have supported the rabbis' position against a judge who differed. He would rather have preferred, where the matter was not immediately relevant to his political or administrative purposes, to allow the judges themselves to decide what the law should be. In a case of family law, the exilarch was apparently prepared to stand aside, while by contrast, in a case involving economic policy, he was not. Enjoying great prestige, Rav and Samuel could denounce a dissident judge, who

rabbinical courts, outside of exilarchic control. The Sasanians would never have permitted it, and they *did* know what was going on in Babylonia. And the sources suggest, quite to the contrary, that Rav, Samuel, Shila', Qarna, and others were working quite closely with the exilarchate, and were officials of that institution. Given the political pressures upon the Jews exerted by the early Sasanians, who owed them nothing and regarded them with great suspicion, the Jewish leaders could not have acted prudently had they ignored or competed with one another.

seemed to them inclined to inforce the law as he saw fit. They thus apparently possessed a measure of freedom of action in some areas of law, but not in others, with moral and religious, but not political, sanctions to enforce their views about laws which the exilarch neglected.

We may, in fact, discern three kinds of law in which the exilarchate and his rabbinical judges involved themselves. The first was law which strictly concerned the Jewish religion and the inner life of the Jewish community, as in the case cited here. Here the rabbis from the very beginning probably had a completely free hand, for the exilarch, using them as judges and agents for other purposes, and respecting their learning, would have been quite content to rely upon their traditional knowledge to decide cases with no practical bearing upon public order. The second involved the economic, social, and political welfare of the community. In this area, the exilarch proved to be quite willing to intervene as he saw fit, and to impose his judgment, based upon practical necessities of his relationship to the Persians, rather than upon traditional precedents. Such a case is represented by the imprisonment of Rav for refusing to supervise the pricing of goods in the market, a refusal based upon ample precedent in Palestine. One may conjecture that the Persians would not have respected the efficiency of an administration unable to control such important matters. The third concerned the relationship between the Jews and the government, as in the collection of taxes, the regulation of land ownership, and the like. Here both the rabbis and the exilarch had to submit to Persian hegemony, but with a major difference. The exilarch was held directly responsible by the Sasanian government, and the rabbis were not, but could foster their opinions among the people without regard to, or in outright opposition against, both the needs of the exilarchate and the will of the imperial power. Therein lay the germs of their later disenchantment with one another. Samuel, for example, regretted that riparian wharfage rights were governed by Persian law, but he enforced that law.[1] In the next generation, we find the following case:

A certain person cut down a date tree belonging to his neighbor. When he appeared before the exilarch, the latter said to him, 'I myself saw the place. Three date trees stood close together and they were worth a hundred zuz. Go, pay thirty-three and one-third zuz.' Said the defendant, 'What have I to do with an exilarch who judges in accord with

---

[1] Bab. Talmud Bava' Meẓi'a' 108a.

Persian law?' He therefore appeared before R. Naḥman [student and heir of Samuel] who said that the valuation should be made in conjunction with sixty.

(Bab. Talmud Bava' Qama' 58b)

When Samuel decreed that the government's law is law, he did not mean to say that it must therefore take precedence in Jewish courts. After his death, the exilarchate may have gone much further than the rabbis approved in bringing into Jewish justice the precedents of Persian law, something the earliest *entente* may not have included. Hence the rabbis would have found themselves progressively more estranged from the less learned, ever more narrowly political, Jewish authority. In future research, I shall explain how it was that R. Naḥman, who was related by marriage to the exilarch, was able to act as a kind of appellate authority, if that is what the above case implies, and to ignore the exilarch's decision.[1])

IV

The bearing of these data on interpretation of the Dura synagogue art is quite obvious. The rabbis were not synagogue officials, but rather carried out wholly different political and social functions. They were teachers, judges, doctors of the law. (They were much else, but that does not concern us here.[2]) But the archisynagogus of Dura, like that of other synagogues, was not a rabbi, nor was the figure whom Goodenough called "the philosopher" of the synagogue. There was no reason why these men *should* have been rabbis. In any event, the rabbis, as we have seen, recognized a tension between their enterprise and that of the synagogue. "We with ours, they with theirs" said Rav Sheshet in explaining why he studied his traditions while the Torah was read in the synagogue. Abaye refrained from leaving his school house to attend synagogue services. Rav Naḥman did not even bother to assemble a quorum. In the earlier generation, Rav and Samuel tolerated the existence, in the synagogues of Dura and Nehardea, respectively, of a mosaic floor and a statue, though neither approved of such iconography. However much the rabbis may have wished it otherwise, they had no great role in third-century synagogue life, and

---

[1]) Compare vol. III, pp. 61-75.

[2]) Except for the sacerdotal function, they provided Jewish equivalents for the social-religious leadership of the Iranian Magi. See my *History*, II, chapter IV, pp. 126-150, and my "Rabbi and magus", *History of Religions*, 6, 2, 1966, 169-178.

the interpretation of synagogue art at Dura must take that fact into account.

If, moreover, the rabbis had wanted to assert their authority over synagogue decoration, what means of enforcement were available to them? The exilarch would surely have found their attempt troublesome, since large numbers of Jews would have been disturbed by rabbinical interference with what they doubtless believed to be ancient and honorable customs and practices. One can hardly suppose that the exilarch would have brought his influence to bear in support of his agents' interference with such delicate matters. He had no reason to do so. Indeed, if, as has been asserted, the *andarta* was a statue of the monarch, then it would surely have been contrary to the exilarchic interest to have tried to remove it from the synagogue building. For their part, the rabbis could have made use of the ban of excommunication, as they did in Parthian times against the inhabitants of a village who violated the Sabbath, and in this time as well. What could have been the result? The effectiveness of the ban depended upon popular acceptance including the virtual ostracism of the excommunicated party. But to excommunicate the Jews of a whole town would scarcely be practicable, (as R. 'Aḥai b. R. Josiah found out earlier), since they could doubtless survive by continuing their regular intercourse with one another and ignoring the rabbis' decree altogether. Its practical effectiveness would thereby have been vitiated. When it was contrary to popular desires, the ban bore no weight at all. It was precisely this fact which would have prevented rabbinical interference. Indeed, the subsequent discussions of Rav's behavior in the Sura synagogue suppose that he had a good, legal reason for refraining from issuing a decree of excommunication, but it seems more reasonable to suppose that his best "reason" was the ineffectiveness of such a decree in a synagogue-setting. During the years when Dura was in Roman hands, from ca. 165 to 256, moreover, the Babylonian rabbis could not have made use of exilarchic support even if it had been available. His power depended upon the Iranians' support. The Romans would not in any event permit its exercise within their borders, any more than the Persians would allow the Palestinian patriarch to govern their Jewish community.

As we have seen, however, it is not correct to phrase the problem in terms of communal discipline. The issue is not whether or not the rabbis had any authority over the Jews. The issue is what *kind* of authority they had and executed, and upon what basis. As I have said, their practical authority was based upon the support of the exilarchate, upon the prestige accruing to their learning, upon their power to issue decrees of excommunication, and upon the acquiesence of the people themselves. In the final analysis, it was the people who decided what they wanted to put on the walls of their synagogues, and, as Goodenough rightly pointed out, one will look in vain in rabbinical literature for proof texts upon which to hang interpretations of the Dura murals. The reason is not that we cannot find significant, relevant material, for we can. It is rather that whatever material we *do* find cannot tell us, standing by itself, which motifs and ideas were meaningful, indeed, which were even available to Dura Judaism. Goodenough has the merit of forcing us to reconsider our conceptions of Judaism in late antiquity, and especially, our view of what was normative and what was sectarian, indeed, of whether these categories even have bearing upon the social, cultural, and religious realities of Jewry and Judaism when viewed as historians must view them.[1]

---

[1] My thanks are due to the following, who offered critical comments on earlier drafts of this paper: Professors Jonathan Z. Smith, Charles Liebman, and Robin Scroggs. I am especially indebted to Professor Morton Smith for extensive criticism.

John T. Pawlikowski | ROMAN IMPERIAL LEGISLATION ON THE JEWS: 313-438 C.E.

The dawn of the Constantinian era represents a landmark in the history of the church. Suddenly freed from persecution Christianity was presented with direct access to the sources of political power. How it used some part of this newly found power is the purpose of this study. We will examine the legislation enacted against the Jews by the Christian emperors under the influence of the church and its theology, and try to explain its genesis. The question is of importance because it marks the beginning of the church's attitude towards using the power of the state to spread the gospel, a practice that has persisted into our own time in some parts of the world. The actions of the emperors in concert with church leaders during the formative period of legislation also defined the political pattern of Jewish existence until emancipation was at least partially achieved at the time of the French Revolution.[1]

The primary source for the legal status accorded Jews under the Christian emperors is the *Codex Theodosi-anus*,[2] a collection of laws passed from the time of Constantine up to 438 C.E. when this code was promulgated as a whole by Theodosius II in the East and Valentinian III in the West. Though there are laws relative to Jews scattered throughout the Codex,[3] the bulk of them (thirty-three in number) are found under sections eight and nine of book sixteen.[4] Juster warns that the Codex does not contain all the laws of the period having reference to Jews.[5] But it does include those in force, or not explicitly withdrawn, at the time of its compilation. Since the Code gives the date of each law, the place in which it was issued (an important consideration in view of the only nominal unity of the Empire and the effect of differing

---

[1] On the gradual segregation of Jewish life from the mainstream of society, cf. Salo Baron, *A Social and Religious History of the Jews* (2nd edition), Vol. II. New York, Columbia University Press, 1958, pp. 172-214; Herman Vogelstein, *History of the Jews in Rome*. Philadelphia, Jewish Publication Society, 1940, pp. 96-97; and James Parkes, *The Conflict of the Church and the Synagogue*. Cleveland, World Publishing Co., 1961, pp. 153-157.

[2] The translation of the Theodosian Code used in this article is that by Clyde Pharr, *The Theodosian Code and Novels, and the Sirmondian Constitutions*. Princeton, Prince-University Press, 1952.

[3] Some laws in the Codex repeal other laws in the Codex or revive laws that had been previously repealed. It should also be noted that not all the laws applied to the Empire at large until the Codex as such was promulgated in 438 C.E.

[4] Twenty-nine in section eight and four in section nine.

[5] "Le nombre des lois perdues concernant les Juifs est au moins aussi, grand que celui des lois conservées; d'ailleurs, celles-ci nous apprennent et la perte des lois et parfois même, le contenu de ces lois perdues." Jean Juster, *Les Juifs dans l'Empire Romaine*, Vols. I & II. Paris, Librairie Paul Geuthner, 1914, Quotation from Vol. I, p. 164.

35

local conditions on the legislation of East and West), and the name of the recipient, it does permit us, according to Parkes, "to reconstruct with a fair degree of certainty the progressive decline in the privileges and ultimately in the security of the Jewish communities of the Empire."[6]

Though this study will confine itself to the legislation of the Theodosian Code, reference should be made to other possible source material on this subject. The Sirmondic Constitutions contain the full text of sixteen imperial constitutions from which certain laws in the Theodosian Code are extracted. Juster dates this document from between 425 and 438 c.e.[7] For subsequent legislation on the Jews one can consult the new laws relating to the Theodosian Code (what Juster calls "les Novelles Théodosiennes"[8]) which reactivate and often strengthen the Theodosian originals. Also of importance is the *Interpretatio* of the Theodosian Code which comes from the same period as the Breviary of Alaric.[9] Finally, there is the Justinian Code which replaced the Theodosian Code. This Code contains modifications of and additions to the Theodosian Code made by Justinian as well as legislation from an earlier period (especially from the Gregorian Code of 294 and the Hermogenian Code from between 314 and

324) that are not found in the Theodosian Code.[10]

The process whereby the laws eventually codified in 438 c.e. came into existence was not always a smooth and consistent one. The emperors were by no means identical in their efforts at promoting Christian interests or protecting Jewish rights. The Arian Constantius proved more rigorous in legislating against Jews than did Constantine himself. Theodosius I went along with unlawful encroachments on imperial policies by Ambrose while Arcadius, on the other hand, exiled John Chrysostom from his see at Antioch probably as a result of exasperation over John's anti-Jewish demagoguery. The pagan emperor Julian attempted to correct the situation of the Jews probably in hopes of gaining Jewish support in his battle with the Christians. But the time was not distant, says Flannery, "when ecclesiastical and imperial legislation concerning Judaism would reflect one another faithfully."[11]

---

[6] Parkes, *op. cit.*, p. 177.

[7] Juster, *op. cit.*, Vol. I, p. 164.

[8] *Ibid.*, p. 165.

[9] Some scholars consider it the work of the same author. cf. *Ibid.*, n. #3.

[10] For a chronological listing (213-527 c.e.) of the principal laws against the Jews found in various sources, cf. *Ibid.*, pp. 168-171. Legislation regarding the Jews from church councils of the fourth century which had at least indirect sanction from the state is summarized by Parkes, *op. cit.*, pp. 174-177. A good summary of the application of the anti-Jewish legislation after the promulgation of the Code till 1096 can be found in Bernhard Blumenkranz, *Juifs et Chrétiens dans le Monde Occidental 430-1096*. Paris. Mouton & Co., 1960, pp. 293-371.

[11] Edward Flannery, *The Anguish of the Jews*. New York, Macmillan, 1965, p. 53.

No precise systematization of the various Jewish statutes devised by the emperors is possible. But four principal areas of concern do appear from an overall survey of the Theodosian code: (1) acknowledgment of the Jew's fundamental rights and freedom under the law; (2) the prohibition of injustices or violence against Jews or their cult; (3) punishment for Jewish activities judged to be anti-Christian; and (4) restrictions imposed on Jewish cult and activities.

Officially under the Christian empire Judaism remained a *religio licita* as it had been under the pagan emperors. Even at the end of the fourth century Theodosius still insists, in reaction to some of the anti-Judaic excesses encouraged by certain segments of the clergy, that Judaism is not a prohibited sect.[12] It enjoys the right of excommunication for its members.[13] This point of view according to Marcel Simon[14] explains not only the maintenance of traditional Jewish privileges, but also the granting of new rights under changed circumstances. An example of this would be the edict issued by Honorius which prohibited the employment of Jews on the Sabbath.[15] A number of Jewish leaders were granted the same privileges as the Christian clergy[16] and the patriarch continued to retain his accustomed rights together with a title of honor until the abolition of the patriarchate in 425 c.e.[17]

Judaism's legal status resulted in several decrees that guaranteed the Jewish people certain protections. Jews were not to be molested so long as they did not cause any disturbances.[18] No one was allowed to interfere with their celebration of the Sabbath and other festivals.[19] Synagogues were not to be attacked, desecrated, burned or confiscated. Several statutes, especially from the time of Theodosius II in the early fifth century, reiterated this injunction.[20]

The third category of Theodosian Jewish legislation, curbs on anti-Christian practices, was probably brought about by the desertion of the synagogue by many Jews in favor of the newly triumphant church which sometimes occasioned violent reactions against them

---

[12] Codex Theodosianus (C.T.), 16.8.9. (393 c.e.)

[13] C.T., 16.8.8. (392)

[14] Marcel Simon, *Verus Israel* (French). Paris, E. de Boccard, 1948, p. 156.

[15] C.T., 2.8.26; 16.8.20 (398 and 412). cf. *Ibid.*, pp. 178-179.

[16] C.T., 16.8.13 (397). Parkes believes that in the first days of the Christian empire state officials were willing to stretch the point to insure that Jews were on an equal footing, for not only was the freedom of religious functionaries repeated twice, it was reaffirmed in a special charter addressed to the persons themselves. Cf. *op. cit.*, pp. 178-179, also cf. C.T., 16.8.4 (331). For a full listing of these privileges, cf. Juster, *op. cit.*, I, pp. 406-408.

[17] C.T., 16.8.15 (404)

[18] C.T., 16.10.24 (423)

[19] C.T., 16.5.44 (408)

[20] C.T., 7.8.2, 16.8.12, 16.8.25-26, 18.8.21 (370 or 373, 397, 423, 396)

by faithful Jews.[21] Jews were forbidden to stone or to use violence against Jewish converts to the church, to interfere with the sacraments, to mock or burn the cross during the feast of Purim, or to outrage Christianity itself.[22]

Legislation restricting the Jewish cult and other religious activities began with the victory of Constantine. The earliest legislation in this area was directed in the main at curbing external Jewish activity, i.e. Judaism's relations with Christians and pagans. Restrictions on internal Jewish life were far less frequent though they did increase in later periods.

One of Constantine's first measures was to ban proselytizing by Jews.[23] Simon says that in itself this restriction did not represent a substantial modification of the pre-Constantinian law, for convert making had never been explicitly recognized as a right of the Jews, but merely tolerated. It is clear, he maintains, that this injunction was religiously rather than politically motivated. It helped to suppress a dangerous situation for the church. The context of this piece of legislation is significant. It stands as the second part of the law mentioned above which protected Jewish converts to Christianity from physical harm. The equilibrium between Jews and Christians, however, had begun to change from the first

days of the Constantinian peace even if the restriction against Jewish proselytizing did not strictly speaking constitute a change in the imperial law. Theoretical equality was giving way to flagrant inequality in practice.[24] Further legislation in this area rendered Christian converts to the synagogue intestate[25] while converted Jewish children, on the other hand, could not be disinherited by their parents.[26] The law of Hadrian, long dormant, had been reactivated. One law in the Codex did allow unwilling Jewish converts to return to the practice of Judaism.[27] It seems on the whole, however, to have been ignored by the civil authorities.

This legislation which in increasing measure curtailed the possibility of interaction between Jews and Gentiles, pagans, and especially Christians tended to isolate the Jews within the Christian society and to make their loss of many previous rights and privileges appear

---

[21] On Jewish desertion, cf. Parkes, *op. cit.*, p. 179.

[22] C.T., 16.8.5, 16.5.44, 16.8.18, 16.8.1 (335, 408, 315)

[23] C.T., 16.8.1, 16.8.7 (315, 352 or 357)

[24] Marcel Simon, *op. cit.*, pp. 156-157, "Liberté de propagande pour le Christianisme, protection officielle aux Juifs convertis, et pour le Judaise interdiction absolue de se répandre: déjà l'égalithéorique tend à faire place à une flagrante inégalité de fait." Blumenkranz, *op. cit.*, p. x, seconds Simon's conclusion regarding the religious primacy of the motivation behind the legislation against the Jews. cf. also I. Baer, "Israel, the Christian Church and the Roman Empire from the days of Septimus Severus to the 'Edict of Toleration' of 313 C.E.," Zion, 21, 1956, pp. 1-49 (Hebrew).

[25] C.T., 16.7.3 (383)

[26] C.T., 16.8.28 (426)

[27] C.T., 16.8.23 (416)

to be the result of a divine chastisement upon a group of unfaithful people.[28]

A series of progressively harsher penalties forbade the circumcision of slaves owned by Jews. Apparently Jews, however, were not prohibited from owning slaves as long as no attempt was made to circumcize them.[29] Initially the penalty for circumcision was forfeiture of the slave. Subsequently it could involve the confiscation of goods or even death.[30]

No laws from the period of Julian remain extant. But a letter of his does imply that he did lighten in some ways the burdens of Jews.[31] The absence of any extant letters may be an indirect proof of his toleration of the Jews, whatever his motives, in contrast to the increasing restrictions from the hands of the Christian emperors. Jovian, Valentinian and Valens appear to have continued this moderate approach enabling the Jews to keep the immunities secured from Julian intact for some twenty years. It was not until the advent of Gratian, the successor of Valentinian in the West, that restrictions began to appear again with great regularity. From 384 onwards Jews were prohibited from purchasing Christian slaves,[32] a statute reiterated in a law

of 423.[33] This later legislation added a further clause to regulations covering Jewish ownership of slaves: slaves in Jewish hands who had been converted to Judaism from Christianity were to be compulsorily sold at a fixed price to Christian masters.[34] The apparent tenacity exhibited by the Jews toward the restrictive slave legislation and the equally strong determination of the empire to enforce it brings to light the deep social and religious implications of the slave issue. On the Christian side there was fear of the potential for conversion to Judaism among the slaves and the resultant harm for the church,[35] while the loss of slaves could force Jews out of agriculture and industry into minor crafts and trades. The full economic effects of this legislation upon Jews of the period cannot be determined because of a complete lack of Jewish sources from this era.[36] Another infringement upon Jewish religious concerns touched the building of synagogues. One of the crimes of the patriarch Gamaliel VI spoken of in a law dated 415 was the erection of new synagogues without authorization. For this he was degraded and the synagogues destroyed.[37] But the first record

---

[28] cf. Simon, *op. cit.*, p. 157.

[29] C.T., 16.8.5 (335)

[30] C.T., 16.9.1-2 & 4-5 (335, 339, 417, 423)

[31] cf. Parkes, *op. cit.*, p. 180.

[32] C.T., 3.1.5 (384)

[33] C.T., 16.9.5 (423)

[34] C.T., 3.1.5 (384)

[35] Parkes, *op. cit.*, p. 180, sees slaves as a potentially rich harvest for Judaism if the supposition is true that an important sector of the slave traders at the time were Jews. He offers, however, no evidence for this supposition.

[36] cf. Vogelstein, *op. cit.*, p. 229.

[37] C.T., 16.8.22 (415)

we have prohibiting such building comes from 423.[38] Parkes suggests that a reference in a work of Zeno, bishop of Verona (d. 380), seems to indicate that such a law existed prior to 423.[39] On the other hand, this statement from Zeno may simply prohibit improvements in existing buildings. The church may have been worried about the beautification of synagogues lest they become an attraction for potential Christian or pagan converts to Judaism. The degradation of Gamaliel, however, should be set within the general conflict in which he was involved with Theodosius II. There was Jewish agitation on the feast of Purim and certain Jewish elements collaborated with the Emperor in his action. The construction of new synagogues may just have been the final link in a chain of events that increased the hostility between the Patriarch and the Emperor leading to the former's disappearance from the scene.[40] Another law enacted in 423 prohibited even the repairing of a synagogue without permission.[41]

Other restrictive legislation, known as *privilegia odiosa,* further curtailed the civil standing of Jews. They were barred from public functions, such as serving in the army, from administrative posts and occasionally from the legal profession.[42] Legislation was drawn up which ruled out marriages between Christians and Jews. These were looked upon as "shameful" and "adulterous" unions. Violation of such laws brought the death penalty.[43] Yet this prohibition must be seen within the social context of the day. Jewish laws and customs discouraged marriage with Christians as strongly as imperial legislation. Juster says that Christianity took up from Jewish law the prohibition of marriage with infidels, placing Jews in this group. This attitude passed into the canons of church councils through the Fathers and then eventually found its way into the law of the Empire.[44] A later marriage law did encroach directly on the rights of Jews by imposing on them the Christian laws regarding affinity and consanguinity in place of the rabbinical laws.[45]

A law of 397 denied Jews the right of asylum customarily granted by the church.[46] This law of Arcadius most likely was economically motivated since it was directed against Jews who sought

---

[38] C.T., 16.8.25 (423)

[39] cf. Parkes, *op. cit.,* p. 182. The passage from Zeno (*Tractatus,* XIV; P.I. XI, p. 354) reads "If Jews or pagans were allowed, or if they wished, they might build more beautifully their synagogues and temples. . . ." Juster, *op. cit.,* I, p. 469, supports this view.

[40] cf. Simon, *op. cit.,* p. 160. The abolition of the Patriarchate was officially sanctioned by a law of 429. cf. C.T., 16.8.29 and Juster, *op. cit.,* I, p. 397.

[41] C.T., 16.8.27 (423)

[42] cf. C.T., 16.8.24 (418) and Juster, *op. cit.,* II, pp. 263-264. On the *privilegia odiosa,* cf. *Ibid.,* I, pp. 230f.

[43] C.T., 16.8.6, 3.7.2 (339, 388)

[44] Juster, *op. cit.,* II, pp. 45-46.

[45] C.T., 3.12.2 (383). cf. *Codex Justinianus,* 1.9.7 (393)

[46] C.T., 8.45.2 (344)

asylum in the church while in debt to the Empire. Yet it is important to mention such laws even though their original motivation may have been just because they remained on the books well after the time when knowledge of their original intent was lost. They became part of the body of legislation which in later ages would be applied as a whole against the Jews.

In 398 Jewish tribunals, in charge of all Jewish affairs up to that time, were invalidated with respect to all matters not purely religious.[47] In 425 when the patriarchate was abolished, the tax collected for the support of this office was not abolished but simply added to the list of Jewish taxes owed to the Empire.[48]

One further comment should be made with regard to the laws contained in the Theodosian Code. It concerns the tone of some of the legislation. Many offensive and degrading references to Jews and Judaism throughout the Code plainly go beyond purely juridical terminology, echoing similar terminology in the conciliar canons. Judaism is called a "wicked sect," "a sacrilegious assembly" while Jews are described as "abominable" people.[49]

Christianity is designated, on the other hand, as the "venerable religion."[50] Marcel Simon has noted in the legislation of the Codex a growing influence of religious considerations over merely political motives.[51]

We conclude from this examination of the legislation on the Jews that the Theodosian Code played an important role in bringing about a new orientation within the Jewish community that was to set the pattern of its existence for centuries. The ghetto, if not actually born during this period,[52] was certainly firmly established. Faced with increased hostility and isolation, the Jews chose to centralize authority and the individual community, became the basic unit wherein life would be directed by the laws of the Talmud and their rabbinical interpretations.[53] The center of Jewish life moved outside of the Empire into Persia. Simon stresses, quite correctly, that the period in which

---

[47] C.T., 2.1.10 (398)

[48] C.T., 16.8.25 (423)

[49] C.T., 16.8.1, 16.9.4, 16.8.6-7 (315, 417, 339, 352 or 357). One term in the Codex that should not necessarily be interpreted in a derogatory sense is "supersitio" as a description of Judaism. In the Codex, as in classical literature, "supersitio" denotes a religion at variance with the state religion

rather than an ignorant and unreasonable belief in superhuman powers. "Judaica Superstitio" was actually one of the official designations of Judaism. cf. Juster, *op. cit.*, I, p. 250 and Simon, *op. cit.*, p. 420.

[50] C.T., 16.8.13 (397)

[51] *Simon, op. cit.*, p. 267.

[52] Some writers, such as Flannery, maintain that the ghetto's roots "sink deeply into pagan antiquity and into the nature of Judaism itself." He believes Jules Isaac's view that the early roots of the ghetto are visible in the restrictive legislation of this period contains only a partial truth. cf. Flannery, *op. cit.*, p. 286, n 41.

[53] cf. Baron, *op. cit.*, p. 200 and Simon, *op. cit.*, p. 161.

the legislation of the Theodosian Code was gradually formulated cannot properly speaking be called an era of persecution. The source of agitation against Jews was of popular rather than imperial instigation. The authorities merely tolerated it and on occasion even repressed it. But they never actively encouraged it.[54] Blumenkranz concurs in this view. He says that the laws of this period were merely preparatory for the persecutions and pogroms of later times. The rupture between Jews and Christians would have to become greater before the full fury of the legislation would be applied.[55]

This period was decisive for Christianity as well as for Judaism. During the century and a quarter between the Edict of Toleration and the promulgation of the Theodosian Code the church slowly decided how it was going to use its newly found political muscle in the service of its mission of evangelization. The laws against the Jews represented a model that the church could now draw upon for its relations with any

other outside religious group, be it non-Christian or heretical.

The question that remains to be clarified is how this legislation gradually arose. No single factor by itself will explain the genesis of the legislation. The answer, if there is a clear-cut answer, will depend on a combination of several factors which we will now examine in some detail.

A survey of several of the historians who have expressed opinions on the causes of the imperial legislation against the Jews beginning with Constantine reveals anything but a consistent explanation. Some of the commentators preface their theories with certain cautions. Marcel Simons insists that we risk falsification of the actual situation by speaking of hostility between Judaism and Christianity in global terms. The problem must be seen in terms of outbreaks between certain groups of Jews and Christians which led to legislation that eventually would be codified.[56] Only after actual codification do the terms Judaism and Christianity become generalized. To apply them haphazardly during the formative period would be to overlook many important factors and often friendly relations on a popular level (cf. below). Most of the legislation in the Codex originally was devised to combat specific local problems. Some of

---

[54] cf. Simon, *op. cit.*, p. 161.

[55] Blumenkranz, *op. cit.*, p. 293. "Les lois ici ne consacrent pas un état de fait, mais le préparent. Il faudra la rupture brutale dans l'evolution des rapports qui caractérisera l'époque des croisades pour fournir le cadre lequel cette législation trouvera, sa peine besoin alors d'être retouchée, renforcée, pour immédiatement être applicable." cf. also G LeBras, *Prologomenes à l'Histoire du Droit et des Instutions de l'Eglise en Occident.* Paris, Editions du Cerf, 1955, p. 106.

[56] Simon, *op. cit.*, p. 154. "Ne parlons pas trop de Judaisme et de Christianisme, mais plutôt de Juifs et de Chrétiens, car des étiquettes trop générales risquent de fausser la réalité."

the legislation dating from the reign of Honorius,[57] for example, very likely was motivated by a severe economic problem in the West (this applies to both his anti-Jewish and pro-Jewish legislation). The same might be said for the period of Arcadius in the East.[58]

Also of significance to this discussion of cautions in interpretation are the popular uprisings staged against Christians by Jews in certain cities. How widespread these were is disputed by scholars. Parkes[59] tends to downplay the Jewish uprisings while Flannery[60] lays greater stress on them. Simon takes a position somewhat in between Parkes and Flannery.[61] Baron distrusts the accounts of Jewish outbreaks against the church, implying they were fabricated to justify Christian outbreaks against Jews (e.g. at Alexandria) which occasionally were unleashed in an attempt to unite warring Christian parties.[62] The exact amount of Jewish hostility is difficult to measure. But from such Codal legislation as the law of 408 against insults to the cross on Purim mentioned above there must have been some. The question here is not to assign responsibility for the outbreaks which might be understood as self-defense reactions on the part of the Jews. Rather,

it is to recognize that occasional Jewish hostility must be seen as an element in the formation of locally inspired laws that eventually took their place in the Codex.

Parkes[63] offers a warning against isolating the situation of the Jews in the early days of Christian imperial power from the general treatment of heretics. It would be wrong to see the legislation of the fourth century as "an attack of a homogeneous population upon an alien minority." This was not to be the case until the Middle Ages. If the Jews were a problem in the eyes of the Christian emperors, so were Christian heretics. In fact, during the reigns of Constantius and Valens, the "Catholics" were themselves heretics, though neither emperor seriously bothered them. The fourth century was an era in which many different groups were in competition with frequent shifts of power. Secular power was used to oppress others and each group resorted to anathemas and excommunication when mere legislation did not work. This situation was hardly of comfort to harassed Jews, but it is important in grasping properly the complexity of the power struggle of the time in order, according to Parkes, "to avoid seeing more definitely anti-Jewish tendencies in the legislation than actually existed."

The abuses endured by Jews and heretics were similar, though the heretics had one advantage in the fact that it was often less of a compromise for

---

[57] C.T., 16.8.16, 23-24. (404, 416, 418)

[58] C.T., 9.45.2,4 (397). cf. Parkes, op cit., pp. 200-202.

[59] Parkes, op. cit., p. 188.

[60] Flannery, op. cit., pp. 56-57.

[61] Simon, op. cit., p. 264.

[62] Baron, op. cit., pp. 189-190.

---

[63] Parkes, op. cit., p. 183.

them to submit to an ecclesiastical anathema than for a Jew to be baptized. In conciliar legislation Jews and heretics were on an equal footing, both viewed as potential corruptors of Catholics. In the secular legislation the Jews did enjoy certain benefits not shared by heretics. The law was able to abolish a heretical community, but Jews, as long as they avoided contact with Christians, constituted a lawful community and enjoyed certain protections. The heretics were prohibited from holding meetings or possessing property, while Jews enjoyed the right to both. Exile was a frequent punishment for heretics and they were not permitted to make wills or receive any legacy. Jews were not subject to these restrictions except in the case of those who were apostates to Judaism. Heretics were liable to a death sentence, but Jews could be executed only in the case of a crime against the non-Jewish community. Books by heretics were burnt, but the Torah generally continued to be regarded as a sacred book by the church. On this basis Parkes concludes that on the whole the Jews had the advantage over the heretics: ". . . the heretics could be forbidden to exist. The Jews could not."[64]

Parkes[65] also warns against seeing the fourth century as one of continual hatred between Christians and Jews. On the contrary, genuine friendship

seems to have existed at various times and places, especially on the popular level. The conciliar canons and the violent attacks by John Chrysostom were, he suggests, both directed against such friendships. Trouble generally was begun by ecclesiastical authorities and not by the general populace. Jewish attacks were generally due to the particular and general political situation more than to any immediate hatred towards Christians. Salo Baron confirms this picture of widespread good-will on the part of the masses.[66] He points to the fact that many Christians continued to show great respect for the Sabbath, including attendance at synagogues and apparent special services in the church on the day (a practice which even the strongly anti-Jewish Council of Laodicaea had to allow), to the continued celebration of Easter on the Jewish Passover (the Council of Nicea and ensuing imperial law notwithstanding), and to requests to Jews for medical and agricultural advice and to bless crops. In some communities, particularly in North Africa, Christians were buried in Jewish cemeteries. Antioch was an especially strong center of Christian interest in Judaism, bringing about the bitter denunciations against this situation by John Chrysostom. Baron, however, does admit that part of this interest in Judaism might have been occasioned by the growing belief (strongly evident among medieval Christians) that the Jew was endowed

---

[64] *Ibid.*, p. 184. Juster, *op. cit.*, I, p. 179, confirms this clear distinction in the Code between Jews and heretics.

[65] cf. *Ibid.*, pp. 189-195.

[66] Baron, *op. cit.*, pp. 187-191.

with superior powers of healing and of blessing crops as a result of his intimate association with demons.[67]

It appears safe to place continuing Christian interest in Judaism on the list of contributing factors to anti-Jewish imperial legislation. This interest no doubt aroused fears on the part of church leaders that newly converted Christians would lapse into Judaism. And given the accelerated rate of conversion to Christianity after 313, added to the fact that many of the new converts had little real grounding in Christianity before baptism, the pressure on church leaders to keep new members "in the fold" was tremendous. This does not necessarily justify the anti-Jewish legislation, but it does help to explain its origins. The problem of the large number of new converts once the church became established as the state religion is only one part of a massive adjustment Christianity was forced to make as its status in the Empire suddenly changed from persecuted to victor. Its subsequent role as oppressor against the Jews also caused the Jewish community to change drastically its life-style. In the fourth century we witness both Christianity and Judaism searching for a new form of existence under conditions considerably different from those to which both had been accustomed in the past. This period of adjustment was marked by great tension within Christianity itself and it is easy to see how this tension could spill over into relations with Jews. Parkes says that reading the lives of Athanasius, John Chrysostom, and others one gets the impression of great confusion in the period. Parts of the Empire continually are disturbed by travelling bishops, the peace of cities is broken by continual wars ranging among civil parties. Mutual intolerance and harsh vindictiveness against individuals was rampant.[68] All in all, the picture was not a pleasant one. Hostility against Jews may have been a way of letting out some of the frustration to which Christians were subject at this time. Often this frustration was converted into canonical and imperial legislation against the Jews which was almost inevitable given the conditions. What the Jews would have done if the circumstances had been reversed is open to dispute, though some Jewish scholars have suggested the results might not have been greatly different. To a historian, however, the latter point is somewhat irrelevant since he can only deal with the way history actually unfolded, not the way it might have been.

Another contributing influence on the anti-Jewish legislation may have been the ascetic strain in Christianity, especially so in some of the polemical writings of the fathers. Flannery offers this suggestion[69] and Simon also speaks of the generally more affirmative attitudes of Jews towards the world and its goods.[70] In the patristic period when

---

[67] *Ibid.*, p. 189.

[68] Parkes, *op. cit.*, p. 190.
[69] Flannery, *op. cit.*, p. 59.
[70] Simon, *op. cit.*, pp. 272-273.

Christian asceticism and monasticism were in the process of formation, Jewish interest in "things of the earth" may have appeared "unholy" to the fathers. On this point, Juster quotes a revealing remark from St. Jerome's writings: "The Jews . . . seek nothing but to have children, possess riches, and be healthy. They seek all earthly things, but think nothing of heavenly things. For this reason are they mercenaries."[71]

In any discussion of the causal factors involved in the Codal legislation something should be said about the beginnings of this legislation with Constantine. It is obviously not within the scope of this presentation to enter into the complex and highly disputed theories about Constantine's motivation and his true attitudes towards Christianity. Constantine's legislation on the Jews centered around three points: treatment of proselytes from Judaism, their relationship to their non-Jewish slaves, and their share of the burdens of the decurionate.[72] The last of these areas involved no real injustice towards the Jews. Their previous immunity had been based on their inability to hold office in the days of the pagan empire be-

causeof the sacrificial offering that was required. But this situation had changed with the coming of Constantine.

Two representative explanations of Constantine's anti-Jewish legislation are those of Frend and Doerries. W. H. C. Frend sees this and other legislation by Constantine favorable to the mission of the church enacted down to Nicea (325) as the expression of a sense of obligation on the part of Constantine for benefits received. Frend says that Constantine "bitterly assailed the traditional enemies of the Christians, the Jews, reviving the prohibition on proselytism decreed by Septimius Severus in 202 under pain of death."[73] Hermann Doerries leans towards a more "theological" explanation. He says Constantine felt he had a mission which was as much religious as political—the religious unity of mankind. Yet Doerries insists that for Constantine, unlike Diocletian, this was not something he maintained or tried to impose at all costs. It was the highest of all goals. Since it was incapable of realization except on a Christian basis, the assistance of the church was indispensable. The decisive feature of this Constantinian approach which gives it its historical status was the dependence on consent from the people rather than

---

[71] cf. Juster, *op. cit.*, II, p. 312.

[72] The decurionate was the office held by a class called the "curiales" who were responsible for the collection of imperial taxes and compelled to compensate for any deficits out of their personal funds. The evasion of taxes by the wealthy and the general economic slowdown made this office an increasingly difficult one. Stiff penalties were imposed on those who tried to evade the task.

[73] W. H. C. Frend, *Martyrdom and Persecution in the Early Church*. Oxford, Basil Blackwell, 1965, pp. 542-543. cf. C.T., 16.8.1 (315); A. H. M. Jones, *Constantine and the Conversion of Europe*. New York. Macmillan, 1949, p. 202; and James Parkes, *Jews and Christians in the Constantinian Epoch*, Parkes Library publication, 1964.

imposition from above. The toleration Constantine originally had proclaimed always remained the basis of his policy.[74] It is interesting, however, that Doerries says almost nothing about the anti-Jewish legislation explicitly. One wonders if his thesis holds up in light of this legislation, although it must be granted that the regulations devised by Constantine seem to aim at protecting Christianity more than forcing the conversion of the Jews.

An issue that must be squarely faced in any discussion of the origins of the anti-Jewish legislation is the Jewish role, if any, in the persecution of the Christians prior to Constantine. Simon says that if one refuses to attribute to the Jews, in the manner of Christian apologetics, a decisive role in the genesis of these persecutions, it is at least necessary to explain in what way they did take part.[75] As in the case of the controversies over Constantine, a full examination of this problem is not possible here. Several historians such as Allard[76] have spoken at length of the central role played by Jews in the persecution of Christians by the pagan emperors, using the patristic writers as support. Parkes strongly disputes this claim. He insists that Jews took no real part in the great persecutions of the

second, third and fourth centuries. The statements of the fathers about Jewish hostility are always in general terms with no concrete examples and are based on theological exegesis and not on historical memory. Strong support for his position, Parkes maintains, comes not from Jewish sources but from the lives of martyrs whose deaths are in question such as Hermagoras, Paulinus, Severus, Justus, Orontius, Priscus, Hedistus, Polycarp and Pionius. In these lives of the martyrs responsibility for the persecution is never assigned to Jews.[77]

If Parkes claim is correct, then an attempt by Christians to "get even" for Jewish collaboration in the pre-Constantinian persecutions does not seem to be a contributing element, at least not to the major legislation of the Theodosian Code. Marcel Simon generally concurs with Parkes' conclusions on Jewish anti-Christian persecution, though he admits certain Jews may have played a secondary part in stimulating popular hatred. But there is no question of a general Jewish involvement or any determinative role in the persecutions. Simon also leans heavily on Parkes' argument from the silence of Christian sources: "L'argument ex silentio est ici d'une valeur incontestable."[78]

In the same line as the pre-Constantinian persecutions, the charge is sometimes made about Jewish influence

---

[74] Hermann Doerries, Constantine and Religious Liberty. New Haven, Yale University Press, 1960, pp. 48; 93-94.

[75] Simon, op. cit., p. 125.

[76] Paul Allard, La Persécution de Dioclétien et Le Triomphe de L'Eglise. Vols. I & II. Paris, Librairie Victor Lecoffre, 1900.

[77] cf. Parkes, The Conflict of the Church and the Synagogue, pp. 125-150.

[78] Simon, op. cit., p. 152.

against Christians during the reign of Julian and Jewish support of the Donatists. The Julian period does furnish us with three stories of Jewish participation in the persecution: the imprisonment of a Christian anti-Jewish preacher named Eliphius to please the Emperor, the condemnation of a Christian woman called Benedicta by a Jewish judge who hated Christ, and the mocking of Bonosus and Maximilianus, two soldiers who had refused to remove the cross from their standards at Antioch. Parkes doubts the authenticity of the first two stories.[79] Among the fathers and historians, we find Ambrose accusing Jews of having burnt down churches during the Julian period, but Gregory of Nazianzen, Socrates and Sozomen are silent about this charge. Parkes concludes that while Jews might have shared in such activities during this period, "it is difficult to assert that they took the initiative in such attacks."[80]

The situation with regard to the Donatist controversy is somewhat different. An examination of the Code confirms the view that Jews had taken some part in the Donatist attacks upon Catholic churches and their services.[81] How large a part remains debatable. Augustine is silent on Jewish partici-

pation which tends to mitigate the extent of Jewish influence. But we have to include Jewish participation as an influence, however small, on the legislation against the Jews.

Another factor that must not be discounted is the pre-Christian anti-Judaism, especially among the Roman nobility, and in such cities as Alexandria. When Greeks and Romans began to enter the church in large numbers after the victory of Constantine, they likely carried over their prejudices into the church and this fact may have influenced some of the legislation.[82]

The final causitive influence on the Codal legislation that must be discussed is the theological. How decisive was it in the period of the Code's composition? There is no quick, simple answer. Flannery sees the imperial legislation as the translation of patristic teaching into statutory form.[83] Flannery seems to hedge on this conclusion, however, in another part of his book when he attributes primary influence to pastoral zeal rather than to orthodox doctrine.[84] Juster also opts for strong theological influence. He insists that the fathers not only inspired the legislation, but directly helped in its formulation and passage.[85] And Simon says that when all is said and done the imperial legislation of the fourth century is only one aspect of

---

[79] Parkes, *op. cit.*, p. 140.

[80] cf. *Ibid.*, p. 188.

[81] cf. the twice repeated law on the matter, C.T., 16.5.44 & 46 (408, 409). Jews also seemed to be involved with another group of Christian heretics called the Caelicoli. On this, cf. C.T., 16.8.19 (409).

[82] cf. Flannery, *op. cit.*, pp. 3-24.

[83] *Ibid.*, p. 80.

[84] *Ibid.*, p. 63.

[85] Juster, *op. cit.*, I, p. 231.

the struggle of Christianity against its religious rival: Le problème qui se pose à nous n'est pas un problème de législation et de politique, mais bien, au premier chef, un problème de concurrence religieuse."[86]

It seems to me that Flannery and Juster oversimplify the problem. Simon's position, on the whole, is sound but needs some further elaboration. Theological anti-Judaism is certainly present in many of the church fathers. But the question remains, how crucial was their theology in shaping the actual legislation. The legislation of church councils in the fourth century does not seem to be greatly affected by their ideas on the Jews. What Jewish legislation there is seems primarily intent to safeguard the faith of the church rather than to emphasize the invalidity of Judaism. That occasionally, as we have seen above, the language of the imperial laws incorporates some of the patristic terminology for the Jews is clear. But this language is not typical of the legislation as a whole and may be due to the tension of local circumstances rather than to strictly theological motives.

After careful examination of the Code it seems Flannery and Juster have overstated their case (but remember Flannery's hedging). The chief motivation behind the imperial legislation seems to have been to keep intact the faith of Christians, many of whom were recent converts with a meagre ground-ing in Christian teachings, rather than the suppression of Judaism on theological grounds. The continuing attraction of Judaism for Christians apparently was a recurring problem for the church, especially at Antioch. The Theodosian legislation on the Jews is thus defensive rather than offensive in nature, it is protectionist rather than conversionist. Though some Christian preachers and clergy undoubtedly were motivated by conversionist aspirations towards the Jews, imperial legislation was more concerned with insuring that the church did not lose its grip on the large influx of pagans and some Jews who recently had joined the church. The negative theology of Judaism did not have the power during the formative period of the legislation that it would hold after the promulgation of the Code.

Though Christianity did stress theologically what Simon calls the *genus tertium* which was to encompass all men (and which may have caused resentment among the pagans and hence account in part for the pre-Constantinian persecutions), it was being applied at this time more to non-Christian Gentiles than to Jews.[87] Yet Simon has a point in his insistence on the over-riding presence of theological considerations in the formation of the legislation. New Testament theology continued to hang over the church, and Christians were reminded of it by preachers and clergy, by the readings

---

[86] Simon, *op. cit.*, p. 162.

[87] cf. *Ibid.*, p. 137.

at the liturgy, and during the celebration of Christian feasts.[88] So it could be called into service in a defensive attitude towards Jews when contact with them was seen as dangerous for the church.[89] The point I wish to make is that theology came into play *after* a problem had developed which produced legislation against the Jews. Theology was used more to justify legislation than to instigate it during this period.

We have enough examples of laws within the Code which aim at protecting Judaism's right to continue to exist as a valid religion and forbidding interference with its internal life. There is even the possibility of the Emperor's participation in Chrysostom's banishment when the latter refused to tone down his attacks on the Jews. Likewise Theodosius ordered the rebuilding of a burnt out synagogue destroyed by Christians despite vehement objections by Ambrose. He also ordered the incendiarists punished. Though the Emperor finally capitulated and annulled his order after he had been threatened in the cathedral itself with refusal of the sacraments, Theodosius' original impulse is indicative of the general spirit of the emperors.[90]

It would seem that generally speaking the Roman notion of religious toleration continued to exercise a controlling influence, though admittedly it was fighting a losing battle. But the battle was not really lost until after the promulgation of the Code. Juster raises the point that protection of the Jews' right to exist by the imperial legislation was primarily due to theological reasons. Jews had to exist, but in a miserable state, in order that the evangelical predictions might come true: ". . . la même théologie, qui enseigne qu'il faut laisser exister les Juifs, a besoin, pour sa démonstration, que leur existence soit misérable. C'est ainsi seulement que la véracité des prédictions évangéliques, la punition encourue par les Juifs en crucifiant le Christ, pouvait être prouvée."[91] Simon also stresses the Christian theological exigency of Jewish existence, though he does not lay as much emphasis on its "miserable" aspect.[92] While it must be granted that there may have been some of this theology operative in the formation of the legislation, the Roman notion of toleration was by far more dominant, Juster notwithstanding. What did occur through legislation aimed at Christian self-defense was the increasing isolation and suffering of the Jews. This brought about the ghetto conditions of the Jews that would provide the basis for the type of theology of which Juster speaks at a later period in the church's history.

In conclusion, we can say that an overarching negative theology of Judaism inherited from the New Testa-

---

[88] cf. Juster, *op. cit.*, I, pp. 290-337.

[89] Considerations of political strength cannot be entirely overlooked as possible causes as well.

[90] cf. Flannery, *op. cit.*, pp. 57-58.

[91] Juster, *op. cit.*, I, p. 229.

[92] Simon, *op. cit.*, pp. 161-162.

ment combined with varying specific causes at different times to produce a series of laws against the Jews during the first century and a quarter of the Christian Empire which left Judaism totally transformed by the middle of the fifth century. The Jewish struggle with the church was lost and the Hellenistic trend in Judaism had disappeared. The national and cultural center of Judaism had shifted to Persia and the Patriarchate was abolished. The Jew increasingly was being viewed, in Flannery's words, as "a guilt-laden unbeliever resistant to grace and a destroyer of souls."[93] In the eyes of the Empire he continued to enjoy citizenship and the protection of the law, but was very much a second-class citizen who was merely tolerated. Faced with the possibility of extinction, Judaism withdrew more and more into itself to preserve its spirit. The Talmud became the center of Jewish life. Commenting on this period, H. Graetz remarks that "For more than a thousand years the external world, nature and mankind, power and events, were for the Jewish nation insignificant nonessentials, a mere phantom; the only true reality was the Talmud."[94]

Jewish propaganda and proselytizing never fully disappeared, but hereafter were only halfhearted and generally unsuccessful. The Theodosian legislation ultimately was responsible for the birth of a new era in the history of Judaism.

[93] Flannery, *op. cit., p.* ET.

[94] H. Graetz, *History of the Jews,* Vol. II. Philadelphia, Jewish Publication Society, 1893, p. 634.

THE JEWS OF NORTH MESOPOTAMIA BEFORE THE RISE OF ISLAM

by

J. B. SEGAL

To my first teacher with gratitude

I

The story of Mesopotamian Jewry under the Arsacid and Sasanid dynasties is mainly the story of the Jews of South Mesopotamia — in particular, the region known in the Talmud as Babylon [1]. It was around the near-confluence of the Tigris and the Euphrates in the vicinity of Ctesiphon and southwards to the Persian Gulf that the Jewish communities were most powerful in both numbers and influence; it was there that were the residence of the Resh Galutha and the great academies of Nehardea, Sura, Pumbeditha and Maḥoza. Of North Mesopotamia — the בין הנהרות of the Talmud — historians have little to tell [2].

The reason lies, of course, in the comparative paucity of contemporary literary material. Yet at this time North Mesopotamia passed

---

1. See S. Krauss, art. "Babylonia", *Jewish Encyclopaedia.*
2. S. Funk, *Die Juden in Babylonien* 200–500, 1902–08; L. H. Gray, "The Jews in Pahlavi Literature", *Actes du XIVe Congrès International des Orientalistes, Alger* 1905, I, 1906, pp. 177 ff.; S. Krauss, *Studien zur byzantinisch-jüdischen Geschichte,* 1914; J. Starr, "Byzantine Jewry on the Eve of the Arab Conquest", *JPOS* XV, (1935), p. 280 ff.; A. Sharf, "Byzantine Jewry in the Seventh Century", *Byzantinische Zeitschrift* XLVIII (1955), pp. 103 ff.; G. Widengren, "Quelques rapports entre Juifs et Iraniens...", *Suppl. VT IV* (1957), pp. 157 ff.; J. Starr, *The Jews in the Byzantine Empire,* 1939, opens with the death of the Emperor Heraclius in 641.

[32*]

through a course of events and experiences by which the south was scarcely affected; and for this reason alone it may be of interest to analyse the impact of these events upon its Jewish inhabitants. Nor are literary sources entirely lacking. From the few direct accounts and from indirect allusions judiciously assembled and evaluated we may evolve a picture of the Jewry of North Mesopotamia between the second century and the early seventh century. The picture may not be sharp in detail, yet I venture to believe that its outline will be clear enough.

As the frontiers of North Mesopotamia we may take the highlands of Armenia to the north, the Euprates to the west and the Tigris to the east; but it is usual to include in this area also the riparian lands to the east of the Tigris whose population was related to that of the western bank by ties of culture and consanguinity. As the southern boundary of the region we may assume an imaginary line drawn eastward from the junction of the Euphrates *Kh*abur with the Euphrates at Circesium, near the 35th degree of latitude [3]. This is a frontier dictated by political rather than physical considerations. By the terms of the peace of 363, the junction of the *Kh*abur and the Euphrates was recognized as a legal point of demarcation between Byzantium and Persia; and the continuous hostilities of the following centuries took place mainly, if not entirely, to the north of this line.

In the second century, and for some time afterwards, the whole of Mesopotamia lay within the sphere of influence of whichever power held the near-confluence of the rivers at Ctesiphon. The country was, to all appearances, largely united in its rejection of more than the outward tokens of Hellenization; and it was, on the whole, hostile to Rome. But there were fundamental differences between North and South Mesopotamia. Aramaic was a *lingua franca* throughout Mesopotamia. In the north, however, it was well-nigh universal; in the south it was only the speech of minorities, Jewish and Christian, and of *literati*, for

3. See map on p. 36*.

[33*]

there the dominant language was Persian. More insuperable was the gulf in temperament between the sturdy people of the north and the prosperous and effete inhabitants of the south. Among Christians this contrast expressed itself in schisms and bickering [4].

Unlike the south, North Mesopotamia was not greatly distinguished by the fertility of its soil. Agriculture gave those who practised it a modest livelihood. Large tracts were barren of crops, the home of Beduins and of semi-nomad Arabs at the first stage of the progress from wandering herdsman to sedentary farmer. The importance of the region lay in an extraneous, almost an accidental, factor. Across it were carried the jewels, spices and drugs from India and the Far East to Asia Minor, Syria and the Mediterranean litoral. But the most valuable commodity was material for clothing. The peoples of the rich and powerful countries of the Mediterranean depended upon the cotton and calico of India and the silk of China — either raw or in tissue form — and their appetite for these materials was insatiable. Even after the establishment of a flourishing silk industry in Asia Minor in the seventh century, the citizens of Byzantium continued to import large quantities of silk.

Two routes for the transport of this merchandise passed through North Mesopotamia. One followed the Euphrates southword to Circesium, and thence along the *Kh*abur to *Th*annurios; there it passed through Singara to Mosul and the East. The latter part of this journey, however, placed caravans at the mercy of hungry Beduin tribes whose rapacity was matched by their ruthlessness. To avoid the blackmail of these nomads, it was found preferable to use a longer but safer route to the north. This passed from Zeugma on the Euphrates to Edessa, and thence to Amid and Nisibis — through a region in which the writ

4.   See the present writer's: "Mesopotamian Communities from Julian to the Rise of Islam", *Proceedings of the British Academy* XII (1955-56), pp. 133ff.

[34*]

382

of law ran. Thence it was a short stage to the Tigris valley and to Mosul [5].

The Jewish settlements of which we hear, lay in the proximity of this northern trade route, and it will be convenient to follow the route from east to west in our account of the Jews of North Mesopotamia in the second century. The Jewish population of Adiabene in the east had achieved prominence already a century earlier. The story of the virtuous proselyte Queen Helena and her two sons who ruled over that kingdom is familiar from the pages of Josephus and the Talmud [6]. It made a striking impression on the inhabitants of Mesopotamia, for three centuries later the biographies of another Queen Helena — the mother of the Emperor Constantine the Great — who was also a generous patron of Jerusalem, were largely modelled upon it. In the second century the Jews of Adiabene were numerous and still powerful. Of a certain Bishop Noah of Adiabene at that period we read that his parents took him as a child to Jerusalem. There he became Christian. Subsequently his parents feared to return to their native city of Anbar [7]; instead, they settled in Adiabene, because, our chronicler explains, many Jews lived in that region [8]. At Arbela, capital of Adiabene, was a Jewish academy [9]. Indeed, Obermeyer suggests that there was considerable intermarriage between Jews and non-Jews not only in Adiabene, but throughout Kurdistan, of which Adiabene is part [10]; for the Talmud

5. See V. Chapot, *La frontière de l'Euphrate de Pompée à la conquête arabe,* 1907, p. 301. A minor road linked Zeugma with Thannurios through Carrhae (Ḥarran) and Resaina (Ras al-'Ain).
6. The material is conveniently assembled in art. "Adiabene" and "Helena", *Jewish Encyclopaedia.*
7. Peroz-Shapur on the Euphrates, due west of the later Baghdad.
8. Chronicle of Meshihazkha, ed. A. Mingana, *Sources syriaques,* 1907, I, p. 13; C.E. Sachau, *Die Chronik von Arbela,* 1915, p. 50.
9. *Jer. Talm. Soṭah* iv. 4 (tol. 19 d).
10. J. Obermeyer, *Die Landschaft Babyloniens im Zeitalter des Talmuds und des Gaonats,* 1929, p. 133.

[35*]

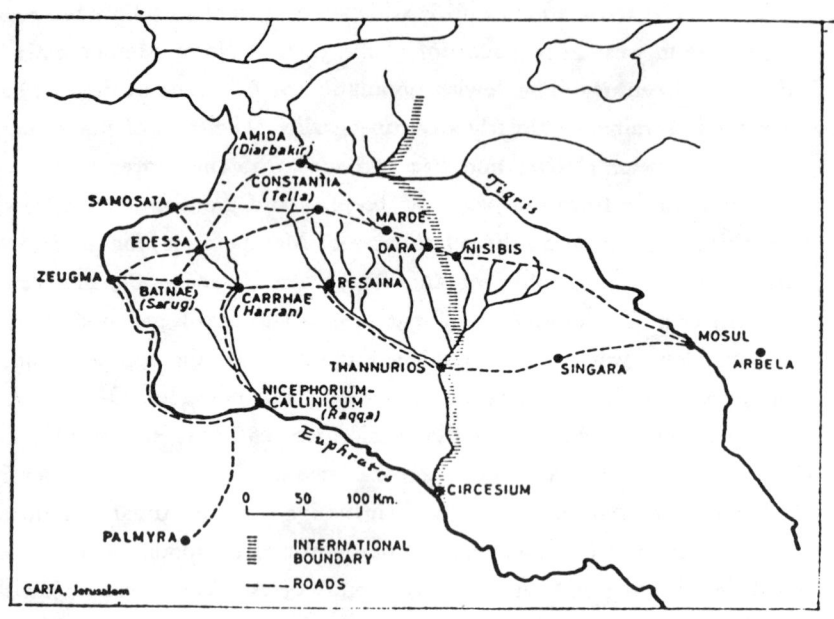

declares that proselytes may be accepted from among the קרדיים, or Kurds [11].

At Mosul, site of the ancient capital of Assyria, Nineveh, there must have been a Jewish community from early times. Yet we have no more than two references to it at this period. The Talmud relates that a severe drought occured during the late summer, and the Jews of Nineveh (that is, Mosul and the district) wrote to Rabbi in Palestine about the procedure for proclaiming a special prayer for rain [12]. Already in the second century or the beginning of the third century — if our chronicles are to be relied upon — there stood on the banks of the Tigris opposite Mosul a fort called the "citadel of the Hebrews" [13]. In the sixth century this was to become a Christian monastery [14]; and it may be identified with the quarter named Maḥallat al-Yahud, "the place of the Jews", when Mosul was captured by the Moslems in 641 [15].

11. *Bab. Talm. Yebhamoth* 16 a. On the Kurds living west of the little Zab, see J.G.E. Hoffmann, *Auszüge aus syrischen Akten Persischer Märtyrer..*, 1880, p. 207, n. 1639.
12. *Bab. Talm. Ta'anith* 14 b.
13. Mingana, *op. cit.*, p. 11; Sachau, *op. cit.*, p. 48 and n. 1.
14. Mingana, *Narsai.. Homiliae et Carmina*, 1905, II, p. 410 and n.; J. B. Chabot, *Le Livre de Chasteté*, 1896, p. 32; O. Braun, *Timothei Patriarchae I Epistulae* (Corpus scriptorum Christianorum orientalium 74, Scriptores Syri 30), 1953, p. 150; E.A.W. Budge, *The Book of Governors*, 1893, II, p. 337 n. 2, p. 461 n. 2; A. Scher, *Histoire nestorienne* (*Chronique de Séert*), ch. xl (Patrologia orientalis, VII, p. 200).
15. Al-Baladhuri, *Kitab Futuh al-Buldan*, ed. Riḍwan Muḥammad Riḍwan, 1932, p. 327. In the 13th century it was called *Ḥisna 'ebra* and the residence of a Re*sh* Galu*tha;* see A. Ben-Jacob, *Kurdistan Jewish Communities* 1961, 33. The explanation of the Syriac name as "citadel of the Hebrews is accepted by Nöldeke, *Die von Guidi herausgegebene Syrische Chronik*, 1893, p. 22 n. 9, and Budge, *loc. cit.* It is preferable to the interpretation of Ḥesna *'ebhraya* as the "citadel on the other side (of the river)", as F. Sarre and E. Herzfeld, *Archäologische Reise im Euphrat-und Tigris-Gebiet*, II, 1920, p. 208, and more recently J. M. Fiey, *Mossoul chrétienne* (Recherches publiées sous la direction de l'Institut de lettres orientales de Beyrouth II), 1959, p. 11 n. 2. The adjective *'ebhraya* normally means "Hebrew"; it seems to have the meaning postulated by Sarre and Herzfeld only where it is used to explain

[37*]

As we follow the trade route to the west, we come to the metropolis of North Mesopotamia, Nisibis. This ancient fortress, with its
powerful river defences, was coveted by Seleucids, Parthians, Armen-
ians, Romans and Persians in turn, and it rarely changed hands without
a struggle. Its importance derived chiefly from its situation on the trade
route; indeed, its Syriac name, Ṣobha, means congregation or meeting-
place, probably of merchants. In the first century it had been annexed
for a time by Adiabene [16]. And in 197/98 the soldiers of Osrhoene in
the west and of Adiabene in the east were laying siege to Nisibis together
— presumably to safeguard the trade route which was of vital concern
to both regions — when they were surprised by the Roman forces of
Septimius Severus [17].

The Jewish community of Nisibis was the greatest in North Mesopotamia. Josephus tells us that the Jews of that area fled to Nisibis
from attacks on them by their neighbours, as in South Mesopotamia
they fled to Nehardea. "There", he writes, "they obtained security...
Moreover, the inhabitants, who were a great many, were all warlike
men" [18]. At Nisibis, too, were stored the contributions of the Jews of
North Mesopotamia to the Temple at Jerusalem [19]. It was the seat of
a Jewish academy whose fame was great even in Palestine [20], and which
was able to attract students not only from South Mesopotamia, but
from Palestine itself [21]. It is unlikely to be a coincidence that it was
in the time of the celebrated Rabbi Judah b. Bathyra — the first of

the etymology of עברי, cf. J.S. Assemanus, *Bibliotheca Orientalis* .., 1719-
28, III, p. 314 a.
16. Cf. Josephus, *Antiquities*, XX.iii.3.
17. Dio Cassius, *Historia Romana*, lxxv.1.
18. Josephus, *op. cit.*, XVIII.ix.9.
19. Josephus *op. cit.*, XVIII.ix.1.
20. *Bab. Talm. Sanhedrin* 32 b, 96 a, *Pesaḥim* 3 b. We may note that R.
Simlai who came to Nehardea from Palestine (*Pesaḥim* 62 b) also taught
at Nisibis ('*Abhodah Zarah* 36 a). Allusions to Nisibis in the Talmud are
conveniently assembled in artt. "Nisibis", "Bathyra", *Jewish Encyclopaedia*.
21. *Siphre* on Deuteronomy, 80.

[38*]

that name in the Talmud — at Nisibis that the ruling house of Adiabene adopted the Jewish faith. Of a later Rabbi Judah b. Bathyra we are told that it was his influence that dissuaded his fellow Jews of Mesopotamia from seceding from Palestine in matters of the calendar [22].

Further along the trade route, to the west of Mardin, was situated the important garrison town of Constantia, called in Syriac Tella, the modern Viranşehir. Among its ruins is a short inscription in Greek that testifies to the presence of Jews at Tella at an early period. It reads:

Isaac, physician

Qaiyuma, merchant [23]

West of Tella we reach Edessa, the modern Urfa, a city of great strategic strength, situated on the edge of the Armenian highlands. Here the east-west road which we have been following meets the road from Armenia that continues southward to the rich cities of Syria. Between Edessa and the Euphrates lies Batnae, or Sarug. The annual fair that took place there in September is vividly described by Ammian in the fourth century. He writes:

Batnae is filled with wealthy traders when, at the yearly festival near the beginning of the month of September, a great crowd of every condition gathers for the fair, to traffic in the merchandise sent from India and China [24] and in other articles that are brought there regularly in great abundance by land and sea [25].

22. *Jer. Talm. Nedarim* vi. 13 (fol. 40a).
23. J.B. Frey, *Corpus inscriptionum judaicarum*, 1936-52, II, p. 342, which gives a bibliography.
24. Latin *Seres*.
25. Ammian Marcellinus, XIV. iii. 3. See further U. Monneret de Villard, "La fiera di Batnae..", *Rendiconti .. dell' Accademia nazionale dei Lincei*, Classe di Scienze morali, storiche e filologiche, Serie VIII, vi, fasc. 3-4, 1951, p. 77. The fair of Batnae may be referred to in *Jer. Talm. 'Abhodah Zarah* i. 4 (fol. 39 d) and *Genesis Rabba* 47 end; cf. S. Krauss, "Der Jahrmarkt von Batnan", *ZAW* XXIX (1909) p. 294 ff.

[39*]

Batnae was the scene of the fair because it was the last halt on this caravan route before crossing the Euphrates and leaving Mesopotamia. But Batnae was dependent on Edessa, and it was Edessa that was the capital and administrative centre of this region.

There was an important Jewish community at Edessa. Indeed, it is, as we shall see, possible that the Arab dynasty that ruled the city already in the second century B.C. had, like the ruling house of Adiabene, come under the influence of Judaism [26]. Certainly, the Jews of Edessa in the second-third century A.D. included merchants in cloth, especially silk, who were clearly men of substance. They lived on easy terms with their neighbours, and they were known at Court [27]. A synagogue stood in a prominent position, near the intersection of the two principal streets of the city; it is this synagogue which later was converted into a church [28], and which may be the site of the Ulu Cami, the chief mosque of modern Urfa [29].

A relic of the early Jewish community of Edessa still remains. Little more than a kilometre to the west of Urfa stands the small village called today Kirk Maǧara, the village of the "forty caves". These caves are tomb-chambers cut in the declivity of the mountains that approach the city on this side. Some have rough carvings, some inscriptions. Most of those buried here were pagans — worshippers of the seven planets that were the deities of ancient Edessa. But three brief inscriptions in Hebrew and one in Greek commemorate Jews of Edessa — a Seleucus son of Izates, a Joseph and a Samuel son of Gordianus(?) [30].

26. P. 44*f. below.
27. See p. 45* below. Knowledge of the silk trade is evident from *Bab. Talm. Shabbath* 20b, 90a, *Soṭah* 48b; see I. Ben-Zvi, *Sefunot* v, 1961, 31 n. 6.
28. *Chronicon Edessenum,* ch. li, ed. I. Guidi, *Chronica Minora,* I (CSCO 1, Scriptores Syri 1), 1955, p. 6 (Syriac text). There seems little reason to adopt (with L. Hallier, *Untersuchungen über die Edessenische Chronik,* 1892, *in loc.*) the reading " 'Audaye" for "Yehudaye".
29. So, for example, F.C. Burkitt, *Euphemia and the Goth,* 1913, p. 38.

[40*]

I have already remarked that, at this time, the whole of Mesopotamia lay naturally within the orbit of influence of the power established at the near-confluence of the Tigris and the Euphrates in the vicinity of Ctesiphon. But Rome sought to safeguard the trade route by extending her occupation of North-west Mesopotamia. She succeeded in exercising direct control only over Osrhoene [31]. In this struggle between Rome and Parthia, the Jews, like the majority of the inhabitants, threw their weight on the side of the native power. When the forces of the Emperor Trajan in 115 moved eastwards and advanced over the Tigris, they were bitterly opposed by the Jews of Edessa and Nisibis, and by the people of Adiabene with its large Jewish element. For their contumacity the Jews paid a heavy price; we are told that the streets and houses of Edessa and Nisibis were strewn with corpses [32].

II

A new factor in the early second century was to have a more lasting effect on the whole of Mesopotamia, and not least on the Jews there. This was the appearance of Christianity and its swift expansion.

It is almost a truism to declare that the advance of Christianity was most rapid in those places where Jews lived firmly established and secure. In North Mesopotamia the ground had been well prepared. The Christian evangelists found in the Jewish communities tools ready to hand for the diffusion of their faith — close-knit congregations, respected by their neighbours, willing to accept the Christians as allies

30. H. Pognon, *Inscriptions sémitiques de la Syrie, de la Mésopotamie et de la région de Mossoul*, 1907-08, p. 78 ff.; see also the bibliography in Frey, *op. cit.*, p. 340 ff. A copy of the "Abhgar letter" was also found in this place, and it is therefore likely that also Christians were buried there.
31. After the campaign of Lucius Verus in 164-65.
32. H. Graetz, *History of the Jews*, II, 1893, p. 398. Eusebius, *Historia ecclesiastica*, iv. 2, writes of the deportation of the Jews from Mesopotamia.

[41*]

against the dominant paganism, well-acquainted with the methods of analysis and reasoning best suited to the theological climate of the country — and well-acquainted, too, with the doctrines of the Old Testament. The last factor is by no means the least in importance. It was probably at Edessa — though some scholars maintain in Adiabene [33] — that the Bible was translated into Syriac, and already in the second century. Parts of it were certainly translated by Jews for Jews; at several points it reflects close knowledge of the interpretations of orthodox Judaism. The holy text had been accepted and diffused through the medium of this admirable rendering into the local speech [34].

The importance of the Jewish community of North Mesopotamia may be measured, then, in some degree by the rapid growth of Christianity there. In one Syriac chronicle it is claimed that there was a Christian congregation at Arbela, the capital of Adiabene, already at about A.D. 100 [35]. Certainly it is to be noted that the first bishops of Arbela — Samson, Isaac, Abraham, Noah, Abel — all bear names from the Old Testament [36]. This new faith must have reached Nisibis early. Nisibis became a centre of Christianity without parallel in North Mesopotamia — with the exception of Edessa; by the time of Julian, in the fourth century, it could be regarded as entirely Christian [37]. It was the seat of the most famous Christian academy in the whole of Mesopotamia. The statutes of this university, with rules of conduct and discipline for both students and staff, are still extant; and we shall prob-

33. See the discussion in F. Rosenthal, *Die aramaistische Forschung seit Th. Nöldeke's Veröffentlichungen*, 1939, p. 199. A different view is held by A. Vööbus, *Studies in the history of the Gospel text in Syriac*, 1951, p. 46.
34. For the influence of Jewish Targumim on Syriac versions of the Pentateuch, see Vööbus, *Peschitta und Targum des Pentateuchs*, 1958. *See further* A. Harnack, *The Mission and Expansion of Christianity in the first three centuries*, 1908, I, p. 15; J. Labourt, *Le Christianisme dans l'Empire perse sous la dynastie sassanide . . .*, 1904, p. 16.
35. Sachau, *op. cit.*, p. 30.
36. Sachau, *loc. cit.;* cf. Mingana, *Sources syriaques*, p. 82 n. 2.
37. Sozomen, *Historia ecclesiastica*, v. 3.

[42*]

ably not err in holding them to have been modelled to some extent on those of the older Jewish academy of the same city [38].

Edessa is likely to have been the first large city through which Christianity entered Mesopotamia, following the trade route from Antioch, but acounts of its origins there are too closely entangled in legend to bear factual analysis. Tradition maintains that Addai, the first evangelist of Mesopotamia, arrived at Edessa within the lifetime of Jesus. He was preceded by the letter of Jesus to Abhgar the Black, king of Edessa, commending his faith and assuring him that his city would remain for ever inviolable to enemy invader [39]. To this legend was added later the story of the sacred *mandelion* which bore the impress of the features of Jesus. The legend of the letter was accepted already by Eusebius in the first half of the fourth century, although it does not seem to have been familiar to Ephraim Syrus at Edessa itself at a somewhat later date. Modern scholarship has exposed the story of the letter and the story of the *mandelion* as unhistorical — indeed, they may be accounted as one of the most successful pious frauds of antiquity [40]. But they received wide credence. Edessa was the goal of pilgrims from even Europe; and the journal of "St. Silvia" recounts how the Bishop of Edessa himself spoke of the efficacy of the letter affixed to the gates of the city [41].

38. See the present writer's article, *Proceedings of the British Academy* XLI, p. 131 and n. 8.
39. G. Phillips, *The Doctrine of Addai, the apostle*, 1876, p. 4 (Syriac text).
40. See in particular E. von Dobschütz, *Christusbilder..*, 1909, ch. v. Copies of the letter have been found in places as far apart as Edessa itself, Egypt, Asia Minor and Macedonia; for the last-named see Ch. Picard, "Un texte nouveau de la correspondance entre Abgar d'Osrhoène et Jésus-Christ..", *Bulletin de correspondance hellénique* XLIV (1920), p. 41.
41. *S. Silviae (Aetheriae) peregrinatio*, ed. P. Geyer (Corpus scriptorum eccles. lat. 39), 1898, ch. xix; cf. H. Pétré, *Éthérie. Journal de voyage* (Sources chrétiennes 21), 1948, p. 158. On the date of this text, see Monneret de Villard, *op. cit.*, p. 90 and the bibliography there; it is ascribed either to the 4th or the 6th century — the latter is more probable.

[43*]

Here we are concerned with one aspect only of the Ab*h*gar legend. A strange passage in an early Syriac treatise tells of "a Jewish woman named Ku*th*bi" who saved from death the "patrician" Bakru. In memory of her deed she was worshipped as a goddess by the pagans of Edessa [42]. The event — if historical — would be assigned to the end of the second century B.C. [43]; but the passage is too brief and strange to be historical. Clermont-Ganneau has proposed an ingenious explanation. He points to the close relations between Edessa and Adiabene — we have seen that the two regions were allies in a siege of Nisibis in the second century A.D. [44] — and he points to the Jewish faith of the rulers of Adiabene. It is possible, he maintains, that the early kings of Edessa also were influenced by Judaism; indeed, an Armenian tradition even holds that Queen Helena of Adiabene was wife of the king of Edessa [45]. The name Ku*th*bi is derived by Clermont-Ganneau from Syriac *Ktb*, "write", and he finds in the name and legend of the deified Jewish woman an echo of a sacred writing associated with the city of Edessa from ancient times. From this arose later the myth of the letter of Jesus as the palladium of Edessa; in pre-Christian days, suggests Clermont-Ganneau, it was derived from the Jewish custom of the *mezuzah* affixed to the gates of a city to ward off foes, as the *mezuzah* is affixed to doorposts of a house [46]. The theory is attractive and plausible. In the Talmud, indeed, we are told of the special reverence paid to the *mezuzah* by the retinue of a Jewish prince of Adiabene [47].

42. British Museum Ms. Add. 14,658, No. 21, fol. 178 a col. 2; see W. Cureton, *Spicilegium syriacum*, 1855, p. 25 (Syriac text).
43. R. Duval, *Histoire politique, religiuse et littéraire d'Édesse jusqu'à la première croisade*, 1892, p. 40 f.
44. P. 35* above.
45. See A. Carrière, "La légende d'Abgar dans l'*Histoire d'Arménia* de Moïse de Khoren", *Centenaire de l'École des langues orientales vivantes*, 1895, p. 411 f.; the error of Moses of Chorene arose from an error of Eusebius.
46. C. Clermont-Ganneau, *Recueil d'archéologie orientale*, III, 1900, pp. 216 ff.
47. *Bab. Talm. Menaḥoth* 32 b.

[44*]

However this may be, it is certain that Christianity was firmly established at Edessa in the middle of the second century. Among its members it appears to have numbered Bardaisan, the philosopher-poet and friend and familiar of prince Abḥgar, later to become Abḥgar the Great [48]. According to Eusebius, the bishops of Osrhoene held a Council in the second century to discuss the date of Easter [49]. A Christian church stood within the walls of Edessa at the end of the second century; in the flood of 201 more than 2,000 persons who passed the night in the church were drowned [50]. It was probably in the reign of Abḥgar the Great, in the year 206 or thereabouts, that the king of Edessa adopted Christianity as the official religion of his kingdom. Edessa was the first semi-independent kingdom officially to accept Christianity, and the city acquired thereby a sanctity without parallel in Mesopotamia.

It is certain beyond doubt that the traditional account of the introduction of Christianity to Edessa in the time of Jesus himself is unhistorical. But the story contains elements that bear the stamp of truth, although we must transfer them to the beginning of the third century at the earliest, and although their present literary form may belong to the early fifth century [51]. It was at the house of the Jew Tobias son of Tobias from Palestine that the first evangelist resided when he came to Edessa; and it was this Tobias who was requested by the king to introduce Addai into the royal presence [52]. The Jews are said to have

48. F. Nau, "Bardesanes..", *Patrologia Syriaca*, I/2, 1907, p. 490. See also H. H. Schaeder, "Bardesanes von Edessa in der Überlieferung der griechischen und der syrischen Kirche", *Zeitschrift für Kirchengeschichte*, LI (1932), p. 21.
49. See the discussion in C.J. Hefele, *Histoire des Conciles..*, I, 1907, p. 141, 149. This Council is probably not historical; cf. art. "Édesse", in F. Cabrol and H. Leclerq, *Dictionnaire d'archéologie chétienne et de liturgie*.
50. *Chronicon Edessenum*, ch. i (viii), ed. Guidi, *op. cit.*, p. 2.
51. A. Baumstark, *Geschichte der syrischen Literatur*, 1922, p. 28.
52. Phillips, *op. cit.*, p. 5.

[45*]

been among the classes of the population summoned by the king to hear the public proclamation of the new faith [53]. We are told, too, that the Christians found many converts among the Jews:

> the Jews also, conversant with the law and the prophets, who carried on commerce in soft (materials), were also persuaded and became disciples and made the (Christian) confession [54].

The second "bishop" of Edessa, the successor, according to the legend, of Addai, was probably a Jewish convert, for he bore the name Aggai [55]. He, too, dealt in silk — not as merchant, but as craftsman. It was he alone who had the right to make the tiara worn by the king of Edessa and some of his nobles [56]. This tiara was part of the royal insignia; and it appears on the coins of Edessa of this period [57]. On the death of king Abhgar the Great, his reprobate son bade Aggai: "make me the golden tiara as thou didst of old for my fathers". Aggai refused and was put to death [58].

At the beginning of the fourth century the Christians of Edessa, like their coreligionists elsewhere in the Roman empire, were persecuted by the Roman authorities. The Christians had the open sympathy of the Jews; we are told that the Jews mourned with them at the funeral of Ḥabib, one of the three martyrs of Edessa [59]. But the church of Mesopotamia owed more than this to the Jews. It is well known that the church of Edessa, the most westerly in Mesopotamia, had a two-

53. Phillips, *op. cit.*, p. 18.
54. Phillips, *op. cit.*, p. 34.
55. Phillips, *op. cit.*, pp. 35, 40, 49.
56. Phillips, *op. cit.*, pp. 35, 42, Cureton, *Ancient Syriac Documents*, 1864, p. 35 (Syriac text), cf. pp. 36, 42, and Phillips, *op. cit.*, p. 33.
57. G.F. Hill, *Catalogue of the Greek Coins of Arabia, Mesopotamia and Persia* .., 1922, pp. 92 f.
58. Philips, *op. cit.*, p. 51; Cureton, *op. cit.*, p. 22. For the early history of Christianity at Edessa see F.C. Burkitt, *Early Eastern Christianity*, 1904, pp. 6 ff., and the brief account in Harnack, *op. cit.*, II, pp. 142 ff.
59. Burkitt, *Euphemia and the Goth*, p. 41 (Syriac text).

[46*]

fold strain in its history, Semitic — that is, Aramean — as well as Greek [60]. At this period it stood remote from the rest of Christendom, perhaps partly because of ignorance of the Greek language [61]. Nevertheless it thrived. This continued strength of the Mesopotamian church — in spite of its isolation — may be ascribed in no small degree to the resources, both moral and theological, of the Jews of the region [62].

The influence of Jewish learning and tradition upon the early Christianity of North Mesopotamia is apparent from the writings of Aphraates, who lived near Mosul in the first half of the fourth century. His tracts are among the most ancient of any Syrian church fathers; they made a deep impression on his contemporaries. Aphraates was acquainted with traditions of the Targums and Talmud, although his acquaintance with them was not necessarily direct. He employs a Jewish chronology, and even his metaphors are, in a few passages, Jewish. It is possible that he had knowledge of Hebrew [63]. Several of his homilies are directed against the Jews. His theological arguments follow familiar lines; he does not spare his attacks upon the Jews — but they are upon Judaism and the Jewish contemporaries of Jesus, not upon his own Jewish contemporaries. He writes without rancour. Several times he addresses himself to a Jewish disputant, calling him "doctor" or "wise man" [64]. Aphraates's attitude towards marriage is closer to that of the

---

60. Burkitt, *Early Eastern Christianity, loc. cit.*
61. The first appearance of a bishop of Edessa at an important synod of clerics outside Mesopotamia was at the Council of Nicaea in 325; see E. Kirsten, art. "Edessa", *Reallexikon für Antike und Christentum,* § 6 d.
62. On the influence of Jewish exegesis in the Aramaic-speaking world, see D. Gerson, "Die Commentarien des Ephraem Syrus im Verhältniss zur jüdischen Exegese", *Monatsschrift für Geschichte und Wissenschaft des Judenthums,* XVII (1868), pp. 15, 64, 98, 141.
63. J. Parisot, "Aphraatis .. Demonstrationes", *Patrologia Syriaca,* I/1, p. XLIV, LVIII.
64. Parisot, *op. cit.,* p. XXV.

[47*]

Jews than the bitter intolerance of many early Christians. God, he declares :

> created marriage, ... and it is good — though preferable is celibacy [65].

III

For centuries North Mesopotamia had been a constant battleground between the armies of Parthia in the East and Rome in the West. In the third and fourth centuries occured two events which were greatly to affect the balance of power between the opposing forces. In 226 the Parthian dynasty of the Arsacids was supplanted by the Persian Sasanids. The new regime drew much of its vigour from a revival of the Zoroastrian religion, and its first monarch Ardashir I persecuted the Christians and restricted severely the autonomy of the Jews [66]. The repression did not continue long, for most Persians — unlike the more fanatical of the Zoroastrian priests — were a tolerant people who treated their minorities with easy liberality. While Christians were harassed by the Romans in the third century, in Persia Christianity was permitted to spread in a discreet manner — just as in the sixth century a Persian king was to welcome to his realm the pagan philosophers of Athens who had fled from the bigotry of Christian Byzantium [67]. The rulers of Persia did not, of course, tolerate any movement that threatened the security of their kingdom; apart from this, however, only one thing was anathema to them in their dealings with religious minorities — open proselytization among Zoroastrians. Here the Jewish minority of Persia were free of offence. Indeed, Zoroastrian and Jew were at one

65. *Demonstratio* xviii. 8, ed. Parisot, *op. cit.*, p. 837.
66. See Funk, *op. cit.*, I, p. 68; S. Krauss, art. "Babylonia", *Jewish Encyclopaedia*.
67. Khosrau Anushirvan, 531-579. When these philosophers found that neither the Persian king nor his state corresponded to the Platonic ideal, Khosrau arranged with Justinian that they should return unmolested to their home.

[48*]

in their opposition to Christian evangelists, for the latter sought converts among the adherents of both religions [68]. We are told that Jews cooperated with Zoroastrians in the fourth century to secure the expulsion from Arbela of a bishop whose missionary ardour had passed the bounds of discretion [69]. But the Persians did not normally vent their disapproval indiscriminately; it was the bishop or priest, not his flock, who suffered their anger [70].

The Jews of Persia were an inoffensive minority; with the course of history the Christians were regarded very differently by the Persian authorities. Almost exactly a century ofter the foundation of the Arsacid dynasty in Persia, the Emperor Constantine adopted Christianity as the established religion of his empire, its capital now at Byzantium. At one stroke the Christians of Persia had become coreligionists of the enemy of their country. The king of Persia of the time, Shapur II, was an energetic monarch who was straining every nerve to drive the Romans from Mesopotamia. The key to the struggle was Nisibis, and three times he invested the city, each time without success. The population of North Mesopotamia, including Nisibis, was now predominantly Christian. It was natural that king Shapur should regard his Christian subjects as a hostile element [71]. The persecution of the Christians that followed was of special ferocity. We may, in spite of Mingana, regard Sozomen's figure of 16,000 martyrs as exaggerated [72]; but certainly a

---

68. See Assemanus, *op. cit.*, iii. 2. p. LXV, on the conversion of a Jew and his family.
69. *Meshihazkha*, ed. Sachau, *op. cit.*, p. 73; Mingana, *op. cit.*, p. 46.
70. Sachau, *op. cit.*, p. 31 f.
71. A different reason for the persecution is offered by Faustus of Byzantium; see P. Peeters, "Le début de la persécution de Sapor . .", *Revue des études arméniennes I*, (1920), p. 15. The statement of Sozomen, ii. 15, that Constantine wrote to Shapur to intercede on behalf of the Christians of Persia is unhistorical, since Constantine had died three years before the persecution began, cf. Labourt, *op. cit.*, p. 43 n. 3.
72. Mingana, *op. cit.*, p. 139 n. 1.

[49*]

great number of Christians, priests and laymen, suffered torture and death for their faith.

Here we are concerned only with the allegations of Christian writers that the Jews — as well as the Manichaeans — had stirred up the animosity of the king of Persia against the Christians [73]. It is highly probable that Persian Jews were bitterly hostile to Christian Byzantium whose rulers had treated their Jewish subjects with calculated malice. In the Talmud one passage appears, too, to reflect the distrust of some Mesopotamian Jews for their Christian neighbours in the fourth century [74]. Yet we may doubt these allegations of Jewish complicity in the persecution of the Christians of Persia. The Jews had apparently themselves suffered persecution at the beginning of the reign of *Sh*apur II, when the king was still a child [75]; and in the Talmud *Sh*apur is shown as having a by no means friendly attitude towards them [76]. Of the writers who make the charge of complicity against the Jews, one — Sozomen — lived outside Persia and in the fifth century; he was therefore divorced both in time and place from the events he describes. Another, Me*sh*iḥazkha, relates incidents — they have the appearance of being based on contemporary accounts — of the persecution in North Mesopotamia. Now, it is in North Mesopotamia that (as we have seen) the onslaught on the Christians was to be expected, for political reasons. And yet the persecution opened in South Mesopotamia in 339, and did not reach North Mesopotamia until 343 [77]. Much, it is true, depended on the degree of vigour and fanaticism of each local governor [78]. But it is doubtful whether much reliance should be placed in the allega-

73. Mingana, *op. cit.*, p. 50 f., Sozomen, ii. 9.
74. *Bab. Talm. Sanhedrin* 96 a: "If thou art singeing (the hair of) an Aramean and he is pleased therewith, set light to his beard; so wilt thou not suffer his mockery". The saying is ascribed to R. Papa.
75. See Krauss, *op. cit.*
76. *Bab. Talm. Taʿanith* 24 b, cf. *Niddah* 20 b.
77. For a general study of the persecution, see Labourt, *op. cit.*, ch. iii.

[50*]

tions of Meshiḥazkha. He writes (in the middle of the sixth century at the earliest) of South Mesopotamia at second hand. And his statements on North Mesopotamia also must be viewed with caution. In one passage he declares that the victims of the persecution there were without number; but the victims whose names he does in fact give — from, apparently, the accounts of eye-witnesses — are few [79]. On the other hand, Aphraates, who lived in North Mesopotamia at the period of these persecutions and who was a reliable and accurate observer, mentions only that the Jews rejoiced at the misfortunes of the Christians [80]. Aphraates would certainly not have hesitated to assert that the Jews were the authors of the misfortunes had this been the case. The evidence for such a charge is, I have suggested, flimsy, and we should acquit the Jews of North Mesopotamia of complicity in the persecution of the Christians [81].

78. See, for example, Mingana, *op. cit.*, p. 52, where it is related that the Christians of Adiabene were spared from persecution for one year by a merciful governor.

79. See Mingana, *op. cit.*

80. *Demonstratio* xxi. 1, ed. Parisot, *op. cit.*, pp. 932-33, cf. xxi. 23, ed. Parisot, *op. cit.*, pp. 988-89.

81. The detailed accusations against the Jews of South Mesopotamia are largely confined to their being privy to the arrest of Simon bar Ṣabba'e and his sister Tarbo; cf. Sozomen, ii. 9. We cannot arrive at the precise facts. There must have been widespread panic, since even Christians denounced their coreligionists to the authorities, Labourt, *op. cit.*, p. 58. The Jews of Seleucia are said to have converted the church there into a synagogue. On the whole, the allegations against the Jews even of South Mesopotamia must be regarded with caution. The friendship between the mother of King Shapur and certain Rabbis may have given rise to a legend of Jewish influence at Court; cf. *Bab. Talm. Ta'anith* 24 b, *Niddah* 20 b, *Zebhahim* 116 b, Sozomen, ii. 12. The Arabic Christian chronicle edited by Scher, *op. cit.*, ch. xxvii (Patrologia Orientalis, IV, p. 297), relates that the mother of Shapur was daughter of a Jew; she was converted, the story goes on, to Christianity, and in anger the king gave order for the persecution of the Persian Christians. But this chronicle is late, and the account there bears signs of being apocryphal.

[51*]

There is no mention in our chronicles of the effect upon the Jews of Byzantine Mesopotamia of the adoption of Christianity by Constantine; this may well be a tribute to the good relations between Jews and their Christian neighbours. During the two years' reign of the Emperor Julian (361-63), the situation was less simple. Christianity suffered a brief set-back, for Julian saw in himelf not only a second Alexander carrying the revived glories of Hellas to the horizons of Persia and the Far East, but also as champion of paganism against Christianity. The story of Julian's arrival in Mesopotamia to lead the attack on Persia, his visit to pagan Ḥarran and his refusal to visit Christian Edessa, the swift campaign down the Euphrates which ended in his disastrous defeat and his death at the hands of the Persians was a never-failing subject for Syrian poets and moralists. Yet the professed pro-Jewish sympathies of Julian seems to have left undisturbed the relations between Jews and Christians in Mesopotamia [82]. Graetz recounts what he calls a trustworthy report that "about this period the Christians of Edessa massacred the entire Jewish population of that city" [83]. His statement is to be regarded with extreme caution. The incident is nowhere to be found in the Syriac chronicles; and they would not have been slow to relate, and to seek to justify, such an incident had it occurred.

IV

The end of Julian's campaign marks the beginning of a new epoch

---

82. We may cite the sage comment of Sozomen, v. 22, that "Julian was not actuated .. by any respect for the religion (of the Jews) .. but he thought to grieve the Christians by favouring the Jews. And perhaps he also calculated upon persuading the Jews to embrace paganism and sacrifices". See J. Vogt, *Kaiser Julian und das Judentum*, 1939.

83. Graetz, *op. cit.*, p. 599. Graetz, *loc. cit.*, on the other hand, rejects out of hand — probably rightly — the story that monks were slaughtered by Samaritans and Jews in the time of Julian; the story is related in the Chronicle of "Dionysius of Tell-Maḥre", on the year 674, ed. Chabot (CSCO 91, Scriptores Syri 43), 1953, p. 178.

[52*]

in North Mesopotamia. In 363 his successor, the Christian general Jovian, concluded a treaty with the Persians. Ammian who was a contemporary of this event describes the "bitter grief" of the people of Nisibis when the shameful peace was made [84]. Under the treaty the frontier line between Byzantine Mesopotamia in the west and Persian Mesopotamia in the east was now fixed by legal sanctions. It ran from Circesium along the *Khabur* towards Marde and the junction of the Nymphios with the Tigris near Maiferkat; all that lay to the east, including the great fortress of Nisibis, was surrendered to the Persians without a fight. This "iron curtain" remained across North Mesopotamia — in spite of intermittent skirmishing — for nearly three centuries [85].

Relations between the Jews and the Persians during that period are part of the general history of Persia, and not peculiar to North Mesopotamia. The Jewish community was, as I have already observed, an inoffensive minority, and they continued — apart from two outbursts of persecution in the middle of the fifth century and one towards the end of the sixth century — to be treated by the Persian authorities with tolerance [86]. More interesting are the relations between the Jews and the Christians who formed the majority of the population of north Mesopotamia. The Persian Christians, embarrassed by the attentions of Byzantine Christendom on the one hand and the suspicions of their fellow Persians on the other, broke away from the church of Antioch to which they owed nominal allegiance; towards the end of the fifth century they formed their own church — the Nestorian church, as it

---

84. Ammian Marcellinus, xxv.
85. See the map on p. 36*.
86. The Jews were persecuted by the Persians in the reign of Yezdegard III (c. 454-55) and his son Peroz, and again under Hormizd IV; the Jews supported the general who deposed Hormizd in 589. See A. Christensen, *L'Iran sous les Sassanides*, 1936, pp. 266 f., 278, 286, 440, and Gray *op. cit.*, *passim*. The opposition of the Jews to the Zendik movement was due to exceptional causes.

[53*]

came to be called [87]. This is no place to discuss complex details of dogma [88]. But in the popular view, the central principle of Nestorianism lay in the stress placed upon the human element in the nature of Jesus; he had human qualities in addition to the divine qualities with which he was attributed. This is far from Judaism, based as it is on the absolute unity of God, but it stands nearer to Judaism than the uncompromising belief of the Monophysites in the wholly divine nature of Jesus. Jews, then, may have felt some less hostility towards Nestorians than towards Monophysites. So, too, in Nestorian practice we find a spirit less remote from that of Judaism. This is shown strikingly in the tolerant attitude of the Nestorians towards women and marriage. In the Nestorian Synod of 486 it was, indeed, laid down that all ranks of the priesthood may by married — a practice wholly repugnant to the Monophysite church [89].

Relations, then, between Jews and Nestorians were not unfriendly. It is true that a Nestorian chronicler at the end of the sixth century writes of the partisans of Paul of Samosata that they "are ill with the opinions of the Jews; like them they confess a single divine nature and a single hypostasis... They say that Christ was a simple man, that his beginning as a son comes from Mary" [90]. The same chronicler writes, with more obvious inaccuracy, of the "Jewish reasoning" of Cyril of Alexandria against Nestorius [91]. These theological arguments are clearly

87. See Labourt, *op. cit.*, ch. vi.
88. The reader may consult J.F. Bethune-Baker, *Nestorius and his Teaching* ... 1908.
89. Chabot, *Synodicon Orientale*, 1902, 56 (Syriac text). This was a formal confirmation of the ruling of Barsauma's irregular Synod of 484; see further the present writer's article, *Proceedings of the British Academy*, XLI, 136.
90. History of Barhadbeshabba 'Arbaia, ch. ii. 7, ed. Nau, *Histoire de Barhadbešabba 'Arbaia* (Patrologia Orientalis, IX, p. 193).
91. Barhadbeshabba 'Arbaia, ch. xxii, ed. Nau, *op. cit.*, (Patrologia Orientalis, IX, p. 535), cf. ch. xxvii (*ib.*, p. 564).

[54*]

at fault. But more significant is the fact that the Nestorian leader Barsauma in the fifth century entrusted his Christian opponents to a Jewish
gaoler [92]. And even when there was friction between Jews and individual Nestorians, Jews were not without powerful friends. When the
Jews brought accusations against Abraham, principal of the Christian
academy of Nisibis, the people of Nisibis supported Abraham, but the
bishop upheld the cause of the Jews. It was only after a direct appeal
to the Persian court that the penalty imposed upon Abraham was res-
cinded [93]. Indeed, throughout the acts of the Nestorian Synods extending over three centuries, I can find only one brief mention of Jews. In
554 the patriarch Joseph declares that pagans and Jews rejoiced because the Christians were refraining from building new churches [94].

Among the Nestorian martyrologies there is, however, one which is
directly concerned with Jews. The scene is laid at Singar, perhaps
towards the end of the fourth century, though it may well be later. An
eleven-year old lad, Asher, son of Levi, a wealthy Jew of Singar, used
to lead his father's sheep to pasture in the company of other boys. The
others were Christian or Zoroastrian, and Asher was compelled to eat
alone [95]. He longed for the company of the Christian lads; and, on their
insistence that he first be baptized, he received at their hands the triple
baptism in the waters of the spring at which they watered their cattle.
The young convert was clad in clean garments, saluted by his com-

92. Labourt, *op. cit.*, p. 136, on the authority of Bar Hebraeus. For an allu-
    sion to a Persian Jewish gaoler in the 6th century, cf. Hoffmann, *op. cit.*,
    p. 111 and n. 1007.
93. Barhadbeshabba 'Arbaia, ch. xxxii, ed. Nau (Patrologia Orientalis, IX,
    p. 626).
94. Chabot, *op. cit.*, p. 106. In the martyrologies of Karka de*Bheth Slokh*,
    the persecuted Christians are said to have been robbed by pagans and
    Manichaeans, but not by Jews; see Hoffmann, *op. cit.*, p. 52.
95. For the rule among the Christians of Mesopotamia against eating with
    Jews, see Ephraim Syrus, "De Fide et Admonitione", ed. T.J. Lamy, *S.
    Ephraem Syri Hymni..*, 1889, III, p. 165.

[55*]

rades with a kiss, and took the Christian Arab name of 'Abd al-Masiḥ. As they sat to eat together, 'Abd al-Masiḥ vowed to abjure the society of Jews thenceforth. To strengthen him in his resolve, his ear was pierced and an ear-ring placed in it — for, we are told, no Jewish free man of this region would wear an ear-ring lest he be accounted a slave in accordance with the Mosaic law [96].

On the return of 'Abd al-Masiḥ to his home at night, his mother remarked on his ear-ring, and the lad confessed to her his new faith. For days he hid from his father, and there came upon him visions and strange presentiments. The end was not far. On the eve of a great festival, the lad proclaimed his religion to his father and his father's guests. His father, transported by rage, pursued the young convert to the place where he had received baptism; and there he slew his son. The martyr's body was buried secretly by his comrades. Miracles followed — in the way of martyrologies; the stone on which the lad had been killed glowed red with blood, and on it appeared the martyr's ear and the fateful ear-ring. And, finally, the father, maddened by remorse, visited the grave of his son, accepted Christianity, and was healed of his sickness [97].

This tale of 'Abd al-Masiḥ — told with a deftness that makes it an admirable example of the art of the Oriental story-teller — does not reflect the normal relations between Christian and Jew in Persian North Mesopotamia. Its setting is far from the towns and hamlets where lived most Nestorians and most of the Jews of this region. Singar is in the

96. Ex. xxi, 6, Deut. xv, 17. Ear-rings were perhaps worn by slave attendants in pre-Islamic times; cf. Muḥammad Ḥusain, *Diwan al-A'asha al-kabir*, 1950, p. 59.
97. For the text see P. Bedjan, *Acta Martyrum et Sanctorum*, 1890, I, p. 173; a Latin translation is given by J. Corluy, "Acta Sancti Mar Abdu'l Masich", *Acta Bollandiana*, V, 1886, p. 5. The study on 'Abd al-Masiḥ by Peeters has not been available to me.

[56*]

harsh, bleak atmosphere of Beduins and the desert[98]. Nevertheless, though the villains of the piece are Jews, there are no denunciations and no calls for revenge.

The picture was very different in the west, the area of North Mesopotamia that lay under the rule of Byzantium. There, the final division of Mesopotamia and the cession of Nisibis to the Persians in 363 marked a turning-point. To the merchants it spelt poverty and decay, to the Christians it meant isolation from the greatest centre of their faith in Mesopotamia at that time. But to the Jews it was a disaster from which they never recovered. They were left leaderless.

Relations between Christian theologians and the Jews of this region began to deteriorate early. We have seen that Aphraates, who wrote in North Mesopotamia at a period of stress for Christians, nevertheless speaks of the Jews at least with respect, if not with sympathy[99]. The Nestorians of Persian Mesopotamia treated the Jews with passive forbearance. It was otherwise in the west. The name Jew had become a term of opprobrium, flung against anyone holding a different religious doctrine. But nowhere was this contempt for Jews deeper and more widespread than among the Monophysites. They levelled the name Jew at their enemies without thought or restraint. Elijah of Dara reviles the Melkite bishops as "impious men, renegades, and new Jews"[100]. Severus of Antioch, the outstanding Monophysite churchman of his day, saw fit to abuse his opponents indiscriminately with the epithet "Jew". He fulminates against the "Jewish Tome of Leo"[101]. Of the Sabellians he declares, "Ye shall avoid the meanness of the Jews

---

98. For the dislike of Jews for the nomads on grounds of immorality, see *Bad. Talm. 'Abhodah Zarah* 22 b, *Qiddushin* 49 b.
99. P. 47* above.
100. John of Ephesus, *Lives of the Eastern Saints*, ed. E.W. Brooks, p. 373 (Patrologia Orientalis, XVIII, p. 575).
101. Brooks, *A Collection of Letters of Severus of Antioch*, p. 149, No. xlvi (Patrologia Orientalis, XII, p. 321).

[57*]

and of Sabellius who restricts the divinity to a single person and to a single hypostasis" [102]. "Against his Nestorian enemies on the other side, he inveighs against "the darkness of the cult of that Nestorian fellow — or rather, the Jewish odiousness and ugliness — I mean the duality of the natures (of Jesus)" [103]. In the same way, the Mono-physite Emperor Anastasius abused the Nestorian clergy of his capital as "you accursed Jews" — and his words were echoed by the mob of Constantinople, who screamed after the Nestorian patriarch, "No one wants (this) Jewish bishop" [104].

It was especially the Nestorians whom the Monophysites reviled as Jews — and not, I have suggested, without logic [105]. The position of Jews in the Byzantine empire generally was unenviable; the position of the Jews in North-west Mesopotamia was pitiable, for that region was dominated by the Monophysites — the most virulent and fanatical ene-mies of the Nestorians, whom they regarded as allies of the Jews; and the Nestorians could be equated, only too readily, with Persia where Nestorianism had its seat. The Jews of Byzantine Mesopotamia had no-where to turn for help. The power of the pagans — unreliable allies in time of need — had been broken with the defeat and death of Julian [106]. In the early fourth century the Christians of North Mesopotamia still

102. M. Briere, *Les Homiliae Cathedrales de Sévère d'Antioche* .., p. 301, No. lxx (Patrologia Orientalis, XII, p. 19).
103. Duval, *Les Homiliae Cathedrales de Sévère d'Antioche* .., p. 80, No. lvi (Patrologia Orientalis, IV, p. 80).
104. Chronicle of "Zacharias Rhetor", vii. 8, ed. Brooks (CSCO 84, Scrip-tores Syri 39), 1953, pp. 43 ff.
105. See, for example, Nau, *Jean Rufus.. Plérophories* .., 430, ch. xiv (Patro-logia Orientalis, VIII, p. 30) and Evagrius, *Historia ecclesiastica*, i. 2, and especially Chabot, *Documenta ad origines Monophysitarum illustrandas* CSCO 17, Scriptores Syri 17), 1955, pp. 105, 107, 317, 321, etc.
106. But paganism continued to exist at Edessa (as well as at near-by Harran); see V. Schultze, *Geschichte des Untergangs des griechisch-römischen Hei-dentums*, 1887, II, pp. 267 ff., and the present writer's article, *Proceedings of the British Academy* XLI, p. 125.

[58*]

retained some Jewish observances; they removed blood from their meat, and they ate unleavened bread at Easter [107]. But barely a generation later, in Byzantine Mesopotamia, St. Ephraim the Syrian at Edessa declared bluntly that circumcision and the laws of the Sabbath need not be observed, for they were Jewish practices, and the Christians no longer required the support of the Jews in the propagation of a monotheistic faith [108]. Towards the end of the fourth century a synagogue was destroyed near Callinicum by order of the bishop. The Emperor Theodosius the Great sought to punish the miscreants; he was roughly abused by Bishop Ambrose, and was powerless to intervene [109]. At Edessa Bishop Rabbula, by order of Theodosius II, converted the synagogue in the centre of the city into the Church of St. Stephen [110]; and he received, his biographer informs us, thousands of Jews into Christianity [111].

There are, it is true, some signs of friendliness between Jews and Christians recorded by our chroniclers — but they are few. The Jews of Edessa, for example, took part in the general mourning on the death of Rabbula in 435 [112]. We are told, too, that they shared the wonder of gullible Christians at the egg that was laid in the town of Zeugma bearing writing that prophesied the victory of the Byzantines over the Persians in 503/04 [113]. But in the general poverty of Byzantine Mesopotamia the Jews suffered perhaps more than their Christian neighbours.

---

107. Aphraates, *Demonstratio*, xiii. 2.
108. J.B. Morris, *Select Works of St. Ephraim*, 1847, p. 390 f.
109. "S. Ambrosii .. Epistola xl", Migne, *Patrologia Latina*, XVI, p. 1101. Similarly at Antioch in the 5th century Simeon Stylites violently dissuaded Emperor Theodosius II from rebuilding the synagogues, Evagrius, i. 13; cf. the letter of Simeon Stylites the Younger to Justinian, Migne, *Patrologia Graeca*, LXXXVI, p. 3216.
110. After 411-12; *Chronicon Edessenum*, ed. Guidi, *op. cit.*, p. 6, and see Kirsten, *op. cit.*
111. J.J. Overbeck, *S. Ephraemi Syri .. aliorumque opera selecta*, 1865, p. 193.
112. Overbeck, *op. cit.*, p. 207.
113. Chronicle of "Joshua Stylites", ch. lxvii—lxviii, ed. W. Wright, *The Chronicle of Joshua the Stylite*, 1882, pp. 65 f. (Syriac text).

[59*]

During the famine of 499/500 at Edessa, Jewish women were permitted by the Byzantine governor to bake bread. Normally bakers bought flour at their own expense and sold the bread at a fixed rate of profit. This purchase of the flour, however, was evidently beyond the means of the Jews of Edessa; and the Jewish women were granted flour from the public storehouse [114].

The lot of the Jews in remote villages, far from the centre of law and authority, was — as always — worse than in the towns. John of Ephesus describes the unsavoury exploits of a certain Sergius, a recluse in a village of the territory of Amid, and he relates his story with expressions of pious praise for his hero. "There were", we are told :

> many Jews in this village, and they went about (their affairs) with great freedom. (Sergius) carried on a continuous contest against them, and every day he used to contend against them as with slayers of God, being fervent in the love of his Lord, and gnashing his teeth, and saying, 'These crucifiers of the son of God should not be allowed to live at all'; and he used to upbraid Christians who had dealings with them in the way of business. And one day he led twenty . . . disciples by night . . . and burned their great synagogue-house with their books and their trumpets and all their furniture . . . (The Jews) lamented bitterly; and because they were settled in the territory of the church of Amid and used to pay many contributions to the members of the church . . . all the members of the church became their supporters.

A deputation of Jews went to Amid to bring a complaint before the city authorities, while the synagogue still burned. In the meantime Sergius assembled a band of his supporters from the village :

> and they took water and put out that fire. And they cleared all the soil, and collected stones, and within three days built

114. "Joshua Stylites", ch. xl, ed. Wright, *op. cit.*, p. 35.

[60*]

a small martyr's chapel in that place ... The Jews assembled
and looked on and lamented, not knowing what to do; and
that synagogue remained a martyr's chapel for ever. Then
the Jews ... saw that all hope for their place of worship
was lost ... and they were no longer able to approach it ...
They took fire by night, and burned down the huts (of
Sergius) ... (He) rebuilt them firmly in a few days.

The Jews began to build a new synagogue. And Sergius :

waited till they were on the point of finishing, and occupied
one night in pulling down the synagogue down stone by
stone ... Again they took courage and built a new place of
worship ... Again he sent his disciples by night, and they
burned it; and so (the Jews) desisted from building all the
days of his life [115].

This was the work of obscure fanatics; but the Byzantine authorities
themselves were less than sympathetic towards the Jews. When the
Persians besieged Tella in 502/03, the Jews were entrusted with the
defence of the walls that adjoined their synagogue. Then, it was alleged,
they sent word to the Persian commander that they would dig a hole
in the tower of the synagogue and admit his troops to the city. The
"plot" was discovered, and the Byzantines :

killed all the Jews they could find, men, women and children.
This they did for several days, and they would scarcely
cease from killing them at the order of the commander ...
and the entreaty of the bishop [116].

---

115. John of Ephesus, *op. cit.*, ed. Brooks, pp. 90 ff. (Patrologia Orientalis,
XVII, pp. 90 ff.).
116. "Joshua Stylites", ch. lviii, ed. Wright, *op. cit.*, p. 55. It is of interest to
note that the "plot" was discovered by the Byzantine general who was
prisoner in the hands of the Persians besieging Tella; he conveyed the information to the Byzantine garrison inside the city by shouting it to them
in Greek. We may deduce that Greek was unintelligible to the Jews inside

[61*]

Had the Jews of Tella conspired to deliver the city? The Byzantine authorities were not unskilled at diverting the wrath of their mobs upon the Jews [117]. We cannot tell what was the truth. Certainly the Jews of North-west Mesopotamia had every reason to prefer the tolerance of Persia to the bigotry of the Monophysites and the insecurity of Byzantine rule; and they might rightly be thought to sympathize with the Sasanids. It was no coincidence that in 610 the Jews of Syria and Byzantine Mesopotamia were accused of plotting to attack the Christians and their churches exactly at the moment that the Persian army was about to move westwards. The Jews were massacred with the approval of the Emperor Phocas [118]. Shortly afterwards, in the reign of Heraclius, the Emperor's brother expelled the Persians from Edessa. "Then", the chronicle continues :

> he ordered the Jews who were at Edessa to be killed, because they had helped the Persians to do harm to the Christians. And when he began to kill them, one of them arose and came to Heraclius (at Tella) and... asked him to spare them and treat them kindly. And Heraclius wrote to (his brother)... and when the letter arrived, he desisted from them [119].

Tella as well as to the Persians outside. At an earlier period, however, there were Greek-speaking Jews at Tella, see p. 39* above.

117. For example, John of Ephesus, *Historia ecclesiastica*, III. iii. 31, ed. Brooks (CSCO 105, Scriptores Syri 54), 1952, p. 159. See further Sharf, *Byzantinische Zeitschrift*, XLVIII (1955), p. 104ff.

118. Agapius (Maḥbub) of Mabbug, *Kitab al-'Unwan*, ed. A. Vasiliev, p. 189 (Patrologia Orientalis, VIII, p. 449), and n. 1.

119. Agapius (Maḥbub) of Mabbug, *op. cit.*, ed. Vasiliev, p. 206 (Patrologia Orientalis, VIII, p. 466). The incident is related also by Michael the Syrian, *Chronicle*, X. 4, ed. Chabot, *Chronique de Michel le Syrien*, II, 1901-04, *in loc.*, and in the anonymous *Chronicon ad annum Christi* 1234 *pertinens*, ch. ci (CSCO 81, Scriptores Syri 36), 1953, p. 235. See also the account of Sebeos in F. Macler, *Histoire d'Héraclius*, 1904, p. 94; S. Krauss, *Zion*, III (1929), p. 17 ff., adds nothing to the present discussion.

[62*]

The clemency of Heraclius at Edessa has been cited as "an indication that he was not irrevocably bent on an anti-Semitic policy" [120]. The argument is open to question. We may prefer to judge from the anti-Jewish actions of Heraclius in Syria where his rule was comparatively secure rather than from his actions in Mesopotamia where he may have wished to win any friends — even the Jews — for his struggle against Persia.

V

But against this background of misery and intolerance, a new power was mounting from the south, to sweep away the effete monarchy of the Sasanids and to curtail the sovereignty of Byzantium. Islam was destined to reunite Mesopotamia into a single land. And the more enlightened among Muslim rulers were to grant all their Jewish subjects some measure of security and autonomy.

120. Sharf, *op. cit.*, p. 108.

CHRONOMESSIANISM

THE TIMING OF MESSIANIC MOVEMENTS
AND THE CALENDAR OF SABBATICAL CYCLES*

BEN ZION WACHOLDER

Hebrew Union College-Jewish Institute of Religion, Cincinnati

THIS paper presents an outline of the evidence in the biblical, Qumran, New Testament, and rabbinic literature for a hitherto unnoticed but apparently at one time widespread belief, that the inevitable coming of the messiah would take place during the season when Israel celebrated the sabbatical year. Sabbatical messianism, or chronomessianism, are appropriate terms for a phenomenon that inspired a search in the scriptural prophecies for the exact date of the redeemer's coming. Although most powerful in the apocalyptic tradition, chronomessianism appears as well in the mainstream of Judaism. The locus classicus of chronomessianic doctrine is found in Daniel 9, particularly in the mysterious verses 24–27. This study will trace the impact of Daniel 9 on the literature of ensuing centuries. A fascinating question arising from this investigation is whether chronomessianic doctrine was a factor in the timing of the launching of certain movements, such as John the Baptist's ministry or Bar Kochba's rebellion against the Romans.[1]

I

The pre-history of chronomessianism may be traced in several biblical pasages. Isa. 23:15–18 predicts that Tyre will be forgotten for seventy

* Professors John Strugnell, Chanan (Herbert) Brichto and Mr. Hershel Statman have rendered valuable assistance in the editing of this paper, for which I wish to express my profound gratitude.

1 For more extensive bibliographical citations, see "The Calendar of Sabbatical Cycles During the Second Temple and Early Rabbinic Period," *HUCA*, 44 (1973), 153–196. The following items should be added: Zuckermann's "Ueber Sabbatjahrzyclus, etc." (*ibid.* p. 156 note 12) is now available in an English translation by A. Lowy, "A Treatise on the Sabbatical Cycle and the Jubilee (New York: Hermon Press, 1974); Nachum Sarna, "Zedekiah's Emancipation of Slaves and the Sabbatical Year," in *Orient and Occident. Essays Presented to Cyrus H. Gordon* (Neukirchen-Vluyn: Butzon & Bercker Kepelaer, 1973), 143–149. To note 97 p. 180, add: A. A. Akavia, *Sinai* 30 (1951), 118–137.

years, at the end of which time the Lord will again remember the famous city.[2] Jeremiah employs the 70-year period for the length of Judah's coming exile in Babylonia (Jer. 25: 11–12; 29: 10).[3] The use of the number 70 might reflect the Jewish affinity for the numeral seven and its multiples, evidenced in weekly and yearly sabbaths (shemittah) and the jubilee; alternately, it might have been a common Near Eastern convention for the maximum life expectancy or the normal span of two or three generations.[4] Whatever that number's function in Jeremiah, Zech. 1:12 regards the number 70 as the precise length of Judah's exile. By fusing Jeremiah's "70-year prophecy" with the assertion in Lev. 26:34–35, 43, that during the exile the land would atone for the sabbaths that Israel had violated, 2 Chron. 36:21–23 suggests not only that Jeremiah's words came true, but explicitly interprets Cyrus' edict as having reference to them.

Whatever the precise meaning of these passages, the credit for inventing sabbatical messianism belongs to the author of Daniel 9.[5] Zech. 1:2 and 2 Chron. 36:21–23 merely repeated Jeremiah's prophecy to account for the length of the exile; the interpretation in Daniel was future-directed. The author of Daniel openly acknowledges that he uses Jeremiah, specifically, and other "books" where the reference may include Zechariah, without question the Chronicler, from whose views he dissents.[6] Stressing the novelty of the discovery in a lengthy introduction (1–23), the author of Daniel goes on in 9:24–27 to present his own chronological exegesis of Jeremiah's 70-year prophecy. Before proceeding with a review of chronomessianic doctrine and movements, it will be necessary to analyze this passage in some detail, particularly to determine how it was generally understood in antiquity.

The ancient Jewish exegesis of Dan. 9:24–27 differs from modern scholarship in two significant ways. With a few exceptions,[7] all medieval and recent commentators translate the key-word shavu'a (supposedly

---

2 For a view that this passage is a postexilic addition, see O. Procksch, *Jesaia* I (KAT, Leipzig, 1930), 305.

3 See W. Rudolph, *Jeremia* (HAT, Tübingen, 1968), 161, 184 f.

4 Cf. Ps. 90:10; Jer. 27:7. For a review of ancient lore in reference to 70 years, see P. Grelot, "Soixante-dix semaines d'années," *Biblica* 50 (1969), 169–186, esp. 173–175.

5 Cf. R. H. Charles, *Critical and Exegetical Commentary on the Book of Daniel* (Oxford, 1929), pp. xxvii f.; D. S. Russel, *The Method and the Message of the Apocalyptic* (London, SGM Press, 1964), 16 f.

6 Dan. 9:2 cites "books." The use of 2 Chron. 36:21 is apparent a) in the word "To fulfill" (לִמְלֹאות), which varies from כִּמְלֹאות in Jer. 25:12 and 29:10. Dan. 9:10–14 also suggests an awareness of the Chronicler's use of Lev. 26 in citing Jeremiah.

7 Grelot, note 4; M. Delcor, *Le livre de Daniel* (SB, Paris, 1971), 194–204.

following the LXX) as heptomad or a "week," seven years.[8] The ancient exegetes, it will be shown, understood *shavu'a* to refer to the seven-year cycle, the last year of which was "the year of the Lord" (Lev. 25:2), the equivalent of the year of shemittah or release (Deut. 15:1–2), when debts were canceled and land lay fallow.[9] The difference between the two interpretations is that, according to the former, any septennial number will do; according to the latter, however, each seven-year period had its fixed place in a series, precise in beginning and end. A second difference stems from the first. Modern exegetes interpret the passage without reference to Jewish chronology current at that time.[10] The ancients, however, took it for granted that the numbers in 9:24–27 had to harmonize with their calendar of sabbatical cycles.[11] No student would undertake to determine the day of the week without reference to the Jewish or Christian calendar; yet none of the nineteenth or twentieth century commentators, I have concluded, tries to harmonize Daniel with the sabbatical cycles as they were uninterruptedly observed during inter-testamental and early rabbinic times. This study attempts to show that such a harmonization is plausible, perhaps even compelling.

That *shavu'a* meant the sabbatical cycle is attested in Qumran, rabbinic and epigraphic documents. In its description of the beginning of rule of Light, the Manual of Discipline mentions the monthly and annual seasons: the period of years "for their weeks" (לשבועיהם); and at the beginning "of their weeks" a period of "freedom (דרור i.e., jubilee)."[12] The so-called Zadokite Document alludes to the Book of Jubilees in these words: "And the exact statement of the epochs of Israel's blindness to all these, behold it can be learnt in the Book of the Divisions of Times into their Jubilees and Weeks" (ספר מחלקות העתים ליובליהם ובשבועותיהם).[13] These and similar passages allude to the sabbatical cycles known to have been observed in Palestine from the post-exilic period to the fifth or sixth Christian century.[14] A recently excavated

---

8. Cf. Schürer, III, 266 f.; J. A. Montgomery, *Daniel* (ICC, New York, 1927), 373, who notes the possibility of *shavu'a* meaning sabbatical cycle, but ignores it in 390–401; A. Bentzen, *Daniel*[3] (HAT, Tübingen, 1952), 73–77; Russel, *Method* (note 5), 195–202.

9 Seder Olam, 28; 30; Yer. Ta'anit IV, 5, 68d; Naḥmanides' *Commentary* on Exod. 12:2 and 20:8.

10 Cf. references cited in notes 5, 7–8.

11 Seder Olam, 28 (p. 65, Ratner ed.); Yalkut Shim'oni on Amos 7:17, no. 547; Dan. 9:24, No. 1066; B. Yoma 54a. Although Saadia, Rashi, and Ibn Ezra diverge widely in the hermeneutics of Dan. 9:24–27, they agree that these verses referred to the traditional calendar of sabbatical cycles.

12 IQS 10:8–9. See also below notes 26–29.

13 CD 16:3–4.

14 Cf. B. Zuckermann (note 1), 5–45; Wacholder, *HUCA*, 44 (1973), 156–

synagogue at Khirbet Susiya contains fragments of a mosaic dated in the "second year of the Week (שלשבוע) .... four thousand years ... after the world was created."[15] This inscription comes from a synagogue probably built not before the fifth Christian century, yet the basic meaning of shavu'a had hardly changed through the centuries.[16]

In contrast to the Chronicler, who had understood Jeremiah's 70-year prophecy literally, Dan. 9:24 interpreted it as 70 sabbatical cycles (שָׁבֻעִים שִׁבְעִים) equal to ten jubilees or 490 years; each of Jeremiah's years being equal to a shemittah cycle, seven of which made up a jubilee, at the end of which the Hebrews in bondage gained their freedom. But Jerusalem's sins have been so grave, in the author's opinion, that ten jubilees "are decreed concerning your people and your holy city, to finish the transgression, to put an end to sin, and to atone for iniquity, to bring in everlasting righteousness, to seal both vision and prophet, and to anoint a most holy place" (v. 24). Daniel never uses the term jubilee directly, but his numbers can be only understood in light of Lev. 25:1–23, which gives seven sabbaticals as the maximum time of sanctioned bondage. Lev. 25:10, to be sure, may be plausibly interpreted to mean that a jubilee cycle consisted of 50 years, not of 49. But a 49-year jubilee is taken for granted by the author of the Book of Jubilees. Even the rabbinic tradition which generally supposes a 50-year jubilee for the period of the First Temple argues a 49-year jubilee for the Second. Moreover, as has been stated above, the observance of shemittah cycles is attested, while the assumption of an extra year for the jubilee year is totally unwarranted by the evidence. This is not to say, however, that during the intertestamental period the Mosaic injunction regarding the jubilee was entirely ignored. The author of Daniel 9 not only assumed the reality of a jubilee period, but without mentioning it directly made it the most significant unit of the divine divisions of time. What appears to have happened is that the seventh shemittah (i.e., the 49th year) was legally considered both a sabbatical and jubilee year.[17]

The Book of Daniel reflects an interest in chronography that is unique in the biblical tradition. This interest, however, reflects not an antiquarian's passion for accurate dating of events, but a purpose to strengthen the author's prophetic vision. The names of the Babylonian

---

196, Cf. J. Jeremias, "Sabbathjahr und neutestamentliche Chronologie." *ZNW*, 27 (1928), 103.

15 S. Gutman et al., "Excavations in the Synagogue at Khirbet Susiya," *Qadmoniot*, 5 No. 2 (1972), 47–52, esp. 51a.

16 M. Nedarim, 8:1, rules that a vow "this *shavu'a*," limits its validity to the remainder of the current cycle, inclusive of the shemittah year.

17 In accordance with the opinion of Judah, who argued, however, that the 50th year counted also as the first year of the next shemittah cycle; the sages differ (Arakhin, 12b; cf. Seder Olam, 15, and passim).

and Persian kings and the fictional dates which are interspersed through-out the Book of Daniel were inserted there to give an appearance of historicity to the prophetic material.[18] In some passages, indeed, the author weaves chronological lore into the very essence of the prophecy. This is the case in chapters 7–8, which relate the sequence of the four kingdoms that was to conclude at "the end of days;" it is particularly evident in 9:24–27, which uses Jeremiah's 70-year prophecy to structure a "chronology" of the future. An analysis of these verses suggests that the author proposed a threefold division of history:

A. The rebuilding of the temple

B. The prophetic epoch, described in our passage;

C. The postprophetic epoch, presumably identical with the messianic age. Thus Daniel's interpretation of Jeremiah's 70-year prophecy trans-cended the antiquarian interest in chronology and chronography, claim-ing as it did, to reveal the schedule of the future. Unfortunately, the author tells nothing of A and C; but we should be grateful that he chose to detail Epoch B which is likewise divided into three periods:

1. The rebuilding of the temple

2. Persecution

3. The bridge between the prophetic and postprophetic epochs.

1. "Know then and understand: from the time that the word went forth that Jerusalem should be restored and rebuilt, seven weeks shall pass till the appearance of one anointed, a prince; then for sixty-two weeks it shall remain restored, rebuilt with streets and conduits" (25: NEB). Daniel defines the first stage of the prophetic epoch (when "the word went forth") as an unmistakable reference to Leviticus' admonition and to Jeremiah's oracle, cited in Dan. 9:2. Our passage points out that from the time of the prophecy, presumably uttered just prior to the exile, until the restoration of Jerusalem and the appearance of the "anointed prince" (evidently a reference to Zerubbabel), there elapsed seven sabbatical cycles (one jubilee or 49 years). But Daniel seems to insist that the time of the exile was to be counted as part of the sixty-two cycles, the period of Jerusalem's rebuilding. A possible justification for regarding the two as segments of a single time-unit is that since the exile was integral to the fulfillment of Jeremiah's prophecy of re-demption it became a part of the period of restoration. Therefore, the subtraction of seven sabbatical cycles (one Jubilee) reduces the period of the 62 sabbatical cycles (8 and 6/7 jubilees) to 55 sabbatical cycles or 7 and 6/7 jubilees = 385 years.

---

18 The fictional nature of Daniel's chronological lore has not prevented scholars of many generations from transforming it into historical chronology. Cf. H. H. Rowley, Darius the Mede and the Four World Kingdoms in the Book of Daniel (Cardiff, University of the Wales Press Board, 1959).

2. "At the critical time, after the sixty-two weeks, one who is anointed shall be removed with no one to take his part; and the horde of an invading prince shall work havoc on city and sanctuary. The end of it shall be a deluge, inevitable war with all its horrors. He shall make a firm league with the mighty for one week; and, the week half spent, he shall put a stop to sacrifice and offering... then, in the end, what has been decreed concerning the desolation will be poured out" (26–27: NEB). The period of crisis, according to our passage, would occur during the final sabbatical cycle of the ninth jubilee, which verse 27 splits into two equal segments, the second more horrible than the first.

3. Daniel makes no explicit mention of the third period of the post-prophetic epoch, but its existence is apparent, as verse 24 listed 70 sabbatical cycles, while verses 25–27 accounted for only 63, leaving 7 cycles as a remainder. It may thus be assumed that the third period of this epoch lasting seven sabbatical cycles = one jubilee, was intended to serve as a bridge between the prophetic epoch and the coming of the messianic kingdom.

Table 1 sums up the chronology implicit in the three periods:

TABLE ONE

DANIEL'S PROPHETIC EPOCH

Dan. 9	Period	No. of Jubilees	No. of Sabbatical Cycles	No. of Years		Remarks
24	1–3	10	49	490		entire epoch
25	1	8 6/7	62	434		exile plus restoration
25a	1a	1	7	49		exile
25b	1b	7 6/7	55	385		restoration minus exile
27	2	1/7	1	7		persecution
27a	2a	1/14	1/2	3 1/2		stage I of persecution
27b	2b	1/14	1/2	3 1/2		stage II of persecution
24–27	3	1	7	49		bridge to messianic age

We are now faced with the question which has confronted every student of Dan. 9:24–27. How are we to identify the chronology underlying this passage? We must further address an additional question: In what respect does our study presume to offer a more satisfactory answer to Daniel's messianic numerology than do the numerous scholarly proposals made hitherto?[19]

19 Consult the bibliographies assembled in the works cited in notes 5, 7–8. As to the dates of the sabbatical cycles, see the tables in *HUCA* 44 (1973), 185–196, cited in note 1. Zuckermann's tables of sabbatical cycles (note 1), presently the consensus, assume a chronology described in note 21.

To address the second question first, the explanations proposed hitherto fail to take account of the obvious link between Daniel's chronology and the then current calendar of sabbatical cycles. As has been stated above, *shavu'a* in the sense of seven years always referred, in ancient texts, to the computing of the shemittah cycle. The chronology proposed here is the first attempt, to our knowledge, to interpret Dan. 9:24–27 in light of the then current sabbatical calendar.

As is now almost universally accepted, any approach that attempts to solve the numerology of Dan. 9:25–27 must presume that our passage refers to the onslaught on Judaism by Antiochus IV Epiphanes. Since verse 27 predicts that this persecution will last a sabbatical cycle, split into two stages, the problem is how to synchronize this sabbatical cycle with the then current calendar. Now since Antiochus IV ascended the throne of Syria (according to cuneiform tablets) between Ululu 11 and the end of the month of 137 (September 4 and 22 of 175) and was murdered in Kislimu 148 S.E. (November 20–December 18 of 164 B.C.E.), the single sabbatical cycle of the Jewish calendar alluded to in verse 27 could only be either 176/75–170/69 B.C.E. or 169/68–163/62 B.C.E.[20]

Which of these two sabbatical cycles does the evidence better fit? Arguments in favor of the first: a) Antiochus IV in fact became king at the end of the first year of the cycle; b) Hellenization of Judaea commenced soon thereafter; and c) Dan. 9:26, "the anointed shall be removed" (וכרת משיח) apparently refers to Antiochus' replacement of the rightful high priest, an event which seems to have taken place in 172 or 171 B.C.E.

Daniel's words, however, become unquestionably more pointed in light of the second alternative: a) "the horde of the invading prince shall work havoc with the city and sanctuary," is a perfect fit for Antiochus' pillage of the Temple in the autumn of 169 B.C.E., at the beginning of the sabbatical cycle; b) the division of the sabbatical into two segments, during the second of which "sacrifice and offering will cease" would not fit into the first but does accord with the second alternative; and c) the same may be said of "the desolations" (שקוצים משומם). As to the reference to the removal of Onias, the date of this event is obscure and cannot be cited to refute the evidence which so strongly supports the cycle of 169/68–163/62 B.C.E. Now if the sabbatical cycle recorded in verses 26–27 alludes to the Julian years 169/68–163/62 B.C.E., which corresponded to the 63rd sabbatical cycle, as well as to the last cycle of the 9th jubilee, Daniel's underlying sabbatical chronology can be reconstructed

20   A. J. Sachs, and D. J. Wiseman, "A Babylonian King List of the Hellenistic Period," *Iraq*, 16 (1954), 202–212, esp. 209. R. A. Parker and W. H. Dubberstein, *Babylonian Chronology 626 B.C.–A.D. 75* (Providence, R. I., Brown University Press, 1956), 23; Wacholder, *HUCA* 44 (1973), 160–163.

as shown in Table 2. (Suppose, however, that the first alternative, or some other exegesis of Dan. 9:24–27, is to be preferred, then deduct from Table 2, seven Julian years, or adjust dates otherwise as needed.)[21]

TABLE TWO

DANIEL'S SABBATICAL CHRONOLOGY

Dan. 9	Epoch	Period	No. of Jub.	No. of Sabb.	No. of Years	B.C.E.	Remarks
24	I					Until 604/03	prepropheticepoch
24	II	1–3	10	49	490	603/02–114/13	propheticepoch
25		1	8 6/7	62	434	603/02–170/69	restoration,includingexile
25a		1a	1	7	49	603/02–555/54	exile
25b		1b	7 6/7	55	385	554/53–170/69	restorationminus exile
27		2	1/7	1	7	169/68–163/62	persecution
27a		2a	1/14	1/2	3 1/2	169/68–166/65	stage I
27b		2b	1/14	1/2	3 1/2	165/64–163/62	stage II
24–27		3	1	7	49	162/61–114/13	end of pro-phetic epoch
24	III					After 113/12	messianic age

A recurring discrepancy between the proposed reconstruction of Daniel's dates and the chronology based on reliable sources presents a problem. Daniel apparently dated the exile in 604/03 B.C.E. but it occurred either in Nisan of 597 B.C.E., if the writer referred to the first Babylonian exile, or in Av of 587, if the second was meant. Cyrus issued his edict in 538/37; not in 554/53, as is suggested in our interpretation of the passage. The answer to these objections is that Daniel's dates, as they related to the remote past, were often approximate or artificial, made to fit into a more or less arbitrary chronomessianic structure, exemplified by the book's chapter headings which date by a fictive Darius the Mede.

More problematical, however, is the inconsistency of the date of the placement of the "abomination" in the Temple. According to I Macc. 1:54, it occurred in Kislev of 145 S.E. = December of 167 B.C.E.; Table 2 seems to date the event in the spring of 165. Although the difference between the two datings is only about fifteen or sixteen months, it does represent a serious objection to the calculation, as it is too large an

21 See note 19. By deducting 1 Julian year from the dates, Table 2 would conform to the sabbatical chronology of the consensus. See Maimonides, Shemittah X, 1–8.

error for contemporaneous chronology. In fact, however, the difference may be reduced by six months, as in Jewish tradtion, half a week is not 3½ days or years, but 3, since the sabbath day or year is not normally part of the computation. If so, Daniel may have dated the second stage of Antiochus' persecution in the fall of 166 B.C.E.; I Macc. 1:54, some ten months earlier. This method of computation would reduce Daniel's departure from the historical date to ten months, perhaps a permissible deviation in a chronomessianic book.

Daniel appears nearest to the historical date in his evident timing of the end of the persecution, presumably in Tishri of 163. For most purposes, however, in the ancient Jewish calendar, the year commenced in Nisan. And if Daniel intended to time, using the customary postdating, the cleansing of the Temple on Nisan 1 149 S.E. = April 163 B.C.E., this timing departs from that of I Macc. 1:54 by only three or four months.

Because Dan. 9:24–27 offers the classical locus of sabbatical chronomessianism, a relatively large section of this study dealt with this passage, permitting now a more abbreviated treatment of the evidence for this belief in subsequent Jewish writings. No matter how divergent their opinions might have been among men such as the author of the First Book of Maccabees, the members of Essene groups, Josephus, or the talmudic sages, they regarded Daniel's numbers as a guide to the date of the redemption. Even Christian chronography, which ultimately developed into a science, had had its foundation in Daniel.[22] To be sure, the ancient Jewish exegetes frequently misapplied or abused our passage; but their understanding, in contrast to that of modern scholarship, that Daniel referred to sabbatical messianism is right. Only with the gradual disappearance of the agricultural laws of shemittah from Jewish life did the link between the calendar and the expectations of redemption finally disappear.

II

Qumran Writings

If Daniel 9 pointed out the messianic implication of the sabbatical cycles, the author of Jubilees elaborated the same divisions of time for the creation of the world and Israel's history until the entry into Canaan. By its very formal title, "The Book of the Divisions of Times into their Jubilees and Sabbatical Cycles," the author shows his indebtedness to Daniel 9, as both *'ittim* and *shavu'ot(im)* were probably inspired by

22   H. Gelzer, *Sextus Julius Africanus* (Leipzig, 1880), I, 24–26.

Dan. 9:25.[23] Although the Book of Daniel never mentions the term directly, the jubilee forms the essence of Dan. 9:24–27. Daniel, we are told, became aware of the meaning of the sabbatical division by studying Jeremiah and Chronicles, with the aid of Gabriel (Dan. 9:2, 21–27). Jubilees' introductory sentence attributes the division of time into sabbaticals and jubilees to the Lord, as he had spoken to Moses on Mount Sinai. The angel of the Presence, according to Jub. 1:29, informed Israel that these periods would prevail from the creation "until the sanctuary of the Lord shall be made in Jerusalem in Mount Zion," i.e., probably to messianic rather than Solomonic times.

During the sabbatical year, according to the War between the Children of the Light and the Children of the Darkness, special sacrifices were ordained. Warfare was prohibited.[24] Thse nature of these sacrifices is obscure; the prohibition of warfare may have reflected a strictly sectarian view. But it seems clear that there existed, confirmed in writings so diverse as Josephus and Tacitus,[25] a tendency to equate the laws of the yearly sabbaths with those of the weekly sabbaths.

The recently published fragments from a partially preserved *pesher* offer a fascinating presentation of sabbatical chronomessianism.[26] Although written in the familiar Qumran style, the *pesher* applied Daniel's insight into what evidently was an anthology of biblical passages related to the sabbatical and jubilee themes, but which also included allusions to the reigns of the Righteous (Melchizedek) and Wicked (Melchiresha^c). After commenting on Lev. 25:13 in regard to the Israelites' return to their patrimony in the year of דרור (jubilee), the remission of debts in Deut. 15:2, and freedom (דרור) to the captives, proclaimed in Isa. 61:1, 11QMelch 3 II continues: "Its interpretation is: that He will proclaim them to be among the children of Heaven and of the inheritance of Melchizedek ... For He will restore (their patrimonies?) to them and proclaim freedom to them and make them abandon all of their sins. This shall take place during the sabbatical cycle (*shabu'a*) of the first jubilee following the ni[ne] jubilees, and on the D[ay of Atone]ment f[alling]

---

23   The term *'eth* is used 13 times in the Book of Daniel. CD 16:3–4.
24   IQM 2:6–10.
25   *A.J.* XIII, 234; Tacitus, *Hist.*, V, 4, 3.
26   A. S. van der Woude, "Melchisedek als himmlische Erlösungsgestalt in den neugefundenen eschatologischen Midraschim aus Qumran Höhle XI," *OTS* 14 (1965), 354–373; M. de Jonge and A. S. van der Woude, "11Qmelchizedeq and the New Testament," *NTS* 12 (1965–1966), 301–326: J. T. Milik, "Milkî-şedeq at Milkî-rešac dans les anciens écrits juifs et chrétiens," *JJS* 23 (1972), 95–144; "4Q visions de 'Amram et une citation d'Origène," *RB,* 79 (1972), 77–97. The citations below follow Milik's transcription of what is labeled as 11QMelch in *JJS*.

at the en[d of the ju]bilee, the tenth;[27] To forgive on it (the day of atonement) for all of (the sins) of all the children of [God and] the men of the lot of Melchizedek."[28] Although its main thought is quite clear, the precise chronology of the *pesher* remains obscure. There is no doubt, however, that the tenth jubilee alludes to the chronology of Dan. 9:24's 70 sabbatical cycles, which equals 10 jubilees, when Melchizedek will overcome Me(a)lchiresha[c]. Any lingering doubt that this is so disappears when one reads in line 18 of our fragment: "And the herald of good tidings (Isa. 52:7a) refers to the messiah, the Spirit concerning whom it was said by Dan[iel (9:25): 'Until the coming of the messiah, the prince, 7 sabbatical cycles...'"[29] Despite the fact that the *pesher* utilizes a long list of biblical passages, Dan. 9:24–27 remained the key to the author's chronology of sabbatical messianism.

Rabbinic Traditions

The Seder Olam, attributed to Rabbi Jose ben Ḥalafta (second century C.E.), but clearly a chronographic anthology of material stemming from several generations of scholars preceding and following Rabbi Jose, represents the rabbinic chronomessianic school. In chronicling the biblical events this treatise often adds the alleged current sabbatical and jubilee dates. The author does this particularly when he deals with momentous occasions, such as the building of Solomon's Temple or the disaster to Sennacherib's army.[30] Chapters 29–30 of Seder Olam, which may be regarded as a kind of midrash on Dan. 9:24–27, tailor the chronology of the burnings of the First and the Second Temples to make them conform to the author's view of Daniel's sabbatical numbers: 10 Jubilees = 70 Sabbatical cycles = 490 years elapsed from Nebuchadnezzar's to Titus' conquests of Jerusalem. To be sure, the Seder Olam, like the Book of Jubilees, formally merely furnished a chronicle of the past, but its deterministic chronology clearly points to a didactic lesson in the divine design of time.

We have place here for only a few of the numerous talmudic allusions to chronomessianic expectations. Of the paragraphs that make up the Eighteen Blessings, a fourth century Palestinian amora, Rabbi Aḥai,

27   This reading differs from that of Milik's rendition of 11QMelch 3 II lines 6–7 (*JJS* 23 [1972], 99): "Et cet événement [*aura li*]eu dans la première semaine (d'années) du jubilé suivant des neu[f] jubilés. El 'le j[our des Expia]tions' (*Lev.* 25:9) est a f[in du] dixième [jub]ilé...."
28   11QMelch 3 II, 4–8.
29   11QMelch 3 II, 18.
30   Seder Olam Rabbah (ed. Ratner), 11, 15, 23, 24, 25, 26, 27. Sennacherib's disaster, for example, is said on the basis of Isa. 37:30 to have occurred in a shemittah year (ch. 23, p. 53a–b).

noted that the seventh blessing (גאולת ישראל) dealt with the redemption of Israel, which he took to show that "Israel would not be redeemed except during the year of the sabbath."[31] An identical motif was ascribed to Ps. 126, relating the return of Zion, to its being the *seventh* of the fourteen psalms of Ascent.[32] A frequently cited Baraita describes the apocalyptic events of the seven years prior to the messiah's coming (all of which would be disastrous, except the years of shemittah) with the redeemer making his appearance during the postsabbatical year.[33] Mishnah Avot (5:8) expresses the link between redemption and the sabbatical year thus: "Exile came to the world because of idolatry, incest, the shedding of blood, and the (non-observance of) shemittah." For just as the observance of shemittah hastens redemption so its violation causes exile.[34]

Furthermore, talmudic computations of the messiah's expected appearance figure dates that coincided with Sabbatical chronology. "Just as the seventh offers a release to the Jew, so the world will be released during the seventh millennium," the epoch of the universal sabbath.[35] Sanhedrin 97b promises that the messiah would appear "after the year 4291 of the creation of the world"; its being in the Jewish calendar a shemittah year evidently played a role in the choosing of this specific date.[36]

Not only did the chronomessianic school claim to date the year when the redemption would come, but it presumed also to predetermine the season of the year. Rabbinic chronographers, including the authors of Seder Olam, dated events such as the angelic announcement of Sarah's impending pregnancy, Isaac's birth and God's covenant with Abraham as having occurred on the night of the 15th of Nisan.[37] The early *payyetan*, Yannai, who apparently flourished in the seventh century, using one line for each biblical incident, filled a twenty-four-line alphabetic acrostic poem, with incidents all of which allegedly occurred on the night of the 15th of Nisan; Abraham's victory over the four kings, Jacob's wrestling with the angel, Gideon's dream, the angel's striking the Assyrian army,

---

31 Yer. Berakhot, II, 4, 4d–5a; cf. B. Megillah 17b.

32 Yer. *ibid.*

33 B. Megillah 17b; Sanhedrin, 97a; Pesiqta d'Rab Kahana, *Baḥodesh* I, 97 f. (Mandelbaum ed.), Songs Rabbah on 2:11.

34 Cf. B. Shabbat, Targumim and Rashi, Lev. 26:34–35, 44. Rabbi Elijah of Vilna's biblical calendar, appended to the Seder Olam (Waxman ed.; New York, 1952), identifies the ten shemittah years neglected by Israel during the preexilic period.

35 B. Sanhedrin 97a; cf. Av. Zarah 9a. See also Gelzer (note 22); Seder Eliyyahu Rabbah 2.

36 Av. Zarah 9b, which gives year 4231 A.M. is apparently a corruption.

37 Seder Olam, 5; B. Rosh Hashanah, 11a.

Daniel in the lions' den, concluding with the expected coming of the redee-mer.[38] These Midrashic datings were of course based on nothing except the parallel with the timing of the Exodus. Their purpose was not so much to time the miraculous incidents as to emphasize the point that, in the words of the Mekilta and Tanḥuma, בניסן נגאלו ובניסן עתידין להגאל, "Dur-ing the month of Nisan they (Israel) were redeemed; they will be re-deemed again in Nisan."[39]

<h1 style="text-align:center">III</h1>

So far I have outlined the chronomessianic lore from Jeremiah to the late talmudic tradition. In this section I propose to show that the sab-batical calendar was probably a factor in the timing of the following messianic movements:

1. the commencement of John the Baptist's ministry; 2. the ascribed date of Jesus' birth; 3. Agabus; 4. the prophet of Egypt; and 5. Bar Kochba's uprising against Rome.

1. John the Baptist's Sabbatical Date

What is the evidence for the likelihood that John the Baptist commenced his ministry during or near the period when the Jews celebrated the year of release? Luke 3:1–2 offers a sixfold synchronism for John's date:

"In the 15th year of Emperor Tiberius, when Pontius Pilatus was pro-curator of Jerusalem, when Herod was prince of Galilee, his brother prince of Ituraea and Trachonitis, and Lysanias prince of Abilene, during the high priesthood of Annas and Caiaphas." It should be noted that this passage makes no mention of a sabbatical date, which might lead to a negative conclusion, that the sabbatical cycle played no or only a minor role in John's timing. Such a deduction is unwarranted because: a) even Graeco-Jewish historians, such as Josephus, customarily did not mention the year of the sabbatical cycle, perhaps since the Jews of the Diaspora did not observe shemittah; b) Luke addressed himself primarily to Gentile Christians; and c) conversely, Luke perhaps had no need to mention the chronomessianic link as it was taken for granted. The question whether John the Baptist's preaching coincided with the period of shemittah can be decided only on the basis of the contemporary calendar.

At first sight it should be a simple matter to convert Luke's "15th year of Emperor Tiberius" into a Julian date since Roman chronology

---

38   M. Zulay (ed.) *Piyyute Yannai* (Berlin, Schocken, 1938), 92 f.
39   B. Rosh Hashanah, 12b; Mekhilta, *Pisḥa*, 14, p. 52 (Harowitz and Rab-bin); Tanḥuma, *Wayyera'*, 17.

during this period is well attested. But the matter is complicated because it is not known which of the divergent calendars or regnal calculations Luke had in mind. Finegan and Hoehner have summarized the extensive scholarship on this point:[40] a) assuming that the reference is to Tiberius' dynastic reign, which commenced on August 19 of 14 c.e., Luke meant the year running from August 19 of 28 to August 18 of 29; b) if Luke's dating was the one customary in Antioch, presumably Luke's home town, the 15th year ran from Tishri 1 of year 27 to the end of Elul of year 28; c) by Babylonian and Jewish convention, the beginning of the regnal year fell in the spring, the 15th year of Tiberius ran from Nisan 1 of the Julian year 28 to the end of Adar of year 29 and d) if Luke followed the usage of Roman historians, such as Livy and Tacitus, Tiberius' 15th year commenced on January 1 and ended on December 31 of the year 28. Whichever of these methods of dating was intended by Luke, the whole or a part of Tiberius' 15th year coincided with the current sabbatical year that ran from Tishri 1 of year 27 to Elul 29 of year 28.[41]

If this synchronism of John's ministry is, or at least was assumed by Luke to have been historical, and if the synchronism was not a sheer accident, only under possibility b) could John have commenced his mission anytime during the year and still coincide with the sabbatical year. Under possibilities a), c), or d), however, his first public appearance could have taken place only during a fraction of the year. The largest fraction would have occurred under possibility d), from January 1 of 28 c.e. to Elul 29 by Jewish reckoning; from Nisan 1 to Elul 29 of 28 c.e., assuming possibility c); but only about a month, i.e. Elul of 28 c.e. under a). Whatever the fraction, if Luke's report of John's ministry in the 15th of Tiberius is historical, it coincided with the "sabbath of the land" in the Jewish calendar. But even if Luke or his sources invented the date, a problem which I do not here attempt to evaluate, the sabbatical calendar probably was a factor in John's timing. The fact that John began his ministry in 27/28, a year that happened to have been a shemittah, does not prove that he had deliberately planned the synchronism. For all we know, since John had to begin preaching sometime, if he was going to do it at all, the coincidence might reflect an accident. But the tradition of chronomessianism since Daniel suggests strongly that John planned the timing of his appearance in a season when preachers customarily called on the people to repent, for the "day of the Lord" was approaching.

If this timing was both deliberate and consistent with popular Jewish

---

40   J. Finegan, *Handbook of Biblical Chronology* (Princeton, N. J., Princeton University Press, 1964), 259–280; H. W. Hoehner, *Herod Antipas* (Cambridge, University Press, 1972), 307–312.
41   Wacholder, *HUCA*, 44 (1973), 190.

chronomessianism, John will have begun his ministry before or during the Passover season. "On Passover they were redeemed and on Passover they will be redeemed again." (It is of course more than a coincidence that Christ rose in the Passover season.) A major festival date for John, assuming Luke's dating was intended to be·precise, rather than approximate, would exclude possibility a) from the above mentioned listings. Thus Passover of 28 C.E. during the period of shemittah appears to be the most reasonable date, from a chronomessianic point of view, for the beginning of John the Baptist's ministry.

2. The Sabbatical Date of Jesus' Birth

Chronomessianic beliefs may also help explain why early Christian writers assigned the birth of Jesus to certain dates. We need not stop here to review the diverse traditions of the ancients and the immense scholarship of the moderns on this point. What ought to be remembered, however, is that the determination of the exact dates of birth, except in royal families or in circles among whom horoscopes were popular, was in antiquity rarely possible even for contemporaries. The date of Jesus' birth became a problem only after he had been proclaimed Christ by his followers. In other words, the question of Jesus' birth became enmeshed in chronographic and historical factors. Hence, it may be assumed that, presented with the problem of assigning the year of birth to Jesus, the early Christian writers, having absorbed the doctrine of sabbatical messianism, would tend to pick a timing in consonance with this belief.

Three sabbatical dates were available to Christian historians while remaining faithful to the Gospels: Tishri of year 9 to Elul of 8 B.C.E., 2/1 B.C.E., or 6/7 C.E. Luke (2:1-2) evidently chose the shemittah of 6/7, since he mentions Quirinius' census. That Sulpicius Quirinius became the procurator of Syria in C.E. 6 is attested by Josephus and possibly by an inscription.[42] A number of scholars posit, however, mainly on the basis of Luke, that Quirinius served in some kind of official post in the Near East also in 4-2 B.C.E.[43] If so, it might still fit with the chronomessianic tradition which would have expected the messiah during the shemittah of Tishri of year 2 to Elul of 1 B.C.E. In fact the earliest Christian chronographers from Clement to Eusebius offer the equivalent of 3/2 or 2 B.C.E.,[44] which tends to support the view that the ancient writers tended to favor a date that fell on the very eve of or during a shemittah.

---

42 Schürer, I, 516 f.
43 *A. J. XVIII*, 1-2. Cf. the literature cited by H. L. Feldman, in the LCL edition of Josephus, ad locum; cf. S. Sandmel, "Quirinius," in *IDB*, III, 975–977.
44 Finegan, *Handbook of Biblical Chronology*, 215–249.

3. *Agabus*

A certain Agabus, who together with other prophets came from Jerusalem to Antioch, according to Acts 11:27–30; 12:25, predicted a worldwide famine which in fact occurred during Claudius' reign. Joachim Jeremias took it for granted that whenever a famine is mentioned in Palestinian sources, it necessarily referred to deprivations caused by sabbatical years,[45] as if famines in Palestine other than during shemittah years or outside Palestine were, in antiquity, rare occurrences. Josephus (*A. J.* XX, 101) reports a famine in Judaea about that time, but divergent readings in the text, epitome and the Latin translation make it doubtful whether the famine occurred under Fadus (c.e. 44–45?) or under both Fadus and Tiberius Alexander (c.e. 45), or only during Tiberius Alexander's sole procuratorship (46–48). Contextually, the last date is the only plausible one under the circumstances.

4. *The Egyptian Prophet*

Little is known of the Jew of Egypt, labeled the prophet, except that Josephus brands him as one of the impostors who had promised to show to his followers "unmistakable marvels and signs...in harmony with God's design."[46] In Jerusalem and elsewhere he collected, according to Acts (21:38) 4,000 men, according to Josephus 30,000; but he was finally defeated by Felix, the Roman procurator, who with a large army slew some 400 of the prophet's followers and captured 200. The prophet himself, however, escaped unhurt, and his scattered believers continued to plague the land for a while.

The timing of this prophet is likewise poorly attested. We know that the procuratorship of Felix lasted from 52 to 60 c.e. Since Josephus records the story of this movement after having mentioned first Nero's accession, which took place in September of 54, and Felix's murder of the high priest, Jonathan, which apparently had occurred in early 55, the timing of this messianic movement coincided with the sabbatical year of 55/56.[47] In light of what has been said so far Nisan of 56 appears to be the likely date of the Egyptian prophet, a date that may have been regarded as "in harmony with God's design."

---

45 Jeremias (note 14) conveniently cites the ancient evidence on contemporary famines.

46 *A.J.* XX, 167 f.; cf. *B.J.* II, 61–63; Acts 32:38.

47 *A.J.* XX, 158 f. dates Nero's gift to Agrippa in the first year of Nero's reign, i.e. 54/55; 20:160–168 relates the rise of the Sicarii and the murder of Jonathan. Cf. *B.J.* II, 250–270.

5. Bar Kochba

Bar Kochba is the popular name (the rabbis called him Bar Koziba; he himself used Shimeon bar or ben Kosebah) of the leader of the second revolt against the Romans in 132–135. His official title was *nasi'*, denoting chief, prince, or king.[48] That his followers regarded Bar Kochba as the messiah of the Jews is almost certain. The very choice of the popular name of Kochba, denoting star (cf. Num. 24:17), instead of Bar Koziba (liar) suggests a claim of messianism. His coins and documents are dated according to a new era, that of "the Redemption of Israel" or "Freedom of Israel." Rabbi Akiba called him king, messiah. Ancient Jewish, Christian, pagan, now reinforced by numismatic and papyrological documents, combine to round out for us a picture of a messiah in action.[49]

As with regard to John the Baptist's ministry and the date of Jesus' birth, the timing of the beginning of Bar Kochba's revolt appears to synchronize with the season of shemittah.[50] Eusebius dated the revolt in 132–135 C.E. and the rabbinic tradition maintains that it lasted three and a half years. A number of scholars have dated the beginning of the revolt during Tishri of 132, but recently found numismatic and papyrological evidence has shown that spring of 132 is the correct date.[51] The nearest shemittah season lasted from Tishri 132 to Elul of 133. In other words, the timing of the uprising evidently coincided with the Passover season, on the eve of the Sabbatical year, in accordance with chronomessianic divine design.

Another point needs to be noted. The Julian date of 132/33, when the Bar Kochba rebellion commenced, happened to have been both a sabbatical and a jubilee year; which may have been an additional factor in the rise of the pitch of messianic fervor. As has been noted above (Dan. 9:24–27), the Qumran, and rabbinic writings, strongly suggest that the celebration of the jubilee year continued to be observed during inter-testamental times, as every 7th shemittah, or 49th year, was proclaimed a jubilee.[52] Unfortunately, unlike the dates of shemittah, none of those of the jubilee has survived. According to the reconstruction proposed

48 J. T. Milik, in *Discoveries in the Judean Desert II* (Oxford, Clarendon Press, 1961), 118–171.

49 Yer. Ta'anit, IV, 7 p. 68d; Aristo of Pella in *FGrH*, 201; Eusebius, *Eccl. Hist.* IV, 6.

50 For the scrupulous observance of the customs of shemittah during Bar Kochba's rule, see *Discoveries in the Judean Desert* II, 125 ff., suggesting perhaps that Hillel's   *prozbol* (M. Shevi'it, 10:3–8) had not been operative at the time.

51 B. Kanael, "Notes on the Dates Used During the Bar Kokhba Revolt," *EJ* 21 (1971), 39–46; Wacholder, *HUCA*, 44 (1973), 155, and passim, 153–184.

52. S. Safrai, "Yovel," in *Encyc. Hebraica* (in Hebrew), says that there is no shred of evidence for the existence of jubilee since the postexilic period. That

above, however, 603/02–555/54 B.C.E. constituted a jubilee cycle in Daniel's calendar, which Table 3 extends to the Bar Kochba period, showing that 132/33 C.E. was a jubilee year.

TABLE THREE

JUBILEE CYCLES

No. of Jub.	B.C.E.	No. of Jub.	B.C.E.	No. of Jub.	B.C.E., C.E.
1	603/02–555/54	6	358/57–310/09	11	113/12–65/64
2	554/53–506/05	7	309/08–261/60	12	64/63–16/15
3	505/04–457/56	8	260/59–212/11	13	15/14–32/35 C.E.
4	456/55–408/07	9	211/10–163/62	14	35/36–83/84
5	407/06–359/58	10	162/61–114/13	15	84/85–132/33

It is evident that the observance of the sabbatical years and jubilees during the intertestamental times played a far larger role in the consciousness of Israel than has been hitherto recognized. Immense as were the effects of the calendar of sabbatical cycles on the agricultural and social life of the people, its influence was no less on the formulation of Jewish religious beliefs. Concepts such as creation, history, apocalypse, and eschatology all became enmeshed with the calendar of sabbatical cycles. In the 7th year debts were cancelled, hard labor in the fields stopped; the voice of freedom was heard throughout the land as the steps of the messiah were believed to have become more and more audible.

---

a specific Pentateuchal commandment was altogether ignored, however, seems unlikely, especially in view of the observance of shemittah. Aside from Dan. 9:24–27 and the literature cited in notes 26–29, see also Yer. Sanhedrin V, 1, 22c; B. Sanhedrin, 40b. In fact, supposedly, the Book of Jubilees is rather inconceivable without the assumed existence of some aspects of the institution of the jubilee.

CHURCH AND STATE IN THE LATER
ROMAN EMPIRE[1]

THE title of this book is more comprehensive than its contents. Notwithstanding the main title, this is not a history of the relations between *Church and State in the Later Roman Empire* but rather a contribution to this topic limited to an account of *The Religious Policy of Anastasius the First* as the subtitle reads. A transposition of the titles would express in an adequate way the contents of the book and the author's main point at issue. But even so the well-known inseparability of religious and secular policy in the Byzantine Empire makes it impossible to isolate one from the other. The picture drawn of Anastasius is based on primary and secondary material, i.e., all the source material and the already·existing research into the subject. Both are dealt with in a special note (pp. 81–89) and enumerated in the bibliography (pp. 91–96). To the latter I add: Otto Bardenhewer, *Geschichte der altkirchlichen Literatur*, vols. IV and V, Freiburg im Breisgau, 1932; E. Merten, "De Bello Persico ab Anastasio Gesto," *Commentationes Philologae*, Jena, 1906, 2nd part, pp. 139–201; A. Vogt, *Constantin VII Porphyrogénète: Le Livre de Cérémonies*, Paris, 1935; W. Ensslin, "Nochmals zu der Ehrung Chlodowechs durch Kaiser Anastasius," *Historisches Jahrbuch der Goerresgesellschaft*, LVI, 1936, pp. 499–507; O. Treitinger, *Die ostroemische Kaiser- und Reichsidee*, Jena, 1938; F. Doelger, "Die Kaiserurkunder der Byzantiner als Ausdruck ihrer politischen Anschauungen," *Historische Zeitschrift*, LIX, 1938–39, pp. 229–50.

Dr. Charanis' excellent treatment itself urges me *not* to accept his main point at issue that there is "little evidence that Anastasius' religious policy was shaped by his own religious convictions" (p. 13), that he was a "pragmatist" (p. 19), and that the main purpose of his policy was "the establishment of ecclesiastical peace" (p. 25). But that Anastasius' own hidden Monophysite religious convictions shaped his entire policy is undeniable. It was not for nothing that the Patriarch

---

[1] *Church and State in the Later Roman Empire.* The Religious Policy of Anastasius the First, 491–518. By PETER CHARANIS. Madison: THE UNIVERSITY OF WISCONSIN PRESS, 1939. Pp. vi+102. $1.50.

261

431

Euphemius agreed to the coronation of the man whose preaching he had forbidden only after having received Anastasius' profession of the Council of Chalcedon where Nestorianism and Eutychianism (which went on slightly modified under the new title of Monophysism) had been anathematized. If Anastasius had been a real pragmatist he would never have tried to impose Monophysism on provinces with strong Chalcedonian inclinations. Furthermore, it was detrimental to the establishment of ecclesiastical peace between Rome and Byzantium when Anastasius honored the Franconian King Chlodewech in the year 508, a very important incident overlooked by the author (see above Ensslin). The book would have gained if the author had tried to sketch the emperor's attitude toward the clearly established Byzantine idea of state and church (see the papers of Treitinger and Doelger quoted above).

Print and format of the book are excellent. The title of Hormisdas as *bishop of Rome* is a paraphrase of the simpler title *pope* and should not appear in a register (p. 100).

LUITPOLD WALLACH

Florence, Alabama

THE THIRD-CENTURY SEAT OF
CALENDAR REGULATION

By Abraham Weiss

I

It is generally maintained that although the seat of the court for the regulation of the leap year — עיבור שנה — had been moved by R. Judah I from Judah to Galilee, the seat of the court for the regulation of the month — קידוש החדש — still remained in Judah for some time, if not for several generations.

The information illuminating this problem comes from a few passages in the Palestinian and Babylonian Talmuds (where Entab is mentioned as the seat of calendar-regulation), and principally from a passage in Y. Sanhedrin 18c, which reads:[1]

Rabbi Eleazar related in the name of Rabbi Ḥanina that the inhabitants of 24 villages of Beth-Rabbi who entered Lydda to regulate the leap year had been struck by an evil eye, all of them dying simultaneously. In that time the regulation of the leap year was moved from Judah to Galilee. It was intended to transfer this סימנא too, but Rabbi Simon said to them: shall we not even leave a memento in Judah?

Here we have an explicit record of the transfer of עיבור שנה from Judah to Galilee. Furthermore, we note that the transfer of the סימנא was also intended, but R. Simon opposed the step.

The meaning of the word סימנא and the identity of the R. Simon herein mentioned constitute the principal difficulties of the passage.

Some passages in the Yerushalmi dealing with calendar-regulation contain the expression אזל לעיין טב לסימנא — he went

רבי אלעזר בשם רבי חנינא מעשה בכ״ד קריות של בית רבי שנכנסו לעבר שנה בלוד ונכנסה [1]
בהן עין רעה ומתו כולם בפרק אחד מאותה שעה עקרוה סיהודה וקבעוה בגליל בעיון סיעקר
.אף אהן סיסנא אסר לון רבי סיסון אין אנו סניחין ביהודה אפילו זכר
267

to Entab for סימנא. Furthermore, in several Talmudic passages, Entab is mentioned as the seat of קידוש החדש. Therefore, it would seem, סימנא signifies the regulation of the month — קידוש החדש. Hence the passage quoted above from Y. Sanhedrin reads: it was also intended to move the קידוש החדש from Judah to Galilee, but R. Simon (who is to be identified with R. Simai, the contemporary of R. Judah I) opposed the action. The authority of קידוש החדש, therefore, remained in Judah — viz. in Entab, which we actually do find in later generations as the seat of קידוש החדש.

This view is held by Graetz[2] and Halevy.[3] Ginzberg in his commentary on the Palestinian Talmud[4] follows it as far as the assumption that סימנא signifies קידוש החדש, and that R. Simon is to be identified with R. Simai. However, he has some doubts as to whether Entab is actually located in Judah.[5] As a compromise, he suggests that Entab be located in Galilee; the transfer of the seat of the court for calendar-regulation was a partial one. At first only the עיבור שנה was moved from Judah to some spot in Galilee, while the court presiding over קידוש החדש still remained in Jamnia in Judah. Later, however, the seat of קידוש החדש was also removed from Judah to Entab in Galilee. Jawets, in his work *Toldoth*[6] follows Schwartz[7] in placing the location of Entab in Galilee, which was, in his opinion, the seat of all calendar-regulation. But as to the time of this transfer, he seems to be very unclear. He merely emphasizes the transfer of עיבור שנה by R. Judah I towards the end of the latter's life. Furthermore, סימנא means, according to Jawets, the sending of secret messages concerning the decided regulation. Hence סימנא in the Yerushalmi equals שלח לי סימנא in Babli R. H. 25a.

Before proceeding to an investigation of the sources, it is worthwhile to call attention to the following two points:

---

[2] Geschichte IV. 199.   [3] Doróth II. 64 f.

[4] III. 125 ff.

[5] L. c. p. 131: וקשה למצוא טעם למה עקר בסוף ימיו מקום קה׳׳ח מיבנה שביהודה לעינטב שביהודה.

[6] VI, Note 11, p. 338 f.

[7] תבואת הארץ, חלוקת הארץ, יששכר, comp. also Halevy l. c. note 34.

It is expressly stated:[8] אין מעברין את השנה אלא ביהודה; nowhere, however, does such a statement occur regarding קידוש החדש. Nevertheless, עיבור שנה was transferred without opposition; over the moving of קידוש החדש there arose opposition which even prevented the action. Indeed, there occurred the death of the 24 קריות, but this was in the face of an interdiction: אין מעברין את השנה אלא ביהודה, while there was no interdiction stating, אין מקדשין את החדש אלא ביהודה.

According to the interpretation of סימנא as קידוש החדש, the statement אין אנו מניחין ביהודה אפילו זכר is hardly appropriate.[9] עיבור שנה takes place once in three years, and קידוש החדש at least 36 times in three years. One could, therefore, hardly cite קידוש

---

[8] B. Sanh. 11b: ת"ר אין מעברין את השנה אלא ביהודה ואם עברוה בגליל סעוברת העיד חנניא איש אונו אם עברוה בגליל אינה מעוברת א"ר יהודה בריה דר"ש בן פזי ס"ט דחנניא איש אונו. א"ק לשכנו תדרשו ובאת שמה כל דרישה שאתה דורש לא יהא אלא בשכנו של מקום But אין מעברין . . . סעוברת העיד חנניה איש אונו לפני רבן נסליאל in the Tos. ibid II,13: שאין מעברין את השנה אלא ביהודה ואם עברוה בגליל סעוברת And Y. Sanh. 18d f.: סעוברת העיד חנניא איש אונו שאם אינה יכולה להתעבר ביהודה שמעברין אותו בגליל . . . אין. Concerning Hananya's testimony we have three different readings. Yet the reading of the Yer. seems to be influenced by the following discussion there: אין מעברין בחו"ל ואם עברוה אינה מעוברת את חמי בנליל אין מעברין בחו"ל מעברין בנליל אין מעברין ואם עברוה סעוברת בחו"ל אין מעברין ואם עברוה אינה מעוברת ביכולין לעבר בא"י אבל בשאינן יכולין לעבר בא"י שמעברין אותה בחו"ל ירמיה עיבר בחו"ל וכו'. The passage: את חמי . . . ואם עברוה אינה מעוברת, is rather difficult and Y. Nedarim 40a has actually: סעוברת העיד חנניא . . . שמעברין אותה בנליל אין סעברין את השנה בנליל ואם עברוה סעוברת אין מעברין את השנה בחו"ל ואם עברוה אינה סעוברת בשיכולים לעברה בא"י אבל בשאין יכולים לעברה בא"י סעברים אותה בחו"ל ירסיה וכו'. One almost has the impression, that Sanh. originally had another reading. But nevertheless the wording of Hananya's testimony is influenced by this discussion. The reading of the Bab. is proved by R. Judah b. R. Simon b. Pasi, and has also a certain support in the Mekilta Bo II end: רבי יאשיה אומר מנין שאין שאין מעברין את השנה אלא בבית דין הנדול שבירושלים ת"ל ראשון הוא לכם. It seems therefore, that we have here at least two different views, an older one presented by the Babli and Mekilta, and a later one in the Yer. and Tosefta. Between Yer. and Tosefta the reading of the Tosefta is certainly the primary one.

Prof. L. Ginzberg called my attention to the fact that העיד usually has an affirmative meaning. In accordance with this the reading of the Babli is very questionable and the right reading should there too be סעוברת and not אינה סעוברת.

[9] Jawets felt this difficulty, but the identification of our סימנא with שלח לי סימנא in B. R. H. 25 is untenable.

החדש in a comparative connection with עיבור שנה, as being only a sign of remembrance, אפילו זכר.

It is appropriate to examine now the passages containing סימנא and Entab together.

In Y. Sukkah II.5 it is stated:[10] R. Honah went to Entab for סימנא. Upon arriving at the highway, he became thirsty, but refused to taste anything until he entered the *Sukkah* of R. Johanan, the scribe of Gufta.

The business at which R. Honah went to Entab hardly seems to be that of קידוש החדש. He went there on Sukkot, and these are very early days for קידוש החדש.

Further attention should be given to the wording: "when he arrived" (מי אתי), on the one hand, and to the two geographical references איסרטא and נופתא, on the other.

What is the meaning of the statement: he went to Entab, and, upon arriving at the איסרטא, he became thirsty? Was he already at the end of his journey? Now, should we be in the position to determine the direction of this highway, and should we be able to say exactly what cities or places it connected, it would be of great help in locating the direction and location of Entab. For the present, however, we only have the name of the place נופתא.

In Y. R. H. II.5, we read: רבי חנינא אזל לעין טב למימנא והה אוירא מעונן אמר כדון אמרין מה נטיל אוירא מהן סבא והקריח לו הקב"ה ככברה ונראה מתוכה.

This passage certainly deals with קידוש החדש, but here instead of סימנא, the reading is מימנא. The word מימנא, from the root מנה or מנא, with the prefix[11] "מ", can be a verbal substantive; it can thus not only mean nomination or ordination, but can signify as well the name of a body, subject, action, or something else which was either to perform or was connected in some way with nomination or ordination.

[10] רב חונה אזל לעיינטב לסימנה מי אתי צחא גו איסרטא ולא קביל עלוי מיטעום כלום עד דעל למטללתא דרבי יוחנן ספרה דנופתא.

[11] Similarly B. Sota 40a: לסמנייה ברישא. Y. Bikkurim 65cd: . . . . הוון בעיין ססניתא, Kohelet r. p. קשע כי העשק has: הוה ססני תרין סנאין and parallels in Yer.: תרין סינויין, קביל עלוי סמניתא.

The reading מימא is here at least no less plausible than סימנא, because his own activities and that of the body in Entab were certainly connected in many ways with both nomination and ordination. However, it must be admitted that here alone the reading of סימנא in the sense of קידוש החדש is also plausible.

Although there are two passages with the reading סימנא against one with the reading מימנא (and in the later, the reading סימנא is also plausible), it is nevertheless not probable, that the סימנא is the correct reading. Summing up the examination of the three passages which have סימנא, we find: that of Sanhedrin contains the wording אפילו זכר, raising some objections to סימנא as קידוש החדש. In Sukkah, it isn't probable that the passage deals with קידוש החדש. The word סימנא seems, therefore, to have a broader meaning than that of קידוש החדש. And the last passage, in R. H., reads מימנא, making good sense there. It, therefore, seems most acceptable to adopt the reading of מימנא, which certainly makes good sense in R. H. and Sukkah, and in Sanh. too, as will be indicated below.

In several passages[12] Entab is recorded as the seat of קידוש החדש. But *when* did Entab become the seat of קידוש החדש?

In Y. R. H. III.5 we read: אבא בר בא שאל לרבי שופר קדוח מהו א'ל כזה תוקעין ביבנה רבי בא בעי קומי רב שופר קדוח מהו א'ל כזה תוקעין בעיינטב. From this passage it is possible to conclude that during the time when Rab had been living in Palestine, the seat of קידוש החדש had in all likelihood already been transferred from Jamnia to Entab. This means that it was moved by R. Judah I.

This is further evidence by the passage in B. R. H. 25a: רבי חייא חזייא לסיהרא דהוה קאי בצפרא בעשרים ותשעה שקל קלא פתק ביה אמר לאורתא בעינן לקדושי בך ואת קיימת הכא זיל איכסי א'ל רבי לרבי חייא זיל לעין טב וקדשיה לירחא ושלח לי סימנא דוד מלך ישראל חי וקיים.

The סימנא herein mentioned naturally has no connection either with our סימנא or מימנא. The expression שלח לי סימנא here means nothing but, "Notify me, by a symbol, of the decision."[13] The

---

[12] So Y. Berakot IV.1, Sanh. I.2.

[13] This was needed, because the formal declaration of קידוש החדש was left to the Nasi as his own privilege. In my article in the volume dedicated to the memory of Prof. M. Schorr I try to prove, that this was an innovation made probably by R. Judah I. See there Notes 52, 53.

question, however, as to whether we have here a narration of
only one or two facts,[14] may for the present remain unanswered.
At any rate, we see here that R. Hiyya was sent by Rabbi to
Entab for קידוש החדש.[15]

II

It remains for us to determine the location of the איסרטא
and נופתא.

We read in Y. Shekalim VII.5:[16] A roasted lamb had been
found at the איסרטא בנופתא and the man who had found it received from the rabbis permission to keep it and eat it. It was
then found to have come from Beth-Rabbi.

Here we find again the איסרטא בנופתא, and it appears to be
near בית רבי. We should, therefore, be looking for some spot in
the vicinity of ציפורי. Indeed, in Babli B. M. 24b we find:
רבי חנינא מצא גדי שחוט בין שיבריה לציפורי והתירוהו לו א'ר אמי התירוהו
משום מציאה כרשב'א משום שחיטה וכו'. Here is doubtless a record of
the identical incident, except that in the second passage, we find
בין טבריה לציפורי instead of איסרטא בנופתא. Furthermore, in
Y. Kilayim IX.4 (= Kethuboth XII.3) we read: "and the voice
of the inhabitants of ציפורי, who rent their garments at hearing
of the death of R. Judah I, was heard in נופתא, a distance of
three miles."[17]

We are now in a position to determine the location of נופתא
and the איסרטא דנופתא as well. נופתא had been established three
miles east of ציפורי. And the איסרטא mentioned in Y. Sukkah,
where R. Honah became thirsty when he arrived there on
his journey to Entab, is certainly the איסרטא דנופתא connecting
טבריה with ציפורי, leading from east to west.

[14] If Entab is in Judah it would have been impossible for R. Hiyya to reach
it on the same day, and it is therefore necessary to assume, that: רבי חייא
חייא לסיהרא וכו', and: א'ל רבי לרבי חייא וכו', are two different facts. Comp.
Ginzberg l. c. 129 f.

[15] About the different versions comp. Ginzberg l. c.
[16] גדי צלי אישתכח באיסרטא דנופתא והתירוהו משם שני' דברים משם מציאה ומשם רוב
מהלכי דרכים . . . ואישתכח דבית רבי
[17] ואזל קלא דקרעון לנופתא מהלך נ' מילין.

Finally, we come to the problem of identifying the R. Simon who defended the prerogative of Judah with his statement: אין אנו מניחין ביהודה אפילו זכר.

Y. Horayoth (end) reads:[18] If there be need to nominate (or ordain) elders, wherefrom shall they be nominated, from טבריה, i. e. Galilee, or from the South, i. e. Judah? R. Simon said: "Judah shall go up." R. Mana replied: this had been said in connection with war (Judges 1:2), but for nomination (or ordination), it is "they who saw the king's face and sat first in the kingdom (Esther 1.4)."

The entire story related here is not quite clear. We have however the explicit statement:[19] רובן של סנהדרין משל יהודה היו. At best this can only be accounted for by the fact that Judah was really for the longest time both the seat of the Sanhedrin and the main center of learning. Even if we should maintain that the sages of Judah had any prerogative to membership in the Sanhedrin, this is hardly understood in this connection. We read here: למנות זקנים, which ordinarily signifies ordination, which, in turn, is radically different from membership in the Sanhedrin. It is too far fetched to conclude from the question, מאיכן ממנים, that we are dealing with a kind of nomination or ordination, in which the number of places is limited. This too could hardly be the case with ordination as we know it to have been constituted.

At any rate, we have again encountered R. Simon as defender of Judah's precedence, whatever the circumstances may have been. Hence, I see no reason to differentiate between the R. Simon of the passage quoted above from Sanhedrin, and the R. Simon cited here in Horayoth. In both instances, his name is spelled identically, and in both instances the same conviction and purpose are manifested in a discussion with others. Moreover, as we shall soon see, these were in all likelihood, two discussions of the same question.

---

[18] ביקשו ליסנות זקנים סאיכן הן ססנים סטבריה או סדרוסא אסר רבי סיסון יהודה יעלה אסר ליה רבי סנא הדא דת סר לסלחסה אבל לסנויי רואי פני סלך היוסבים ראשונה בסלכות.

[19] Bereshit R. 98.

We can, therefore, quite assuredly identify R. Simon in
Sanhedrin with R. Simon in Horayoth. Hence, R. Simon in
the former passage is not R. Simon the contemporary of R.
Judah I but a later sage contemporaneous with R. Mana.

III

After this clarification, we return to the sources in an attempt
to reclarify them in the light of our explanation.

a) If R. Simon is not R. Simai, the contemporary of R.
Judah I, we have in Y. Sanhedrin 18c two different accounts:
1) concerning the 24 קריות and the transfer of עיבור שנה from
Judah to Galilee, which took place during Rabbi's lifetime;
2) that it was desired to remove the סימנא as well, which actually did happen during the days of R. Simon, the contemporary
of R. Mana.

But what is the סימנא, which they had then wanted to remove? We have already seen that the reading מימנא is not only
a possible one in the other two passages, but a very likely one
as well; we will, therefore, attempt to read מימנא here too and
test its acceptability. We read anew: בעיון מיעקר אף אהין מימנא —
they also wished to remove from Judah the privilege of ordain-
ing or nominating (or both). In this context, it would mean
that they wished to remove from Judah the prerogative to membership in the court of calendar-regulation. The nature of this
privilege has already been explained by Halevy;[20] namely, the
greatest number of the sages mentioned as members of this
court were from the South, i. e. from Judah. This privilege in
a comparison with the entire sitting of the court in Judah could
have very well been called אפילו זכר. The reading is appropriate
here too, and it should, therefore, be substituted as the correct
one.

b) Now it should not appear too presumptuous for us to
assume that we have in Horayoth the almost identical situation.

The question מאיכן ממנים was not concerning ordination, but
concerning the nomination of members for the court of calendar-

[20] L. c.

regulation. Their members were periodically nominated *ad hoc*.[21]
The number of those nominated was limited, and the position
was greatly coveted by the sages.[22] From this point of view,
this passage assumes clarity and intelligibility in its own
light. It seems, moreover, to discuss the same matter as that
mentioned in Sanhedrin, to wit, the membership of the court
for calendar-regulation, which was defended by R. Simon.

We now come to the geographical problem to which Entab
is central.

a) The following observations may be recalled: נופתא is in
Galilee, a distance of several miles from ציפורי on the highway
to טבריה.

The seat of עיבור שנה was moved by R. Judah I from Judah
to Galilee.

During the lifetime of R. Judah I, Entab was already the
seat of קידוש החדש.

R. Honah probably went to Entab for a purpose other than
that of קידוש החדש.

Going to Entab, R. Honah used the highway leading from
east to west, and not from north to south, which would be the
simplest route if Entab had been in Judah.

Arriving in נופתא, R. Honah seems to have been at the end of
his journey to Entab.

b) Considering all these observations, the most plausible conclusions are the following:

Entab was in Galilee, being very close to נופתא, and, hence, to
ציפורי as well. Perhaps Entab is even to a certain measure to be
identified with נופתא, i. e. there was a particular spot in the
vicinity of נופתא called Entab, which served as the seat for
calendar-regulation.

Entab was not only the seat of קידוש החדש, but of the entire
calendar-regulation, i. e. קידוש החדש and עיבור שנה.

In accordance with this explanation, the passage in Y. Sukkah
II.5 would mean that R. Honah went to Entab for עיבור שנה.

---

[21] So Sanh. 10b: אין מעברין את השנה אלא בטוסנין, Y. *ibid.* 18c: יקרוני שבעה
זקנים.

[22] See Yer. Sanh. 18c bottom.

He went there on סוכות, which is occasionally the time for consideration of עיבור שנה. Arriving in נופתא, he was actually at the end of his journey, since Entab is to some measure identical with נופתא.

This is further evidenced by a passage in Pesik. R.,[23] in which it is said of Entab, that there: היו יושבים ומעברים השנים והחדשים. This passage is based on reliable sources and may be taken literally.

Not only the עיבור שנה, but קידוש החדש was also removed by R. Judah I from Judah to Galilee. Moreover, both acquired their seat simultaneously in Entab, in the vicinity nearest to the Nassi.

Accordingly, we have in Babli R. H. 25a but one continuous account.[24] R. Hiyya saw the moon on the 29th day of the month, and on this same day he was sent by Rabbi to Entab for קידוש החדש, since Entab was only one or two hours' walking distance from the residence of Rabbi.

c) Hence, the conclusion would be that at the beginning of the third century, the seat of all calendar-regulation was moved by R. Judah I from Judah to Galilee. The immediate reason for this change seems to have been a political one, as evidenced by the death of the 24 קריות, and also hinted at in external sources.[25] It is very probable, however, that in addition to these considerations, it must have been largely motivated by the fact that the Nassi had been living in Galilee.

---

[23] Pes. 41. But see also Ginzberg l. c. p. 128. Yet in my above mentioned article I tried to prove that the reading עיבור חדש, known to Yer. as well as to Babli, in the Mishna San. I.3, is the right one.

[24] See above note 14.

[25] See the quotation by Graetz, M.G.W.J. 1884 p. 481 f.

ENCYCLOPAEDIA JUDAICA:
THE STATUS OF JEWISH SCHOLARSHIP

By SOLOMON ZEITLIN, Dropsie University

THE IDEA OF PUBLISHING a Jewish Encyclopaedia *de novo* was originated by Dr. Nachum Goldman. Dr. B. Netanyahu was designated as the editor-in-chief of this undertaking. As far as I know, he assembled a staff and was working in one of the buildings at Dropsie University. When Dr. Netanyahu told me about the publication of a Jewish Encyclopaedia, my reaction was negative. I told him that we have no reservoir of Jewish scholars, able to publish a worthwhile scholarly encyclopaedia. My opinion was that there should be supplements of one or two volumes to the *Jewish Encyclopaedia* which appeared in the beginning of the century. The supplements should have items of Jewish history in America, which in the last seven decades became the largest Jewish community in the world, items about the Jewish history from the first World War up to the present. The supplements also should have an item about the so-called Dead Sea Scrolls, but that article had to be nonpartisan and should present the ideas of the protagonists of the antiquity as well as the ideas of those who denied the antiquity.

Modern days are the age of public relations, and this is used to its utmost. The appearance of the *Encyclopaedia Judaica* was heralded as a major event in the world of Jewish scholarship and literature. The great accomplishment of the work was spread all over the Anglo-Jewish press. Copies were presented to President Nixon and to Pope Paul VI. These presentations remind me of the history of the Jews in Russia, when the Czar visited a city which had a large Jewish population, the Jewish leaders presented him with a *Sefer Torah*. However, the backgrounds of these presentations are radically different.

I

The publicity about the scholarly importance of the *Encyclopaedia Judaica* intrigued me. I thought maybe I under-estimated modern Jewish scholarship. Maybe we do have a reservoir of Jewish scholars of whom I was not aware. They are dwelling in ivory towers and do not publish, just as we are told that every generation has thirty-six pious people, whom the world does not know.

Since I am very engrossed in my work on the history of the Second Jewish Commonwealth and I cannot spare much time to go over the sixteen volumes of the Encyclopaedia I decided to read some of its items dealing with the history of the Second Jewish Commonwealth and Talmudic studies. The first item which I read was "Shavuot". Reading this item, I was dismayed to see how the article is inadequate and full of misstatements. To my regret, I saw that I did not under-estimate the scholarly abilities of our times. To be more objective, I did not look at the names of the authors. Some of them I may know and greatly respect—so in my reviews of the articles in the Encyclopaedia, I do not know who are the authors.

The author of the item "Shavuot" states: "It is possible that the Pharisees insisted that Shavuot be observed on a fixed day, for they wished to affirm that the festival comme-morated the Sinaitic theophany which occurred on the 50th day after the Exodus." The entire statement is fallacious. The Pharisees never held that the festival of Shavuot, Atzeret (the festival of Weeks) had to be observed on a fixed day or date. As a matter of fact, Shavuot, Atzeret, had no fixed date until the fourth century of the common era, when the present Jewish calendar was established. According to the Tosefta Arakhin and the Palestinian Talmud, R. H., Shavuot, Azeret, could fall on the fifth, sixth and seventh day of the third month, Sivan. The statement, "they (the Pharisees) wished to affirm that the festival commemorated the Sinaitic theo-phany which occurred on the 50th day after the Exodus", is either due to carelessness or to a lack of comprehension.

According to the Pentateuch, the festival of Shavuot should be on the 50th day after the offering of the *omer*. According to the Pharisees, the *omer* was brought on the sixteenth day of the first month, Nisan. The Exodus took place on the fifteenth day of that month, so, the festival of Shavuot would be on the fifty-first day after the Exodus. Neither the Pharisees nor the early Tannaim ever connected Shavuot with the Exodus. The author's statement is unfortunate.

In the article *Am Ha-Arez*, we have the following assertion: "In Hagigah 2:7, where the amha-arez appears on the lowest rung of the ladder of ritual purity. 'The clothes of the *am Ha-Arez* are *midras* (unclean) for Pharisees.' " Apparently, the author followed the faulty translation of the Mishne by Danby, where he rendered the word פרושים Pharisees. If the author had studied the text of the Mishne, he would have realized that the word פרושים has the connotation of separatists. The rendering of the Mishne is as follows, "The garments of the *am ha-aretz* are *midras* to the פרושים i.e., to those who maintain levitical purity. The garments of the *perushim*, the separatists, are *midras* to those who eat *Terumah*, i.e., priests. The garments of the priests are *midras* to those who eat hallowed food. The garments of those who partake of the hallowed food are *midras* to the sin offering." Each represents a higher level of sanctity and requires a higher degree of purity.

בגדי עם הארץ מדרס לפרושין בגדי פרושין מדרס לאוכלי תרומה
בגדי אוכלי תרומה מדרס לקודש בגדי קודש מדרס לחטאת. M. Hag. 2.4.

That the Mishne deals with the degree of purity can be proven by the previous Mishne.

חטובל לחולין והוחזק לחולין אסור למעשר טבל למעשר .Ibid. 5
והוחזק למעשר אסור לתרומה טבל לתרומה והוחזק לתרומה אסור לקודש
טבל לקודש והוחזק לקודש אסור לחטאת.

Cf. also Talmud B.B. 60 כשחרב הבית בשניה רבו פרושין בישראל
שלא לאכול בשר ושלא לשתות יין.

תניא יהודה בן דורתאי פירש הוא ודורתאי בנו והלך וישב לו 70 .Pes
.בדרום .... אמר רב אשי ואנן טעמא דפרושים ניקו ונפרש

The term Perushim in the meaning of Pharisees never occurs either in the Mishne or in the tannaitic literature. It only occurs in the dialogues between the Sadducees and the Pharisees. The Sadducces said: "We complain against you Pharisees", and the Pharisees retorted: "We complain against you Sadducces." Or, it occurred also in the mouths of their opponents. Cf. Talm, Kid. 66, Sota 22b.

The item on the Pharisees is both meager and confused. Apparently, the author read some literature which he did not fully digest. It seems from the article that he did not make a study of the sources. The author writes: "Pharisees, *Perushim*, a Jewish religious and political party or sect during the Second Temple period which emerged as a distinct group shortly after the Hasmonean revolt, about 165-160 B.C.E." In another paragraph, the author states: "The Pharisees' first bid for power was made in a period two centuries after the Babylonian exile during the struggle to remove the Temple and religious control from the sole leadership of the aristocratic Sadducees." The Judaeans were exiled by the Babylonians in the year 587-86, two hundred years after the exile would bring us to 387-86. Thus it is a flagrant contradictory statement. Did the Pharisees come into existence in the year 386 or in 165? It is a difference of over two hundred years. It is surprising that the editor did not notice this blunder.

According to the author, the inception of "synagogue worship" is to be traced to the period of the Pharisees and came into being two centuries after the Babylonian exile. This is false. The synagogue as a house of worship came into Jewish life after the destruction of the Second Temple.

The author makes the following statement: "Under John Hyrcanus the Pharisees were expelled from membership in the Sanhedrin and branded with the name *Perushim*, 'separated ones'. They took the name as their own but under its alternate Hebrew meaning, 'the exponents' ''. From this statement we may assume that the name *Perushim*, separatists, was applied to them at the time of John Hyrcanus, while Josephus tells us that at the time of Jonathan, there were three sects, the Pharisees, Sadducees and Essenes. Furthermore, the author says that they, the group, adopted the name *Perushim* under the meaning of exponents, i.e. they expounded the law. This is again wrong. We do not find in the entire tannaitic literature that the *Perushim* expounded the law, but we have the phrase, "the sages say it."

According to the author, the Pharisees believed in the coming of the Messiah. This is historically untrue. Neither in the Talmud nor in the writings of Josephus it is ever mentioned that the Pharisees believed in the coming of the Messiah.

The author further says: "The Pharisees spoke of God as 'the Creator of the World' (*Bore Olam*), 'the Place' (*Ha-Makom*), 'the Divine Presence' (*Shekhinah*), and so forth." The Pharisees never used the term *Bore Olam*. It is a late cipher for God, neither did they use *Ha-Makom*. The term *Ha-Makom* as a cipher for God came into usage after the destruction of the Second Temple. The Temple was termed τόπος, place, *Makom*. The first of the sages who used the term *Ha-Makom* as a cipher for God was Akabya b. Mahalael who lived at the time of Rabban Gamaliel the second. The term *Shekhinah* came into vogue long after the destruction of the Second Temple.

The Talmud never quotes any *halakha* in the name of the Pharisees. The term used in the tannaitic literature is "the sages said." However, we do have some dialogues between the Pharisees and the Sadducees. These dialogues shed light on their different attitudes towards *halakha* and institutions. In an article on the Pharisees in a Jewish Encyclopaedia, these dialogues should have been quoted and expounded.

The article on the Pharisees is disappointing to say the least. It is not only brief, but sophomoric and deceptive.

In the article on the Messiah, the author states: "The title 'Messiah' as a designation of the eschatological personality does not exist in the Old Testament." It is quite true. We may add that the term משיח as a noun does not occur in the Hebrew Bible. The author further says: "However, for ancient Judaism the idea of eschatological salvation was more important than the concept of Messiah. Hence, there are books from the Second Temple period where the Messiah does not occur, even if they refer to eschatological salvation. Such a book, for instance, is the Book of Tobit in which the salvation of Jerusalem, the return of the Diaspora, and the conversion of nations to the God of Israel is described, but a personal Messiah is lacking." The statement made by the author is entirely faulty and has a christological connotation. The *Oxford Dictionary* defines the term salvation in the following words: 'the saving of the soul; the deliverance from sin, the admission of eternal bliss, wrought for man by the atonement of Christ." The concept of salvation is foreign to Judaism. The author refers to the book of Tobit but does not give the chapter. I believe he refers to chapter 14 where it is stated: ". . . God will bring them back to the land of Israel; and they will again build the Temple, but not as the first, until the term of the appointed time will be fulfilled; and afterward, they will return, all of them, from their captivity, and build up Jerusalem in glory, and God's Temple shall be built in her even as the prophets of Israel spoke concerning her. And all the nations of the earth shall turn and fear God in truth." Neither the term *salvation* nor the term conversion to Judaism is found in Tobit. The author of Tobit says that all the nations of the world will fear God. There is a big difference between fearing God and becoming a convert to Judaism. The author's statement is deceptive.

Further, the author states: "The Old Testament of Zechariah already makes mention of two messianic figures, the high priest and the messianic king." The book of Zechariah does not make any mention of the idea of Messiah. It is true that the Church Fathers interpreted V. 12, Ch. 6, as referring to Jesus. The Targum according to Jonathan in refuting the idea of the Church Fathers said that this verse refers to the Jewish Messiah. Rashi on the other hand claimed that it had nothing to do with the term Messiah.

The author made the following statement: "A further proof of the expectation of the Davidic Messiah can be found in the New Testament, where Jesus is identified with the Davidic Messiah . . . From the first century C.E. there were messianic movements centered on messianic pretenders. Such a list of messianic pretenders occurs in Acts 5:36-37. One of the names there is Judas the Galilean, who was the founder of the Zealots." The entire passage is tendentious and a distortion of historical facts. In the book of Acts it is related: "After this man (Theudas) rose up Judas of Galilee in the days of the taxing, and drew away many people after him; he also perished." In the book of Acts it does not say that Judas considered himself a Messiah. The author's assertion that Judas was the founder of the Zealots does not square with the truth. Josephus in his book *Jewish War* IV, 295; V, 5, states that Eliezer son of Simon was the founder of the Zealots.

The article on the Messiah is not only ambiguous and faulty, but has the aura of a christological overtone.

The problem of proselytes and proselytism occupies the minds of modern Jews, especially in the land of Israel. The term for proselyte is *ger*. However, this term had another connotation in the Pentateuch. It meant a sojourner, one who came to live in the country for a while. The Pentateuch as well as the early prophets did not recognize conversion. Yahweh was held to be an ethnic god, the God of the Children of Israel, the children of Abraham, Isaac and Jacob, with whom He made a covenant. Yahweh was the God of the descendants of those whom He had brought out of the land of Egypt, the land of slavery. Hence, those who were not descendants of Abraham, Isaac and Jacob and whose ancestors were not slaves in Egypt, could not worship Yahweh. Therefore, they could not become a member of the community of the Children of Israel.

During the time of the Second Commonwealth, the Judaean religion went through a revolutionary transformation, due to the influence of the prophets and the teachings of the Pharisees. Yahweh was no longer believed to be an ethnic god, the God of the Judaeans alone; now He was held to be the God of the entire universe. Anyone could accept Him. Hence, conversion not only became possible, but desirable. Were any ceremonies attached to conversion to Judaism? From the story given in the book of Ruth, it seems there were no ceremonies attached to conversion. Ruth simply said: "Thy people shall be my people, and thy God my God". Also from the story in the Talmud Shabbat 31 about the proselyte who came to Hillel it is also evident that there were no ceremonies required to convert to Judaism. During the later part of the Second Commonwealth, it was required of a convert to Judaism to be circumcized and immersed, and also to offer a sacrifice of two doves. Later, the rabbis added more laws in connection with conversion.

In the item of proselytes, the author does not give a historical development of the laws of conversion. He lumps together all the laws, the tannaitic, amoraic and the laws given by Maimonides.

The author states that Rabbi Eliezer and R. Joshua: "disagreed as to whether someone who immersed himself but was not circumcized or vice versa could not be considered a proselyte. According to R. Eliezer, he is a proselyte, even if he performs only one of these commandments." Thus, according to the author, R. Eliezer was of the opinion that if a convert to Judaism just immersed himself but was not circumcized, he is a *bona fide* proselyte. This is not true. This is not the opinion of R. Eliezer. R. Eliezer held that if a convert to Judaism circumcized himself but did not immerse himself, his conversion is valid. However, if he immersed himself but was not circumcized, his conversion is not valid. Cf. Yeb. 46.

גר שמל ולא טבל רבי אליעזר אומר הרי זה גר שכן מצינו באבותינו שמלו ולא טבלו, טבל ולא מל הרי זה גר דברי רבי יהושע.

Cf. Yer. Kid. 3.   תני גר שמל ולא טבל טבל ולא מל הכל הולך אחר המילה דברי רבי אליעזר.

The author was either careless in quoting the opinion of R. Eliezer, or simply misunderstood the text of the Talmud.

There are more ambiguous statements by the author. To give one example of many, the author states: "They (the rabbis) tried to equalize the statutes of the proselytes and that of the Jew; certain differences stemming from the origin of the convert, however, remained. According to an anonymous Mishnah a proselyte may not confess himself after taking out the tithes since the statement occurs in the confession 'the land which Thou hast given to us'." The fact that the proselyte cannot confess because he cannot say "the land which Thou hast given us", does not mean that he is not a fullfledged Jew and that he is not equal to a native Jew. A tenant of a field can neither bring the first fruits nor confess, since the land is not his, but it does not make him less of a Jew.

With the discovery of the so-called Dead Sea Scrolls, the name Zealots became fashionable among certain scholars. Articles and books were written about the Zealots. The *Encyclopaedia Judaica* also gave three columns to the item ZEALOTS.

Josephus is the only historian who provided us with the party of the Zealots and their activities. Everything that is known about the Zealots is from the writings of Josephus. He is the only Jewish historian who described the war against the Romans and the functions which the Zealots performed during the revolt against the Romans.

The author of this item states: "He (Josephus) preferred to describe them (the Zealots) as *lestai*, 'brigands' or as *sicarii*, 'dagger-men'. His indiscriminate use of the latter term for the Zealots is particularly confusing, for it would seem that he purposely called the main resistance party by an opprobrious term more appropriate to the terrorist organization." Josephus does not indiscriminately use the term *Sicarii* for the Zealots, nor is he confusing the subject. The author of this item is confused and distorts the writings of Josephus. Josephus referred to the Zealots as a party fifty-one times in the *Jewish War*, while he referred to the *sicarii* fifteen times in the *Jewish War*, ten times before the burning of the Temple and five times after. He clearly differentiates between the Zealots and the *sicarii*. Anyone who made a study of Josephus' writings can readily see his differentiation between the two groups. In book VII of the *Jewish War*, where he described the criminal acts of the different groups whom he considered responsible for the burning of the Temple and the fall of Jerusalem, he first mentioned the *sicarii*: "For in those days the *Sicarii* clubbed together against those who consented to submit to Rome and in every way treated them as enemies . . . The *Sicarii* were the first to set an example of the lawlessness and cruelty to their kinsmen, leaving no words unspoken to insult, no deed untried to ruin the victim of their conspiracy." He also refers to them as they who occupied the fortress Masada and were attacked by Flavius Silva. Josephus goes on to describe what he calls the other criminals: "Yet even they (Sicarii) were shown by John (of Gischala) to be more moderate than himself. For not only did he put to death all that proposed just and solitary measures, treating such persons as bitterest enemies among all the citizens." Then Josephus describes the criminal acts of Simon son of Gioras. After that he describes the madness of the Idumaeans whom he called the most "abonimable wretches". Then in the last of the groups, he describes the Zealots: "In this the called Zealots excelled, a class which justified their name by their actions, for they copied every deed of ill, nor was there any previous villany recorded in history that they failed zealously to emulate." Thus, it is crystal clear that Josephus does differentiate between the so-called *Sicarii* and the so-called *Zealots*.

Again, in book IV, Josephus relates that the high priest Ananus expelled Simon the son of Gioras from the province of Acrabetene. When Simon later learned that Ananus died, he assembled an army and over-ran not only the province of Acrabetene but the whole district extending to greater Idumaea. He further said when the Zealots were alarmed of Simon's designs, and went to attack Simon, but Simon had the upper hand and with an army of twenty thousand men, marched to the frontiers of Idumaea. Josephus states that the Idumaeans assembled an army of twenty five thousand men, to defend their country. They left a considerable number of people in the country: "To protect their property against the incursion of the *Sicarii* of Masada." So here again Josephus clearly differentiates between the Zealots who made war against Simon and the Sicarii of Masada who made frequent, sudden attacks aginst the Idumaeans.

The author of the item says that in *Antiquities* when he referred to Judas of Galilee, he does not use the adjective Zealot: "In a further descriptive note (Ant. 18:23-25), which he (Josephus) still studiously refrains from using the name Zealot." The reason that Josephus never referred to the Zealots in the book *Antiquities* is because the history given in the book terminates with the year 65, while the Zealots as a group came into being in the year 66-67, thus, it is axiomatic that Josephus could not have used the term Zealot in his book *Antiquities*.

The author connects Jesus with the Zealots. He said that Jesus was crucified "between two *lestai* (Mark 15:27; John 19: 18) since *lestai* was the official Greek designation for the Zealots, the fact probably indicates that the Romans viewed Jesus as a Zealot leader." Where did the author get the idea that *lestai*

was the official Greek designation for Zealots? That is pure
fancy. The Gospel according to Matthew and the Gospel of
John mention a few times the term *lestai* and they designate
it as brigands, criminals. Furthermore, the Gospel according
to Luke 23:33 relates that Jesus was crucified between two
kakourgous, criminals, malefactors. Thus, apparently, *lestai*
had the same designation as *kakourgous*. According to the
Gospels, Jesus said: "Render to Caesar the things that are
Caesar's, and to God the things that are God's." These words
could not come from a Zealot or a Sicarii. The author did
not explain this utterance of Jesus, unless he thinks that the
account given in the Gospels is not historical. But he did
not say so. He passed over it in silence.

The author states that Eliezer, who initiated the revolt by
ending the daily sacrifice for the Emperor and the Roman
people, was the "*segan* of the Temple". Josephus named him
strategon, the captain of the guard. The Hebrew term *segan*
has the connotation of second to the high priest. The phrase
כהן המשנה is rendered by the Targum סגן כהניא.

Under the subtitle "Zealots at Masada and Perhaps
Qumran", the author states: "The final proof of the Zealot's
faith and fortitude was given at Masada in 73 C.E., where
the Zealot garrison, under Eliezer b. Jair defied the Romans
as long as it was physically possible and then, rather than
surrender, killed their families and drew lot to slaughter
themselves (*Wars* 8:275-401)." Josephus clearly states that
the people in Masada were the *sicarii, not the Zealots*. He
repeats this a few times in *Wars* IV, 400-516. He writes:
"Not far from Jerusalem was a fortress of redoubtable
strength, built by the kings of old as a depository for their
property and a refuge for their persons during the vicissitudes
of war; it was called Masada. Of this the so-called Sicarii
had taken possession." Again, in book 27 V:253, Josephus
said: "This fortress was called Masada and the Sicarii who
had occupied it had at their head a man of influence named
Eliezer." So it is crystal clear that Josephus said that the

people who were in the fortress of Masada were the Sicarii, not the Zealots. We already mentioned that Josephus definitely distinguishes between the Sicarii and the Zealots. He does not confuse them. The author of the item about the Zealots not only confused the subject, but presented a false panorama of the period of the pre-war against the Romans, by a distortion of Josephus' writings.

The Sicarii and the Zealots were two distinct groups hostile to each other. It may be compared to the hostility which raged between the Bolsheviki and the Mensheviki during the Russian Revolution.

The author's statment that the Zealots "defied the Romans as long as it was physically possible" does not square with the account given by Josephus. According to the historian— who is the sole source of the last days of the Judaean State— the Sicarii did not counterattack to protect Masada, they offered no resistance. They did not kill even one Roman soldier. They delivered Masada to the Romans without a fight. Masada did not fall to the Romans by committing suicide, Masada was delivered to the Romans. A pseudo historical article on the Zealots, the Sicarii and Masada is being foisted.

In reading the item on *economic history* "Second Temple Period", I was dismayed to see the author constantly using Palestine: "substantial funds they had collected for Palestine", ". . . continued to send to Palestine groups of pilgrims", "in Jewish Palestine", "for in its part Palestine had a sort of monopoly on the balsam tree". Does the author not know the simple fact that the land where the people lived was called Judaea and the people were called Judaeans? The Greek and Roman historians recognized the country as independent and called it Judaea. The geographer and the historian Strabo, the historian Diodorus, Dio, Pliny the Elder, Tacitus and Suetonius, all named the country where the Judaeans lived Judaea. In later days, the Church called this country Palestine and claimed that the Jews have no right to this country. It would be tantamount to writing about the economics of Tel Aviv and say that Tel Aviv is situated in Palestine, ignoring the country of Israel.

The article does not present the true picture of the economic life of the Jews in Judaea during the period of the Second Commonwealth.

To have a full comprehension of the economic life of the people we must first know what kind of taxes they paid. The author does not give the form of taxation levied on the people. He made one statement: "In Jewish Palestine, (Sic!) moreoover, according to the biblical law the farmer was expected to set aside a first tithe to the Levite." At the time of John Hyrcanus I, a Takkanah was introduced that the tithe which the farmer was supposed to give to the Levite was now transferred to the consumer. The reason was twofold. First, the farmers were suspected of not giving the tithe to the Levite. Furthermore, economic necessity forced the sages to relieve the farmers from paying the tithe because the farmers of the neighboring state, Syria, were not supposed to give the tithe to the Levite. Thus, in selling their produce, they could charge ten percent less than the Judaean farmers. Thus the competition was too acute for the Judaean farmers. Therefore, they were relieved from paying the ten percent and the consumers were obliged to pay the tithe.

The author does not deal with the land tenancy which highly developed during the Second Commonwealth. The royal land engaged many farmers who were tenants. There were different types of *aris*, tenants. Some worked in the field for a certain share in the harvest, but if there was a loss, they bore a share of the loss. There was another type of tenant who paid the landlord a definite rental in kind, irrespective of the yield. We also know that a man hired himself out for particular periods to work on the fields. So, we see that a proletarian class came into being. The article about the economics does not reflect at all the economic situation of the Jews in Judaea.

Josephus relates that upon the completion of Herod's Temple reconstruction, over eighteen thousand workmen were thrown out of employment. Agrippa II engaged the men to pave the streets of Jerusalem, probably the first instance in history of the use of public works to alleviate the economic condition of the country.

The author rightly said that the main wealth of the country was the balsam trees. There were other materials which the Judaeans exported, like perfumes which were manufactured from the extract of the balsam, honey from the bees, and particularly fish, which they pickled and exported. The inhabitants of the city Tariedchaea, on the Galilaean lake, specialized in pickling fish and exporting them. The name of the city is derived from the Greek word *taricheiai*, factory for the pickling of fish. We also know that during this period, the industry of manufacturing of glass, and glass-blowing was highly developed in Judaea. It was a great stimulus to the economic development of the country. The author does not say a word about it. Neither does the author deal with slavery during that period, a great factor in the economic development of the country.

The author makes the statement that Judaea was poor in metal. However, during the time of Herod, copper was brought from Cyprus, where Augustus Caesar had given Herod the management of the copper mines.

Some of these statements are unwarranted. He stated that the Jews "even participated in Mediterranean piracy." From where did he learn this?

We know that the Romans, who maintained that the Mediterranean was their lake, held that anyone who was engaged in maritime navigations not beneficial to the Romans, was named pirate.

The author says: "The Dead Sea region supplied the country with a variety of minerals; it was renamed by the Romans the 'lacus asphaltites'." This is a very ambiguous statement and I do not comprehend it. The original name

of the Dead Sea was called by the Jews the Sea of Salt. The
Greeks called it *lacus Asphaltites* because it contained asphalt.
The first who mentioned the name Dead Sea was, as far as I
know, the Roman historian Justin.

The item "Economic History" does not present the
economic condition of the Judaeans during the Second
Commonwealth and certainly not the history and development of the economic life of Judaea.

Jewish identity is a very popular subject discussed in
modern Jewish intellectual circles. The item on "Jewish
Identity" is a very ambitious one. First, the author deals
with Jewish identity during the time of the first Temple.
I do not know what kind of identity there was. There were
two states: the land of Judaea, where the people were
Judaeans and the king was called the king of Judaea, and
in the north the land was called Israel, the people Israelites
and the king the king of Israel. There were no *gerim* at that
period. The term *ger* at that period had the connotation of
sojourner, and not that of a convert.

During the Second Commonwealth, the Jewish religion was
revolutionized. Hitherto, Yahweh was considered an ethnic
God. However, after the Hasmonean period, Yahweh was
considered the God of the universe. Thus, anyone could
accept the God of Israel and conversion became not only
acceptable but expedient. During the period of the Second
Commonwealth, a Diaspora came into being, i.e., many
Judaeans migrated to other countries, a great part of the
Judean people lived outside of Judaea. Those who lived in
Babylonia were designated as Babylonians, those who lived
in Alexandria were named Alexandrians, similarly, those
who lived in Antioch were called Antiochians. They, themselves, in some localities, called themselves Hebrews or
Israelites. In the Hellenistic world they were known as
Judaeans. Both Julius Caesar and Augustus Caesar in their
decrees to the different cities in Asia Minor ordered the
authorities that the people who followed the Judaean obser-

vance should not be tampered with and the customs they followed should not be interfered with. They should have religious freedom. Dio in his history of the Romans, relates the events that occurred in Palestine and said: "They (Judaeans) have also another name that they have acquired; the country has been named Judaea and the people themselves Judaeans. I do not know how this title came to be given to them, but this applies also to all the rest of mankind, all those of alien race, who affect their customs. This class exists even among the Romans . . . They are distinguished from the rest of mankind in practically every detail of life, and especially by the fact that they do not honor any of the usual gods but show extreme reverence for one particular god."

The identity of the people of the Diaspora who called themselves Hebrews or Israelites was with their co-religionists in Judaea, by observing the Judaean laws and sending gifts to the Temple and making pilgrimages to Jerusalem. They observed the holidays which were regulated by the *Beth Din* in Jerusalem. Thus, the Jews who lived in Judaea had a simple Jewish identity because they lived in the land of Judaea. The Jewish identity of their co-religionists who lived in Diaspora was because they affiliated religiously with their brethren in Judaea. The outside world designated anyone who followed the Judaean religious customs, as a Jew.

Similarly, in our days, the Jews who live in Israel have a very simple Jewish identity, by observing the holidays which are now of a religious character. The Jews who live outside of Israel have a Jewish identity of an affiliation with Jewish education or any other Jewish cause. For the outside world, their Jewish identity consists of one thing. If a person is born a Jew, he is a Jew, regardless if he observes the Jewish precepts or belongs to a synagogue, Orthodox, Conservative or Reform, or if he is an atheist. To the outside world, a Jew ceases to be a Jew when he converts to another religion. However, according to the *halakha*, a Jew who converts to another religion is still a Jew. If such a person marries a

2

Jewish girl and later she wants to divorce him and remarry a Jew, she must have a religious writ of divorce from her husband. Although he converted to another religion, he is considered recording to the *halakha* a Jew.

Speaking about the animosity between the Greeks and the Jews, the author says: "there was no major venom in these encounters until the Maccabeans raised the standard not merely of a national independence but of a need to purify the national religion." I do not know what he meant by purifying the national religion. After the Hasmonean revolt, Judaism was no longer a national religion, but became a universal religion. There was no venom against the state of Judaea, the neighbors feared the Judaeans, that they would conquer their cities and a Judaean King would rule over them. Judophobia began with the Diaspora; it was not, however, the Diaspora which brought about the hatred toward the Jews, but the Jewish idea that God was universal and the only God, and that the deities of all other nations were abominable idols which ought not to be worshipped. The Jews refused to worship and to bow to the god of the state. They would not participate in the libations in honor of the king. Their conception of the universality of God, in fact, their intolerance of polytheism aroused the venom against them.

There are many ambiguous statements and some of them are not warranted. In writing about the Judaeo-Christians, the author says: "By the end of the first century, the rabbis included a new prayer in the *Amidah*, 'and for the *minim* let there be no hope'. By that time the Roman imperial authorities were recognizing Christianity officially as a new religion, because the emperor Nerva (96-98) exempted Christians from the *fiscus judaicus*."

Where did the author get the idea that in the time of Emperor Nerva Christianity was recognized as a new religion? Where is the source? Again, where is the source that Emperor Nerva exempted the Christians from the *fiscus judaicus*? Dio, in his history relates that Emperor Nerva had forbidden anyone to inform who had adopted the Jewish mode of life. It is possible that it refers also to those who adopted Christianity. In his time, Christianity was considered a segment of Judaism.

With regard to *fiscus judaicus*, according to Suetonius, as well as to Dio, the *fiscus judaicus* was levied upon all Jews, regardless of where they lived. Nerva did not exempt the Christians from paying this tax. The Romans still considered the Judaeao-Christians as an heretical sect of the Jewish people.

I picked these articles only at random. They are only a specimen of the other articles dealing with the history of the Second Jewish Commonwealth. Because of lack of space, I have to eliminate other items. However, I want to call attention to only one other article: "CHRONOLOGY". In this article, the author writes: "This Seleucidan era was in vogue among the Jews until the Middle Ages; in the East it lasted until the 16th century." This is historically wrong. The Seleucidan era was abolished in Judaea with the establishment of a free Judaean State in the year 141 B.C.E. Since then, it was never used by the Jews in Judaea and later by the Jews in France and Germany. The Seleucidan era was used only by the Jews of Babylonia and was also used by the Jews of the Orient: and in Egypt, Syria until the 16th century. Maimonides who lived in Egypt employed the Seleucidan era and the era of the Creation, while the rabbis in France and Germany employed the era of Creation and the era to the destruction of the Second Temple. It is puzzling that the item "Chronology" is in the sixteenth volume, and not in the sixth volume, following the item "Chronicles".

The articles dealing with the Halakha are not better than those dealing with history. They are again full of mistakes and misunderstandings of the rabbinic texts.

The question confronting modern scholars has been what form of law came first. Some maintain that the laws which are

given in the Mishne preceeded the Midrash form, while others
maintain that the Misdash form is older. In the item"INTER-
PRETATION", the author states: "From early tannaitic
sources it may be inferred that Midrash already served as a
creative legal source of the *halakhah*. Thus, the description
is given of how the judges should deliberate the relevant
scriptural passage in each case before they gave judgement,
'And if he had committed murder, they deliberated the passage dealing with murder; if he had committed incest, they
deliberated the passage dealing with incest' (Tosef. Sanh.
9:1)." First, let me note that the Mishne says that they
deliberated among themselves about the case. נושאין ונותנין
בדבר ... There is no mention about deliberating the passage
dealing with murder. Furthermore, the word פרשת in the
Tosefta may mean subject or case, but not the scriptural
passage. The author continues: "Similarly, as regards the
legal order of succession. The Pentateuch prescribes the
order as son, daughter, brother, brothers of the father, and
then the nearest kin of the deceased (Num. 27:6-11); the
father is not mentioned as an heir but this omission is rectified
with the Mishnah, where his place in the order is determined
as falling after the children of the deceased and before the
latter's brothers (B.B. 8:1)."

This Mishne definitely proves that the *halakha* preceeds the
form of Midrash, because the Mishne does not cite any
Pentateuchal passages of inheritance. It is only the later sages
who explained this law in interpreting a biblical passage.
As a matter of fact, the laws of inheritance as testimental
succession and the principles of possession and many other
ancient laws in connection with injury belong to great
antiquity and they preceed the method of Midrash. Cf. also
the first Mishne of Kid. 1, 1. It is to note that the author did
not give the views of the scholars who held that the *halakha*
preceeds the Midrash. The reader of a Encyclopaedia is
entitled to know all the theories regarding the *halakha*.

The author writes: "DORESHIN LESHON HEDYOT ('interpreting human speech') Interpretation of document was originally referred to as *doreshin leshon hedyot.*" *Leshon hedyot* is not to be interpreted as human speech, but refers to the aramaic language. In contrast to Hebrew, which was called the sacred language. The sages interpreted the biblical verses which are written in the sacred language. However, Hillel introduced a law, that the *Ketubah* written in aramaic could likewise be interpreted. The same was law applied to documents of business transactions which were written in the aramaic language to be legally interpreted.

Jewish laws are not static but plastic, and applicable to the change of time. Therefore, some laws could be characterized as progressive, while others can be regarded as regressive. The laws which came into vogue after the destruction of the Temple do not have the stamp of progressiveness as do the laws which were enacted during the Second Commonwealth. There is certainly a difference between the laws of the tannaitic period in Judaea and those laws which were enacted in the amoraic period in Babylonia and the laws which were enacted by the rabbis in Europe during the Middle Ages.

Takkana is a source for law. Many *takkanot* were introduced during the Second Commonwealth as well as during the amoraic period and during the Middle Ages. The author of the item TAKKANOT lumped together all the *takkanot* during the entire Jewish history. There is no historical development. He does not differentiate between the *takkanot* of the Second Commonwealth and the *takkanot* of the Middle Ages. This blurs the article. In defining the term *takkana*, the author writes: "A *takkanah* is a directive enacted by the halakhic scholars, or other competent body (*see Takkanot ha-Kahal*), enjoying the force of law." This may be true in regard to *Takkanot ha-Kahal* but not to the *takkanot of* Tannaim. A *takkana* is an amendment of earlier law, either pentateuchal or halakhic, introduced by the Tannaim generally for the purpose of harmonizing religion and life. (Cf. the Takkana of Erubin, Takkanot of Ezra; the Takkanot of R.

Gamaliel). It is most surprising that the author never refers to the *takkanot* which were instituted during the Second Commonwealth. To have a proper conception of the history of the Jewish people, one must deal with the *halakhah* historically, since law is the foundation of society. The *takkanot* which were introduced in the Second Commonwealth were for the purpose of bringing religion into consonance with life. Hence, a *takkana* has a lenient tendency. The author, in lumping together all the *takkanot* without any historical explanation, marred the article.

The author made the following statement: "The legislative activity of the halakhic scholars is sometimes termed *takkanah* and sometimes *gezerah*." The author in defining the term *gezerah* writes: "The term *gezerah* is generally applied to the determination of directives aimed at deterring man from the prohibited, at making 'a fence around the Torah', i.e., directives of a negative nature prohibiting the performance of a particular act." Again, that may be true to the decrees of the Middle Ages, however, during the Second Commonwealth, a *gezerah* was not a directive for some other reason, but *per se*, as the Eighteen Decrees which were adopted at the conclave in the year 65 CE, or the decree of defilement of the land of the heathens. A *gezerah* is a decree of the authorities, absolutely independent from the Torah and may be for a certain period. A *takkana*, on the other hand, is universal and applicable to all classes.

According to the author, a *takkana* is sometimes rendered *tenai bet din*. He supports himself on the Mishne Ket. 4:12. The term *tenai bet din* in the said Mishne does not refer to the *takkana* of the Ketubah but to the gloss: "You shall dwell in my house and receive maintenance from my property until you will remarry." If this gloss was not inserted in the Ketubah, the woman can collect her money from the ex-husband's property because that is a *tenai bet din*. Similarly, there is a law that if a person marries a virgin, upon divorce or the death of the husband, she is entitled to 200 *zuz*. If he

marries a widow she is only entitled to 100 *zuz*. If this gloss
was not included in the Ketubah, the woman, upon divorce, is
entitled to collect 200 *zuz* if she was a virgin when she married,
because it is a *tenai bet din*. So the term *tenai bet din* does not
refer to the *takkana* of Ketubah.

As was to be expected, there is a lengthy article on the Dead
Sea Scroll and also an article on the Qumran community.
These articles are written from a partisan point of view, from
the point of view of the protagonists of the antiquity of the
Dead Sea Scrolls. A few lines are devoted to the views of this
writer: "S. Zeitlin has vigorously maintained that the Scrolls
belong to a much later date and have no substantial scholarly importance. However, the discovery of analogus material in the excavations at Masada, which are certainly
not later than 73 C.E., seem to establish the *terminus ad quem*
positively." The present writer has endeavored to show that
many materials found at Masada are of a later period, the
Byzantine period, and that the fragments of ben Sira also
belong to that period.

There is a touch of vulgarism in this undertaking of the
Encyclopaedia. There is an item about Louis (Lepke) Buch-
alter, who was an American gangster executed for murder.
There is also an item about another gangster, Siegel (Butsy)
whose motto was: "Don't worry, we only kill each other"
(New York Times, Sunday, August 20th 1972). However,
there is no item about well known Jewish scholars, like
Dr. J. Teicher and Prof. S. Hoenig, and others. I dare-
say that the inclusion of gangsters and the exclusion of
Jewish scholars is an affront to learning and Jewish scholarship. It is a sad reflection on the editorial policy. (My
attention was called to these inclusions and exclusions).

One may wonder at the editors' sense of proportion. The
item on the Kabbalah consists of eighty-three pages. The
Pharisees molded Jewish life. The institutions of today are
to be traced to the Pharisees. Judaism as we know it, is the
creation of the Pharisees. We also know that they influenced

the origins of Christianity. The item on the Pharisees received only three columns. I do not question the propriety of the editors. On the contrary, the article on Kabbalah which is indeed a monograph, is to be welcomed. It is skilfully presented and the intelligent reader will certainly greatly profit from it.

In this article, Prof. G. Scholem presents a concise history of Kabbalah and Messianism, with great insights. Although many times I radically disagreed with his interpretations, his facts are unquestionable. Reading this article, one can see that it came from one of the great authorities on the subject. The brevity of the item on the Pharisees may be a blessing.

The American Academy of Jewish Research received a brief item, I believe of twenty lines. It is not a question of brevity, but there are also many inaccuracies. The author apparently did not even read the book by Prof. Eli Ginzberg, *Keeper of the Law: Louis Ginzberg*, in which he gives a short account of the organization of the Academy, based on a memorandum of his father's files, it also has some inaccuracies.

The present writer is the only surviving member of the group which founded this Academy. Thus, I believe it is my duty to give a concise account of how the Academy was founded.

In 1918-1919, after the Bolshevik Revolution, when the Russian Jewry had been destroyed as a factor in Jewish culture and life and the institutions of Eastern Europe had been shattered, I was of the opinion that the center of Jewish learning would be shifted to America. I was of the opinion that an institution of scholars should be founded for the purpose of advancing Jewish learning and to formulate standards of Jewish scholarship. When I discussed this with Prof. H. Malter, he was very enthusiastic about this idea. However, Prof. M. Margolis was skeptical. He said that Cyrus Adler would not join this organization and without his goodwill, this idea could never be realized. This opinion was shared by Profs. L. Ginzberg and I. Friedlaender.

Once I had a long conversation with Dr. Cyrus Adler about the situation in Europe and during the conversation I expressed the idea of organizing a group of Jewish scholars for the furtherance of Jewish scholarship in this country. Dr. Adler not only expressed full-hearted approval, but he said he was ready to help. He believed that such an organization could be of great encouragement and enhancement of Jewish scholarship in this country. I told my friends, that they misjudged Adler. He expressed readiness to do anything possible to help this organization.

After a lengthy discussion with my peers, I persuaded them to have a meeting of Jewish scholars to see if it was feasible to organize an academy of Jewish scholars. I succeeded to arrange a meeting in the late spring of 1920 in the home of Prof. Ginzberg at Avon-On-The-Sea. It was attended by Prof. H. Malter who was living at Bradley Beach and by Prof. D. Neumark who was also vacationing at Avon-On-The-Sea, and by Prof. A. Marx who was vacationing in Belmar as well by Prof. J. Lauterbach, who was nearby; Prof. Friedlander and I came from New York. Thus, the meeting consisted of seven men, the founders of this organization. I suggested that the organization should be called the Jewish Academy of America, which Friedlander supported. However, the other five men were opposed. They were apprehensive that Dr. Adler and Louis Marshal, whose support was sought, would object. Thus, the name the American Academy of Jewish Research was finally accepted. The seven scholars who organized this Academy were members of the faculties of the Jewish Theological Seminary, the Hebrew Union College, Dropsie College, now Dropsie University and of the Rabbinical College, now Yeshiva University. The seven members who organized this Academy invited three other scholars to join them, Profs. G. Deutsch of the Hebrew Union College, I. Davidson of the Jewish Theological Seminary and M. Margolis of Dropsie. They gladly accepted. Thus, the original founding members were ten scholars. It was the consensus of the members who attended the meeting to nominate Prof. Friedlander as the President. He was a man of great scholarship and organizational ability. As he was leaving America for Russia on an errand of mercy, Prof. Ginzberg assumed the Presidency; however, it was the opinion of the scholars that Friedlander would assume the Presidency upon his return. To our great grief, Friedlander did not return, he was murdered in the Ukraine. Prof. Ginzberg, therefore, continued as President for many years. Malter was appointed as Secretary. It was decided that the original members of the Academy should be designated as Fellows. It was also decided to have elected honerary members, These first Fellows of the Academy elected Dr. Kohler, the President of the Hebrew Union College and Dr. Adler, the President of Dropsie College and the acting President of the Jewish Theological Seminary. They also elected Judge Mayer Sulzberger as an honorary member. Dr. Bernard Revel, who was President of the Rabbinical College, was not elected as an honorary member. The decision of the members was that to elect an honorary member, the vote must be unanimous. Dr. Malter had a personal grudge against Dr. Revel; they had a dispute about a particular manuscript. Thus, one President of a great institution was not elected as an honorary member. With regard to new Fellows, two negative votes were enough to blackball. It was also agreed that no one should ever be elected a Fellow unless he published a significant contribution to Jewish scholarship. It was decided that practicing rabbis should not be nominated as Fellows. One of the purposes of the Academy was to publish scholarly projects. For this purpose, funds had to be secured. It was voted that another category of members should be added, paying certain annual dues. Thus, the Academy came to have three types of members, Fellows, honorary members and regular members.

In the Fall of 1922,—I believe—the first regular meeting

was held—at Dropsie College. The different scholarly projects which the Academy should undertake were discussed: 1) An Index to the Responsa Literature and 2) The Jews in Patristic Literature.

Since the original meeting of 1920, the Academy had lost two of its founding members, Friedlander and Deutsch. At that meeting, the following scholars were elected as Fellows: D. Blondheim, B. Halper, I. Husik and H. Wolfson. President Morgenstern was elected an honorary member to succeed Dr. Kohler. After the death of Judge Sulzberger, Louis Marshall was elected as an honorary member.

In July of 1918, the cornerstone for a Hebrew University in Jerusalem was laid. It was the consensus of the Fellows of the Academy "to express their views as to what the Hebrew University should be like." A committee was appointed, headed by Ginzberg. Its members consisted of Drs. Adler, Lauterbach, Malter, Marx and the present writer. In 1925, the Hebrew University opened on Mount Scopus. The present writer was a representative of the Academy as well as of the Yeshiva. When the Institute for Jewish Studies was organized under the chairmanship of the Chief Rabbi of England, Dr. Hertz, the members of the Academy took part in its guidance.

I must express with great regret that the Academy did not live up to the ideas and ideals of the founders. The scholarly publications which the founders thought to be a must for the history of the Jewish people are still wanting, neither was the standard of Jewish scholarship enhanced.

The publication of the *Encyclopaedia Judaica* is not a major accomplishment in the world of Jewish scholarship. On the contrary, it reveals the paucity and the decadence of Jewish learning. Many articles are below the standards of a good encyclopedia, they are sophomoric. The items dealing with the early history of the Jews are replete with distortions of historical facts. They may misguide the reader. In the articles on the Halakha and Rabbinics we note the lack of understanding of the text. The contributors are not to be reproved. A person cannot give more than he possesses. Many of the contributors are scholarly benighted. The blame is with the publishers and the editors. It seems that they were more concerned with public relations than with scholarship. The multiplicity of identical photographs is another indication for "good public relations". The *Encyclopaedia Judaica* is indeed inferior to the *Jewish Encyclopaedia* which appeared almost seven decades ago and is even more inferior to the Russian-Jewish Encyclopedia. The publication of the Encyclopedia Judaica was a waste of effort and money.

The physical production of the *Encyclopaedia Judaica* is excellent and praiseworthy. The cover design is superb and imaginative. Israeli printing is highly commendable.

JUDAISM AND
PROFESSORS OF RELIGION

By Solomon Zeitlin, Dropsie University

Since the supposed discovery of the Hebrew Scrolls professors have engaged in writing books on Jesus. Those who maintain that the Hebrew Scrolls have been written by the Zealots associate Jesus with the Zealots. Prof. S. G. F. Brandon, in his book *Jesus and the Zealots: A Study of the Political Factor in Primitive Christianity*,[1] made Jesus a member of the Zealot party. Prof. Brandon ignores the historical fact that the Zealots as a party appeared on the Jewish scene many years after the death of Jesus. He errs in combining the Zealots with the Sicarii. He does not distinguish the word zealot, referred to by Josephus as an adjective, from the word Zealot as a noun, the name of a particular group. It may be compared to one who in writing a history of the United States would not distinguish between democrat with a small d and Democrat with a capital D. Thus Prof. Brandon's thesis is based on a faulty foundation. The Zealots as a party arose in the year 66 CE. while the Sicarii had been active long before.

Prof. David Flusser, Professor of Religion in the Hebrew University at Jerusalem, is of the opinion that the Hebrew Scrolls were composed by the Essenes. In his recent book *Jesus*[2] Prof. Flusser asserts that Jesus was an Essene, He ignores the fact that the term Essene does not occur in the New Testament nor does this nomenclature occure in the Hebrew Scrolls. Any serious historian would question if Jesus was an Essene why this term does not occur in the

[1] Charles Scribner's Sons, New York. 1967.
[2] Herder and Herder, New York, 1969.

13

471

New Testament. We do find that the other two groups, the Pharisees and the Sadducees in the Gospels, with whom Jesus had discussions and arguments. It would be historical fallacy to assume that Jesus was an Essene and this term does not occur in the New Testament. The fact that the term Essene does not occur in the New Testament militates against the unwarranted theory that Jesus was an Essene.

The book *Jesus* which is supposed to be a historical account of the life of Jesus contains many passages of Christian theology. I must say with absolute candor that one who does not know that the author is a professor of the history of religion in the Hebrew University would assume that the book was written by a Christian fundamentalist. To cite a few passages. On page 44 the author wrote, "This episode in Paul's mission to the heathen was of enormous importance; it was the will of God to spread Christianity to Europe. Thus Christianity became at first a Graeco-Roman, and later, a European religion. In contrast to Judaism and the religions of eastern Asia, that originated in ancient Persia, Western culture sets no store by ritual or ceremonial prescriptions ... Had Christianity spread first to the eastern Asiatic regions, it would have had to develop a ritual and ceremonial law based on the Jewish law in order to become a genuine religion in that part of the world."

On page 122 the author wrote, "There can be no doubt that the Crucified appeared to Peter, and then to the twelve." On page 17 we have the foollwing, "If one accepts the virgin birth as historical, and also concedes that the brethren of Jesus were his true brethern and sisters, the conclusion must be accepted that Jesus was Mary's first-born child." On page 30, "We are to believe the words of the archangel reported by Luke (1:36), Mary was related to John's mother." On page 96, "Jesus' sonship leads then not to life, but to the death that many prophets before him had suffered." This is Christological theology. Where are the historical proofs that many prophets suffered death for their prophecies?

On page 56 we have the following, "Obviously, there were some petty minds among the Pharisees—such people are found in all societies—who were suspicious of this wonder-worker, and who would gladly have caught him in some forbidden action so that they could blame him before the rabbinic court." This is again theology. At that time there were no rabbis and hence there was no rabbinic court. On page 59 the author wrote, "When in 62 A.D., the Lord's brother James, and apparently other Christians, were illegally put to death by the Sadducean High Priests the Pharisees appealed to the king, and the High Priest was deposed." The source for this is Josephus.[3] *Antiquities* 20. 9. 1 (200-203), who states, "And so he (Ananus, the High Priest) convened the judges of the synedrion and brought before them a man named James, the brother of Jesus who was called the Christ and certain others. He accused them of having transgressed the law and delivered them up to be stoned. Those of the inhabitants of the city who were considered the most fair-minded and who were strict in observance of the law were offended by this." The name Pharisees is not mentioned in this passage. Furthermore "the Lord's brother James" does not occur in Josephus' passage. (Some times the author uses the term Lord for Jesus when he does not quote the New Testament) Elsewhere I have pointed out that we have reason to question if the words "He was called the Christ" are authentic. We have the right to assume that these words were interpolated later.

That the author was careless in the use of sources is evident in another passage. On page 122 he states, "When he (Jesus) answered the high priest's question about his Messiahship with the words, 'From now on the Son of man shall be seated on the right had of the power of God.'" In Mark 14. 62 the text has τῆς δυνάμεως "on the right hand of Power." Matthew 26. 64 has the same words. Luke 22. 69

---

[3] Josephus on Jesus, 1931, p. 70.

has τῆς δυνάμεως τοῦ θεοῦ "the right hand of the Power of
God." However Sys omits τοῦ θεοῦ "of God." The word
"Power" is a rendering of the Hebrew נבורה which is a
cipher for God.

I shall not comment on the theological views of Dr. Flusser.
As an individual he is entitled to his views. I do believe that
the words of an author reflects his mind. I shall review his
citations from rabbinic sources.

On pages 19-20 the author wrote, "External corroboration
of Jesus' Jewish scholarship is provided by the fact that,
although he was not an approved scribe, men were accustomed
to address him as 'Rabbi', 'my teacher'. The form of address
'Rabbi' was in common use in those days, and was specially
in favor to describe scholars and teachers of the Torah." The
title rabbi came into vogue after the destruction of the
Second Temple. It was not used in the time of Jesus. The
title Rabbi prefixed to a name is not possessive, it is anoun.
(Cf. the writer's article "The Title Rabbi in the Gospels is
Anachronistic." *JQR* Oct. 1968, pp. 158-160.)

On p. 20 the author, rendered the phrase אהוב את המלאכה
ושנא הרבנות, Aboth I. 10 "Love manual work and hate
rabbinism." When I read this I did not believe my eyes that
a professor should render ושנא הרבנות "hate rabbinism." At
first I thought that the author's translation is due to *lapsus
calami*. Even Danby, in his translation of the Mishneh has
"Hate mastery." Upon rereading this page I became convinced that this unpardonable rendering could not be
ascribed to *lapsus calami*. The author wrote, "Jesus did not
approve the pleasure so many Pharisees·took in being addressed as rabbi ... In many generations before Jesus, a scribe
has said much the same thing; 'Love manual work and hate
rabbinism.' Many shared this view. Arrogance may often
have been found among the scribes but they were
not effete academicians." Dr. Flusser wants to show that
some of the scribes as well as Jesus hated rabbinism.
Such rendering is unforgivable and reminds me of another

professor who translated דורש ברבים "expounded for the rabbis."

On p. 13 the author has, "Today it would be almost impossible for a Jewish child to be named after his own father, were he alive." Does he not know that the Sephardic Jews name their sons after themselves while they are still living? The custom not to name a son after his father who is still living came into vogue among the German and Polish Jews after the thirteenth century. Rabbi Judah heChasid who lived in the thirteenth century in his book *Sefer Chasidim* mentioned this prohibition. This was due to superstition.

On p. 116 the author made the following statement, "The Sanhedrin was the Jewish supreme court and numbered seventy-one members. To pass sentence of death, the presence of twenty-three judges sufficed." The supreme court of seventy-one never tried individual cases involving capital punishment. It was a legislative body. Cases involving national importance, if they ever occurred, were tried by the supreme court. Ordinary cases which involved capital punishment were tried by the court of twenty-three which had its seat in Jerusalem and the Temple Mount. The statement, "To pass sentence of death, the presence of twenty-three judges sufficed", reveals the author's lack of knowledge of the Jewish judiciary system during the Second Commonwealth.

According to John 19. 39, after the crucifixion of Jesus, Nicodemus brought a mixture of myrrh and aloes. Dr. Flusser states on p. 119, "We know from rabbinic sources that Nicodemus' son, Gorion, was one of the Jerusalem councillors and one of the three richest patricians in the city." According to the Talmud, Nicodemus was the son of Gorion. There is no mention in rabbinic sources that Nicodemus had a son Gorion.

On p. 126 the author made the following statement, "The Roman governor was in the habit of releasing a Jewish prisoner on the Passover. From rabbinic literature we know that this amnesty often went by default." In rabbinic literature we do not find any reference to a custom of releasing a Jewish prisoner on the Passover by the Roman authorities. The author's statement to rabbinic reference that "this amnesty often went by default" is not true historically.

On p. 93 the author writes, "Jesus is portrayed in the gospels as a miracle-worker. Rabbinic literature tells us of four such men who operated before the destruction of the second temple. Two of these were Galileans, and of them we are told, in passing, that they were very poor men. One of these two was a laborer Abba Hilkia. On one occasion when two scribes had been sent to ask him to pray for rain he behaved very strangely towards them."

The story about Abba Hilkia is told in the tractate Taanit 23. According to the Talmud Abba Hilkia was the grandson of Ḥoni the Circle-Drawer. However from internal evidence we must conclude that the entire story about the man Abba Hilkia is legendary. The story was composed in the amoraic period not earlier than the end of the third century CE. In this story is told that there was once a drought and a pair of *rabbanon* were sent to abba Hilkia to ask him to pray for rain. The term רבן was never used in the tannaitic literature. It came into vogue after the codification of the Mishneh, i.e. in the middle of the third century CE. The term used for scholars in the tannaitic literature was סופרים or חכמים. The cipher for God used in this story was, "the Holy One, blessed be He," הקדוש ברוך הוא. This cipher for God came into usage in the Amoraic period. Another cipher for God was used in this story מקום, "Place". The cipher מקום for God came into usage after the destruction of the Temple. During the Second Commonwealth the term τόπος Place, was applied to the Temple. After the destruction of the Temple the term מקום became a cipher for God. There is no doubt that this talmudic story about Abba Hilkia is legendary and originated in Babylonia during the amoraic period.

The following story about Ḥanin ha-Nehba, the son of the daughter of Ḥoni the circle-drawer, is also a legend as can be ascertained by internal evidence.

The Talmud may be compared to a primeval, dense forest in which a person will lose his way without a skillful guide.

The Babylonian Talmud comprises many sections,—some are of the tannaitic period and even go to antiquity, before the destruction of the Temple. Other sections are of the amoraic period. Some of the sections are of Palestinian origin while the bulk of the Babylonian Talmud is the creation of the Babylonian Amoraim. A historian who utilizes the Talmud for research must be a Talmudist. He must have analytical capacity to recognize which passages have historical value and which are of legendary character. He must have a thorough knowledge to distinguish which are tannaitic and which are amoraic passages, which are Palestinian and which are Babylonian. Without adequate knowledge of the Talmud the person who utilizes it for research will be lost and will come to faulty conclusions. It must be emphasized again and again that for research the Talmud has to be used in its original language and not depend on translations.

Dr. Flusser's statement, "Rabbinic literature tells us of four such men (miracle workers) who operated before the destruction of the Second Temple. Two of these were Galileans", is based on a lack of historical comprehension of the Talmud. Apparently he had no skillful guide. The book is full of talmudic misstatements.

The book was badly edited. On p. 16 is stated, "Jesus, then, was a Galilean Jew, probably born in Nazareth ... He was born either in 27/28 A.D. or 28/29 A.D." On p. 96, "Jesus said to Peter "Rabbi" instead of "Peter said to Jesus "Rabbi". On p. 60 the page from the biblical manuscript, codex Aleppo, is up side down.

There are a number of illustrations in the book which have no place in a scholarly work on the life and mission of Jesus. On p. 12 is the following illustration:

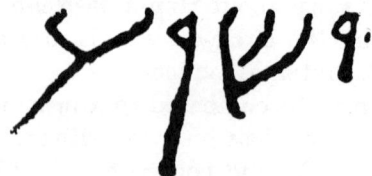

"This is how Jesus wrote his name in Hebrew."

The innocent reader would assume that this is the auto-graph of Jesus. ישׁע is not Hebrew. In Hebrew the name is written יהושׁע.

At the end of the book there is an appendix called "Reflec-tions", consisting of different views about Jesus. It begins with Paul and ends with Spengler. In this table are recorded the views of Sigmund Freud and Martin Buber. The following passage is quoted from Freud

> The Jews had to bear the reproach from the new religi-ous community, that they had murdered God. Unabridged, this reproach reads thus: They refuse to admit that they murdered God, whereas we admit it and are thereby clean-sed from its guilt. It then becomes easy to understand how much truth lies behind this reproach. The reason the Jews have been unable to make the progress implied in admission that they murdered God would be a subject of special study. By this they have burdened themselves with tragic guilt; and they have been allowed to perform a very heavy penence for it.

The Jews do not have to admit any guilt in connection with the crucifixion of Jesus. Jesus was crucified by the Roman authorities as a political offender. I am puzzled over the purpose of quoting Freud in a book which is supposed to be a scholarly treatise on the life of Jesus.

I am more perplexed over the purpose of quoting from Buber in this book about Jesus:

All my life I have felt that Jesus was my elder brother. My own open brotherly relationship to him has become even stronger and purer, and today I can see him with surer and purer vision than before. I am more certain than ever that he merits a greater place in the history of Israel's faith, and that this place cannot be defined in terms of the usual categories.

Many Christians and Jews regard Buber as a Jewish theologian. His theology is diluted. It is neither Jewish nor Christian theology. Incorporating Christian thoughts in Jewish theology he distorted true Judaism. Buber was born in Lemberg, Galicia, and spent a lot of time in Bukovina, nearby Sadagora where primitive Hasidism flourished. He was fascinated by the stories of the Hasidim about the *Zaddikim* whom they regarded as miracle-workers. Buber was deeply impressed by the unwavering devotion of the Hasidim to their leaders the *Zaddikim*. Possessing a warm poetic soul he was attracted by the primitive Hasidism. In it he saw a challenge to the old establishment of Judaism. It may be that he compared it to the early Judaean Christian who were devoted to Jesus who challenged the old establishment of Judaism. Buber grasped only the outer aspects of primitive Hasidism. He did not penetrate into its inner philosophy. He probable did not read the works of Jacob Joseph of Polonnoye and Dov Baer of Meseritz not to speak of the works of HaBaD. Buber speaks of *Der Grossee Maggid*, Baer of Meseritz. I wonder if he read his work. In his writings he uses the phrase "Christ, Hasidism, Gnosis", as having relationship, a common philosophy. The fact of the matter is that Buber dilutes Hasidism, Judaism and Christianity. In his so called Jewish theology he blurs Hasidism and Judaism.

In propounding a true Jewish theology one must not only know the Bible but be well versed in the historical development of Judaism from the canonization of the Hebrew Bible until the time of the medieval Jewish theologians. A comprehensive knowledge of the ideas of the sages from the time of the Second Jewish Commonwealth to the Middle Ages is *sine quo non* for one who wants to present a Jewish theology in modern times.

Many sincere and well-meaning presidents of universities and deans of faculties have included the study of Jewish religion in their curricula to present a good historical knowledge without bias for Jewish and Christian students. With regret we must note it was not a success. Many of the professors of Jewish religion had no historical knowledge of Judaism and some of them are even hostile. Thus the lectures of these professors are a disservice to Jewish religion. The book under review is a case in point, "A scribe has said much the same thing (as Jesus said) 'Love manual work and hate rabbinism'".

In recent times many theologians have propounded the idea of dialogues between Jews and Christians, i.e. between Judaism and Christianity. Some Jewish theologians and laymen have applauded this idea. Elsewhere I have stated (*Prolegomenon, The Jewish Sources of the Sermon on the Mount*, G. Friedlander, pp. XXXI-XXXIII, Ktav Publishing House, 1969) that dialogues between Jews and Christians on religion is contrary to the history of true Judaism. The Jews never engaged in dialogues with Christians on religion. The Jews do not wish to convert the Christians to Judaism, nor to be converted to Christianity. The dialogues and disputations which took place between Jews and Christians during the Middle Ages were forced upon the Jews.

Upon reading the transcriptions of the dialogues which took place between the Jews and Christians I was dismayed to note the lack of knowledge displayed by the Jewish participants of Judaism at the time when Christianity came into being. It was disheartening to note their lack of comprehension of the historical causes which brought about the *Parting of the Ways*. To such participants in dialogues on Jewish religion and to the professors of religion in universities and seminars it must be said *Disce aut discede*.

SPURIOUS INTERPRETATIONS OF RABBINIC SOURCES
IN THE STUDIES OF THE PHARISEES [AND PHARISAISM

THE LITERATURE concerning the Pharisees is growing by leaps and bounds. Lately, I came accross two works, one, *Jesus and the Pharisees* by John Bowker, and another one, by Jacob Neusner, *The Rabbinic Traditions about the Pharisees Before 70*.

The sources for the Pharisees are the books of Josephus, the synoptic gospels, Acts, and most important the tannaitic literature. Josephus primarily deals with the Pharisees concerning their ideas as opposed to those of the Sadducees. The synoptic gospels record the disputations between Jesus, or rather his disciples, and the Pharisees regarding the tradition of the elders, i.e. the halaka. Acts states that the Pharisees believed in resurrection and angels, while the Sadducees denied both.[1] In the tannaitic literature as well as in the entire Talmud, the term Pharisees is not found. When it occurs in the Talmud, the term Perushim is used by their opponents. As we have pointed out elsewhere, the term Pharisees is a term of reproach employed by their opponents who reproached them for propagating the ideas of the universality of God, reward and punishment, and the validity of the oral law along with the written. They were called Perushim, separatists, who separated themselves from the Torah and the Judaeans, while the Sadducees were those descendants of the family of Zaddok, the high priest, who believed himself to be the vicar of God, the guardian of the Torah and thus opposed to any innovations. The tannaitic literature records dialogues between the Sadducees and the so-called Pharisees with regard to the halaka. From these dialogues we can learn their different attitudes concerning the oral law, i.e. the development of the halaka.

Josephus uses the term Pharisaioi, and so also it is used in the gospels. In the Talmud, the term *Perushim* is employed. Mr. Bowker writes, "The basic problem can be stated, once more, quite simply: those whom Josephus referred to as Pharisaioi are to some extent linked with, or related to, those whom the later rabbis regarded as their legitimate predecessors. But the rabbis scarcely ever refer to their predecessors as *perushim* ... what, if any, is the connection between Pharisaioi of Josephus and the *perushim* of the rabbinic sources?"[2] There can be no question that the Pharisaioi in Josephus

---

[1] Acts 23.8.
[2] P. 4.

and the *perushim* in the Talmud are identical, and refer to the same group of men. Josephus records a story of a conflict between the Pharisaioi and John Hyrcanus I.[3] The same account as is given in Josephus appears in the Talmud where the term perushim is used.[4] Hence, it is crystal clear that Josephus and the Talmud are referring to the same people—Josephus is using the term Pharisaioi while the Talmud is using the Hebrew word, *perushim*.

The author further states, "The rabbinic sources contain attacks directed *against perushim*—attacks which are almost as violent as the attacks on the Pharisaioi in the Gospels." [5] As was said before the term *Perushim* has the connotation of separatists. There was a group of people whom the Sadducees called perushim, separatists. The Talmud does not record any attack against these *perushim*. The attacks we do find are against the Perushim who separated themselves from mundane life. Those who deal with the Pharisees must differentiate between these two nomenclatures.[6] To give an example, the term democrats refers to persons who maintain the social or political equality of men, while Democrats refers to a definite political party. One may write about senators Schweiker and Javitz as being democrats, but this does not mean that they belonged to the Democratic party, but rather, that they upheld the principles of democracy. In the English language we note the difference between a capital "D" and a small "d". In Hebrew no such differentiation in spelling exists. The differentiation must be made by means of the internal evidence, that is to say, by the text of the Talmud.

The author advanced a novel but unfounded theory that the Pharisaioi mentioned in Josephus and in the Gospels are not identical with the *Perushim* mentioned in the Talmud. He writes, "There is an obvious strength in the argument that the *perushim* are not to be confused or identified with the Pharisaioi." [7] He identified the Pharisaioi with the *Hakamim*. This theory is based on the fact that the rabbis in the Talmud never refered to their predecessors as *perushim*. He writes, "A particularly good example of this occurs in 4.10, since here both the verb and the noun (*perushim*) are used; and it is quite clear that the word *perushim* is used by a rabbi of those who detached themselves from the Hakamim, not of the predecessors of the rabbis." [8] The author refers to the account of

---

[3] *Ant.* 13, 10. 5-6.
[4] Kid. 66.
[5] P. 4.
[6] Equivocal expressions are frequently misleading even to scholars.
[7] P. 6.
[8] Pp. 67-6-7.

Pes. 70b where it is stated that Judah the son of Durtai and his son separated פירש הוא ודורתא themselves and they settled in the south. They complained against Shemaiah and Abtalyon who were great Hakamim and great *Darshonim*, interpreters—who never said that the sacrifice of Hagigah could take precedence over the Sabbath. Rab asked, what was the reason for the statement given by the son of Durtai? To which R. Ashi replied, do we have to explain the statements of separatists (perushim)? The author continues to write, "Even more dramatic than these examples are the instances in which *perushim* are strongly attacked in the rabbinic sourses—condemnations which are scarcely likely to have been made if the *perushim* were regarded as the predecessors of the rabbis—i.e. as the Pharisaioi of Josephus." [9] The fallacy of the author's view is due to the fact that he does not distinguish between the word *perushim* and the term Perushim as applied by the Sadducees and other opponents. As was said before, in the Talmud *perushim* as a group does not occur, unless it is used by the Sadducees. If the author would have been versed in the Talmud, he would have known that the Pharisees referred to by the Sadducees were Hakamim, the sages—the predecessors of all the later rabbis. In the complaints of the Sadducees against the Pharisees in the question of the halaka, we know that the views and theories of the Pharisees became the laws as well as the tenents of the later rabbis and Judaism. The Sadducees called the leaders of the Jews who did not agree with them, who propagated the universality of God and so forth, *Perushim*. Not all who were called Perushim were Hakamim, but all the Hakamim were Perushim.

According to the author the Pharisaioi in Josephus are to be identified with the *Hakamim* and he dates the emergence of the *Hakamim* and the Pharisaioi to the time of John Hyrcanus I. However, he overlooked the fact that Josephus mentioned the three philosophical groups, *Saddoukaioi, Pharisaioi*, and *Essenoi* in the time of Jonathan [10] long before the time of John Hyrcanus I. Josephus never refered to *Hakamim*, sages.

In the tannaitic literature the term, סופרים, *sopherim* occurs. The term *Sopherim* refers to the sages who interpreted the Torah and previous halaka for the purpose of amending old laws and introducing new laws. It began shortly after the time of the Restoration and lasted to the destruction of the Temple. The term *Sopherim* has the connotation of Scribes. There were scribes of the court and scribes of documents. The first is with a capital "S", the latter, with a small

[9] P. 7.
[10] *Ant.* 13. 3. 9.

"s". The author employs the same pattern of error, lack of differentiation between *Perushim* and *perushim*, the in his usage and interpretation of *Sopherim* and *sopherim*. The author writes, "After John Hyrcanus excluded the Hakamim, Pharisaioi, they were compelled into a degree of isolation. They could nevertheless continue to extend and implement their interpretation of Torah because of their direct contact with the people. It also seems likely that they became increasingly influential in courts of law for pragmatic reasons. Here the connection of Scribes (*sopherim*) and Hakamim is of great importance." [11] The term Sopherim has the connotation of a title of those who had the authority to introduce new laws, while the *Hakamim* are sages without title. .As was said before, the term *Sopherim* ceased with the destruction of the Temple while the Hakamim flourished. The term Hakamim was applied even to one person. There are numerous instances in the tannaitic literature where the phrase "the sages said" was used for the opinion of only one sage.[12] The author confuses the whole idea of *Sopherim* and *Hakamim* due to his apparent lack of knowledge of the Talmud. The word Hakamim in the Talmud is a generic term.

On the following pages the author deals with Jesus and the Pharisaioi, and the offense and trial of Jesus. On page 38, the author writes, "The attack on *perushim* as extremist, and particularly on their attention to details of Torah ... is similar to some of the attacks of the Pharisaioi in the gospels. These are strongest ... in Matthew and Luke, but they are present in Mark. In ii. 16 describes how the Pharisees are criticized by Jesus when they express an attitude to the *'amme haArez*." First let me say that in Mark ii. 16 the term *'amme haAretz* does not occur. What is stated is a complaint by the Pharisees and Scribes against Jesus because Jesus has been eating with publicans and sinners καὶ πολλοὶ τελῶναι καὶ ἁμαρτωλοί. The Perushim never opposed association with the *'amme haArez*, only the *Haberim* were so strict in their observance of the laws of purity that they did not participate in a meal with *'amme haArez* (farmer) because the *Haberim* suspected them of not observing the laws of tithe not being careful in the laws of purity.

As to the author's statement that the strictures of the authors of the gospels against the Pharisees are similar to the attacks found in the Talmud against the perushim, this is simply absurd. The Talmud is against those perushim who separated themselves from mundane life in an ostentatious and hypocritical display of piety. Nowhere in the

---

[11] P. 21.

[12] Cf. Yeb. 46, מאן חכמים ר יוסי, passim.

Talmud is the term *Perushim* used unless it is by their opponents.

It is regretable to note that this absurdity is found in many books about the Pharisees; it is even recorded by a professor of religion who fell victim to this theory. He wrote, "Jesus did not approve the pleasure so many Pharisees took in being addressed as rabbi ... In many generations before Jesus, a scribe has said, much the same thing; 'Love manual work, and hate rabbinism' אהוב את המלאכה ושנא את הרבנות, (Aboth I. 10). Many shared this view. Arrogance may often have been found among the scribes, but they were not effete academicians." The author wants to show that some of the scribes as well as Jesus hated Rabbinism. This distorted view was paroted by the author of the item "the Pharisees" published in the *Encyclopaedia Judaica*. I am certain that the authors of this false view did not conceive it in malice but rather out of ignorance of the Talmud.

In dealing with the offense and trial of Jesus, the author wants to inject his view that Jesus was tried by the Sanhedrin as a Rebellious Elder. Bowker writes, "The main point of this argument is not to suggest that Jesus was arraigned as a rebellious elder according to the definitions and procedures which the rabbis later elaborated. This is certainly and univocally not the case. But the category of 'rebellious elder' long pre-exists the eventual definition of the rabbis." [13] The conception of the Rebellious Elder was introduced in Jabneh after the destruction of the Temple. A Rebellious Elder refers only to a member of the Sanhedrin who revolted against the decision of his colleagues. The word זקן, Elder, has the connotation of a member of the Sanhedrin.[14] Jesus was never a member of the *Bet Din*, Sanhedrin. (Why this concept of Rebellious Elder arose in Jabneh, I hope to deal with at length in the third volume of *The Rise and Fall of the Judaean State*.)

In an "Additional Note" the author enumerates twenty-six controversies between the Pharisees and the Sadducees. Some of them, such as number 10, "Ransom in place of execution," and number 20, "Proof of virginity," [15] never took place between the Pharisees and the Sadducees.

At the end of the book the author cites talmudic passages where references are made to the Pharisees. It is a conglomeration of citations. In many passages the term Pharisees does not occur. Furthermore, the author does not differentiate between tannaitic sources, amoraic

---

[13] P. 51.

[14] Cf. Tal. Yer. Sanh. 1 חברים מהו ליכנס לעיבור השנה · · · מעשה ברבן גמליאל שאמר יקרוני שבעה זקנים לעלייה ונכנסו שמנה אמר מי הוא שנכנס שלא ברשות עמד שמואל הקטן על רגליו ואמר אני· · ·

[15] P. 54.

sources and the rabbinic sources of the seventh and eighth centuries. He quotes the scholia to the *Megillat Taanit* as a source for the Pharisees which it certainly is not. Some translations are totally wrong. On page 149 he quotes the Talmud Men. 65a, "From the eighth of the same until the close of the Festival (of Passover), during which time the date of the feast of Weeks was re-established, fasting is forbidden." It is true that in some texts of the Talmud the phrase חגא דשבועיא the festival of week i.e. from the eighth day of Nisan to the festival of Passover constituted one week. To have these words חגא דשבועיא translated as the Festival of Weeks is erroneous. In the entire Talmud the phrase חג שבעות the festival of Weeks is never mentioned unless the Pentateuchal passages were quoted. The term used for the festival of Weeks in the Talmud was עצרת *Azereth* and Josephus employed the same term, *Azartah*. Thus the translations on page 149 show the author's unacquaintance with the Talmud and Josephus.[16]

The same shortcomings as were noted in Bowker's book are regrettably found in the *Rabbinic Traditions About the Pharisees Before 70* by Dr. Neusner. This work consists of three volumes. It is a very ambitious work and the author undoubtedly invested many days of hard work. It is well written and even convincing for those readers who do not know the rabbinic traditions as found in the Talmud. The author first quotes the texts of the Mishne and Talmud, then he gives his own "Comment". However, from the outset I must say that many of his "Comments" reveal the lack of comprehension and proper understanding of the Talmudic passages with which he deals. There are numerous examples which may be cited. But I must limit myself to only a very few examples due to my limited time. These few examples, however, will clearly demonstrate the author's being insufficiently equipped to deal with the Talmud, and that he is not well versed in the development of the halaka. On page 63, in vol. I, he quotes M. Hag. 2:7 according to the translation of Danby,

[16] Mr. Bowker, on p. 10, n.1 makes reference to one of my articles, "see S. Zeitlin, "The Origin of the Pharisees Reconsidered," *JQR*, LIX, 1969, 255-67", I never wrote an article by this title. The correct title of my article is, "The Origin of the Pharisees Reaffirmed." The title given by the author may be misleading. The reader may think that I reconsidered my former position on the origin of the Pharisees and changed my mind. I never reconsidered. An article bearing the title, "The Origin of the Pharisees Reconsidered" was written by Finkelstein who really did reconsider his position. To this article, I replied with an article, "The Origin of the Pharisees Reaffirmed," *JQR*, 1969.

"For perushim (Pharisees? Separatists?) the clothes of Am ha arez counts as suffering *Midras*-uncleanness. For them that eat heave-offering, the clothes of the Pharisees count as suffering *Midras*- uncleanness. For them that eat of Hallowed things, the clothes of them that eat heave-offering count as suffering *Midras*-uncleanness. For them that occupy themselves with sin-offering water, the clothes of them that eat hallowed things count as suffering Midras-uncleanness.

Yosef b. Yoezer was the (most) pious (HSYD) in the priesthood yet for them that eat of Hallowed things his apron counted as suffering *Midras*-uncleanness."

To this Neusner comments, "Like the foregoing, this is to be classified as a reminiscence concerning Yosi Yosef b. Yo'ezer. Here Yosi serves as an example of an ancient pious priest. Even the best of the virtuous old priests still serve as a source of *Midras*-uncleanness. Any other name e.g. Simeon the Just—would have served just as well." Dr. Neusner's statement that Yosef b. Yoezer was brought into the Mishne as an example and that any other virtuous priest would have served as well, betrays his lack of knowledge concerning the Talmud, and the history of the laws of uncleanness. According to the Pentateuch, one who touched a corpse shall be unclean for seven days and is called *ab* אב הטומאה. One who touches this man becomes the first degree of impurity, and anyone who touches an object of first degree impurity becomes a second degree impurity, and anyone touching a second degree of impurity becomes a third degree of impurity. And if a third degree touches *terumah*, then it becomes unfit for the priest to eat. And anyone who touches an object having the third degree of impurity becomes a fourth degree impurity and defiles holiness קודש. Some sages decreed a law that the sword which killed a person had the same degree of impurity as the corpse.[17] Those that touched the sword thus became an *ab* and he is impure for seven days. Yosef b. Yoezer opposed this law and declared that the sword who killed a person is not of the same degree of uncleanness as the corpse.[18] He who touches the words becomes only of the first degree of impurity. What to the sages was a fourth degree of impurity and defiled holiness, was for Yosef b. Yoezer a fifth degree impurity and did not defile holiness. There was a difference between that concerning the degree of purity; what was pure to Yosef b. Yoezer was impure to the sages. Yosef b. Yoezer was brought into the Mishne not as an example chosen at random.

[17] Cf. Pes. 14. בחלל חרב חרב הרי הוא כחלל·

[18] Cf. Ab. Zar. 35 ודיקרב במיתא מסאב וקרי · · · · העיד יוסי בן יועזר
ליה יוסי שריא·

The term perushim in the Mishne Hag. does not refer to the Pharisees but to those who separated themselves from uncleannesses. The Mishne discourses on the different degrees of impurity, and states that the garments of the *Amme ha aretz* are unclean to the *perushim*, i.e. those who separate themselves from uncleanness. And the garments of the perushim are unclean to those who eat *terumah*, *terumah* being more sacred that *maasser*. The garments of those who eat hallowed things are unclean to those who occupy themselves with sin offerings i.e. sacred. Since Yosef b. Yoezer disagreed with the sages regarding the degrees of purity and impurity, what to him was pure was to them impure, thus his handkerchief, his garments were considered unclean to those who occupied themselves with sin offerings. This Mishne is a continuation of the previous Mishne, which reads, in part, as follows, "If a man immersed himself to render himself fit to eat unconsecrated food חולין he may not eat *maasser*. If a man immersed himself to eat *maasser* (i.e., a priest) he may not eat *terumah*. If a priest immersed himself to eat *terumah* he may not eat hallowed things. If he immersed himself to eat hallowed things, he may not sacrifice sin-offerings." These two texts are a unit, one Mishne, dealing with purity and impurity.

טובל לחולין והוחזק לחולין אסור למעשר טבל למעשר והוחזק למעשר
אסור לתרומה טבל לתרומה והוחזק לתרומה אסור לקודש· טבל לקודש
והוחזק לקודש אסור לחטאת בגדי עם הארץ מדרס לפרושין בגדי פרושין
מדרס לאוכלי תרומה בגדי אוכלי תרומה מדרס לקודש בגדי קודש מדרס
לחטאת יוסי בן יועזר היה חסיד שבכהונה והיתה מטפחתו מדרס לקודש·

On page 347 of the same volume, the author quotes the M.R.H. 25-6 following the translation of Danby, "There was a large courtyard in Jerusalem and it was called Bet Yaazoq, and to there all the witness would assemble. And there the court examined them. And they prepared large meals for them so that they might make it a habit to come. Before time they did not stir from there the whole day. Rabban Gamaliel the Elder ordained that they might walk within two thousand cubits in any direction."

To this the author adds his "Comment", "The decree of Gamaliel is given in the Yavnean form: *At first . . . when the Temple was destroyed, Rabban X decreed . . .* The form here makes good sense, however, unlike its use in connection with Hillel's decrees, for it is entirely plausible that the witnesses earlier remained in the courtyard, once they had reached it on the Sabbath. But we have no information on the provocation for changing the law; in the Yavnean form it is invariably specified." Here again he displays his lack of perception not only in the Mishne but also with regard to the development of the laws of Sabbath as given in the tannaitic literature. According to

the Pentateuch, the ancient Hebrews had no right to leave a place
on the Sabbath. The Septuaging renders "his place" as "his house"
οἴκους ὑμῶν. This, however, was a hardship for any Jew. It certainly
could not be considered a "Sabbath pleasure" to stay in the house
all day. The sages amended this law to say מקום "his place" as "his
city". Thus the Jews were allowed to walk on the Sabbath through
the city. This law, however, was granted only to city dwellers. The
man who saw the birth of the new moon was allowed to travel even
on the Sabbath to testify about the birth of the new moon. The
witnesses being non-city dwellers in Jerusalem were not allowed to
walk through the city. Gamaliel the Elder amended this law so that
the witnesses could share in the same privilege as the city dwellers
and were allowed to walk two thousand cubits within the city of
Jerusalem on the Sabbath.

Neusner maintaining that it was in the Yavnean form said, "But
we have no information on the provocation for changing the law."
Apparently he did not know of the Mishne Er. 4. 1 where it is stated
that if a Jew were forcibly taken into another city on the Sabbath
day i.e. kidnapped by pagans, he could walk only four cubits but not
throughout the city because it was not his abode.[19] The men who
saw the new moon were obligated to go to Jerusalem to testify and
the sages permitted them to travel even on the Sabbath for this
purpose. However, they did not have the privileges of the inhabitants
on the city concerning travel in the city on the Sabbath. That is what
the Mishne states, בראשונה. Prior to the time of Rabban Gamaliel,
witnesses were kept in the courtyard all day since they were not
inhabitants of the city. Rabban Gamaliel the Elder amended the old
law by declaring them as dwellers of Jerusalem. Thus they had the
privilege to walk two thousand cubits in the city on the Sabbath. To
place this Mishne in the time of Yavne is absurd and points out his
lack of comprehension concerning the laws of Sabbath. In the period
of Yavne there was already the law of the Sabbath journey, תחום שבת
i.e. that a Jew was allowed to walk two thousand cubits outside of
the city and the law of Erub had already been introduced in order
that one might be able to walk four thousand cubits outside of the
city. The author states "the *decree*, of Gamaliel". He confuses a *gzera*
with a *takkana*. *Gzera* is a decree, and there is a vast difference between
a *gzera* and a *takkana*.

A decree, *gzera*, was promulgated for a particular reason and when
the reason for it disappeared the *gzera* became void. *Gzera* is always a
stricture of the law. On the other hand, a *takkana* is an amending of

[19] מי שהוציאוהו גוים או רוח רעה אין לו אלא ארבע אמות.

the Pentateuchal law or the *halaka*, and liberalizes the law. It was introduced by the sages for the purpose of harmonizing religion and life. Rabban Gamaliel the Elder introduced a *takkana* giving the witnesses who came to testify of the birth of the new moon the same privilege as that of an inhabitant of the city allowing the witness to walk two thousand cubits on the Sabbath.

Dr. Neusner raises the following question, "Who took the sightings of the moon and there upon decreed the calendar?" Certainly, the *Bet Din*. Apparently Dr. Neusner is not acquainted with the history of the development of the calendar during the second commonwealth nor with the Pharisees, otherwise he would not have raised this question.

The author continues, "So long as the Temple stood, the Temple administration held full responsibility for the declaration of the sacred calendar important in determining the proper Temple sacrifices for each day. It is hardly likely that the Pharisees would have told the priests when the festival and Atonement offerings were to be made." This paragraph again reveals the author's unacquaintance with the Pharisees, the Temple, and the history of the Second Commonwealth in general. He speaks of the "sacred calendar", what kind of nonsense is this? The calendar is neither sacred nor profane. There is no question of sanctity in the reckoning of the calendar. When the sages changed the solar calendar to a lunar-solar calendar, the year began with the Fall, the month of Tishri, however the months were counted from the Spring, Nisan, since the Pentateuch says that the Spring month is the first of the months.[20] There existed other reckonings such as the era reckoning i.e. the reckoning of the independence of the State of Judaea. Similarly in America, there is a general calendar which begins with the month of January, and there is another reckoning in America starting with the day of independence, July 4, 1776. In the same manner, in modern Israel, while the lunar-solar calendar is in vogue, there is also the era reckoning i.e. from the fourth of Iyyar, 1948 when the state of Israel was established. There was also a reckoning according to the years of the reign of the king which began in the Spring with the month of Nisan, i.e., if a king ascended to the throne more than a month before Nisan, then it was counted as a full year, and the second year of the reign began with the year following Nisan.[21]

The statement, "it is hardly likely that the Pharisees would have told the priests when the festival and Atonement offerings were to

[20] Ex. 12. 1.
[21] See M. R.H. 1.1.

be made", is not borne out in the tannaitic literature nor by the writings of Josephus. From the tannaitic literature we know that the priests had to follow the Pharisees' doctrine. There was a dispute between the Sadducees and the Pharisees concerning the libation of the water on the altar during the Festival of Tabernacle. Once it had happened that a priest who had opposed the doctrine of the Pharisees poured the libation on his feet and the people pelted him with their *etrogim*.[22] From this Mishne we can see that the priests in the Temple had to follow the teaching of the Pharisees otherwise the people would not tolerate them. [23] This is corroborated by Josephus where he says, "Sacred rites of divine worship are performed according to their (Pharisees) exposition." (*Ant.* 18.1.3 (15)) Thus the author's assertions are not in accord with the true history.

In book II, page 185, Dr. Neusner quotes M. Hag. 2. 3-4 according to the translation of Danby, "If the Feast of Pentecost fell on the eve of the Sabbath, the House of Shammai say, 'The day for the slaughtering is after the Sabbath.' And the House of Hillel say, 'The day of the slaughtering is *not* after the Sabbath.' But they agree that if (the Feast) fell on the Sabbath, the day for slaughtering is after the Sabbath." The Mishne has עצרת *azeret*, while the author has the Feast of Pentecost. That is a wrong rendering. The innocent reader, not having before him the text of the Mishne, would have readily to conclude that the text has חמישים, *fifty*. The term Pentecost never occurs in the entire rabbinic literature. It is found only in Josephus, Acts and in two books of the Apocryphal literature, the Second book of Maccabees and Tobit. It is well said that translators are traitors. The rendering of the word *azeret* into Pentecost is a betrayal. The author in his "Comment" writes, "Hag. 2:4, concerns the slaughter of the *Re'iyyah*—sacrifices. The House of Shammai say that they must be sacrificed on Sunday since they do not override either the festival or the Sabbath. The House of Hillel say that it may be done both on the Sabbath and on the festival itself." Here is another distortion. No sacrifices could be brought to the Temple on the Sabbath, except the daily and the Sabbath sacrifices. The House of Hillel never rendered such an opinion that a sacrifice could override the Sabbath.

The history of the Eighteen Measures which were decreed shortly before the destruction of the Second Temple is very intricate since there are different versions in the Mishne, the Tosefta, the Palestinian

---

[22] Cf. Tosefta Suc. 3.16; Yer. ibid. 14.
[23] Cf. also Y M. Yoma 1. 1-5, אנו שלוחי בית דין · · · משביעין אנו עליך
במי ששיכן את שמו בבית הזה שלא תשנה דבר מכל אשר אמרנו לך · · ·

Talmud and the Babylonian Talmud. Only a skilled Talmudist who is also well versed in the development of the halaka could harmonize all the different versions. Some of the decrees which were accepted before the destruction of the Second Temple were with the consent of the Shammaites and Hillelites, while on others, the Shammaites opposed the Hillelites. In expounding on the Eighteen Measures, Dr. Neusner confused and confounded the views of the House of Shammai and House of Hillel and thus presented a distorted perspective which once again shows his incapability to deal seriously with Talmudic passages.

Among the Eighteen Measures which were finally adopted, there were different controversies between the school of Shammai and the school of Hillel. One such controversy goes back to Shammai and Hillel themselves. It was with reference to grapes, which were gathered for wine-press. Shammai said that they were susceptible to levitical uncleanness because of the juice that runs out of the grapes. Hillel, however, held that they do not become susceptible to levitical uncleanness. הבוצר לגת שמאי אומר הוכשר והלל אומר לא הוכשר In the Talmud Shab. 15 three controversies between Shammai and Hillel are enumerated. The exact number of the controversies was challenged as there existed another controversy between them "concerning grapes". It was replied, "This controversy does not count," as Hillel did not retort to Shammai's contentions, he remained silent. והאיכא הבוצר לגת שמאי אומר הוכשר והלל אומר לא הוכשר בר מיניה דההי דהתם קא שתיק ליה הלל לשמאי

On page 318, vol. I, Dr. Neusner writes, "I do not copy Freedman's translation, *Hillel was silenced by Shammai*. My text (sic!) reads STYQ LYH HLL LSMY, which can only mean *Hillel silenced Shammai*." Here Dr. Neusner not only wrongly translated the phrase, קא שתיק ליה הלל לשמאי which should be rendered: Hillel was silent before Shammai, but he also did not properly understand the Talmudic passage. The controversy about the grapes which is given in Shab. 15 b is discussed in greater detail on ibid. 17. There it is stated that Shammai opposed Hillel and to this the Talmud adds that Hillel was sitting in front of Shammai as a disciple הבוצר לגת ••• ואותו היום היה הלל כפוף ויושב לפני שמאי כאחד מן התלמידים, which means that Hillel did not reply. As was practiced among the sages, a student could not contradict his superior, a teacher. Thus the phrase in Shab. 15 b that Hillel was silent before Shammai is actually based on the passage on p. 17 of the same tractate. It is regrettable to note again that the author of "the rabbinic traditions" did not fully comprehend the Talmudic passages. It is one among too many to enumerate.

I said in my review of his book, *A Life of Yohanan Ben Zakkai*, that Dr. Neusner writes lucidly and demonstrates that he had ideas. This work in three volumes, *The Rabbinic Traditions About the Pharisees before 70*, as well as his volumes on *A History of the Jews in Babylonia* contain many distortions about the rabbinic traditions concerning the Pharisees and the history of the Jews in Babylonia. (Since my time is limited, I can not review his volumes on the history of the Jews in Babylonia because this would be a waste of time for me. I refer, however, to an article by Dr. Leo Landman, "R. Shila and the Informer." *JQR*, LXIII, p. 136, ff.)

I wrote this review with a heavy heart. As I said before this author is a gifted young man and a prolific writer, but apparently he never had a proper guide when studying the Talmud. His hypotheses are based on an inadequate knowledge of the Talmud. Thus he is both confused and confounded. I follow the axiom of Kohelot, "there is a time to speak out." He writes lucidly and presents his statements with self assurance and even with arrogance. Innocent readers, Jews and Christians, who are not versed in the Talmud would accept his conclusions and thus be misguided. This type of writing is harmful to scholarship. As I have said in my review of *A Life of Yohanan Ben Zakkai, disce aut discede*. I reiterate this phrase again.

I would like to take the liberty of restating what I wrote in 1942 in *JQR*, p. 36,

> In this country Jewish scholarship is still a field of new research, as it does not have the tradition of the old centers like Russia and Germany, ... which have been utterly destroyed by Nazism and Communism. Especially in the rabbinic field, scholarship is still in a state of *tabula rasa*. Some of the books written by authors in this field are based on the use of translations ... many of the theories and hypotheses are founded upon secondary literature ... it was my duty as a student of Rabbinics to expose such books without bias or favor. I saw in many works a danger to scholarship, since the intelligent laity and particularly our Christian colleagues are inclined to accept any book coming from Jews dealing with Rabbinics and appended with notes as *ex cathedra* pronouncements.

It is regrettable to state that in over thirty years, Rabbinics in America has not been enhanced, on the contrary, it has worsened and is in a state of paucity. Thirty-two years ago we still had some rabbinic scholars who came across the Atlantic with sufficient knowledge of Rabbinics. Maybe the present status of Jewish scholarship in America is due to the shortsightedness of the Jewish leaders who have not fully encouraged Jewish scholarship and have not possessed the far-ranging vision for building a strong and healthy Judaism in the Diaspora.

Dropsie University   SOLOMON ZEITLIN

While my review was in the press another book from this prolific author, *An Invitation to the Talmud*, was brought to my attention. On page 26 the author states, "I am not a 'Talmudist'. I do not engage in the classical disciplines of Talmudic study. I have not mastered the medieval commentaries."

The author confirms my contention that he is not a Talmudist and is not versed in rabbinic literature. There is a Talmudic axiom,

הודאת בעל דין כמאה עדים דמי.

I wonder what a scientist would think of a person who is not a mathematician and writes on algebra and geometry, or one who is not a biologist and writes on biology. We may say that such writings are at best journalism, not scholarship.

In the article, "Talmud" in the *Encyclopaedia Britannica*, I stated that the Talmud "may be compared to a primeval, dense forest in which a person will lose his way without a skillful guide".

Dr. Neusner ventures into the forest without knowing the different trees and colors. When he studied the Talmud he did not have a skillful guide. We must say that he has lost his way in the primeval, dense forest. Thus by his confession he admits his lack of knowledge of the Talmud. By his writings innocent readers are misled.

S. Z.

THE ENCYCLOPAEDIA JUDAICA
A SPECIMEN OF MODERN JEWISH SCHOLARSHIP

IN THE *Jewish Quarterly Review* Vol. LXIII, p. 1-28, I published a
review entitled "*Encyclopaedia Judaica*: The Status of Jewish Scholarship." where I reviewed a few articles which appeared in this Encyclopaedia, dealing with the history of the Second Jewish Commonwealth
and talmudic studies. The articles which I reviewed were taken at
random, and I did not know who were the authors. Apparently my
review did not please the publishers and the editors. Dr. L. Rabinowitz, Deputy Editor-in-Chief, sent in a so-called refutation.

On the first pages, the Deputy Editor-in-Chief uses insinuations and
innuendos which have nothing to do with the subject and are only
personal. I shall certainly ignore them. My reviews were not written
against any of the contributors as such, but only against their statements. I followed the principle *amicus Plato sed magis amica veritas*.

Dr. Rabinowitz states, "Before we proceeded to plan the *Encyclopaedia Judaica*", he and his colleague visited Professor Urbach to
invite his cooperation. "He pointed out that the name Pharisees applied
to the sages is most inappropriate, though it has been widely adopted
merely as a result of the New Testament reference to "Scribes and
Pharisees".

In my article, "The Sadducees and Pharisees" published in 1936 (in
Hebrew), I pointed out there was no sect among the Jews called
Pharisees. The word was coined as a nickname by the Sadducees, a term
of contempt of those who innovated Oral Law. Those Jews were
nicknamed *Perushim* Pharisees—this group did not call themselves
Perushim. The term *Perushim* in the meaning of Pharisees never
occurs either in the Mishne or in the tannaitic literature. It only occurs in
the dialogues between the Sadducees and the Pharisees. The Sadducees
said, "We complain against you Pharisees", and the Pharisees retorted,
"We complain against you Sadducees". Or, it occured also in the mouths
of their opponents. Cf. Tal. Kid. 66, Sota 22b. The term *Perushim*
appears a few times in the Talmud, but not in the sense of a party,
group or sect. It has rather the general meaning of separatists, of people
who separated themselves from one thing or another.

An analogous use of a contemptuous name may be found in Jewish
history of the eighteenth century when the sect of Hasidim came into
existence; those who did not accept their theories and views were
nicknamed by them *Mitnagdim*, i.e. who opposed not only Hasidism,

but even from their viewpoint, Judaism. Another example may be found in the rise of the Reform Movement in the sixteenth century against the pope. The Catholics at that time contemptuously called opponents of the pope Protestants—implying that they are opposing the essence of Christianity. History is replete with examples of this nicknaming propensity.

Although the term *Perushim*, in the sense of a group, never occurs in tannaitic literature, the people at large called these men who propagated the idea of the universality of God and that the Oral law is on a par with the Written law, *Perushim*. The nickname *Perushim* became later a name of distinction. Similarly, the term *Mitnagdim* was originally a nickname of reproach, ·but became in due time a term of distinction.

Josephus tells us that he joined the Pharisees to learn their ideas. He also relates that Rabban Simon ben Gamaliel was a Pharisee. He records that in the delegation which was sent by the provisional government there were three Pharisees. Thus we can see that the Judaean people took cognizance of the fact of a particular group known as Pharisees, were learned and interpreters of the law.

Again the Gospels record dissentions between the Pharisees and Jesus and also between them and his disciples. There also occur some halakic controversies between Jesus and the Pharisees; thus, it is understandable that an article on the Pharisees is a *must* for any Jewish encyclopaedia. The article had to be substantiated by historical facts. It is regrettable to say that the item Pharisees in the *Encyclopaedia Judaica* is confused and full of errors. I shall reiterate what I said in my review. "The author states: the Pharisees' first bid for power was made in a period two centuries after the Babylonian exile during the struggle to remove The temple and religious control from the sole leadership of the aristocratic Sadducees. The Judaeans were exiled by the Babylonians in the year 587-86, two hundred years after the exile would bring us to 387-86". In another passage, the author writes, "Pharisees, *Perushim*, a Jewish, religious and political party or sect during the Second Temple period which emerged as a distinct group shortly after the Hasmonean revolt, about 165-160 BCE". Thus it is a flagrant contradiction. Did the Pharisees come into existance in the year 386 or in the year 165 ? It is unfortunate that the editor did not notice this blunder.

The author states, "While the Pharisees, as a whole, set a high ethical standard for themselves, not all lived up to it. It is mistakenly held that the New Testament references to them as 'hypocrites' or 'offspring of vipers' (Matt. 3, 7; Luke 18.9 ff. etc.) are applicable to the entire group. However, the leaders were well aware of the presence of the insincere among their members described by the Pharisees themselves in the Talmud as 'sore spots' or plagues of the Pharisaic party (Sot. 3, 4 and 22b)''. The Talmud (Sot. 3, 4 and 22b) refers to separatists, but not to the *Perushim* Pharisees. He confused separatists and *Perushim*. The author apparently was influenced by Dr. D. Flusser's book *Jesus* when he writes on page 20, ''Jesus did not approve of the pleasure many Pharisees took in being addressed as rabbi, 'And, he said, 'Call no man your father on earth, for you have one Father who is in heaven' (Mt. 23.6-12). In those days 'Abba' was another common form of address. In the generation before Jesus, a scribe had said much the same thing: 'Love manual work and hate rabbinism' (The author appended no. 13: *Sayings of the Fathers* 1, 10). Many shared this view. Arrogance may often have been found among the scribes, but they were not effete academicians''. The text in *Sayings of the Fathers* has אהוב את המלאכה ושנא את הרבנות. Reading this paragraph, I didn't believe my own eyes, that a professor of religion should render this phrase, ''Love manual work and hate rabbinism''. To translate the phrase שנא את הרבנות hate rabbinism is unbelievable. Such a statement of the author in his article ''Pharisees'' and Dr. Flusser's theory not only delude the readers but are also sowing bitter herbs for the students.

The Deputy Editor-in-Chief explains why the item Pharisees is brief because Professor Urbach wrote a comprehensive article, ''The Sages'' in which there is a reference to the Sadducees and the Pharisees. When I wrote my article in the JQR, I did not see Professor Urbach's article, ''The Sages''. As I said before, I read the articles in the Encyclopaedia at random. However, I went to the Dropsie Library, and I read Professor Urbach's article ''The Sages''. It is indeed a comprehensive article (about which I may write some time in the future), however, there is less than one column on the Pharisees. There is no mention of the dialogues between the Sadducees and the Pharisees which are of great importance not only for the proper understanding of the views of the Sadducees and the Pharisees, but also for the history and development of the halakah. Neither is there any mention of the difference between the Sadducees and the Pharisees regarding the Red Heifer. The controversy between the Sadducees and the Pharisees about the ''Holy scriptures defiled the hands'' is not mentioned in the item Pharisees nor is there any reference in the item Sages. All this is a *sine qua non* for a proper understanding of early Judaism.

As I said in my review the dissentions between Jesus and the Pharisees should be related and expounded. It is a must for a Jewish Encyclopaedia. I did not criticize the briefness of the item Pharisees. I even said it is a blessing. What I contended was that as short as it is, it is full of distortion and deception.

Regarding the institution of the synagogue, Dr. L. Rabinowitz writes, "Zeitlin's dogmatism knows no bounds. He denies the almost universally accepted view that the inception of synagogue worship came into being centuries after the Babylonian exile... he categorically states 'this is false'; the synagogue as a house of worship came into Jewish life after the destruction of the Second Temple". Apparently the Deputy Editor-in-Chief does not know the difference between dogmatism and historical analysis. In my essay "The Origin of the Synagogue" after an analytical study of the tannaitic literature as well as external sources, I came to the conclusion that the synagogue as a house of worship, came into being after the destruction of the Second Temple. My contention was not refuted. Dr. Rabinowitz states "He denies the almost universally accepted view". It is not a universal view. It is Zunz's view, which almost everybody copied. He further states, "How does Zeitlin explain the fact, curious though it is, that the first mention of a synagogue service as such is in the New Testament where Jesus' participation in one is referred to with details of the service (Luke 4.17; Acts 3.15)". My explanation is simple I would advise him to read the text carefully. In Luke 4.15-16, the text reads, "and he taught in their synagogues being glorified of all. And he came to Nazareth where he had been brought up; and as his custom was, he went into the synagogue on the sabbath day, and stood up for to read". Acts 13.14-15, the text has "They came to Antioch in Pisidia, and went into the synagogue on the sabbath day, and sat down. And after the reading of the law and the prophets"... There is not a word in Luke or in Acts about worship in the synagogue. What is stated is that the Torah and the Prophets were read in the synagogue.

The Synoptic Gospels refer many times to the synagogue as a house of instruction, of study, but not as a house of worship, prayer. Mark wrote that Jesus went to the synagogue on different occasions. In 1.21, he states that Jesus and his disciples "went into Capernaum; and immediately on the sabbath he entered the synagogue and taught". In 6.1-2, Mark wrote, "He ...came to his country and his disciples followed him and on the sabbath, he began to teach in a synagogue ..." In Luke 6.6 it is stated that Jesus "On another sabbath ... entered the synagogue and taught". Matthew 9.35 tells us that "Jesus went about all the cities and the villages teaching in their synagogues". In Luke 4.44 "And he preached in the synagogues of Galilee; Acts 17.1-2 "They came to Thessalonica where was a synagogue of the Judaeans. And Paul as his manner was, went in unto them, and three sabbath days reasoned with them out of the scriptures". In the Synoptic Gospels, many references are made to Jesus praying. He prayed on the mountain, and in the other places in the open. In Luke 9.28, "He took

Peter and John and James and went up into a mountain to pray"; Mark 6.46, "When he had sent them away, he departed into a mountain to pray". Act 10.9, "Peter went up upon the housetop to pray about the sixth hour". It is never mentioned that Jesus or his disciples went into a synagogue to pray.

The only place where the synagogue is referred to as a house of prayer is in the Sermon on the Mount as given by Matthew, "And when thou prayest thou shalt not be as the hypocrites, for they love to pray standing in the synagogues and in the corners of the streets", Matthew 6.5. This however is not mentioned in the Sermon on the Plain recorded by Luke. Hence we must conclude that the section "On Prayer" in the Sermon on the Mount belongs to a later period, after the destruction of the Temple when the synagogue became a house of prayer.

The Sermon on the Mount is a conglomeration of the sayings of Jesus. We must stress that the sayings of Jesus as given in the Sermon on the Mount, were recorded at least two generations after his death. His followers had different traditions of his sayings and so we find confusion and contradictions in the sayings of Jesus as recorded in the Sermon on the Mount and in other passages in the Synoptic Gospels. There are several terms supposedly used by Jesus which were not in vogue during the lifetime of Jesus, they came into usage after the destruction of the Temple. The word *Gehenna* as a place for punishment after death was first used in the Judaean literature after the destruction of the Temple. Similarly the saying in the Sermon on the Mount, "You cannot serve God and mammon" Matthew 6.24, could not have been uttered by Jesus since the word "mammon" was not in vogue in his lifetime. The word "mammon" is Hebrew *mamon* meaning money, wealth. During the Second Commonwealth, the word used for money was *kesef*; and the word *nekhasim* had the connotation of property, wealth. The word *mamon* came into usage after the destruction of the Temple.

In my essay, "The Origin of the Synagogue", I endeavored to show that during the early part of the Second Commonwealth, the Judaeans were divided into twenty-four divisions called *maamadot*. The members of each *maamad* were supposed to go to Jerusalem to the Temple to take part in the ceremony of the slaughtering of the daily sacrifices. But not all the Judaeans of the division could go or wished to go to Jerusalem. It was arranged that the members of the division who remained at home gathered in their respective cities and towns on the days on which they were supposed to be in Jerusalem and read portions from the Petateuch relating to the sacrifices. They assembled every morning and every afternoon throughout the year and three times on Sabbath. It is axiomatic that since the members of the division had to assemble regularly, they had to have a permanent place of assemblage. This place of assemblage was called *kneseth*, synagogue, assemblage.

Thus the *kneseth*, the synagogue came into being as an institution where the Pentateuch was read. In later days, the sages took advantage of the opportunities offered by the assemblage to propound their ideas to interpret the Pentateuchal passages. In the course of time, the reading of the prophetic books was introduced. The synagogue was not instituted for the purpose of prayers. Prayers were offered everywhere. The Temple was regarded as the appropriate place for prayers. There was no particular place in the Temple where prayers were offered, nor were there organized prayers. People prayed and besought God to grant their needs anywhere. After the destruction of the Temple, when prayers were organized and standardized, the sages thought that the proper place should be the synagogue where the Torah was read. Thus the synagogue became a house of prayer, and this took place after the destruction of the Temple.

Thus I am not dogmatic. My theory that the synagogue as a house of worship came into vogue after the destruction of the Temple, is based on historical investigation of the tannaitic literature as well as the external sources. I may add that the Deputy Editor-in-Chief read the New Testament too hastily, to say the least.

The Deputy Editor-in-Chief also takes objection to my statement, "We may add that the term משיח as a noun does not occur in the Hebrew Bible". He asks, "Does he really deny that in the frequent references to משיח in the Bible, the word is not a verbal noun meaning 'the annointed one'? e.g., 1 Sam. 26.33, Hab. 3.13, Ps. 84.10 and the mention of Cyrus as God's משיח?" In all these cases, the word משיח is an adjective. In I Sam. 26.16 "the *mashiah* of Yahweh"; Is. 45.1 "Thus said Yahweh to his *mashiah* to Cyrus"; Hab. 3.13 "Thine *mashiah*". In all these cases, the term *mashiah* has the connotation of being annointed.

In the book of Psalms the word *Mashiah* is found a few times. It appears in chapters 84.10; 89.39, 52; 105.15. The term used is משיחך and משיחי thine anointed and my anointed. In the book of Lamentations the words *Meshiah* of *Yahweh*, are found, these words refer to king Josiah "of whom we said under his shadow we shall live among the nations". In the book of Daniel the word *mashiah* occurs twice. In ch. 9.25 the author designates *mashiah* as *nagid*, ruler. This is a reference to the high priest who, during the Second Commonwealth, was the spiritual leader as well as the secular leader of the people. In ch. 9.26 the author wrote "And after three score and two weeks shall the *mashiah* be cut off". Here the author refers to the assassination of the High Priest Onias at Daphne, near Antioch. (Cf. II Mac. 4.30-35).

The term *mashiah-christos* as a noun appears only in the apocalyptic literature. The early Church Fathers, to prove that Jesus was the true *mashiah-christos*, maintained that there were references to Jesus as the *mashiah* in the Pentateuch and in the other books of the Bible. To combat the views of the Church Fathers, the sages interpreted the same verses as containing prophecies of the Jewish *mashiah*. Hence the interpretation of the biblical verses as referring to *mashiah* was theological and came after the destruction of the Temple. That the Jews during the first part of the Second Commonwealth had no expectation of a personal messiah is evident from the literature written during that period. The word *mashiah* does not occur in the book of Ben Sirah nor does it occur in the other apocryphal literature—Tobit, Judith, the Wisdom of Solomon, I Maccabees. In the latter it is stated that when the high priesthood was given to Simon, the Hasmonean, a clause was inserted, "Until a true prophet will arrive in Israel". From this we may deduce that the Judaeans believed prophecy would be restored, but there is no indication that they expected a messiah. Even in II Maccabees, wherein physical resurrection and the hope that all Jews would be gathered in Judaea are given prominence, the word *mashiah* does not occur—the author believed that this would be accomplished through the intervention of God.

After the destruction of the State and the burning of the Temple, particularly after the tragic collapse of the Bar Kokba revolt, the believe in a supernatural messiah who would rebuild the Temple and restore the Jewish State, gained sway over the minds of the people.

Regrettable to note that the scholars did not fully comprehend the ideas of the sages. The sages injected the idea of *mashiah* in the Bible as a weapon to combat the propaganda of the Church Fathers. The scholars took as historical fact, that the concept of *mashiah* is found in the Bible. The histories of the Second Commonwealth are vitiated with the idea of messianic expectations.

Dr. Rabinowitz did not dispute my other strictures against the item Messiah, where I said that the author's references to the book of Tobit regarding salvation and conversion are deceptive. His reference to Acts is also faulty. I shall repeat what I said in my original review. The article has an aura of a christological overtone, thus he confirmed my original statement that the article on the Messiah is not only ambiguous and faulty, but has an aura of christological overtone.

Rabbi L. Rabinowitz, in his reply, revealed the name of the author of the article on Shavuoth, Rabbi M. L. Jacobs. In his reply to my criticism, Rabbi Jacobs writes, "I wish I knew what on earth Zeitlin is on about. Of course there was no fixed day for Shavuoth before the present Jewish calender was established . . . . nor does the article say that the Pharisees connected Shavuoth with the Exodus, but with the theophany at Sinai". Zeitlin wrote about the author's statement that the Pharisees connected Shavuoth with the theophany at Sinai. The connection of the festival of Shavuoth with the Revelation on Mount Sinai was introduced after the revolt of Bar Kokba when there were no longer Sadducees and Pharisees, so Dr. Jacob's statement is faulty.

The author further states that his theory, "as a mere possibility". Possibility has the connotation of a fact being possible. Anyone who is aware of the Jewish history knows well, that there is no possibility to assume the Pharisees connected Shavuoth with theophany.

The author makes the following statement: "The rabbinic name is 'Azeret'. This word of uncertain meaning was generally translated as 'solemn assembly' ". The reason for calling the festival of Shavuoth *Azeret* is as follows. This festival was not celebrated by all Judaeans since only those living in Judaea could participate, and of these, only those who owned land. The sages who strove to unite all the Judaeans, regardless of whether they dwelled in the land or in the Diaspora, changed its name to Azeret. (Josephus called this festival *Azarta*), the conclusion of the festival of unleavened bread. The term Shavuoth never occurs in the Talmud unless it is a quotation from the Pentateuch; the term Azeret is used instead.

The author of the article on Shavuoth writes, "It is also extremely revealing that Zeitlin takes the Encyclopaedia to task for failing to have an item on Sidney Hoenig and on Teicher. Why these two?" The answer is, as I said in my article, that my attention was called to these exclusions. I recently learned that more names of scholars were omitted. Rabbi Jacobs supplied the motive for the exclusion of these two scholars, "The answer is that they alone, albeit very tentatively, side with Zeitlin in his unacceptable notions regarding the Dead Sea Scrolls". So, these two scholars, who side with me in my "unacceptable notions" were declared heretics and were penalized, and instead, they included the names of two Jewish American gangsters. (My attention was called to these inclusions.) I wrote in my review and I restate that "the inclusion of gangsters and the exclusion of Jewish scholars is an affront to learning and Jewish scholarship". It has a touch of vulgarism.

The Rabbi wrote that my notions regarding the Dead Sea Scrolls are unacceptable. I dare him to refute my proofs that the Dead Sea Scrolls are of the Middle Ages and have no value for the history of the Second Jewish Commonwealth.

In my criticism of the article "Proselytes", I said "In the item of Proselytes, the author does not give an historical development of the

6

laws of conversion. He lumps together all the laws, the tannaitic,
amoraic and the laws given by Maimonides". I also remark that the
author's statement that, according to Eliezer, a proselyte who performed only one of these commandments, i.e. either circumcision or
baptism, was acceptable is not true. In his reply, he says that I did not
go to the end of the Talmudic passage or "if you have read it, you have
not gone over it". He further states, "He apparently has overlooked the
statement of the Talmud (Yeb. 46, a and b) 'there is no difference of
opinion (between R. Eliezer and R. Joshua) when he immersed himself
but did not circumcize' ". I read the end of the passage, and I didn't
overlook anything. Reading a Talmudic passage is not sufficient and
not a virtue. We have to apply analytical scrutiny and to ascertain
what is tannaitic, and what is amoraic, and what is even saboraic in the
Talmud. The passage reads as follows, 'תנו רבנן גר שמל ולא טבל ר
אליעזר אומר הרי זה גר שכן מצינו באבותינו שמלו ולא טבלו, טבל ולא מל
רבי יהושע אומר הרי זה גר שכן מצינו באימהות שטבלו ולא מלו וחכמים
אומרים טבל ולא מל מל ולא טבל אינו גר עד שימול ויטבול ורבי יהושע נמי
נילף מאבות ורבי אליעזר נמי נילף מאימהות וכי תימא אין דנן אפשר משאי
אפשר והתניא רבי אליעזר אומר מניין לפסח דורות שאין בא אלא מן החולין
... אמר לו רבי עקיבא וכי דנין אפשר משאי אפשר אמר לו אף על פי שאי
אפשר ראייה גדולה היא ונלמד הימנה אלא בטבל ולא מל, כולי עלמא לא
פליגי דמהני, כי פליגי במל ולא טבל רבי אליעזר יליף מאבות ורבי יהושע
באבות נמי טבילה הוה...רבי יהושע טבילה באימהות מגלן סברא הוא דאם
כן במה נכנסו תחת כנפי השכינה,
Rabbi Eliezer said one who was circumcized but was not immersed,
is a גר, a proselyte. Then comes an explanatory remark that the
patriarchs were circumcized but not immersed. Eliezer could not have
said this because Isaac and Jacob were not proselytes. They were
circumcized because God commanded Abraham that all his descendants
should be circumcized. Rabbi Joshua held that one who was immersed
but not circumcized, is a proselyte. This is followed by explanatory
remarks that the matriarchs were immersed only. First, Rebeka, Ra-
chel and Leah were not proselytes, and second, where is the proof that
they accepted Judaism by immersion? As a matter of fact, the Talmud
says that that is only an opinion of Rabbi Joshua, and there are no
proofs. Rabbi Joshua could not have said this. The Book of Ruth relates
that when Ruth joined the Israelites, she only said, "Thy people is my
people, and thy God is my God". Immersion is not mentioned. The
entire passage is either late amoraic or even saboraic and was taken
from the Talmud Men. 82. The phrase בטבל ולא מל כולי עלמא לא
פליגי דמהני is not in accordance with Eliezer's point of view. The
difficulty of this passage was already noticed in Tos. 46b. Rabbi
Eliezer's point of view, as stated in Yer. Kid. 3 is that circumcision is

a prerequisite for conversion, but not immersion. גר שמל ולא טבל טבל ולא מל הכל הולך אחר המילה דברי רבי אליעזר. Thus my criticism on the item proselytes stands. The talmudic aphorism לקרות אתה יודע לדרוש אין אתה יודע. (Yer. Git. 5) may be applied to some of the editors and contributors.

The author of the article states, "They tried to equalize the status of the proselyte and that of the Jew; certain differences stemming from the origin of the convert, however remain. According to an anonymous Mishnah, a proselyte may not confess himself after taking out the tithes since the statement occurs in the confession, 'The land which thou has given us as thou has sworn to our fathers' ". In my criticism, I pointed out that the fact that the proselyte cannot confess, does not indicate that he is not a full-fledged Jew and that he is not equal to a native Jew. In the same way, a tenant of a field cannot confess since the land is not his, which means there is nothing wrong with himself. The author calls my comparison nonsense and cites another example—that a robber cannot confess either. Either the author is quibbling, or he simply does not understand. A proselyte cannot confess because he cannot say the land which You gave to us and which You swore to our forefathers. Similarly, a tenant cannot do this because he has no land. A robber cannot confess because he is a wicked person, since he robbed the land from a fellow Jew. A proselyte and a tenant are not wicked. No blemish can be attached to them. Only outside circumstances prevent them from confessing. You cannot compare them to robbers. Unfortunately, the author did not see the difference.

Rabbi Judah was of the opinion that a proselyte, when offering the first fruit, has to confess, and the Halaka is in accordance with Rabbi Judah's point of view. By the way, the author states in his article in the *Hebrew Encyclopaedia* he "gave the opinion of R. Judah, of the Palestinian Amoraim, and of the Rishonim". Rabbi Judah was a Tanna, and *not a Palestinian Amora*. According to Rabbi Simon, a priest may marry a proselyte who was converted when she was not yet three years and a day, albeit according to the book of Ezekiel, a priest may marry only a virgin of the seed of the house of Israel (Ez. 44.20). Thus according to Rabbi Simon, she was equal to a native Jewess. According to Josephus, Izates King of Adiabene when he converted to Judaism was circumcised. No immersion was mentioned. According to the book of Judith, Achior the Ammonite when he converted to Judaism, was circumcised. Again, immersion is not mentioned. Circumcision, beside being a precept which God commanded Abraham, became a symbol of the unity of the Jewish people and a mark of differentiation from the pagan world. Immersion, baptism, was not required for conversion. This rite was introduced after the

adoption of the eighteen decrees in the year 65 C.E. Rabbi Joshua
was the first to demand immersion, baptism, as a *sine qua non* for
conversion to Judaism.

When I reviewed the two talmudic articles INTERPRETATION
and TAKKANOT, I did not know who were the authors. Now the
Deputy Editor-in-Chief tells me that both articles were written by
Professor M. Elon, and he wrote a detailed reply of my criticism. "It is
available to anyone who may be interested to see it. In it, Professor
Elon answers every single point of Professor Zeitlin, but it is too long
for reproduction". I am very anxious to see what Professor Elon
wrote, but I cannot express an opinion since I did not see it; however,
he sent in some extracts. He maintained that he gave the opinions
with regard to the Halaka. My criticism on the article, "Interpretation" was not based on his omissions, but on his commission, what
was said in the article. In stating that the "Midrash already served as a
creative legal source of the Halakhah", he is basing it on a Tosefta
Sanh. 9:1. In my review, I pointed out that he simply misunderstood
the tannaitic text. He further writes that it is my contention that
progressive development of the laws took place during the Second
Temple, while after that period it became less liberal and retrogressive.
On this he states, "It is useless to argue with a statement like this,
which does not stand up to any criticism. I have devoted scores of
articles (including a three-volume book which will appear next week)
which completely refute this statement". I have not yet seen the book,
but I may say at the outset if he really argued in his book that the
Amoraic Halaka and the Halakot which came into vogue during
the Middle Ages, are as progressive as the Halakot of the Second
Commonwealth, he did not make an historical study of the Talmud as
well as of the writings of the rabbis during the Middle Ages. It is true
that some laws in the Talmud, as well as in the Responsa, are liberal
and progressive. Rashi and Rabbenu Tam, on many occasions, interpreted the Talmudic laws liberally, especially with regard to יין נסך, but
that was not the trend of the rabbis. As I see from Professor Elon's
writings, he studies Jewish law in dogmatic form, not historic form. He
lumps the laws of the Second Commonwealth together with Maimonides' interpretations. Here we see his shortcomings which are evident
also in his item, *Takkanot*.

To my criticism that the author does not refer to the takkanot which
were instituted during the Second Commonwealth, he replied that I
did not read the pages beyond Col. 720. I read the whole article
including the pages after Col. 720. On Col. 721 the author states,
"Takkanot pertaining to procedural rules and other fields of the
Halakhah are attributed to Ezra the Scribe". That is what he said

about the Takkanot of Ezra. He calls them procedural, while in truththe Takkanot which were ascribed to Ezra are very important for the study of the development of the Halaka. These Takkanot were not enacted at one period or by one man, they were instituted during the period of the Second Commonwealth. They show how the sages stroveto bring religion into consonance with life and to ammend the Pentateuchal law, if such were life's demands.

On Col. 721 the author devotes more than half of a page to the periods of the Sanhedrin and the Tannaim. He gives the names of the sages who enacted takkanot but does not elaborate and explain the significance of the takkanot except of the takkana enacted by Rabban Gamaliel. However, he does not mention his takkana in reference to the laws of the Sabbath. (Cf. R.H. 2, 5).

On Cols. 721-722, the author deals with the Amoraic Period. He writes, "Another legislative principle of the amoraim is that stated by them in matters of marriage and divorce that 'a man who marries a woman does so subject to the conditions laid down by the rabbis and his marriage is annulled by the rabbis'. The meaning of this is that since every marriage takes place according to 'the law of Moses and Israel', it takes place subject to the consent of the scholars who laid down the relevant laws and therefore the scholars have the power, in circumstances deemed proper, to annul the marriage and hold it to have been invalid *ab initio*' ". The term takkana does not occur in this Talmudic passage. It is legislation, not a takkana. Again the author states, "A man who marries a woman does so subject to the conditions laid down by the rabbis". The text reads כל דמקדש אדעתא דרבנן מקדש". What conditions the rabbis laid down when a man marries a woman he does not spell out. He apparently copied Rashi and the Tosafot (Git. 33: Ket. 3) who maintained that the term Israel meant the rabbis.

Copying the Talmudic interpretations of the rabbis of the Middle Ages is important for the decision of the halaka, but a scholar must apply a critical analysis of their interpretations. As a matter of fact, during the Second Commonwealth, the marriage document read "according to the law of Moses and the Judaeans" משה ויהודאי כדת. Cf. also Mishne Ket. 7.6 העוברת על דת משה ויהודית Only after the destruction of the Temple, the term Judaean was changed to Israel due to the fact that the early Christians maintained that they were the true Israelites with whom God made a covenant, but the Judaeans are not the descendants of Israel with whom God made a covenant. To combat the contention of the early Christians, the sages changed the name of Judaeans to Israelites. They coined the term *Kneset Israel*. The term Judaeans does not appear in the Talmud after the destruction of the Temple; instead, the term Israel is used. Hence the phrase "according to the law of Moses and Israel" could not have the connotation of rabbis. (In my article, "Who is a Jew?", *Bitzaron*, April-May, 1973, I endeavored to interpret the meaning of "according to the law of Moses and Israel".) The item takkanot will not give the reader a clear panorama of the development of the takkanot because it placed together all the takkanot during the entire Jewish history. There is no differentiation of the takkanot of the Second Commonwealth and the takkanot of the Amoraim. In the case of the legislation of marriage, he merely copied uncritically the rabbis of the Middle Ages.

Regarding the item, "Jewish Identity" I stated that it contained many ambiguous statements, and some of them are wrong. I called attention to the author's statement, "By that time the Roman Imperial authorities were recognizing Christianity officially as their new religion, because the Emperor Nerva (96-98) exempted Christians from the *fiscus Judaicus*". To this, I ask where did the author get the idea that in the time of Emperor Nerva, Christianity was recognized as a new religion. I also question his statement that Nerva exempted the Christians from *fiscus Judaicus*? I wrote that the historian Dio relates that Emperor Nerva had forbidden anyone to inform who had adopted the Jewish mode of life. I said further, "It is possible that this prohibition refers also to those who adopted Christianity. In his time, Christianity was considered a segment of Judaism". The Deputy Editor-in-Chief writes, "In the article Judaeo-Christians (read Jewish Identity) as Zeitlin points out, the author makes the apparently unsubstantiated statement that the Emperor Nerva exempted the Christians from the *fiscus Judaicus*. The article on the *fiscus Judaicus* does not mention this. (Then I may question why he gave space to the unsubstantiated fact about *fiscus Judaicus* in this item). But if, as Zeitlin says, 'it is possible that it was imposed on Christians' ...". The Deputy Editor-in-Chief simply misread and misconstrued my statement. I wrote that it is possible that Emperor Nerva prohibited to inform on those who adopted Christianity. I did not refer to *fiscus Judaicus*. Dr. Rabinowitz continues, "It is not equally 'possible' that Christians were not regarded as 'proselytes to Judaism' who had to pay the tax?" What kind of nonsense is this? During the first century, the Christians were considered a segment of the Jews. They cannot be considered proselytes to Judaism, they were Judaeo-Christians.

The Deputy Editor-in-Chief continues, "It is indicative of Zeitlin's prejudices that whereas he roundly denounces the author of the article on Shavuoth for putting forward a suggestion introduced by these same words 'it is possible', he expects us to accept it when he uses it". Apparently the Doctor is lacking in discrimination. The term "possible" has the connotation that it may be, nothing is known to the contrary. In the item on Shavuoth, we know to the contrary that the Pharisees did not connect the festival of Shavuoth with the sinaitic theophany. However, in the case that the Emperor Nerva prohibiting to inform on the Jews, my statement "it is possible" is in order, because we have no fact to the contrary. It is regrettable that Dr. Rabinowitz did not comprehend the difference.

The rabbi said if he has to decide between the views of the author of the item Jewish Identity and mine, he would choose the author's. Certainly it is·his prerogative. The author made the following statement: "Those who did· not participate in that glorious tragedy (the revolt of Bar Kokba) could no longer lay any claim on being Jewish". Not all the Jews believed that Bar Kokba was a messiah and were opposed to his revolt against the Romans. The author of *Assumption of Moses* which was written in the year 140 C.E. called the followers of Bar Kokba "deceitful and impious men". Rabbi Joshua, as well as Rabbi Johanan ben Torta, were opposed to the Bar Kokba revolt. Would the Deputy Editor-in-Chief exclude them from the Jewish people?

In my review, I wrote that the item "Economic History" does not present the true economic condition of the Judaeans during the Second Commonwealth. The author did not deal with labor; he did not deal with taxation; he did not deal with the exports, that of fish, or the industry of glass blowing. I also mentioned that the author did not mention that Augustus Caesar gave to Herod the management of the copper mines in Cyprus, and thus it was a great factor in the economy of Judaea. Dr. Rabinowitz, in his reply, writes, "And what is one to make of the sentence in Zeitlin's criticism of the article on economic life. 'The author makes the statement that Judaea was poor in metal. However, during the time of Herod, copper was brought from Cyprus?' It is on a par with criticizing a statement on the economic situation of Israel that 'Oil had not been found in any significant quantities in Israel.' on the ground that there is a large import of oil from Israel!" Apparently the Deputy Editor-in-Chief is not a student of history of economics. If one should write on the economic life of Israel after 1967, certainly he would have to deal with the discovery of oil in the desert of Sinai as well as the import and export of oil to and from other countries. Similarly, a student who writes on the economic life of Judaea during the Second Commonwealth had to refer to the copper of Cyprus, which had a dominant effect on the economic life of the country. I repeat the item Economic

History does not give the economic condition of the Judaeans during the Second Commonwealth. It is jumbled together without historical perspective.

The item on the American Academy of Jewish Research, according to the Deputy Editor-in-Chief, "is an excellent and comprehensive article". According to him, it consists of twenty-nine lines. The question is how could it be a comprehensive article if it consisted of only twenty-nine lines? By the way, only four lines longer than the item on the gangste rSiegel (Butsy). Dr. Rabinowitz said it was objective and factual and was written by Professor Abraham Halkin. Professor Halkin, whom I respect greatly, is undoubtedly a serious scholar.

Giving twenty-nine lines, he reveals what he is thinking of the Academy and of the Encyclopaedia. The writing is not factual. As the only surviving member of the scholars who founded the Academy, I thought it is my duty to give a factual history of the founding of the Academy which is lacking in the article.

In the item Zealots, I stated that the description given in this article does not square with the truth. I wrote, "A pseudo historical article on the Zealots, the Sicarii and Masadais being foisted". The Deputy Editor-in-Chief, in replying, wrote a proem. He writes, "In one point Zeitlin puts himself completely out of court (sic!). Denying, as he does the authenticity of the Dead Sea Scrolls, he consequently denies that they throw any light on the Zealots and adamantly maintains that 'Josephus is the only historian who provided us with the party of the Zealots and their activities...' ". He actually repeats what he wrote in a previous page, "But Zeitlin has put himself out of court (sic!) in scholarly circles by his persistence, in spite of the vast material which has accumulated to the contrary, that the Dead Sea Scrolls and other discoveries in the Judean Desert are fakes (I never maintained that they are fakes) belonging to a later period. The Encyclopaedia might have been excused if it had passed over his views in silence as an exploded theory". *Pace* Rabbi! (The Deputy Editor-in-Chief is also a rabbi). To support my contention that the Dead Sea Scrolls are not of the pre-Christian period but belong to the Middle Ages, I adduced many arguments and proofs that the scrolls could not have been written during the Second Commonwealth. My arguments are based particularly on internal evidence. I was never refuted. The protagonist for the antiquity of the scrolls took refuge in silence.

In my letter to the *Jerusalem Post*, May 3, 1969, where I refuted Albright's allegations, I said, "I challenge Professors Albright and Yadin to refute my proofs against the antiquity of the Scrolls, one by one, openly and in a scholarly fashion. If they succeed, I shall readily surrender my position. But under no circumstances will the case be lost by default. Ultimately truth will prevail". Many times I appealed to the protagonists of the antiquity of the scrolls if they could, to refute my argument to the contrary. But they always lapsed into silence. The Rabbi, in his reply, made a wild allegation that my theory is "exploded". A rabbi, more than any ordinary human being, has to possess the following qualities: knowledge, integrity, and truthfulness. I challenge the Rabbi to substantiate his statement by refuting my arguments. I shall quote here a few.

מורה צדק ,בית המשפט ,קץ האחרון ,גמר קץ ,תוגר ,כהנא רבא עקביא ,בית השתחות,

All these terms came into usage after the Bar Kokba period. The Scrolls contain physical marks, *parentheses* in order to indicate that words should not be read; *hyphen* was used to indicate that words were connected. The use of hyphen between words, which is known in rabbinic literature by the term *makef,* came into usage in Hebrew literature in the seventh or eight century, when the rabbis introduced accent signs in the Bible. Some scrolls have *ellipses* to indicate that a word or words have been omitted. These physical signs used in some of the scrolls are unimpeachable proof that they were composed during the Middle Ages. Again, in *The Zadokite Fragments,* the phrase ברית אברהם, the Covenant of Abraham as synonomous with circumcision, was used. We do not find in the tannaitic and in the hellinistic literature of the pre-Christian period the term Covenant of the Abraham used as synonomous with circumcision. The first person who applied the term Covenant of Abraham to circumcision was Eleazar of Modein who lived during the Bar Kokba period. The application of the term Covenant of Abraham to circumcision was made in opposition to Paul and his followers who denied the necessity of circumcision. Thus we may say with certainty that *The Zadokite Fragments* could not have been written during the pre-Christian period.

The Deputy Editor-in-Chief tried to show that the *Encyclopaedia Judaica* was objective regarding the Dead Sea Scrolls, by giving my opinion against the antiquity of the Scrolls. He quotes, "S. Zeitlin has vigorously maintained that the Scrolls belong to a much later date and have no substantial scholarly importance. However the discovery of analogous material in the excavations of Masada, which are certainly not later than 73 C.E. *seem* to establish the *terminus ad quem* positively". And he states, "This objective statement Zeitlin calls a 'partisan point of view' ". This is not only a partisan point of view, but it was brought to kill my point of view. My opinion against the antiquity of the Scrolls was purposely quoted in order to kill it by stating that the excavations of Masada established that my opinion is totally wrong. It did not refer to the proofs that the findings in Masada are definitely and unequivocally of the Byzantine period of the seventh or eighth century. The fragments of the book of Leviticus and of Ben Sirah are of that period.

In the bibliographies, not only were my writings not included, but also none of the writings of the scholars who maintain that the Dead Sea Scrolls are not of great antiquity. The editors were apparently apprehensive that a reader may learn from them that there are some scholars who maintain that the Scrolls are of the Middle Ages, and hence, have no value for Judaism and early Christianity.

I certainly think that the rabbi, who alleged that my theory against the antiquity of the scrolls "was exploded", has the obligation to show it by refuting my arguments (if he can), one by one, in a scholarly manner. "The court" may assist him. Otherwise, the future historians will classify him as having uttered slanderous words. It is well known that Judaism considers slander as a capital sin.

The Rabbi states, "Zeitlin puts himself completely out of court". This is repeated twice. Who made up the court ? Who are the members of the court ? I am not isolated, I do not stand alone, many scholars hold the same opinion. Furthermore, I believe that one and the truth constitute a majority. He further states that I denied that the Scrolls "throw any light" on the Zealots. I emphatically deny that the Scrolls have any reference to the Zealots. The term קנאים Zealots never occurs in the Scrolls. Those who maintain that the Scrolls were written by the Zealots are distorting the Jewish history of that period.

Certainly Josephus, in his writings about the Zealots and the Sicarii, reveals a strong prejudice against them. They were anathema to him. He held them responsible for the destruction of the State. The facts however are reliable and truthful. He never confused the Zealots and the Sicarii. The Zealots and the Sicarii were two distinct groups, hostile to each other. The Sicarii were idealists and fanatics. In the name of liberty, they raided and plundered the Judaean towns and villages. They killed the High Priest Ananus. It is well said that idealists, fanatics, are more dangerous to society than ordinary criminals.

The Deputy Editor-in-Chief takes exception to my idea that what was needed was one or two volumes, supplements to the Jewish Encyclopaedia, which was published seventy years ago, and also to revise some items. Regrettable to note, the old Encyclopaedia is also full of gross errors and deluded some of our historians, who used it as a source. He claimed there is a massive contribution of Jewish scholarship both in America and especially in Israel. Of course, there are some advances in research, particularly in archaeology, demography and sociology.

There are also some new studies in the Bible, particularly in philology. Regrettable to state that 'The research in the Talmudim, rabbinics in general, inter testamental literature and medieval history and literature is very scant. The *Encyclopaedia Judaica* presents a good specimen.

Since I wrote my review, I read some more articles, again at random. I found some of them marked by gross inaccuracies, while others I found downright bad. I also noted that two of the most renowned biblical scholars, Professors H. Orlinsky and R. Gordis, are not found among the contributors. By the way, both of them are graduates of The Dropsie University and serve on the editorial board of the *Jewish Quarterly Review*.

Dr. E. Shulman, an authority on Yiddish literature, in an article in the *Forward*, charged that his item on Zinberg was doctored and even distorted. Dr. Trude Weiss-Rosmarin, on *EJ* in *Jewish Spectator*, October 1972, wrote that "there are thousands of mistakes". She also remarked, "the waste of *Encyclopaedia Judaica* is staggering". Her conclusion was "Unfortunately, the 16-Volume *EJ* is another 'non-Encyclopaedia' ". Georges Weill, in *Cahier*, also criticized the *Encyclopaedia Judaica*. He writes, "*Que l'E.J. ne fait pas honneur à la science juive, parce que, affirme-t-il, il n'y a pas d'érudits juifs; un autre qualifie l'ouvrage de non - Encyclopedie...*"

Mr. Philip Slomovitz, the fearless and gallant editor of the Detroit *Jewish News*, made the following remarks, "Many wanted to say it and some are saying it: that the newest *Encyclopaedia Judaica* is a faulty work, that it has many errors and its importance is exaggerated. It took the courageous Prof. Solomon Zeitlin of Dropsie University, to put this down in writing and to provide the evidence". (*The Jewish News*, Feb. 2, 1973).

I received many letters regarding my review. One came from Dr. Habib Levi a Jewish leader in Tehran, Iran, in which he charged that the modern history of Iran, in the *Encyclopaedia Judaica*, is confused and distorted. One of the many letters I received from the readers of the *Jewish Quarterly Review*, was from a rabbi in Pittsburgh who writes, "In almost every area where I have used the *Encyclopaedia*, I have found gross errors, many misinterpretations and woeful commissions". This letter is typical of the many letters which I received.

In sum, as I wrote in my review, the *Encyclopaedia Judaica* is not a major accomplishment. On the contrary, it reveals the paucity and the decadence of Jewish learning. Many articles, even dealing with the Bible, are below the standards of good encyclopaedias.

The items on the history of the Second Commonwealth and tannaitic literature are faulty and ambiguous. According to the Talmud Ket. there is an injunction against having at home books that contain errors.

SOLOMON ZEITLIN

THE PLAGUE OF
PSEUDO-RABBINIC SCHOLARSHIP

By Solomon Zeitlin, Dropsie University

In a recent issue of *Judaism* an article entitled "The Best Kept Secret of the Rabbinic Tradition" by Samson H. Levey the author made the following bold statements: Ben Zoma was a Christian; he adopted Christianity formally. The Tannaim who were Ben Zoma's contemporaries and colleagues, have known this. However, they decided that it might be best to keep the matter as quiet as they could, so as not to lend strength to the aggressive evangelism of the early Church. The author continues by saying "It is precisely this that became the best kept secret of the Rabbinic tradition-that Ben Zoma had converted to Christianity and became a professing Christian." He bases his assertions on talmudic passages. He claims that the passage in Hag. 14b is the most revealing document "the main key to solving the riddle which confronts us". The author says, "The text as found in the most widely used editions of the Talmud, the Vilna, Romm and related editions read thus: 'They asked Ben Zoma, Is a virgin who has become pregnant eligible to marry a High Priest? ... He answered them ... It is possible that she became pregnant while bathing'." The author continues "This question sounds like one of Halakhah and so does Ben Zoma's answer .. Light on this aspect of the problem is shed by a variant reading found in a manuscript dating from the 12th century, in the British Museum, supported by the Munich manuscript of the Talmud, in the *Dikdukei Soferim*, in *loc*. ... According to these versions the question propounded to Ben Zoma was, 'What of a virgin who is pregnant?' This is not a question of Halakhah but of theology. The question can be rendered, 'Do you believe in the Virgin

16

Birth?' And the reference is unmistakable, dealing with the birth of Jesus, one of the fundamentals of Christian dogma as found in the Gospel of Matthew 1:18-21." The author continues to say "Ben Zoma's reply is brilliant and clever. He does not provide a forthright answer, but only an oblique and implicit one. By saying that she may have become pregnant while bathing, what he said, in effect, was that a virgin birth is possible."

The author who asserts that he found the riddle of the well-kept secret that Ben Zoma was a Christian and believed in a virgin birth is totally wrong and betrays his lack of understanding of the Talmud. The text reads as follows: שאלו את בן זומא בתולה שעיברה מהו לכהן גדול (לכהן גדול Some Mss, omit the words) מי חיישינן לדשמואל דאמר שמואל יכול אני לבעול כמה בעילות בלא דם או דילמא דשמואל לא שכיחא אמר להו דשמואל לא שכיחא וחיישינן שמא באמבטי עיברה.

The author accepts the readings of the mss. where the phrase "to a High Priest" is omitted. Thus he thinks that the question was not a halakhic, but a theological one. The question propounded to Ben Zoma according to him was "what of a virgin who is pregnant". He ascertains "the question can be rendered 'do you believe in the Virgin Birth?' And the reference is unmistakably dealing with the birth of Jesus, one of the fundamentals of Christian dogma as found in the Gospel of Matthew 1:18-21."

The correct talmudic text is in accordance with the reading of the mss. where the phrase לכהן גדול is omitted. There were no high priests during the time of Ben Zoma. However, there is no doubt that the question propounded to Ben Zoma was not a theological, but a halakhic one. According to Rabbi Eliezer, an unmarried woman who had an affair with a man is considered to be a harlot.[1] The question was asked of Ben Zoma, what is the status of a virgin who is preg-

---

[1] אמר רבי אליעזר פנוי הבא על הפנויה שלא לשם אישות עשאה זונה. Yeb. 59b, 61b; Yer. Ibid. 7.4.

nant, is she a harlot? According to the Pentateuch, an ordinary priest may not marry a harlot.[2] The question to Ben Zoma certainly has nothing to do with the Virgin Birth and does not deal with the birth of Jesus.

The author continues to say, "Ben Zoma's reply is brilliant and clever. He does not provide a forthright answer, but only an oblique and implicit one. By saying that she may have become pregnant while bathing, what he said, in effect, was that the Virgin Birth is possible."

The talmudic text is somehow confused and anachronistic. After the question was propounded to Ben Zoma, it is stated: can we take into consideration Samuel's view that coition can be performed with a virgin without causing bleeding and thus a virgin who became pregnant must have had an affair with a man and therefore considered a harlot, or is Samuel's point of view uncommon: מי חיישינן לדשמואל ..... יכול אני לבעול כמה בעילות בלא דם או דלמא דשמואל לא שכיחא. He said to them Samuel's point of view does not occur and we have to take into consideration that she may have gotten pregnant while she was bathing in the bathtub where a man left animatic sperm. Ben Zoma could not have said אמר להו דשמואל לא שכיחא, since Samuel lived a century after Ben Zoma.[3]

Dr. Levey did not fully comprehend this talmudic text and thus he erred by stating that Ben Zoma was a Christian and he refers to the birth of Jesus.

The author continues with his faulty imaginary assumptions. He writes, "But this is not the only clue which the Rabbinic tradition has left us, pointing to Ben Zoma as a Jewish Christian. Another key passage is the version in the Babylon-

---

[2] Lev. 21.7. אשה זנה וחללה לא יקחו.

[3] There is a legend that Ben Sirah was the son of the prophet Jeremiah. His daughter became pregnant while she was bathing in the bathtub where her father, Jeremiah, left animatic sperm. וכן בירמיהו הנביא זה אמרו עליו כי הרהר והפיל זרעו במרחץ ... דרכה בתו ביה ביה שעתא וישבה באותו המקום במרחץ להתרחץ בו מטמאתה ומשכה רחמה אותן טפות הזרע ונתעברה ממנו ... גלה להם בר סירא קראו שמי כמנין אותיות ירמיהו הנביא, כי אבי הוא וכמנין אותיות שמו ככה יהיה שמי, וכן קראו לו בר סירא כלומר בן ירמיהו הנביא. (אשכל הכפר סס״ג)

516

nian Talmud of Ben Zoma's encounter with his master,
R. Joshua b. Hananiah ... In that passage there are several
items of indisputable evidence [sic!] that Ben Zoma was,
indeed, a Christian. First, Ben Zoma does not show his
master the respect due to a teacher, for he does not
rise to greet him, thus indicating that the Jewish sage and
what he represented were no longer of primary interest to
him." I am greatly dismayed to read the author's conclusion that Ben Zoma was a Christian because he did not rise
to greet his teacher. First, let me state that there are different
versions, in the Babylonian Talmud, in the Palestinian Talmud
and in the Tosefta. The text in the Babylonian Talmud reads
as follows: מעשה בר׳ יהושע בן חניה שהיה עומד על גב מעלה בהר הבית
בין מים . . . וראהו בן זומא ולא עמד מלפניו אמר לו מאין ולאין בן זומא
. . . עליונים למים התחתונים . . . אלא ג׳ אצבעות . . .

Rabbi Joshua b. Hananiah was standing on a step on the
Temple Mount and Ben Zoma saw him but did not rise in
front of him. In the Palestinian Talmud, the story is told that
R. Joshua was walking on the road and Ben Zoma came
across and he saluted him and he did not reply.[4] The Tosefta
has this version: מעשה בר׳ יהושע שהיה מהלך באיסטרטא ובן זומא
בא כנגדו הגיע אצלו ולא שאל בשלומו אמר לו מאין ולאין בן
זומא. It once happened that R. Joshua was walking on the
street and Ben Zoma met him and did not greet him. The
text in the Palestinian Talmud and the Tosefta is more
correct. After the destruction of the Temple, R. Joshua could
not stand on the step of the Temple Mount. It cannot be
assumed that the story refers to the period before the destruction of the Temple since R. Joshua was very young at the time
of the destruction and certainly Ben Zoma was either not
yet born or a young child, Ben Zoma did not greet R. Joshua,
not because he became a Christian and did not respect him.

---

[4] מעשה ברבי יהושע שהיה מהלך בדרך ובן זומא בא כנגדו שאל בשלומו
ולא השיבו אמר לו מאין ולאין בן זומא אמר לו מסתכל הייתי במעשה
בראשית ואין בין מים העליונים למים התחתונים אלא כמלא פותח טפח.
Yer. Hag. 2.

He was absorbed in Cosmogony, מעשה בראשית. Then R. Joshua asked him, "from whence and whereto Ben Zoma?" The reply of Ben Zoma was "I was looking between the upper waters and the lower waters and between the one and the other there is nothing but three fingers."

The Midrash Genesis gives another version of the story of Ben Zoma. כבר היה שמעון בן זומא עומד ותוהא עבר ר יהשוע שאל בשלומו פעם ופעמים ולא השיבו בשלישית השיבו בבהילות אמר לו מה זו בן זומא מאין הרגלים אמר לו לא מאין רבי אמר לו מעיד אני עלי שמים וארץ שאיני חז מיכאן עד שתודיעני מאין הרגלים אמר לו מסתכל הייתי במעשה בראשית ואין בין מים העליונים לתחתונים כב' וג' אצבעות. Simon Ben Zoma was standing and wondering, R. Joshua passed by and greeted him once and twice and Ben Zoma did not acknowledge, and on the third time he replied hastily, Joshua said to Ben Zoma, "from whence and whereto?" Ben Zoma answered from nowhere Rabbi. Rabbi Joshua said to Ben Zoma I testify upon me heaven and earth that I will not move from here until you will let me know "from where?" Ben Zoma replied, "I was observing the Mystery of Creation and there is nought between the upper waters and the lower waters, but two and three fingers". From all these versions, we may see that there were different traditions about the story of Ben Zoma. From all accounts, it is clear that Ben Zoma was very much absorbed in Cosmogony.

According to the version given in the Babylonian Talmud, Ben Zoma said that "between the upper waters and the lower waters there are three fingers." Upon this phrase, the author concludes "that there is a Godhead consisting of three entities, that in the heaven and in the earth there are but three Gods." The author based this assumption on *Gezerah Shawah*, verbal congruity. He writes, "The key to this phraseology is to be found in Ex. 8:15, in the context of the plague of vermin. When Pharaoh's magicians marvelled at this feat of Moses and Aaron, they said to Pharoah, 'This is the finger of God' " ... With subtlety in mind, Ben Zoma's reply to R. Joshua was that in all the universe, both upper

and lower, there are but three fingers, that is, there are three
Gods, the Christology being quite obvious to one who understood the exegetical base of his remarks."

To apply verbal congruity to historical facts is very
dangerous. The Talmud well said אין אדם דן גזירה שוה מעצמו.
No one should invent theories on verbal congruity. There
is no historical discipline or logic in such analogy. It is applied
only by those who could not substantiate their theories by
history or by factual argument. It was applied by the
theologians in the Middle Ages to prove their theological
points of view. It is regrettable to state that this method is
applied by the professors, the protagonists of the antiquity
of the Dead Sea Scrolls. Since they had no proof to substantiate their contentions, they applied the analogy of verbal
congruity. By verbal congruity, one can prove anything one
wishes.

By the way, the phrase "three fingers" is not found in the
Palestinian Talmud or in the Tosefta. The word *tephach* occurs.
The word *tephach* has the connotation handbreadth, i.e. four
fingers. The text in Tosefta has that there is nothing between
the upper water and the lower water even a *tephach*,[5] that is
three fingers. The text in the Babylonian Talmud is based on
the reading of the Tosefta.

The author to substantiate his view that Ben Zoma was a
Christian writes: "But there is even more convincing evidence
in Ben Zoma's continuing statement wherein he cites Gen. 1:2
as a proof-text: 'And the spirit of God hovered over the face
of the water, like the dove which hovers over its offspring'.
This cannot be other than a reference to Mark 1:9-11 ...
The spirit of God of Gen. 1:2 is equated by Ben Zoma with
the Holy Spirit in the Christian tradition as found in Mark,
and the reference to the dove is clear and unmistakable."

I am puzzled how the author came to such a fantastic
conclusion which he emphasizes as "unmistakable" that Ben

אפילו טפח [5]

Zoma alludes to Mark 1:2. Is it not more likely that he refers to the dove mentioned in connection with the Deluge? The dove was a symbol for good tidings and peace, the dove in the story of Ben Zoma and Mark had the meaning of good tidings. It may refer to the dove who brought good tidings to Noah. It is to note that in the text of the Palestinian Talmud as well as in the Tosefta, *dove* is not mentioned, but they make reference to an eagle.[6]

Bizarre ideas often lead to absurdity. The author continues to say, "The reference to 'waters' by Ben Zoma also becomes obvious, since it points to the narrative of baptism of Jesus and, hence, to one of the cornerstones of the Christian faith. The parallel which Ben Zoma draws, connecting the upper and the lower waters, is an exegetical way of indicating the divine, universal nature of the Christian baptismal rite, not only in relation to Jesus but which Ben Zoma apparently had accepted upon himself. This, too, explains the cryptic reference to 'water, water' in the PRDS incident."

Reading this paragraph reminds me of the founders of Christianity and the Christian theologians of the Middle Ages who in their endeavor to prove that Jesus was the true Messiah, recited verses from the Bible to prove that Moses and the Prophets had prophesized of the coming of Jesus as the true Messiah.

The author was so preoccupied with his fixed idea that Ben Zoma was a Christian that he did not pay sufficient attention to the story of the Creation given in the Book of Genesis where it is related that God separated between waters and waters. The Midrash of Genesis in interpreting the passage of the Creation, states that God separated between the upper waters and the lower waters and the רקיע heaven was between the two waters. The sages who studied Cosmogony naturally speculated about the upper waters and the lower waters.

The author makes the following statement: "Which Ben

<hr>

[6] ‫נאמר כאן ריחוף ונאמר להלן כנשר . . . ירחף‬.
In Midrash Gen. reference is made to a bird, ‫מרחפת כעוף שפרות‬.

Zoma apparently had accepted upon himself". According to the author Ben Zoma became a convert to Christianity by "Christian Baptismal Rites". That a convert to Christianity has to be baptized is found only in the Gospel according to Matthew 28:19. "Go ye therefore, and teach all nations baptizing them in the name of the Father, and of the Son and of the Holy Spirit". The rite of baptism for converts to Christianity came into practice in the middle of the second century C.E. The Christians adopted this rite from the Jews. The Jews did not demand baptism for converts to Judaism before the time of R. Eliezer and R. Joshua.[7]

In connection with the story of Ben Zoma, it is related that four men entered the *PRDS*.[8] The author comments, "The traditional vocalization of the word is *Pardes* from the Greek *paradeisos* meaning garden, hence, the garden of speculative theosophy, or esoteric philosophy. My hypothesis is that there is a reference to Christianity in this Baraita. Assuming that Ben Zoma's dereliction was his adoption of Christianity, which the Rabbis sought to conceal, something startling emerges from this passage ... I propose that instead of *Pardes* it be read *Parados*, the Hebrew rendering in apocopated form of the Greek word *Paradosis*, which was the term used extensively by Christians, in the second century and thereafter, to apply to the authoritative tradition of transmission of authentic doctrine concerning the life of Jesus and the early teachings of the Church ... What the Baraita tells us is that the four made a probing study of Christian origins and beliefs." What kind of absurdity! Among the four who entered the *Pardes* was Rabbi Akiba, thus the author assumed that the Rabbi Akiba studied Christian origins and beliefs.

---

[7] Cf. S. Zeitlin, "The Halakhah in the Gospels and its Relation to the Jewish Law at the time of Jesus" *HUCA*, I (1924).

[8] ארבעה נכנסו בפרדס ואלו הן עזai בו זומא אחר רבי עקיבא ... בן עזאי הציץ ומת ... בן זומא הציץ ונפגע ... אחר קיצץ בנטיעות, רבי עקיבא יצא בשלום.

The word פרדס *Pardes* occurs in the Bible.[9] The Septuagint renders *paradeisos* garden. In the Jewish apocalyptic literature *Paradeisos*, paradise, is designated as the enclosure where God dwells.[10] In IV Ezra *paradeisos* refers to a heavenly paradise.[11] In the Testament of Levi *paradeisos* is a place where the saints and the righteous will live."The great *paradeisos* will be their shelter ... They (the righteous) shall no more bear the lawlessness and those on earth.[12] The four sages entered the *Pardes*, the heavenly paradise, where they speculated about מעשה בראשית Cosmogeny, regarding the creation of the world. The author's hypothesis is unfounded, to say the least.

Rabbi Joshua said regarding Ben Zoma that he is מבחוץ, outside. The author asserts that R. Joshua meant that Ben Zoma "is still unquestionably a Christian." Where did the author get the idea that R. Joshua knew that Ben Zoma was unquestionably a Christian? The term חוץ outside was never applied in the Talmud to Judaeo-Christians.[13]

On p. 463 the author declares "that Ben Zoma had converted to Christianity and became a professing Christian." What does the author have in mind by saying Ben Zoma was a professing Christian? Had Ben Zoma visited Church every Sunday? Or maybe he participated in the Eucharist?

The third proof that Ben Zoma was a Christian the author deduced from the Mishne Menaḥot 11:4. He writes, "What treatment did Ben Zoma receive at the hands of his colleagues seeing that he was a Christian? The Gemara to M. Menahot 11:4 which contains a Christological reference by Ben Zoma." In n. 68 the author writes, " 'God has a face', i.e., He has the physical form of a human being, He became

---

[9] Cf. Song of Songs, 4.12; Koheleth, 2.5.

[10] Cf. 2 Enoch.

[11] 4 Ezra 4.8. Neither to heaven have I ever ascended, nor entered Paradise. ... *aut qui sunt exitus paradisi.*

[12] 18. 10.

[13] The word מבחוץ probable refers outside of the Beth Midrash, Academy. Cf. Yer. Tan. 4.1. שמונים ספסלים של תלמידי חכמים היו שם חוץ מן העומדים מאחורי הגדר.

incarnate in Jesus." So according to the author, Ben Zoma believed that God was incarnated in Jesus, (that Jesus was indeed the son of God in incarnation). The text of the Mishne reads as follows: שתי הלחם ארכן שבעה טפחים ורחבן ארבעה טפחים וקרנותיה ארבע אצבעות לחם הפנים ארכן עשרה טפחים ורחבו חמשה טפחים וקרנותיו שבע אצבעות רבי יהודה אומר שלא תטעה ז'ד'ד'י'ה'ז' בן זומא אומר ונתתה על השולחן לחם פנים לפני תמיד לחם פנים שיהו לו פנים. The Two Loaves were seven handbreadths long and four wide and their horns were four handbreadths high. The Shewbread were ten handbreadths long and five wide and their horns were seven handbreadths high. Rabbi Judah says in order not to make a mistake, keep in mind the following letters: ז ה י ד ד ז.[14] Ben Zoma says 'And you shall set upon the table shewbread in my sight always', It shall have a visibility." What Ben Zoma meant was that the Shewbread shall be longer, wider, and higher than the Two Loaves, and thus they will be distinct.

To the author's inquiry how Ben Zoma was treated by his colleagues, he quotes the Gemara (Men. 98b) "Rabbi Simeon b. Lakish says, A *Talmid Hakham* who has become wayward in his faith must not be publicly put to shame (variant,— excommunicated), as is said (Hos. 4:5), you shall stumble by day and the prophet also shall stumble with you by night. Conceal it as the darkness of the night'. i.e., keep it a secret." The aphorism of Simeon b. Lakish has nothing to do with the statement of Ben Zoma given in the Mishne.

In the Gemara Menaḥot 99b it is related that the tablets which Moses broke when he descended from heaven and saw that the Israelites made a golden calf were kept together with the second tablets which Moses gave to the people. As is the custom in the Talmud to collate the sayings of a particular sage, so in the Gemara Menahot 99b a few aphorisms of Simeon b. Lakish were brought together. אשר שברת מלמד שהלוחות ושברי לוחות מונחין בארון . . . אמר ריש לקיש פעמים שביטולה

---

[14] The six letters have, respectively, the numbers 7, 4, 4, 10, 5, 7.

של תורה זהו יסודה דכתיב אשר שברת . . . ואמר ריש לקיש תלמיד חכם
שסרח אין מבזין אותו בפרהסיא שנאמר וכשלת היום וכשל גם נביא עמך
לילה, כסהו כלילה, ואמר ריש לקיש כל המשכח דבר אחד מלמודו עובר
בלאו שנאמר השמר לך ושמור נפשך מאד פן תשכח . . .

From the aforequoted passage of the Gemara we must
conclude that the aphorism of Simeon b. Lakish has no relation
to the Mishne, and it does not refer to the homily of Ben Zoma.

Talmid Hakham is a generic term applied to a sage, scholar.[15]
The word שסרח cannot be rendered ''who has become wayward
in his faith.'' The word תחטא in Numb. 15:27, is rendered in
the Targum according to the pseudo Johnathan ''כד סרח''.[16]
The aphorism of Rabbi Simeon b. Lakish is to be rendered:
a *Talmid Hakham* who sinned shall not be publicly put to
shame . . . cover him like the night, i.e. like the darkness of
the night that covers the earth and people don't see each other,
rebuke him privately and quietly in the darkness and not
publicly. Cf. Ber. 19a. ''If you saw a *Talmid Hakham* committing a sin (transgressing the law) do not think evil of him the
following day . . . he certainly repented.'' [17]

To connect the aphorism of Rabbi Simeon b. Lakish with
a homily of Ben Zoma is incredible. Again, the author's
pronouncement with absolute certainty that Ben Zoma
''became a professing Christian'' is a perversion of the truth.
In asserting that Ben Zoma's homily שיהו לו פנים '' 'God has
a face', i.e. He has the physical form of a human being, He
became incarnate in Jesus'' the author simply misunderstood
the saying of Ben Zoma. The meaning of the saying of Ben
Zoma as I said before was that the Shewbread shall have
visibility, i.e., that it should be longer, wider and higher than
the Two Loaves.

The phrase שיהו לו פנים refers to the Shewbread that should
have a פנים visibility.

[15] Yer. M.K. 3.7. אי זהו תלמיד חכם חזקיה אמר כל ששנה הלכות
יעשו כל אדם עצמן תלמידי חכמים Ibid., Prs. 4. 5. ועוד תורה
[16] Numb. 15: 25. חטאתם is rendered סורחותהון
[17] אם ראית תלמיד חכם שעבר עבירה בלילה אל תהרהר אחריו ביום
שמא עשה תשובה . . .

If indeed Ben Zoma was an apostate renegade who became a Christian, no *halakhot* would be quoted in his name.[18] Elisha b. Abuyah who was one of the four who entered the *Pardes* and was the teacher of Rabbi Meir, who later became an apostate, no *halakhot* were ever quoted in his name. He was called by the epithet of אחר, i.e. "other one," he does not belong anymore to the Judaeans. We also have to bear in mind that at the time of Ben Zoma a special prayer was composed and inserted in the *Shemoneh Esreh* against the apostates, the Judaean-Christians.[19] If indeed, Ben Zoma was a Christian, the Mishne would not have said, "When Ben Zoma died there were no more דרשנים," interpreters of the Torah and of the halakhot.[20]

---

[18] M. Nazir 5.1. אמר לו [לרבי יהושע] בן זומא . . . אמר רבי יהושע נמצא זה מבי קרבנותיו לחצאים אבל הודו לו חכמים לבן זומא.
Yer. Nazir. 8.8. כיצד עושין לו כדברי בן זומא.
Tosefta Toh. 6.17. שאלו את בן זומא מפני מה ספק רשות היחיד טמא
Ibid. Yoma 1. 16. שאלו את בן זומא מה לטבילה זו
Ibid. Sann. 3.5. שמעון בן זומא אומר . . . כך נתנה תורה מחיצה בין הבכור למעשר שני
Yer. Shek. 5.1. תני סנהדרין שיש בה שנים שיודעין לדבר וכולן ראויין לשמוע הרי ראויה לסהנדרין, שלשה הרי זו בינונית, ארבעה הרי זו חכמה, וביבנה היו בה ארבעה בן עזאי בן זומא בן חכינאי ורבי אלעזר בן מתיה.
[19] The sages regarded the Judaean Christians a menace to the unity of the Judaeans and to Judaism. Rabban Gamaliel asked the sages to compose a prayer against the Judaean Christians, apostates. According to the Talmud (Ber. 28) Samuel the Little composed the prayer. אמר להם רבן גמליאל לחכמים כלום יש אדם שיודע לתקן ברכת (הצדוקים) מינים עמד שמואל הקטן ותקנה. Justin Martyr, who lived during this period, accused the Jews of "cursing in your synagogues those that believe in Christ." *Dialogue with Trypho*, 16.
[20] Cf. M. Sotah 9.15. משמת בן זומא בטלו הדרשנים.
M. Ber. 1. 8. אמר להן רבי אלעזר בן עזריה הרי אני כבן שבעים שנה ולא זכיתי שתאמר יציאת מצרים בלילות עד שדרשה• בן זומא . . .
M. Hulin, 5.5. יום אחד האמור באותו ואת בנו היום הולך אחר הלילה, את זו דרש בן זומא . . .
Midrash R. Gen. אמר רבי לוי יש מן (הדרושות) הדרשנים שהן דורשים כגון בן עזאי ובן זומא קולו של הקב"ה נעשה מטטרון על המים ה"ה קול ה' על המים.
Ibid. ויעש אלהים את הרקיע זה אחד מן המקריות שהרעיש בן זומא את העולם ויעש אתמהא, הלא במאמר, הן בדבר ה' שמים נעשו וברוח פיו כל צבאם.

The article is simply a distortion of historical facts and the title does not square with the truth. I am sorry to see an author of certain ability a victim of such blunders.

It was after great hesitation that I decided to write this article. I deem it was my duty to refute the thesis pronounced by the author. I always followed the well known maxim: *Amicus Plato sed magis amica veritas.*

This article was published in a popular magazine under the auspices of a reputable establishment. The editors of this magazine enjoy great esteem. It is surprising to see such an article appearing in *Judaism.* The readers of this journal are not all well versed in the Talmud, thus they may follow blindly the idea propounded by the author.

In the United States of America Jewish scholarship is still a field of new research, as it has not the tradition of the old centers like Russia and Germany which were destroyed during World War II. Rabbinic scholarship is still in a state of a *tabula rasa.* The few rabbinic scholars whom fortunately we do have here came from across the Atlantic. Most of the books written in the field of rabbinics by some professors show that they had no guidance in the Talmud; most of them use translations. Apparently they are unable to use the originals. As a student of rabbinics, I considered it my duty to expose such books without bias or favor.

It appears that it became a fashion among professors of religion to show that many of the sages of the Talmud either were Christians or shared with the early Christians their hatred towards the Pharisees. I had occasion in another review to show the flagrant errors of a professor of religion who maintained the sensational idea that the sages also disapproved the arrogance of the Rabbis. He wrote, "Jesus did not approve the pleasure so many Pharisees took in being addressed as Rabbi ... In many generations before Jesus a scribe has said much the same thing: 'Love manual work and hate rabbinism.' Many shared this view. Arrogance may often have been found along with the scribes but they were not effete

academicians," The author simply misinterpreted the phrase
אהוב את המלאכה ושנא את הרבנות by "love manual work and
hate rabbinism." To render the phrase ושנא את הרבנות by
"hate rabbinism" is unbelievable.

In the last few decades the study of Jewish religion has
been included in the curriculum of many universities and
colleges for which indeed we should be very thankful to the
sincere and well meaning presidents and deans of the universities. But unfortunately it became a plague upon Judaism.
Some of the professors of Jewish religion are not only biased
against Judaism but definitely unqualified to teach. Their
teachings are a menace to Judaism because they delude the
students on the campuses who already are under the sway of
the Evangelists, "Jews for Jesus." The well meaning presidents
of the universities as well as the leaders of the Jewish
establishment think that the inclusion of Judaism in the
curriculum in the different universities will serve to spread
true Judaism on the campuses. To our great shagrin we must
note that these professors are only sowing bitter herbs for
the students.

In some universities, professors of Jewish religion instead
of teaching the theology of Maimonides, Judah Halevi,
Crescas, and others, concentrate on the theology called
Buberism. Buber's theology is deluded; it is neither Jewish
nor Christian theology. To quote one paragraph of his
writings:

> All my life I have felt that Jesus was my elder brother.
> My own open brotherly relationship to him has become even
> stronger and purer, and today I can see him with surer and
> purer vision than before. I am more certain that he merits
> a greater place in the history of Israel's faith, and that this
> place cannot be defined in terms of the usual categories.

It is no wonder that on some campuses signs were hoisted
with the inscription "Jesus is kosher." The professors of
religion with their teaching Jewish religion not only delude

the students but they are making them a ready prey for the *Key* 73 Movement that has set out to evangelize.

Lately I encountered two young men, students of a certain university who also attended ecumenical dialogues and said to me that it is high time for the Jews to seek a rapproachment with the Christians and accept Christianity. They argued that there is no great division between the Christians and the Jews. The Christians believe that Jesus was the Messiah while the Jews believe that the Messiah did not come. According to them as they understood from their professors, "Jesus is kosher." Why then, they say, should the Jews not accept him and cease their isolation?

I tried to explain to them that while it is true that Jesus was a Jew by birth, his twelve apostles were Jews, and the first seventy bishops were Jews.[21] In the first two centuries, Christianity was an offshoot of Judaism. Most of the Christians were Jews. I tried to enlighten them on the *Parting of the Ways*, the underlying reasons of the break between Judaism and Christianity. At the Nicene Council in 325 C.E. Christianity broke entirely with Judaism. It became a different religion and hostile to Judaism. Now Judaism and Christianity are definitely two religions. Jews and Christians are members of one human society. Having a common interest in the welfare of their country, they are members of one human society. Having a common interest in the welfare of their country, they are members of one fellowship but they are separate in their religions. The Jews do not wish to convert the Christians to Judaism nor be converted to Christianity. The Jews follow the eternal words of the prophet Micah,

> Let all the people walk each one in the name of his God, but we will walk in the name of Adonai our God forever and ever.[22]

[21] Eusebius, The *Ecclesiastical History*.
[22] 4.5.

I am certain that Judaism will endure the faulty teachings of the professors of Judaism in the universities, but at the same time I think that the Jewish people will sustain some harm due to the teachings of the professors. It is already known that on some campuses Jewish students of traditional Jewish homes were caught in the net by the Evangelists and accepted Christianity. This should be a cause for concern to all Jews who believe in the eternity and unity of the Jewish people.

Beside the plague of the pseudo-scholarship of Judaism propagated in the universities, we are also witnessing a growing mysticism in a new garb. Some of the writings of the mystics are more in accord with Christian theology than with Judaism, although they clothe themselves in a Jewish garb. Judaism is based on knowledge and learning.

Judaism, as was formulated and cemented by the sages during the Second Commonwealth, is a religion controlled by law which we may call nomocracy, the rule of the law. The Hebrew term for the Jewish religion is דת *dat* which has the meaning of custom, law. The belief in God, according to the sages, is not sufficient; God's precepts had to be observed. The sages who framed the laws never meant that the laws should be rigid, but plastic. Many of the sages held that the laws were meant for man and not man for the laws, that the laws were given to man for his benefit, not for his destruction. The sages strove to bring the religion in consonance with life, and even to amend the pentateuchal law if such were life's demands. They strove to make Judaism a living religion.

In the Talmud it is related that the sages argued among themselves what is more important, the observance of the laws or the study, knowledge. They unanimously arrived at the conclusion that the study, the knowledge, takes precedence over the observance.[23]

[23] Kid. 40 נשאלה שאילה זו בפניהם תלמוד גדול או מעשה גדול נענו כולם ואמרו לימוד גדול.
Yer. Pes. 3.7. נמנו בעליית בית (ארוס) נתזה בלוד התלמוד קודם למעשה.

The present writer is the only surviving member of the scholars who founded the American Academy of Jewish Research, hence I deem I have the right to say a few words about the present status of the Academy. The Academy was founded over a half a century ago. It was founded with the idea to enhance scholarship and to serve as a guardian of Jewish scholarship in America. There was already a fear in the minds of the founders, since America has no tradition for Jewish scholarship, particularly in the field of rabbinics, pseudo-scholarship may flourish. How right they were! These principles regrettable to note, were not followed by the present leadership of the Academy. The Academy did not live up to the ideas and the ideals of the founders. The founders were strongly of the opinion that one who did not publish a scholarly work cannot be considered a candidate for a Fellow. We note that there are Fellows in the present Academy who never published scholarly books. Some did publish books, but those publications do not present a contribution to scholarship. On the contrary, they reveal the inadequacy of the authors. On the other hand, some young men, whose publications are marked by originality and scholarship, were never nominated as Fellows. The American Academy of Jewish Research lost its original mission and became a society. Some of the papers published in the *Proceedings* are below the standard of an Academy.

To fulfill the ideas and the high ideals of the scholars who founded the Academy, the American Academy of Jewish Research must be completely reorganized. A Jewish Academy in the full sense of the word in order to enhance scholarship and be a guardian of true learning, is a paramount need now, even more than it was in 1920.

17

Volume Index

2:1. The Pharisees and Other Sects

Joseph D. Amusin, "The Reflection of Historical Events of the First Century B.C. in Qumran Commentaries (4Q 161; 4Q 169; 4Q 166)."

Albert I. Baumgarten, "Josephus and Hippolytus on the Pharisees."

Roger T. Beckwith, "The Pre-History and Relationships of the Pharisees, Sadducees and Essenes: A Tentative Reconstruction."

Shaye J. D. Cohen, "The Significance of Yavneh: Pharisees, Rabbis, and the End of Jewish Sectarianism."

Dan Cohn-Sherbok, "The Mandaeans and Heterodox Judaism."

Samuel S. Cohon, "Pharisaism, A Definition."

Victor Eppstein, "When and How the Sadducees Were Excommunicated."

Enslin, Morton S., "The Samaritan Ministry and Mission."

Louis Finkelstein, "The Pharisees, Their Origin and Their Philosophy."

Henry A. Fischel, "Story and History: Observations on Greco-Roman Rhetoric and Pharisaism."

David G. Flusser, "The Social Message from Qumran."

Norman Golb, "Literary and Doctrinal Aspects of the Damascus Covenant in the Light of Karaite Literature."

A. M. Haberman, "The Dead Sea Scrolls—A Survey and a New Interpretation."

John Kampen, "A Reconsideration of the Name 'Essene' in Greco-Jewish Literature in Light of Recent Perceptions of the Qumran Sect."

Kaufmann Kohler, "The Origin and Composition of the Eighteen Benedictions, with a Translation of the Corresponding Essene Prayers in the Apostolic Constitutions."

Ralph Marcus, "Pharisees, Essenes, and Gnostics."

Ralph Marcus, "The Pharisees in the Light of Modern Scholarship."

Ralph Marcus, "Philo, Josephus, and the Dead Sea Yahad."

Jacob Neusner, "From Exegesis to Fable in Rabbinic Traditions about the Pharisees."

Jacob Neusner, "History and Purity in First-Century Judaism."

Jacob Neusner, "'Pharisaic-Rabbinic' Judaism: A Clarification."

Jacob Neusner, "The Rabbinic Traditions about the Pharisees in Modern Historiography."

Jacob Neusner, "The Use of the Later Rabbinic Evidence for the Study of First-Century Pharisaism."

Cecil Roth, "The Zealots in the War of 66–73."

2:2. The Pharisees and Other Sects

Jacob Z. Lauterbach, "A Significant Controversy Between the Sadducees and the Pharisees."

Jacob Z. Lauterbach, "Sadducees and Pharisees. A Study of their Respective Attitudes Towards the Law."

Jacob Z. Lauterbach, "The Pharisees and Their Teachings, Part I, The Pharisees."

Jacob Z. Lauterbach, "The Pharisees and Their Teachings, Part II, The Pharisees' Attitude toward Law and Tradition."

Jacob Z. Lauterbach, The Pharisees and Their Teachings, Part III "The Pharisaic Ideas of God and Israel."

Saul Lieberman, "The Discipline in the So-Called Dead Sea Manual of Discipline."

Saul Lieberman, "Light on the Cave Scrolls from Rabbinic Sources."

Jacob Neusner, "'Fellowship' in Judaism."

Jacob Neusner, "The Rabbinic Traditions about the Pharisees before A.D. 70: The Problem of Oral Transmission."

Ellis Rivkin, "Defining the Pharisees: the Tannaitic Sources."

Ellis Rivkin, "Pharisaism and the Crisis of the Individual in the Greco-Roman World."

Cecil Roth, "Qumran and Masadah: A Final Clarification Regarding the Dead Sea Sect."

Cecil Roth, "The Pharisees in the Jewish Revolution of 66–73."

Roth, Cecil, "The Religious Nature of the Zealots."

Cecil Roth, "The Zealots—A Jewish Religious Sect."

Lawrence H Schiffman, "Communal Meals at Qumran."

Lawrence H Schiffman, "The Eschatological Community of the Serekh Ha-'Eda."

Daniel R. Schwartz, "Josephus and Nicolaus on the Pharisees."

Morton Smith, "The Description of the Essenes in Josephus and the Philosophumena."

Abram Spiro, "Samaritans, Tobiads, and Judahites in Pseudo-Philo."

Solomon Zeitlin, "The Account of the Essenes in Josephus and in the Philosophumena."

Solomon Zeitlin, "The Origin of the Pharisees Reaffirmed."

Solomon Zeitlin, "The Pharisees and the Gospels."

3:1. Judaism and Christianity in the First Century

Leo Baeck, "Haggadah and Christian Doctrine."

Leo Baeck, "Judaism in the Church."

Herbert W. Basser, "Allusions to Christian and Gnostic Practises in Talmudic Tradition."

Herbert W. Basser, "Tannaitic References to Christian Fast Days."

Elie Benamozegh, "Judaism and Christianity in the Light of Noachism."

Ludwig Blau, "Early Christian Archaeology from the Jewish Point of View."

George Alexander Kohut, "Abraham's Lesson in Tolerance."

Jacob Neusner, "A Zoroastrian Critique of Judaism: (Skand Gumanik Vicar, Chapters Thirteen and Fourteen: A New Translation and Exposition)."

Jacob Neusner, "Jews and Judaism Under Iranian Rule: Bibliographical Reflections."

Jacob Neusner, "The Jews in Pagan Armenia."

Jacob Neusner, "New Perspectives on Babylonian Jewry in the Tannaitic Age."

Jacob Neusner, "Politics and Theology in Talmudic Babylonia."

Jacob Neusner, "The Phenomenon of the Rabbi in Late Antiquity."

8:2. History of the Jews in the Second through Seventh Centuries of the Common Era

Saul Leiberman, "The Martyrs of Caesarea."

Saul Leiberman, "Palestine in the Third and Fourth Centuries."

Saul Leiberman, "Roman Legal Institutions in Early Rabbinics and in the Acta Martyrum."

Saul Leiberman, "The Martyrs of Caesarea."

Jacob Mann, "Changes in the Divine Service of the Synagogue Due to Religious Persecutions."

A. Marmorstein, "Judaism and Christianity in the Middle of the Third Century."

Jacob Neusner, and Jonathan Z. Smith, "Archaeology and Babylonian Jewry."

Jacob Neusner, "Babylonian Jewry and Shapur II's Persecution of Christianity from 339 to 379 A.D."

Jacob Neusner, "Rabbis and Community in Third-Century Babylonia."

John T. Pawlikowski, "Roman Imperial Legislation on the Jews: 313–438 C.E."

J. B. Segal, "Jews of North Mesopotamia Before the Rise of Islam."

Ben Zion Wacholder, "Chronomessianism: The Timing of Messianic Movements and the Calendar of Sabbatical Cycles."

Luitpold Wallach, "Church and State in the Later Roman Empire."

Abraham Weiss, "The Third-Century Seat of Calendar Regulation."

Solomon Zeitlin, "Encyclopaedia Judaica: The Status of Jewish Scholarship."

Solomon Zeitlin, "Judaism and Professors of Religion."

Solomon Zeitlin, "Spurious Interpretations of Rabbinic Sources in the Studies of the Pharisees and Pharisaism."

Solomon Zeitlin, "The Encyclopaedia Judaica: A Specimen of Modern Jewish Scholarship."

Solomon Zeitlin, "The Plague of Pseudo-Rabbinic Scholarship."

9. The Literature of Formative Judaism: The Mishnah and the Tosefta

Shaye J. D. Cohen, "Jacob Neusner, Mishnah, and Counter-Rabbinics: A Review Essay."

Shamma Friedman, "Two Early 'Unknown' Editions of the Mishna."

Louis Ginzberg, "Tamid: The Oldest Treatise of the Mishnah."

Judah Goldin, "The First Chapter of Abot de Rabbi Nathan."

Mayer I. Gruber, "The Mishnah as Oral Torah: A Reconsideration."

Alexander Guttmann, "Tractate Abot—Its Place in Rabbinic Literature."

Alexander Guttmann, "The Problem of the Anonymous Mishna: A Study in the History of the Halakah."

R. Travers Herford, "Pirke Aboth: Its Purpose and Significance."

Hyam Maccoby, "Jacob Neusner's Mishnah."

Henry Malter, "A Talmudic Problem and Proposed Solutions."

Samuel K. Mirsky, "The Mishnah as Viewed by the Amoraim."

Jacob Neusner, "The Mishnah and the Smudgepots."

Jacob Neusner, "Transcendence and Worship Through Learning: The Religious World-View of Mishnah."

Joshua Starr, "A Fragment of a Greek Mishnaic Glossary."

P. R. Weis, "The Controversies of Rab and Samuel and the Tosefta."

Ernest Wiesenberg, "Elements of a Lunar Theory in the Mishnah, Rosh Hashanah 2:6, and the Talmudic Complements Thereto."

Meir Ydit, "A Case Study in Mishnaic Theodicy."

10. The Literature of Formative Judaism: The Talmuds

Moshe Aberbach, "Educational Institutions and Problems During the Talmudic Age."

Ludwig Blau, "Methods of Teaching the Talmud in the Past and in the Present."

Gerson D. Cohen, "The Talmudic Age."

Nina Davis, "The Ideal Minister of the Talmud."

Lewis N. Dembitz, "Babylon in Jewish Law."

Ian Gamse, "The Talmud of Babylonia, XXIII: a Review."

Judith Hauptman, "An Alternative Solution to the Redundancy Associated with the Phrase Tanya Nami Hakhi."

Louis Jacobs, "Are There Fictitious Baraitot in the Babylonian Talmud?"

Hyman Klein, "Gemara and Sebara."

Hyman Klein, "Gemara Quotations in Sebara."

H. Klein, "Some General Results of the Separation of Gemara from Sebara in the Babylonian Talmud."

Saul Lieberman, "A Tragedy or a Comedy."

Author Index

1A refers to Volume 1, Part 1, etc.

Lightning Source UK Ltd.
Milton Keynes UK
13 March 2011

169173UK00001B/9/P